THE NIXON TAPES

THE NIXON TAPES

1971–1972

Edited and annotated by

DOUGLAS BRINKLEY *and* LUKE A. NICHTER

Mariner Books
Houghton Mifflin Harcourt
BOSTON   NEW YORK

First Mariner Books edition 2015
Compilation and annotation © 2014 by Douglas Brinkley and Luke A. Nichter

For information about permission to reproduce selections from this book,
write to trade.permissions@hmhco.com or to Permissions, Houghton Mifflin Harcourt
Publishing Company, 3 Park Avenue, 19th Floor, New York, New York 10016.

www.hmhco.com

Library of Congress Cataloging-in-Publication Data
The Nixon tapes / edited and annotated by Douglas Brinkley and Luke A. Nichter.
pages cm
ISBN 978-0-544-27415-0 (hardcover)   ISBN 978-0-544-57033-7 (pbk.)
1. Nixon, Richard M. (Richard Milhous), 1913–1994 — Political and social views.
2. Nixon, Richard M. (Richard Milhous), 1913–1994 — Archives. 3. United States — Politics and
government — 1969–1974 — Sources. 4. United States — Foreign relations — 1969–1974 — Sources.
5. Presidents — United States — Archives. 6. Audiotapes. I. Brinkley, Douglas. II. Nichter, Luke.
E856.N59 2014
973.924092 — dc23
2014011209

Printed in the United States of America
DOC 10 9 8 7 6 5 4 3 2 1

To our wives, Anne Brinkley and Jennifer Nichter,
and the townspeople of Perrysburg, Ohio

CONTENTS

Contents

INTRODUCTION

Four decades later, we have all but forgotten that in late 1972 President Richard M. Nixon was at a political high point. That year, he made historic peace overtures with America's Cold War enemies, first with China, then with the Soviet Union. The Vietnam War, which had long divided the American public, seemed to be drawing to a close. Nixon walloped Democratic rival George McGovern in his November reelection bid, 520 electoral votes to 17, capturing 61 percent of the popular vote. In recent memory, such levels of approval had been achieved only by Franklin D. Roosevelt in 1936 and Lyndon B. Johnson in 1964. Even though questions about Watergate hung in the air, the scandal never emerged as a major issue during the 1972 campaign. As Nixon hoped, the break-in remained a story of interest mainly inside the Washington Beltway — it would explode only in 1973.

On December 14, relaxing in the Oval Office, Nixon discussed his legacy, as it promised to develop at that point. He tried out ideas with White House Chief of Staff H. R. "Bob" Haldeman:

HALDEMAN: There are a lot of good stories from the first term.

NIXON: A book should be written, called *1972*.

HALDEMAN: Yeah.

NIXON: That would be a helluva good book. . . . You get in China, you get in Russia, you get in May 8 [his dramatic decision to bomb and mine Hanoi and Haiphong just before his summit in Moscow], and you get in the election. And it's a helluva damn year. That's what I would write as a book. *1972*, period.

By and large, that is the subject of this book: the public policy that drove the most significant year of the thirty-seventh president's first term. The events of that "hell of a damn year" are presented just as they were recorded on Nixon's taping system, uncensored and unfiltered.

Richard Nixon's legacy is inseparable from his tapes, but White House taping started much earlier. In 1940, Franklin Roosevelt ordered that the thick wooden Oval Office floor be drilled to install wiring that would be used to record his press conferences. Harry Truman inherited FDR's system, adding a microphone to a lampshade on his desk. Dwight Eisenhower installed a new system that included a bugged telephone in the Oval Office. John Kennedy and Lyndon Johnson used recorders provided by the U.S. Army Signal Corps that were capable of capturing hundreds of hours.

Despite the fact that other presidents also recorded, today it is Nixon who is known for bugging the White House. As far as we know, no president since Nixon has taped the way he did. He recorded more than all the rest combined, approximately 3,700 hours. At first, he had no plans to tape anything. Shortly after he was inaugurated on January 20, 1969, he ordered the dismantling of Lyndon Johnson's recording system. A bit of a klutz, he did not want the headache of dealing with electronics. Johnson's system required someone to monitor it and to turn it on and off each day.

Two years later, he changed his mind. Halfway into his first term, Nixon mused that none of his predecessors had employed sound-activated devices to capture everything. He wanted to be the first. Nixon presumed that his White House tapes would be an invaluable source for his memoirs. He believed, however, that in order to create an accurate record of his presidency, he should record everything, without discretion. What Kennedy did — taping moments of crisis like his ExComm meetings during the Cuban Missile Crisis — struck him as window-dressing history. "I thought that recording only selected conversations would completely undercut the purpose of having the taping system," Nixon said. "If our tapes were going to be an objective record of my presidency, they could not have such an obviously self-serving bias. I did not want to have to calculate whom or what or when I would tape."

Tapes of his meetings, he believed, would help set his administration's record straight and allow him to maintain the upper hand on history. "The whole purpose, basically," Nixon told Haldeman during the first recorded conversation, "is that there may be a day when . . . we want to put out something that's positive, maybe we need something just to be sure that we can correct the record."

On Nixon's instructions, the Technical Services Division of the U.S. Secret Service planted mini microphones throughout the Oval Office in February 1971. Five were concealed in the president's desk, and two others were installed around the fireplace. Telephone lines in the Oval Office and the Lincoln Sitting Room were also recorded. Two more microphones were placed in the Cabinet Room. A central mixer, housed in a decrepit locker room in the White House basement, was the switchboard that coordinated the recording machines, Sony TC-800B open-reel models. Very few people knew about the taping system besides Nixon, Haldeman, Alexander Butterfield (who was responsible for its operation), and members of the Secret Service.

Soon after the system's initiation, Nixon liked it enough that he expanded its reach. The fact that everything he said was being saved appealed to his narcissistic sense of grandeur. He believed himself a world leader of great geopolitical insight and military strategy, like Churchill. Indeed, as this book's sampling suggests, he was obsessed with foreign policy with suprisingly little interest in domestic issues. Fewer than 10 percent of the available tapes touch on domestic policy, and sadly, most of those conversations were in the Cabinet Room, where crosstalk and poor microphone placement rendered them among the most difficult to transcribe.

In April 1971, Nixon had four hidden microphones installed in his hideaway in the Executive Office Building, a private office in Room 180 where he could work away from the ceremony of the Oval Office. A year later, Aspen Lodge at Camp David was similarly outfitted, both the interior of the cabin and the telephone that Nixon used frequently when there.

The taping system gave Nixon an accurate record of his meetings and phone calls without the need for someone to sit in and take notes, which had been the practice before taping. It was simple. Nixon wore a pagerlike device provided by the Secret Service, and when it was within range of one of the taping locations, recording started automatically. There was no on or off switch. On some days we have recordings of almost his entire day as he moved between locations for different meetings or events. While not all are decipherable due to intermittently poor audio quality, the Nixon tapes represent a trove for historians unlike any record left by other presidents during the nation's history. To fully transcribe Nixon's tapes would take perhaps 150,000 pages, a task that may never be completed.

The vast majority of people recorded on the Nixon taping system did not know they were being recorded. The existence of the taping system was disclosed on July 16, 1973, by Alexander Butterfield during testimony before the Senate Select Committee on Presidential Campaign Activities, as part of the Watergate investigation. "Mr. Butterfield, are you aware of the installation of any listening devices in the Oval Office of the president?" Republican counsel Fred Thompson asked. It was an unexpected question. Under oath, Butterfield had no choice but to answer honestly. "I was aware of listening devices. Yes, sir," he answered. The testimony changed the course of the Nixon presidency and American history. As Senator Howard Baker said, the purpose of the Senate investigation into the June 17, 1972, Watergate break-in and subsequent White House cover-up was to find out "what the president knew and when he knew it." The tapes provided a way to answer those questions accurately, but they needed to be intact. On the reel for June 20, 1972, the recording was erased at a crucial point, an action for which Nixon's secretary, Rose Mary Woods, largely took responsibility.

As a matter of fact, Nixon was advised by many to burn the tapes while he had the chance. Some — most notably Henry Kissinger, William Rogers, Melvin Laird, and even Billy Graham — felt betrayed by their existence. For Nixon, the secrecy of the system and the value of the record outweighed the privacy concerns of those recorded. Others, including Ray Price, Charles Colson, and John Ehrlichman, believed the president was entitled to a record of his private meetings. George H. W. Bush, Pat Buchanan, Alexander Haig, Donald Rumsfeld, Paul Volcker, and George Shultz went on to have their own political careers. Yet the long shadow of the Nixon tapes, capturing comments they all made privately — and the president's own observations about them — never allowed them to have public careers fully independent of Nixon. The tapes may have been intended to secure Nixon's legacy, but their existence influenced the reputations of many others as well.

The Nixon Tapes is a direct beneficiary of Nixon's refusal to destroy the 3,700 hours of recordings. Nixon made that decision out of consideration for his legacy. Once the hullabaloo of Watergate died down, he thought his diplomacy with China, a milestone in the history of American foreign policy, would resuscitate his standing in history. He had long admired Winston Churchill's *The Second World War,* published in eight volumes between 1948 and 1953. He recognized the importance of leaving a verifiable record.

It is a loss to history that Nixon did not start taping earlier. We have no private recordings of Nixon calling the *Apollo 11* astronauts during their lunar landing on July 20, 1969, nothing touching on the antiwar protests that caused the White House to be ringed with buses on November 15, 1969, in case protesters breached the fences, no taped telephone call to request his limo when Nixon spontaneously visited protestors at the Lincoln Memorial during the predawn hours of May 9, 1970, no recording of Nixon's famous Oval Office meeting with Elvis Presley on December 21, 1970.

After the disclosure of the existence of Nixon's tapes in 1973, they became the talk of the nation. At first, the president flatly refused to hand them over on the grounds of executive privilege and national security. Nixon always assumed that the tapes belonged to him. He most likely never intended to open them up to public scrutiny. The U.S. Supreme Court believed otherwise, ruling, 8–0, on July 24, 1974 that Nixon turn over subpoenaed tapes. Beyond the question of the tapes, or Nixon, the decision was a significant check on presidential power. No one would be above the law, not even the chief executive. The decision was a fatal blow to the Nixon presidency and led to Nixon's resignation only fifteen days later, on August 9. The tapes had damaged Nixon badly. They were a key source of evidence used against him in the Watergate affair, the "smoking gun" that shot lethal holes in his reputation. Under a cloud of shame, he fled the White House for Casa Pacifica, his home in San Clemente, California. There, he continued to fight for ownership of his tapes. Nixon died on April 22, 1994, never having recovered his tapes or his reputation, despite the admonition in President Bill Clinton's eulogy: "may the day of judging President Nixon on anything less than his entire life and career come to a close." In fact, Nixon's death removed the final major obstacle to the public release of his tapes.

In doing the tapes, journalists and historians share a debt to the University of Wisconsin historian Stanley Kutler. In 1992, Professor Kutler and the advocacy group Public Citizen sued to compel the National Archives and Records Administration (NARA) to expedite its review and release of the Nixon tapes. They argued that NARA had been too slow in adhering to its own release timetable. The lawsuit was settled in 1996, and approximately two hundred hours of tapes documenting abuses of governmental power were made public. Following that hotly contested decision, additional tape releases began in 1997 with the first batch of the Cabinet Room tapes. As coeditors of *The Nixon Tapes,* we are the direct beneficiaries of Kutler's advocacy.

Since the key Watergate tapes have been published, we have decided to focus this volume on 1971 and 1972, when non-Watergate topics dominated the conversations. This is not to deny the critical importance of the scandal that destroyed Nixon's presidency — rather, it is our desire to reveal everything that was recorded during his administration. The first two years of taping were heavy on foreign policy and electoral politics, primarily because that is what Nixon dwelled on the most. When it came to domestic policy, Nixon believed it could be delegated largely to John Ehrlichman, who ran the Domestic Council. Foreign policy, on the other hand, was what Nixon wanted to be remembered for. Nixon believed his tapes would prove that he was the key architect of the historic détente with the Soviet Union and the opening of diplomatic relations with China — not National Security Advisor Henry Kissinger or Secretary of State William Rogers (as they and the press often insisted). The Nixon tapes offer scholars an unparalleled opportunity to listen to Nixon's encounters with the principal world leaders and political confidants during his presidency. It is impossible to write seriously about the Cold War and the 1970s without consulting the tapes.

Nixon explicitly told both Haldeman and Butterfield that the tapes were not to be transcribed without his express orders, minimizing the chance that people could suspect that they were being taped. At least initially, the political uses of the tapes and a desire to control the depictions of meetings were also on the president's mind. Nixon wrote in his 1978 memoirs that he quickly "accepted [taping] as part of the surroundings." Our transcripts confirm that Nixon was not consciously aware of the taping system most of the time, at least not after the first few weeks. By 1973 Nixon couldn't even remember that Alexander Butterfield had supervised the installation of the system (or so he said), and he and Haldeman were sometimes unsure about exactly which locations were being taped.

The demise of the taping system in July 1973 was quick. Within hours of Butterfield's testimony, and with Nixon hospitalized with viral pneumonia, Chief of Staff Alexander Haig ordered the deactivation and removal of the taping system.

Other than Nixon, Kissinger had perhaps the greatest stake in the tapes after they became public. He questioned their benefit in *Years of Upheaval* (1982):

> What could anyone uninitiated make objectively of the collection of
> reflections and interjections, the strange indiscretions mixed with
> high-minded pronouncements, the observations hardly germane to
> the issue of the moment but reflecting the prejudices of Nixon's youth,
> all choreographed by the only person in the room who knew that the
> tape system existed? . . . The significance of every exchange turns on
> its context and an appreciation of Nixon's shifting moods and wayward

tactics. Remove these and you have but random musings — fascinating, entertaining, perhaps, but irrelevant for the most part as the basis for the President's actions.

Kissinger's warnings to the contrary, if one cannot accept the observations, justifications, and decision-making by primary American policymakers in the moment, what historical source can be considered truly valid? All historical sources contain flaws and bias. It is difficult to believe Kissinger's overwrought argument that Nixon choreographed all or even most of his conversations soley for the sake of posterity via the tapes. On the contrary, Nixon is sometimes recorded as forgetful about things that happened minutes before. This is not to say that Nixon did not on occasion manipulate conversations to get certain viewpoints on record. But while it is true that Nixon purposely laid down audio to promote his innocence in the Watergate debacle, that wasn't his modus operandi when it came to foreign policy.

The richness of the Nixon tapes is undeniable. We listened to them in real time and painstakingly transcribed the audio — which ranges in quality from clean to fuzzy to downright unintelligible. Many aspects of Nixon's personal idiosyncrasies and working style come into play when attempting to produce reasonably accurate transcripts of conversations. Problems such as the notorious ticking clock in the Executive Office Building, Nixon's penchant for listening to classical music while he worked, movements in the office, ineffective microphone placement, and poor recording materials have meant that some conversations will never be intelligible — no matter how much time, energy, or technological wizardry is at one's disposal. Stuttering, mumbling, verbal tics, low or quiet talking, accents, the occasional recording of foreign languages, and place names only increased the difficulty of producing faithful and accurate transcripts.

The National Archives and Records Administration has now released approximately three thousand hours of the tapes. The remaining seven hundred hours are still classified either because of national security concerns or to protect the privacy of individuals, including Nixon, his heirs, or people still alive who were secretly recorded. We have done our best in this volume to give a fair sampling of what was on Nixon's mind during his first term. We heard a lot of embarrassing, goofy, and comical moments on the tapes but included only a smattering. More seriously, we could have made this a compendium of "gotchas," as the tapes contain myriad bigoted slurs, put-downs, cursing, and off-color gossip, by Nixon and by others. We have included some of those moments (for example, Nixon's trashing of Indira Gandhi, Ted Kennedy, Henry Kissinger, Jews, military officers, and gays, among others). But our aim as presidential historians was to be fair-minded. We have not set up straw men just to knock them down. And we have not edited this volume in the hope of making Nixon look either "good" or "bad." We have left that determination up to the reader. We instead consider this volume a collection of accurate transcriptions on which future scholars and fellow citizens can rely.

As editors our process was fairly simple. Once we decided which conversations to include — no easy task — we typically trimmed them somewhat. Nonetheless, if you have fifty conversations about the timing of the Soviet summit and have room for one or two, difficult decisions have to be made. There is no question in our minds, after listening to thousands of hours, that Nixon was a ruthless political operator, fully in control of his White House foreign policy agenda. It is unlikely that an effort such as elevating the global position of China would have blossomed so early without his hubristic persistence. But peeking behind the curtain of Nixon's attempts to usher in the Grand Realignment is not always pretty. Throughout the tapes Nixon boasts that he is the defender of the U.S. Armed Forces in an age of antiwar doves. He truly feared that if he did not win reelection in 1972, a weak pacifist like Ted Kennedy or George McGovern would slash defense budgets to the detriment of American security. And yet Nixon, in private, regarded most of the military establishment with antipathy. That Nixon had little use for Democrats — except John Connally of Texas and a few others — is clear on these tapes. His disdain for the liberal press lashes out in anti-Semitic rants on occasion.

The publication of *The Nixon Tapes* coincides with the fortieth anniversary of Nixon's resignation. We hope this volume, at the very least, answers once and for all questions about why Nixon started taping in the first place and why he did not burn the tapes when he had the chance, and that it will illustrate the types of issues Nixon grappled with during his first term. The handling of a crisis — like Eisenhower in the U-2 affair or Johnson in the Dominican Republic intervention — can be reported on by the press daily. A Grand Realignment of the magnitude Nixon was aiming for — nothing short of a Wilsonian overhaul of the Great Powers — takes time to develop, as well as fully comprehend. These tapes provide the grist.

CAST OF CHARACTERS

Abrams, Creighton Commander, Military Assistance Command, Vietnam (MACV)
Abrasimov, Pyotr Soviet Ambassador to East Germany
Agnew, Spiro Vice President of the United States
Aiken, George U.S. Senator (R-VT)
Allison, Royal Member, U.S. delegation to the SALT talks
Alsop, Joseph Syndicated columnist, *Washington Post*
Alsop, Stewart Columnist, *Newsweek*
Andrews, John White House speechwriter
Antonov, Sergei Official, Soviet Committee for State Security (KGB)
Atherton, Alfred "Roy" Deputy Assistant Secretary of State for Near Eastern and South Asian Affairs
Bahr, Egon State Secretary, West German Chancellor's Office
Baker, Howard U.S. Senator (R-TN)
Barzel, Rainer Chairman, Christian Democratic Union Party (West Germany)
Beam, Jacob U.S. Ambassador to the Soviet Union
Bentsen, Lloyd U.S. Senator (D-TX)
Bhutto, Zulfikar Ali President of Pakistan
Biden, Joseph U.S. Senator-elect (D-DE)
Binh, Madame See Nguyen Thi Binh
Brandt, Willy Chancellor, West Germany
Brezhnev, Leonid General Secretary, Soviet Union
Bruce, David K. E. Chief, U.S. delegation to the Paris Peace Talks
Buckley, William F. Editor in Chief, *National Review*
Bundy, McGeorge President, Ford Foundation; former National Security Advisor
Bunker, Ellsworth U.S. Ambassador to South Vietnam
Burns, Arthur Chairman of the Federal Reserve Board
Bush, George H. W. U.S. Ambassador to the United Nations
Butterfield, Alexander Deputy Assistant to the President
Calley, William Former U.S. Army officer found guilty of the My Lai massacre
Carver, George Special Assistant for Vietnamese Affairs to the CIA Director
Ceausescu, Nicolae General Secretary, Romania
Chancellor, John Anchor, *NBC Nightly News*

Chapin, Dwight Deputy Assistant to the President
Chapman, Leonard Commandant, U.S. Marine Corps
Chiang Kai-shek President of the Republic of China (Taiwan)
Chiles, Lawton U.S. Senator (D-FL)
Church, Frank U.S. Senator (D-ID)
Clark, Ramsey Former Attorney General
Clifford, Clark Former Secretary of Defense
Colson, Charles Special Counsel to the President
Connally, John Secretary of the Treasury
Cooper, John Sherman U.S. Senator (R-KY)
Cronkite, Walter Anchor, *CBS Evening News*
David, Edward, Jr. Science Advisor to the President
Davison, Michael Commander in Chief, U.S. Army, Europe
Dean, John Counsel to the President
De Gaulle, Charles Former President of France
DeLoach, Cartha "Deke" Former Assistant Director of the FBI
DePuy, William Assistant Vice Chief of Staff of the Army
Dewey, Thomas Former Governor of New York (R)
Diem, Ngo Dinh Former President of South Vietnam (assassinated in 1963)
Dobrynin, Anatoly Soviet Ambassador to the United States
Dole, Robert U.S. Senator (R-KS); Chairman, Republican National Committee
Dulles, John Foster Former Secretary of State
Duong Van Minh, aka "Big Minh" Former ARVN general and South Vietnamese leader
Ehrlichman, John Assistant to the President for Domestic Affairs
Eisenhower, Dwight 34th President of the United States (1953–61)
Ellender, Allen U.S. Senator (D-LA)
Ellsberg, Daniel Former RAND analyst, coauthor of the Pentagon Papers
Farland, Joseph U.S. Ambassador to Pakistan
Farley, Philip Deputy Director of ACDA
Finch, Robert Secretary of Health, Education, and Welfare
Fisher, Max Philanthropist and advocate of Jewish causes
Ford, Gerald Minority Leader, U.S. House of Representatives (R-MI)
Frankel, Max Chief Washington correspondent, *New York Times*
Fulbright, William U.S. Senator (D-AR); Chairman, Foreign Relations Committee
Furtseva, Yekaterina Soviet Minister of Culture
Gardner, John W. Former Secretary of Health, Education, and Welfare
Giap, Vo Nguyen North Vietnamese Commander in Chief
Goldwater, Barry U.S. Senator (R-AZ); 1964 presidential candidate
Goodpaster, Andrew NATO Supreme Allied Commander, Europe
Graham, Billy Chairman, Billy Graham Evangelistic Association
Grechko, Andrei Soviet Defense Minister
Green, Marshall Assistant Secretary of State for East Asian and Pacific Affairs
Gromyko, Andrei Soviet Foreign Minister
Haig, Alexander Deputy National Security Advisor
Haldeman, H. R. "Bob" White House Chief of Staff

Halperin, Morton Former National Security Council staff member
Harriman, W. Averell Former head of the U.S. delegation to the Paris Peace Talks
Hatfield, Mark U.S. Senator (R-OR)
Heath, Edward Prime Minister of the United Kingdom
Helms, Richard Director of the CIA
Hilaly, Agha Pakistani Ambassador to the United States
Hirohito Emperor of Japan
Hoang Duc Nha General, ARVN
Hodgson, James Secretary of Labor
Hoover, J. Edgar Director of the FBI
Hua, Huang Chinese (PRC) Ambassador to the United Nations
Hubbard, Henry White House correspondent, *Newsweek*
Hughes, James Donald Deputy Commander, U.S. Air Force
Humphrey, Hubert Former Vice President
Hunt, E. Howard Former CIA officer; member of the White House "Plumbers"
Jackson, Henry "Scoop" U.S. Senator (D-WA)
Jarring, Gunnar Swedish diplomat; UN Special Envoy to the Middle East
Johnson, Lyndon B. 36th President of the United States (1963–69)
Judd, Walter Former U.S. Representative (R-MN)
Kalb, Marvin Reporter, CBS News
Kennedy, Edward U.S. Senator (D-MA)
Kennedy, John 35th President of the United States (1961–63)
Kennedy, Richard National Security Council staff member
Kerry, John Spokesman, Vietnam Veterans Against the War
Khiem, Tran Thien Prime Minister of South Vietnam
Khrushchev, Nikita Former General Secretary, Soviet Union
Kiichi, Aichi Japanese Minister of Foreign Affairs
Kissinger, Henry National Security Advisor
Kleindienst, Richard Deputy Attorney General, later Attorney General
Korologos, Thomas Deputy Assistant to the President for Congressional Relations
Kosygin, Alexei Premier, Soviet Council of Ministers
Kraemer, Fritz G. A. Pentagon analyst and Kissinger mentor
Kraft, Joseph Columnist, Field Newspapers Syndicate
Kuznetsov, Vasily First Deputy Soviet Foreign Minister
Ky, Nguyen Cao Former Prime Minister of South Vietnam
Laird, Melvin Secretary of Defense
Lake, Antony Former National Security Council staff member
Le Duan First Secretary, North Vietnamese Workers' Party
Le Duc Tho Special Advisor, North Vietnamese delegation to the Paris Peace Talks
Liddy, G. Gordon Member of the White House "Plumbers"
Lodge, Henry Cabot Director, U.S. delegation to the Paris Peace Talks
Lon Nol Prime Minister of Cambodia
MacGregor, Clark Counsel to the President for Congressional Relations
Malraux, André Former French Minister of Culture
Mansfield, Michael Majority Leader, U.S. Senate (D-MT)

Mao Zedong Chairman, People's Republic of China

Matskevich, Vladimir Soviet Minister of Agriculture

Mazurov, Kirill First Deputy, Soviet Foreign Ministry

McCain, John Commander in Chief, U.S. Pacific Command (CINCPAC)

McConaughy, Walter U.S. Ambassador to the Republic of China (Taiwan)

McCracken, Paul Chairman, Council of Economic Advisors

McGovern, George U.S. Senator (D-SD); 1972 Democratic presidential nominee

McNamara, Robert Former Secretary of Defense

Meany, George President, AFL-CIO

Mitchell, John Attorney General

Moorer, Thomas Chairman, Joint Chiefs of Staff

Murphy, Robert Former American diplomat; informal advisor to Henry Kissinger

Muskie, Edmund U.S. Senator (D-ME); 1972 Democratic presidential candidate

Nguyen Phu Doc Special Assistant to South Vietnamese President Thieu

Nguyen Thi Binh Chief Delegate of the PRG in South Vietnam

Nguyen Van Thieu President of South Vietnam

Nitze, Paul Member, U.S. delegation to the SALT talks

Nixon, Patricia "Pat" First Lady of the United States

Nixon, Richard 37th President of the United States (1969–74)

Noyes, Crosby Reporter and editor, *Washington Star*

O'Neill, John Leader, Vietnam Veterans for a Just Peace

Osborne, John F. Columnist, *New Republic*

Packard, David Deputy Secretary of Defense

Panetta, Leon Former Assistant to Secretary Robert Finch

Patolichev, Nikolai Soviet Minister of Foreign Trade

Pearson, Drew Former syndicated columnist

Pegov, Nikolai Soviet Ambassador to India

Percy, Charles U.S. Senator (R-IL)

Peterson, Peter Assistant to the President for International Economic Affairs

Pham Van Dong Prime Minister of North Vietnam

Podgorny, Nikolai Chairman, Presidium of the Supreme Soviet

Pompidou, Georges President of France

Porter, Sylvia Financial reporter and journalist

Porter, William Chief, U.S. delegation to the Paris Peace Talks

Price, Raymond White House speechwriter

Rabin, Yitzak Israeli Ambassador to the United States

Rather, Dan White House correspondent, CBS News

Reagan, Ronald Governor of California (R)

Reston, James "Scotty" Vice President, *New York Times*

Richardson, Elliot Secretary of Health, Education, and Welfare

Roberts, Chalmers Chief Diplomatic Correspondent, *Washington Post*

Rockefeller, Nelson Governor of New York (R)

Rogers, William Secretary of State

Rostow, Walt Former National Security Advisor

Rowen, Hobart Financial editor, *Washington Post*

Rumsfeld, Donald Counselor to the President

Rush, Kenneth U.S. Ambassador to West Germany

Rusk, Dean Former Secretary of State

Ryan, John Chief of Staff, U.S. Air Force

Sadat, Anwar President of Egypt

Safire, William White House speechwriter

Scali, John Special Counsel to the President

Schecter, Jerrold Moscow Bureau Chief, *Time* magazine

Schumann, Maurice Former French Minister of Foreign Affairs

Scott, Hugh U.S. Senator (R-PA)

Semenov, Vladimir Deputy Soviet Foreign Minister

Sevareid, Eric Journalist, *CBS Evening News*

Shakespeare, Frank Director, United States Information Agency

Shen, James Republic of China (Taiwan) Ambassador to the United States

Shultz, George Director, Office of Management and Budget

Singh, Swaran Foreign Minister of India

Sisco, Joseph Assistant Secretary of State for Near Eastern and South Asian Affairs

Smith, Gerard Director, ACDA

Smith, Howard K. Co-anchor, *ABC Evening News*

Snow, Edgar American pro–Chinese Communist journalist

Stalin, Josef Former General Secretary, Soviet Union

Stans, Maurice Secretary of Commerce

Stein, Herbert Member and later Chairman, Council of Economic Advisors

Stennis, John U.S. Senator (D-MS)

Stephens, Melville U.S. Army Vietnam veteran

Stevenson, Adlai U.S. Senator (D-IL)

Sullivan, William Deputy Assistant Secretary of State for East Asian and Pacific Affairs

Symington, Stuart U.S. Senator (D-MO)

Thieu, Nguyen Van See Nguyen Van Thieu

Thompson, Llewellyn Member, U.S. delegation to the SALT talks

Thompson, Robert British military officer and counterinsurgency expert

Thurmond, Strom U.S. Senator (R-SC)

Tito, Josip Broz President of Yugoslavia

Tower, John U.S. Senator (R-TX)

Train, Russell Chairman, Council on Environmental Quality

Tran Kim Phuong South Vietnamese Ambassador to the United States

Tran Van Lam South Vietnamese Foreign Minister

Tri, Do Cao ARVN general

Trudeau, Pierre Prime Minister of Canada

Vogt, John Deputy Commander, Military Assistance Command, Vietnam (MACV)

Volcker, Paul Undersecretary of the Treasury for Monetary Affairs

Volpe, John Secretary of Transportation

Vorontsov, Yuli Soviet Minister Counselor to the United States

Wallace, George Governor of Alabama (D)

Walters, Vernon Military Attaché, U.S. Embassy in Paris; Deputy Director of Intelligence

Warren, Gerald Deputy White House Press Secretary
Watson, Richard "Dick" U.S. Ambassador to France
Weinberger, Caspar Deputy Director, Office of Management and Budget
Westmoreland, William Former Commander, Military Assistance Command, Vietnam
  (MACV)
Weyand, Frederick Commander, U.S. Military Assistance Command, Vietnam (MACV)
Whitehouse, Charles Deputy U.S. Ambassador to South Vietnam
Xuan Thuy Chief, North Vietnamese delegation to the Paris Peace Talks
Yahya Khan President of Pakistan
Young, David National Security Council staff member
Young, Milt U.S. Senator (R-ND)
Zhou Enlai Premier, People's Republic of China
Zhou Shukai Republic of China (Taiwan) Ambassador to the United States
Ziegler, Ronald White House Press Secretary
Zumwalt, Elmo Chief of Naval Operations

ABBREVIATIONS AND TERMS

AA Antiaircraft
ABA American Bar Association
ABM Antiballistic missile
ACDA Arms Control and Disarmament Agency
AID Agency for International Development
AP Associated Press
ARVN Army of the Republic of Vietnam (South Vietnam)
CBU Cluster bomb unit
Central Committee Soviet high-ranking policy committee
ChiCom Chinese Communists (see PRC)
China Lobby Special-interest groups acting on behalf of the Republic of China (Taiwan)
ChiNats Chinese Nationalists (Taiwanese)
CIA Central Intelligence Agency
CINCPAC Commander in Chief, U.S. Pacific Command
COMINT Communications intelligence
CV U.S. Navy hull designation for aircraft carriers
DIA Defense Intelligence Agency
DMZ/DMZL Demilitarized zone
DRV Democratic Republic of Vietnam (North Vietnam)
FBI Federal Bureau of Investigation
GAO U.S. Government Accountability Office
GATT General Agreement on Tariffs and Trade
GCI Ground-controlled interception (of incoming aircraft)
Glassboro Reference to a 1967 U.S.-Soviet summit in Glassboro, New Jersey
GVN Government of Vietnam (South Vietnam)
HEW Department of Health, Education, and Welfare
ICBM (or IC) Intercontinental ballistic missile
JCS Joint Chiefs of Staff
LDP Liberal Democratic Party (Japan)
LOC Line of communication
LORAN Long-range navigation systems
MACV Military Assistance Command, Vietnam

MBFR Mutual and Balanced Force Reductions

MFN Most favored nation

MiG Mikoyan and Gurevich, a Russian aircraft manufacturer

Minuteman American land-based intercontinental ballistic missile

MIRV Multiple independently targetable reentry vehicle (ballistic missile)

NATO North Atlantic Treaty Organization

NCA National Command Authorities (Washington and Moscow)

NLF National Liberation Front (North Vietnamese political and military organization)

NSC National Security Council

NVA North Vietnamese Army

OP Observation post

PF North Vietnamese Popular Forces (irregulars)

POL Petroleum

Polaris/Poseidon American sea-based ballistic missile systems

Politburo Soviet executive committee composed of top Central Committee members

POW Prisoner of war

PRC People's Republic of China

PRG Provisional Revolutionary Government (Communist government in waiting)

PRO Public relations officer

Quadriad Nixon's economic kitchen cabinet (Connally, Shultz, McCracken, and Burns)

RF North Vietnamese Regional Forces (irregulars)

Safeguard American defensive missile system

SALT Strategic Arms Limitation Treaty (SALT I)

SAM Surface-to-air missile

SDS Students for a Democratic Society

Sihanoukville Location in Cambodia of intense fighting during the Vietnam War

SIOP Single Integrated Operational Plan (U.S. plan for nuclear war)

SLBM (or SL) Submarine-launched ballistic missile

TASS Russian state-run news syndicating agency

Trident British sea-based ballistic missile system

U-2 American reconnaissance aircraft

UAR United Arab Republic, which included the political union of Egypt and Syria

ULMS Undersea long-range missile system

UN United Nations

UP United Press International

VC Viet Cong

Vienna Location of public SALT talks

WSAG Washington Special Actions Group (subcommittee of NSC)

PART I

The Start of Taping to the China Announcement

February–July 1971

The start of taping

February 16, 1971, 7:56 a.m.
Richard Nixon and Alexander Butterfield
OVAL OFFICE

When Richard Nixon entered the White House on January 20, 1969, he rejected Lyndon Johnson's suggestion to secretly record his meetings and telephone calls. Presidents had taped for over thirty years, beginning with Franklin D. Roosevelt's Oval Office press conferences in 1940.

Two years later, in early 1971, Nixon changed his mind. He wanted an accurate, private record of his conversations. He did not want a system that had to be turned on and off, or was difficult to operate. The system the Secret Service installed was sound activated, so it recorded everything whenever Nixon was within range.

Taping started in the Oval Office and was later expanded to locations where the president spent time: various White House telephones, Nixon's office in the Executive Office Building, the Cabinet Room, and Camp David. The taping system was one of the most closely held secrets in the Nixon White House. Even many of Nixon's most senior assistants did not know they were being recorded. The existence of 3,700 hours of Nixon tapes was not revealed until July 1973, during Alexander Butterfield's sworn testimony before the Senate Watergate Committee.

Immediately following the installation of the taping system on February 16, 1971, Alexander Butterfield briefed Nixon on its operation. Nixon inquired if it would be possible to expand the system, which at the time operated only in the Oval Office. Butterfield acknowledged that it was possible to expand the system to include other locations, and that he had reviewed with Chief of Staff Bob Haldeman the potential use of the tapes for note-taking purposes.

• • •

NIXON: How does it work in here?

BUTTERFIELD: Well, they're [the Secret Service] sorting it out now. What activates it [unclear] locator on [unclear] the machine starts. [unclear] You might not be surprised by this [unclear], locator on. It tells us where you are, including [unclear] the office [unclear]. It's automatically working, so it's working now. [unclear]

NIXON: The system stays off, no? It's working?

BUTTERFIELD: You're wearing the locator right now and you're in the office [unclear] it depends on voice activation —

NIXON: Right.

BUTTERFIELD: — so you don't have to turn it on and off.

NIXON: Oh, this is good. Is there any chance to get two? You see, the purpose of this is to have the whole thing on the file —

BUTTERFIELD: Yes, sir.

NIXON: — for professional reasons.

BUTTERFIELD: Right, but if it were voice activated in the Cabinet Room, because there's so much going on there all the time —

NIXON: Yeah.

BUTTERFIELD: [unclear] it'd be using up stuff so fast [unclear], so —

NIXON: Yeah.

BUTTERFIELD: I mean you can come in but [unclear] chance that you turn it off and you've got no record. I can tell when it's on and off, but only from my office. There's no way of telling that [unclear]. When it is going on, you just have to remember we selectively [unclear].

NIXON: All right.

BUTTERFIELD: It could be used to make notes [unclear]. I was going over this [unclear] this morning with Bob.

NIXON: Uh-huh.

BUTTERFIELD: And we're going to monitor it. [unclear] He called my attention to this.

NIXON: How does that work, Alex? Does it work with you here?

BUTTERFIELD: Uh, no. I'm going to monitor this [unclear].

NIXON: I don't want it monitored, you see?

BUTTERFIELD: [unclear]

NIXON: What happens when a record is made — a tape?

BUTTERFIELD: A tape is made, yes, sir.

NIXON: And then it's, well —

BUTTERFIELD: There are only five people that know about it, outside of Haldeman, Ziegler, you, and me. Only five people in our office, [and] Secret Service — none of Taylor's people [Robert H. Taylor, the Secret Service special agent in charge of the White House detail for both Presidents Johnson and Nixon].

NIXON: No. No.

BUTTERFIELD: None of Taylor's people. They're all [unclear].

NIXON: Yeah, then it's used for, uh —

BUTTERFIELD: They only change the spools. They cannot monitor it.

NIXON: Yeah.

"I will not be transcribed."

February 16, 1971, 10:28 a.m.

Richard Nixon, Bob Haldeman, and Alexander Butterfield

OVAL OFFICE

In one of the first recordings made in the Oval Office, Nixon stated that the purpose of the system was that a record of every conversation would "be put in the file." This new system of recording meetings and phone calls was to replace the prior practice of having a note taker sit in on every meeting and prepare a memorandum for the president's files.

• • •

BUTTERFIELD: You don't have any questions on this other business that you might want me to answer now? This, this voice, I explained to the president that the secretary can't —

NIXON: No. Mum's the whole word. I will not be transcribed.

BUTTERFIELD: Correct.

NIXON: This is totally for, basically, to be put in the file. In my file. I don't want it in your file or Bob's or anybody else's. My file.

HALDEMAN: Right.

NIXON: And my [unclear] today. The whole purpose, basically, is [unclear] so there may be a day when we have to have this for purposes of, maybe we want to put out something that's positive, maybe we need something just to be sure that we can correct the record. But we're going to [unclear] that's all. And also, though, because I won't have to have people in the room when I see people —

HALDEMAN: That's right.

NIXON: — which is much better. I can have my personal conversations, which I want to have, and don't have the people there, you know, which I'd much rather do anyway, unless I feel that I need them there to carry out something or as buffers. Then I'll have them, of course. So I think it'll work fine. It's a good system.

HALDEMAN: Just don't tell anybody you've got it and don't try to hide anything [unclear] —

NIXON: [unclear]

HALDEMAN: Anytime that anything gets used from it, it's on the basis of "your notes" or "the president's notes" —

NIXON: That's right.

HALDEMAN: — or "my notes" or —

NIXON: [unclear] For example, you've got nothing to use from this today. Just forget it. File it. Everything today will be filed.

HALDEMAN: Yes.

NIXON: Fair enough?

BUTTERFIELD: I think it's gonna be a very fine system.

A Soviet nuclear submarine in Cuba

February 16, 1971, 10:48 a.m.
Richard Nixon and Henry Kissinger
OVAL OFFICE

In the late summer of 1970, Richard Nixon faced a situation that he and most other observers compared to the Cuban Missile Crisis of 1962. Intelligence reports and U-2 spy plane photographs indicated that the Soviet navy was not only servicing nuclear submarines at the small Cuban port of Cienfuegos but expanding the port there. Any such installation was unacceptable according to U.S. policy. In response, Nixon plied a course that he described as "strong but quiet diplomacy," although it was soon racked by leaks that made the news anything but quiet. Nixon chose not to comment on the reports of Soviet activities in the press, leaving them to circulate as unconfirmed rumors. He then used the press reports to spur his strategy, directing his security advisor, Henry Kissinger, to privately inform Soviet ambassador Anatoly Dobrynin that the president would allow Moscow to withdraw the plans for Cienfuegos before he turned the situation into a public confrontation — and a detrimental one — like the Cuban Missile Crisis. Within weeks, construction of the port stopped.

Nixon and Kissinger congratulated themselves on handling a dangerous situation with cunning, but in mid-February 1971 they had to measure yet another response, when the Soviets visited Cienfuegos again.

. . .

KISSINGER: The Russians now have put a tender back —

NIXON: Yeah, I saw that.

KISSINGER: — in Cienfuegos and a nuclear submarine next to it.

NIXON: Yeah.

KISSINGER: And that really is a kick in the teeth in the light of what you said on your —

NIXON: Yeah.

KISSINGER: — television program. Of course, it was produced by all these leaked stories that came out early in January saying that no one — well, that's not the story now.

NIXON: The Soviet Union [unclear] that was exactly what they did.

KISSINGER: That's right. But I then told —

NIXON: Isn't that what the understanding was?

KISSINGER: That is the understanding. But I told Ehrlichman early in January. There were two stories in the *New York Times* saying State didn't think — that State thought we exaggerated it and there was no problem. I told him — I said they'd be back there in six weeks and here they are. I think I ought to tell Dobrynin that until this damn nuclear submarine leaves I can't continue talking to him.

NIXON: Yeah. Well, now do you consider [unclear]? Do you consider that a violation of the understanding?

KISSINGER: I would think you should say something very enigmatic: "The Soviets know the understanding and the consequences."

NIXON: Yeah, I saw that. All right. You could say that. But as a matter of fact, they —

KISSINGER: This comes very close —

NIXON: They better not — it's servicing a nuclear submarine.

KISSINGER: Well, it says that when they have a nuclear submarine next to a tender —

NIXON: Mm-hmm.

KISSINGER: It's also — if we then say this is a servicing unit — if they can establish that, then —

NIXON: Yeah. Okay.

KISSINGER: Mr. President, they're really putting it to us. If they put a submarine into Havana and a tender into Cienfuegos, it would be rough but we could close our eyes. But I think on this one, I hate to run any risks on the thing that's going on now, but our experience with them is whenever we've played it hard — if they really want that summit and that agreement, particularly now that we're giving them their goodies on Berlin —

NIXON: Well, we have to do it because we said so, Henry.

KISSINGER: So —

NIXON: Don't you understand?

KISSINGER: Mr. President, what is —

NIXON: What are [unclear]?

KISSINGER: That's what they — sort of, yes. They're probably going to make the distinction between port visits and servicing. But — and it's all right if they have a port visit without the tender and the tender next to the —

NIXON: Well, when do we find out? You have to make the distinction if it's real. This is not a — this is what kind of a submarine?

KISSINGER: It's a nuclear-powered submarine.

NIXON: I know. With missiles?

KISSINGER: I don't know if it's an attack submarine.

NIXON: Yeah. But we consider that — oh, I know what we said: "nuclear submarine free."

KISSINGER: That's right.

NIXON: You didn't say anything about the other. Remember, I had to raise the question.

KISSINGER: That's right.

NIXON: As you'll recall, all the others said no, right?

KISSINGER: Well, because the British, the navy, everybody felt that that distinction —

NIXON: Is meaningless?

KISSINGER: — is practically meaningless. No, it's one of their games. They are just a bunch of thugs.

NIXON: They just are. And then — what else? Well, play it tough with the Soviet, too.

KISSINGER: And —

NIXON: [unclear] Yeah, I saw that and I said, "Well, here we go again." What a jerk.

KISSINGER: I'll just tell him until that submarine leaves Cienfuegos I won't continue my conversations with him. I think it will leave.

NIXON: Just tell him he started this thing.

KISSINGER: Right. I think it's the only thing he respects. I've got the whole thing set but I think if we let them put it to us and continue talking as if nothing were happening —

NIXON: I know. [unclear]

KISSINGER: You have publicly said "servicing in or from Cuban ports."

Afterword: The Soviet visit did not develop into further activity in Cienfuegos.

Lack of trust in the SALT negotiations
February 18, 1971, 9:56 a.m.
Richard Nixon and Henry Kissinger
OVAL OFFICE

By early 1971, President Nixon was growing impatient with the lack of progress in the negotiations over the Strategic Arms Limitation Treaty (SALT) talks between the United States and the Soviet Union.

During the 1968 presidential campaign, Nixon had promised to make SALT a top priority. Starting in his first year in office, the talks received continual attention as a proving ground for his international views and abilities, yet he was frustrated by the slow, detail-oriented process. The negotiations, staged in Helsinki and Vienna, soon formalized into semiweekly conferences between teams of up to a dozen diplomats. Overall, the personnel on each side numbered about one hundred. The American delegation was headed by lawyer Gerard Smith, who was also then serving as director of a federal agency called the Arms Control and Disarmament Agency (ACDA). During SALT, Smith later wrote, "White House suspicion of ACDA officials was often apparent." ACDA officials, however, should have been more suspicious in return, as Nixon and Kissinger began negotiating arms control directly with Moscow through secret memos, without telling the members of the SALT team.

• • •

KISSINGER: Well, what these guys want, they are afraid we — that this section is holding them to your position and they want a free hand to negotiate an ABM-only agreement.

NIXON: Who? Who's "they"?

KISSINGER: The ACDA people. And today they have — they leaked a column to Kraft, which I'm afraid is going to blow up my negotiation with Dobrynin because they put in there that — they put the whole debate on the arms control section, which I thought was entirely editorial. I didn't take it seriously, in there. And they said, it's, the reason is that I want to hold them to an option which they want to change. And, in effect, they said Rogers, which isn't true, and Smith, but we've got to think it through. I don't think Rogers has studied the problem with our position, but Rogers and Smith want to give them — have an ABM-only agreement. Now here, the Russians have already accepted your proposal. And now, they get this column. I would bet they are going to back off now, to see whether they can't get more.

NIXON: [unclear] the Russians very sanguine about what else but the [unclear].

KISSINGER: But it's one of the most irresponsible things that I've seen —

NIXON: [unclear] been through it with the Senate.

KISSINGER: And now, I couldn't really give a damn about that section, but they've now turned it into a damn extra distraction. On the negotiating position, which I didn't even realize it, Kraft has more detail in his column in three paragraphs than we have in ten pages. But I'm going to still try to because I don't want a huge fight on the report. But this —

NIXON: It's an act of spite.

KISSINGER: I thought, frankly, Mr. President, it was an issue of pure vanity. That they wanted to get credit, and they didn't want you to get credit.

NIXON: Yeah. But you think [unclear].

KISSINGER: That's right. [unclear] What is so revolting to me is that last August, when we could have had an ABM-only agreement, and when it could have helped you at the elections, they fought it, saying it was an election stunt.

NIXON: Hmm. Yeah. That I did what?

KISSINGER: Last August, we could have had an ABM-only agreement. The Russians offered it, and I checked with Smith. He said, "No, it would be an election stunt."

NIXON: Huh. Whose side is he on?

KISSINGER: That's what I'm beginning to wonder. I've got the correspondence —

NIXON: I'd just get Smith out of there if we can. I think we should send him to Vienna in the next few days. But, on this I want him out. And, he —

KISSINGER: No, what he wants is a completely free hand, so that he gets the credit for whatever is achieved. We've got the Soviet agreement to your secret memo, and —

[STAFF member interrupts.]

NIXON: All right.

KISSINGER: But I'll just get out.

"We can lose an election, but we're not going to lose this war."

February 18, 1971, 6:16 p.m.
Richard Nixon and Henry Kissinger
OVAL OFFICE

As of mid-February in 1971, 332,900 American troops were in Southeast Asia, down from a high of 536,100 at the end of 1968, the year Nixon was elected. The Americans were fighting to defend South Vietnam against the intention of the North Vietnamese to unify the two nations into a single Communist state. North Vietnam was supported in varying degrees by the Soviet Union and the People's Republic of China, yet the war was more than a proxy battle between superpowers.

As Nixon and Kissinger recognized, it was the resolve of the North Vietnamese and their loyalists in the South, the Viet Cong, that made victory elusive. Yet some scholars argue that Nixon and Kissinger's strategy in Vietnam was never more than securing a "decent interval" between American withdrawal and Communist takeover, a point that other scholars dispute, as have Nixon and Kissinger.

When reviewing the broad arc of Nixon and Kissinger's conversations related to Vietnam, it becomes clear that their moods on a given day were a direct reflection of how the war was going. Their feelings about the war evolved, just as the war itself evolved. For example, in this conversation late on another day of frustrating war news, the president made his views on the end of the war clear.

• • •

KISSINGER: Because they couldn't get a large number of troops that far south, they're not — the North Vietnamese are not limited by troops, by manpower. They're limited by the, by the difficulty of access.

NIXON: That's right.

KISSINGER: And they, that problem is solved by putting the Chinese in there. If we went north, if we landed in Haiphong, or if we landed in Vinh or someplace like that, then it's conceivable. But I don't think under present circumstances, they cannot.

NIXON: But the battle is shaping up on [unclear]?

KISSINGER: Yeah.

NIXON: Well, they're moving their divisions?

KISSINGER: Oh, yeah. But they are practically committing their entire strategic reserve force —

NIXON: What does the intelligence say? Are they still confused? Are they [unclear]?

KISSINGER: Now, they're pretty —

NIXON: What do the intercepts [unclear] when you were there?

KISSINGER: No. Well, now, they're pretty sure of what it is, and they're moving in whenever they can.

NIXON: Our diversionary tactics aren't fooling them much now?

KISSINGER: Well, they're fool — still fooling them some. They're holding some, but they're not moving anyone from the coast. [unclear] But, again, they —

NIXON: The South Vietnamese tried this torpedo boat to attack ships? [On the evening of February 17, two South Vietnamese torpedo boats out of Da Nang, on interdiction patrol in the South China Sea opposite Quang Binh province in southern North Vietnam, engaged and destroyed a North Vietnamese gunboat and a tanker.]

KISSINGER: They tried one, and they're trying another one tonight. They did one; they're doing another one tonight.

NIXON: Right.

KISSINGER: Now, some people scream that that's a violation of the understanding.

NIXON: By the South Vietnamese?

KISSINGER: Yeah, because they are technically part of the — but, I think you should just state that he — they violated the understanding on it they had with us.

NIXON: Oh, I see. The point being that they're part of the understanding?

KISSINGER: Yeah, but all attacks would stop on North Vietnam.

NIXON: What'll they do when you [unclear]?

KISSINGER: We think that this—

NIXON: Mm-hmm?

KISSINGER: — they've actually claimed they sank eight ships last time. I don't know whether that's true. Well, they've got one more scheduled. It's probably already over today, and that's all that's authorized [unclear].

NIXON: Well, how do you feel your people will think? WSAG and the rest? Are they all reasonably staying [unclear]?

KISSINGER: They're feeling fine.

NIXON: They're not getting jumpy? Do you know if Laird is a bit?

KISSINGER: Well, Laird is a little bit jumpy, but I had breakfast with him this morning.

NIXON: He told me he was going to see you.

KISSINGER: Yeah, I had breakfast with him, and he's all right.

NIXON: He's calmed down a little?

KISSINGER: Yes. Laird is a funny guy; he maneuvers like a maniac, but when the chips are really down, he's amazing, and he's also loyal to you—

NIXON: Depending on this.

KISSINGER: So I—

NIXON: Well, he is. He's a—

KISSINGER: I rather like Mel.

NIXON: He's a rascal, but by golly, he's our rascal—

KISSINGER: That's right.

NIXON: — and those kind of rascals [unclear]. I think, too, that on this thing, now, thank God, we're not going to lose it. That's all there is to it.

KISSINGER: In Laos—

NIXON: We can't. We can't lose.

KISSINGER: No, Mr. President—

NIXON: We—but, I can't. I am thinking more in terms of Vietnam. For us, the objective of all these things is to get out of there and [unclear] it's not going to be done. We can't lose. We can lose an election, but we're not going to lose this war, Henry. That's my view. Do you agree with it?

KISSINGER: I agree, Mr. President—

NIXON: I have a feeling about Laos as well.

KISSINGER: That's right.

NIXON: It isn't a question of losing it, but we might. I mean, that's it. This can make a hell of a difference. You say that the air is really pounding them pretty good?

KISSINGER: I thought the weather has been off and on, but for the next three days, it's expected to be perfect. It's perfect now, and they're pounding them. They're putting every B-52 they've got in there. They're putting [unclear]. They are pounding them around the clock.

NIXON: As far as on the ground, is there any way we can determine?

KISSINGER: They've set up special radars on the ground, things they can bomb within, I think, 150 yards of these, of the frontline troops. And —

NIXON: [unclear] —

KISSINGER: — [unclear] the South Vietnamese.

NIXON: 'Cause they're lining up these B-52s?

KISSINGER: Then, it's going to be awfully tough for them to take this pounding. They — they took a direct pounding in Khe Sanh three years ago.

NIXON: Did they? And that turned out all right for us.

KISSINGER: That worked out all right. We chewed up a lot of their troops. I've got a feeling, if things build up, I don't doubt that the press is going to try to, to cut us up. Now, the major work should be over. And they should stay out if they keep the roads cut. They already determined the Chup operation [a South Vietnamese operation to neutralize enemy headquarters and base area in the Chup plantation in Cambodia running parallel to Operation Lam Son 719 in Laos] is going extremely well.

NIXON: It seems to me, everybody's agreed. That's what I understand.

KISSINGER: Well, and Laos — we expected Laos to be much tougher. If they would roll over and play dead ten miles from their border, then they'd be completely through. On the other hand, all of the units they're going to lose up there [unclear] will not be ready for an offensive next year, or later this year.

NIXON: The main thing I'm interested in is just to be sure the South Vietnamese fight well —

KISSINGER: That's right.

NIXON: — because they're going to be battling in there for years to come. I guess if they fight well, North Vietnam can never beat South Vietnam. Never. And it's because our South Vietnam has more people, and more —

KISSINGER: And more equipment.

NIXON: What happens?

KISSINGER: North Vietnam will be at the end of their supply lines. The geography will work against it. And in the meantime, in Cambodia, for example, what they have done in the Chup plantation area is to introduce Cambodian troops behind the Vietnamese troops, so that they're beginning to take over some of the territory. And —

NIXON: The Cambodians are not becoming hysterical over Lon Nol['s increasingly authoritarian rule]?

KISSINGER: No, no. No. That's gone very smoothly. And also, it's interesting — of course, now, they don't report it anymore — there haven't been any road cuts — roads cut since the Chup plantation operation started.

NIXON: Did we draw them off?

KISSINGER: Oh, yeah. We are occupying them all. They can't move around the country now.

NIXON: Did they fight in there? Three hundred thousand that are in reserve, though, that's — Abrams believes is an adequate reserve for whatever North Vietnam —

KISSINGER: Yeah. I understand there's another division he's got in reserve, too. We've just got to stay cool now and, and shove in whatever reserves are needed. It's going to be tough, and we'll need strong will the next few weeks; there'll be panicky moments. But I think, having made strides, we ought to stay in there now through the rainy season — until the rainy season starts, and just chew them up.

NIXON: We've got to develop a position in terms of being able to stay as long as we're needed there.

KISSINGER: And Moorer gave me some statistics today on helicopter losses, that, actually, they, they lost only six more helicopters last week than in a normal operating week for all of Southeast Asia, and less than they did in a comparable week last year. That, even with the Laos operation, and even with all these horror stories, they lost fewer helicopters last week than they did in the comparable period —

NIXON: I wonder if the — that's good. I wonder what the situation is with regard to fellows like goddamn Gardner and Kennedy going. Kennedy started — you know, they started to press buttons, and the libs kind of all get together and go. But, this time, they aren't all going together [unclear].

KISSINGER: What I'm beginning to think —

NIXON: [unclear]

KISSINGER: — is that those who are, who are subject to Communist influence are all going nuts.

NIXON: Exactly.

KISSINGER: And —

NIXON: I think Gardner is subject to Communist influence —

KISSINGER: Yeah, I'm afraid so. And he's got this bastard Halperin, who used to be on my staff for three months. He was — he's become —

NIXON: He's got Halperin now?

KISSINGER: Yeah, who's his chief aide, apparently —

NIXON: Gardner's?

KISSINGER: Yes. But, at some moment, I'm going to surface some memos that Halperin wrote for me when he was trying to butter me up.

NIXON: Jesus! We still have Halperin. [unclear] Son of a bitch. What's happened to him?

KISSINGER: Well, I fired Halperin in July of '69 —

NIXON: Muskie is the man with Lake?

KISSINGER: He's —

NIXON: I noticed Muskie is reorganizing his staff, because Lake is still [unclear].

KISSINGER: I haven't seen him. Well, he's certainly not as sharp with policy research, which is what he said — he thought he was going to be. And, I don't think Lake is —

NIXON: He's not that gifted.

KISSINGER: (a) He isn't that heavy. (b) His knowledge is very out of date. Halperin doesn't have any insight on this, anyway, because he was across the street writing think papers for me; he didn't even see any documents. In fact, as I said, I got rid of him in July '69. But, Halperin is probably very much on the list in influence.

NIXON: Yeah, I know. I heard that he is.

KISSINGER: And, I think those are the guys —

NIXON: [unclear] overconceited. [unclear]

KISSINGER: And those are the guys that are going now.

NIXON: Like Gardner is? Who'd want that fool anyway?

KISSINGER: Well, it's a tragedy. At one stage, I thought Gardner had pot — potential presidential caliber.

NIXON: You ever hear Johnson's strategy? Gardner came in — I guess Johnson called him and Gardner came in — he said he just couldn't go with the emotional energy, you know, with Vietnam, and Johnson says, "Well, that's just fine. You can resign." He kicked him out. Just think. He shouldn't have done it. I mean, these guys [unclear]. If not, you kick 'em out. We can't just do it. One of these guys —

KISSINGER: Yeah. But, you know, to say your policy is a policy that leads to more war — what is their alternative? If they had the guts to say, "Just get out," but that they don't have the guts to say. I may have to ask John Dutton [unknown acquaintance of Kissinger's] for lunch sometime because he used to be an old friend and just ask him, as a friend, "Now, what the hell would you do if you'd been in this whole thing?" It's a pity to see a man of his caliber go to hell.

NIXON: Henry, [unclear] no hard feelings. You've got to see who finances [unclear]. It may be that. I've noticed that that's the fellow from Dreyfus [Corporation], [Howard] Stein is financing it. Stein is way left, you know.

KISSINGER: Yeah. Howard Stein —

NIXON: I think maybe he's just a pacifist. He's not to the left of these other financiers, who may be left, too.

KISSINGER: Yes —

NIXON: Well, Stein is. Isn't it amazing? Here is Stein, one of the richest men in the country, and he is so goddamn liberal.

KISSINGER: Well, but what you should see — Mr. President, you've changed the political landscape. I'm —

NIXON: I'm convinced of that.

KISSINGER: I am absolutely convinced that you [unclear] Vietnam, as you are now eighty percent of the way to doing, no matter what happens —

NIXON: [unclear] if we get knocked out of Laos, they'll succeed on that —

KISSINGER: Yeah, but we won't get knocked out of Laos. [unclear] —

NIXON: [unclear] The South Vietnamese are going to fight. They're going to stand and fight. Aren't they?

KISSINGER: Oh, yeah. So far, they have. They are, right now, moving cautiously to reconnect, so that they can cover each other with artillery. That's fine. We don't care, as long as they've got the roads cut. And, the — but I think we can win in '72. These guys won't be able to stand four years in the wilderness. More, you can fight them off cheap.

NIXON: [unclear]

KISSINGER: I know, but I —

NIXON: I'll get a new establishment.

KISSINGER: You can create your new establishmnt.

• • •

KISSINGER: Agnew would like to go to Asia again to visit some of our friends.

NIXON: Yeah. This is a question of honor, isn't it?

KISSINGER: I think it's not. I think we don't need any additional covenants on paper, now.

NIXON: I don't think it's the time. I think we should do it if we get anything in Laos.

KISSINGER: That's what I think. It would just —

NIXON: [unclear]

KISSINGER: Well, I just wanted to —

NIXON: We have been a little tentative, Henry, considering [unclear] —

KISSINGER: [unclear]

NIXON: You know what that is — you know what I mean? That's —

KISSINGER: Well, it's partly human. He likes to be in places where he gets a nice human reception.

NIXON: Yes, of course, Henry. He's [unclear] very sensitive [unclear] he gets a hell of a good reception. But, I must say, you know, after seeing Hubert [Humphrey] today with all his good qualities, can you really imagine Hubert —

KISSINGER: No way —

NIXON: — being, being here?

KISSINGER: Mr. President, I, I told Chancellor this. I said, "I love Hubert." And, I said, "But, can you really feel that if there was a Democrat here, this country wouldn't be torn to pieces?" He asked me what your — I said, "The thing you never get credit for is you've kept the Right in this country related to this, to the government, where, in all normal situations, if anyone else had had to do this difficult thing, and — so, you'll still turn out to be the best protection of the students who are rioting against you, even though they'll never thank you for it, because the alternative to you in 1968 was not a liberal Democrat, but a Wallace or a Reagan. And, I think that if this country is radicalized, it will not be from the Left. The Left will start it, but the Right will take it over."

NIXON: Yeah, maybe. But, right now, the important thing is to see this miserable thing through. They [unclear] the North Vietnamese [unclear] settle the thing. In fact, there it is. And, I suppose it's a long shot, it may just be the Chinese government saying it.

KISSINGER: No, that's against their national —

[unclear exchange]

KISSINGER: I mean, Duc called them their "hereditary enemy." What I think we can do, what I would recommend, Mr. President, in our game plan is if we get through this [unclear] bomb September, close to the election, I ask for a meeting with Le Duc Tho. Then have it October 15, and tell him, "Look, we're willing to give you a fixed deadline of total withdrawal next year for the release of all prisoners and a cease-fire." What we can then tell the South Vietnamese, "You've had a year without war to build up." And, I think, then, we can settle. We may have a fifty–fifty chance to get it.

NIXON: We should be able to get it. What the hell is their choice? [unclear]

KISSINGER: I think they may take it. But it's too early, because it would panic the South Vietnamese. But, after Thieu's election, I think we may be able to do that.

NIXON: Okay.

"There's an insurmountable problem between the two of them."
February 23, 1971, 10:05 a.m.
Richard Nixon, Bob Haldeman, and Henry Kissinger
OVAL OFFICE

Richard Nixon's distrust of the State Department went back at least as far as his energetic investigation of employees there in 1948–51, when he was a member of the House Un-American Activities Committee. He led the effort to implicate Alger Hiss for disloyalty and had several clashes with Dean Acheson, then secretary of state, or what Nixon termed the "Cowardly College of Communist Containment." During his first term as president, Nixon looked to an old friend and early supporter, William P. Rogers, to be secretary of state. Like Nixon, he came from humble beginnings, though he later attended some of the finest colleges in the East on scholarships. Rogers was a lawyer, not a career diplomat, but he was an articulate man and open-minded. He should have made a successful colleague for Nixon. By 1971, though, Nixon's attitude toward the Department of State had become more strained than ever. One complicating factor was the presence of Henry Kissinger in the White House.

At once shy and aggressive, Kissinger was a difficult personality for Nixon to control. The president unburdened himself on the subject of Kissinger in a brief talk with Chief of Staff Bob Haldeman, as the two were waiting for Kissinger to join them in a meeting.

• • •

NIXON: [The trouble] with Henry's personality, Bob, is it's just too goddamn difficult for us to deal with. I mean, let me just put it out there for a minute, for this reason. If we — you know, I have, I beat him over the head time and again, you know, to get him to — you see, he's trying to get involved in the Mideast again. I said, "Don't do it." I mean, I just don't encourage him, because I don't know whether that's going to come out or not. He's praying every day they'll have a war out there, because, you know — and I know that. [unclear] I went over that speech. That's why I sent Safire to see Rogers. But I use that only as an example.

We also have the problem too, that in these other areas, he is just so damn jealous of letting even Haig come in. You know, I had — I've called Haig a couple of times. And last night, I called Moorer, you know, to keep an eye on this myself. Keeping up on things — I should. I've got to. But I only mention that as a problem. He's a — maybe he was wrong, you know, in those negotiations, you know, to go to Paris and those trips.

HALDEMAN: Yeah.

NIXON: Not all the time, about it. That doesn't prove anything. I mean, many of us have been wrong.

HALDEMAN: Mm-hmm.

NIXON: He's always tried. He was wrong; he tried. But he was wrong in the sense of saying, "Well, they're ready to start jiggling," or "They're — I think they're going to twitch," or "We can just hope." You know, all that sort of thing. He has always felt that. His big pitch last night to me was: he was talking to Dobrynin, and Dobrynin raised the point today — yesterday that they [North Vietnamese] would be willing to talk again to him.

HALDEMAN: Mm-hmm.

NIXON: Now, I don't believe that at all. I think what has happened is that Henry has planted the idea again. Henry said, "This is the time." I said, "No, it isn't." It's not. I've got to tell him to waste no time. You see, the problem is that, let me put it: Henry's not a good negotiator. He just is not. He does not know — shit, he does not know how to — you've got to keep him the hell out of that sort of thing, because he's a — he's in negotiation just like he is in your staff meetings.

HALDEMAN: It's an attitude.

NIXON: He's an admirable worker, he's a superb writer, he's absolutely loyal to the country, to us, and so forth and so on. But in a deeper sense, a very, very difficult problem in working with these people that I must work around. We just can't have a blowup, you know.

I mean, I can't have a blowup with Rogers — or Laird, for that matter. And once Connally gets in there, he could blow up with him. I don't know. Maybe it's just a matter of — at the present time, of course, we're kicking around the possibility of wanting a letter to Kosygin.

HALDEMAN: Well, we're back on a sticky wicket there, because on the plane down to Florida, Rogers said he wanted to talk to you about it.

NIXON: About the summit?

HALDEMAN: He said, "You know" — you see, he doesn't —

NIXON: He thinks that we should have it next year.

HALDEMAN: He raised the scenario yesterday that — he said, "We aren't going to get a SALT agreement." Of course, Henry thinks we have one.

NIXON: Yeah.

HALDEMAN: And, therefore, we — then we might as well forget that and we ought to work to a summit next year. He raised it. I was over there for lunch yesterday going over personnel stuff with him. And he raised that whole thing again, that Moorer said; so then, he thinks the Russians will go along because they need this as much as we do. They've got their own —

NIXON: Reasons?

HALDEMAN: Mm-hmm. And I — well, I can't — you know, don't say anything to him at all —

NIXON: Letters.

HALDEMAN: — whatever he's talking about. And get —

NIXON: Henry's only reason, Bob —

HALDEMAN: This puts it — I don't know. It's this problem there that —

NIXON: It's a very difficult problem, because I can't conduct these negotiations, conduct, you know, independent discussions here without — Henry is — goddamn it, Bob, he's psychopathic about trying to screw Rogers. That's what it really gets down to. He wants to have a SALT agreement and a Berlin agreement. And I keep him out of the Mideast with, just by tugging. But he wants to do that without, so that — I don't think I'm overestimating the problem. I think it's a very serious one.

HALDEMAN: Oh, it is.

NIXON: He's just goddamn hard. I mean, I can't — don't you agree?

HALDEMAN: And we kept, you know, patching it over with Band-Aids and airbrushing it, but — which we do. Maybe we keep on doing that now. But I'm not sure. It flares up and down and — the problem really is, though, at least I think, and as I found when — if you face that there's an insurmountable problem between the two of them, Henry is clearly, to me at least, more valuable than Rogers is.

NIXON: That's true.

HALDEMAN: And more irreplaceable than Rogers is.

NIXON: True. True. Because I don't trust the State Department.

HALDEMAN: But if Henry wins the battle with Rogers —

NIXON: That's right.

HALDEMAN: — and resulting in Rogers going, then I'm not sure Henry's going to be livable afterwards, livable with afterwards.

NIXON: He's going to be a dictator.

HALDEMAN: And —

NIXON: You got to remember, too, the need for Henry becomes less as time goes on. Do you really realize that? He divides us. And you know —

HALDEMAN: But it takes — you see, he's right on a lot of things —

NIXON: I know.

HALDEMAN: — like procedurally, that don't interest you and —

NIXON: That's right.

HALDEMAN: — that we don't want to be bothered with and shouldn't be.

NIXON: That's right.

. . .

NIXON: You've got to remember that Henry is a terribly difficult individual to have around, you know, in terms of our, just our whole general morale. I mean, he just really is, Bob. It's too damn bad. But he's making himself so, and I think it's because of his, this psychotic hatred that he has for Bill. What the Christ is the matter with him? What the hell is it? I mean, he — hardly anybody believes that — is Rogers out to get him? Is that it? He's constantly saying, "I don't want to — I can't go into it." Then he shouldn't mention it to me. He says, "I can't go into it now, but —" Well, Christ, then he shouldn't tell me. I shouldn't be worried about things that he can't go into now. He just says —

HALDEMAN: Did he raise that with you?

NIXON: Every day. It's something or other. Well, you know about what's, the way State's cutting him out, cutting us up, the things they are doing, the horrible things they are doing.

HALDEMAN: Yeah.

NIXON: And then I find it in Joe Kraft's column [Kraft's February 18 column stated that Kissinger was "in the thick of a furious internal fight about the next American move in the arms control negotiations"]. Now, what the Christ bit of difference does that make?

HALDEMAN: Well, they leak something big they're going to want to hit you on today.

NIXON: Sure.

HALDEMAN: I don't know if you saw that story today, put out that State had triumphed over the NSC and got SALT removed from the State of the World message, the basis on which the SALT talks are [unclear]. Not a lot on that other story.

NIXON: Kraft?

HALDEMAN: No, it's not a piece of his.

NIXON: Just say — I want you to send a memorandum to Rogers and just say that "the president's on this and he thinks this is not helpful. He says it makes the task exceedingly more difficult. Really believe that you —" Well, why don't you call him? Say, "Look, that's it. That's a real tough thing." You know, "We have enough [with] our routine to do anything about whether someone would do such a thing." You see, Rogers overlooks a lot of his damn people too. He will not discipline them. It doesn't make a goddamn bit of difference whether SALT's in the State of the World or not. You know it's — nobody gives a shit, except Henry.

. . .

[KISSINGER joins the conversation.]

NIXON: Let me ask this: where does everything stand now? Do I understand that — did we, with regard to a letter to Dobrynin — to Kosygin, have I sent a letter to Kosygin?

KISSINGER: No, but —

NIXON: That wasn't a letter.

KISSINGER: No, what I have done is —

NIXON: Is to suggest —

KISSINGER: No. I have given a draft letter —

NIXON: Oh.

KISSINGER: — to Dobrynin —

NIXON: Yeah.

KISSINGER: — which Kosygin will approve.

NIXON: Yeah. And then —

KISSINGER: Or not.

NIXON: And then he will clear that through the bureaucracy? Is that the goal?

KISSINGER: Then, if he approves it, then we'll know what his answer will be too.

NIXON: Yeah.

KISSINGER: He will give me a copy of his answer and I'll edit that.

NIXON: Mm-hmm. Mm-hmm.

KISSINGER: That Dobrynin is sharp as a tack. The way that he edited that letter of yours —

NIXON: Good.

KISSINGER: — actually strengthened it.

NIXON: Yeah. Now, the point is, that having done that, then when we get it back, we just bring in the people and say, "Look, here's the" — what do I do?

KISSINGER: If they accept our proposal, you're going to have more trouble with Smith. Smith will tell you they won't accept it.

NIXON: That's all right, because I'll just say that I — that I've decided to take an initiative here and I'm going to do it. And that's that. I'm not going to screw around with Smith on SALT anymore.

KISSINGER: And, of course, today they have another story that they made me back off SALT.

NIXON: I saw that.

KISSINGER: And —

NIXON: I saw it. Let me first —

KISSINGER: And it's going to hurt me again with Dobrynin.

NIXON: Is it? That's a screw-up. That's — that doesn't make any difference, a long op-ed on this whole — but it's interesting. We have a section on SALT.

KISSINGER: Yeah, but I yielded and I —

NIXON: You gave in?

KISSINGER: For the sake of peace with Rogers, I yielded on it.

NIXON: Did you?

KISSINGER: It was frivolous. Well, because I don't want to come to you —

NIXON: No, but how much did you —? You had something, but you didn't take the whole section on SALT?

KISSINGER: Oh, no. But I took out much of it. And it's pure mischief. They had me on the phone ten times in one day. And then they demanded to see you. I didn't want to put you in the position where you would have to rule either for me or for Rogers.

NIXON: Yeah.

KISSINGER: Because I don't think it's the right position for you to be in.

. . .

NIXON: Getting back to the other thing.

KISSINGER: But I —

NIXON: On Berlin. How do we do the —? Don't worry about this one now. But on Berlin —

KISSINGER: Well, on Berlin, we —

NIXON: There — the deal there, it's all in channels —

KISSINGER: Yeah.

NIXON: — so we don't have to worry about that.

KISSINGER: With the Berlin deal, the only pity is you won't get the credit.

NIXON: Yeah. Well, let's try.

KISSINGER: Well —

NIXON: Let's leak a story.

KISSINGER: But we can leak it. I'll tell you when we get the — after the agreement is signed.

NIXON: No. No, I don't want it before — I want it before the agreement is signed.

KISSINGER: Well, before the agreement is signed —

NIXON: I'm going to leak the story that we're doing it. Screw them.

KISSINGER: That's right. Of course —

NIXON: We've got to leak stories that we — well, then, why not leak it now?

KISSINGER: Well, because it's too early. But this is going to be obvious long before there's a signature. We'll have plenty of opportunities.

NIXON: When do you think Berlin will come off?

KISSINGER: Depending on how quickly we can move the Germans, within two months.

NIXON: All right. Send a letter — send a message to Rush and say that he should indicate that the president is playing a personal role in these negotiations.

KISSINGER: Right. To whom?

NIXON: The press. When he's talking to them, you know, on this background.

KISSINGER: Yeah.

NIXON: That the president is personally in charge of these negotiations. Let's just get that in.

KISSINGER: I think if — well, Mr. President, if we could wait a week —

NIXON: All right.

KISSINGER: — until we could get some answers —

NIXON: All right, fine. As soon as you get the answers —

KISSINGER: Otherwise, if it fails —

NIXON: As soon as you get the answers, and you think it's on stream, have him put out the fact that the president is personally — and have him put it out. It's much better than having it come from here.

KISSINGER: Because at this point —

NIXON: Then, you see, then we could — then the people, the other people in the government, they can't claim they did it. But I want them to know that we did it.

KISSINGER: Because at this point, Mr. President, we're not — this is not like SALT. SALT, you can make one big play.

NIXON: That's right.

KISSINGER: And they'll accept it or not.

NIXON: And then have the State Department trying to —

KISSINGER: And I think they'll —

NIXON: Now, on this one — on SALT — my view on that is that, if they come back and accept this thing — and you think they may now.

KISSINGER: Oh, yes. I think —

NIXON: If they come back and accept it, then my view is that, I just call in — well, I'd have to have that son of a — I have to have Smith in too, don't I? What do I do? We'll have an NSC meeting or what? Or just have him —

KISSINGER: Well, I'd call in Rogers and Smith and I'd say, "I've thought about it."

NIXON: Yeah. Yeah.

KISSINGER: Actually, the *New York Times* yesterday had an editorial suggesting you write a letter to Kosygin.

NIXON: Yeah. Yeah.

KISSINGER: So you say, before they go you want to break the deadlock. And this is the letter you're going to write. Now, Smith is going to have a heart attack at that point.

NIXON: Smith? I'll call in Rogers to tell him.

KISSINGER: And tell Rogers then.

NIXON: And he just tells Smith. And that's it. I'm going to tell Bill that's the way it's going to be.

KISSINGER: Right.

NIXON: That's better. I think with Rogers along, I could say that I have strong feelings about this.

KISSINGER: And I can get Laird aboard.

NIXON: I'm so sick of that Smith anyway. I don't like him. I don't trust him.

KISSINGER: Well, I think we can get Laird aboard. The only thing that's going to cause trouble — there are two things that are going to cause trouble. One, they can't surface. That's why they didn't want the long SALT section, because they didn't want to get you — the section is long but not as detailed as it was. But [that's] not important. They don't want you to get the credit for it, but they can't say that. The second thing they won't want is the change in the position on the ABM, because they'll say the Russians won't accept it.

NIXON: Could you get Laird to agree to that?

KISSINGER: But Laird will back that. I've already talked to Laird, because we couldn't do it without Laird.

NIXON: [unclear] Well, go ahead and work that out.

KISSINGER: But to show you something of this labor of Dobrynin: when I gave him the letter to Kosygin —

NIXON: Mm-hmm.

KISSINGER: — he didn't say, "I have to refer that to Moscow." He said that too, but he immediately started editing it to see what would be easier for them to take and what wouldn't. And I had a section in there about MIRVs. And he said, "Why don't we both drop that one, since it's embarrassing for you?" And he's got a good point. I had in the letter, "MIRVs would be permitted." He said, "Of course, they'll be permitted."

"The whole damn Defense Department is PR crazy."

February 26, 1971, 5:15 p.m.
Richard Nixon and William Rogers
OVAL OFFICE

The Soviets pressed to divide the definition of "strategic" weapons into separate categories: defensive, including mainly the new antiballistic missile (ABM) systems, and offensive, including an array of various warheads. Nixon was in favor of the division. The U.S. negotiating team didn't want to cede anything until all of the points had been addressed. Nixon discussed the matter with Rogers, treating it as a public relations matter.

• • •

NIXON: I'm not ready to tell you, but I've been doing a little thinking about the SALT thing, and I'm — I want to, before they go back on March 15, it may be that I may want to either say something or write a letter or something else, [unclear] to have some outcome [unclear]. Let me put it this way: I think the — I'm not as bearish about this as some who are willing to do something. I'm inclined to think that right now they want to do something. Now, let me say on that, for your information, I [unclear]. I want to talk, I want to think about it for a while. I just wanted to tell you about it now. It would have to be before March 15, if anything I've said here that — but I would like to do it in terms of a, where, if I do it, here, where you inform [unclear] to tell Smith but on a, on an absolutely — I don't believe him, I don't have any confidence in him, basically, as a — and particularly his shop [the Arms Control and Disarmament Agency], naturally. And, now, understand, I think he does as well as he can, considering the people that are there. But I, I feel that he looks at this thing [unclear] but, as anybody who would be involved in long negotiations, are personally, sometimes in minuscule terms. And also that, he just has too much of a tendency sometimes, he doesn't want to fight with his own people.

ROGERS: Hmm.

NIXON: Now, this is a big play, you know, when you really come down to it, if there's any agreement with the Russians, this might be it, you know, the ABM and something else. But if we do it, I think we've got to get the credit here. I don't believe it should be in Vienna. You know what I mean?

ROGERS: Sure.

NIXON: So give some thought to that, but I sense he — I don't know what I'm going to do, but I would particularly suggest that we, we ought to keep that very closely held to ourselves, you know.

ROGERS: I was asking Bob Haldeman the other day, what you — I felt, sort of, basically, my own feeling is that if we could get an agreement which became effective at the end of this year. By "effective," I mean "signed." It would be effective sometime this year or the beginning of the next, and as long as it didn't cause us to have — be at any, be at any disadvantage, as long as we have —

NIXON: Right.

ROGERS: As long as we have, we have the opportunity to develop all the things we would develop anyway —

NIXON: Mm-hmm.

ROGERS: — and really stop the things that we probably would stop anyway —

NIXON: Well, I'm on the same track. I've been thinking a lot about it. I've told Haig and Kissinger [unclear] the steps that I can think of, and yourself, and now we really have studied it, but I think something could come of it. I think something might come of it, because I think maybe they could use something, too. What the hell?

ROGERS: It's just a matter of saving some money. That's all [unclear].

NIXON: Say that we do.

ROGERS: Well, I've been thinking along the same line. As a matter of fact, I —

NIXON: But also, it could be an enormously good thing to have if we could get something said or done, or at least some indications of progress this spring, well, which would take the heat off some of this press thing, too [unclear].

ROGERS: Well, I think — I really — I don't think Mr. Brezhnev [unclear] these people left out. I think what we should —

[unclear exchange]

NIXON: [unclear] the damn television and, incidentally, they're absolutely right. [unclear] I don't look at it, but I read it and I know how horrible it is. Bill, the whole trouble is, I think you can't blame Mel [Laird]. You can't. The whole damn Defense Department is PR crazy.

ROGERS: Hmm.

NIXON: And I personally think he felt, I would have been a lot more tough on this end. Let 'em squeal. Let 'em squeal. Look at Woody Hayes after a football game.

ROGERS: Yeah.

NIXON: Vince Lombardi—whenever he lost a game, he wouldn't let anybody in for thirty minutes. Ted Williams?

ROGERS: Of course.

NIXON: You know, he never lets the press in after the foot—the baseball players lose a game for a half-hour. Oh hell, this is war.

ROGERS: Well—

NIXON: And, so, the press squeals at Ted Williams. And most of the people say he's right. What do you think?

ROGERS: Sure.

NIXON: I tell you, God, I just think we're just going crazy to get ourselves beat over the head, bloodied. I talked to Moorer afterwards, after you had, and I said, now [unclear]. And he's good. He said, "Now, I'm going to do everything I can." And he will. Jesus, you're absolutely right. In a war, you'd never let a guy talk to the press after he'd been in a battle, would you?

ROGERS: No.

NIXON: When he's shell-shocked?

ROGERS: What we used to do is, afterwards, we took them—

[unclear exchange]

ROGERS: [unclear] when I was in the—

NIXON: Naval Intelligence?

ROGERS: Yeah. And what we used to do is, when we were ready, then we would let them go and talk to the press. You see, we didn't do it under orders, we just did it—

NIXON: Yeah.

ROGERS: It made sense. I mean, that was the choice we had to make. So, we just didn't go out and talk to the press until we were ready.

NIXON: Look, on the SALT thing, let us develop our own strategy. Let Smith continue to work on table support. We must do better, 'cause it has to be done that way. Well, I'll see you.

ROGERS: All right, Mr. President.

"This whole SALT mess."

February 26, 1971, 5:47 p.m.
Richard Nixon and Henry Kissinger
OVAL OFFICE

Two minutes after Rogers left the Oval Office, Kissinger walked in. The contrast in Nixon's conversations with the two is striking, in terms of the level of discourse and the decisions made.

• • •

NIXON: Hello.

KISSINGER: Hi.

NIXON: I thought you were going to see him.

KISSINGER: I'm seeing Dobrynin at—

NIXON: Right.

KISSINGER: —six. And I have an answer from Rush on Berlin. And I'll just put that to him.

NIXON: Where are you going to see him? Over here?

KISSINGER: In the Map Room here.

NIXON: Right. Because—

KISSINGER: I have two—three items—and one other thing.

• • •

NIXON: As far as I'm concerned, I'm not too—

KISSINGER: And also—

NIXON: I just thought that psych—I wasn't doing it because we lost the hill [Hill 31, a key defensive position in Laos, overrun by North Vietnamese troops on February 25]. I just thought that psychologically it was a damn good thing to keep banging them there.

KISSINGER: And also, I must then say, the day after the TASS statement, to then hit them—

NIXON: Yeah.

KISSINGER: I'd just like to see whether we get an answer from Kosygin to your letter.

NIXON: What is the—what's your evaluation of the TASS statement? I think what you did was written last night.

KISSINGER: My evaluation is that that was the—

NIXON: Why did they move it two weeks? And why did they make it? Because they're—?

KISSINGER: I think it's the minimum that they could do. They would have had a hell of a lot of explaining—

NIXON: You mean they must have had a lot of argument before they decided to make it?

KISSINGER: Well, I think they must have had some hell from Hanoi. Why—

NIXON: Oh.

KISSINGER: —why it is this that they didn't make any statement of support.

NIXON: I see.

KISSINGER: And China must have attacked it. And I think it's the minimum that they can do. But maybe it indicates that they're shifting to a tougher line. I just—

NIXON: I doubt it.

KISSINGER: You couldn't draw the conclusion—after Cambodia [the Cambodian incursion, the American–South Vietnamese sweep into Cambodia that began on April 29, 1970, for the South Vietnamese and the following day for the Americans and ended on June 30] they made an immediate statement. They held a press conference. They went into high gear. This time they said nothing officially—

NIXON: I wonder if they're doing it because they think that maybe they'll get public support — try to stir up, gin up support in this country.

KISSINGER: I think that's one of the factors.

NIXON: That's what I was thinking it would be.

KISSINGER: And I think that the public support is —

NIXON: They always react to that, Henry.

KISSINGER: Yeah.

NIXON: But as a matter of fact, it's interesting to note, as they said to me, the doves have one hell of a time getting — they're split without Symington, Aiken, and all these other faces, it'll be faceless.

. . .

NIXON: Well, how did you feel your — what's your conversation supposed to be about with him today?

KISSINGER: Berlin.

NIXON: Oh.

KISSINGER: And I just wanted to — he might, might have an answer from, well, on the letter, but we'll have to see.

NIXON: Probably not. I've prepared the way, incidentally, for the summit thing. Not just the summit, but the SALT thing. I told Rogers I didn't have any confidence in Smith. I didn't want him to have any discussions with him until I had him in. But I said, "I've been thinking a great deal about this whole SALT mess. I might want to make a statement or I might want to write a letter or something." And I said, "If I do, look, I'll tell you, and you're going to tell Smith, but I'm not going to go let him in."

KISSINGER: No. Excellent.

NIXON: Now, you see, I've figured we really don't need him. If he doesn't come in, forget it. My view is that we get it, then I'll get the letter, and I'll write it out because I've already decided on it. This is it. I'm going to do this on my own.

KISSINGER: No, I think, Mr. President, if he doesn't come, you ought to make a public statement offering it publicly.

NIXON: That's what I was thinking, Henry.

KISSINGER: I mean, if Kosygin —

NIXON: Oh, I know.

KISSINGER: If we don't get an answer, then I would make a very forthcoming offer.

NIXON: And before it, so people — so that we can — I told Bill, I said, "We have got — I've got to take credit," I told him, "for anything that happens in arms control." And I said, "It can't be Smith who's going to get the credit." I said, "He's a small player and I don't trust him." I put it right to him. I said, "Therefore, I'm going to make a statement or" — I didn't indicate a letter to whom — but "I've decided I might want to write a letter and make a statement before the thing begins. And then we're going to go back. I won't — I will not discuss it with Smith." So we're all set on that.

KISSINGER: Okay.

NIXON: Now, "The ball's in your court and it can go over if you can." I hope it's a letter.

KISSINGER: Oh, that would be spectacular.

NIXON: That would be great.

KISSINGER: And that would shut up the doves a bit.

An offensive in Laos

February 27, 1971, 9:18 a.m.
Richard Nixon, William Rogers, Melvin Laird, Richard
Helms, Thomas Moorer, and Henry Kissinger
OVAL OFFICE

Even as Nixon reduced American troop strength in Vietnam, he expanded the war geo-graphically with a 1970 strategic bombing campaign over Cambodia. Early in 1971, he was faced with related decisions regarding Laos, where the South Vietnamese were poised to begin an offensive called Operation Lam Son 719. The ultimate goal of the offensive was to cut the North Vietnamese supply network of routes known as the Ho Chi Minh Trail by capturing key bases in the neighboring nation. By law, American soldiers could not fight in any country beyond the Vietnam border, but Nixon made a bold decision to offer mas-sive noncombat military support to South Vietnamese troops, an overall shift known as Nixon's "Vietnamization" of the war.

On February 27, about two weeks after the operation began, Nixon met with his ranking advisors to discuss the fighting and its ramifications on the home front. Secre-tary of Defense Melvin Laird was a proponent of Vietnamization, as a means of moving Americans out of harm's way. The chairman of the Joint Chiefs of Staff, Admiral Thomas Moorer, was not intrinsically any more interested in Vietnam than was Laird, but he did believe that if the United States was in a war, it should make an all-out effort to win.

• • •

NIXON: All right, so what the main, main point is: what about all the hills we lost yes-terday, and what's the situation? At any rate, are we ready to bug out, and so forth and so on, or not? I think I know the answers, but quickly tell us what has happened overnight, since — in the last twenty-four hours? Is it up, down, or sideways?

MOORER: All right, sir. First, this week we had this operation [Operation Toan Thang during January] down in the south in Cambodia and, as you know, there was very heavy fighting right there at [unclear] where over two hundred of the enemy were killed —

NIXON: Good.

MOORER: — very light casualties on the part of the South Vietnamese. The operations are continuing on schedule. As you know, sir, this operation will go till 1 July, and then making a —

NIXON: Yeah.

MOORER: — deliberate, thorough —

NIXON: Yeah. Tom [Moorer], with regard to that operation, is it — could it be fairly safe to be said at the present time the death of Tri has not, to an appreciable extent, reduced the effectiveness — the verve of the operation [Lam Son 719]?

MOORER: Oh, that's right. That's quite true.

NIXON: In other words, they were able to change commands.

MOORER: We had the one report —

NIXON: This is not unimportant —

MOORER: — that the —

NIXON: In one, they thought it was Tri, only it didn't —

MOORER: Yes, sir. We, we had one report that the — of course, the — that some of the senior commanders actually were —

NIXON: Yeah?

MOORER: — upset about his —

NIXON: [unclear]

MOORER: — actions. On the other hand, what they want is contact, they say, and then they are [unclear] go right back to —

NIXON: Yeah.

MOORER: — the very top [unclear].

NIXON: You've already answered this question. That's —

MOORER: I think the answer to that's no, sir —

NIXON: [unclear] agree on the answer to this question. You know, we all know from, from the historical thing. Everybody, everybody — I'll ask it — almost everybody agrees that [unclear] had Stonewall Jackson been at Gettysburg, the South might have won the war. So, the general does make a difference.

ROGERS: That's right.

LAIRD: It would have made a difference —

MOORER: Mr. President —

NIXON: Huh?

LAIRD: It would have made a hell of a difference there.

NIXON: Because Stonewall Jackson would have, instead of marching those poor bastards across that [unclear]. [laughter] He'd have gone around and taken them from the rear. Go ahead.

MOORER: Yes, well, now I wanted to describe to you, I guess, a pretty significant thing we got over the evening. One is, as I told you when I briefed you on this plan, I think we left a — the idea for the First Regiment of the First Division to move prior on this highway here, 914, and for the Third Regiment to come across here. They are grouping these battalions now into — so that they'll have their whole organization intact, of the — with the — this is what these movement flags mean as they move the First and the Third Regiments up into position. They're moving there, as you know, they already — then there are reporters traveling this road, though, operating along this road, and there's nary a bomb-free area from here, down to here. We're not bombing in there because the ARVN is patrolling that road. Next, up here, where there's been quite a bit of COMINT about Fire Support Base 31A. It was an area called Hill 31. And there's some very heavy fighting in this area.

NIXON: Well, the score last night: they had lost 450 South Vietnamese killed?

LAIRD: No, sir, that's not correct.

MOORER: That's not right. We don't have reports. This battle is still going on, and they report as follows: that the South Vietnamese are, are dug in two hundred meters from their previous position, and that the North Vietnamese have taken a part of the hill; that they are still fighting. [unclear] the fact is reported that 250 North Vietnamese dead, 100 along — right on the base, I think in the center of the base, and another 150 or so in the vicinity. Two kilometers to the east, they reported another 200 dead. And I think the radio this morning was talking about very large numbers of North Vietnamese casualties. That's the first time that I've heard anything at that — in that direction. But, there's been a, a series of attacks — tank fights. They've —

NIXON: What about Laird's [unclear]?

MOORER: They reported ten tanks destroyed: one by artillery and nine by Tactical Air. And then, there was a tank fight by — between the ARVN tanks and the North Vietnamese tanks along this Road 92, just at dusk — which would be just a day like this morning — where there were three North Vietnamese tanks destroyed and one South Vietnamese tank destroyed. So, the issue is a stalemate down there, but I think the significant thing is that the South Vietnamese are staying there and fighting. As you know, they brought the armored reinforcements up here, and they have linked up with one company, but the enemy has landed two or three kilometers from the group of North Viet — South Vietnamese that have dug in right adjacent to this position. And they're still fighting, and I think that the, the fact that they are still there and holding on under this intensive fighting is an indication that they are certainly fighting well. The casualties are very heavy on the North Vietnamese side. I'm — I'm sure the forces of the South Vietnamese will suffer casualties, but the — in other words, I think the most encouraging part is that they didn't break and, and blew 'em away —

NIXON: Those people on Hill 31, they have been the survivors of that other hill we lost and moved in with them. Is that right?

MOORER: No, sir. No, sir. That was — this was independent of that. That operation was back over here. This is a separate operation.

NIXON: Yeah. Yeah.

MOORER: What they did, and you're quite correct, the Thirty-ninth Battalion, in the first action that you were reported to, did join up with the Twenty-first —

NIXON: Yeah?

MOORER: — but they were not related to this action over here.

NIXON: Now, with regard to General Abrams's plan to replace the Airborne with the Marines — that'll take about a week, or —?

MOORER: Yes, sir. I think so. I've asked him, though, what time then that's going to be. If you look over here, you'll see where these Marines are. You see, the green —

NIXON: Yeah?

MOORER: — indicates the position of the South Vietnamese. There are some of the Marines here. Some of them are back here in reserve; they'll be brought forward —

NIXON: Uh-huh.

MOORER: — but, he'll, he'll move them in there in a few days, I'm pretty sure.

NIXON: Fine.

MOORER: And then at [unclear]. Also, he wanted to bring up that one brigade which would be moving in there to replace this one. I think it would come across. [unclear]

NIXON: What about the balance of the reserves that he has in South Vietnam? He still has — after he moves these — he will still have [unclear] reserves in South Vietnam? But the point that Mel raised after our meeting yesterday was that — or maybe it was during the [unclear] meetings — the North Vietnamese must be making a major effort to, to cut off those, go to the rear of our force — the South Vietnamese forces that are on Route 9, and cut 'em off. Is that action, what does our intelligence show in that respect?

MOORER: Well, there was an intelligence report to the effect that two regiments were moving almost directly south.

NIXON: Right.

MOORER: On — just down the line, more or less.

NIXON: Right.

MOORER: As you know, the —

NIXON: What are we doing? Just punishing them with air, or —?

MOORER: Yes, sir. We're doing more than that. We're putting out patrols, and, of course, when they get over there to the South Vietnamese side, then they are up against [unclear] forces. But we have right here a very large fire support base, and we have artillery, and we are covering this with twenty-four-hour attacks. With all of that, General Abrams, of course, has all the intelligence. And, here again, there may be some enemy fire, but I think that — Mr. Helms will back me up — here, for the first time in a long time, we have the North Vietnamese willing, apparently willing, to commit as much as a battalion, which they haven't done in a long, long time.

NIXON: Well, what the North Vietnamese are obviously doing, it seems, is to make a major effort —

MOORER: I think —

[unclear exchange]

NIXON: Now they're trying to conserve their forces. Not fighting in the Giap fashion, but going all out to break the back of this thing. Is that correct?

ROGERS: That's correct. Did we get any intercepts that [unclear]? Do we have any conversations?

MOORER: Yes, sir.

ROGERS: You know what I mean?

HELMS: Well, we do have some conversations. Conversations saying, "Stand and fight." I mean, definite orders to these units. This is the first time we've seen this in, oh, literally years.

MOORER: Not only that, but they're establishing headquarters —

[unclear exchange]

NIXON: You said what?

MOORER: They've established headquarters down here, sir, 70B they call it, to control the entire operation. Heretofore, they've been leaving the actions in the different base areas up to the local commanders. And, now, they have headquarters —

NIXON: Right. I assume that our air force, as usual, does not have the capacity to know how to hit such headquarters, is that correct?

MOORER: Well, sir, if they get the top men over at the headquarters, of course, they will lay the B-52 strikes on this target. [unclear] have to recognize that these generals move —

NIXON: Is that right —?

MOORER: — every day. They move from one place to another. By the time you know they're, uh —

NIXON: Yeah.

MOORER: [unclear] are reported to be down there in the Lam Son — or rather the Chup operation, we did pick up the headquarters, laid down a B-52 strike, and killed the Twentieth Headquarters area here a few days ago.

NIXON: One point, Dick, that concerned me, and I saw on television and so forth, and the news summaries, that our intelligence people are saying that our intelligence is inefficient, inadequate, bad, and that that's the reason that we're, we're running into more resistance than was expected —

HELMS: Mr. President, resistance is precisely what we expected. It's been there, we outlined it before the plan ever kicked off —

NIXON: They both quote, "A high official said —"

HELMS: What if that high official doesn't know? When we were in here briefing you long before this operation kicked off, we identified all of those units surrounded on the map, and [unclear].

MOORER: We thought [unclear].

NIXON: I don't suppose [unclear] find the high official who said this —

HELMS: [unclear]

NIXON: All right. Go ahead.

MOORER: Well, sir, that's our — that's about it. As I say here, of course, it's night over there, now. They'll start in, again, first thing in the morning. General Abrams reports that General Lam is very resolute and —

NIXON: Yeah.

MOORER: And, now, one other interesting aspect of this is the sensors indicated, indicated in the last twenty-four hours, which just confirms what we talked about yesterday, I think, in the sense that if you look at what's happening on these fire bases. You see, here on [Route] 922, which is a route in through Base Area—

NIXON: Mm-hmm.

MOORER: —611, the traffic is down by nine trucks. In [Route] 9G, which, of course, is the one that they had tried again, is—well, they've got zero yesterday, and two northbound and five southbound today. This could have been, we do know that there's something going on to put a strike in. We do know that there's some enemy forces on that road, and so, these five trucks could have been, I suppose, anything. Let me turn to Route 99, which goes off to the south, whereas we had, three or four days ago, 86 and 80, yesterday, we had fourteen trucks and some of them were knocked off by air.

NIXON: Very important.

MOORER: But only thirty. Then, you go to Route 914B, which is the one we've all been so interested in. They—the one that comes down here.

LAIRD: Yeah.

MOORER: It was a—

[unclear exchange]

MOORER: —the twenty-third [of February]—

LAIRD: Going up the "Kissinger Trail."

[laughter]

MOORER: The twenty-third was a hundred, the twenty-fourth was eighty-four, yesterday twenty-eight, and today seventeen. And so, I think that, overall, there's no question about the fact that they have slowed this, it appears. Now, I just had a briefing on the input through the passes.

NIXON: Yeah, and one aside: that very little figure is still valid, but [unclear]. The press will get it out, and so forth. In other words, there's so many traps before this began and so many now [unclear]. These are things people understand, right?

MOORER: Well, we haven't enough. I could give you some better charts and that's it to show that and make that point, but not, now, our intelligence indicates, also, that—and this is about five days old now, because it takes that long to accumulate. In any event, the input through those passes has been high. So, the point up to this, there's still a tremendous amount of material north of this area we're operating in.

ROGERS: But that, Tom, is what I said is a source of confusion. You read in the papers, somebody says the—

NIXON: [unclear]—

ROGERS: —it's a lot more traffic—

[unclear exchange]

ROGERS: Now, what it is: it's traffic in, but not out. What we're trying to do is cut it off. I mean, the traffic below Tchepone is greatly reduced.

MOORER: That's right.

ROGERS: But that, as you read — sometimes read in the papers —

NIXON: That's what it's all about.

. . .

NIXON: A question, with regard to the DMZ: the major purpose, of course, of statements in which we have deliberately left fuzzed up, with the North Vietnamese — the South Vietnamese, what they do in North Vietnam. The purpose of that, of course, is not because they're going north. We all know that. They can't do it without our support. But, I don't think at this point, I think the main purpose of that is to tie those forces down. Isn't that true, what I said?

MOORER: Exactly.

NIXON: That they have a free shot. They just move our guys out of there and come on over here.

MOORER: As you see, they have not reduced the total number of forces, at least going back there, though, right on the DMZ they —

NIXON: How many Americans — how many Americans across that section are facing the DMZ approximately?

MOORER: Well, in this general area, we have about nine thousand.

NIXON: I see. Huh? Only nine thousand?

MOORER: Yes, sir —

LAIRD: American combat troops.

MOORER: American combat forces right there, sir.

NIXON: Right.

MOORER: We're talking about the helo operations, and support people, and add those people on Khe Sanh.

NIXON: Okay, at Khe Sanh. Did you mean the total at Khe Sanh, and clear across that whole bottom half of the DMZ, there're only nine thousand American forces?

MOORER: There's about nine —

NIXON: I know about combat. I want to know about all Americans. How many are in the region?

MOORER: [unclear]

NIXON: Oh, I mean the whole goddamn bunch. What is it?

[unclear exchange]

NIXON: Fifty thousand?

LAIRD: [unclear] to Da Nang and through there —

MOORER: That's right. It depends on how far you go, go south —

NIXON: All right.

[unclear exchange]

MOORER: But they, traditionally, they have eight thousand up here, and we have about nine thousand in this blocking position.

NIXON: Now, the point I'm making has nothing to do with how many combat, military, or any of that. It has to do with: how many Americans might be vulnerable, in the case that the people are going to be there when those in North Vietnam thought they had a free shot at coming across? Now, is it nine thousand combat? Or is it twenty-five thousand or fifty thousand —

MOORER: [unclear]

NIXON: — Americans? Forget combat —

MOORER: Yes, sir. I think it's about, well, I think the figure's twenty-nine thousand based on my knowledge —

NIXON: I'd like to verify it again. Get that figure —

MOORER: Should we go all the way down to — it depends on where you stop, Mr. President.

[unclear exchange]

MOORER: If you include all of Military Region I.

NIXON: Fine, Military Region I. That's great. Just get me that there [unclear] below the DMZ. That, really, is what this is all about. [unclear] Now, the second point is that, with regard to the whole business about [unclear] and so forth and so on. It, as we all know in this room, the purpose of that is [unclear] just like your little running, your boat up there with five thousand Marines on it, sending them for a field trip, with boats and the rest, to keep them worried over there, and at least tie down a few of their people, so that they don't come running around over here and get these guys. Is that true?

MOORER: Yes, sir.

LAIRD: Now, we were, during the meeting with [unclear] said he wants more this week —

NIXON: Good.

LAIRD: — and —

NIXON: That's all right.

LAIRD: — there is, we've been watching those pass areas up there and getting the best kind of intelligence that we can. Both CIA and DIA have been working closely together.

NIXON: Well —

LAIRD: There is a substantial amount up there, but I think it would be worthwhile, maybe, but I didn't think it was going to be —

NIXON: [unclear]

LAIRD: — this weekend.

NIXON: We've got another week to go.

LAIRD: Because —

NIXON: I'm sorry, but we will present that, though. I'm going to talk about that. But, understand: it's militarily that can have the effect of tying those people down. That's all.

MOORER: It's already doing it, sir. We've got intercepts —

NIXON: I know, I know, but I'd keep hitting that pass area.

• • •

NIXON: Don't give 'em news. I told Ziegler, for example, when they ask about, "What, what is the American position about supporting the North — South Vietnamese if they go north?" He says, "Gentlemen, I have nothing new on that. The president covered that completely at his press briefing. What's the next question?"

ROGERS: Hmm.

NIXON: Because I did cover it. I said, "Well, obviously, I don't have anything with what the South Vietnamese are going to do [unclear]. As far as our policy, it will be solely dictated in terms of whether or not there's a threat to our forces in the South." And that's true, we all know. Which, really, is, in effect, saying that we won't. And then, if somebody did ask a question. He says, "Well, what if there were such an operation, and it required a combined thing, and so forth? What would you do?" And I said, "Why, of course, we have no plans to do anything like that." But, you see, the point is, Mel, it makes news —

LAIRD: Yeah.

NIXON: — whenever a press secretary, and he does a good job, but whenever a press secretary, in answering a question, tries to give the answer directly, rather than telling the son of a bitch in the press, "Gentlemen, I refer you to the secretary's comment on that. What's the next question?" You see, but that's not news, sir, because there is nothing new. Don't you agree, Bill?

ROGERS: It's very tough for them to say that, but that's what they should —

NIXON: I do it all the time.

• • •

NIXON: You know, the, the other thing is, which I'm sure Abrams was shooting at, up there in Laos, the South Vietnamese could just win one cheap one, just a cheap one. Yeah. Take a stinking hill. Carefully bring back a prisoner or two, anything. I'm sure that has all been brought up.

MOORER: [unclear] I mean, there's a seizing of men, seizing of prisoners, and killing the 250 survivors —

NIXON: No, but they don't believe those figures.

ROGERS: Tom, there's no sign of any —

NIXON: Prisoners.

ROGERS: — demoralization — deterioration of the South Vietnamese?

MOORER: No —

[unclear exchange]

NIXON: That's the point that I'm worried about.

ROGERS: I think we've got to, you've got to be sure that everybody out there's very [unclear]. Even a sign of it, because we can get on it right away —

NIXON: Right.

ROGERS: — so that it doesn't [unclear].

NIXON: We mustn't have nothing. The South Vietnamese demoralization has been terribly important.

MOORER: Yes, sir. Well, we, we recognize —

NIXON: The North Vietnamese, I think they'd be getting it when we hit 'em —

[unclear exchange]

NIXON: What do you think, Dick?

HELMS: That's right. I think — the North Vietnamese are having a rough time. This time, the South Vietnamese stand their ground, and the operation will run out [unclear] when Mel came back from his trip. But they'll stand and fight, and we can really clobber them, and so forth. They'll not only take losses in men, but they'll take losses in supplies.

"His people were crucified over there. . . . five million of them, popped into bake ovens!"

March 9, 1971, 5:36 p.m.
Richard Nixon, Bob Haldeman, and John Ehrlichman
OVAL OFFICE

National Security Advisor Henry Kissinger was the point man on every major foreign policy during Nixon's first term of office. The president set the policy and Kissinger carried it out. Sometimes Nixon had to mediate between Kissinger and Secretary of State William Rogers when turf battles popped up, and they did from time to time. Nixon felt that if there was one area of the world that Kissinger should not lead American policy, it was the Middle East. Nixon worried that Kissinger's well-known Jewish heritage could create the perception that the United States showed favoritism in the region.

• • •

NIXON: In regard to Henry, he was in talking about his problems, you know. This is only for your own information, you know. He's — I don't know why he reads all this . stuff. Apparently *Newsweek* has an article this week that talks about his —

HALDEMAN: At a press —

NIXON: — religious background, or something, or his being in an [unclear] —

HALDEMAN: That's what I was saying, Jewish.

EHRLICHMAN: Jewish.

NIXON: Yeah, he was talking about that. Safire had given it to him. He's terribly upset. He feels now that he really ought to resign. You know, he mentioned that little [unclear] when he came in, and so forth and so on. He took the position that [unclear]. The position that I have taken, and this is very, I said, "All right, look, I am just not going to talk about it now. We've got several very big things in the air. Laos, and the possibility of some deal with the Soviets, and SALT." [unclear] And I said to him, "We cannot allow this to be a situation where it worries him." Besides, I said, but the difficulty in Henry's case, it's very simple. He's somewhat more, I must say, I think somewhat more honest than Rogers in that Henry knows his ego problem. And so he says, "I've got an ego," he said, "when Rogers is around." Rogers is a different problem. Rogers is a vanity problem. Henry's is not a vanity problem. Henry has an ego for reasons that [unclear] vanity.

What apparently set him all off on this, State is in the process of preparing a paper on the Mideast. If only, God, if Henry could only get, even have that one issue, if he could have that not handled by himself! My [unclear] behind it is true. Anybody who is Jewish cannot handle it. Even though Henry's, I know, as fair as he can possibly be, he can't help but be affected by it. You know, put yourself in his position. Good God! You know, his people were crucified over there. Jesus Christ! And five million of them, popped into bake ovens! What the hell does he feel about all this?!

HALDEMAN: Well, what he ought to recognize is even if he had no problems at all on it, it's wrong for the country, for American policy in the Middle East, to be made by a Jew.

NIXON: That's right.

HALDEMAN: And he ought to recognize that. Because, then if anything goes wrong —

NIXON: That's right.

HALDEMAN: — they're going to say it's because a goddamn Jew did it rather than blame Americans.

EHRLICHMAN: We've just been through this on health.

HALDEMAN: Yeah. You, as a Christian Scientist, shouldn't be making health decisions, either.

EHRLICHMAN: Well, that's why I farmed it out.

Crisscrossing negotiations with the Soviets on SALT

March 11, 1971, 4:00 p.m.
Richard Nixon, Bob Haldeman, and Henry Kissinger
OVAL OFFICE

In early March, Ambassador Dobrynin tried to make clever use of the secret communications from Nixon and Kissinger over the ABM aspect of SALT. He contacted Smith, the chief negotiator, and played him against the president. Dobrynin pressed Smith for the possibility of an ABM-only agreement, which could be negotiated in 1971, while an offensive/defensive agreement could not. Smith told Dobrynin that he must follow the president's guidance, which stressed the relationship between offensive and defensive weapons control.

• • •

KISSINGER: I think, incidentally, that the Russians are feeling that. I read now the Smith record of the Dobrynin conversation. That son of a bitch is just taking your letter, without telling Smith he's got it, and feeling out whether Smith is willing to give more.

NIXON: Sure.

KISSINGER: Because Smith's nearly dropped his teeth, because Dobrynin had — he had always said the Russians will never accept trading Washington — and the Washington system in for, for ABM. Here, Dobrynin offered it to him yesterday for nothing. And that actually helped us, because if they do come back now with the letter, it doesn't look like an arbitrary decision of yours. We've positioned it at the NSC meeting with Laird —

HALDEMAN: And it's easy to cover now —

KISSINGER: Dobrynin has come in, and you were — and it's much better for us. Scoop Jackson called this afternoon, and he said if we screw him on this Washington defense after all the pleading he's done for us on —

NIXON: We're not going to do that.

KISSINGER: — on Safeguard, he'll never forgive us.

NIXON: Well, you told him we weren't?

KISSINGER: I told him we weren't, and he should come in. I'm seeing him Saturday, and I'll —

NIXON: Sure.

KISSINGER: — I'll tell him.

NIXON: Because after all, he is a decent man.

KISSINGER: I think he's a decent guy.

NIXON: Oh, sure.

"An ABM-only agreement. It's fine, as far as you could do it, but that would be a disaster."
March 12, 1971, 8:50 a.m.
Richard Nixon and Henry Kissinger
OVAL OFFICE

Nixon was at first willing to accede to the Soviet suggestion of signing an agreement for defense systems (ABM), while continuing talks about offensive systems. On March 9, Secretary of Defense Laird sent Nixon a stern warning: "We should not accept a formal agreement on defensive weapons only, even with an informal agreement on offensive systems." On March 12, Nixon heard via Dobrynin that Leonid Brezhnev, leader of the Soviet Union, insisted that there would be no agreement beyond the anticipated ABM treaty. Nixon had no intention of acquiescing, so he had to decide who would write whom how long a letter, and when.

• • •

KISSINGER: Well, I saw our friend [Dobrynin].

NIXON: Oh, yeah.

KISSINGER: And he brought me a reply, a draft letter, which they would give you. And now we're in a bit of a negotiation. I don't know if at first you want to hear the details. They want a shorter letter from you.

NIXON: Mm-hmm.

KISSINGER: In fact, there was a lot of detail —

NIXON: Yeah.

KISSINGER: — in mine.

NIXON: Yeah.

KISSINGER: And Dobrynin says —

NIXON: Well, at least, it's a reply though.

KISSINGER: Oh, they're dying to reaffirm the summit meeting.

NIXON: All right. All right.

KISSINGER: And they're saying —

NIXON: They want that announced now?

KISSINGER: No.

NIXON: They don't want it announced?

KISSINGER: Not now. [That would be] too fast, Mr. President.

NIXON: Fine. Look, I'm just trying to feel them out.

KISSINGER: But —

NIXON: All right. But on this, do they want this exchange of letters to occur now?

KISSINGER: Well, yeah. Oh, yeah.

NIXON: Do you think we can? Why don't you just summarize it for me?

KISSINGER: Well, the exchange of letters is that I have proposed with him, in the draft of your letter, a very detailed agreement on freezing.

NIXON: All right.

KISSINGER: They don't want to do that. They, and Dobrynin says frankly they don't want to do it because he thinks that the preparation for the party congress they can't all get together —

NIXON: Yeah. Yeah. Fine. So what?

KISSINGER: So they gave us a much shorter reply and they recommended we give them a much shorter letter, which just talks about the principles rather than the technical details.

NIXON: But does it mention offensive and defensive?

KISSINGER: Yes. Now, there we had one point —

NIXON: Yeah.

KISSINGER: — which we have to settle with them.

NIXON: Yeah.

KISSINGER: They, of course, are driving their usual hard bargain. They say, "Let's negotiate in detail defensive first and then we will discuss the freezing." I told him that I didn't know your thinking —

NIXON: Mm-hmm.

KISSINGER: — but that that was too vague. I think what we have to ask them is this, Mr. President: that they agree to the principle of the freezing of deployments. Then we will authorize Smith to discuss ABM limits. And then, before the whole thing gets wrapped up, we will agree to the specifics of the freezing. I don't think with this new Soviet missile buildup we can afford to sign an ABM-only agreement—

NIXON: No.

KISSINGER: —that isn't very specific.

NIXON: Yeah.

• • •

NIXON: My view is you get what you can get in the beginning and then you do whatever to have an agreement together. It's nice for their—I don't mean—you see what I mean? Particularly with an ABM-only agreement. It's fine, as far as you could do it, but that would be a disaster.

KISSINGER: Disaster. Well, on that kind of language, they are—

NIXON: That would be a mistake. Well, I don't know what you can get.

KISSINGER: On this one, too, they prefer Moscow and Washington rather than—

NIXON: What?

KISSINGER: Rather than two sites. These are—

NIXON: Well, they can't compare these things in significance, Henry.

KISSINGER: Exactly, Mr. President. I think the significance of this is that they've gone this far. This is their first position on the inspection. Obviously, they're going to try to get the best possible deal.

NIXON: Yeah.

KISSINGER: I don't believe that he expected for a minute that we would accept this draft, as I said before.

NIXON: Yeah. Keep you both working on it—did he agree to that?

KISSINGER: That's right.

• • •

KISSINGER: Smith won't, can't do any damage, because he's frozen for four weeks—

NIXON: Yeah.

KISSINGER: —into position. We'll have this settled in two weeks, leaving only two topics left to go.

NIXON: Yeah.

KISSINGER: We'll be done within ten days in my view.

NIXON: Your view is that we might have the exchange of letters in ten days?

KISSINGER: Within two weeks. If—unless there's a total deadlock, which I don't believe.

• • •

NIXON: Listen, we've got to stick to our guns but, I think, running this thing now could have an enormous effect. We need something like this about now.

KISSINGER: Well, we'll have this—

NIXON: Just make any kind of a damn deal. You know it doesn't make a goddamn bit of difference. We're going to agree to settle it anyway. Just drive the hardest deal you can.

KISSINGER: Push the letter. I think, Mr. President —

NIXON: You drive it and I'm going to write the letter.

KISSINGER: Oh, yeah. What we can do is probably, after being — we may have to give on Moscow and Washington.

NIXON: But what about Scoop Jackson?

KISSINGER: Well, he's only a senator.

NIXON: Don't tell him that.

"They say we're being obstinate by linking offensive and defensive weapons."
    March 16, 1971, 9:30 a.m.
    Richard Nixon and Henry Kissinger
    OVAL OFFICE

On March 15, the official SALT negotiations began again in Vienna — the fifty-fifth such session. At the same time, Washington and Moscow were in public discussions over a planned summit, with private haggling over just what would be concluded there.

• • •

KISSINGER: Mr. President, if I could just bother you with that letter so that —

NIXON: Yeah.

KISSINGER: — I can get it to Dobrynin today.

NIXON: Okay.

KISSINGER: They have a Politburo meeting on Thursday, which means he's got to get it out by four this afternoon.

NIXON: Sure.

KISSINGER: [showing Nixon several drafts] This is the one where we stand now.

• • •

KISSINGER: This is what they want to say, so you see it's a lot more. This was his counterproposal to the previous draft. [pause] Notice it says nothing about a freeze.

NIXON: [reading] "Negotiations and to reach an agreement on the limitation of strategic offensive weapons."

KISSINGER: I think they'll accept this one because —

[NIXON reads several drafts of his letter to Kosygin.]

KISSINGER: [unclear]

NIXON: Mm-hmm. Fine.

KISSINGER: We'll know by Friday if we can't get an agreement.

NIXON: However that would be seen, do you think we're going to get it?

KISSINGER: I think we may have better than a fifty–fifty chance.

NIXON: I wonder if, well, if we put ourselves in the [unclear], saying that we shall reach an agreement before we know for sure.

KISSINGER: And then we have the freeze. Oh, you mean on the ABM?

NIXON: Well, on the both, Henry. You see, a freeze may — it's just a document. [unclear] to cover MIRVs. I mean it's a —

KISSINGER: We didn't ask for a MIRV even in our formal proposal.

NIXON: I know, but I, I'm getting at — the point I'm getting at, the point here, is whether we just — puts us any worse off than we are now.

KISSINGER: I think it would show an initiative of trying to break the deadlock. If they then deadlock on technical — I have the impression that they want an agreement.

NIXON: What we're doing is — say we negotiate an agreement in Vienna that has the opposite effect. It's still worth doing. With ABM we could still not get, get together on that. Then we would have a freeze on offensive weapons and agree to negotiate more at a later time.

KISSINGER: Well, what it would do, Mr. President — right now the deadlock is — for example, we have a long *New York Times* editorial again today, not that that matters, but in which they say we're being obstinate by linking offensive and defensive weapons. And this is your way to break that deadlock. Whatever we put in the letter would still — you couldn't possibly cover all the bases because —

NIXON: The *New York Times* just wants a SALT agreement [to] agree to an ABM limitation.

KISSINGER: That's right.

NIXON: They want it, because that's the drive of everybody who's opposed to ABMs, is simply to go back and be done with it. Correct?

KISSINGER: That's right. But in that case, we're doing better than what the *New York Times* recommended. They accept it because we're getting an offensive freeze also. You'll get an ABM limitation with a good chance of one different from what they want, which is Washington —

NIXON: Mm-hmm. Do you see anything [unclear] —?

KISSINGER: I mean, we were just —

NIXON: Do they want us to stop?

KISSINGER: Yeah. We would instruct Smith to stick with —

NIXON: Three [missile sites].

KISSINGER: — our present program. But, his present instructions are four, and we could let him fall back to three. Of course, what we really need is the radar, and the radar does the same for three and four. Only we'll get — three gets us fewer launchers.

NIXON: Fine. Well, let's go on that. We'll do it that way.

KISSINGER: Okay, Mr. President.

NIXON: Fine.

• • •

KISSINGER: I think that every time we've tried to meet, to placate these liberals, they've gotten nastier —

NIXON: A lot worse.

KISSINGER: As I see it, every time we've met them frontally, they've started wailing.

NIXON: Damn. I don't think we need to worry about them now —

KISSINGER: I don't think that's —

NIXON: —I think what the problem right now is this: I'm not so sure the SALT thing is going to be all that important. I think it's basically what I'm placating the critics with. Maybe it's just as well.

KISSINGER: Well, I think — I met with a group of senior businessmen yesterday.

NIXON: Yeah.

KISSINGER: I think it would be considered a generally hopeful thing. And it would be a run-up to a summit. I think, if we got that and the summit — and Rush sent me a cable that some of the stuff Dobrynin and I have been talking about is beginning to be reflected where he is.

NIXON: Mm-hmm.

KISSINGER: I consider it — in Berlin, all we can do is cut our losses. But Brandt has, in effect, has practically given away the ball game there already. So —

NIXON: Sure. Nothing we can lose.

KISSINGER: No.

NIXON: There's nothing to lose that he hasn't lost already.

• • •

NIXON: Laos was the right thing to do. Cambodia was the right thing to do. But my point is, we did both of those for the purpose of getting to another point. Now we've reached the other point.

KISSINGER: That's right.

NIXON: And once we reach it — now, every decision is now made not in terms of, well, what's the effect going to be on Saigon. The decision has got to be made on what's the effect on us.

KISSINGER: Absolutely. I agree.

NIXON: Now —

KISSINGER: One thing too —

NIXON: We have to remember that our giving to the Russians — everything is all tied to this. And we have — now, about Thieu, we have to remember that our view of the Russians, everything, is all tied into this, and we —

KISSINGER: If we could — the advantage of a summit, even if it gets a sort of half-baked SALT agreement, whatever the SALT agreement is, it's a lot better than the nuclear test ban.

NIXON: Of course. Of course. Of course.

KISSINGER: And it —

NIXON: I agree with you. It would stop —

KISSINGER: —it would defuse people. They can't very well attack their president when he's getting ready for a summit meeting.

NIXON: No.

KISSINGER: And that would get us a few months of, of, of, you know, of quiet here. One thing we might consider that's in the summer, a meeting with Thieu in which Thieu asks us to end our combat role. That would be an —

NIXON: Well, we've got to figure all those things out. The combat thing, no draftees —

KISSINGER: Right.

NIXON: — a whole series of announcements for the purpose of getting the thing cooled off.

KISSINGER: That's right.

Afterword: Nixon directed Kissinger to negotiate an agreement that both types of military systems would be included in the SALT treaty.

"Announce the whole damn thing, and that's that. The war is dead as an issue."
March 18, 1971, 6:25 p.m.
Richard Nixon, Bob Haldeman, and Henry Kissinger
OVAL OFFICE

One of the continuing issues of 1971 was the need for a renewed agreement on the situation in Berlin. Since the end of World War II, the city had been divided, the original four sectors evolving into East Berlin (Soviet-protected) and West Berlin (U.S.-protected). The entire metropolitan area was located in East Germany, a Soviet satellite state, making West Berlin an island of Western-style culture and government. As such, it was a highly charged symbol of U.S. support of non-Communists along the Iron Curtain. Nonetheless, servicing West Berlin with food and other essentials was awkward and the Soviets wanted to erase access to the isolated city. Meanwhile, Nixon and Kissinger groped for substantive information about the progress of the war in Vietnam.

• • •

KISSINGER: Dobrynin sent over a message.

NIXON: Yeah.

KISSINGER: They've come up with a draft agreement on Berlin, which on first reading is acceptable. I sent it to Rush on my private channel to him for his analytical comment. But in the two areas that I've discussed with him, Federal presence and — it's a major, there's some major concessions.

NIXON: Hmm.

KISSINGER: He just called ten minutes ago to say he hoped he'd have a response by — a preliminary response from me by Monday, that they're very anxious to move ahead.

NIXON: Hmm.

KISSINGER: And I said, "Well, you know, as you know, there are parts of it that are totally unacceptable." He recognized that.

NIXON: On Berlin?

KISSINGER: Yeah, on Berlin.

NIXON: Yeah.

KISSINGER: But he said, "But, as you know, none of the parts that are unacceptable to you are worse, and a lot of the parts are better" — which is true. I think we should use Berlin just to keep him talking —

NIXON: Yeah.

KISSINGER: — and to do the —

NIXON: But he also expects you to — does he still feel he'll have some answer on the other proposition on Monday, too?

KISSINGER: Yeah. I won't give him an answer on this until —

NIXON: Of course not.

KISSINGER: — he gives me an answer on the other.

• • •

KISSINGER: We had another two-hour session on these —

NIXON: Yeah.

KISSINGER: — logistics, and it's a hopelessly complicated subject. I'm writing a memo for you to read over the weekend, without figures, just to —

NIXON: Well, I don't want to read any memos, because I'm going to be preparing for the [Howard K.] Smith thing next week —

KISSINGER: No, no, but I thought you might use it for the Smith thing —

NIXON: Oh. Oh, I see.

KISSINGER: Not use figures, but show some of the factors why we are so confident that this has been a success. And now, I really am very confident, now that I've worked through these things.

• • •

KISSINGER: So, they put in fifty thousand troops where, last year, they had seven thousand troops. If you just add the rice consumption for fifty thousand troops —

NIXON: Mm-hmm.

KISSINGER: — you create a totally new consumption pattern, and no one had done this before.

• • •

KISSINGER: Some of this stuff, because when you add it, the figures of what it takes to feed fifty thousand people in southern Laos, as compared to eight thousand last year, and —

NIXON: [unclear] Let me tell you, Henry, I have that feeling. There are other reasons. I just know that going in there and knocking the livin' bejeezus out of those in Laos [unclear] —

KISSINGER: It scared them.

NIXON: And it scared 'em. And part of it — and it sent the international establishment into such a tizzy, and these people are deeply proud. The other thing — and I think your point is — these bastards, they've got to look at their hole card now. We'll find out. If they're going to negotiate, they're going to negotiate in the next three or four months.

KISSINGER: That's right. Well, Walt Rostow was in today.

NIXON: Oh, yeah.

KISSINGER: Of course, he's often wrong, but he's —

NIXON: No, I — he's not really —

KISSINGER: Actually, his judgments have been —

HALDEMAN: Pretty right.

NIXON: No. Hell, no! I agree with Rostow. He makes good speeches, everything.

KISSINGER: Walt —

NIXON: He should have been in to come and say hello.

KISSINGER: Well, Walt Rostow said —

NIXON: He knows we're doing the right thing, doesn't he? Huh?

KISSINGER: Absolutely. He, he —

NIXON: Hmm?

KISSINGER: — he said something today — he said — and that really takes a lot for him — he said, "If we could have put your president together with our cabinet, we would have really done something."

NIXON: [laughs] [unclear]

KISSINGER: Yeah.

HALDEMAN: That's kind of interesting.

NIXON: Well —

KISSINGER: This is an interesting —

NIXON: Well, he had Rusk, of course, who is a tower of strength.

KISSINGER: Yeah. And McNamara, in his way —

NIXON: He did what he was told.

KISSINGER: What?

[unclear exchange]

KISSINGER: McNamara would never have leaked.

NIXON: Never.

[unclear exchange]

NIXON: But what, what did Walt say?

KISSINGER: Well, Walt says his gut feeling tells him they're getting ready to negotiate, and, to him, the Zhou Enlai visit to Hanoi —

NIXON: Yeah?

KISSINGER: — was the beginning of a political process rather than the opposite.

HALDEMAN: Hmm.

KISSINGER: And, today, the Russians attacked China on the radio for being willing to sell out in Vietnam.

NIXON: [laughs] Sell out?

KISSINGER: Yes.

NIXON: There is the problem, I think. I think the problem with both — the reason the Russians can't help us there is that they can't be timid, and they can't be accused of selling out. The reason the Chinese can — they can't be accused of it, so the hardliners in Hanoi —

KISSINGER: Of course, the, the trouble for Hanoi is —

NIXON: Yeah?

KISSINGER: — that they've now fought for ten years against us. They must've lost at least seven hundred thousand men.

NIXON: Yeah.

KISSINGER: They've had a whole young generation that are neither productive in North Vietnam, or, for that matter, even breeding.

NIXON: Yeah.

KISSINGER: I bet their birthrate — I'm serious —

NIXON: [unclear]

KISSINGER: — their birthrate must be way, way down.

NIXON: Why — good God, there's no men!

KISSINGER: There are no men there.

NIXON: Yeah!

KISSINGER: And, all it — if it ends now, they'll have very little to show for it. The fact that we can now run two big operations — at this moment there are five and a half North and South Vietnamese divisions outside of the country, and they haven't been able to get a guerrilla movement started. And that is —

NIXON: They haven't got one in Cambodia. Incidentally, what's happening in northern Laos?

KISSINGER: Nothing.

NIXON: What the hell's the trouble there, though?

KISSINGER: Well, we laid in some B-52 strikes a few weeks ago.

NIXON: Aren't we — but, but, you know —

KISSINGER: They all told —

NIXON: — Helms told us five weeks ago, we're going to lose it again.

KISSINGER: That's right.

NIXON: Maybe we'll lose it next month?

KISSINGER: We may lose it, but every month, week we gain brings that rainy season closer.

NIXON: When is their rainy season? Theirs is early, isn't it?

KISSINGER: It starts in the middle of June.

NIXON: Middle of June?

KISSINGER: Yeah.

NIXON: May? Because it varies over there, doesn't it?

KISSINGER: Yeah. And the — and in Cambodia, there are next to no incidents.

NIXON: Yeah.

KISSINGER: Route 4 is open. You see, when Route 4 was cut, it was reported every day. Now, unescorted convoys go from Sihanoukville to Phnom Penh every day. And there's no report in the newspapers —

NIXON: No —

KISSINGER: — that there are no incidents.

NIXON: — good news is never reported.

KISSINGER: So —

NIXON: It's all right. It comes out in the end, when we're done.

KISSINGER: But, I must say, this analysis, I found very encouraging, because I, I didn't go in with that expectation, particularly. I didn't know what the —

NIXON: But, this analysis — they've got it, too, Henry. And they've got to look at their hole card. What the hell can they do?

KISSINGER: They have only — they have two hopes, now. The one hope is that —

NIXON: Get Thieu out —

KISSINGER: — that Thieu would collapse with the election in October. So, he may not be so wrong in playing it closely.

NIXON: Yeah.

KISSINGER: And, the other one is our election. But our election, in my judgment, is a double-edged sword for him —

NIXON: Yeah.

KISSINGER: — for them, because if you get reelected — because you've demonstrated, from their point of view, unpredictability — and now, not having to be elected again —

NIXON: Yeah.

KISSINGER: — there's just no telling what you'll do.

NIXON: Yeah. So damn true.

KISSINGER: That's one problem. The second problem is: if we don't give them a date before, and if you leave it in fairly good shape, and you should get defeated, would a Democrat dare to sell it out and take the opprobrium? So —

NIXON: Right.

KISSINGER: So, I'm not sure that the '72 election is as clear a signal to them as the '68 one was. In '68, they thought if they would get rid of Johnson, they'd have it made.

NIXON: Hmm. They thought they'd get Humphrey.

KISSINGER: And they thought they'd get Humphrey. But, in '72, this isn't so, so clear to them. And, if we get into a negotiation with them on a very private basis, this is a point —

NIXON: Yeah.

KISSINGER: — that should be made to them.

NIXON: Yeah, yeah, yeah, yeah.

KISSINGER: I actually think this summer, if we — if our domestic situation holds reasonably well, and we don't give the deadline away, the deadline is our best bargaining chip—

NIXON: Sure it is. Well, maybe that little memorandum will help.

KISSINGER: If we give it away in November or December or October — if we — if we don't get a negotiation by November—

NIXON: We'll do it then.

KISSINGER: — then it doesn't make any difference—

NIXON: No, that's right.

KISSINGER: Then we can do it—

NIXON: That's right.

KISSINGER: Then we should do it.

NIXON: What we should — we've got to, then. That's the time to give it away. Right after Thieu's election, we'll have a little meeting — assuming he gets elected—

KISSINGER: That's right.

NIXON: — and announce the whole damn thing, and that's that. And the war is dead as an issue.

KISSINGER: No problem.

NIXON: [snaps his fingers] Like that. Out! That's the time to do it.

KISSINGER: But, if you do it now, you'll just get into the [unclear].

NIXON: Well, if you do it now, the main problem is right now, if you do it it's a little bit more important, you — there is still a chance that you could negotiate something. And, boy, that would be the best of all worlds—

KISSINGER: [unclear]

NIXON: — to get it done. And I had chances. You know, I never thought it was very good, but there's some, now. There was none before. So, what the hell?

KISSINGER: And now, what — we wouldn't put to them the political proposition. Now, we would just negotiate military arrangements.

NIXON: Military arrangements. Mutual withdrawal.

KISSINGER: That's right.

NIXON: What about Cambodia and Laos?

KISSINGER: Well, they'll have to stand down there, too.

NIXON: Yeah. All right, well, if it's something—

[unclear exchange]

NIXON: — or, or, or the cease-fire, at least.

KISSINGER: Yeah, we can do it in one of two ways. We can either not have mutual withdrawal, but just negotiate a cease-fire for our withdrawal and the prisoners, which would give everybody another year to gear themselves up without Communist attacks.

NIXON: Yeah.

KISSINGER: And, since we're going to get out anyway in, in a year and a half, it doesn't make any difference whether we agree to get out in a year.

NIXON: Sure.

KISSINGER: Once we are below one hundred thousand troops we have no combat effectiveness left —

NIXON: None.

KISSINGER: — and —

NIXON: Well, the air.

KISSINGER: The air. Yeah, but we could do a lot from Thailand and from carriers if they break the agreement.

NIXON: Oh, I see what you mean. Yeah. Okay.

"The Chinese really blasted Russia."

March 19, 1971, 11:45 a.m.

Richard Nixon and Henry Kissinger

OVAL OFFICE

On the hundredth anniversary of the Paris Commune, Chinese newspapers harshly criticized the Soviet Union as an unworthy heir to the revolution, an imperial nation that was both overly militaristic and expansionist. Implying that Brezhnev was "a traitor to the proletariat," the editorialists lambasted the use of police to oppress people in the Soviet Union and armies to control citizens of other nations around the world. The Soviets responded to the attack by accusing China of merely trying to curry favor with the United States.

• • •

KISSINGER: The Chinese really blasted Russia.

NIXON: The Chinese did?

KISSINGER: Yeah. And —

NIXON: About what?

KISSINGER: About, oh, bourgeois — a real all-out blast just before their party congress. So —

NIXON: It's a real fight.

KISSINGER: Yeah.

"Let this country go up in flames."

April 6, 1971, 1:00 p.m.

Richard Nixon and Henry Kissinger

EXECUTIVE OFFICE BUILDING

Nixon and Kissinger continued to read the political tea leaves as they considered their approach to talks with the Soviet Union.

• • •

KISSINGER: One interesting thing happened this morning. That vulture McGeorge Bundy called up.

NIXON: Yes?

KISSINGER: And he's a great weathervane for them.

NIXON: Is he?

KISSINGER: Yeah.

NIXON: They were giving money to Muskie all the time, you know. Did you know the Ford Foundation has financed all of Muskie's trips to Africa? Now that's a foundation for you. Now, Muskie is a presidential candidate. I traveled for eight years by myself. I paid it all out of my own pocket. I earned the money by writing for the *Reader's Digest,* Henry. And with a two-hundred-fifty-thousand-dollar law firm practice, and I made two hundred fifty thousand dollars on my book, I financed the whole goddamn thing. Did I ever hear a word from the Ford Foundation? How many foundations suggested, "Look, Nixon, the former vice president, is going to make this trip abroad. You're going on a nonpartisan basis. We'd like to help"? No. They finance this son of a bitch Muskie. Boy, and he's had his [unclear].

KISSINGER: Well, he [Bundy] was very cagey again. And —

NIXON: What's he cagey about?

KISSINGER: Well, he said, "Well, it's a tough one." And —

NIXON: Yes, yes.

KISSINGER: — there's more support than you think. Well, he will never say so. But what — but he did say that when he returns —

NIXON: More support than you think. I think there is more than we think. I don't —

KISSINGER: Well, one thing he said was: there's a fellow at the UN, with whom he — the Soviet mission to the UN — with whom he was working when he was assistant to the president. And he said he called him yesterday, or over the weekend, and he said, "We want you to know that Brezhnev is deadly serious about wanting to improve relations with the United States." He wanted to know if we had an answer to give to this fellow. Well, I —

NIXON: [laughs]

KISSINGER: I didn't give him an answer because —

NIXON: What?

KISSINGER: I made the statement, we're deadly serious too. And —

NIXON: Well, Brezhnev is going every which way. And he probably doesn't trust Dobrynin's word and so forth.

KISSINGER: It's very interesting. It's typically Russian to try to handle it through another channel too.

NIXON: Yeah. Yeah. Yeah. Yeah.

KISSINGER: But I don't think — my instinct is that the reason they were holding out until spring is what this [party] congress is doing in terms of Brezhnev's preeminence. And I —

NIXON: Well, when will they know? When will they know? The end of the week?

KISSINGER: About what happened?

NIXON: The congress. When will that be over?

KISSINGER: Well, it probably will be over —

NIXON: Or is it over?

KISSINGER: No, no. It will be over no later than a week from today.

NIXON: All right.

KISSINGER: And then he'll [Dobrynin] be back within a week after some time.

NIXON: Well, things better start to happen or — you know, I'm — you probably don't believe me, but I can perfectly turn, I'm capable, that is — even my own, even Haldeman wouldn't know — I'm perfectly capable of turning right awful hard. I never have in my life. But if I found that there's no other way — in other words, hell, if you think Cambodia had flower children fighting, we'll bomb the goddamn North like it's never been bombed. That's why we've had these planes gotten ready, Henry. They're not getting ready just to get these people over there.

KISSINGER: Well, I will —

NIXON: We'll start doing it, and we'll bomb those bastards, and then let the American people — let this country go up in flames.

"There will come a time when there ain't nothing more to negotiate."
April 7, 1971, 3:15 p.m.
Richard Nixon and Henry Kissinger
EXECUTIVE OFFICE BUILDING

The year 1971 continued to be a difficult one for Nixon and Kissinger. The war was not going the way they wanted, the Soviets were not being as responsive as they had hoped — secret talks had been going on for nearly two years at this point — and a breakthrough somewhere was desperately needed.

• • •

NIXON: Look, Henry, the difficulty with our position is this: you've got to know that there will come a time when there ain't nothing more to negotiate. In January of next year, what the hell are you going to negotiate about?

• • •

NIXON: Do you think if America loses, what this country is going to do? I don't understand why the intellectuals, they really just —

KISSINGER: They don't mind losing. They don't like America, and that's the difference.

NIXON: They don't, huh? That's nice. Isn't that's just great? I wish to Christ they had to live someplace else. I wish they did.

KISSINGER: They don't have the patriotism.

"You even threw ol' Dan Rather off balance."
April 7, 1971, 9:52 p.m.

Richard Nixon and Billy Graham
WHITE HOUSE TELEPHONE

Following a major speech, Nixon often received congratulatory phone calls and instant analysis from friends and major figures in the administration late into the night. His Vietnam speech on the evening of April 7, 1971, was no exception, when Reverend Billy Graham was one such caller. Graham counseled Nixon from time to time not only on spiritual matters, but also on policy and politics. Graham's international ministry came in contact with millions of people, and his insight was valuable. Here, the subject is Graham's view on how the United States got into the war in Vietnam.

• • •

GRAHAM: I want to tell you that that's by far the best anybody has done on Vietnam. You had me in tears. I really feel that —

NIXON: Well I was in tears myself, you know. Every time I think of that little Kevin, and he saluted, it just broke me up.

GRAHAM: I think you even threw ol' Dan Rather off balance. [laughs]

NIXON: Yeah.

GRAHAM: I thought it was just tremendous, and I just wanted to tell you that —

NIXON: Are you in Knoxville?

GRAHAM: No, I'm still in Vero Beach, Florida.

NIXON: Oh, yeah.

GRAHAM: I've been down here for about five weeks.

NIXON: When are you going for your crusade in Kentucky?

GRAHAM: Yes, that starts in about two weeks.

NIXON: Oh, yeah. I see.

GRAHAM: But I go to California to deliver a couple of speeches first.

NIXON: That's right. But you felt it was the right — of course we're fighting a very tough battle here. You know, everybody wants to pull out, but I have to fight against the tide. I have to do the right thing.

GRAHAM: I think you defused a lot of it tonight, though. I don't see what in the world they can say after tonight. I think that you've given some of, people like me, you've given me something to hold on to, and to really say, and I've got an editorial in the *New York Times* on Friday, which I wrote this morning —

NIXON: Good for you.

GRAHAM: — which I wrote this morning. They asked me to do it yesterday.

NIXON: Good.

GRAHAM: And I'm putting all the blame of this whole thing on Kennedy.

NIXON: That's right! He started the damn thing!

GRAHAM: Well, I —

NIXON: He killed Diem!

GRAHAM: Right.

NIXON: And he sent the first sixteen thousand combat people there himself!

GRAHAM: Well, I'm saying that the first time I heard about involvement was four days before he was inaugurated, playing golf with him. He said, I quote, "We cannot allow Laos and South Vietnam to fall to the Communists." And then I —

NIXON: [laughs]

GRAHAM: I said when President Johnson took over we had sixteen thousand troops — there.

NIXON: That's right!

GRAHAM: And I said the political climate in the United States —

NIXON: And Diem had been murdered. You see, Billy, the key thing here was Kennedy's, and I must say our friend Lodge's, agreement to the murder of Diem. Diem, that's what killed the, opened the whole thing.

GRAHAM: The whole thing. And I said this sentence, I said, "Many of the present doves in the Senate were not then so dovish. Even Senator Fulbright, who introduced the now-famous Tonkin Resolution." And I got all that in there. They've taken it. They're going to print it Friday morning.

NIXON: Good. Well, anyway, I appreciate —

GRAHAM: But I thought it was —

NIXON: Yeah.

GRAHAM: Your sincerity and manner of presentation was just excellent.

NIXON: Yeah.

GRAHAM: It was just wonderful. I was —

NIXON: One thing, incidentally, I threw away the text at the last and talked about this little boy that came there. That little Kevin, when he saluted me, I damn near broke up.

GRAHAM: I am sure you did.

NIXON: You know how it is.

GRAHAM: I sure do.

NIXON: It's awful tough, isn't it?

GRAHAM: Well, God bless. You've got a lot of people praying for you and pulling for you.

NIXON: Believe me, Billy, it means an awful lot. And you keep the faith, huh?

GRAHAM: Ah, you betcha.

NIXON: Keep the faith.

GRAHAM: Yes, sir. Bye.

NIXON: We're going to win.

"There ought to be a way to get him [Kennedy] covered."

April 9, 1971, 11:40 a.m.

Richard Nixon, Bob Haldeman, and Ron Ziegler

OVAL OFFICE

Long before the Democratic Party named a nominee in the 1972 presidential election, Nixon feared that a Kennedy-Nixon rematch was inevitable. It had been almost a dozen years since his defeat by John F. Kennedy, and this time his attention was focused on Edward Kennedy. While Kennedy clearly was the most recognized name among possible rivals, the senator from Massachusetts was still recovering from Chappaquiddick, an incident during July 1969 in which Mary Jo Kopechne, a passenger in Kennedy's car, was killed when he accidentally drove off a bridge. Nixon was eager for regular updates on Kennedy's political intentions, and he was willing to use questionable means to obtain them.

• • •

NIXON: Well goddamn it, there ought to be a way to get him [Kennedy] covered. I wouldn't bother with McGovern. Certainly, I think with Teddy, the reason I would cover him is from a personal standpoint. You're likely to find something on that [Chappaquiddick].

HALDEMAN: He's covered on that.

NIXON: You're sure?

HALDEMAN: Pretty much.

NIXON: You watch. I predict something more is going to happen.

HALDEMAN: They're keeping an eye on that one and in [unclear].

NIXON: I mean, it's a matter of judgment. I mean, he's just gonna —

HALDEMAN: Did you see his wife [Joan] came into the White House again all done up in some crazy outfit?

NIXON: What, did Pat [Nixon] [unclear] something?

HALDEMAN: Yeah, a Senate wives' luncheon.

NIXON: What did she [Joan] wear?

HALDEMAN: Some —

ZIEGLER: Body stocking.

HALDEMAN: — gaucho, leather gaucho —

ZIEGLER: With a leather gaucho over it.

HALDEMAN: — with a bare midriff, or something.

ZIEGLER: Well, no, they put on a body stocking, which is flesh tone.

HALDEMAN: Oh, is that it?

ZIEGLER: And then they wrap the leather, you know, gaucho-type thing around it. So you look at it from a distance, and you think, "My God —"

HALDEMAN: You think she's naked.

ZIEGLER: [laughs] "— there she is." But she has a body stocking.

NIXON: Weird.

HALDEMAN: She was going to wear hot pants but Teddy told her she couldn't.

ZIEGLER: They're weird people. They really are. I mean, even the —

NIXON: It's crude. What the hell's the matter with them? What's she trying to prove?

HALDEMAN: Whatever it is, she ain't gaining many votes, because they've got, the super-swinger jet-set types are going to be for them and not for you no matter what happens.

ZIEGLER: I don't know, the super-swingin' jet-set types don't even relate to that type thing. It's a very, very small group.

HALDEMAN: That's right.

NIXON: Hmm.

HALDEMAN: Middle American folk, they don't think they like, that's desecration of the White House to most Americans [unclear].

ZIEGLER: Oh, sure.

HALDEMAN: She does it every time she comes. That's why she does that.

NIXON: I know.

ZIEGLER: She has to have some sort of hang-up herself personally. She knows what Teddy was doing out there with that girl [Mary Jo Kopechne] running her into the water, you know, and what he's been doing.

HALDEMAN: But that family's used to that.

NIXON: They do it all the time.

HALDEMAN: That's the price you pay when you join that club. They all know that. Ethel, Jackie, and all the rest of them.

NIXON: They gotta expect that.

HALDEMAN: That's the game you play. If you want to get in their ball game, you play by their rules.

"On the UN membership issue . . . some people say, 'Let's find a clever way of doing it,' but there is no clever way of being defeated."
April 12, 1971, 11:28 a.m.
Richard Nixon, Taiwanese Ambassador Zhou Shukai, and Henry Kissinger
OVAL OFFICE

During World War II, Chinese and Americans fought side by side against the Japanese. After 1948, however, when mainland China became a Communist state — the People's Republic of China — the two nations had little or nothing to do with one another. Occasionally they staged limited conferences, but there was no travel, no trade, very little communication, and no diplomatic relations. For decades, the United States sided with the former Chinese leaders, President and Madame Chiang Kai-shek, who took up residence on the island of Taiwan. Many Americans, especially in the conservative ranks, were highly emotional on the subject of the two Chinas, siding entirely with Democratic, capitalistic Taiwan.

After assuming office, Nixon indicated that he was open to efforts to improve relations with the mainland. The Chinese responded in subtle ways, but the greatest leap of progress was made in spring 1971, when two Ping-Pong players representing the feuding nations made friends at a meet in Japan. Mao Zedong, the leader of the PRC, took an interest and allowed the U.S. Ping-Pong team to travel to his country for a tournament. That small event was a sensation in diplomatic circles and across the United States.

The sobering decision facing Nixon concerned Chinese representation in the United Nations. Taiwan had a seat there, and mainland China had been excluded since the founding of the UN. A compromise "two-China policy" was widely discussed but had little hope of being implemented, presenting Nixon with major problems in 1971.

• • •

NIXON: One interesting thing is that we're saying goodbye to him on the day that the Ping-Pong team, waited, you know, Ping-Pong team makes the front page of the *New York Times.*

KISSINGER: They are very subtle though, these Chinese.

NIXON: You think it means something?

KISSINGER: No question.

• • •

KISSINGER: Mr. President, one more thing I want to mention, about the Chinese ambassador. He's going to be the Chinese foreign minister, and we're going to announce the relaxation of our trade restrictions [with the PRC]. He's going straight back to Taipei. I wonder whether you could just mention that to him, so that he doesn't arrive there with a severe loss of face after seeing you and not having been told about it. Now this first group, there are actually three groups of relaxations. The first one is minor, the entry of Chinese, currency controls, bunkering, some shipping restrictions.

• • •

[ZHOU joins the conversation.]

NIXON: I want you to convey my warmest greetings to Generalissimo and Madame Chiang. We will stick by our treaty commitments to Taiwan; we will honor them. I said so in my State of the World report. We will do nothing in the trade and travel field which is in derogation of friendship to your president and to Madame Chiang. On the other hand, we will take some steps in the next few days that are primarily to be seen as part of our world perspective, particularly vis-à-vis the Soviet Union.

On the UN membership issue, some of our friends have deserted us. We are prepared to fight for you but we want to do it in an effective way. I have many proposals on various schemes such as dual representation. I will make this decision, not the State Department. Some people say, "Let's find a clever way of doing it," but there is no clever way of being defeated. There is no change in our basic position, but there may have to be some adaptation of our strategy.

We, however, before we make a decision want to talk to you. I am sending Ambassador Murphy to Taiwan; he is going there on business anyway, and the Generalissimo should talk to him as he talks to me. Taiwan and the UN is a fact of life for us and we will do nothing to give it up, but we have to be intelligent and we want to hear your views.

ZHOU: We appreciate your special attention; above all, don't spread the impression that all is lost.

• • •

NIXON: I want you to know that the relaxation of trade that we are planning is mostly symbolic; the important issue is the UN. We will be very much influenced by what the Generalissimo will think. As long as I am here, you have a friend in the White House and you should do nothing to embarrass him. The Chinese should look at the subtleties. You help us and we will help you. I want Murphy to bring his report personally to me. We will stand firm as long as we can, but we must have an army behind us.

"Everybody in the government, in the NSC, is not told everything."

April 13, 1971, 11:19 a.m.

Richard Nixon, Bob Haldeman, Henry Kissinger, and John Scali

OVAL OFFICE

Thanks to "Ping-Pong diplomacy," Nixon suddenly found himself in the driver's seat of a fast-moving car. He talked with his advisors about how to handle the many possibilities, especially in terms of the reaction from the Soviets. Included in the meeting was John A. Scali, a former journalist and special consultant to the president, who became a regular advisor on U.S.-China relations.

• • •

NIXON: Now, one area that is particularly — it will be particularly important too. And I noticed that, I mean, I was eager to hear your comment on the China thing. And, I think, Henry, that it's important that you have a talk with John about how all this began —

KISSINGER: We're going to get together. We're going to get together this afternoon —

NIXON: — how all this began. There's much more than meets the eye here. For example, you probably were under the impression, and much of the press corps is, that the China initiative came from State.

SCALI: Right.

NIXON: It may surprise you to know that the China initiative I undertook started twenty months ago. The first announcement made thirteen months ago was utterly opposed by the Foreign Service. You know why? Well, they're not — they're for it now. You know why? The Kremlinologists. [Former U.S. Ambassador to the Soviet Union] Chip Bohlen wrote in a memo.

HALDEMAN: Llewellyn Thompson.

KISSINGER: Tommy Thompson.

NIXON: Tommy Thompson did. The State Department Foreign Service people — not Bill. I'm not referring to Bill.

SCALI: Bill Rogers?

NIXON: Bill Rogers plays the game the way that he's supposed to. In other words, by [unclear]. They opposed it because they said it's going to make the Russians mad. Sure, it made the Russians mad. We didn't do it for that purpose, although it may be a dividend. Who knows? It depends. If it makes them mad, it helps us. But the point is, State, from the beginning, opposed it. They only came around on it in the past, perhaps, two or three months. Now, the reason being, that is, that they have the idea that we need a détente with the Russians; we must do nothing that irritates the Russians. Every time Kosygin came to see anybody at State, or anybody in the White House, he raised holy hell about what we were doing with China. And he scared them off — but not me. I deal with the China things for long-range reasons — very, very important reasons.

Now, that brings us to the present thing: Ping-Pong. It's very important now — we're going to have another announcement tomorrow, which you should fill John in on — it's very important now that we, while we want to get every dividend we can on this, that we not appear to exploit it. Now, the reasoning is that, much as we want the publicity, we're playing for much higher stakes. We're playing for much higher stakes with the Russians — and this thing is sending them right up the wall, the Ping-Pong team. And we also are playing for high stakes with the Chinese. It makes good — it's very good copy here for us to appear to be the people that are, have opened up the Chinese thing, and so forth and so on. But our major goal is to open it up. And whenever a propaganda initiative will have the effect of hurting that goal, we can't do it.

SCALI: Sure.

NIXON: Now, the reasons why, at this point, what I think we can get when we — and this is where subtlety is involved — where we can get maximum benefit here. When this announcement is made tomorrow, everybody's going to read into it a hell of a lot more. Incidentally, this announcement that's going to be made tomorrow, we've been planning for months. It just happens to fall right after the Ping-Pong team. See, we didn't know the Ping-Pong team was going to happen like that.

KISSINGER: We had some feeling that something was going to happen. They —

NIXON: Oh, yeah. Because they have been dropping little hints around the world at the various embassies, and for months we've been expecting some thaw. We didn't expect — but I suppose we were looking more to the fact that the thaw might come in Warsaw. But the Chinese, with their usual subtlety, had the thaw — we'll call it a "thaw" for lack of something else; the press will all write it that way anyway — it comes in another area. Right?

KISSINGER: That's right.

NIXON: You never can predict how the Chinese are. They're much less predictable than the Russians. The Russians are predictable. The Chinese are not predictable.

KISSINGER: But they're subtler.

NIXON: Because they are Chinese, not because they're Communists. The Russians are more predictable because they're doctrinaire, but you can goddamn near tell how the Russians will react to the Chinese Ping-Pong thing. I can almost tell you what Dobrynin will say when he comes back — and particularly on this announcement.

KISSINGER: Well, if Dobrynin were here, he'd be over here already.

NIXON: So — but my point is, and this is the thing where John can probably get the word out, we — now, let me say: we don't want to start a fight with State about this — actually, with the career guys. We're not trying to, even though they constantly may try to cut us out, but — at the White House. And we don't want to embarrass — we don't want to, particularly, have anything with regard to the — with regard to Rogers, you see, because that's very important to maintain that.

SCALI: That's right.

NIXON: But on the other hand, we cannot allow the myth to exist, to get [unclear], that this whole thing, which was mine alone —

KISSINGER: Yeah.

NIXON: Henry, you recall I put it out. It didn't come from the NSC staff either. I put the whole damn thing out twenty months ago, starting that trip around the world.

KISSINGER: Right.

NIXON: He'll give you the chapter and verse. It's a fascinating story, and someday it's going to be written. But anyway — and maybe now, maybe a little bit of it now. A little bit of it now, before it's announced, just to see if we can't —

KISSINGER: I think we should get a little further. It's — the danger is that this whole operation will stop again. And we've had it started once and it stopped.

NIXON: And it stopped. That's right.

KISSINGER: We shouldn't crow too early.

NIXON: We don't want to crow. We don't want to crow. We simply want to say we're watching with interest and all that sort of thing. The point is that I think that it's important, Henry, for John to know what the game is.

KISSINGER: I'll give him the picture this afternoon —

NIXON: Now, John, the main thing that you have to know is that first, everybody around here, and everybody in the government, in the NSC, is not told everything. They are not. But I told Henry that I want you to know anything that — in these critical areas. But you must remember that when we are telling you these things, as I'm sure you know, that, usually, there's an awful good reason not to tell others.

SCALI: I understand.

NIXON: And so, you know what I mean. And that's the reason on the — I use the China thing as an example; I don't know of a better one. It's a very delicate situation. Maybe in three weeks we'll want to tell a little more of the story. Maybe not this week. Maybe a little of it comes out this week. As I suggested to you this morning, I may have to remind you —

KISSINGER: We can get a little out. Well —

SCALI: I want to be in the position of knowing so that I can recommend to you, perhaps, when.

NIXON: That's right.

HALDEMAN: That's —

NIXON: Sure.

• • •

[HALDEMAN and SCALI leave the conversation.]

NIXON: I don't think you'll have any — I know you'll have no problem with leaks from him [Scali]. None.

KISSINGER: I won't tell him, though, about the summit game yet.

NIXON: Oh, God no. I don't want anybody to know about the summit game —

KISSINGER: Right.

NIXON: — that hasn't been told. The only one that knows is Haldeman.

KISSINGER: Yeah.

NIXON: Shultz doesn't know.

KISSINGER: No.

NIXON: Ehrlichman doesn't know.

KISSINGER: No.

NIXON: Jesus Christ! If that ever gets out, it's down the drain.

KISSINGER: Right.

NIXON: The summit game should be absolutely between us.

KISSINGER: That's right.

NIXON: Until Dobrynin gets back. And also the SALT game.

KISSINGER: That's right.

NIXON: Don't tell him about the SALT game — the SALT game, the summit game. But the China game is something else again. He should know that background. Tell him why we don't want a broker.

KISSINGER: Incidentally, I thought I'd have Dobrynin's replacement in for five minutes this afternoon, because there's a meeting — it's just a technical thing — between Rush and Abrasimov that I've set up for Berlin for Friday. And I'll just review the arrangements with him. It will take five minutes, but it's — it shows them that this channel has some uses for them. I won't say anything else except the technical arrangements of that meeting.

NIXON: Yeah. Fine. Whatever you want.

• • •

KISSINGER: But now, if a few good things happen, people will say, "He [Nixon] knew all along what he was doing."

NIXON: Yes—

KISSINGER: And, of course, if we pulled off a spectacular and—

NIXON: I know.

KISSINGER: — settled it this year—

NIXON: Well, let's not even think about that.

KISSINGER: Right.

NIXON: The only good thing that I would like to see—

KISSINGER: It could happen, Mr. President.

NIXON: Well, it could.

KISSINGER: I really think it could—

NIXON: It could. But the good thing that I would like to see—I mean, I'm shooting low. At the lowest, I want the summit.

KISSINGER: Yeah. I think that will—

NIXON: Even without SALT. Just the summit.

KISSINGER: I just don't see how they cannot have a summit.

NIXON: Yeah.

KISSINGER: I mean—

NIXON: If we have the summit—

KISSINGER: — looked at from their cold-blooded point of view, they may—after all, you don't like Brezhnev and you would just as soon screw Brezhnev. But why would you expend your capital on somebody who is irrelevant to you? They may not like you. If this were '72, they probably would hang on. But the fact that Brezhnev has just been elevated to the top spot, and you would be the first president to come to Moscow—the Russian people are pro-American. It would mean one hell of a lot of symbolism to them if they can get a SALT agreement signed in Moscow, so that the—

NIXON: The Russian people are pro-American.

KISSINGER: Yeah. It's a Moscow treaty. He can claim credit for it all over the Communist world.

NIXON: Incidentally, could I—could you make a note, and I know that it's a silly thing to even think about, but why not—why don't we consider the possibility of a, which you raised with Dobrynin, of a nonaggression pact? Why not?

KISSINGER: No. That's dangerous because that would be the end of NATO.

NIXON: No, I mean with NATO.

KISSINGER: Well, that's what they've always offered.

NIXON: No, no, no, no. What I meant is the whole wax—the whole ball of wax.

KISSINGER: Yeah, but the danger—

NIXON: Not with America in, not the Soviet Union and the United States in—

KISSINGER: No, but the danger—

NIXON: Now, look, I know that—

KISSINGER: The danger is that then they'll say you don't need a NATO. But what we can do is have a European security conference next year.

NIXON: Well, we agree to that next year.

KISSINGER: No, we agree to it at the summit for next year, so you have had—

NIXON: And that's got to come for a reason.

KISSINGER: — a big conference next year.

NIXON: Have that next year, but what the hell comes out of that? Hope?

KISSINGER: Nothing but a conference.

NIXON: Well, we can have a lot of nice little truisms about travel.

KISSINGER: Well, it just keeps things moving. I mean, at this stage of the game, if we can play a cold-blooded game, in which we don't give anything away, we can make them work for it, because I really think your reelection is essential for the country. There just isn't anybody else.

NIXON: Except Connally.

"Brezhnev has two choices. . . . He's got to break out, one way or the other, just as we do."

April 14, 1971, 9:10 a.m.

Richard Nixon and Henry Kissinger

OVAL OFFICE

As much as Nixon and Kissinger hoped their friendly signals to China would be reciprocated, even they were caught off guard by Premier Zhou Enlai's unprecedented private comments to the U.S. Ping-Pong team in Beijing. This might just be the breakthrough that Nixon and Kissinger were looking for.

• • •

KISSINGER: Zhou Enlai gave an interview to that Ping-Pong team — he's such a subtle guy—

NIXON: Yeah.

KISSINGER: — in which he said that this begins a new era of Chinese-American relations.

NIXON: Really?!

KISSINGER: Yeah.

NIXON: [laughs] To a Ping-Pong team?!

KISSINGER: [laughs]

NIXON: You know, what they're really—

KISSINGER: Right—

NIXON: — they're really trying to drive at: irritating the Russians.

KISSINGER: Right.

NIXON: Two questions: I don't know, but are we unnecessarily irritating the Russians about this right now?

KISSINGER: Well, I am slightly — I'm thinking this, Mr. President. Well, first of all, my call to Dobrynin was a good move.

NIXON: Well, you think that may have been too eager?

KISSINGER: Oh, no.

NIXON: No, I wondered, in light of this, that whether or not you —

KISSINGER: No, I just called him to congratulate him on the Central Committee election and —

NIXON: Yeah, but I mean, you call him and then today we — wham!

KISSINGER: Well, I think what I might do is to get this fellow Vorontsov over here again and say, "Now, look, our top priority is the relation with you."

NIXON: That's right. And that this is something that's been in the works for six months.

KISSINGER: And now let's not miss the opportunity.

NIXON: Yeah.

• • •

KISSINGER: He [Vorontsov] said that he had noticed I had said some friendly things about the Brezhnev speech and that pleased him very much. And he slobbered all over me. And he said the ambassador would come back with new instructions on Sunday. And they hope —

NIXON: He said we should pay attention to Brezhnev's speech?

KISSINGER: Yes. And he said, "Now, you noticed that we were paying constructive attention." Because I had said on *Air Force One* —

NIXON: Oh, yeah.

KISSINGER: — that it was a conciliatory speech, coming, when I was coming back from California.

NIXON: And he said we should know?

KISSINGER: Right. Then I said as a joke, I said, "You know, your ambassador gave me his phone number in Moscow, and I lost it, and it's too late in the day now anyway to call him" — there's an eight-hour difference — "otherwise, I'd congratulate him for his, on his election to the Central Committee. Why don't you do it for me?"

NIXON: That's fine.

KISSINGER: A half-hour later, they called over and they said, "The time difference doesn't, is of no account. Why don't you call him? It would please him very much," and gave me the Moscow phone number —

NIXON: Oh, the phone number. Good.

KISSINGER: — which, as you know, they don't give out Moscow phone numbers.

NIXON: No, no.

KISSINGER: Well, I called him in Moscow. I said, "I just want to congratulate you." And I said, "I just want to tell you I discussed some procedural things with your man here." And he said, "Was it about the exchange of letters? Because I'll have something to say about that." I said, "Oh, no. They're just purely technical things." And he said, "Well, I'm coming back with new instructions on Sunday." He was very — Haig listened in to it, on it. And he said it was —

NIXON: Of course, the instructions — well, we've been through this before, Henry.

KISSINGER: Well, it looks —

NIXON: The instructions could turn the other way too.

KISSINGER: I doubt it. They could but I doubt it. I'm looking at it from Brezhnev's point of view. Now, Brezhnev has two choices. He can't continue the way he's going. He's got to break out, one way or the other, just as we do.

NIXON: Mm-hmm.

KISSINGER: So he's going to go either very tough, which I think is premature for him, or he's going to go the way we want him to go. Not to help — certainly not to help us out. You see, I'm beginning to think we can get that ambassador into Beijing before the year, before another calendar year has passed.

• • •

NIXON: Be sure that this one — they [Department of State] have been screwing us so much on leaks. Now, we're about to screw them on this one. For this thing, just a little lightly.

KISSINGER: Yeah. Well, I think this China thing is completely confusing our opponents also. That's a tremendous break that —

NIXON: You really think it is?

KISSINGER: Oh, yeah. They just can't tell what else is going on. And, of course, they're right.

NIXON: What's going on —

KISSINGER: I think, Mr. President, this is going to have a significant backwash on Hanoi.

NIXON: That's the point that I think you — that I hadn't thought of, but you're right. They've got to worry about our looking at China. They don't — no Communist trusts another Communist. He doesn't trust his own mother. Isn't that right?

KISSINGER: They — and no Vietnamese trusts any foreigner, so they must think that they could become an insignificant plaything.

NIXON: Hmm.

KISSINGER: And they must figure, as they correctly do, that unless the Chinese, who are very worried about the Russians — see, I think if Brezhnev jumps anyone, it will be the Chinese. Not us.

NIXON: He's not going to jump us —

KISSINGER: If —

NIXON: — as we get reelected.

KISSINGER: Yeah. And if he's not going to jump us, he's got to go the other way with us. Anything else will look like stagnation. And he needs some sort of big leadership ploy. It's a — in my view, it's a coincidence of needs.

NIXON: And his aim—

KISSINGER: We need a leadership ploy and he needs one.

NIXON: Yeah. Yeah. Yeah.

• • •

NIXON: On ABM, I must say, throw at them what we know privately. But that means that in our discussions with this son of a bitch [Dobrynin] when he comes back, you've got to—if there is just—you've got to remember, there isn't much to deal with. To me, the worst of both worlds would be for us to get nothing.

KISSINGER: That's right.

NIXON: Nothing. To be beaten in the House—in the Senate on the thing. We could just forget any kind of thing, you know. Then SALT is dead. Absolutely dead. I think you should know that, while you must play the game, that we're going to go forward with the ABM in your talks with him. You got to assume, they're for immediate agreement on it.

KISSINGER: Oh, I recognize that, Mr. President.

NIXON: Well, let me say, now, we have to recognize it not because it's right but because we can't get it otherwise. That's all there is to it. That's all. We've got it figured out.

KISSINGER: Yeah. I thought they'd give us one more year of—they just—you see, if—

NIXON: Henry, if you get any kind of a letter or any kind of a, even a half-assed statement, you could get another year. That's good.

KISSINGER: Well, we'll get a half-assed statement by June 1.

NIXON: How do you do that? We can say—

KISSINGER: I think—

NIXON: We can say—

KISSINGER: I don't know why I'm so confident, because if they figure we're going to lose it anyway, why should they make a deal?

NIXON: Yeah, well, maybe they're not so sure. They—we've surprised them before. I think maybe that's part of it. But I think you should know it's awful tough. The ABM one is very tough because of the way the damn split has come. If we were—just figure—if we could just figure what happened on, in our states, it'd be fine. But the two southerners that we lost—

KISSINGER: Yeah.

NIXON: Goddamn.

KISSINGER: Lawton Chiles.

NIXON: And Lloyd Bentsen. Then they may be better, better than they seem so far.

KISSINGER: He may vote with us on that.

NIXON: Might they? They were very mad.

KISSINGER: I think he'll vote with us on that.

NIXON: Put the heat on but—Bentsen may. I think you ought to—I think that when he [Dobrynin] gets back, he probably will have something to say. But I don't want this damn Chinese action to infuriate them so damn much—

KISSINGER: No, well —

NIXON: — that they figure they got to keep us waiting a month.

KISSINGER: They are tough customers, Mr. President. They don't play it that way.

NIXON: Right.

KISSINGER: And I think from — our experience with them now has been that whenever we put it to them — I'm — when he comes back, I'm going to tell him that if we don't settle it in two weeks, I'll send him back to the State Department. Might as well go for broke on it.

NIXON: That's right.

KISSINGER: That I won't deal with him anymore. If we can't settle a simple matter like a SALT exchange of letters in this channel, there's nothing worth doing.

NIXON: That's right. That's right.

KISSINGER: Now, if it fails, it fails.

NIXON: That's an impediment.

KISSINGER: With this luck, they'll — but I don't think it will fail. And really, I think these Russians are so tough that if we —

NIXON: Yeah?

KISSINGER: — if they have any sense of insecurity on our part — they will be impressed by this Chinese thing —

NIXON: Mm-hmm.

KISSINGER: — if we give them a way out.

NIXON: Mm-hmm.

KISSINGER: We'll get them that message to say that our priority is Soviet relations and that it's really up to them —

NIXON: I think you could get that to Vorontsov.

KISSINGER: Yeah, I'll — just so — because they're meeting tomorrow.

NIXON: He'll dutifully report it.

KISSINGER: Yeah. Thursday is the Politburo meeting there.

NIXON: Right. The Politburo meeting.

KISSINGER: Yeah.

NIXON: Another thing: they did launch that raid yesterday, or they're going today, or what's —?

KISSINGER: They've started the movement, yes.

NIXON: Mm-hmm.

KISSINGER: The first part of it is inside South Vietnam —

NIXON: Mm-hmm.

KISSINGER: — down the A Shau Valley.

NIXON: Well, you're right about one thing. We are not interested, Henry, at this point — particularly at this point too — [in] anything, whenever they've got to take any risks on our casualties.

KISSINGER: Yes.

NIXON: It just isn't worth it now.

KISSINGER: No.

NIXON: We've got too many other fish to fry.

KISSINGER: No, no. We've got — you know —

NIXON: Yeah, but even there, we could —

KISSINGER: — I've always been for a tough policy on Vietnam —

NIXON: So have I. Already —

KISSINGER: — but we've got to cool it a bit there now.

NIXON: We always have — actually, Henry, we've given them everything now.

KISSINGER: I know.

NIXON: I mean, they've fouled everything up. We just got to — we have to do a little bit, little bit different game.

KISSINGER: Yeah. I told him that. We can't have it. We can't have many helicopter losses, because we're now, if we get — this Chinese thing is deflating matters. With half a break, we should get that SALT thing wrapped up in two weeks.

NIXON: The SALT thing, huh? You think the China policy — the SALT thing will have one enormous wallop.

KISSINGER: That's two weeks more, and then, if the SALT thing works, we'll have the summit by the middle of May, and then we have the summer free.

NIXON: [The] whole thing will pack a wallop such as you can't imagine.

KISSINGER: Well, that's good. And on SALT, State won't be able to leak a damn thing because they won't know it —

NIXON: Sure.

KISSINGER: — until you're ready to do it.

NIXON: And the summit, they won't be able to leak a thing, because —

KISSINGER: Right.

NIXON: — they won't know it either. You know, I think we should — while on the summit, just as soon as it gets down to any kind of an understanding, we ought to get it out. Do you understand?

KISSINGER: No — oh, no question.

• • •

NIXON: The main thing: what pace it is, is not important now. That will set them talking. I mean, the press corps here will be writing spec stories, and so forth, fighting to get out, over there, and trying to, you know, determine who's going to get to go, and who's going to cover it and all — an American president to visit Russia. If it comes, do you realize what that's going to be? The damnedest show you ever saw in the world.

KISSINGER: One thing — maybe another thing I ought to tell Vorontsov, which I haven't told Dobrynin yet, just so that we get it into the system, that August is no longer possible for a summit. We've got to have it in the first half of September.

NIXON: After Labor Day.

KISSINGER: Right.

NIXON: We can leave — that I have a very important — I have a schedule right through Labor Day, but I can leave the day after Labor Day. You know, let's just put it that way.

KISSINGER: So that we don't waste any exchanges of —

NIXON: Yeah. I wouldn't fall on that but that's a good point [unclear].

KISSINGER: Just — one reason why it's a pleasure to deal with these sons of bitches is you know that you can't hurt their feelings.

NIXON: No. No.

KISSINGER: And you can — you can get them mad. And that's why perhaps it would be useful if I saw this guy today.

NIXON: That's quite interesting.

KISSINGER: All our experts were again wrong. All of them said it would hurt us with the Soviets — Laos would hurt with the Chinese, with the Soviets, and with everybody else. It hasn't. It — if anything, it's helped with the Chinese.

"Kennedy was cold, impersonal, he treated his staff like dogs."
April 15, 1971, 8:59 a.m.
Richard Nixon, Bob Haldeman, and Henry Kissinger

The Kennedys were one of Richard Nixon's favorite conversation topics. "Obsession" might be an overstatement, but Nixon often compared their achievements with his own political career. He criticized the myth of Camelot and drew a contrast between their public image and what he believed was the private reality. Long before the term "frenemy" entered our lexicon, Nixon spoke of the Kennedys with a combination of admiration and disgust.

• • •

NIXON: Kennedy was cold, impersonal, he treated his staff like dogs, particularly his secretaries and the others. He was not a beat man, he didn't read, all these other things. His staff created the impression of warm, sweet, and nice to people, reads lot of books, a philosopher, and all that sort of thing. That was a pure creation of mythology. We have created no mythology. The one thing, Bob, that has not gotten across, and I come back to it again. Henry's beginning to get some of it across now. For Christ's sakes, can't we get across the courage more? Courage, boldness, guts? Goddamn it! That is the thing.

• • •

NIXON: What is the most important single factor that should come across out of the first two years? Guts! Absolutely. Guts! Don't you agree, Henry?

KISSINGER: Totally.

NIXON: Intelligence? Maybe, but a president is expected to be intelligent.

KISSINGER: Well, complexity and guts.

NIXON: Well, complexity. But a president is expected to be intelligent, so wash that out.

I mean, I may have a little more than most, but not as much as some. But on the other hand, just sheer unadulterated guts, and boldness stand alone. And coolness under fire. Now goddamn it, can't we just try to get one point across, Bob? That's all. What do you think, Henry, or do you agree?

KISSINGER: No, I think that should get across.

• • •

KISSINGER: I was thinking today, the *Washington Post* editorial, he had to find something to slam.

NIXON: So?

KISSINGER: So they said, they don't understand why you said that the trade, lifting the trade restrictions, easing up on China, why is it you had to say it was planned a long time ago. It would have been much better if you had said it was in response to the Ping-Pong trip.

NIXON: Oh, shit! Really? Oh, God!

HALDEMAN: They didn't put it exactly that way, but what they did was take a cheap shot. They said it was a good thing to have done, but they couldn't understand why you were so concerned with making the point that it had been decided before the Ping-Pong.

KISSINGER: Because you don't make a major addition of your policy—

NIXON: Because of a Ping-Pong team.

KISSINGER: —because of a Ping-Pong team. It makes you look trivial. Because you don't want to scare the Russians out of their mind.

NIXON: We don't care what they say.

KISSINGER: If Kennedy had brought China policy a tenth of the way to this point, they'd be throwing bouquets at me [unclear].

HALDEMAN: The overall thing out of there is, what bothers them is that they don't like the fact that Nixon is going to get credit for it.

KISSINGER: That's right. That's right.

"You know, when you stop to think of eight hundred million people, and where they're going to be. Jesus, this is a hell of a move."
April 15, 1971, 7:33 p.m.
Richard Nixon and Henry Kissinger
WHITE HOUSE TELEPHONE

Even as the reality of a potential breakthrough with China set in, Nixon and Kissinger returned to reality. The outcome remained an unknown, and the impact on the Vietnam War or U.S.-Soviet relations was also an unknown.

• • •

NIXON: Henry, you know, we don't realize—I think China, more than Moscow, is a goddamn nerve thing for these people. What do you think? I don't know.

KISSINGER: Because it's so new.

NIXON: Yeah.

KISSINGER: And, of course, there's —

NIXON: And, of course, let's face it, in the long run, it's so historic. You know, when you stop to think of eight hundred million people, and where they're going to be. Jesus, this is a hell of a move.

KISSINGER: Of course, I don't want to get our hopes up too much, but one of the things that has occurred to me, that I did not tell to this fellow [Henry Hubbard of *Newsweek*] —

NIXON: Yeah?

KISSINGER: — is that it is conceivable — indeed, it is very possible — that they know Hanoi's going to make a peace move and they don't want to be left out.

NIXON: Mm-hmm. Yeah. Well, that'll take care of itself. Getting back to the Russian thing, I was concerned about the TASS thing. [On April 15, TASS reported that "reciprocal gestures" between the United States and the People's Republic of China had taken place.] I don't know how — how are you — are you concerned that much? Are we — let's — or do we — can you call Vorontsov again and — or that would be too much?

KISSINGER: No, I think that would make us look too eager, Mr. President.

NIXON: Well, I don't want them to think, though, that — you know what I mean? Maybe you should call Dobrynin.

KISSINGER: No, Mr. President —

NIXON: Yeah?

KISSINGER: I've called Dobrynin once.

NIXON: All right.

KISSINGER: I've had Vorontsov in.

NIXON: All right.

KISSINGER: I've called Vorontsov this morning.

NIXON: Mm-hmm.

KISSINGER: And I've had Ziegler put out a statement.

NIXON: Right, that's enough. Okay.

KISSINGER: And I think any more would really be overeager —

NIXON: Yeah. And now, at this point, they're basically, TASS is simply — but TASS, that shows that they must be hysterical about this damn thing.

KISSINGER: That's right.

NIXON: Huh?

KISSINGER: That's right.

NIXON: [laughs] Because they said, "This removed the mask of U.S-China" — [laughs] shit, we don't have any relations with the Chinese.

KISSINGER: Well, they're also —

NIXON: They must think we're doing something.

KISSINGER: Well, they're also using it against the Chinese.

NIXON: Oh, how's that?

KISSINGER: Well, because one of the things in which the Chinese have been driving them crazy, is by claiming they were revolutionary purists while the Russians were opportunists —

NIXON: Yeah, I see.

KISSINGER: So this is part of their internal problem.

NIXON: I see. So they're saying that we are the — they are, the Chinese, colluding with the capitalists.

KISSINGER: That's right. I think this was more directed at them.

NIXON: You know, I would say this: the columnists and the rest, they should have enough to write about for at least two weeks. I don't say it's a month —

KISSINGER: Oh, yes —

NIXON: — but two weeks —

KISSINGER: — but, of course, at the end of those two weeks, we may have something else to tell them.

NIXON: Yeah.

"Because the American people are so peace-loving, they think agreements solve everything."
April 17, 1971, 2:36 p.m.
Richard Nixon, Bob Haldeman, and Henry Kissinger
OVAL OFFICE

Nixon often spoke of wanting to erase the Vietnam War from his agenda. In calm or frustrated moments, he spoke of all-out bombing of North Vietnam in order to end the war once and for all, and with a victory. Demonstrations against the war rocked college campuses, reaching a peak in 1970 after the May 4 shooting at Kent State University where Ohio National Guardsmen killed four students. In the aftermath of Kent State there was a fury of protest not seen since the Johnson administration. For a brief time in 1970, the Nixon White House was even ringed bumper to bumper with buses to prevent protesters from breaching the grounds of the White House.

A steady sequence of troop withdrawals by Nixon, beginning in his first year in office, was planned in part to defuse the antiwar movement. Nonetheless, plans for major antiwar activity leading up to May Day 1971 were in the works, and Nixon knew it. The new, angry season of protests was set to begin on April 23–24 with massive demonstrations in Washington, and students were planning a May Day march on Washington on May 5.

• • •

NIXON: That's right, but they say, "Well, by God, we're going to keep —" It — well, the main thing it does: it tells the enemy that in no uncertain terms that, by God, you're going to do — we're going to stay right there, and also, I've thrown out something there, as you noticed: that we're going to bomb 'em, which we damn well will. If we've withdrawn and they haven't returned a thing, we'll bomb the hell out of North Vietnam. Get my point? Just bomb the living bejeezus out of it, and everybody would approve of it. Well, I don't know about that.

· · ·

[KISSINGER joins the conversation.]

NIXON: We're not moving too fast on that [China]. We're moving goddamn slowly.

KISSINGER: That's right.

NIXON: We're going to continue to move slowly, Henry.

KISSINGER: I don't think we have to hurry now.

NIXON: If we push—

KISSINGER: First of all, we now have to hear from the Russians. We have to hear what they've got to say.

NIXON: That's right, if anything. And also what Chiang has to say.

KISSINGER: No, the Russians, after that first bleat, I think we've quieted them down with our statement. See, that Ziegler statement—

NIXON: —was very good.

KISSINGER: —was front page in the *New York Times* and they reported it in Moscow.

NIXON: Mm-hmm. And you, of course, calling him—

KISSINGER: And my calling Dobrynin.

NIXON: That's right.

KISSINGER: And my calling Vorontsov.

NIXON: That's right.

KISSINGER: And while I'm sure they're spinning like crazy—

NIXON: Mm-hmm.

KISSINGER: And we've got their paranoia working for us. No matter how much we protest, they don't believe it anyway.

NIXON: They particularly won't believe me.

KISSINGER: Yeah. But on the other hand—

NIXON: You see, they really think I'm a tricky bastard. And they're right.

KISSINGER: Well, you're the toughest president they've dealt with.

NIXON: You see, the others—

KISSINGER: If you had the nuclear superiority—

NIXON: You see, the sentiment that—if they thought I was sentimental, you know, if they thought I was really like I was talking last night [at a "panel interview" during the annual convention of the American Society of Newspaper Editors at the Shoreham Hotel], you know, about wanting to visit China and the whole joke, you know, and all that crap, then [laughs] there's nothing—but they know that—

KISSINGER: No, they know you.

NIXON: They know that's cosmetic.

· · ·

KISSINGER: And—

NIXON: [unclear]

KISSINGER: —with the Chinese, the Russians, there is an enormous respect. And in this respect—from this point of view, your April 7 speech—

NIXON: Helped?

KISSINGER: —was crucial.

· · ·

KISSINGER: If you analyze—I've become convinced, Mr. President, we cannot accept the Soviet proposal. Their proposal is Moscow versus Washington, and no offensive limitations—

NIXON: You haven't told him anything? Dobrynin doesn't know you're not going to accept it then?

KISSINGER: No, I've told him we want Safeguard. He knows we want Safeguard.

NIXON: Oh, yeah. Yeah.

KISSINGER: But the proposal that Smith is pushing is the following: we would have to tear down the only thing we're building with the right to build something that Congress will never appropriate, namely a Washington defense. And they can continue to keep what they already have.

NIXON: Which—which defends some of their missiles, right?

KISSINGER: Which defends five hundred of their missiles. Plus—plus, permitting them to continue their offensive buildup. Once the American people understand that, I think—

HALDEMAN: What, what do we get from them in this respect?

NIXON: Clever bastards, aren't they?

KISSINGER: I mean it's a really ridiculous proposal. But of course—

NIXON: On our part, it's ridiculous? Oh—

KISSINGER: Yeah. Well, what I've told Dobrynin, what Smith doesn't know, is that we won't accept it. What we want is Safeguard. That at least enables us to keep what we've already got, and it protects some of our missiles. Next week, if they accept our—

NIXON: If we find that out next week, then we got to start the big push for more national defense. That also means, of course, then we've got to go for more taxes. It's a tough row.

· · ·

NIXON: The real point here, what you're talking—what we're really talking about here, though, is something different. And I know that this kind of an agreement isn't worth a damn.

KISSINGER: That's right.

NIXON: Any kind of agreement with the Soviet—

KISSINGER: I agree.

NIXON: We're having it for political reasons.

KISSINGER: That's right.

NIXON: Because the American people are so peace-loving, they think agreements solve everything. If we can do it for political reasons — this is where I would disagree with Buckley, who won't understand it — if we can do this, and get sort of the peace issue going with us, we — the Democrats —

KISSINGER: No, no. Buckley isn't against a SALT agreement.

NIXON: The Democrats — I know. But I'm a lot more hard-line than he is on this kind of thing. Once we get it in, and then, should we then survive in the election —

KISSINGER: Then it's separately —

NIXON: — then by God, we have got to lay the facts before the Soviet and before the American people and go all out —

KISSINGER: I agree.

NIXON: — on more defense. That is really what —

KISSINGER: That's how I see it, Mr. President.

NIXON: The whole point of this, as you know, that —

HALDEMAN: Well, and that's the argument to the defense, to the hard-line sophisticates, is that that's their only hope. Because —

NIXON: Yeah, Bob —

HALDEMAN: — if Nixon's defeated, you know damn well —

NIXON: Well, there the point is, the reason that we can't get the defense now is that the goddamn Congress won't give it to us.

HALDEMAN: It won't give us the money.

NIXON: That's right. We're having a hell of a time. They're going to be cutting this defense budget —

KISSINGER: But, what it may suggest, Mr. President, is that we'd be better off having the Democrats cut us than compromising with them ahead of time on some of these defense items.

NIXON: Oh, hell. I wouldn't compromise.

KISSINGER: Simply as a strategy.

NIXON: That's right. And vote against the cuts.

KISSINGER: And vote against the cuts and then accept them.

NIXON: And I'll simply say that the cuts in defense are, are — endanger our national security. Let them be against national security —

• • •

KISSINGER: I think the China story has driven Vietnam into a secondary rank.

NIXON: For what?

HALDEMAN: Although going into Laos has been — we've got to watch that, too. I think that's been the view of —

KISSINGER: Who's going into Laos?

HALDEMAN: The South Vietnamese.

KISSINGER: Oh, but that's just in and out.

NIXON: I mean, these little — they've already done that.

KISSINGER: Uh —

NIXON: Those raids? Is that what you mean?

KISSINGER: Yeah, yeah.

NIXON: The raids?

HALDEMAN: Yeah.

NIXON: We've been in twice, and they didn't make a blip.

HALDEMAN: Now they're talking about the buildup in A Shau, and all that stuff —

KISSINGER: Yeah, but A Shau is in — on the Vietnamese side.

NIXON: But that is —

HALDEMAN: It still leads to Laos, doesn't it?

NIXON: I know.

KISSINGER: Yeah, but they clean that out once a year, in order to prevent an attack on Hue. They're not going deep into there. They'll — that won't go.

HALDEMAN: That's the only, only area where you've got any activity in Vietnam that's gonna, you know, make a blip.

KISSINGER: I know, but there isn't much —

NIXON: I do not think that will be too big. I — my guess is that I don't think it'll make that big an operation. Does it, Henry?

KISSINGER: No. And, they're not — the South Vietnamese aren't going anywhere where they're going to suffer casualties right now. Doing that for their own [unclear].

HALDEMAN: They did good at Fire Base 6. They finally — even the media has finally got [laughs] has given us that.

KISSINGER: That was a big victory.

HALDEMAN: Sure. But it took a long time before they admitted it. They didn't call it that. They —

KISSINGER: Oh yeah, they're now give —

HALDEMAN: [unclear]

KISSINGER: — fifteen hundred enemy killed, three battalions —

NIXON: By the ARVN.

KISSINGER: By the ARVN.

NIXON: And a little air power. The A Shau Valley, I don't think it's the same thing as Laos, Bob, for the reason that it doesn't involve a tremendous exposed flank, and all the rest. I mean, they're just going to —

HALDEMAN: It is the same thing, though —

NIXON: Incidentally —

HALDEMAN: [unclear] the media [unclear] I think you're gonna — any chance they get, like they're picking up Abrams's statement that he wouldn't rule out another invasion of Laos.

NIXON: Yeah.

HALDEMAN: That's — they're, they're going to look for any little thing —

NIXON: Yeah.

HALDEMAN: — like that to try and regenerate. I don't think they'll succeed. I think you're right.

NIXON: Yeah. Well —

KISSINGER: Besides, I told Osborne, you know —

NIXON: Yeah.

KISSINGER: You remember now, six weeks ago, everyone told us that we are bringing China into Southeast Asia.

HALDEMAN: Yeah. That's the one that's fun to throw at them.

NIXON: Yeah. What did he say?

KISSINGER: And I said, "Now, look —"

NIXON: Because he wrote it, too —

KISSINGER: Yeah. I said not a word that they haven't mentioned Vietnam once on this whole trip of this Ping-Pong team, and to the journalists. The Hanoi people put out a statement in Paris today saying that China stands unalterably behind them. I consider that a sign of weakness. They have to put out a statement —

NIXON: Yeah.

HALDEMAN: And they put it out, not China?

KISSINGER: No, no. Hanoi put it out in Paris.

NIXON: We just know that means that they're, they're defensive —

KISSINGER: That they're defensive, and they announced in Hanoi a railway agreement between China and North Vietnam with big fanfare — the sort of thing they do once every six months.

NIXON: Hmm.

• • •

KISSINGER: You see, the way we are setting up the Hanoi thing, we'll be in a position where we either get a settlement, or announce, together with Thieu, not a complete terminal date, but something in which, for a cease-fire and — and a prisoner exchange, we will give a terminal date.

NIXON: Mm-hmm.

KISSINGER: So, if we will either get Hanoi to agree, or we'll announce it during the summit —

NIXON: Remember, at the same — at that time, too, we will then announce the end of the American combat role.

KISSINGER: At the same time —

NIXON: At the very least.

KISSINGER: Yeah.

NIXON: What I think we ought to do on that, if we — if it turns out that way, is not to put it all in one announcement. I'd have it — I'd make it a two-day meeting. Let's let 'em come one day, and then come the other. And we could get maximum bang out of it.

KISSINGER: That's right.

NIXON: Knock everything for what it's worth.

• • •

KISSINGER: But we'll know by Wednesday, I would think, what — where the Russian thing is going. I mean, if we know that the week after next we have a SALT announcement —

NIXON: Well —

KISSINGER: — then that's going to be a tremendous thing —

NIXON: And, hell, that'll take — that will take care of China for a while? And —

[laughter]

KISSINGER: If we get this —

NIXON: If we could get — to be perfectly frank with you, Henry, maybe we want it after the [May Day] demonstrations.

KISSINGER: I think it's better that way.

HALDEMAN: I would.

KISSINGER: Well, we couldn't.

NIXON: Why is it better? Why have the demonstrations afterwards?

HALDEMAN: Let them have them. Let them run their course through May 5. We can't make it by then anyway. Can you?

NIXON: Yes —

KISSINGER: No. I think you can get the SALT announcement, not next week; I think you could get it the week after next by around the thirtieth.

NIXON: You mean before the demonstration?

KISSINGER: No —

HALDEMAN: No. No, you've got one demonstration — the big demonstration's on the twenty-fourth. Then you have —

NIXON: When's that?

HALDEMAN: This — a week from today.

NIXON: Right.

KISSINGER: That's —

NIXON: Well, it's my view that, I've just decided — I told you, Henry — I decided, Henry, not to do — I was going to have an office press conference next week. Then, I decided not to —

KISSINGER: I think —

NIXON: I think this serves as two press conferences. [unclear]

KISSINGER: That's right.

NIXON: Don't you agree?

KISSINGER: Absolutely.

NIXON: Now, two weeks, however, from now, I'll have a press conference.

KISSINGER: Yeah.

NIXON: I'm not getting frozen into it, but I — about the time, I'll want to hit television.

HALDEMAN: You won't be — we are just about getting to the point where you have to do one on TV.

NIXON: TV? That's right. You get back to TV leadership. Now —

HALDEMAN: And that'll have been three weeks after your —

NIXON: That's right.

HALDEMAN: — your troop announcement.

NIXON: Three weeks after the troop, which is about right. See, we're trying to hit about every three weeks.

KISSINGER: No, that's — that fits very —

NIXON: Now, if that — by that time we might have SALT.

KISSINGER: Yeah. Or at least we would know whether we won't have it —

NIXON: We'll know. We'll know if we won't have it.

HALDEMAN: If we do have it —

NIXON: Yeah.

HALDEMAN: — I sure wouldn't announce it at the press conference.

NIXON: Oh, hell no! Come to think of it, you know what I could do? [laughs] Well, we — it depends on how we want to play it. Rather than having a press conference, we may just go on —

HALDEMAN: TV.

NIXON: — go on TV for five minutes at night.

HALDEMAN: Yeah.

NIXON: See, Henry?

KISSINGER: Yeah.

NIXON: Five minutes at night at prime time to, to make an announcement —

HALDEMAN: All from here.

KISSINGER: Another possibility — but I think Bob is right. The more likely thing is that it would be around May 7. This stuff probably will have to go back and forth once, and they [the Soviet Politburo] meet every Thursday.

NIXON: Okay. Right.

KISSINGER: But we'll know all of this when Dobrynin is back.

• • •

NIXON: I think you can tell me when he [Dobrynin] gets back whether he's going to diddle you.

KISSINGER: I'm not going to let him diddle me. My judgment, Mr. President, if you agree, is that we should go for broke with this fellow now. And then —

NIXON: Oh, hell yes.

KISSINGER: I'll just tell him this is — I'll break the contact, I won't see him anymore, because if we can't settle a simple exchange of letters, then let him work with the State Department.

NIXON: That's right.

KISSINGER: I mean, that's a daring ploy, but they want this contact.

• • •

KISSINGER: He [Brezhnev] needs some successes. He, Mr. President, in his way, he's got a domestic situation as complex as you have and more intractable. He's got to do something that he did. And he's got a lot of opponents in the Politburo, and he's got to make the same decision. He's got to get — I think he needs you in Moscow at least as much as you need to be there. The best thing the Chinese have done for us is not so much in domestic opinion, which is good enough, but it's given us the maneuvering room with the Russians. The thing that worried me with the Russians was that they might think you are so vulnerable —

NIXON: Right.

KISSINGER: — that they're doing you a personal favor that they wouldn't have done.

NIXON: So what if maybe they couldn't. But now they may have to do it for themselves.

KISSINGER: That's right.

NIXON: In other words, they figure that the Chinese — the race to Beijing is on. Well, just so we can keep Beijing from slapping us. Well, it isn't — well, we can't control that either. They might. Do you think they might?

KISSINGER: No, but we should just — insofar as possible, if we could just be a little more disciplined. The government has been superb.

NIXON: Yeah, but the —

KISSINGER: What you said yesterday was —

NIXON: Well, but what about the press shitting and the rest? Should we —?

KISSINGER: But there's nothing we can do.

NIXON: That's right. They're going hog-wild.

KISSINGER: Well, after that first orgasm, I think they've got to quiet down. And they can't keep sending telegrams.

NIXON: Let's see. They're probably thinking [unclear] hay out of the China policy again. Because, as I said last night, implied, if you try to make hay out of it, it won't work.

HALDEMAN: With all we've done, you don't really need to make much hay out of it.

NIXON: I think what we do —

HALDEMAN: It makes hay out of itself.

KISSINGER: That would —

NIXON: We should just let it rest. And, well, also, there's this other danger: you might make hay out of it and then —

KISSINGER: Could I make a [unclear] —

NIXON: — and it'd be a disappointment.

KISSINGER: Yeah.

NIXON: They could turn on it.

KISSINGER: That —

NIXON: Well, we're prepared for that. We're prepared.

KISSINGER: Well, you're, publicly — you have been less enthusiastic than some of the people who have been praising it.

NIXON: That's right.

"There wouldn't be a chance of a Russian play now, a year before the election, if we didn't have the Chinese warming."

April 20, 1971, 1:12 p.m.

Richard Nixon and Henry Kissinger

OVAL OFFICE

Awaiting Brezhnev's response to the week's events between the United States and China, Nixon hoped that they might spur him to compromise on SALT, Berlin, and other issues. If, however, the Soviets came back with a hard line, Nixon was ready with an aggressive stance of his own.

• • •

NIXON: You say Dobrynin will be back tomorrow night?

KISSINGER: Tomorrow late afternoon. I've got it — we've — I've got the FBI checking passenger lists.

NIXON: You expect, then, to hear from him probably Thursday, don't you?

KISSINGER: No later than Friday. He may have to translate something he's bringing back.

NIXON: Translate. All right.

KISSINGER: Oh, he'll bring something back.

NIXON: Now, hold the horses: he's going to bring something. He said he had a message.

KISSINGER: Well, if not, I'll call him.

NIXON: If not, you say, "What the hell is the message here?"

KISSINGER: Yeah. I'll tell him —

NIXON: I mean, don't —

KISSINGER: — either now or we'll break the channel. I think we —

NIXON: Hell, no. No fooling around. But I think it's got to be, it's got to well be understood — I mean you, for your bargaining purposes — that if they, if he ain't going to play, then we'll explore the Chinese one to the hilt if there's any way of exploring it.

KISSINGER: Yeah —

NIXON: The other way — the other thing is, Henry, if he isn't going to play, even though probably it's going to get a little — it will cost us, however, our electoral future — by God, we're going to wake this country up to the danger. And I'll do it. I'm going to tell the country that things are — that we've got to get re-armed.

KISSINGER: I'm not sure it's going to cost us.

NIXON: I'm not sure. It may be — it may, it may.

KISSINGER: It would put the other side into a hell of a position.

NIXON: The country is so, you know, weary trying to get peace.

KISSINGER: But I think —

NIXON: Our problem —

KISSINGER: But I think they're going to play, Mr. President. I can't imagine —

NIXON: No.

KISSINGER: I think the best explanation for the Russian — for the Chinese behavior is that they're — that they had to get in before Brezhnev did.

NIXON: [unclear]

KISSINGER: Because then, on any other ground, they could have waited a month or two.

NIXON: Let me tell you this though, Henry. If they play, God knows — we all know — but if they play, it will be because you and I planned the whole goddamn thing. It wouldn't — listen, there wouldn't be a chance of a Russian play now, a year before the election, if we didn't have the Chinese warming. There wouldn't be a chance. You know that. Is that right?

KISSINGER: And there wouldn't be a chance with the Russians if we hadn't played them so cool all along.

NIXON: Yeah.

KISSINGER: Hell, they were going to give SALT away the first year.

NIXON: That's right. Oh, sure. SALT. Yeah, they would have given the Mideast away — not the Mideast but Berlin.

KISSINGER: Berlin.

NIXON: They were going to give Berlin away. They'll do anything for Willy Brandt.

KISSINGER: Absolutely.

NIXON: Right. To hell with them. Don't give them a thing.

KISSINGER: And if we hadn't — if you hadn't done Cambodia —

NIXON: Ha!

KISSINGER: Basically, we gained with the Russians with these tough moves. They screamed a bit, but that's something they understand.

NIXON: Yeah.

KISSINGER: We'll know by Friday what he's come back with.

"What was Zhou Enlai like? Tell me about him."

April 21, 1971, 11:35 a.m.

Richard Nixon, Graham Steenhoven, Ron Ziegler, John Scali, and Henry Kissinger

OVAL OFFICE

Few Americans had met Zhou Enlai in the previous two decades. Fewer still conservative anti-Communist Republicans had met him or had visited the People's Republic of China. Graham Steenhoven was the lone exception. Steenhoven, a Republican from Detroit, was

the coach of the American Ping-Pong team that visited China the week before and was received by Premier Zhou Enlai.

• • •

STEENHOVEN: I came here from England when I was thirteen and a half.

NIXON: Or you were born in England?

STEENHOVEN: Born in England, yeah. And that's why I said, this group that we took, that were invited, couldn't be any more representative of the United States.

NIXON: Tell me a little about it, will you?

STEENHOVEN: Well, just background-wise, we have a seventeen-year-old girl, who was born in Hungary —

NIXON: Do you pick them?

STEENHOVEN: No, these people were selected on the basis on their ability to play, to go to Japan. And we all go on our own money —

NIXON: Yeah.

STEENHOVEN: — you know, so that was the type of thing. We were completely independent.

KISSINGER: Did you pay for yourselves?

STEENHOVEN: All of us paid for ourselves. Not to go to China.

KISSINGER: No, no.

STEENHOVEN: But to go to Japan.

NIXON: Well, that's the big piece of it.

STEENHOVEN: That's why we had to go.

NIXON: Did you say, what, a fifteen-year —

STEENHOVEN: No, the fifteen-year-old girl [Judy Bochenski]'s from Eugene, Oregon. We had a seventeen-year-old girl [Olga Soltesz] born in Hungary, that lives in Orlando, Florida. We had a twenty-three-year-old housewife [Connie Sweeris] whose baby was two years old a couple of days, just a day before we got home. It was a bad day for her, she wanted to be home with her child. She's our national champion, a marvelous girl from Grand Rapids.

NIXON: Mm-hmm.

STEENHOVEN: Then we had myself, born in England, and Rufford Harrison's born in England. And we had a, the term is "black," not "colored" anymore, but the black man [George Braithwaite], who's a real gentleman, you might have seen him on *The Tonight Show.*

KISSINGER: I saw him.

NIXON: Mm-hmm.

STEENHOVEN: He's in a shirt and tie when the rest look like bums, right? He's from British Guyana.

NIXON: God, this is an international group!

STEENHOVEN: We had one from the Dominican Republic.

NIXON: Did you?

STEENHOVEN: Yes, Errol Resek is from the Dominican Republic.

NIXON: Isn't that something.

STEENHOVEN: So you couldn't have had, and then we had a guy with hair down to here.

NIXON: Yeah. Who was he?

STEENHOVEN: Frankie Allen from California.

NIXON: California, that's my state!

[laughter]

• • •

NIXON: Let me ask a question that you've probably responded to, but I would like to get your evaluation. What was Zhou Enlai like? How did he look physically? I know he is very intelligent, because I have mutual friends, even though we're on this side [unclear]. But George Yeh, the respected ambassador, knows Zhou Enlai. What was he like? Tell me about him.

STEENHOVEN: First, let me explain how, we went into a room and there were now five countries there, and we weren't alone. So there were five countries all over China, but they kept us separated until we met Zhou Enlai.

NIXON: Mm-hmm.

STEENHOVEN: We went into this tremendous room. What was it, you know, the equivalent of the White House?

NIXON: Sure.

STEENHOVEN: And they had us alphabetically, and of course that made the USA last. Because when they put up signs, we were America, but when we were seated, we were USA.

NIXON: Sure, sure. It's like the UN.

STEENHOVEN: Well anyhow, he talked with Marge Baldwin of Canada. Now, we know the Canadians very well, and I know Marge Baldwin, and he talked with her, and of course —

KISSINGER: In English?

NIXON: He does know English though?

STEENHOVEN: I'm positive he knows better English than the interpreter.

NIXON: Oh!

KISSINGER: Oh no, he speaks English.

NIXON: He didn't speak English to you?

STEENHOVEN: No, not to us. He spoke Chinese.

NIXON: Hmm.

STEENHOVEN: But when the interpreter was interpreting to us, in English, and made a mistake, he corrected her.

NIXON: Hmm.

STEENHOVEN: And it didn't take long to pick that up. But he's very bright. And anyway, he'd be talking, and he knew everything about each group. He was so thoroughly briefed, and an immense memory. And he kept asking for criticism. "Please criticize us. We want to do better. Let us know your criticisms." You know.

NIXON: You mean of the country?

STEENHOVEN: Anything, he didn't care. And, nobody crit—

NIXON: He asked you that kind of question?

STEENHOVEN: He asked all of us this, as a group. He said—

NIXON: More importantly, what did he ask you? Because you're the Americans.

STEENHOVEN: So he got around to sitting with me. And he commented about the various things we had done, and how pleased he was to see us, and so on. And he asked some of the same questions again. And I said, "Well, I've been thinking that, because you've been asking about that. Nobody has criticized you, but I have one." "What is it?" I said, "Well, you feed us too much." He answered just like this, and he said, "Well, that's not your fault. That's the fault of your host. He should have provided you with a menu." So I had to get the host off the spot, because, you know, so I said, "It's not his fault, either. Because you put out the cold meat, and we thought that was the whole course. We thought that's the lunch. We have cold meat in the United States. We were so busy filling ourselves with that cold meat, we failed to see that there was a menu right by our place with ten other courses! And, however, I want you to know we ate them all." [laughter] He kind of grinned at that.

NIXON: Was the food good?

STEENHOVEN: Excellent.

NIXON: The Chinese are great cooks.

STEENHOVEN: Oh, well, they must have—

NIXON: They were there, too.

STEENHOVEN: If somebody was a gourmet, they would have [unclear], because we just got everything, everything!

NIXON: Had you ever been to any Chinese cities—

STEENHOVEN: Never. Never been to China.

NIXON: —or, ever been to the Far East?

STEENHOVEN: Not at all, sir. No, never. It was all new to us.

"I'm getting sick of the military, anyway. They drag their feet about everything."
April 21, 1971, 12:50 p.m.
Richard Nixon and Henry Kissinger
WHITE HOUSE TELEPHONE

Operation Lam Son 719 in Laos was a temporary victory for the South Vietnamese, but as soon as the combat was over in early April, North Vietnam put more traffic than ever on the Ho Chi Minh Trail. Nixon was left with a very partial victory that had no permanent effect, except to fuel the suspicion among Americans that he was expanding the war rather than stopping it.

. . .

NIXON: The war presents a very serious problem. You see, the war has eroded America's confidence up to this point. The people are sick of it, and, and so, therefore, our game here, of course, must be to deal with it. And we've played it right to the hilt with no support and got — and, as far as the last Laotian thing, goddamn poor execution on the part of the military. No support from anybody else and a poor excuse militarily. On the other hand, we also have to realize that simply ending the war in the right way may not save the country. At this point, if it goes too far — let's put it this way: let's suppose the war ends; let's suppose that it isn't known until next year; and then the war is over, and then, politically, we go down — the country. No way. You understand?

KISSINGER: Oh, yes.

NIXON: Everything has to be played, now, in terms of how we survive. It has to be played that way due to — not because of the war, and not because of Asia, but because of defense. Goddamn it, nobody else is going to be for defense. Who the hell else is going to be for defense? It's the point I make there. Who's going to be sitting there?

KISSINGER: Well, of course, it depends entirely on how one interprets ending the war. I think your strength is that you've been a strong president.

NIXON: That's true, and I agree. I agree. I'm simply saying —

KISSINGER: Right.

NIXON: — saying that we realize, though that —

KISSINGER: Even the, I think, the polls if you had announced a cave-in on April 7, I think in —

NIXON: It'd move the other way.

KISSINGER: — two months, you would've been the way that —

NIXON: Johnson.

KISSINGER: — Johnson was after Glassboro. You would have had a big rise, and then a sharp — but, I'm no expert at that.

NIXON: Let me put it this way: I had no intention of announcing a cave-in, as you know. I had no intention of it. As a matter of fact, we took the Laotian gamble solely for the reason that —

KISSINGER: Absolutely.

NIXON: — we had one more. The Laotian gamble cost us. It cost us very, very seriously, because we probably did — well, let me put it this way: had it not been done — I think the comfort we can take from it — had it not been done, there certainly would've been a big summer offensive by the Communists this summer. All right, on the other hand, doing it did — as, as Baker put it pretty well. He thought the war issue was finished last fall. A lot of people thought it was finished, and everybody was relaxed. And that's why we held up rather well in the polls. The action in Laos, itself, dropped us ten points in the polls. You know that?

KISSINGER: No question.

NIXON: Just the action. And then, the coverage of the action continued to drop us. We held it off just a little by our press conference. Then, of course, the, the night after night on television continued to drop us — a little. Then, then came the defeat weekend, which took us along. Then came Kalb, which shook the stuff all up. And then, for the first time, we get a little bit up from — a good boost by reason of doing something that the people wanted in Calley. But, even after the speech, we have to realize, we're only back to where we were. Not to where we were before we went into Laos, but when we — but where we were after we had taken the bump going into Laos.

KISSINGER: Yeah.

NIXON: See my point? Now, what I'm getting at is that from now on, we have to ruthlessly play for the best news that we can.

KISSINGER: No question.

NIXON: That's why I would have — we — Henry, that's why I was disturbed about Abrams's statement about supporting Thieu —

KISSINGER: Oh, it was outrageous.

NIXON: You see, it's that — it's what we have to realize: that, from now on, Henry, the people have got to be reassured.

KISSINGER: I —

NIXON: I've got to have good news —

KISSINGER: On that, I agree, and we can do — well, see, a lot would depend — supposing Hanoi bites at this proposal. Then, of course, we'll settle the war —

NIXON: [unclear]

KISSINGER: — then we'll settle the war this year, and then we have no problem. But, assuming Hanoi rejects the proposal —

NIXON: That's right. There's where we go.

KISSINGER: Well, but then —

NIXON: [unclear] I want us to reexamine, though, the — it, if it — but, let's assume rejection. We've got to examine the strongest possible thing we could do this year. That's my point —

KISSINGER: Well, that's something —

NIXON: Or, because we may erode so much, that next year won't matter.

KISSINGER: No, but that's what I'm asking —

NIXON: Don't assume — you see, Henry, you've been calculating, and we've all been calculating, "Well, we'll make a final announcement in April or May of next year."

KISSINGER: No. No, no, I —

NIXON: The final announcement must be made later this summer. That's when it must be made.

KISSINGER: Well, the —

NIXON: People have got to know. People have got to know. I don't mean you put the date on, necessarily. People have got to know the war is over. They've got to know that —

KISSINGER: Well, preferably, it should be made after the Vietnamese election. But, we —

NIXON: Well, we can, we can make it go that long.

KISSINGER: But we can wait. We can do —

NIXON: [unclear] I'm just saying, you've got to examine it. Let's remember, if we're going to make the final announcement, don't hold it. I mean, don't worry so goddamn much about the Vietnamese election. You'd better worry about our own.

KISSINGER: Well, I think the final announcement should certainly be made this year, and it should be a part of the next announcement — your — well —

NIXON: The No — November 15, you mean?

KISSINGER: Well, or it could be November 1. Well, whether it's the fifteenth or the first of November, or October 20, that's no —

NIXON: Yeah.

KISSINGER: — makes no difference as long as the Vietnamese election is behind us —

NIXON: [unclear]

KISSINGER: Secondly, we can, during the summer —

NIXON: We'll take a look at the Vietnamese election. We'll see how it comes out, who shapes up, who's getting into it, and the rest. Let's see.

KISSINGER: Well, we can —

NIXON: This summer, we could do —

KISSINGER: This summer, we can announce the end of American ground combat, and we can probably announce — and I'm just going to drive it — announce the end of draftees being sent.

NIXON: I think you've got to drive that.

KISSINGER: And —

NIXON: I'll say that I think that has to be. Look, when a guy as hawkish as Bill Buckley —

KISSINGER: No question.

NIXON: — is hitting it, goddamn it —

KISSINGER: Well —

NIXON: — let's just do it. Now —

KISSINGER: [unclear]

NIXON: — I have to tell you, I'm getting sick of the military, anyway. They drag their feet about everything, and they — the bastards want everything, and they're selfish. They [unclear].

KISSINGER: Well, you see, for example, if you had a meeting in Midway with, with Thieu —

NIXON: Mm-hmm?

KISSINGER: — at which you announce the end of American ground combat, plus the end of American draftees —

NIXON: Those two things.

KISSINGER: — that would be a pretty big —

NIXON: That would be a good thing —

KISSINGER: — story. It would be a — that would take the mothers off your back immediately. If you could announce that after July 1, no more draftees would be sent to Vietnam, uh —

NIXON: Can you drive that?

KISSINGER: I'm driving it like crazy. Laird is fighting it, probably because he wants to leak the thing himself.

NIXON: Aren't — aren't you planning to have him in for breakfast, one day here?

KISSINGER: Yeah, tomorrow or Friday.

NIXON: Want me to work it out now? Or —

KISSINGER: Yeah, that would be a good one to work out. I forgot to raise it with Haldeman in the morning.

• • •

KISSINGER: Another thing we could do, Mr. President, for the summer: if — supposing Hanoi turns us down.

NIXON: Yeah.

KISSINGER: Then, I think, out of the Midway thing we should offer a deadline. We know they're going to turn it down, anyway.

NIXON: Well, we've offered a deadline, but not — never publicly, huh?

KISSINGER: By that time, we'll have offered the deadline, privately. They'll have turned it down —

NIXON: Yeah.

KISSINGER: — then, we'll offer it, publicly. By that time, that will get the, the —

NIXON: Mm-hmm.

KISSINGER: — the doves off our back for the rest of the summer. Then, you can do it unilaterally. At that time, the offer would be release prisoners —

NIXON: Mm-hmm.

KISSINGER: — cease-fire, and a deadline. They will then refuse that.

NIXON: Not bad.

KISSINGER: I mean, we'll know —

NIXON: It's about as far as we can go. I mean, I'm just asking, Henry, how far we could go short of —

KISSINGER: Now, on the other hand, if they —

NIXON: — a bug-out.

KISSINGER: — if they have accepted our propositions, so we are not —

NIXON: Oh, if they accept it, it's a different case.

KISSINGER: Then, we don't announce it at, at Midway, we'll just get it done during the summer. And, if they've accepted our proposition, the more squealing our opponents do, the better off you are.

NIXON: That's right.

KISSINGER: Because you know you're going to pull the rug right out from under them —

NIXON: That's right. That's right. That's right —

KISSINGER: So, so either way, once we've made the proposition to them, and they've rejected it, we can have a very successful Midway meeting —

NIXON: Yeah, we'll see.

"I think you'll find Kerry is running for political office . . . the way he's building himself."

April 23, 1971, 9:15 a.m.
Richard Nixon and Bob Haldeman
OVAL OFFICE

On Friday, April 23, while Nixon, Haldeman, and Kissinger were chatting in the White House, thousands of veterans were collecting at the Capitol. In protest against the Vietnam War, they threw their medals away. As a former air force sergeant said, throwing a certificate onto the pile, "I consider that I am now serving my country." Vietnam Veterans Against the War, including their spokesperson, John Kerry, had been congregating all week in Washington.

• • •

NIXON: Kerry is goddamn pretty well wound up. [unclear] A group like that, you're bound to find [unclear] World War II.

HALDEMAN: I think you'll find Kerry running for political office. I mean —

NIXON: Yeah.

HALDEMAN: — the way he's building himself.

NIXON: He's from Massachusetts.

HALDEMAN: Oh!

NIXON: Mm-hmm.

"Despite all the way we put the cosmetics on, Henry, they know goddamn well that what our policy is, is to win the war."

April 23, 1971, 11:56 a.m.
Richard Nixon and Henry Kissinger
OVAL OFFICE

As war demonstrators arrived in Washington, it was the only news story that mattered. All Nixon and Kissinger could do was watch and wait, and hope that the protests would not lead to a repetition of the massive demonstrations seen during the Johnson presidency, but also as recently as 1970.

• • •

NIXON: If it's not television, it's gone. You see, the point is that you have to realize that that's what really matters in terms of the public thing. After all, the television at the present time is — has zeroed in on these people. It'll zero in on the demonstrations Saturday [a rally in Washington by antiwar groups and labor unions that attracted an estimated two hundred thousand to five hundred thousand demonstrators]. And then they'll try to play it with the next two weeks. They're stringing it out, and it's highly unconscionable reporting on the part of television.

KISSINGER: Oh, it's awful.

NIXON: Highly unconscionable. They're just —

KISSINGER: Well, they want to destroy you and they want us to lose in Vietnam.

NIXON: I really think that it's more, it's more the latter. If they destroy me, I think it's — if they think, they know, they know that they're both the same.

KISSINGER: That's right.

NIXON: But deep down, basically, you want to realize that critics of the war are furious, that when they thought they had it licked, when they threw Johnson out of office, they thought, "Well, now, we've won our point on the war." Now, we've come in and it looks like we're going to — they know what it is.

KISSINGER: Right.

NIXON: They do, because, despite all the way we, look, put the cosmetics on, Henry, they know goddamn well that what our policy is, is to win the war.

KISSINGER: Yeah.

NIXON: And winning the war simply means —

KISSINGER: But it —

NIXON: — that South Vietnam survives. That's all.

KISSINGER: To come out honorably —

NIXON: That wins the war.

KISSINGER: That's right.

• • •

NIXON: We always said that. And now, you see, we — I think it's good we forced them out now, so that they're finally saying that, that they want — they say, "We must give up on the right of the South Vietnamese." Even the *Christian Science Monitor*, I know, has an editorial to that effect. Well then, if we did, then nobody — there wouldn't be any recrimination in this country, because nobody really cares what happens to South Vietnam. They're crazy as hell.

KISSINGER: They're crazy as hell.

NIXON: They're crazy as hell because, afterwards —

KISSINGER: That's what the radicals understand: they want to break the government. They want to break confidence in the government. They don't give a damn about Vietnam, because as soon as Vietnam is finished, I will guarantee the radicals will be all over us — or all over any government for any of it — for other things. These tactics of confrontation aren't going to end it. And, our tremendous national malaise — right now, the Establishment has the great excuse of Vietnam.

NIXON: [unclear]

KISSINGER: No matter what goes wrong, they blame Vietnam.

NIXON: That's right. Well, I told you what the college presidents, at the time of — do you remember, they were just — they were really relieved, really. That, as they say, their campuses were politicized. Do you remember the torrents —

KISSINGER: Oh, yeah.

NIXON: — of frustration because of Cambodia? But, they were relieved, because it took the heat off of them.

KISSINGER: Well, they told you, "If you go on national —"

NIXON: [unclear]

KISSINGER: "— television, don't talk about university problems, talk about international affairs." When you asked, "What should I talk about?" they said, "Don't talk about university problems, talk about international affairs —"

NIXON: And one day, when the war is over, then they've got to look in the mirror. And, they don't want to do that, do they?

KISSINGER: That's right.

NIXON: That's the real thing.

KISSINGER: And face the real issues. I remember four — three years ago when Arthur [possibly Arthur Schlesinger Jr.] first flew up. I told the liberals there that two years from now it will be infinitely worse with all the concessions you've made. You meet every one of these points, you'll be worse off. Last year when the radicals smashed every window in Harvard Square, one of those professors was honest enough to call me up and say, "Yes, now I see."

NIXON: Did he?

KISSINGER: Yeah. But, it got — now, now they have big riots at Harvard. They're not reporting them, or big to-dos —

NIXON: Are there riots going on, now?

KISSINGER: Well, they have a tremendous campaign on against professors they consider right wing, with a slogan: "No Free Speech for War Criminals." In other words, the movement that started as a free speech movement in Berkeley is now a "No Free Speech" movement for war criminals. And they're after —

NIXON: Oh, boy.

KISSINGER: — some of my colleagues —

NIXON: Isn't that a shame?

KISSINGER: Sam Huntington, who would be —

NIXON: Yeah, I know — liberal.

KISSINGER: Liberal — well, he's honest.

NIXON: I know him, I know him. I know who he is.

KISSINGER: And they want to force him off the faculty.

NIXON: I hope he doesn't go.

KISSINGER: No, but I — the dean of the School of Public — the Kennedy School — called me yesterday and said, "We're holding a meeting, and we're convincing our faculty to vote for him." I said, "Why do you have to have a meeting to affirm that you are against the 'No Free Speech,' and that — and why do you have to convince anybody? That ought to be taken for granted —"

NIXON: Who is "they," when they say "No Free Speech for War Criminals"?

KISSINGER: That's the SDS chapter. The —

NIXON: But, my God, does that represent the whole school? [unclear]

KISSINGER: No, but it's the ten percent of the activists, and the others are cowardly. But, I think it's the macrocosm of our society, Mr. President. I think the big problem in this country — I feel that as a historian, it's going to happen after the war is over. They know the war is over —

NIXON: Even if we end it right well?

KISSINGER: No. No —

NIXON: [unclear]

KISSINGER: — but that's why the radicals — the radicals understand what they're doing. You cannot win for two reasons: one because it's you; you're so anathema —

NIXON: Yeah.

KISSINGER: Two —

NIXON: They never — they know that they never will influence me.

KISSINGER: And, and, therefore, you don't panic. You're not Johnson. And, secondly, because they think the war is a magnificent opportunity to break the self-confidence of this, of this country.

NIXON: And the system, really —

KISSINGER: And of the system. So, they use both of it. But, they'll be back next year with the war over, and they'll find some other issue. These conference — if the war is over next year, or whenever it will be —

NIXON: Hmm?

KISSINGER: — or two years from now, when it'll surely be completely over — and they'll find enough in Vietnam for a good long time, because —

NIXON: And then, we will be supporting the Thieu-Ky government with military assistance —

KISSINGER: They're already starting that.

NIXON: — economic — oh, I know, and I know they will, Henry. Just like they do in Cambodia.

KISSINGER: In fact, I am wondering, Mr. President, if — it can't be done this minute [unclear] shouldn't go on the offensive against them. Whether one isn't —

NIXON: Yeah, I know. I know.

KISSINGER: — on the wrong wicket, batting back the balls they throw? Whether one shouldn't accuse them of turning the things over to the Communists? I just don't have the sense that this is a soft country.

NIXON: I think I have been on the offensive as much as I can be.

KISSINGER: You have been the —

NIXON: Yeah.

KISSINGER: You have —

NIXON: You know, everything I have said in my speech, in that meeting with the editors was hard-line —

KISSINGER: You couldn't do —

NIXON: Hell, there's — what, what more could I — I couldn't [unclear] —

KISSINGER: You can do no more. You can do no more.

NIXON: — a thing. Do you think? Or should I do more? I think —

KISSINGER: Not right now.

NIXON: — I can hit them harder.

KISSINGER: Not right now —

· · ·

KISSINGER: Well, I'll be interested to see what the North Vietnamese are going to do. I — I think if we — as long as you stay in your present posture, I think we are — we may have a chance of breaking it this year.

NIXON: We'll see.

KISSINGER: Or getting [unclear]. Or getting them to turn it down, and if they do, we can — we'll surface that, because then we don't need anything from them.

NIXON: Well, what I was going to tell you is that I think when you go to Paris that you've got to present it in a way — listen, I want it to be done in a way so that everybody — so that, so that — that with the assumption that we will want to be able to tell Rogers and everybody else that you've gone.

KISSINGER: Right. Oh, I'm going openly.

NIXON: Openly, that's what I mean. Then you — but when you — you're meeting them, as you already know —

KISSINGER: No.

NIXON: And then you have your meeting, and then we will say nothing about it in the event that anything's going to come out of it. If something does not come out of it, however, then let's say something about it and say, "Well, I was over there, and we knew it." And have in mind the fact that we'll surface those portions of it that will serve our interests.

KISSINGER: Right.

NIXON: And, and — in other words, make an offer. Make an offer. Now —

KISSINGER: Mr. President —

NIXON: I — in other words, try to think in terms of, of — if you get to the point where you're talking to them, and they're dancing around, make an offer that is so outlandish — you know, not outlandish in terms of it — that they really ought to accept it. In other words, move the date and, right after, say, "We've offered this." You see what I'm getting at?

KISSINGER: Yeah.

NIXON: And they won't. If — they're either going to make a deal, or they've determined to sit it out. If they're not going to make a deal, then, the thing to do is to make an offer that makes them look absolutely intransigent. See?

KISSINGER: Right.

NIXON: And then, with the idea that the purpose is, is not to get them to accept the offer — we hope to Christ they don't; we know they won't — but that the purpose is to make an offer that is —

KISSINGER: What I thought is, in the first meeting, I wouldn't give them any date, so that it can't fail on that. I'd say, "We'll give you a date, if you're willing to do — have a cease-fire and a repatriation of prisoners." So then, they can't say we gave them a, a lousy date.

NIXON: Hmm.

KISSINGER: If they accept that in principle, then, we can go ahead. If they don't accept it in principle — if they say, "You've got to overthrow Thieu, Ky, and Khiem, too —"

NIXON: It's out [unclear].

KISSINGER: — then we can give them any date.

NIXON: Yeah. Then I'd off — then I would simply say, "All right, here's our date. This is it. We offer it," and I'd make it awfully good. I'd make —

KISSINGER: But one thing we might consider, Mr. President — it just occurred to me this week — as long as we're playing it this way —

NIXON: Yeah.

KISSINGER: — whether it — depending — if they don't accept it, or if they keep it in abeyance — if, at the end of the meeting, I don't tell Xuan Thuy to talk to me alone for five minutes with just his interpreter present.

NIXON: Good.

KISSINGER: If I tell him, "Now, look, this president is extremely tough. You've been wrong every time. If you think you're going to defeat him, if you don't accept this, he will stop at nothing."

NIXON: That's right.

KISSINGER: And imply that you might do it —

NIXON: That's right.

KISSINGER: Use nuclear weapons —

NIXON: And then you could say —

KISSINGER: Do the Dulles ploy —

NIXON: You can say that. You can say, "I cannot control him." Put it that way.

KISSINGER: Yeah. And imply that you might use nuclear weapons.

NIXON: Yes, sir. "He will. I just want you to know he is not going to cave."

KISSINGER: If they, then, charge us with it, I'll deny it.

NIXON: Oh, sure.

"Without China, they never would have agreed to the SALT."
April 23, 1971, 2:52 p.m.
Richard Nixon, Bob Haldeman, and Henry Kissinger
OVAL OFFICE

In the early afternoon, Kissinger had a critical conversation with Dobrynin, which went surprisingly well, as he reported to Nixon. The Soviets were beginning to drop what Kissinger later called the "essentially meaningless preconditions" that had delayed the scheduling of the planned summit in Moscow. The implication was that the major thrust of the SALT treaty was acceptable. From Nixon's point of view, the immediate concern was practical: how to agree to the basic terms without appearing relieved or, worse yet, eager.

• • •

KISSINGER: Hello, Mr. President.

HALDEMAN: Who won?

KISSINGER: It was a draw. To sum it up, Mr. President, they've, to all practical purposes, given in on this SALT thing. They've come back with a letter from Kosygin, and they're willing to have the exchange of letters published. Up to now, they wanted it secret. There's still one point, which I will raise in a minute. On the summit, they reaffirmed the invitation, and they want it in September. I mean, they agreed with us that it should be in September. They do not want an announcement now. And, they say there has to be some progress in Berlin [talks about the status of Berlin began in March 1970 among the Four Powers and ultimately led to the Four Power Agreement, also known as the Quadripartite Agreement, during September 1971]; they can never explain it to the Politburo. And I — when he said that, I blew my top. I mean, deliberately. I said, "Now," I said, "you're making a terrible mistake." I said, "If we have a goal, then the president, who never plays for little stakes, would recognize that it has to fit into this framework. If you're trying to hold him up with Berlin as a means to get to the summit, you don't understand him. I'm not even sure if he'll let me continue talking to you on Berlin under these circumstances." I thought this —

NIXON: Sure.

KISSINGER: — this was the only way of doing it, because we really cannot promise to be able to deliver on Berlin.

NIXON: No.

KISSINGER: I mean, the Germans have screwed it up to such a fare-thee-well that they may not be prepared to yield anything. I'm seeing Bahr this weekend. He's up there. And I'll have a better estimate at that Woodstock conference. [Kissinger planned to travel to Woodstock, Vermont, to attend the weekend-long Bilderberg Conference, an annual meeting of a private group of the world's wealthiest and most influential people.] My estimate is — oh, he was really — then he started explaining, "Oh, they're enthusiastic. Don't you realize what a tremendous thing it is for us, the first American president in the Soviet Union? That we have four new members in the Politburo? I try," he said, "you have only one man to convince. I had to talk to all fifteen."

NIXON: Mm-hmm.

KISSINGER: He said, "To sell this was almost impossible." That I even believe —

NIXON: Sure.

KISSINGER: — because on this one they have yielded ninety-eight percent. They've practically accepted our position on the SALT. They're giving us a hell of a lot more than —

NIXON: What is left? Well, let's look at where we start from here. What about the SALT position? What's —?

KISSINGER: Well, they [unclear] —

NIXON: What is the timing?

KISSINGER: Well, that we can settle next week. We could publish the exchange of letters within a week.

• • •

KISSINGER: Well, now, the only point is this, Mr. President: what they want, the only disputed point — there are some other nitpicks, which I'll explain to you in a minute — but the disputed point is on the limitation, Moscow against Washington, which will drive Scoop Jackson right up a wall —

NIXON: Hell, that's true.

KISSINGER: — and, on the other hand, Dobrynin says that it is almost impossible to explain to their military that we can protect our missiles, and they have to protect their population. Well, I told him, "Well, they have five hundred missiles protected by their Moscow system."

NIXON: Yeah.

KISSINGER: Well, he denies that. So, what I could propose to him on Monday is that they take out that one sentence which limits it to that, and that we throw that to the negotiators, with the understanding that if they can't settle it, we'll just have to yield. If that's what you want. I think if they freeze their offensive weapons, that's the big thing. If they freeze their offensive weapons, which they've agreed to do in this, then we can be —

NIXON: Yeah?

KISSINGER: — then we can agree to this. Then we can agree to this. If they don't freeze their offensive weapons, it's too dangerous.

• • •

NIXON: Look, let me put it this way: all this is a bunch of shit, as you know. It's not worth a damn. But the point is that in terms of our public relations, we can use something like this at this time. I —

KISSINGER: Right —

NIXON: — don't want to have anything wrong for public relations reasons, but I don't want to horse around and put it out three weeks from now when it doesn't make a goddamn bit of difference.

KISSINGER: Right.

• • •

KISSINGER: Yeah, I thought, they're — they're a cool bunch. I thought, they are dying to get you to Moscow, Mr. President, and I think it would be a mistake for us to promise them a Berlin agreement. In fact, what I'm inclined to say, when I see him, is to say, "Your reaction was just what I predicted." That you just make no commitments until then, when they are ready for the summit. I said, "You think you're doing the president a favor about the summit, you're absolutely wrong —"

NIXON: That's right —

KISSINGER: "— we're not going to pay any price for the summit. We make agreements in our mutual interests or not at all." But they want you there. About that there's no doubt. Because as soon as I got tough —

NIXON: Yeah.

HALDEMAN: The sooner —

KISSINGER: Because as soon as I got tough, he started pulling back. He said, "No, no, no, you misunderstood. You have to tell the president we are renewing the invitation. September is an excellent time. It's a good time, still good weather —"

NIXON: Yeah, but when do they want to announce it?

KISSINGER: Well, then I said, "Look, we would like to make the announcement four months ahead of time. That's what we always do with state visits." He said, "Well, two months is a little better." I think they have a massive problem of getting their government to [unclear].

NIXON: Make it three months.

KISSINGER: And I think they really want it. They probably may need some progress on Berlin. But I think — I'm seeing Bahr this weekend, and I think they know there'll be progress on Berlin, and they're using this to —

NIXON: Mm-hmm. [unclear] So it came out pretty well? Didn't it?

KISSINGER: Well, I think this one, I think the SALT agreement, Mr. President —

NIXON: Without China, they aren't going to [unclear] —

KISSINGER: The SALT agreement is going to drive Berlin.

NIXON: Let me tell you something: without China, they never would have agreed to the SALT.

"If those POW wives start running around . . . we are in trouble."
April 26, 1971, 11:46 a.m.
Richard Nixon, Bob Haldeman, and Henry Kissinger
OVAL OFFICE

By 1971, it was easy to forget about the Paris Peace Talks. They were the public ongoing meetings that brought North Vietnamese, South Vietnamese, Viet Cong, and American negotiators together to seek an end to the war. The talks had gone on for three years, with only minimal progress. Unbelievably, several months were devoted to the shape of the table at which the representatives would sit. As with the SALT talks, Nixon generally left the peace talks on a back burner while he worked a broader agenda through his own private channels, in concert with Kissinger.

In April, the peace talks were moved into the headlines by a group of one hundred women, the wives of prisoners of war held captive by the North Vietnamese. The women said nothing and did nothing except stand in vigil on the sidewalk outside of the building in which the peace talks were staged. According to the best records, 339 Americans were held as prisoners of war, though thousands more were missing in action with the possibility of imprisonment. The North Vietnamese stance was that it would not discuss the release of the Americans that it held until Nixon set a date for withdrawal of all U.S. troops from the region.

• • •

KISSINGER: Now, Lodge collared me on the way in, and he said he's developing some awfully strong feelings on the POWs, and he wants to talk to you.
NIXON: No, I'm not going to [unclear].
KISSINGER: Which is his way of saying he wants to bug out. But I told him he had to have another time; you were terribly busy.
NIXON: No, no, no [unclear].
KISSINGER: I'm seeing Dobrynin at noon, and I wanted to check with you before I did.
NIXON: Yeah.
KISSINGER: I believe, Mr. President, that your instinct on Saturday is the right one, that I ought to be —
NIXON: Oh, yes —
KISSINGER: — tough with him.
NIXON: Tough as hell. So what — you can't do anything?
KISSINGER: No, I — what I was —
NIXON: Let me come to a couple of points before you get to that. It seems to me that — that's all I have, Bob [unclear]. And I'll talk to you about that press thing after I finish these —

HALDEMAN: [laughs]

NIXON: — odds and ends. First, I think it — I think in view of that shelling [unclear] yesterday, we ought to hit those sites that, normally, we can't bomb now.

KISSINGER: I think we ought to think about it very carefully.

NIXON: Why think, when I don't think you need to think about it? My point is, you've got to show them right after these demonstrations, that we're not going to be affected by them. I know a lot [unclear] —

KISSINGER: I'm for it.

NIXON: Too much of this stuff —

KISSINGER: I —

NIXON: Too much of this stuff indicating we're going to be affected by it.

KISSINGER: I'm for it.

NIXON: Now, the only thing to do is to bang 'em.

KISSINGER: I agree.

NIXON: So, you tell them to just do it — and protective reaction. Call it "protective reaction."

KISSINGER: Right.

NIXON: But, let 'em have it.

KISSINGER: Right.

NIXON: Understand?

KISSINGER: Absolutely.

NIXON: This is the time to do it.

KISSINGER: Absolutely.

NIXON: So, they killed seven Americans at this base by random shelling? Correct?

KISSINGER: There — that's the only thing they'll understand.

NIXON: Yeah. And, also, you know, I mainly want them to know that we [unclear] demonstrations.

KISSINGER: Mr. President, I'm —

NIXON: Yeah.

KISSINGER: — thrilled by it.

NIXON: Hit 'em [unclear] —

KISSINGER: What I saw this weekend [at the Bilderberg Conference], Mr. President —

NIXON: Up there in New York? [unclear]

KISSINGER: This country needs —

NIXON: I was —

KISSINGER: In Woodstock. What — that's what I mean.

NIXON: [unclear]

KISSINGER: If we don't —

NIXON: [unclear]

KISSINGER: If we don't do it, no one will do it.

NIXON: [unclear] no doubt, no doubt they're going to do it. And the main point is, this is just a — we're going to crack 'em this week — protective reaction — but, I mean, hit all three sites, now.

KISSINGER: Yeah.

NIXON: I mean, I — or two or three. I don't know. Whatever is militarily feasible.

KISSINGER: Let's hit all of them —

NIXON: You know, I told Laird, "Whenever you're ready, let's go." Now, the chokepoints are about ready; let 'em have it.

KISSINGER: Right.

NIXON: We're protecting American withdrawals. Second point is this: we do need something — I need something that Bruce can say on POWs on Thursday. Now, we've got to get something that he can say.

KISSINGER: Absolutely.

NIXON: I don't know what he can say, but what I mean is when you've got two — stupid [Senator Marlow W.] Cook [R-KY], you know, and that jackass [Republican Senator Jack R.] Miller from Iowa — both joining in this, "We'll — we'll predict — we'll end the war nine months after the POW thing." Well, of course, they're goddamn nearing our ballpark. They're — anyway, but the point is —

KISSINGER: Well, they're tougher than we will be.

NIXON: What? The congressmen are [unclear]?

KISSINGER: But, they want the con — POWs released first.

NIXON: Yeah. My whole point is, though: I think that we ought to have Bruce make a cosmetic offer on POWs, which we can publish. We said we will. You see what I mean? Make the offer. It isn't going to affect your negotiation one damn bit.

KISSINGER: Well, what offer are you thinking of?

NIXON: Anything.

KISSINGER: All right.

NIXON: Just for the purpose — one, one we know they're going to turn down. You know what I mean? So, you could say — well, I was thinking of — you could think of something like this: "That we will — we are prepared to do — we're — we are prepared to discuss a, discuss a deadline, as soon you discuss POWs. We're prepared to."

KISSINGER: That would give away this, the [unclear].

NIXON: Oh, I'm not sure.

KISSINGER: That would — that you should do on television, if anyone does it.

NIXON: Well then, "We're prepared —"

KISSINGER: If you're willing to do that.

NIXON: Well, put it in that — put it in the context of what we — of what we have said, then. "We're prepared to —"

KISSINGER: I mean, we can press any number of [unclear].

NIXON: Well then, say that. Then, separate it out. The — then make the POW–cease-fire —

KISSINGER: That we can do.

NIXON: — make that on Thursday.

KISSINGER: That we can do.

NIXON: He says, "We'll — we will separate those things out." Even when I do it later, you're going to do it privately, of course.

KISSINGER: You'll do the cease-fire —

NIXON: Because you're going to give them the date. He's not going to give them the date.

KISSINGER: No, if he, however, says, "We're prepared to give a date — deadline," that's exactly what I planned to tell them.

NIXON: Well —

KISSINGER: And then, if you want, you can go this route, but it would — that would really look like yielding to the demonstrations. Then, you should do it. Why let him do it?

NIXON: Uh, no. I'm not going to give a date. We're — we — look, we're going to discuss it —

KISSINGER: But that, they'll accept.

NIXON: Hmm?

KISSINGER: They'll accept that.

NIXON: No, I don't think they will.

KISSINGER: Certainly.

NIXON: Cease-fire?

KISSINGER: Well, I think, Mr. President, that's such a big step. To take that at an ordinary session, in the middle of a demonstration —

NIXON: What can we really offer them?

KISSINGER: We can say —

NIXON: Figure something out.

KISSINGER: Yeah. I'll —

NIXON: Work on it —

KISSINGER: — I'll try to have something for you —

NIXON: Something that they can turn down, but something where — and let's, and let's just build it up. Give it to Scali and say, "Now, build the hell out of this thing." That's the way I want to do it, Henry.

KISSINGER: Right. We can have some unilateral withdrawal for prisoners.

NIXON: Yeah.

KISSINGER: We can —

NIXON: And don't let — incidentally, I'm really tired of Lodge, anyway. Goddamn it, I sent him over there, fartin' around there with the pope, and he comes in here on this thing and, now, he wants to take a trip to Vietnam. Goddamn it, leave me alone!

KISSINGER: Yes.

NIXON: He's never come in and showed any — he didn't —

KISSINGER: Yeah.

NIXON: When he was here last time, he didn't say anything about what the hell I've been doing. Where's he been? Why doesn't he stand up a little? I'm going to do this goddamn meeting; I'm going to get out of there. And I'm — don't you feel that way?

KISSINGER: Absolutely.

NIXON: I mean, and the idea is, Henry [unclear]. You talk to him. He can tell you about it.

KISSINGER: Right.

NIXON: Can he?

KISSINGER: Oh, yes. He already has.

NIXON: Now, with regard to Dobrynin, I know that right now he's as tough as hell. Let me tell you why you've got to have the POW thing: it's purely a delaying action. Henry, [unclear] we've got to realize that we have got to keep them from running off. The POW wives may endorse this damn thing. You understand that?

KISSINGER: Right.

NIXON: It's too, too tantalizing for them. Bruce — we've got to indicate that we are at least doing something on POWs.

KISSINGER: Actually, Mr. President, this [proposal to end the Vietnam War by Senator] Miller thing is — unless he's changed it — isn't such a bad one, oh, from that point of view. They —

NIXON: It says as soon as they're released?

KISSINGER: They, first, have to release them, and a year afterwards, we'll withdraw our troops.

NIXON: A year afterwards?

KISSINGER: It used to be a year.

NIXON: Or, nine months?

KISSINGER: Well, maybe he's changed it to nine months, now.

NIXON: Yeah.

KISSINGER: But that means they'd have to give up all their prisoners, first.

NIXON: Mm-hmm. Well, we could almost buy that [unclear] —

KISSINGER: Well, not yet.

NIXON: I mean —

KISSINGER: You see, as soon as we've made the offer to them, Mr. President, and we know whether they'll buy it or not, then we can play it any way we want.

NIXON: I know. I know. But right now —

KISSINGER: And it won't be a big deal until the result of it —

NIXON: — right now, let me say that we've got to put a stopper in the POWs stuff. That's the only thing that worries me at this time.

KISSINGER: Right.

NIXON: The only thing.

KISSINGER: I'll —

NIXON: And I don't think everybody around here is aware of that problem. You see —

KISSINGER: Well, I'll have a suggestion —

NIXON: — because it's our Achilles heel. If those POW wives start running around, coming onto this general election, and veterans, you're in real — we are in troubles like you wouldn't — and you must tell all of them —

KISSINGER: Well, let me talk to the leader of these wives. I know her [likely reference is to Carol North, then chairman of the board, National League of Families]. She was on national television the other day. She was very good. She is very fond of me.

NIXON: I know.

KISSINGER: And I think — I quieted them down —

NIXON: I know, I know. But they — they're still worried, though —

KISSINGER: Oh, they're def —

NIXON: [unclear] you just talk to them every day, you know, and they're, they're a worried bunch. Yeah?

• • •

NIXON: Now, before we leave, you have advised that — just think about — understand: I'm just looking for a gimmick.

KISSINGER: I know.

NIXON: I don't give a goddamn. I don't want to, Henry, to accept it, but don't assume when you talk to 'em — Colson is very close to it. There're a [unclear] number of groups Colson can use. Be sure you talk to them, too, to see what groups are ready to take off. You see?

KISSINGER: Right.

NIXON: To see that they're holding firm. See, Henry?

KISSINGER: Right.

NIXON: We — don't assume when you talk to one that you get them all, because there are about eighteen different — like it's with veterans. We got ninety percent of the veterans — ninety-five percent of the veterans, but five percent go around and give you hell. See?

KISSINGER: Right. Right.

NIXON: I think we can hold 'em, but I think we've got to get it to them, and if we can make some kind of an offer, or even tell them that we are going to make an offer, fine. They have to get some assurance, Henry. They've got to get some assurance —

KISSINGER: I'll talk to the wives —

NIXON: — on what they want to know.

KISSINGER: What I should do —

NIXON: Don't assume the one woman, though. She's just one of many.

KISSINGER: No — but I want to talk and get her advice, because I trust her. And then, I'll do — she's, she's tough enough. It isn't — I don't want to give the impression that she's easy, but she's been —

NIXON: Right.

KISSINGER: Let me talk to her, first. She was on national television the other day —

NIXON: Yeah.

KISSINGER: — and she was pretty firm.

NIXON: Well, we've got to have something new on POWs Thursday. It's got to sound new. That's all. Just put — have Bruce put something out, some gobbledygook. You know, take your pick.

"When we talked about 'linkage,' everyone was sneering."
April 27, 1971, 8:16 p.m.
Richard Nixon and Henry Kissinger
WHITE HOUSE TELEPHONE

When Zhou Enlai, premier of the People's Republic of China, wrote to Nixon proposing a meeting in Beijing, it was a turning point that Kissinger termed "the most important communication that has come to an American president since the end of World War II." The invitation mentioned an envoy making the trip. Part of the discussion that Kissinger and Nixon had about the letter focused on the person who might serve as the first representative of the United States to visit the PRC. They bluntly reviewed many possible figures, though the identity of the envoy may never really have been in doubt. The new probability of talks between the United States and China materially changed the other strains of U.S. foreign policy — the complex of challenges that Nixon called the "linkage."

• • •

NIXON: I had a couple of thoughts on this. One with regard to the Bruce thing [Bruce was under consideration as Nixon's envoy] which seems to me may pose to them a difficult problem because of him being directly involved in the Vietnam negotiations. Secondly, let me think of whether there is something else — how about Nelson [Rockefeller]?

KISSINGER: No.

NIXON: Can't do it, huh?

KISSINGER: Mr. President, he wouldn't be disciplined enough, although he is a possibility.

NIXON: It would engulf him in a big deal and he is outside of the government, you see.

KISSINGER: Let me think about it. I might be able to hold him in check.

NIXON: It is intriguing, don't you think?

KISSINGER: It is intriguing.

NIXON: How about Bush?

KISSINGER: Absolutely not, he is too soft and not sophisticated enough.

NIXON: I thought of that myself.

KISSINGER: I thought about Richardson but he wouldn't be the right thing.

NIXON: He is still too close to us and I don't think it would sit well with Rogers. Nelson — the Chinese would consider him important and he would be — could do a lot for us in terms of the domestic situation. No, Nelson is a wild hare running around.

KISSINGER: I think for one operation I could keep him under control. To them a Rockefeller is a tremendous thing.

NIXON: Sure. Well, keep it in the back of your head.

KISSINGER: Bush would be too weak.

NIXON: I thought so too but I was trying to think of somebody with a title.

KISSINGER: Nelson has possibilities.

NIXON: A possibility, yeah. Of course, that would drive State up the wall.

KISSINGER: He would take someone from State along but he despises them so much he will take our direction and I would send someone from our staff to go along.

NIXON: Send Haig. Really, he's really tough.

KISSINGER: And he knows Haig.

• • •

NIXON: All in all, of course, the whole thing that you can take some comfort in, you know, when you talk about how this happened, that it wouldn't have happened if you hadn't stuck to your guns through this period too, you know. We —

KISSINGER: Well, Mr. President, you made it possible. It's —

NIXON: We have played a game, and we've gotten a little break here. We were hoping we'd get one, and I think we have one now. If we —

KISSINGER: Well —

NIXON: — play it skillfully. And we'll wait a couple weeks and then —

KISSINGER: But we set up this —

NIXON: Yeah.

KISSINGER: — whole intricate web over —

NIXON: Yeah.

KISSINGER: When we talked about "linkage," everyone was sneering.

NIXON: Yeah. I know.

KISSINGER: But we've done it now.

NIXON: That's right.

KISSINGER: We've got it all hooked together.

NIXON: And —

KISSINGER: I mean, we've got Berlin hooked to SALT.

• • •

NIXON: Henry, it wouldn't have happened if you hadn't stuck to your guns. We played a game and we got a little break. It was done skillfully and now we will wait a couple of weeks.

KISSINGER: We have done it now, we have got it all hooked together; Berlin is hooked to SALT. Nelson might be able to do it, particularly if I sent Haig.

NIXON: Oh, we would have to have Haig; and a State guy but not that Green guy.

KISSINGER: Oh, Green could go. On foreign policy, Nelson would take my advice.

NIXON: He would be a special envoy in a sense.

KISSINGER: Actually, Mr. President, that's a very original idea and he's tough.

NIXON: Particularly if you get him in right at the mountaintop and say, "Look, it will make or break you, boy."

KISSINGER: Oh, he would do it and I could tell him on this one. On the long operation he would be hard to control but on this one he would be good.

NIXON: If Dewey were alive, he could do it.

KISSINGER: Nelson would be better.

NIXON: But Dewey isn't alive.

KISSINGER: If you can hold on a minute, I can get you — I have the oral note that the Pakistanis sent me. Here it is — the Pakistan note to Yahya [Khan] which Yahya passed on to the Chinese.

· · ·

KISSINGER: Well, Mr. President —

NIXON: Yeah?

KISSINGER: —the difference between them [the Chinese] and the Russians is that if you drop some loose change and try to pick it up, the Russians step on your fingers and fight you for it. The Chinese don't do that. I've reviewed all the communications with them. And all of it has been on a high level. I mean, if here you look at the summit exchange, they haven't horsed around like the Russians.

NIXON: No, they haven't.

KISSINGER: And compared to what the game was, the Russians squeezing us on every bloody move —

NIXON: Yeah. Yeah.

KISSINGER: — has been just stupid.

NIXON: Yeah.

KISSINGER: And so I think that they probably figure they cannot trick us out of Taiwan, but they have to have a fundamental understanding.

NIXON: Yeah. Well, put Nelson in the back of our minds as one possibility.

KISSINGER: That's right.

NIXON: Incidentally, what'd Haig think of this?

KISSINGER: Oh, he thinks this is one of the great diplomatic breakthroughs.

NIXON: Does he really? Yeah?

KISSINGER: Oh, yeah. And he thinks if we play it coolly and toughly and with the same subtlety we've shown up to now —

NIXON: Yeah —

KISSINGER: — we can settle everything now.

NIXON: He thinks we go — he goes that far [unclear]?

KISSINGER: Oh, yeah. I have absolute — I've never said this before. I've never given it more than one in three. I think if we get this thing working, we'll end Vietnam this year. The mere fact of these contacts is one of —

NIXON: Another thing, of course, that is important is [laughs], you know, we do have a little problem of time, in terms of wanting to announce something in this period of time. And —

KISSINGER: Yeah, but we ought to be able to announce this by the end of the first week of June anyway.

NIXON: Well, we'd have to if you're going to be there in June.

KISSINGER: And if we have the SALT —

NIXON: If we could get it earlier. Now, the thing is, is SALT going to turn them off? No. No?

KISSINGER: No.

NIXON: No, particularly — yeah, but, I must say, we're going to drag our feet on that summit with the Russians, though. They're —

KISSINGER: Well, nothing can happen on that for a while now.

NIXON: No, no. They — that's — the ball's in their court and —

KISSINGER: Yeah.

NIXON: — they're sitting there piddling around. All right, they can piddle. And —

KISSINGER: They won't move fast.

NIXON: No?

KISSINGER: And they'll be confused by the protests in this country. A more sophisticated analysis of the report was made by Zhou Enlai.

NIXON: His analysis in effect realized what we were doing.

KISSINGER: A very subtle analysis of the international situation.

NIXON: Well, anyway, there is another player we can keep. Bruce is another possibility, too. It would be quite dramatic to pull Bruce out of Paris and send him to Beijing.

KISSINGER: For that reason, they might not take him.

NIXON: In terms of Bruce, he is our senior ambassador and we feel he is the best-qualified man.

KISSINGER: They would jump at Rockefeller, a high-visibility one.

NIXON: Visibility and it would be enormous. Can't you just see what that would do to the libs in this country, oh, God. Rockefeller over there, Jesus Christ.

KISSINGER: That has great possibilities.

NIXON: Here is Rockefeller — he is lined up with us all the way; he has lined up with us on foreign policy all the way. Anyway, that is something to think about.

KISSINGER: That's a good problem to have.

NIXON: It is a good luxury to have.

KISSINGER: Once this gets going — everything is beginning to fit together.

NIXON: I hope so.

KISSINGER: You will have to hold hard on Vietnam on Thursday.

NIXON: I intend to hold it hard. What's happening on the prisoners?

KISSINGER: I have three proposals which I am putting in writing — they will release one thousand, they are opening their camps and calling on the North Vietnamese to do the same, and proposing that all prisoners be held in a neutral country. This should be announced by Bruce in the morning —

NIXON: Good.

KISSINGER: And you can hit it in the evening.

NIXON: They might hit that play if we build it up a bit. They will all think it is about bugging out but it will be on prisoners.

KISSINGER: We are beginning to hold the cards.

NIXON: That's true but we are going to hold it. The demonstrators may overplay their hand.

KISSINGER: John Chancellor, whom I had lunch with today, thinks the tide has turned.

NIXON: What turned it?

KISSINGER: He thinks what happened this week has ruined them.

NIXON: John Chancellor —

KISSINGER: Absolutely. He doesn't exactly know what you have up your sleeve but —

NIXON: I am not saying anything about China except that the proposals are at a very sensitive stage and I don't intend to comment on the future and next question, gentlemen.

KISSINGER: Right.

NIXON: I don't want to get into the proposal of a two-China policy, UN membership, Taiwan, and so forth. I am going to finesse all questions by saying that developments here are significant and I don't think the interests of the nation will be served by commenting on it further.

KISSINGER: I think that would be the best position to take, Mr. President.

NIXON: Haig was pretty pleased.

KISSINGER: If anyone had predicted that two months ago, we would have thought it was inconceivable.

NIXON: Yeah, yeah. After Laos —

KISSINGER: After Cambodia, the same thing —

NIXON: Yeah. But look at after Laos, the people over two to one thought it had failed and yet here comes the Chinese move, the Ping-Pong team, and something more significant that pales that into nothing. It can have an enormous significance. Well, look, Nelson's tongue made that statement to Snow. How can we get the Mansfield [Amendment] thing turned off? I don't know how we can do it but one way we could do it is to invite him to go along.

KISSINGER: No. Why give this to him?

NIXON: He could go along with me.

KISSINGER: He can go along with you when you go.

NIXON: We could invite Mansfield and Scott.

KISSINGER: If you want to share it with the Democrats.

NIXON: Share it; the Chinese will treat them very well but they will know where the power is.

KISSINGER: But they actually haven't invited anyone yet.

NIXON: Could you get a message to him?

KISSINGER: Think I can get some oral message to him.

NIXON: Two weeks away and I wonder if they will move on Mansfield before then.

KISSINGER: No, but they may.

NIXON: As a temporary action, can you say that the president will be in California and —

KISSINGER: I have already told them and that a constructive reply will be coming.

NIXON: If you could add to that, that any other visits should be held in abeyance until we give our reply.

KISSINGER: I will get that across.

NIXON: There will be many requests and we feel that political requests —

KISSINGER: Right.

NIXON: Good idea. Okay, Henry.

KISSINGER: Right, Mr. President.

"That's a lifestyle I don't want to touch."

April 28, 1971, 9:28 a.m.

Richard Nixon, Bob Haldeman, and Henry Kissinger

EXECUTIVE OFFICE BUILDING

For over seventy years, the White House sponsored an annual conference on children and youth. The last year this conference was held was 1971, in the middle of Nixon's first term. In Nixon's view, there was a good reason it was the last.

The conference was organized by Counselor to the President for Urban Affairs Pat Moynihan's former staff (after he had left the administration to return to Harvard University), in particular Stephen Hess, and was held in Estes Park, Colorado. A series of proposals came out of the conference, including the demand for the immediate resignation of President Nixon, Vice President Agnew, and all of their staff members, as well as other proposals on lowering the age of consent and more formal government recognition of homosexual relationships. These proposals led to an Oval Office discussion about homosexuality and society.

• • •

NIXON: Let me say something before we get off the gay thing. I don't want my views misunderstood. I am the most tolerant person on that of anybody in this shop. They have a problem. They're born that way. You know that. That's all. I think they are.

Anyway, my point is, though, when I say they're born that way, the tendency is there. But my point is, that Boy Scout leaders, YMCA leaders, and others, bring them in that direction, and teachers. And, if you look over the history of societies, you will find of course that some of the highly intelligent people — [unclear], Oscar Wilde, Aristotle, et cetera, et cetera, et cetera — were all homosexuals. Nero, of course, was, in a public way, in with a boy in Rome.

HALDEMAN: There's a whole bunch of Roman emperors.

NIXON: [unclear] but the point is, look at that, once a society moves in that direction, the vitality goes out of that society. Now isn't that right, Henry?

KISSINGER: Well —

NIXON: Do you see any other change, anywhere where it doesn't fit?

KISSINGER: That's certainly been the case in antiquity. The Romans were notorious —

HALDEMAN: The Greeks.

KISSINGER: — homosexuals.

NIXON: The Greeks.

KISSINGER: The Greeks.

NIXON: The Greeks. And they had plenty of it [unclear]. By God, I am not going to have a situation where we pass a law indicating, "Well, now, kids, just go out and be gay." They can do it. Just leave them alone. That's a lifestyle I don't want to touch.

KISSINGER: Well, it's one thing —

HALDEMAN: I'm afraid that's what they're doing now.

NIXON: Just leave them alone.

KISSINGER: It's one thing for people, to, you know, like some people we know, who would do it discreetly, but to make that a national policy.

• • •

KISSINGER: But something this profoundly offensive to the majority of the population, to flaunt it as an act of public policy. That seems to me to be the issue involved here.

HALDEMAN: It's like any of those other things. You make the public policy, and then you reduce one more barrier that keeps some kids —

NIXON: This is what it really comes down to. The point is now, Henry, drinking at eighteen. Because, well, seventy-five percent of the kids might drink at eighteen, most kids, twenty-five percent that drink at eighteen would probably go off their rockers. It's not a good idea. I mean, you've got to stop at a certain point. Why is it that the girls don't swear? Because a man, when he swears, people can't tolerate a girl who is a —

HALDEMAN: Girls do swear.

NIXON: Huh?

HALDEMAN: They do now.

NIXON: Oh, they do now? But, nevertheless, it removes something from them. They don't even realize it. A man drunk, and a man who swears, people will tolerate and say that's a sign of masculinity or some other damn thing. We all do it. We all swear. But you show me a girl that swears and I'll show you an awful unattractive person. You know, really.

HALDEMAN: Yeah.

NIXON: I mean, all femininity is gone. And none of the smart girls do swear, incidentally. That's why you should tell a dirty story about a girl. The reason is, basically, that once you start [unclear] on just as crude as the man. And believe me, they call it the theory of ethics. The hell with it. It's what made this country. Hell, it goes, Henry, back to the Jewish religion. That's where most of it is, you know. You read the Old Testament, this is Old Testament stuff, not New Testament stuff.

HALDEMAN: You lose the distinction between the sexes, which is one of the main —

NIXON: That's right. [unclear] But the thing about drinking is there, the thing about, that's right. Let's come to the other thing. Then you get, frankly, the public houses of prostitution, that are legalized. Well, frankly, the question there is, well, they're cleaner, the French legalize them, and all that sort of thing. And they're going to have them anyway, and so forth, and there are houses of prostitution everywhere. The moment you move in that direction, you break another barrier down. You say, well, all the whores are over here, and the good girls are over here. Well, the point is that all girls, almost all girls, are potentially interested in some sort of relationship with a man one way or other and they're going to have it. Goddamn it! You don't put it all out there! You just make it too common, too crude. It's everything, really. I think it's a, I must say, I don't do it to say it out of any sense of prudeness, or purity, or anything. I can't buy a lot of the — but I do think that as a society starts to tell all the decent, God-fearing people in this country, and there are still a hell of a lot of them, that the homosexual, the sixteen-year-old that drinks, the public houses of prostitution, you'll have a decadent society. You'll have a decadent society. Now, let's take a look at the Communist societies, for whatever they're worth. Let's take a look at them. All revolutionary societies, for whatever they're worth. They're goddamn pure.

KISSINGER: Oh yes.

NIXON: Pure in their public ethics, on any issue. And pure in their private lives. They don't stand for anything.

"Before I get there, the war has to be pretty well settled."
April 28, 1971, 4:51 p.m.
Richard Nixon, Bob Haldeman, and Henry Kissinger
EXECUTIVE OFFICE BUILDING

Sino-U.S. relations posed the danger of moving too smoothly and quickly, leaving serious problems, notably the Vietnam War and Taiwan, unaddressed before any meetings. The potential summit with the Soviets presented exactly the opposite challenge, seeming to

falter over every point, even ones previously covered time and again. Kissinger lobbied to
position himself as Nixon's point man on both initiatives.

                              • • •

KISSINGER: Actually I don't want to toot my own horn, but I happen to be the only one
    who knows all the negotiations.

                              • • •

NIXON: Well my point is that he [Rockefeller] does not have the subtlety of moving
    around. He is the kind of a guy that wants to make a quick shot, dramatic, you know,
    bold. Now goddamn it, we're going to do things bold, but we don't want to fall down
    doing it. You can do it. The best thing, the best thing to do is this: set up a secret
    negotiation. But the way I would start the telegram, I would say the president has
    considered, and he would like to arrange a visit to Beijing. He believes, he would
    like to come to Beijing. He thinks, however, that the best way to arrange that is for
    his — must be arranged at the highest level, the agenda, the modalities, et cetera
    should be arranged by Dr. Kissinger and whatever.

                              • • •

NIXON: What we are playing for basically is the Chinese summit, that's my plan. That
    is the big play. Now, that's only half of it; the other part of the play is to do something
    about this war. That's the other half of it.
KISSINGER: With that, I think, those guys in '54 they needed peace, and they settled
    Vietnam then. They need peace now, it's got to have an effect on Hanoi. That's one
    advantage of a public emissary.

                              • • •

NIXON: Well, let me say, before I get there, the war has to be pretty well settled. I'd just
    simply say, we can't come there until we have some idea. The fact must be known in
    the United States that the war is settled. I can't come to China before that.

                              • • •

KISSINGER: They're [the Chinese] so scared of the Russians that they're better off hav-
    ing your visit next May or April and keeping it hanging and keep daring the Rus-
    sians to attack them with the presidential visit. That's what I think they want. I do
    not believe they want you now. That would be too quick a turnaround time for them.

                              • • •

NIXON: We've got to deal with the Russians. The Russians can cause us too goddamn
    much trouble. Between now and 1972, I feel, if there's any place in the world, they
    can screw us in Cuba. They can screw us in — in Berlin we can screw them. We got
    the ball there. We got —
KISSINGER: Well, oh, we can certainly wreck the Berlin —
NIXON: I mean, as far as SALT is concerned, it's dead. I mean, the Russians, let us
    suppose that they come back, you know — the Soviet summit is still possible. Did
    Dobrynin raise the summit today? Or you just didn't raise that?

KISSINGER: Well, I said, "Anatol, you remember the —"

NIXON: You just mentioned it to him.

KISSINGER: To him. "Now, look," I said, "you know, the big issue, the only reason there's any movement on Berlin at all is because of me." And I said, "The president" — a minute later, I said, "Anatol, of course, the president believes [I should break] this contact, if it doesn't work out on SALT." Instead of —

NIXON: His position is going to be that —

KISSINGER: Instead of Rogers —

NIXON: Don't call —

KISSINGER: Well, I had to give them a name. I told him.

NIXON: I'd add something else: you have decided [against the] summit. Say, I know with Bill, bureaucratic problems here, that you — the problem you weren't at the State Department, the problem with the Russians — you figure the Russian game is over. You know, that's just sticking it right to them, right? I don't know if they're going to be upset. But that's my approach. Nice to have these phrases.

• • •

KISSINGER: Having gotten to this point, Mr. President, they're not going to bail.

NIXON: Yeah.

HALDEMAN: But the Russians didn't get diplomatic relations —

NIXON: Of course, you want to — that's right, that's right. You want to — if we're going to get a summit with the Russians, then you were wrong.

KISSINGER: I wasn't wrong. We're going to get a summit, [Mr.] President.

NIXON: Well, we're certainly not sucking after it, believe me.

KISSINGER: I'm not so sure we want it in this way.

NIXON: That's right. Yeah.

KISSINGER: My instinct tells me we're going to get the SALT and the summit. Look at their choices: what — where else are they going to go?

"All that really matters is the talk that's going on in that Senate."
May 6, 1971, 11:00 a.m.
Richard Nixon, Bob Haldeman, and Alexander Haig
OVAL OFFICE

Spurred by the May Day protests that brought four hundred thousand more protesters to Washington than the one hundred thousand originally envisioned, the Senate was engaged in debate over two antiwar amendments to the bill extending the military draft. The first amendment under discussion, written by George McGovern (D- SD) and Mark Hatfield (R-OR), called for the withdrawal of U.S. troops from Vietnam by the end of the year. The second, promoted by Frank Church (D-ID) and Sherman Cooper (R-KY), would allow the president to use defense funds in Vietnam only for the removal of the troops. The mood in the Senate had changed, and the possibility of passing such amendments was realistic for the first time since the war began.

. . .

NIXON: I think that, Al, we're going to have to come — to plan that trip on the eighth. You know, the Thieu trip.

HAIG: Yes, sir.

. . .

NIXON: We can haggle around through the summer. I mean, you've got the Chinese game, and we've got the Soviet game, and we've got the, the other game, and so forth and so on. Because I know the domestic game at this point. At the present time, we have got to move decisively [unclear] for domestic reasons. Not, not to — we're not going to change in terms of withdrawal, or anything like that, but we've got to move on the Thieu meeting if we're going to.

If that's going to be our big announcement for the summer, get it over with and get it over fast, because that's the only way you can stop. See, Henry has no, no concern or, certainly, no understanding of the situation in the Senate. Now, the votes are going to start coming around the eighth, ninth, and tenth. We'll have one in the House next week on the appropriations bill with a terminal date. The Senate votes are the ones I'm concerned about. I've got to have something, something more than simply, "Well, and — well, we offered the South Vietnamese — or the North Vietnamese, a terminal date, we've got a date." You know what I mean. It won't be that way in a cease-fire, and so forth, but it's too complicated. It's a good offer, I mean. I agree, and Stewart Alsop will understand it, Chalmers Roberts and a few others, but the guys up there that are — will not. So, on the other hand, the announcement from — after meeting with Thieu, the American combat role ends at a certain time; that'll have some impact. Right?

HALDEMAN: Sure.

NIXON: [unclear] my view.

HALDEMAN: That's just an offer that's turned down.

NIXON: Well, now look. Here's the point —

HALDEMAN: Except that —

NIXON: We have offered everything else. I noted already that — we all know the technical difference. That here, we are not — that here, we are separating out the political settlement, we're separating out the element of the China peace conference, and, and we are saying, "As of a certain date, if you'll give us a cease-fire and release our prisoners, we'll be out." That's new, and we all know that it's new. And it's very significant. We all know it's very significant. But, Al, to the average person in the country, that's just another [unclear] gobbledygook like the one we made before. See?

HAIG: Well, it's not going to mean anything, no.

NIXON: See? You make my point.

HAIG: That —

NIXON: You see, what they need, now, is something, Al. We've got to have something that means something to domestic people, here. That, that, that's — that's why the, the Thieu vote, if we don't have another vote, has got to be thrown — shot on the eighth. And the other vote isn't going to come out of Paris in my opinion. I don't know.

• • •

HAIG: I think a SALT agreement would be a substantial move —

NIXON: Well, well, but we'll have that soon, if we're going to get a SALT agreement. That — I agree, I agree. If we get that, and we announce it, and if we — that's a, that would be a [unclear] —

HALDEMAN: It will confuse them. It isn't gonna — it isn't going to undo your Vietnam thing —

NIXON: But it is — the point is, it'll confuse them just like China —

HALDEMAN: China did.

NIXON: — but it will not have the impact that's needed. The American people — we polled all this and so forth. It's too complicated. Intelligent people, it will confuse the hell out of them. We — but we must not ever confuse ourselves by thinking that that's the way that folks are.

• • •

NIXON: The people — the people that Henry sees —

HALDEMAN: — and know it's a hell of a [unclear] —

NIXON: — are obsessed with SALT, and the rest. I — we all know, you and I know, it's the most important goddamn thing. It's more important than whether we have eternal aid to Vietnam, or combat troops, or anything else. But you see, Al, in terms of the kind of clowns we're dealing with in the Congress, it just doesn't, doesn't have any time to sit. It'll help. It'll help. But what do you — what we do, on that one, we can appraise it. If my judgment is wrong we can embrace it. I can damn well assure you, in terms of — we'll have a chance to appraise it, because if we announce it next week, and it must be — incidentally, if we're going to do it, as I put in a note to you today, we're going to do it. It has to be done Wednesday of next week, or then put it off two weeks.

Now, there's a reason for that: there's a critical vote in the House on Wednesday. And, and otherwise, we should let it go two weeks. Screw it. I mean, there's no real reason to — no reason to get it out any sooner. We might as well drag it along and go through all the process, and inform all the embassies and talk to all the columnists, and all that bullshit. By Friday — but, otherwise, get it out on Wednesday. Thursday's too late — Thursday or Friday. So, that's, that's where we have it there. To do us any good in Congress, you see, I would rather have SALT come out two weeks later to affect the Senate vote. But you see these things wash out. All of a sudden they're forgotten. So, we either have to do it Wednesday or just fart around, which we probably will do, and not do anything about it, and let it get screwed up in Vienna. You know it will be. It probably will be. Now, it could be ready next week, of course, if he [Dobrynin] comes back with some kind of an answer.

HAIG: If he has an answer.

NIXON: If he has an answer. If he doesn't have an answer—it probably isn't going to be ready anyway for two weeks, so it's probably a moot question. Now, what could happen, what could have an effect? I will agree what could have an effect is an announcement of a summit with the Russians. That would have an effect on this whole thing. However, they aren't ready to do much else—

HAIG: They're not—

NIXON: —and we're not going to press them for an announcement. They're—we've told them already, "When you're ready, you tell us." Now, they'll tell us. If they should come in, unexpectedly, and say, "Look, we'd like to go forward with an announcement, and so forth"—because we're not going to ask; no more, no more; we can't appear anxious—that could have a very dramatic effect. See, that's the kind of announcement, though. And that's what an announcement will be with the Chinese—of a meeting, you understand, as distinctive from—well, that the president will receive the table tennis team when it comes over, and we're going to release some more items for trade with China. See? These—so, here's the things that will happen.

· · ·

NIXON: See my point? I don't want to have actions taken which appear to be in reaction to duress, or to the Senate. And the—that's why the Thieu thing very well may have to be the eighth, because there could God-well be an action in the Senate, which—it's hard to phrase all this very well, now, because we can't tell what their reactions will be to the recent demonstrations, and the rest. And some of them may start to harden up a bit, and maybe the House will be better next week than we [unclear] thought, but, it's really the Senate we're worried about. But I do know, I do know this: that, now, it's a cold-turkey proposition.

· · ·

HAIG: Of course, the China thing, I think, has the greatest impact.

NIXON: It has an impact. But there, they're going to need [unclear exchange]. But the China thing, the China thing, which—a China—an open meeting by a presidential emissary, or actually a presidential visit. You see, the difficulty with our whole China thing, though, is that there we have the Russian game. We can't announce that, that, "Well, there will be a presidential visit to China." First, there can't be a presidential visit to China as long as they're supporting South Vietnam—North Vietnam. So that's the deal. It's got to be a straight cold-turkey deal on that. Second, we don't want to throw the China thing, until we get the Russian thing, one way or the other. Because, once you do that, you knock off the Russian summit. And the Russian summit is more important. It may be that we don't want it, but my point is you've got to play, you've got to let both strings play out a bit.

HALDEMAN: The Russian summit is more important substantively. It sure isn't more important, I don't think, in public drama in this country.

NIXON: Could be.

HALDEMAN: We get more out of China, [unclear].

HAIG: The China thing, I think, means more in terms of the war in Southeast Asia —

NIXON: To the postwar order?

HAIG: Yes, sir.

• • •

NIXON: Now, the other thing, of course, that I thought of, was that in view of their turndown of our prisoner thing, you know what I mean? Normal reaction was that it was — that it would have been a hell of a good time to, to hit those three passes in North Vietnam. But, on the other hand, since he has this damn offer hanging out there — I want to get that over with for that reason, too, Al.

HAIG: Yes, sir.

NIXON: You understand, with Henry bouncing back and forth with Paris and those goddamn trips, I mean, that'll — they'd like to string it along, because they know very well that we don't do anything when those — when that's going on. We're going to hit 'em. I mean, they can't turn down an offer like that, and they can't make some of the jackass statements they make without paying some consequences, and that's the only thing we've got left. We're just about ready to hit 'em again, so I — so they — see, that's another reason for you, when you're talking to Henry, must be pressing Thieu. I mean, we — look, we can't diddle anymore. That's the whole point.

HAIG: Exactly.

NIXON: We've got to cut the diddling. Oh, the idea that, well, we can't do this, or that, or the other thing, because of the fact that it might disturb our talks with the Chinese; it might disturb our talks with the Russians; or it might disturb what talks we might have with the South — North Vietnamese. Just let me say: all that really matters is the talk that's going on in that Senate at the present time.

HAIG: Yes, sir.

• • •

HAIG: You know, I think your problems in the Senate, sir, are really your intellectual people.

NIXON: Yeah.

HAIG: And SALT does mean something to these men. These are — these are the leaders that are impressed by that.

NIXON: That's true. [unclear]

HAIG: I think the popular problem we're having now is dialectic, as it was last year. It's a — the swing is a little higher, but it's gonna recede the same way. So, we have to hold these, these real conscientious doves that are in the Senate. And I think the SALT would mean a hell of a lot to those people. I really do.

• • •

HAIG: I think actually, sir, you've got everything postured just beautifully in timing it, with the exception of this Senate —

NIXON: Yeah?

HAIG: — Senate problem, which is where we have a short fuse on it. But, the other things are ideal.

NIXON: You just have to have something when it comes off.

HAIG: They want a summit. I think they don't want us to move with the Chinese. We can't — that's the other reason why we can't move too quickly with the Chinese —

NIXON: Oh, now that's — you understand, I'm not saying we're going to move to the Chinese or the Russians. And on ABM, I'll delay that goddamn thing till hell freezes over, if necessary. But I do say that we have to do something —

HAIG: We have to get it —

NIXON: — tangible on Vietnam. And since we don't have — if we can't do it with regard to the draftee thing, then we'll have to move the Thieu thing up to the eighth. That'll work, and that's good enough. It's the best we got. It'll help.

HAIG: A little bit of a mixed package with Thieu's visit. The — they'll be —

NIXON: [unclear]

HAIG: The doves will say that you're propping up his election, too.

NIXON: That's right.

HAIG: That's — that's one of the criticisms we'll get.

NIXON: I guess you will. So, we will. But he wants to come over. Let's say that, look, if he, after that, announces that he will assume the full combat responsibility at a certain time, that's pretty goddamn good news, isn't it?

HAIG: I think it's very good. I think it'll help.

HALDEMAN: [unclear] you're not being accused of propping up the Thieu government, because you are.

NIXON: And, Al, that's accurate —

HAIG: [unclear]

NIXON: — and everybody thinks we're propping up the goddamn Thieu government, and I don't think — I just think we just, just do it and do it well. That's the point. Good God, you'd have thought we were propping up [unclear].

HAIG: You can talk about, at that meeting, also, about the peaceful development of Vietnam later. [unclear]

NIXON: The most important thing is that announcement, though. If we can get the, if we can get the — if we can get the SALT thing, that will set a warmer climate for the Thieu visit and everything else that comes among the intellectuals. I agree with that. But then, don't let, don't let the little junket to Paris. I mean, that's the one thing I [unclear].

HAIG: I don't see anything.

NIXON: Look, Al —

HAIG: I never have.

NIXON: Yeah. Henry has been too bullish [unclear] he thinks that — as you know, as he's said, because of the Chinese thing and the Russian — particularly the Chinese thing — he thinks there's a fifty percent chance, now, that maybe they'll talk. They aren't going to talk. Why the hell should they?

HAIG: No.

NIXON: We're going to get out anyway. You see my point?

HAIG: And they read. They read our problems here, too —

NIXON: Yeah. Oh, sure. He talks about 'em.

"They think we're caving in to the students?"

May 10, 1971, 12:57 p.m.

Richard Nixon and Henry Kissinger

OVAL OFFICE

During a wide-ranging talk, Kissinger cheered his boss by assuring him of his support from Americans beyond the capital region. He even reported the comments of Ronald Reagan, the governor of California, whom Nixon considered a spokesman for the Right.

• • •

NIXON: Hi, Henry.

KISSINGER: Mr. President.

NIXON: How are you?

KISSINGER: Okay.

NIXON: You look good.

KISSINGER: Yes, I had a good vacation.

NIXON: You have a meeting as soon as you get back?

KISSINGER: Yeah, I'm seeing the head of the Institute of World Politics in Moscow [Georgi Arbatov, director of the Institute for the USA, USSR Academy of Sciences] —

NIXON: Oh, I see.

KISSINGER: — and he's well connected at the Politburo. But — but they really are playing a rough game with us on that SALT business, and —

NIXON: Oh, I expected they would.

KISSINGER: Because what they're doing now is, they've put into Vienna the proposal which we turned down. They made us a formal proposal.

NIXON: Mm-hmm.

KISSINGER: And, I had Haig call in Dobrynin and raise hell with him last week, as he probably told you.

NIXON: Yeah.

KISSINGER: And Dobrynin said, "Oh, it was all a mistake." But, of course, they're — what they may do is they may finally accept our proposal.

NIXON: Mm-hmm.

KISSINGER: But deprive you of the credit for it by putting it into Vienna.

NIXON: Huh?

KISSINGER: I mean, they won't deprive — it's such a cheap little stunt.

NIXON: They'll try, and if anything happens at Vienna, they'll take the credit for it.

• • •

NIXON: Getting back to the Russians. I think that the — I think that when he [Dobrynin] came back, they watched the demonstrations and the rest. You noticed Joe Kraft's been worming around to the effect that the Russians don't want Nixon and so forth. I think the Russians may be playing a strict political game.

KISSINGER: That's right.

NIXON: And if they are, they can't play it with us.

KISSINGER: Well, that's what I mean, Mr. President. I don't think we should get into a position where we are caught between the doves and the hawks.

NIXON: No.

KISSINGER: And where the Russians are whipsawing us.

NIXON: So, how do you avoid that?

KISSINGER: Well, what I think, if they — what I would suggest is the following: if they don't come through with an answer by next Monday —

NIXON: Right. One week.

KISSINGER: One week. We tell Rush he's no longer authorized to talk on Berlin, except in formal channels. No private meetings with the Russians on Berlin —

NIXON: Good. Do you think that will hurt them?

KISSINGER: Oh, yeah.

NIXON: All right. Good.

• • •

KISSINGER: Haig told me he talked to the agricultural people on my behalf on Friday. There was only one question on Vietnam. I — if I heard a hundred times out on the West Coast, "Why won't the president get up and fight these people? Why does he keep turning the other cheek?" That we may wind up in a —

NIXON: They think we're caving in to the students?

KISSINGER: Yeah.

NIXON: On what?

KISSINGER: On —

NIXON: Demonstrations, you mean?

KISSINGER: Well, not on demonstrations, so much. I mean, I had a long conversation with Reagan on, on Saturday who was [unclear] —

NIXON: Who does he think we're turning it to? That's the point.

KISSINGER: Well, no, Reagan made a — well, he made a point that was actually not so bad. He said he listened to your television speech on April 7, and he said the end of it was superlative.

NIXON: Hmm.

KISSINGER: The body of it, he said he thought, was too defensive. I'm just giving you his reaction.

NIXON: Mm-hmm. Well, that's the reaction of the Right, yeah?

KISSINGER: And, a number of people who are not as far right as he is —

NIXON: I mean, we thought the body was pretty strong, you know?

KISSINGER: That's right. Right —

NIXON: Well, most of the people back here wrote that it was strong. They, they were —

KISSINGER: Oh, yes. Yes.

NIXON: So, you see, it shows you, though, that there's a hell of a lot of people in the country that want you to move a little further.

KISSINGER: I'm not —

NIXON: Yes?

KISSINGER: This wouldn't have been my view —

NIXON: But, it's — it's important, you know.

KISSINGER: But I've been really struck out there by —

NIXON: It's good to be out there, isn't it?

KISSINGER: Yeah. First of all, how much support you've got —

NIXON: [unclear] people.

KISSINGER: How much support you've got.

NIXON: We've got some.

. . .

NIXON: Coming back to this, the Russian thing, the other play we have to do is on Vietnam. See, that's the game, though. Let's forget the Russian thing and the rest at the present time. The game is where it is. All that matters here is Vietnam, though. Well, it seems to me, all we've got to play is the combat role, but what about making the offer sooner?

KISSINGER: I think it would bring Thieu down. I think the way to do it is to [unclear].

NIXON: All right, that's a reason not to do it. In other words, you don't think we can sell it to Thieu?

KISSINGER: I think you can sell it to Thieu, but no one else.

NIXON: I have to tell him we're going to offer a cease-fire, and — but we wouldn't do it there.

KISSINGER: No, you'd do it as soon as you — within a week of coming back.

NIXON: After he goes back, and we do it simultaneously?

KISSINGER: Yes. Something may come out of this Le Duan visit to Moscow, Mr. President. It's three weeks —

NIXON: Mm-hmm.

KISSINGER: — and that — they may be getting ready to settle it. I've still — a three-week visit for the leading North Vietnamese in Russia —

NIXON: Maybe he's sick?

KISSINGER: No. It's highly unusual. In fact, four weeks he's stayed on after the party congress. He's never left, and—

NIXON: Is he the big man?

KISSINGER: Yeah.

NIXON: You consider him to be one?

KISSINGER: Yeah, he's the party—he's the number-one man.

NIXON: I think that's one way, but then, let's understand: the least we have to do is to go there. I mean, we planned to go to—let's just plan to go to Midway on the eighth.

KISSINGER: I think that's a good idea—

NIXON: I—see, we've got to start planning that, now.

KISSINGER: I—I've thought about it all last week—

NIXON: We'll go on the eighth, and let's get it done. And then—

KISSINGER: In fact, there's a lot to be said to get—

NIXON: And then it's early, before the election.

KISSINGER: —to do it before. It's good to have it before the election; it's good to have it in a way before the Chinese answer.

NIXON: I know. Coming just two years after Vietnamization and making the announcement that the American combat role will end on—what is it? What's he going to say? The first of December? The first of January?

KISSINGER: Yeah. End of this troop withdrawal, the first of December.

NIXON: Yeah. Well, we could make it spring pretty soon.

KISSINGER: Oh, yeah. And then, if a week later, you come up with a—

NIXON: What were the casualties this week?

KISSINGER: Thirty-two.

NIXON: I thought they'd be down.

KISSINGER: Cut in half—

NIXON: I mean, I thought they'd be lower than that.

KISSINGER: Thirty-two is pretty low. Once you get below—

NIXON: Fifty?

KISSINGER: Fifty, it's really—

NIXON: Forty? [unclear]

KISSINGER: That's cut in half—

NIXON: There's still probably some carryovers from—

KISSINGER: Yes.

NIXON: —helicopter pilots, the poor guys. That's one bit of good news, isn't it?

KISSINGER: Yeah.

NIXON: All right. Then, in the other part—so, that's the Vietnam. In the meantime, Henry, we've got to keep our goddamn troops in the Senate. Do you notice, for example, if you read the weekend news summary, that all these people are, you know, yelling around about what they're going to do, and this, or that. Or Church says the shared responsibility with the House — with the Congress, you know. Responsibility? You know what they're petrified at?

KISSINGER: That you'll succeed.

NIXON: We'll end the goddamn war and blame — and say, "We ended it, they started it."

KISSINGER: Yeah.

NIXON: And that's exactly what we're going to do.

KISSINGER: Yeah.

NIXON: I think we can beat them on that issue. I think — but, provided we keep one step ahead. Now, unfortunately, I was hoping we'd have a SALT thing. Let's assume we don't have it. Let's assume we don't have a summit thing. That means we just — I think, at the very least, we've got to figure that what we've got, we're going to have a June 8 announcement, and then we've got to come back with another announcement of a new negotiating offer and our final negotiating offer. Right?

KISSINGER: Right —

NIXON: And we make it publicly?

KISSINGER: Right.

NIXON: What date would you put?

KISSINGER: I'd put September 1, '72. Well, I don't think that makes a hell —

NIXON: I don't think it makes a lot of difference. They're not going to take it.

KISSINGER: That's right.

NIXON: Cease-fire, and all the rest. I'd make it July 1. If you put it September 1 it looks like you're doing it just before the election, and for the election. See my point?

KISSINGER: Right.

NIXON: I think it's — I think you got to move [unclear]. Well, you don't have to negotiate too much. We've got to sell Thieu on it. Just say, "Let's do it July 1," and then see what happens.

KISSINGER: Right.

NIXON: He knows goddamn well we're not going to agree. You know, on the prisoner thing, their attitude is a cold-blooded deal. They're not going to do a damn thing on prisoners. You know why? They know they've got us by the balls.

KISSINGER: But — no, they're going to use the prisoners. As soon as we give a deadline, they'll insist that we stop military —

NIXON: You don't want to — you don't think we, we should consider any more bombing at the present time?

KISSINGER: I think we should consider it, seriously.

NIXON: As of now?

KISSINGER: Wait till we get their answer.

• • •

NIXON: You haven't heard anything. I don't think they'll give it. They might not even answer at all.

KISSINGER: No, but then, we're in great shape.

NIXON: Well, [unclear]. In other words, we made an offer, and they refused.

KISSINGER: Right.

NIXON: Bruce, he made an offer and they refused in all the private meetings and the rest. They've been hurt by Laos, and the rest, despite everything they tell him —

KISSINGER: Oh, yeah. Or — and, of course, they think they've got us on the run with all these demonstrations, which they're misreading.

• • •

KISSINGER: And, then, I think, Mr. President, if we know we are going to be in trouble with the Russians, you might consider —

NIXON: The Chinese thing?

KISSINGER: Well, the Chinese anyway — going on television with, with the facts of the military situation and just put it to our opponents.

NIXON: Mm-hmm.

KISSINGER: And, and play very tough in SALT. What we mustn't do is yield in SALT —

NIXON: No.

KISSINGER: — beyond the point, which we've already given them in my channel, because that will just encourage them to whipsaw us.

NIXON: What have they offered? Have they offered in — they offered in SALT — they offered in Vienna the National Command Center?

KISSINGER: No, they've done two things in Vienna. They've offered the National Command thing.

NIXON: Mm-hmm.

KISSINGER: And they've offered the construction freeze after the ABM agreement, which while we — we have insisted on —

NIXON: Simultaneous?

KISSINGER: — on simultaneous, and on Safeguard. Now, we could conceivably give on Safeguard but we cannot do it —

NIXON: After?

KISSINGER: — afterwards, because there'll be nothing left for us to negotiate —

NIXON: That's right. Yeah.

KISSINGER: If they're not willing to give us a freeze before an ABM agreement, they sure as hell aren't going to give it to us after an ABM agreement.

NIXON: They've offered to discuss it afterwards. Is that it?

KISSINGER: They've offered to discuss it afterwards. They're trying the Hanoi tactic.

NIXON: That's right.

KISSINGER: And that, Mr. President, I really think would be disastrous to national security —

NIXON: You're not going to do it.

KISSINGER: Also, we have told —

NIXON: You told Smith not to do anything on it, am I right? Haven't we told him? Does he know?

KISSINGER: We told him. He's coming back for consultation anyway —

NIXON: Good.

KISSINGER: Nothing can happen.

NIXON: Well, he'll understand.

. . .

NIXON: Let's just think about that a minute. Did you give this to the Pakistan ambassador this afternoon? [Before this meeting with Nixon, Kissinger met Agha Hilaly at 12:10 p.m. to deliver the reply to Zhou Enlai's latest message.]

KISSINGER: I've already told the essence of it to Farland, who's giving it to Yahya. Yes. This is going with the packet.

NIXON: You've already given it to him. Okay.

KISSINGER: But we could have, if this comes off —

NIXON: Right.

KISSINGER: — we could have a public — that's why I put in this idea of a special emissary.

NIXON: Yeah, I know. I saw that. That was to follow the secret meeting. You see what I'm getting at is that the Russians are going to play this kind of game with us, so we may have to play the public — if we only had a man to send over there. Goddamn it. I'll try to do this tomorrow. A half-hour thing won't work, will it?

KISSINGER: No.

NIXON: It won't work.

KISSINGER: I think it's the best way to get results, because —

NIXON: You can talk turkey.

KISSINGER: I could talk turkey and we could announce this, if it works at all, say, August 1, and then have an emissary, and then have you go.

NIXON: I wouldn't have the emissary if that was the case.

KISSINGER: No. Well, you might, but —

NIXON: Well, if we're going to announce me going, why have somebody else take the cream off?

KISSINGER: Well, if we sent an inconspicuous — if we sent a guy like Bruce, he wouldn't take any cream off.

NIXON: Hmm. Maybe.

KISSINGER: Or even Murphy. Just in case the Chinese want some public demonstration.

NIXON: I see. Well, we've got other plans. We'll see what happens. I'm not — I think — I'm inclined to agree, to say a little bit. We have weathered this storm of demonstrations and so forth, extremely well.

KISSINGER: Yeah.

NIXON: We — it's to the consternation of all the intellectual, all of the intelligent critics of our policy. They're worried as hell about it, that we didn't cave for — by God, I just don't know, Henry, whether — how you can be a lot tougher now. Right now — I mean, I don't know what we can do at the moment. We're certainly prepared to do something.

KISSINGER: Well, we can —

NIXON: We've got to turn on the goddamn Russians though.

KISSINGER: We've got to turn on the Russians.

NIXON: With Russia, there's no question, and that's why the public surfacing, the surfacing of the visit to the Chinese, it's quite apparent, is worrying the hell out of them.

KISSINGER: Yeah.

NIXON: I wouldn't diddle it away, though. I think that's —

KISSINGER: I just think that once — what we absolutely have to have to the Chinese is a reliable contact and a game plan, which they and we follow. And if we can get — once we get that visit set up —

NIXON: [unclear]

KISSINGER: — we may still get — the secret meeting has the other advantage. Of course, you're assuming we won't get the SALT —

NIXON: Yeah.

KISSINGER: I'm not so sure on that yet.

NIXON: Yeah. Yeah.

KISSINGER: We've got to do it —

NIXON: Well, anyway, we'll see. [laughs] I'll see you later.

KISSINGER: Right.

NIXON: Have a good time.

"A little package for bombing the North."
May 13, 1971, 9:28 a.m.
Richard Nixon, Bob Haldeman, and Henry Kissinger
OVAL OFFICE

Nixon, perhaps frustrated by the response to Operation Lam Son 719, spoke of aggressive bombing against North Vietnam.

• • •

NIXON: Cambodia [the 1970 Cambodian incursion] was right.

KISSINGER: Oh —

NIXON: And — well, not public-opinion-wise. Laos [Operation Lam Son 719] was right, too.

KISSINGER: Mr. President —

NIXON: The best thing about Laos that, Bob, you ought to have in mind is, you know, when all these people complain about it and then they vote. We'll never get any credit till later. But, if opponents see through [unclear] the casualties and the level of military activity since Laos — no, from Laos, and since — there has been no spring offensive. And that's when they have the offensive.

KISSINGER: That's right.

NIXON: Now, something had to happen. What happened? The South Vietnamese went in and kicked the hell out of a lot of North Vietnamese —

KISSINGER: No spring offensive, despite the largest input of materiel in any period, including Tet.

NIXON: That's right. Now, one thing else, get the [unclear] — get, get, get that fellow Laird — well, no, no, Moorer. Tell him I want a, a little package for bombing the North.

KISSINGER: Right.

NIXON: And I want it goddamn fast. Now, I don't think we should — I don't think you need to wait for Bill [Rogers]. I think maybe this weekend's a good time. I don't think [unclear] —

KISSINGER: Well, unless —

NIXON: — to think why, why does it, why does it have any relationship with the Russians? You think it has some relationship with the Russians?

KISSINGER: Well, I think we shouldn't put it to the Russians [unclear].

NIXON: Well, then, when can you? But we always — there's never a good time. [unclear]

KISSINGER: No, after we've made this announcement. No, no, after the twentieth. Let's get the [SALT] announcement under the belt. Let's not get that —

NIXON: See, your problem, see, too, with any kind of a summit announcement: once it's out, it's going to tie our hands. You see? When you've got to do anything you're going to do, we want to be in a position to bang 'em. Look, we've got to bang 'em somehow, Henry. We cannot have them —

KISSINGER: [unclear]

NIXON: — turn down our prisoner offer, you know, and just kick us around in Paris. We've got to do something.

KISSINGER: I agree completely, and I think — but, I just think, Mr. President, to be — having come this close, we can wait five days. After the twentieth, a week after —

NIXON: We've been waiting five months.

KISSINGER: Oh, no, we've hit them in March.

NIXON: Not much.

KISSINGER: Oh, no, that was a pretty good jolt. But, we haven't held up with bombing them. There was this damn air force —

HALDEMAN: And we hit some last weekend. There was a thing that was in the news about the [unclear] —

KISSINGER: Yeah, but that was just three airplanes.

HALDEMAN: Antiaircraft [unclear].

NIXON: Well, just, just have no illusions. We're not going to go till we hear from the North Vietnamese, and we end up banging them. Having that in mind, we play out this string [unclear] —

KISSINGER: They — there's something funny going on, though. Le Duan, who was four weeks in Moscow, now, he's in Beijing.

NIXON: Oh.

KISSINGER: There's something. Something is cooking —

NIXON: You think they're getting ready for a big offensive?

KISSINGER: No. No, they — to them, what's going on — to them, there's some — this SALT thing is going to be a jolt, because no matter what the Russians tell them they can't be sure of what side deals are being made.

"This is just a terribly bureaucratic government, Mr. President."
May 18, 1971, 9:41 a.m.
Richard Nixon and Henry Kissinger
OVAL OFFICE

On May 12, the Soviets submitted an outline of the SALT agreement with a plan for the summit. It was hardly the first one, but it was finally acceptable to Nixon, who began to make plans to announce it as a breakthrough in the long, hard Cold War stalemate between the two powers. The outline called for continuing the SALT negotiations, in order to complete a working agreement covering both ABM systems and offensive weaponry before the summit, which would remain unscheduled for the time being. The announcement would be mostly an agreement to try to agree, yet it had taken Nixon more than half a year to bring even that much to fruition. As of May 18, however, Dobrynin was asking for more time in which to circulate the plan in Moscow.

• • •

KISSINGER: I called Dobrynin, Mr. President, and Vorontsov picked up the phone.

NIXON: Yeah.

• • •

KISSINGER: He thinks there's no — he is in the box that, until he gets the word, he can't say yes. But he just doesn't think there is an issue. I just don't want to speculate, Mr. President, because —

NIXON: Well —

KISSINGER: — there may be a hundred reasons why in their bureaucracy —

NIXON: Yeah. I think — it seems to me — I can't see why — or I can't see one reason in a thousand why they aren't going to do it. But the point is, you see —

KISSINGER: I can't see any.

NIXON: — you've got to — I can't see. As I said, one in a thousand. I don't know. Except —

KISSINGER: If they had wanted to stop it, Mr. President, the easy way to stop it was last week, to tell us our proposal is unacceptable.

NIXON: Yeah.

KISSINGER: To get an agreed text and then, at the last minute — we've got too many things hanging over them: China, Berlin —

NIXON: There's nothing he can do to find out what the hell the story is?

KISSINGER: No, he said he sent a cable last night. He said it — and he said it's too early for him to have heard today.

NIXON: Yeah? Too early? Hell.

KISSINGER: Well, there's a two-hour transmission time, because —

NIXON: The problem is that we need to go — we need to know, well —

KISSINGER: Well, I think — I have canceled —

NIXON: — whether we go Thursday or not. That's the point.

KISSINGER: Well, I've canceled Smith for now.

NIXON: Yeah.

KISSINGER: And you might consider canceling —

NIXON: I canceled Rogers.

KISSINGER: — canceling Rogers.

NIXON: I did.

KISSINGER: But —

NIXON: I'm not going to tell him though that we're, of course, we're doing this thing.

KISSINGER: In concrete —

NIXON: If the son of a bitch [Rogers] should turn back on us, this would be a — we just can't —

KISSINGER: No, your —

NIXON: — let him know. You know what I mean, Henry?

KISSINGER: Your one —

NIXON: Never take such a chance.

KISSINGER: Your one thousand — if there's even —

NIXON: Yeah.

KISSINGER: — one chance in ten thousand —

NIXON: Sure.

KISSINGER: — why make ourselves look bad?

NIXON: That's right. That's right. Well, because then they'll think we're — we give away the game without getting anything for it.

KISSINGER: Right.

NIXON: So would a —

KISSINGER: Well, we've kept the Smith appointment with you for three [p.m.].

NIXON: Yeah.

KISSINGER: If we haven't heard, we can say you got locked in the congressional battle.

NIXON: Yeah.

KISSINGER: I'd like to get him out of town, quite frankly.

NIXON: But you think you can get him out?

KISSINGER: Of course, we can get him out of town without telling him anything.

NIXON: I think I'd get him out of town without telling him anything and then come back and tell him. You could even —

KISSINGER: Or we get Farley in and have him tell.

NIXON: Why don't you get Farley in and tell him?

KISSINGER: All right.

NIXON: I think it would be better to get Smith out of town.

KISSINGER: Right. Then I just —

NIXON: It's too late to react.

KISSINGER: Then I just have to make sure that Semenov doesn't say anything to him. And I can handle that.

• • •

KISSINGER: And I think after the SALT announcement, which —

NIXON: If —

KISSINGER: — after all, we'll have within a week —

NIXON: If we get it. If we get it.

KISSINGER: Oh, Mr. President, I cannot — if they negotiate for four months, make that many concessions, and then kick it over when an agreed text exists, that would be so unconscionable. They paid such a price for it. They also — they have a truck plant they are negotiating with us, and I arranged for Peterson to see their man on it. And I — we're holding that.

NIXON: [unclear]

KISSINGER: It can't fail. This is just a terribly bureaucratic government, Mr. President.

NIXON: I know. I think it's going to come, but my point is —

KISSINGER: No —

NIXON: — I'm just taking that extra degree of caution that I know in dealing with this, in dealing with —

KISSINGER: You're a thousand percent right.

NIXON: In dealing with Smith and Rogers, we must never go unless we got them by the balls.

KISSINGER: You couldn't be more right.

NIXON: We got them by the balls, then we go, right?

KISSINGER: You couldn't be more right.

• • •

KISSINGER: As Scali said to me yesterday, that if you would have put this proposal into the bureaucracy, they would have all accused you of sabotaging the SALT talks. It would have leaked all over town. Because we really did something on these negotiations. We pulled away from our own proposal on ABM and got the offensive link. Well, it's —

NIXON: It's a hell of a job. I read the, your memorandum. It's a hell of a job.

KISSINGER: Well, Mr. President, if it fails —

NIXON: And I know the hours that went into it.

KISSINGER: Oh, God, but —

NIXON: Well, if it fails, we —

KISSINGER: It cannot fail.

NIXON: Eight years [unclear] —

KISSINGER: It cannot fail.

NIXON: If it fails, listen, we'll burn the house down ourselves. If it fails, I don't see anything else to do but to fight on everything. I mean, then we'll have to go out and — and if the Russians turn this, we're going to have to go out and say, "To hell with elections and the rest. Let's build up American forces."

KISSINGER: It can't fail.

NIXON: "There has to be more taxes —"

KISSINGER: They're not that stupid, Mr. President. If they wanted it to fail, after having made six major concessions, for them to let it fail now, would be nuts. It —

NIXON: Did they make them? Or did Dobrynin make them?

KISSINGER: Oh, no. They are — Dobrynin always has a note. This is why I'm so confident, because Dobrynin, if he had the slightest doubt about the date —

NIXON: Mm-hmm.

KISSINGER: — would tell me there's a problem. All he is telling me — what he says is, Gromyko — he says Brezhnev was out of town, Gromyko can't set the date alone, and he's now going around town talking to the senior government officials because they don't want to call a new government meeting. That would be too time-consuming.

• • •

NIXON: By God, if we can get this SALT thing, this will really make these bastards look like a bunch of cheap politicians and cowards —

KISSINGER: Oh, that's why it's so important, Mr. President, because —

NIXON: That's why we've got to get — I wish [unclear] — I know I was the one who wanted that word changed but —

KISSINGER: I don't think that's the thing.

NIXON: — that's denial or the —

KISSINGER: I think Dobrynin — I don't think Gromyko has the —

NIXON: It may be that they, however, they could be — the only danger we have is this: they could be looking at the — they have people. Look, they're Communists. They have an American section analyzing American opinion. They also have American agents over here. You got a fellow like Joe Kraft, who's a slimy son of a bitch, constantly saying, "Nixon can't get along with the Russians." Now, it just may be they decided they could — that is what could move them, those great historical facts.

KISSINGER: Yeah, but if they do that, they also know that they won't get a [Berlin] agreement.

NIXON: Well, if they know that. That's —

KISSINGER: If [laughs] — Mr. President, I'm going to do a memo for you summing up what we did on Berlin, because if you think this is —

NIXON: Do they think — does Dobrynin know that we'll flush it?

KISSINGER: Oh, yeah.

NIXON: Listen, don't worry. There ain't going to be no doubt about flushing it. I'm not going to —

KISSINGER: Dobrynin — Dobrynin said to me last week that, that I'm the toughest fellow he's negotiated with since he's come here, and he says his government is just up a tree, because they'll — because I fight over every word. Now, basically, you know, I'm sure they're irritated with me. On the other hand, that's what they respect.

NIXON: That's what they do. They fight over every word.

KISSINGER: I don't — it's that word, Mr. President. Maybe we should have let it go. But I think for them to announce — what I am afraid happened is not the word. Basically, that announcement, which they drafted themselves, is a mistake —

NIXON: [unclear]

KISSINGER: — from their point of view. The word is nothing. But the announcement is where they made their mistake. And I am afraid what happened is that Semenov came back to Moscow from Vienna, saw that announcement, and said, "You idiots, you gave away too much." That's what worries me, because that announcement gives us more than we asked for. Even I didn't have the heart to say — to use the word "agree," "agree."

NIXON: Mm-hmm.

KISSINGER: That's the —

NIXON: Oh, well, I think — I don't think they can —

KISSINGER: But I don't see —

NIXON: I doubt that they can screw around on the announcement.

KISSINGER: But I don't see how they can pull off from an announcement, which is verbatim the text they gave us. That's not — I didn't change a word in the announcement, except put it into English. But I'd worked that out with his own man, with — I mean, with Dobrynin. We'll have it. It's too far down the track.

• • •

KISSINGER: By this time tomorrow, we will have heard. No question. They just cannot not do it.

NIXON: Well, we will have heard what, though? You can't tell.

KISSINGER: We'll have heard —

NIXON: You'll hear?

KISSINGER: — that they want to announce it either Thursday or Friday.

NIXON: I think you're probably right.

KISSINGER: I just —

NIXON: And if they say no, though, then we know what we're up against. We're up against a hell of a —

KISSINGER: Mr. President, if they say no, then we know that we're dealing with an insane government.

NIXON: That's right.

Sadat approaches Rogers

May 19, 1971, 9:05 a.m.

Richard Nixon and William Rogers

OVAL OFFICE

When Egyptian President Gamal Nasser died in late 1970 and a military officer took his place, little real change was expected in the national outlook. That assumption was proven wrong within months, as the new president, Anwar Sadat, presented American officials with a strong initiative to negotiate peace with Israel. Secretary Rogers was dispatched to discuss the possibilities with Sadat, and he reported the details to Nixon as soon as he returned. Nixon, however, was already working a second channel to Sadat and his representatives, the secret meetings being conducted personally by Kissinger, who was far more pessimistic than Rogers about the viability of an agreement.

• • •

ROGERS: Now, Sadat is a very forceful man. He has a lot of strength. He is nationalistic as the devil. He probably is untrustworthy, so I don't want you to think that I'm trusting him.

NIXON: Sure.

ROGERS: But he has decided to — I am convinced — to change his position. He is determined to become closer to the West for economic and political reasons. He's got a hell of a situation there. He's spending his money on his arms; he knows his people can't operate them, can't fly the damn airplanes. He's surrounded with Russians; he doesn't like that very much. Now, what I wanted to say to you, and he told me this in private and then he told Joe [Sisco] the same thing — and he didn't say it unequivocally; he said it as categorically as you possibly can. And I haven't briefed, I haven't told anybody at the State Department or anywhere else because it would be a disaster if we did —

NIXON: [If it] got out.

ROGERS: He said, "I have to have the Soviet agreement."

NIXON: Sure.

ROGERS: "It's important for me to have the new agreement. You're the only one who can help us get it — you, the United States."

NIXON: Mm-hmm.

ROGERS: "I don't like the presence of the Russians. I am a nationalist but I have no way of defending our country — we had no way of defending our country — except to get Russian help. You wouldn't give it to us; nobody else would. It's costing me a lot of money. I'm paying the salaries of the Russians. I'm paying cash for the equipment I get."

And he said, "I want to give you this promise: that if we can work out an interim settlement — and it will take me six months to open the canal — I promise you, I give you my personal assurance, that all the Russian ground troops will be out of my country at the end of six months. I will keep Russian pilots to train my pilots because that's the only way my pilots can learn to fly. But insofar as the bulk of the Russians are concerned, the ten or twelve thousand, they will all be out of Egypt in six months, if we can make a deal."

NIXON: On Suez?

ROGERS: On the interim — Suez.

NIXON: "Interim" means Suez in other words.

ROGERS: Suez.

NIXON: I see.

ROGERS: The final peace agreement is —

NIXON: [unclear]

ROGERS: [unclear] The interim is — we're talking about the Suez Canal. Now — and I said, "Well, Mr. President, you know, based on that, we may be able to work it out." I said, "The complicating factor is the Russian — the presence of the Russians' troops. If you can assure us that they'll be out in six months, that makes our problem a lot easier." I said, "You tell us that we shouldn't be so pro-Israeli. We have to be supportive of Israel's position because you got the Russians here in large numbers." I said, "For as much as we would like to be friendly as hell with you, we can't as long as you have this number of Russians here. You might as well realize that." I said, "We have to supply Israel with arms as long as you've got a large number of Russian troops in your country. On the other hand, once that is not the case, once they've left, or most of them, it's a different ball game."

"I just have a hunch here."

May 21, 1971, 11:29 a.m.

Richard Nixon and William Rogers

OVAL OFFICE

Nixon's career-long reputation as an anti-Communist zealot has given rise to the modern saying, "Only Nixon could go to China." Yet there was another reason why "only Nixon could go to China": he had an instinct for Maoist strategy. As seen in the following exchanges and other short excerpts that follow, Nixon had a clear sense of direction in turning U.S.-Chinese relations around, after a generation of mutually assured antipathy.

· · ·

NIXON: Now, it's something that we should keep very much, now one thing I've done that you should know, Maurice Stans wants to take a commercial mission, Ted Kennedy suggested he could drop over from there [the PRC] on his trips, and so forth. And I said none of you even approach it, don't even suggest it, we're not going to get into [unclear]. Any visits must be at the highest level. It would have to be you or me or both. And it might come, it might come. I just have a hunch here, a feeling that there's something going on there. I think that this Russian thing has a hell of a lot more to do with China than anything else. They're scared of them.

ROGERS: Yeah, no doubt about it. I think we want to be careful, that's why I want to mention today in my speech, on not appearing that we've turned them off. I think we've got to soften, to downplay a little bit so we don't get too eager.

"Both cannot have seats in the UN."

May 21, 1971, 5:26 p.m.

Richard Nixon and Alexander Haig

OVAL OFFICE

Even as Nixon continued to argue publicly for Taiwan remaining in the UN, privately he knew that would not happen. The key, then, was for Taiwan to have a graceful exit — graceful for Taiwan, but also for the United States and the People's Republic of China.

. . .

NIXON: There's only one way to do this; it's either up or down. In my opinion, it's got to be one or the other. Both cannot have seats in the UN. I don't think so.

HAIG: It won't work.

NIXON: It's not going to work. Now, under those circumstances, it's going to be Communist China at some time, [it's] inevitable, it's got to be. But let them do it, don't let us do it. That's the way I feel about it.

"Except in Vietnam."

May 25, 1971, 8:28 p.m.

Richard Nixon and Henry Kissinger

WHITE HOUSE TELEPHONE

As the details continued to be addressed on the SALT agreement, on the developing Quadripartite treaty on Berlin, and on Soviet relations in general, Nixon looked for public appreciation of his progress in foreign relations. As he admitted to Kissinger, though, he knew that he couldn't have it and he knew why.

. . .

KISSINGER: By the end of the month — by June 25, you will see your cards much more clearly.

NIXON: Yeah.

KISSINGER: Mr. President, one thing I was going to suggest to you tomorrow—we ought to give the Russians an ultimatum in about two weeks. If they don't deliver now, we will just delay till next spring on the summit.

NIXON: This is June—in two weeks you say we would do this?

KISSINGER: Yes. We have announced a summit or know we are going to get a summit.

NIXON: I don't know if you can get anything out of them on that.

KISSINGER: We have just given them the Gleason [gear contract], a huge package on economics they want—

NIXON: I spoke to these editors down there today—I talked generally about the whole thing. I said it could open to other things but a lot of negotiating to go forward and so on.

KISSINGER: They are trying to play Berlin. If we get a commitment out of them, [unclear] pressure on SALT.

NIXON: A commitment isn't enough.

KISSINGER: I mean an announcement. They are going to harvest everything and we will end up losing.

NIXON: You didn't talk about SALT today?

KISSINGER: No, no; on Monday. He said if these things work out, bigger things will follow.

NIXON: What the hell bigger can follow?

KISSINGER: We can speed up the Berlin negotiations. If there isn't a summit—there is no earthly reason to refuse a summit now.

NIXON: And we have settled on SALT—I mean [unclear].

KISSINGER: We have given them the economic package. Mr. President, if you agree, fairly soon—after the first of June, around the fourth or fifth—I will say we have been horsing around for a year that we would be glad to come to Moscow but will delay. On SALT, I gave him forty-eight hours—and he came back in twenty-four.

NIXON: We will just say we will have to postpone it indefinitely.

KISSINGER: Then let's just forget about it.

NIXON: As far as this year is concerned.

KISSINGER: That's what I mean. We have all the cards in our hands. We will know yes or no from them. We will have the Chinese answer and see Thieu and they won't scream so much.

NIXON: Yeah. Well, that doesn't bother me any to push them on that. The only thing that worries me is that it appears we are begging for the goddamn summit. I would think they would want it too.

KISSINGER: They want it. They are playing a cute game. I think this way if we keep giving them economic aid—

NIXON: Gleason is all we are going to give them.

KISSINGER: And the computer. You had already given them your approval when Heath was there.

NIXON: The computer, yeah.

KISSINGER: We have a chance to give them more economic things —

NIXON: I would do it in a week then.

KISSINGER: On the second or third of June.

NIXON: Right after Memorial Day, Tuesday or Wednesday of next week.

KISSINGER: Exactly.

NIXON: All right.

• • •

NIXON: Anything else new — you think the SALT thing is eventually going to get understood by everyone?

KISSINGER: It is understood now.

NIXON: By people that know anything about it.

KISSINGER: By people that don't know anything, they think you have achieved something they don't understand. The whole press, very positive. Henry Brandon had a very good article in the London *Sunday Times* although I don't know what distribution is here — a very good response.

NIXON: It is kind of like the China thing, it has the same positive response.

KISSINGER: Everyone feels in foreign policy you know what you are doing.

NIXON: Except in Vietnam. Really the problem — our enemies and press, people like [Stanley] Resor [the outgoing secretary of the army who recently expressed his personal doubts to the press about the war in Vietnam] keep hacking away. We are carrying a burden, then we have to make a sale nobody will buy.

KISSINGER: People will buy it.

NIXON: Except in Vietnam. The polls are pretty rough and they have some effect on the jackasses that read them. Well, we will hope for the best. Go right ahead with the Thieu thing and get it out of the way. I don't mind putting it off.

KISSINGER: Right, Mr. President.

"When you go to two-China, that's going to appear awfully reasonable."

May 27, 1971, 2:42 p.m.

Richard Nixon, William Rogers, and Henry Kissinger

OVAL OFFICE

During the first half of 1971, students of diplomacy noticed a well-orchestrated campaign to pave the way for mainland China to enter the UN. In fact, the impression was that Beijing wanted a seat at the UN even more than normalized relations with the United States. Nations all around the world were aware that China expected a vote to occur in the au-

tumn. The question was what the U.S. president thought about the most widely discussed possibility, a "two-China" UN that included both Beijing and Taipei.

• • •

NIXON: Frankly if we start out fresh, we would put, I mean, Communist China in the UN, right?

ROGERS: Mm-hmm.

NIXON: And, we wouldn't dream of letting Communist China take over fifteen million Taiwanese any more than we'd let North Korea take over South Korea. That's another point.

ROGERS: That's another point.

NIXON: And a defense treaty and all the rest.

ROGERS: This doesn't relate to our relations with Taiwan at all, this is just representation in the UN.

NIXON: Could I suggest a line, which you could do? [unclear] How, first what is — we're talking now on the twenty-seventh of May, how long will you be, until you are back? You'll be over two weeks in Europe?

ROGERS: No, ten days.

NIXON: Ten days. Well, of course, the time, and incidentally, I think you should handle it pretty much yourself on a very, very close basis, indicating that we have reached a position. You can say that we have talked, you know what I mean? And that we frankly are examining our position. We tend, we are examining our position at this point, and you are trying to determine — now I wonder if you can do that. I'd just, or perhaps [unclear] on the British before they say, "You put them all on that basis."

ROGERS: Yeah, I can't do it.

NIXON: Well —

[unclear exchange]

NIXON: What I meant is, could you put it up in this term. I know you've got to have something to say to them. Could you say to them, "Look here," because, you see, since you've returned, we've had Murphy come back. And Murphy has said that Chiang says that they'd accept two-China provided we give them the Security Council seat. We can't do that, it won't work. Nobody can guarantee the Security Council seat.

ROGERS: [unclear]

NIXON: Well, he didn't understand. Anyway, that's done. The point I made, we now know Chiang's position, which is very clear. And he's, he says, "Either go down fighting, or I'll take two-China but you've got to give me a Security Council seat." Well, we can't do that. But on the other hand, knowing now what our problem is there, could you give us the time [unclear], because I think time is going to be extremely important in terms of — I'm going to have to, on this one, if we make a move on the two-China thing, I've got to move on the right wing myself.

I've got to get Walter Judd in and talk about this issue. I may be able to do something with him. But I want to do it by, I want to be able to move now. I think if you could, if we could confirm [unclear], discuss with the various — I figured you could discuss this matter for this period of time, then come in and, I realize you probably already have. But there's still, it's further along and it's crystallizing all over the bullets. I think that's, that would then allow me to have the chance to sort of figure out how exactly to do it. I wouldn't want to have, for example, on your trip, I wouldn't want to have the whole thing come out.

The United States has changed its position and is trying to develop the support for it. I think it's premature to do that. When we change the position, I think that we ought to try to involve — I'd like to compose a message. I'm not concerned about [unclear]. We'll take the heat on the international stuff. You can handle that. But I've got to handle these domestic people — the hardliners in the House and Senate, some of the columnists, and people, frankly, who are part of the China Lobby, which is still a considerable group. I think that if you can get a verdict in the next couple weeks, if it were to come out that the U.S. has actually changed its position and is consulting with its allies to get support for a new position, that would be very difficult. If, on the other hand, you can discuss it in a way that we, you were trying to explore the position that they would take, in other words, "Here are the options, where will you end up?" Having in mind the fact that in the final analysis we will have to take a position one way or the other. Could you do that? Can you handle it that way?

ROGERS: I don't think that's [unclear].

NIXON: You see, the things seeping out is what I'm concerned about. I'm concerned about having to come out because [unclear] I don't want them to descend on me like a pack of little jackals and I have to say, then I'll have to lie to them, and [unclear] lie to the press conference and say, "Oh no, we're not considering, we haven't decided anything yet and so forth." See what I mean?

ROGERS: I don't see how there's any problem with me. I think it's going to be a problem of, as far as our policy is concerned, because so much has gone on with the delay that no policy is going to succeed. In other words, other nations are making, they've been waiting for us to tell them.

NIXON: Yeah. Well now wait a minute. Let me ask you, when we talk about delay, I'm not talking about a delay of two months. I'm talking about a delay of [unclear].

ROGERS: [unclear] talk to him about it? I know, you know, [unclear]. The present course as agreed to by everybody is disastrous, even Chiang Kai-shek. So what we're talking about is suicide as far as they're concerned. I mean, it's doomed to failure. And they know that and everybody that talks about the subject knows that. Really what we're asking them is, "Do you want us to go down in defeat in this way or would you rather have us try something else?"

NIXON: Well, what you're suggesting is that, what you would like to do, or what you would recommend is that you go over and —

ROGERS: What I'd like to do is to —

NIXON: See, if you do that, that will get out —

[unclear exchange]

ROGERS: I don't have to when we get there, but I, what I think we ought to do is to decide now what we want to do. Then I think all, whoever we want to talk to, the Walter Judds and the others, put it on the line. And say, "Lookit, are you prepared, do you want us to go down to defeat this way? We don't think this is a good thing for Chiang Kai-shek and for us." Now they'll all have to come to that conclusion.

NIXON: I think the way we ought to handle that is, the best way to handle that, probably it's the best way anyway, remember you've got to have [unclear]. You do not feel — now wait a minute, leaving out the Walter Judds and the rest for a moment. What I'm getting at is what is going to come out between now and the next couple of weeks? What is going to come out is that, this is a, this isn't, even announcing two Chinas is a monumental decision. And it is a monumental decision, it's a hell of a news story.

ROGERS: Oh, sure.

NIXON: Now, if that comes out in a way, that well, that the United States is privately or secretly discussing the, is trying to enlist support for the two-China thing, it seems to me that that's, I'd rather, I think maybe the proposition of doing it through a speech, as you suggested, at a later time, more frontally [unclear] is better than doing it through consultations.

See my point? You see what I'm afraid of, you talk to the British and you talk to the French or all these other people, now this is the way to do it. I think when it's done, it ought to be done in an orderly —

[unclear exchange]

NIXON: I had a feeling myself, I don't know, it's just a thing, Bill will do this and it's the kind of a thing that he ought to handle.

KISSINGER: Well, he could, I don't see, he could do the consultation and still give the speech in July.

NIXON: Yeah.

KISSINGER: I mean, he wouldn't —

ROGERS: Well the president's giving [unclear]. I'm not — see, everybody knows we're talking about [unclear] all over the world.

NIXON: That's true.

• • •

NIXON: I said, "Here is the proposition. We examined the situation. It appears that we are certain to lose if we consider the present course. For that reason, we are seriously considering this proposition." What do you think of it?

ROGERS: That's the way I feel.

NIXON: How's that sound, Henry?

ROGERS: That's what I think.

NIXON: Don't you think that's good?

KISSINGER: Yes.

NIXON: "We're seriously considering it."

KISSINGER: That's right.

NIXON: What do you think [unclear]? And as you go down and then, you can —

ROGERS: Now, in other words, [unclear] we can sort of get a count now that we find out the number of votes. But in the meantime, I think we should start talking to [unclear].

NIXON: Yes, I know. I know. Well, my inclination with them is to hit them pretty hard and frontally, when it's due, just before it's done, and then just say, "All right. The [unclear]." I think if you, the trouble is, you see, you hit them over a period of time though. I know this will hurt extremely well. What happens? They go home and they [unclear], and they talk about it and the rest, and then they gin up a lot of columns, and raise hell, letters and all that sort of thing. I'm inclined to think, once we decide, I like the idea of decisive motion, decisive motion. We get them all in, we hit them and say, "Here we go." Henry, you know some of these people there? [unclear]

KISSINGER: Just to be the devil's advocate and express [unclear], on this one I go back and forth. [unclear]

NIXON: [unclear]

KISSINGER: It's really a very close vote. What would we lose if we delayed another six weeks without having a vote?

ROGERS: Well, we'd lose a lot of votes. We'd get a lot of people [unclear]. What do we gain by it? Aren't we just sort of —

KISSINGER: Well —

ROGERS: [unclear]

NIXON: That's really —

KISSINGER: Well, no. [unclear] We cut six weeks off the public discussion.

ROGERS: Oh, no. We need the public discussion. The public discussion is [unclear]. Allows us to get nations to support us.

KISSINGER: Well now —

NIXON: He's referring to public discussion on that.

KISSINGER: Taking also the fact that [unclear] this new position.

ROGERS: [unclear] You think that's the way to look at it, if you do what you're doing you're going to die? Do you think we should state our position? How can they [unclear]? Even Chiang Kai-shek recognizes this. [unclear] Everybody knows that what we're doing, our present course is doomed to failure. So how can anybody be unhappy if you say, "Well, should we try something else?"

KISSINGER: Why would you try something else six weeks later? I mean, to whom did he [unclear]?

NIXON: What we're talking about basically is a moot question in a sense but [unclear] come down to is this. That I think that it would be best just to, [unclear] that we should, after you completed that process [unclear]. But, I think the idea, Henry, of building the thing that the ABA is building—

KISSINGER: But that speech offered—

NIXON: I think his idea—

ROGERS: By that time we'll know the vote [unclear] too. [unclear]

NIXON: I think if he makes the announcement there, and he can make it there. But then that also, it also will [unclear] that much of a crack in the door in other words. And I'm considering it from this standpoint. That then we can evaluate the events and so forth.

ROGERS: I would like it—

NIXON: But you think [unclear]—

ROGERS: Well, I think it will hurt you. I really do think it hurts you. I think it'll—

NIXON: You mean get rolled?

ROGERS: I think you'll get rolled. I think your conservative friends will think that it's a terrible defeat and you followed a policy that's doomed to failure.

• • •

[ROGERS leaves the conversation.]

KISSINGER: I don't see the sense of urgency that Bill feels, because it's a purely tactical embarrassment we are suffering from not having a position. But this way is the best we could get out of it.

NIXON: [unclear]

KISSINGER: It's my own, you know, it isn't worth overruling the secretary of state on it. I think tactically the best would have been just to keep it hushed up for another two months.

NIXON: He doesn't think he can do that.

KISSINGER: Well I think he believes that—

• • •

KISSINGER: I suspect they're going to sell the living bejeezus out of it.

NIXON: What?

KISSINGER: I suspect they're going to sell the living bejeezus out of it.

NIXON: Oh, sure.

KISSINGER: What I find so interesting in the State Department is that they have no strategic sense. All they worry about is their personal embarrassment and not having a position. So now they can [unclear]—

NIXON: That's the whole point, that is, of his concern was that I've already told them that I don't have any position. Well Christ almighty, so we've got no position, just go out and say so. Goddamn it, I do it every day in a press conference. But, or every week.

KISSINGER: Well, he follows Green's advice. It isn't, he doesn't, but it's, it's really—we can handle it.

NIXON: Let him go. As a matter of fact we can handle it. After all, Henry, there is a lot of discussion about the two-China thing. It's probably what we're going to end up with. [unclear] I am greatly tempted to stand on principle and get rolled and get them out. I am concerned about one thing: we've got to think very selfishly. But—

KISSINGER: But another way of getting rolled, Mr. President, is to delay our position as long as possible. Then, fairly late, go to a two-China position and then lose on that. Then we've done everything.

NIXON: Well—

KISSINGER: But that's—

NIXON: But that's another thing. The main thing—

KISSINGER: It's really not important enough.

NIXON: When you go to two-China, that's going to appear awfully reasonable to a hell of a lot of people.

KISSINGER: Oh, yeah.

NIXON: Awfully reasonable.

KISSINGER: Actually, the way he's formulated it now is better.

NIXON: Yeah.

KISSINGER: If he then gets off the universality one which will drive everybody, will drive the German situation. He just says, "Communist China in by majority vote; Taiwan expelled only by a two-thirds vote."

NIXON: [unclear]

KISSINGER: Then we don't make a general principle. And that we can, I think—

NIXON: I like that formula, the expulsion by two-thirds vote. And that [unclear], but I'm going to pull this. I want to know what the hell our problem is in the domestic politics before we do it. And I also will have to determine whether or not I am announcing it myself or have him do it. I think there is much to be said for letting him do the announcement.

KISSINGER: Yeah.

NIXON: It's a technical matter. There's a hell of a lot of people who are going to say we'll get the credit for it anyway.

• • •

NIXON: Now on the China thing, we're back exactly around the time he needs.

KISSINGER: That's right. Because—

NIXON: Now if the China [thing] doesn't come back, they should be back—

KISSINGER: They'll be back within ten days to two weeks.

NIXON: You think so? Has Yahya delivered the message?

KISSINGER: He delivered the message on May 19. It took five days. I've now got a good channel, but I told his ambassador to send it by pouch, didn't want it on a Pakistan wire. I've now set up a wire to Karachi for our ambassador, which goes only through Moorer. Nobody knows it. And it's got a special code, which only Haig knows, so even Moorer can't read it. And which only, and so now we can deliver messages in twenty-four hours. It took five days to get there, then it took, then Yahya was in Lahore so he didn't deliver it until the nineteenth. So they've only had it for seven days. And my guess is that they'll reply the first week of June.

NIXON: You think they'll reply in the positive or negative?

KISSINGER: Almost certainly, yes.

NIXON: There's a lot of things in there about a presidential visit and all that kind of stuff.

KISSINGER: We offered them a presidential visit. We told them I'd be authorized to arrange the visit of a public emissary if it was thought useful; it's hedged a little bit. And —

NIXON: In addition to a presidential visit?

KISSINGER: Yeah, in addition to a presidential visit. And for them, Mr. President, after all, they are revolutionaries. But you think of this peasant, former peasant, Mao, the Great March, and then the president of the United States comes to Beijing at the end of his life. That's —

NIXON: Well that's why this former [unclear] Brezhnev has goddamn well got to decide whether he wants to come or not. And —

KISSINGER: I think that, Dobrynin again this morning talked about that trade deal, that five-hundred-million-dollar trade deal.

NIXON: Yeah.

KISSINGER: We just don't have enough information to act on it.

NIXON: Well, but he didn't raise the summit. He never raises it, does he?

KISSINGER: No.

NIXON: Well, he must have a reason, you know.

KISSINGER: Well, no. They are very cute. They figure you're very eager, so they figure they're first going to make you pay on Berlin. Then they're going to make you pay on trade, and after that they give you the summit.

NIXON: What the hell are we going to talk about there?

KISSINGER: But I think, well, we can have, we need the summit for a number of reasons. It will discipline them during SALT.

NIXON: Yeah. Well, we've got to have, we need the summit for the reason of getting the deal on SALT.

KISSINGER: That's what I mean.

NIXON: So then we've got to hammer them.

• • •

NIXON: Are we going to have a summit at all with the Russians? You got a deal with the Chinese, we'll go to China earlier. Why not?

KISSINGER: It also has the advantage that then we know where we stand.

NIXON: You notice the hard line the Chinese are taking on Taiwan. Predictable, right?

KISSINGER: Yeah.

NIXON: The Nineteenth Province [PRC reference to Taiwan] and all that sort of crap?

KISSINGER: Yeah.

NIXON: [unclear]

KISSINGER: Oh, I know. No, what they have asked from us up to now —

NIXON: Basically, to remove the Sixth Fleet.

KISSINGER: — is to remove our military forces from Taiwan. If they would help us make peace in Vietnam —

NIXON: We'll do it.

KISSINGER: — we could do it early in your new term.

NIXON: Just put it in the terms, "Yes, we will do it. We made a private [unclear] to do so."

KISSINGER: But Taiwan, except for the sentimental thing, is really the least significant American [unclear].

NIXON: I'm afraid it is. I'm sorry.

KISSINGER: It's a heartbreaking thing. They're a lovely people.

NIXON: I hate to do it, I hate to do it, I hate to do it, I know. And they've been my friends. [unclear] I still think, I can't believe Bill is right when he says the Koreans don't care, Kiichi doesn't care, and the rest of them don't care about Taiwan.

KISSINGER: Totally wrong.

NIXON: Somebody is selling him a bunch of shit.

KISSINGER: Totally wrong. Totally wrong. Your instinct is absolutely right.

Leon Panetta, and human rights in other countries

May 27, 1971, 4:28 p.m.

Richard Nixon, Bob Haldeman, John Ehrlichman, and Henry Kissinger

OVAL OFFICE

Nixon's dim view of the State Department was not improved by a statement it made in May in support of Soviet Jewry. His annoyance with any encroachment on his evolving diplomacy with the Soviets led to a discussion of the validity of the position offered in the statement.

First, however, was the problem of Leon Panetta. In the early 1970s, Panetta was a Republican staffer assigned to Secretary Robert Finch in the Department of Health, Education, and Welfare. By March of 1971, his views on civil rights had diverged from the administration's. He quit, wrote a scathing critique of government policy, and switched political parties.

• • •

EHRLICHMAN: This damn Panetta book [*Bring Us Together: The Nixon Team and the Civil Rights Retreat*] is really a revelation about the Finch administration over there.

NIXON: Is it really?

EHRLICHMAN: It really is. This guy, apparently, was keeping notes.

NIXON: How does Finch come out?

EHRLICHMAN: Bad.

NIXON: Does he?

EHRLICHMAN: Very weak, very [unclear]. Yeah. He comes out very weak, I come out some kind of a heady — the whole thing is on civil rights, of course. And, he lies in his teeth about five different places, and particularly about his resignation.

NIXON: Yeah.

EHRLICHMAN: And then he quits, just before the March 24 statement on civil rights [Nixon's public statement on the administration's policy with respect to public school desegregation]. The book gives you no credit for civil rights. It's a real ax job. But I told my staff to all read it, because I want them to understand what happens inside a department, and how the department courts us, and how they use us, and how they play us. It's a damn good textbook on that.

· · ·

KISSINGER: The State Department issued a terrific blast against the treatment of Jews in —

NIXON: Yeah.

KISSINGER: — the Soviet Union.

NIXON: Oh, why — didn't we stop that? Goddamn, I thought we just had that little —

KISSINGER: I had thought — I reaffirmed — I may ask you to sign —

NIXON: All right. I'll sign a letter.

KISSINGER: — that they — any statement concerning the Soviet Union for the next two months has to be cleared here no matter how trivial.

NIXON: I think you should get the memorandum to me today. I mean —

KISSINGER: Yeah.

NIXON: — first thing in the morning, Henry. It's so important.

KISSINGER: Because it's a —

NIXON: Yeah.

KISSINGER: — it gets us nothing to —

NIXON: Yeah. But I don't want to — because of very high considerations, indeed, I want no statement concerning the Soviet Union of any kind, public statements, to be made without clearance with me. [unclear]

HALDEMAN: Unless somebody comes —

KISSINGER: With all — you know, I'm Jewish myself, but who are we to complain —

EHRLICHMAN: [laughs]

KISSINGER: — about Soviet Jews? It's none of our business. If they complain — if they made a public protest to us for the treatment of Negroes, we'd be —

EHRLICHMAN: Yeah.

NIXON: I know.

KISSINGER: You know, it's none of our business how they treat their people.

NIXON: Yeah. Well, we — that's why I think your — that's why I couldn't see Max Fisher and that other fellow, Schecter. Christ, I can't see these people about the treatment of — we're — they know how we feel, for Christ's sakes.

"In terms of world peace."

May 28, 1971, 9:50 a.m.
Richard Nixon, Bob Haldeman, and Henry Kissinger
OVAL OFFICE

In late May, when Dobrynin brought word of a further delay of the Moscow summit, Nixon saw easily that the scheduling was becoming a weapon.

• • •

KISSINGER: You have to decide what's worth more to you: the announcement of a visit, and then the anticipation of it; or whether you want to actually have the visit this year, which would be a very dramatic turnaround.

NIXON: Just as long as I have the visit. Again: one or the other.

KISSINGER: Right.

NIXON: Let me put it this way: don't wait. Next year is a political year. Everything will be cast in a political connotation. Everything we do.

KISSINGER: Right.

NIXON: It is not good, therefore — and also, if you get into next year, nothing can occur after July 1, when the Democrats nominate. Because after that time, all the goddamn press will insist that the Democratic candidate had to go along. You understand?

KISSINGER: Right.

NIXON: That's the other problem.

KISSINGER: That's —

NIXON: Or his advisor will want to go along. Now, Johnson didn't do that. The son of a bitch didn't tell me about the bombing pause, except on the telephone. Nevertheless, that's what they're going to say. So, therefore, all of our foreign policy initiatives have to be completed by the first of July. There ain't nothin' else that could be done.

KISSINGER: Absolutely.

NIXON: You see what I mean?

KISSINGER: Absolutely.

NIXON: So there's our — there's the deal. That's why, Henry, what we've got to think of: I prefer a Russian summit this year, and a Chinese next year. But it would have to be in the spring.

KISSINGER: Oh, yes. Absolutely in the spring.

NIXON: Not in July. You see, beginning —

KISSINGER: Oh, no. April or so — or May, or whenever you want it.

NIXON: Sure. Maybe March.

KISSINGER: Or March.

NIXON: What I'm getting at is, the further away from the election —

KISSINGER: Sure.

NIXON: You know how these damn bastards react to everything. Even now, they say it's all political. Now, that doesn't bother me particularly, except that, as you get to the point where they have selected a candidate, or where it's quite obvious there's going to be one, the pressure is going to be enormous.

· · ·

KISSINGER: Yeah, but if a summit were announced, in the interval between its announcement and your going there, they don't want to irritate you, I think. Well, let's see what Dobrynin brings back. I'm going to give him the ultimatum very shortly and tell him if it isn't now, we can't do it this year. That's the only way they'll believe it. I cannot — if I just ask him for an answer —

NIXON: Mm-hmm.

KISSINGER: — then we'll look like plead — it'd look like pleading and nervousness. If I tell him it's now or never — so far, brutality has been the only — and daring, gambling have been —

NIXON: Just put it — you have to put it on the basis that our — "the president has got varying constituencies, you know."

KISSINGER: I said we just will not be in the position —

NIXON: "He can't be in the position. He's filling it out for the balance of the year — state visits, and so forth and so on," and —

KISSINGER: "And we just won't let you play this game. You know as much now as you're going to know from us. And if you can't make up your mind, then let's wait for a time when you can make up your mind, which cannot, then, be this year." That's — that language, he'll understand.

NIXON: Then —

KISSINGER: It has a lot of advantages, because if —

NIXON: It may be that you ought to have both do it now — it may be that — actually, the best of both worlds would be to have the China card in your pocket before the —

KISSINGER: That's why I hope — that would be —

NIXON: But you aren't going to get that this week. You aren't going to get the message?

KISSINGER: No, the Chinese will wait two weeks. That's their system, Mr. President. There's just no way they —

HALDEMAN: Has it been one week?

KISSINGER: Nineteenth, twenty-sixth, it could happen next week. It could happen by the end of next week. Very soon next week.

· · ·

NIXON: We got to milk the publicity out of every achievement. And everything has got to be a presidential initiative. Now, as far as Berlin is concerned, we did it. And we're going to —

KISSINGER: We've got to leak that, because, really, that is a —

NIXON: Well —

KISSINGER: — it sounds as if —

NIXON: When will it come?

KISSINGER: It's moving. Now, we can — I'm slowing it down a little bit —

NIXON: Yeah.

KISSINGER: — just to get the summit.

NIXON: Yeah. Yeah.

KISSINGER: July, I think.

NIXON: All right. That's got to be a presidential initiative too. I might announce it.

KISSINGER: You may get credit, Mr. President. I set up that procedure, on your instructions, on an airplane. I got Bahr invited to the moon shot in January —

NIXON: Yeah.

KISSINGER: — so that I'd have an excuse to see him.

NIXON: That's right.

KISSINGER: I rode up on a plane with him to New York, and we worked out that whole procedure. And we've got a file this thick —

NIXON: Right.

KISSINGER: — of back-channel traffic to Bahr and Rush.

NIXON: Right. Yeah.

KISSINGER: And the Russians —

NIXON: It's a hell of a job. I know.

KISSINGER: And, actually, that was a trickier one, because we had another party involved, than —

NIXON: I know.

KISSINGER: — than SALT. And that —

NIXON: It's a hell of a job.

KISSINGER: Now, if that happens in July, we can say they had a Berlin crisis and we solved it.

NIXON: [unclear]

HALDEMAN: They had an escalating war and we brought it down. They had a missile —

KISSINGER: The Berlin thing — actually, and the way it —

NIXON: The Berlin thing is really more important, really, in terms of world peace, than either the Mideast or — I mean, in order of magnitude, the least important is Vietnam. It never, never, never has risked world war.

HALDEMAN: Right.

NIXON: You know that. Hell, we all know that. I mean, I've been making that speech for twenty — for ten years. You know it's true. China's going to intervene? Russia's going to intervene? None of them will ever intervene. Second, the next is the Mideast. That has the elements that could involve the major powers, because it's important. But, compared in the order of magnitude, the Mideast to Berlin, Christ, it's light-years' difference. Berlin is it. Shit, if anything happens in Berlin, then you're at it, right?

KISSINGER: Right.

NIXON: That's why Berlin is so enormous, and also —

KISSINGER: And —

NIXON: — it's more important to the Russians.

KISSINGER: And, what we —

NIXON: The Russians will let — they'd let Egypt go down the tubes. They will never let Berlin go down the tubes.

KISSINGER: And we got a number of very significant concessions out of them. For example, they had always insisted that we call — these are minor things — that we describe in the document —

NIXON: Uh-huh.

KISSINGER: — Berlin as "Berlin (West)." We've insisted that they say "the Western sectors of Berlin," so that it shows —

NIXON: Yeah.

KISSINGER: — that, the Four Power responsibility. They've now accepted this.

NIXON: Right.

KISSINGER: Secondly, which is more important: they had insisted all along on legal justifications that gave East Germany control over access.

NIXON: Yeah.

KISSINGER: They've now accepted legal formulations in which they have a responsibility for access, which they never did even in the forties. That's more than Truman or Roosevelt got out of them.

NIXON: Right.

KISSINGER: And, under those conditions, the Berlin agreement — which I always told you, we had to cut our losses — will actually be a small net plus on the ground. I would like to call Dobrynin to discourage him from — he's going over to State today — from mentioning a foreign ministers' meeting on Berlin.

NIXON: Foreign ministers?

KISSINGER: Because —

NIXON: Now, Bill didn't raise this point at his crazy meeting with —

KISSINGER: No.

NIXON: He's — well, he can —

KISSINGER: He can't float it. It's too complicated —

NIXON: Oh, it's the silliest thing I ever heard of. Gromyko?

KISSINGER: I think if there are high-level meetings, Mr. President, for this year and next, they ought to be yours.

"'We've horsed around long enough.'"

May 29, 1971, 9:08 a.m.

Richard Nixon, Bob Haldeman, and Henry Kissinger

OVAL OFFICE

The implication that the Soviets would host the summit without completing the SALT agreement pressed Nixon and Kissinger to prepare an ultimatum. As their discussion continued, Kissinger expressed an ever-stronger rationale for Nixon winning the 1972 election.

. . .

KISSINGER: Now, I had a cable from—

NIXON: Rush.

KISSINGER: —from Rush. And [laughs] we are in the ridiculous position, Mr. President, that—

NIXON: Yeah. What did he want?

KISSINGER: —the Berlin talks are going so well that we may not be able to slow them down enough. I think we'll have the Berlin agreement, unless there's a snag, by the middle of July, which makes it imperative that I talk to Dobrynin and tell him—

NIXON: Yes.

KISSINGER: —"This is it, now." And actually the Russians are making two-thirds of the concessions.

NIXON: Mm-hmm.

. . .

KISSINGER: Well, Mr. President, if we get Semenov over here to sign the hot line agreement—it doesn't mean a goddamn thing. It just—

NIXON: It helps.

KISSINGER: It helps. If—the Berlin thing is going to break—

NIXON: Yeah.

KISSINGER: —in the next two or three weeks.

NIXON: I think that what we've got to figure, in the least, is that we get those two. But, on the other hand, the Berlin—can we keep Berlin from breaking if they don't agree to a summit?

KISSINGER: Well, I'm going to give him [Dobrynin] an ultimatum on the summit a week from Monday. The next—

NIXON: It might work but I'm just asking, in order to go, whether we can mess it up.

KISSINGER: Yeah. We can keep it—

NIXON: You see?

KISSINGER: —we can keep it from breaking.

NIXON: All right.

KISSINGER: We have to be bastards but we just—

NIXON: All right. We'll be bastards. That's right. Just say the president—all right, and when he gets to that say, "We're not going to agree to Berlin. It's up to you."

KISSINGER: The next time they're going to meet is on June 4. And that's mostly technical stuff.

NIXON: Mm-hmm.

KISSINGER: Then Brandt and Rush are going to come over here.

NIXON: Then we see Brandt?

KISSINGER: And we see Brandt. And before Brandt gets here, I'm going to tell Do-brynin, "That's it now. We've horsed around long enough."

NIXON: We have.

KISSINGER: "We have to make our basic decisions." The only thing is, the only way we'll make it plausible is to say, "If you reject it now, that's it for this year." That's the one thing—

NIXON: The submarine that's in Cuba is not nuclear, is it?

KISSINGER: It is nuclear.

NIXON: Huh?

KISSINGER: It is a nuclear-powered submarine. It doesn't have missiles on it. It's one of these cheap gangster shots. At first, I thought it wasn't nuclear.

HALDEMAN: Did you know it wasn't?

KISSINGER: No, that was another conversation. No, it is nuclear.

NIXON: Hmm. Is that right?

KISSINGER: That's what I found out yesterday.

NIXON: I read something incorrectly.

KISSINGER: No, that's right. He told me it wasn't.

NIXON: I told him that although the submarines were not nuclear—

KISSINGER: Yeah. Our information was wrong.

NIXON: —there was a submarine at a base in Matanzas.

KISSINGER: And I corrected that. I called him back and said that—

NIXON: [unclear] All right.

KISSINGER: —we had gotten new photography, and it was nuclear.

NIXON: Yeah. So?

KISSINGER: Well, he says they announced it. It's at the very edge of the understanding. It's just at the edge of it. And they're not in Cienfuegos. It's a gangster thing to do. And I think if it comes up in the press conference, as it may because now the word will get out, I wouldn't get into the question of whether it violated the understanding. But I'd be very tough on what we're—

NIXON: I'd just say, "There is an understanding and we expect it to be complied with. The Soviets are quite aware of it," and let it go with that.

KISSINGER: Right.

NIXON: And that I—

KISSINGER: I won't comment on every single trip—

NIXON: "I'm not going to comment on it. The Soviets are quite aware."

KISSINGER: Right.

NIXON: Is that enigmatic as hell?

KISSINGER: Much better.

• • •

NIXON: The problem here, though, with the Russians and the Chinese, what really helps us, is that they have an enormous problem between each other. They try to cut us, our balls off, and here we are —

KISSINGER: I think they've never had as tough an opponent in here, as you've turned out to be.

NIXON: Mm-hmm. In a minute here you've got to give Thurmond a call, right? And have, I mean, the Russian line that we'd agreed to quit — to give up ABM before we had an offensive limitation. But, it's rather awkward language of the communiqué to have at all.

KISSINGER: It says "together with."

NIXON: "Together with." Goodness, if — aren't these people stupid up there, though? We say, "We shall concentrate this year on negotiating —"

KISSINGER: But, of course —

NIXON: "— an ABM agreement." And then, it goes on, in the next sentence —

KISSINGER: "Together with, we will agree on."

NIXON: — "together with this, we will agree with that." You see? That's all we have to do: say, "Look, you're off base, Senator."

KISSINGER: They are — but, what is happening is, Mr. President, I really think that the Communists are beginning to dominate some of our media. Six weeks ago, they were —

NIXON: Oh, on that, I agree with you —

KISSINGER: Because, now —

NIXON: I've been saying it for years.

KISSINGER: I saw a *New Republic* article in which they castigated you for the SALT thing, because you maintained the relationship between offensive and defensive limitations. Here the Russians have already agreed to it, and they're still hitting away at it, which is, of course, what the Russians really want. And that's what, if they babble away enough, of course the Russians will pick it up at the next Helsinki thing. That's why we should get this summit date fixed.

NIXON: Yeah.

KISSINGER: Because then they'll be reluctant to be too —

NIXON: Well, Henry, no summit, however, under any circumstances, unless we do have a — an interim SALT agreement to put it to, to put it on the finish there. We have to do that, Henry. To go there without doing that, that's not even worth our time.

KISSINGER: They agree to it now, because we can't be sure. But —

NIXON: Perhaps.

KISSINGER: — we've got to gamble, I think. We can always sign the accidental war agreement. We can announce some progress on SALT. If there is a deadlock in Vienna we can break it at Moscow —

NIXON: Why do you have the summit, then? Fisheries?

KISSINGER: Frankly, for — partly for domestic reasons, and partly — I frankly feel, Mr. President, at this point, that to keep the Democrats out of office next year —

NIXON: Is the main thing.

KISSINGER: — is a major national necessity.

NIXON: That's right. It'd be terrible if they got in.

KISSINGER: And —

NIXON: Terrible. You know, really, really, with the irresponsibility that they have displayed, it —

KISSINGER: The [Democratic] Party is unfit to conduct foreign policy. These are the radicals.

NIXON: Well, it's just the Eastern establishment.

KISSINGER: Right.

NIXON: That's where the damn radicals are.

KISSINGER: Yeah.

NIXON: Basically.

KISSINGER: And another argument for the summit is we have a better chance of getting the SALT with the summit that —

NIXON: I agree. I agree. They've got reasons as well as we have, to have something come out of the meeting. So, we can be sure on that. I'll put this — the other side of the coin. That we're not going to have a summit and come out without an ABM agreement.

KISSINGER: Out of the question. That we can't do.

NIXON: [unclear] Never, never, never.

KISSINGER: That we cannot do.

NIXON: I don't think it's all that difficult. They can get — we can have an ABM agreement, and a limitation on offensive weapons —

KISSINGER: It's on offensive weapons, so it shouldn't be so hard —

NIXON: It's all we're asking.

KISSINGER: Mr. President, for us to get Berlin, SALT, China, the summit, all into one time frame, and to keep any of these countries —

NIXON: To keep Europe happy.

KISSINGER: — to keep Europe happy, to keep Vietnam from collapsing —

NIXON: Yeah. [unclear]

KISSINGER: — that takes great subtlety and intricacy.

NIXON: All of this, everything is close. But on the whole, everything worthwhile in the world is close. Nothing is easy. Nothing is easy in these times.

KISSINGER: To get this Berlin thing is, I now consider, practically certain. We've got that where we had SALT in March —

NIXON: I ought to get into that, don't you think?

KISSINGER: I beg your pardon?

NIXON: I probably ought to get into that act sometime.

KISSINGER: Berlin?

NIXON: Yes.

KISSINGER: Still —

NIXON: Get a little credit.

KISSINGER: When Brandt is here, you may be able to do something with that —

NIXON: Well, we'll see.

"This boy O'Neill, who's, God, you'd just be proud of him."

June 4, 1971, 2:34 p.m.

Richard Nixon and Charles Colson

WHITE HOUSE TELEPHONE

Greater and greater numbers of Vietnam veterans were returning home. While many stayed out of politics, some expressed opinions about the war, their experience, and the draft. As a counter to John Kerry and the Vietnam Veterans Against the War, John O'Neill started the pro-administration Vietnam Veterans for a Just Peace. The Nixon White House could not officially offer O'Neill any support, but Nixon understood the importance of a pro-administration veterans group. O'Neill was encouraged to take part in public events and speak in favor of government war policy, and to debate John Kerry in highly public venues.

• • •

COLSON: I had the most refreshing experience, Mr. President, I've had in a long time this week with the group of Vietnam veterans who are organized for us.

NIXON: They're doing a great job.

COLSON: Oh! Well, they came in to see me after their —

NIXON: Yeah.

COLSON: — after their press conference, which, by the way, got remarkable press coverage.

NIXON: Yeah! Haldeman and I saw it.

COLSON: This boy O'Neill, who's, God, you'd just be proud of him. They were ten of them. One of them, by the way, had been arrested for tearing down a Viet Cong flag a year ago.

[laughter]

NIXON: Great!

COLSON: They're just marvelous kids! And one hundred percent behind you. They talked about the drug problem in Vietnam. They said it's a problem, but no worse than in the high schools.

NIXON: That's what I think.

COLSON: They're going out, in fact, the Marines in the outfit, in that group, said it was much less in Vietnam. He said that this is all another one of the press exaggerations. These fellas are going out speaking in various parts of the country for us.

NIXON: Yeah.

COLSON: They were invited on *Face the Nation* this week for a debate with Kerry, but Kerry turned them down, refused to debate, refused to debate O'Neill.

NIXON: Aha!

COLSON: Which is a point we'll get out to the press.

NIXON: Yeah. Yeah.

COLSON: They're just a grand bunch. And a few more like this and we can —

NIXON: Yeah.

COLSON: — get people thinking in different terms.

NIXON: Yeah, yeah. Well, of course, they can get equal time, I think, as they move around. And that's good. Kerry may start to wear a little thin in time.

COLSON: Well, there have been some fascinating stories about him, you know. There's one out now that his own organization's going to dump him. And we've gotten out to the wire services the fact that he refused to debate O'Neill.

NIXON: Mm-hmm.

COLSON: I think he's beginning to tarnish. I think his image is tarnishing.

NIXON: Mm-hmm.

COLSON: And these young fellas, we've had some luck getting them placed.

NIXON: Have you?

COLSON: Yes, sir.

NIXON: Good.

COLSON: They'll be on, we'll start seeing more of them.

NIXON: Oh, boy, that's great. And they really, they haven't given up then, these guys?

COLSON: They would give you the greatest lift. I told them that I couldn't recommend their going in to see you because —

NIXON: I know. It would look like a fix. But sometime I want to thank them.

COLSON: I said that later in the summer, after they've done more of what they're doing, that they ought to come in. And I was thinking of it almost as much from your standpoint as from theirs.

NIXON: Sure!

COLSON: They're just believers.

NIXON: They think we've done the right thing.

COLSON: We're doing the right thing, and continue to do the right thing. And they claim that all of their friends, they say, O'Neill said to me, "I don't know how you fellas survive here in Washington," he said. "When you get out in the country, you'll find that people think like we think." And he said, "When you come here, and you watch what you have to watch every night and you listen to this constant chatter and this constant bickering at you," he said, "but let me tell you, it just isn't that way out in the country."

NIXON: Hmm! Isn't that something? Well!

"By the end of the summer, we will know whether we have broken Vietnam."
June 4, 1971, 4:47 p.m.
Richard Nixon and Henry Kissinger
OVAL OFFICE

Nixon and Kissinger had high expectations for the summer months of 1971. They were close to making a breakthrough with either the Soviet Union or China, or both. It was not yet clear how the one would affect the other, or how talks with the North Vietnamese would be affected.

• • •

KISSINGER: By the end of the summer, we will know whether we have broken Vietnam.
NIXON: Or, or SALT.
KISSINGER: Or SALT.
NIXON: Or China.
KISSINGER: Or China.
NIXON: Once we know we're going to do that, we'll know which is which.
KISSINGER: Well, it'd be nice if we could make them all work together.
NIXON: As well as a summit.
KISSINGER: But China, we've got, and that we can —
NIXON: Yeah, if we can get one more, I mean —
KISSINGER: Yeah.
NIXON: — then we could get two out of three. That's pretty good.

• • •

KISSINGER: In terms of achievements — this sounds self-serving — but, who has had a three-year period like this? If you had said on January 20 that you would get four hundred thousand troops out of Vietnam in two years, open the way to — of a visit to Beijing, a visit to Moscow, a SALT agreement, you'd have all of that done at the end of your third year —
NIXON: That'd be incredible, wouldn't it?
KISSINGER: — they would have said, "That's insanity!"

The value of reduced casualty statistics
June 11, 1971, 9:37 a.m.
Richard Nixon, Bob Haldeman, and Henry Kissinger
OVAL OFFICE

The Nixons were looking forward to the wedding of their daughter Tricia to lawyer Edward Cox on June 12 at the White House. Four hundred guests were expected at the first wedding ever held in the Rose Garden. Kissinger met with the president on the morning of June 11, having procured a transcript of a June 8 interview of North Vietnamese official Xuan Thuy by journalist Chalmers Roberts. Despite the relative clarity of Thuy's answers, his intentions were as shrouded as ever. Based on the wording, Nixon and Kissinger decided that either the North Vietnamese war effort was collapsing or it was poised for greater aggression than ever. They could at least point to firm figures on the marked shrinkage of U.S. combat losses and wondered how to use that fact more publicly.

• • •

KISSINGER: You know, one of the problems with the — that the Vietnamese have is if they give us anything at all in Paris, even if it leads to another stalemate, if we could get any movement at all —

NIXON: Yeah?

KISSINGER: — that looks like a serious negotiation —

NIXON: Yeah?

KISSINGER: — that would be a tremendous shot for public opinion.

NIXON: [chuckles] Yeah, you mean if they did it publicly.

KISSINGER: So, that's — that's the tough problem they're up against for June 26 [Kissinger's next secret meeting with the North Vietnamese].

NIXON: [unclear] They know. They must know that —

KISSINGER: Now, they are — I have had an analysis made, and I'll send it in to you —

NIXON: Mm-hmm.

KISSINGER: — taking the Xuan Thuy interview as against what I said to them —

NIXON: Mm-hmm?

KISSINGER: — and they are obviously talking to us in their crooked way —

NIXON: [unclear]

KISSINGER: I mean, this idea, for example, of separating military and political issues — which no one here in town will understand because —

NIXON: Yeah.

KISSINGER: — they don't know what we've said to them, but that's all through that interview. I've got the full text now. Not in an acceptable way, but the mere fact that they're talking about it is, is interesting. But it may not — this is just a bitter pill for them to swallow; they may not be ready to do it. And then they're pushing their infiltration very hard, even in the rainy season —

NIXON: [unclear]

KISSINGER: But, that could mean two things. That could mean that they're in desperate shape, too.

NIXON: Then we hit 'em. [unclear]

KISSINGER: At the middle of the week, it's always tough to tell, but it's — I would say it's certainly not above thirty [casualties in the past week] —

NIXON: Mm-hmm.

KISSINGER: — and it's more likely to be at the low twenties.

NIXON: Where we were before?

KISSINGER: Yeah, it's —

NIXON: [unclear]

KISSINGER: There's no significant difference from last week. But you can never tell whether there's one helicopter down, or whether some people died in a hospital —

NIXON: Yeah, that's right.

HALDEMAN: Because we've brought them down to such low numbers that each [unclear].

NIXON: Yeah, yeah, yeah. [unclear] My God, before if you shot down a helicopter and lost nineteen, it wouldn't make any difference.

HALDEMAN: Well —

NIXON: Nineteen in relation to a hundred twenty is nothing.

KISSINGER: But —

NIXON: Nineteen in relation to nineteen doubles it.

HALDEMAN: Doubles it.

KISSINGER: But, if you look, for example, at the month, if it hadn't been for these thirty-three —

NIXON: Mm-hmm?

KISSINGER: — we would have had below twenty-five every week —

NIXON: Yeah. I sure want them to — I sure want to get some sort of work done. I mean, get the — Scali to get out the — play the casualty line. And, it's that what we said has happened. We said it would go down after Cambodia. It did. We said it would go down after Laos. It did. Now, just keep pointing. In other words —

KISSINGER: That's right.

NIXON: — it's a good point to, to go.

"At least he didn't have it from within his administration."
June 12, 1971, 10:32 a.m.
Richard Nixon and Henry Kissinger
OVAL OFFICE

On Saturday's rainy morning, as the rest of the Nixon family fretted about whether or not to proceed with an outdoor wedding, the president met with Kissinger for a survey of the many irons that they had in the fire. The strategy that he and Kissinger had devised was layered in so much secrecy that it came to the point where they were the only people in whom either could confide.

Later in the morning, when Tricia asked her father whether to move the wedding indoors, he conferred with meteorologists attached to the air force and told her there would be a break in the clouds at about 4:00 p.m. The wedding was held then, under clear skies.

• • •

KISSINGER: Mr. President, Le Duc Tho is on the way west, stopping in Beijing and Moscow.

NIXON: Mm-hmm.

KISSINGER: He's allegedly going to the East German party congress. You can bet your bottom dollar he'll be in —

NIXON: [unclear]

KISSINGER: He's not at the meetings. He's stopping in Beijing and Paris — and Moscow.

• • •

KISSINGER: This is as close as — Le Duc Tho never shows up. They may say no, Mr. President.

NIXON: You think he'll show up at your conference?

KISSINGER: Certainly. Almost certainly. Eighty percent. If not, he'll show up there to give them instructions.

NIXON: Well, it's very good that he's going to Beijing.

KISSINGER: But he is going through Beijing and Moscow. [unclear] Le Duc Tho is the third man in the hierarchy there, the only man who can take independent decisions on negotiations. He travels only when there are crucial matters. He was there for the bombing halt, and he was there for the —

NIXON: Was he there for the bombing halt?

KISSINGER: Yeah. He was there for the early discussions with — until the fall of Siha-nouk, and then he left. You remember those meetings we had in the spring of —

NIXON: Oh, yeah.

KISSINGER: — of six — of '70 [Kissinger's 1970 meetings with Le Duc Tho in Paris, on February 21, March 16, and April 4].

NIXON: Oh, yeah. He was there, yeah.

KISSINGER: And he is formidable.

NIXON: Yeah. I was reading a news summary, and just thinking of the public that we have. As you say, Johnson's was nothing compared to this. 'Cause Christ almighty, at least he didn't have it from within his administration.

KISSINGER: Yeah.

NIXON: You know what I mean? While Gardner left, he never said anything. He was no-body. He was the secretary of HEW [John Gardner resigned his position in January 1968 because of his opposition to the war]. My God, we've got, as you know — but, the way these people are rushing around with this Clifford thing is unbelievable.

KISSINGER: Yeah. But, I actually think that Clifford —

NIXON: You don't think he's getting through?

KISSINGER: No, Mr. President. I really believe that —

NIXON: What's he up to? Is he trying to fork — trying to recircuit the wires? Is that it?

KISSINGER: Yeah, but Mr. President, the North Vietnamese, with Le Duc Tho on the move, sure, they're trying to —

NIXON: Mm-hmm?

KISSINGER: — to draw blood, and they're trying to see whether they can trigger us into —

NIXON: Yeah?

KISSINGER: — into making concessions before he gets there.

NIXON: There ain't going to be any.

KISSINGER: He does not have anything. I will bet my bottom dollar on it that he has nothing of any significance. He may have some Delphic hints by some low-level guy.

NIXON: Mm-hmm.

KISSINGER: It doesn't — they don't do business that way.

NIXON: The probability that they're trying to do something that they don't — they wanted to do it through somebody else. In other words, not let us do it. And there's always that possibility, Henry.

KISSINGER: There's always that slight possibility, Mr. President. But, even then, we're not in a bad position, because we can say on May 31 we made this proposal. And, I mean, we've got him outflanked. That if they're screwing us —

NIXON: Mm-hmm?

KISSINGER: — you can say that. Whenever you decide you can — whenever you decide that this thing isn't getting anywhere —

NIXON: Yeah?

KISSINGER: — you can decide on May 31, on the highest level, we made this proposal. While it was under consideration in Hanoi, we were forced into — Clifford came in with his variation of it. And, you can use it either as — in — as an example of independent negotiation by Clifford, or as an example of, of Hanoi's treachery.

NIXON: Mm-hmm.

KISSINGER: I think we've got them outmaneuvered, but my impression is that the press — I saw Henry Hubbard and Schecter yesterday, and I took a very tough line. I said — I reminded them that on March 25, after Laos, when they were all sneering at us, on the patio of my office in San Clemente, I expressed your conviction and my conviction that this — there might be negotiations this year.

And that, at that time, everyone was saying negotiations were senseless; all that's left to do is to get out. I said to them, "Do you people really believe that we're missing a bet? Do you really believe we don't look into all these things? If you do —" I said, "I admit it. We won't give you any facts. We won't confirm or deny anything. And if you write that we're missing them, it even helps what we are trying to do. So, you just go ahead and write it. I am not going to negotiate publicly with, with them — with them." They were really shaken. They didn't know what to do. Because, on the one hand, they had this — I mean, after all, it isn't plausible, that we, who — no one has talked more about negotiations than you, or I in my backgrounders, here. This is not a Johnson phenomenon.

NIXON: Yeah.

KISSINGER: And I don't think they're going to — they haven't hit us in the press very hard. In fact, they haven't hit us at all. Even the *Washington Post* had a very ambiguous editorial, yesterday, which for [them] it was really quite moderate. They said both are wrong, both Clifford and we. Well, that's pretty good for them.

NIXON: Why'd they say Clifford was wrong?

KISSINGER: Well, because he was implying that there was a solution without giving it, and we were wrong by refusing to recognize that there may be movement. Hell, if there's movement, we produced it. We will be able to show that this break of Xuan Thuy about Thieu was a direct outgrowth — you remember, I spotted it before they even saw it, and told you that this is an answer to what we said to them on May 31. I really think we have, we have a fighting chance, now, for a serious negotiation this summer. Le Duc Tho wouldn't be there unless they really wanted to look it over. He may say no, as he did in March —

NIXON: Suppose it does start to open up: what do you do? Then you put it in the Bruce channel?

KISSINGER: Well, then, we have to decide how to do it, Mr. President. Whether — I really believe —

NIXON: You just can't keep running over there.

KISSINGER: No, no. I can't do it. That's —

NIXON: Why? We can't do it without a — who could do it if we, if we —

KISSINGER: Well, I've worked out —

NIXON: — dispose of it? But, we've got to have something. You — we can't just continue to do this, you know?

KISSINGER: No, no. No, the choice we have to make is — incidentally, I've worked out a way, now, by which I can get over there with great safety. The British have a courier plane that lands at an RAF base, and they will take me anytime I want to go, so we don't have to use American planes.

NIXON: Mm-hmm.

KISSINGER: And they are absolutely secure. [unclear] I might have to go once more — or at most, twice more — to do it, to get it done. The question we have to decide is whether we should let Bruce surface it, or whether we should get you to write a letter? My strong instinct is, Mr. President, that if they —

NIXON: I'd better do it.

KISSINGER: — that you do it. This is what I meant. That's the decision we have to make —

NIXON: [unclear] Hell, we could let Bruce do it. [unclear] both Laird and Rogers would be in saying, "Hey, great."

KISSINGER: Well, that's why I think, Mr. President, that, as soon as we know a serious negotiation is starting, you have to get out in front and break the deadlock. Or make something that breaks — do something that breaks the deadlock. And that can be easily arranged.

NIXON: We can arrange that.

KISSINGER: I think that's better than just letting it trickle out in Paris.

NIXON: Work on it a bit, how long these general principles [unclear] —

KISSINGER: I think, Mr. President, that if there is going to be an agreement, and there —

NIXON: It'll come quickly.

KISSINGER: It will come this summer. That's the funny thing.

NIXON: That's always the theory you've had. Is it —?

KISSINGER: Well, I've always had the theory, but I think the Vietnamese elections are helping us that way.

NIXON: What's your view of the [South Vietnam anti-Thieu opposition leaders] Big Minh–Ky deal I noticed in the paper this morning?

KISSINGER: They actually made it?

NIXON: Well, it said that they had made a deal. I don't know, maybe see if it's true.

KISSINGER: Well, my view of the —

NIXON: It's just as well; put 'em over there. But I want them to really ride hard on those bastards and let them know they aren't going to get anything.

KISSINGER: Well, my view of the Big Minh–Ky deal is that it gives the opposition to Thieu a viable combination —

NIXON: Hmm.

KISSINGER: — but that Thieu will, almost certainly, will win.

NIXON: Well, suppose they won? There's not much difference, would it?

KISSINGER: Mr. President —

NIXON: They, they live at our sufferance, anyway. They'd have to come along. They'd have to.

KISSINGER: If — Ky is actually a friend of ours. Ky behaved with great dignity —

NIXON: That's right.

KISSINGER: — on the occasion that I saw him to turn off his trip, yeah —

NIXON: Right.

KISSINGER: Uh —

NIXON: Big Minh is just dumb.

KISSINGER: Big Minh is just a front man.

NIXON: Yeah.

KISSINGER: And — so, I — I would think that if we get our deal, and if then Thieu is defeated in the election, so be it. It's the major thing. But, I don't think that will happen. If it does happen —

NIXON: Mm-hmm? What is your [unclear]? What's your — any judgment on the, the Cambodian action? I noticed they were trying to build that up now, at least at the present time.

KISSINGER: Well, uh —

NIXON: How significant is it?

KISSINGER: Well, it's significant in the sense —

NIXON: Not as significant as the press obviously feels about it?

KISSINGER: No, but it's significant in the sense that this damn — that the death of Tri obviously kept us from knocking them out in that area. And that may have been the worst loss, because we did gain in Lam Son 719 —

NIXON: Yeah.

KISSINGER: — sixty to eighty percent of what we wanted, but after Tri's death — as I told you then — that Cambodian operation just petered out. I don't think they're going to topple the situation there. What they're trying to do is to create — reconstitute the sanctuaries based on a northern supply route this time.

NIXON: Mm-hmm. Well, that's enough.

KISSINGER: And that's — that, I think, they're in the process of. But, another problem, of course, is — another — one reason for it is that Thieu is economizing his forces now, because of the election.

NIXON: Not trying to have too many casualties?

KISSINGER: No.

• • •

NIXON: Getting back to this Clifford/Gardner, et cetera. I noticed Gardner was on —

KISSINGER: Yeah, I saw that.

NIXON: — against our fellow [unclear]. But anyway, [unclear] miserable prick, isn't he?

KISSINGER: Gardner —

NIXON: Right?

KISSINGER: — he is as petty —

NIXON: [unclear] He's not an admirable person.

KISSINGER: He's an effeminate — I mean, after all, he does not know a goddamn thing about Vietnam.

NIXON: Or about anything else.

KISSINGER: Uh —

NIXON: I mean, about anything else in foreign policy.

KISSINGER: At least education he's given some thought to, but —

NIXON: Yeah.

KISSINGER: — for him to say he — that you might still be there ten years from now, that is so — I told these guys yesterday from the press —

NIXON: Jesus Christ.

KISSINGER: — I said, "We've withdrawn steadily for two years. We've never lowered the withdrawal rate. We've never stopped withdrawing. What do you really think?"

NIXON: Well, that's what I told Cooper. I said, "Now, John, you know damn well what the situation's going to be next year, don't you?" And I says, "You're — you goddamn — you're our opponents, now. Maybe you'd want to get on board? And you —" That's it, Henry. They know damn well where we are.

KISSINGER: But I see now, Mr. President, why —

NIXON: Hmm?

KISSINGER: — Le Duc — why they couldn't come to the meeting: because there's the East — on the twent[ieth], or the thirteenth, or the twentieth — because there's the East German party congress from the fourteenth to the twenty-first. Xuan Thuy undoubtedly will be there to talk to Le Duc Tho. And —

NIXON: Yeah?

KISSINGER: — so, the twenty-sixth is the earliest they could possibly be there.

NIXON: In terms of reaction to this Cambodian thing, is there — are we doing adequately there? Part of the problem with Laird is holding back on the —

KISSINGER: Well —

NIXON: — air strikes?

KISSINGER: — not — no, the real problem is that MACV is just not on top of its job. That, either because Laird has a private deal with Abrams, or because Abrams has just quit, they're not making their extra-special effort, Mr. President, that makes the difference between success and failure. I think that, that is the — that is one of the major problems.

NIXON: Just sitting out there like the French used to sit.

KISSINGER: And —

NIXON: [unclear] Goddamn it, we just need a general. I agree with you: we'll take that little DePuy — he's a cocky little bastard — and let him go out there and to shape them up.

KISSINGER: I think that is one of the big problems: that we're just not —

NIXON: We'll be — it'll be easy after the next announcement to bring Abrams home.

KISSINGER: Yeah.

NIXON: I mean, just say, "We're finished there." Hand DePuy with what we have left. That there's been no deal, and tell him don't worry, he'll — he'll be looking for our opportunities to smack 'em.

KISSINGER: I just have an instinct that we — I don't know whether they'll make it, but this is as close as we've ever been. It's less — it's still far. It's at best one in three, Mr. President. I don't want to —

NIXON: I know. I know.

KISSINGER: — to mislead you, but —

NIXON: Don't worry, I'm not. I'm not being hopeful, but, nevertheless, there's a chance.

KISSINGER: There is a chance.

NIXON: And there has never been before. So, we'll see. Hell, these, these people will — you can be sure, too, that every stinking political fellow like Clifford will try to get in on that chance. You realize what this would do to them politically?

KISSINGER: They'd be dead.

NIXON: If we pull off the negotiations, they'd be absolutely dead.

KISSINGER: If we are ruthless enough.

NIXON: [unclear]

KISSINGER: If we don't let them get off the hook, again.

NIXON: [unclear] off the hook — I'd never. On this one, we're not going to bring them in on it, we're not going to [unclear].

KISSINGER: Because that's the mistake we made after October 7 [Nixon's speech of 1970 in which he announced a five-point peace proposal].

NIXON: That's right.

KISSINGER: Now that I look back, I was part of the mistake —

NIXON: I think we shouldn't have even made the speech.

KISSINGER: We shouldn't have made the speech, but instead then of wallowing in their approbation —

NIXON: Yeah.

KISSINGER: — we should have reminded the country that these were the guys who were rioting against us.

NIXON: That's right.

KISSINGER: Who were encouraging them and against whose opposition we got to that, that point.

• • •

KISSINGER: The thing we need for the next two months is quiet, because we don't want to get the Russians lining up with the Egyptians and get everybody steaming up with a big Mideast crisis. And I think we should just slow that process down a little bit for the next two or three months and not get so much out front. Frankly, I think we have two ways we should have done it: either the way I suggested, by working out again with the Israelis, or to do it together with the Soviets.

NIXON: Sure.

KISSINGER: After the brokering around without objective and floating plan after plan, which puts us right into the middle of it, it's going to — the problem now is to keep the Middle East from blowing up until the end of August. If we can get the other things going, then they will play back on the Middle East.

NIXON: Yeah, of course. Apparently, in terms of trying to — as far as the Soviet is concerned, there isn't much of a problem. They won't —

KISSINGER: No, they're mad that they —

NIXON: They may come back. No, what I meant is, if they come — I'm speaking of a summit —

KISSINGER: Oh, the summit.

NIXON: If they come back, I'm happy just to have him [Dobrynin] come in and offer it to me.

KISSINGER: The summit?

NIXON: Yeah.

KISSINGER: Oh, the summit is easy.

NIXON: It's the easiest, because, I mean, he just comes in and says, "I have instructions from my government to invite you." I'll just tell everybody. I'm just going to do it that way.

KISSINGER: [That's] how it should be.

NIXON: That's right. Then —

KISSINGER: And that doesn't involve me at all.

NIXON: Well, it doesn't have to be done — what I mean, if you had suggested we do that, you know what I mean, go over and suggest it to State and so forth —

KISSINGER: No.

NIXON: The difficulty, if they do it over there, I have no control over the damn thing. It will get out in the press and screwed up beyond belief. So I'll just have him come in here. It's no problem.

KISSINGER: Exactly.

NIXON: Call Bill in —

KISSINGER: And then we'll announce it out of here.

NIXON: — just call Bill in and tell him. That'll be that. The Chinese thing — that's a tough one. That is really something. You see, we're playing with fire, playing with fire. [On] Dobrynin, I guess we could do the — I think it's — your thought is that when you're there, I should send a message to arrange for you to have a meeting with Haig. My talk with — do you see? I mean, how do we get there? How do we get Bill informed?

KISSINGER: Well, I think once I am on the way, you might tell Bill that Yahya offered to arrange for me to talk to the Chinese when I'm there.

NIXON: Exactly. Without saying: what, how, when, who?

KISSINGER: That's right.

NIXON: Right.

KISSINGER: And then blame, you know —

NIXON: Yeah.

KISSINGER: Then just say that I improvised everything once I got there.

NIXON: Right.

KISSINGER: And I mean, his concern — my impression of Bill is that he doesn't give a damn what I do as long as I don't get any credit for it. And as for what we could still consider, it depends on what the Russian game is. If the Russians don't have a summit, then we would just announce a Chinese summit —

NIXON: Right.

KISSINGER: — and we wouldn't have to explain how it was arranged.

NIXON: Sure.

KISSINGER: We would just say, "As a result of high-level contacts —"

NIXON: Sure.

KISSINGER: "— Prime Minister Zhou Enlai has —"

NIXON: No, I think we could tell Bill in that case. We'd just say that —

KISSINGER: Oh, we can tell Bill, but —

NIXON: No, Bill, I think you could just say that when you were there you saw the Chinese. You don't tell him about seeing Zhou Enlai or anything. Or I guess you'd have to then, don't you?

KISSINGER: I don't think that Bill cares as long as we don't let it out.

NIXON: Mm-hmm.

KISSINGER: And we've now proved with SALT—

NIXON: Yeah.

KISSINGER: —where my name is—

NIXON: But you could just then say that when you got there, Yahya said Zhou Enlai would like to you see here, and you went over and saw him.

KISSINGER: That's right.

NIXON: After you leave, I guess the thing to do is to say, now, you're going to Pakistan, Yahya is very interested for you to see the, talk to the Chinese ambassador, I'll say, while you're there. Then it develops beyond that—

KISSINGER: Right.

NIXON: —and I say not to go ahead—

KISSINGER: Right.

NIXON: —off this trade event, so then you just go on as it was. Then it comes from there. Right?

KISSINGER: If I—

NIXON: You know, there's too goddamn much been going on. That's the problem.

"A devastating security breach of the greatest magnitude of anything I've ever seen."
June 13, 1971, 12:18 p.m.
Richard Nixon and Alexander Haig
WHITE HOUSE TELEPHONE

When Alexander Haig first told Richard Nixon about the leak of the Pentagon Papers to the New York Times *and the newspaper's decision to publish the highly classified study of the Vietnam War, Nixon did not fully grasp the situation. Nothing approaching the scale of the Pentagon Papers had been leaked before. The forty-seven-volume study, all seven thousand pages of which were finally declassified in 2011, focused primarily on the actions of Nixon's Democratic predecessors, including Presidents Kennedy and Johnson.*

On another occasion, this could have been a chance to score a political victory. However, Nixon's Department of Justice launched a vigorous yet ultimately unsuccessful defense of government secrecy and the records documenting private war deliberations that went all the way to the Supreme Court. The event played a direct role in creating the White House "Plumbers," the group tasked with preventing leaks to the press whose existence became popularly known during the investigation into Watergate.

• • •

NIXON: Hello?

OPERATOR: General Haig, sir. He's ready.

NIXON: Hello?

HAIG: Yes, sir.

NIXON: Hi, Al. What about the casualties last week? Have you got the figure yet?

HAIG: No, sir, but I think it's going to be quite low.

NIXON: Mm-hmm.

HAIG: It should be last week or better.

NIXON: Yeah. Should be less than twenty, I would think. Yeah.

HAIG: It should be very—

NIXON: When do you get that? Do you know?

HAIG: We don't get it officially until Monday afternoon.

NIXON: Mm-hmm.

HAIG: But we can get a reading on it.

NIXON: Right. Well, Monday afternoon, officially? Well, let's wait until then. Fine. Okay. Nothing else of interest in the world?

HAIG: Yes, sir. Very significant. This goddamn *New York Times* exposé of the most highly classified documents of the war.

NIXON: Oh, that! I see. I didn't read the story. Do you mean that was leaked out of the Pentagon?

HAIG: Sir, the whole study that was done for McNamara, and then carried on after Mc-Namara left by Clifford and the peaceniks over there. This is a devastating security breach of the greatest magnitude of anything I've ever seen.

NIXON: Well, what's being done about it then? I mean, I didn't — did we know this was coming out?

HAIG: No, we did not, sir.

NIXON: Yeah.

HAIG: There are just a few copies of this whole multivolume report.

NIXON: Well, what about the — let me ask you this, though: what about Laird? What's he going to do about it? Is —

HAIG: Well, I —

NIXON: Now, I would just start right at the top and fire some people. I mean, whatever department it came out of, I'd fire the top guy.

HAIG: Yes, sir. Well, I'm sure it came from Defense, and I'm sure it was stolen at the time of the turnover of the administration.

NIXON: Oh, it's two years old then?

HAIG: I am sure it is. And they've been holding it for a juicy time. And I think they've thrown it out to affect Hatfield-McGovern, that's my own estimate. But it's something that is a mixed bag. It's a tough attack on Kennedy. It shows that the genesis of the war really occurred during '61.

NIXON: Yeah. Yeah. That's Clifford! Yeah, I see.

HAIG: And it's brutal on President Johnson. They're going to end up in a massive gut fight in the Democratic Party on this thing.

NIXON: Are they?

HAIG: There's some very—
NIXON: But also massive against the war?
HAIG: Against the war.

"The real issue is the Two-Power relationship."

June 15, 1971, 2:39 p.m.
Richard Nixon, Anatoly Dobrynin, and Henry Kissinger
OVAL OFFICE

Ambassador Dobrynin personally delivered a message to the president and remained for a rare conversation with him about the future of relations between their two countries. Afterward, Kissinger and Nixon compared notes.

• • •

DOBRYNIN: As is obvious, the Soviet Union is asking for a conference of nuclear powers to discuss the question of general and complete nuclear disarmament. The place can be wherever is convenient and the agenda is open. A preparatory meeting is acceptable. The Soviet government hopes that your reply will be positive. Of course, Soviet-U.S. talks will continue bilaterally outside the conference as part of the SALT talks. The note is being delivered today in Paris, London, Beijing, and Washington.

• • •

NIXON: Let's be realistic. The key to this sort of thing is what the two major nuclear powers will do. It is a question of leadership at the top — I don't mean at the top of the governments, but at the top of this group of five.
DOBRYNIN: Do you have anything in mind, Mr. President?
NIXON: We will consider your proposal seriously. The way our two governments can make the most progress is through the talks that you and Kissinger have been having. They are completely confidential with nobody leaking. Your government has confidence in you; Kissinger has a special relationship with me. Apart from the cosmetics of a Five-Power discussion, the real issue is the Two-Power relationship.
DOBRYNIN: Well, how shall we do it?
NIXON: We will make a formal reply. Then you have a little talk with Henry Kissinger.
DOBRYNIN: What do you think of U.S.-Soviet relations in general?
NIXON: We can make a breakthrough on SALT and Berlin, and then our whole postwar relations will be on a new basis. The whole relationship can, indeed, be on a new basis. The press last week spoke of the failure of Berlin. You know better. We are at a point where we should make some agreement. If we culminate one, it will have a massive effect.
DOBRYNIN: Are there any other areas of discussion?
KISSINGER: Mr. President, he is trying to lead you into the Middle East.
DOBRYNIN: [laughs]

NIXON: As for the Middle East, there is, of course, a fear of a U.S.-Soviet condominium. Of course, Soviet and U.S. interests are quite different. We both have constituents we may not be able to control, and this makes the situation very explosive. The Middle East is very much on our mind and, at some point, discussions between us will be possible.

"Something's going to happen."

June 15, 1971, 3:19 p.m.

Richard Nixon and Henry Kissinger

OVAL OFFICE

Would the Soviets or the Chinese agree on a summit first? Either option would require American maneuvering with the other.

• • •

KISSINGER: Something's going to happen.

NIXON: Henry, can you wait to see their faces, though, if they do not give us the summit?

KISSINGER: And you announce [China]? [laughs] Mr. President, no matter what we do — what they do, we are so, for once, we are ahead of the power curve with them.

"Things are going, going great."

June 16, 1971, 10:39 a.m.

Richard Nixon, Ellsworth Bunker, and Henry Kissinger

OVAL OFFICE

In 1967, Lyndon Johnson appointed Ellsworth Bunker as the ambassador to South Vietnam, a position that was, effectively, the president's personal ambassador to the war. As can be seen in the June 16 conversation in the Oval Office, Bunker saw the war in the same light as President Nixon; either that or he considered it part of his job to tell Nixon what he wanted to hear. Bunker's rather sunny conclusions about the war were at odds with those of many others who had been in country.

• • •

NIXON: Our goal is clear: our goal, now, is that, as we come to the — near the end of this long road is to succeed. We can succeed. You agree?

BUNKER: Yes.

NIXON: Well, now, we can.

BUNKER: Yes.

NIXON: We can, but, on the other hand, we must not give our enemies — and I'm not referring to our enemies in North Vietnam, but our enemies in this country — we cannot give them the weapons to kill us with. Now —

BUNKER: Yeah.

NIXON: — I think that, for example, any meeting with Thieu, by me, at this point — that's why I was trying —

BUNKER: Yes.

NIXON: — to get it June 8, that early —

BUNKER: Yes.

NIXON: — though we've had that washed out. But, any meeting, at this point, will — it'd be inevitably hyped into a blatant attempt on our part to strengthen his political position —

BUNKER: I agree. I agree.

NIXON: That will hurt him here.

BUNKER: Yes.

NIXON: It also could hurt him there.

BUNKER: It could hurt him in there, too.

NIXON: Now, I think he must be really — he must be told that in substitution for that, he will have our — he's had as much support as he has, and God knows, nobody's given him support as we have.

BUNKER: Certainly not.

NIXON: Second, that Henry's going to come out and look the thing over. Now —

BUNKER: Yes.

NIXON: — can you sell that to him?

BUNKER: I think so. Yes, sir. I will. He — I think, yes. I think that he'll —

NIXON: You can tell him that you've —

BUNKER: He said [unclear] —

NIXON: — looked over American public opinion —

KISSINGER: That's right.

NIXON: — and you've looked over the Senate.

BUNKER: Yeah.

NIXON: And that, right now, the best thing is to let it ride through the Senate.

BUNKER: I think —

KISSINGER: Because it's all over the front pages.

BUNKER: You know, I think in the interest of the elections there, if this took place, Minh, for example, might use this as an excuse just to pull out, you know? And, as I've said to Thieu, "You can't run alone. [chuckles] You can't run for office alone. You've got to have some other competitors, and Minh is just that sort of fellow." I'm afraid he'll pull out, anyway, at the end.

NIXON: Is Ky running with Minh now, or not?

BUNKER: No. Ky's running separately, independently.

NIXON: Yeah.

BUNKER: And, I have —

NIXON: So, Ky definitely is? Ky will get enough of the deputies to be able to run?

BUNKER: Oh, I think he'll get the provincial — I think he and Minh have got a deal that Minh will work the assembly, and Ky will work the counselors. And Minh will get —

KISSINGER: Oh. Oh, so they don't take away from each other —

BUNKER: They don't take it away from each other. I have a —

NIXON: Well —

BUNKER: I have an interesting document I'd like to show you and Henry.

. . .

NIXON: Just keep it —

BUNKER: Yeah.

NIXON: — and we'll have to hope for the best.

BUNKER: Yeah.

NIXON: Well, right now, he is ahead. He's very well advised not to press it.

BUNKER: Exactly.

NIXON: By the same token, I don't know what else could keep him ahead. Getting back to this problem that we had yesterday in the drug thing, as you can see, that is a — that is just an enormously potent issue [reference is to a congressional report on the growing heroin problem among U.S. servicemen in Vietnam].

BUNKER: Oh, precisely —

NIXON: It's — Young — Milt Young has never voted against us on Vietnam, he's gonna vote against us on McGovern-Hatfield, solely because of drugs. Solely because of drugs.

BUNKER: Yeah.

NIXON: He went back to Bismarck, South [North] Dakota, and found out that people could buy shots for two dollars at Bien Hoa airport or Tan Son Nhut or some damn thing, and so he's gonna vote against [unclear]. And, of course, there're these stories about, well, the brother of the prime minister is involved; they don't know that the prime minister is not Thieu, it's somebody else. They think, "Well this is Thieu," and then — and so forth and everything. It has a — it smacks of everything that's wrong. What the hell is it? We all know that. The Turks have the same problem: their relatives are all in the business — the, the rest. But — but, I just can't emphasize too strongly that —

BUNKER: Hmm?

NIXON: — that — I don't know. Maybe our own people just go in and shoot up those drug places. I don't know why, but we've got to get — and this hurts us. It has to be done, or we've got a massive investigation on our hands.

BUNKER: Yes. He knows that, and I'll —

NIXON: Yeah. I know you talked to him. In your briefing, you put it into him. And I don't want to belabor the subject. You're keenly aware of it.

BUNKER: Oh, yes.

NIXON: Just put it at the top of the agenda —

BUNKER: Yeah.

NIXON: — and don't, don't —

BUNKER: And Thieu is aware of it. He's [unclear].

NIXON: Don't give the press a chance to [unclear]. [laughs]

BUNKER: Yeah, yeah. And, it's a tremendous problem. You see, as I said on Monday, they were not users. I mean —

NIXON: No.

BUNKER: — we brought it there and, and provided the market. And now, they're scared, worried it's going to spread to their own troops [unclear] and concerned that when we're out, if it has spread to their troops, when we pull out, that they're going to be in a real mess. So, let's see. This morning, this report came in that he'd put in this colonel. He told me he was going to put in a new director-general for customs for South Vietnam, a big shakeup. So, we'll get at — keep at it, and keep the pressure on.

NIXON: Well, the — with regard to other problems, what do you see then at the present time? Is there anything that you want to —

BUNKER: Well —

NIXON: — emphasize to Thieu?

BUNKER: President Thieu asked me, of course, to give you his regards, and as he said, which I've already reported, there are three things only that he's concerned about and had one to take up with me. One was immediate economic assistance, long-term economic assistance.

NIXON: Well, he has our assurance on that. And Kissinger, when he is there will reassure him.

BUNKER: Yes. Now, the second thing —

NIXON: Why don't you put it on the basis that Kissinger — that's one of the points: that Kissinger is prepared —

BUNKER: Yes. Fine —

NIXON: — to discuss substantively with him at that point.

KISSINGER: That's right, and [unclear] —

NIXON: Speaking — and that he can speak with total authority.

BUNKER: Good. The second thing, Mr. President, was the acceleration of the ARVN improvement and modernization program. They've asked for some improved weapons. As a result, Thieu said what they learned in the Lam Son operation, what the enemy had: they had longer-range artillery, they had bigger tanks, and they — these are things they want. And I think they want some more helicopters, probably. The —

NIXON: Hmm.

BUNKER: — the — Abrams and I talked to him a week ago and went over some of these things with him. Abrams told him, he said, "Well, it wouldn't have made a difference if you had bigger tanks because of the command problem [more] than your armor. The result would have been the same." Well that's true. But, as I said —

NIXON: Hmm.

BUNKER: — they've got to fix up the command problem, but then when — if they do, they've still got —

NIXON: What if they got tanks?

BUNKER: — smaller tanks. [laughs]

NIXON: Listen, there can be no excuse about that, and Henry will be very forthcoming on that. Incidentally, I don't care what's out there. Leave it there. This business of just picking up a lot of stuff and hauling it home, it doesn't do anything except for bookkeeping. I didn't know they take it out to Arizona and let it rot and rust in the fields. Leave it in Vietnam. Let 'em sell it, put it on the black market, anything they want. Leave it in Vietnam if it'll help.

BUNKER: Then the third thing, Mr. President, is assurance of continued air support. You see, on this basis, the — Thieu feels, and I think, we think, he's right, too — that Lam Son and our better air position has taken care of this year. When it comes to the dry season again in the fall, November, they'll begin to try to build up supplies —

NIXON: Mm-hmm.

BUNKER: — for a push in the March–May period —

NIXON: Mm-hmm.

BUNKER: — and again in the August–September period.

NIXON: Yeah.

BUNKER: Around our elections. And we can't let anything go wrong next year before our elections here.

NIXON: Yeah.

BUNKER: And, therefore, they'll need air support, because they can't. Their planes, what we've given them, are really not, not much good for interdiction. They're small jets that don't carry bombs. The one thing they complain about is that they can't carry enough bomb load; they have to go back and rearm so, so often that they lose time. But our interdiction has been improved tremendously this year. Last year —

NIXON: Mm-hmm.

BUNKER: — the throughput was about thirty-seven percent of the input. So far this year, because of Lam Son and the interdiction, it's been about fifteen point seven percent. It's been a vast improvement, and it's made a tremendous difference. And this is going to be a factor next year. And this is why both Abrams and I think Thieu is right about this; that he does need air support. And when Secretary Laird [unclear] he told us about the reduction in the budget proposal for air, for two hundred million dollars this coming year, and five hundred million dollars the next. Well, how, how that's going to affect us? I don't know, but I do think it's an important thing.

NIXON: Mm-hmm. Mm-hmm.

BUNKER: I think those are the three. Those are — he says those are the only three points that he's concerned about —

NIXON: Well, now, on the air support, there's certainly no problem this year.

BUNKER: No.

NIXON: I mean [unclear] in October — in November and December, and so forth and so on, I mean, just drop everything there is. The real problem we get driven down to, the budgetary problems, I suppose, is what we're going to have left by August and September of next year. And also what the situation is.

BUNKER: Well, he said it seems to be a question, then, of priorities. I mean, where they're shifting from something else to this.

NIXON: Hmm. What's your view on this, Henry?

KISSINGER: My —

NIXON: Your —

KISSINGER: My view is, first of all, we should force Defense to program full air support through next year, because if we don't, they'll just yank it out of there.

NIXON: Mm-hmm.

KISSINGER: Even if we don't use it.

NIXON: Mm-hmm.

KISSINGER: And, secondly, as long as we can keep the interdiction bombing going, they are in bad shape for launching a big offensive. If we started — I think after September next year, or, in fact, even earlier, that their supply effort for the August– September period is during the spring.

BUNKER: Yeah.

KISSINGER: So, we've got to keep it going through the spring in Laos, in southern Laos —

NIXON: Hmm.

KISSINGER: — the northern part is, is less —

NIXON: It [unclear].

KISSINGER: Because of weather.

BUNKER: Yeah. And I think [unclear]. I think we can't let anything go wrong before our elections next year.

NIXON: Yeah. Henry is right. As far as the air support is concerned, what really counts, insofar as their offensive in September, or August and September, it's got to be — you've got to knock 'em off in the spring [unclear].

BUNKER: Yeah, that's right. Yeah.

NIXON: Well, we'll do that. We can commit to that.

BUNKER: And they —

NIXON: They just have to do it.

BUNKER: Yeah. The interdiction has been — it's been a tricky job this year. They've got some improved equipment, these new C-130 gunships —

NIXON: Yeah.

BUNKER: — are doing a good job —

NIXON: You mean they are doing better?

BUNKER: Oh, yeah. That's the main thing, Mr. President. The economic situation, I think, is, at present, it's better than I thought it would be, you know, with these —

NIXON: Mm-hmm.

BUNKER: — reforms we've put in. Now, prices have only increased since the end of December about two point eight percent.

NIXON: Mm-hmm.

BUNKER: And in the last twelve months, only eight point two percent, which is a pretty good, a pretty good record considering we used to think thirty percent a year was good. So, it's been done pretty well. Their minister of economy is here, now —

NIXON: Yeah.

BUNKER: — who is first-rate, the best man they've got in the cabinet —

NIXON: Mm-hmm.

BUNKER: — and Thieu has given extremely good backing. But, those are the main things. The — Thieu, as you know, has suggested — has said that observer groups would be welcome, and —

NIXON: Hmm?

BUNKER: — I think —

NIXON: Then get [unclear]. Get on the offensive on that.

KISSINGER: But we have a group. We have a —

NIXON: [unclear] get on the offensive [unclear].

KISSINGER: Oh, yeah, we're putting one together.

BUNKER: Are you?

KISSINGER: Yeah.

BUNKER: Good.

NIXON: Both sides? Democrats and Republicans?

KISSINGER: [unclear]

BUNKER: Fast.

NIXON: We've got to do it in order to — because, you know, some of these people are asking that a special committee be set up. Well, let's — well, put one together, but put one together that's representative. Let them go out and look.

BUNKER: As a matter of fact, Adlai Stevenson is coming to see me this afternoon.

NIXON: Well, he's wanted to put in a resolution —

BUNKER: Yeah.

NIXON: — in that respect.

KISSINGER: Of course, what he really wants is something that means he really —

BUNKER: He wants to — he wants to monitor me.

NIXON: Yeah.

BUNKER: Yes.

NIXON: Exactly.

BUNKER: [unclear]

NIXON: Well, to see that the Americans do not play a role in it. Well, you just say we're not going to play any role.

BUNKER: That's what I'll give him the — that's just something to put out to the Mission.

NIXON: Why, of course. We've got to keep it out of the Mission, and it's sensible [unclear]. He, then, will look at the past history and that he's on a bad wicket here.

BUNKER: Yeah.

NIXON: Say, "You — you're welcome to come; we have nothing to hide."

BUNKER: Yeah.

NIXON: But, let them — invite him as an individual to come. But put him on that committee, Henry. [unclear] Put him right on. In other words — what — who is on it, now? Who are they trying to — got any names?

KISSINGER: I have, but I don't have the list here.

NIXON: But MacGregor is getting together a list, is he?

KISSINGER: Yes.

NIXON: Understand: this should not be an in-house deal. It should be a —

KISSINGER: No, no. It's bipartisan.

NIXON: A bipartisan group. Go out and look at the elections. Let's get it out. I'd like to have an announcement on that soon.

BUNKER: And we had two very — three good experts on it last time. We had Dick Scammon [political scientist and election analyst, who was an official U.S. observer of South Vietnam's 1967 presidential election].

KISSINGER: Excellent.

BUNKER: And we had Professor [Donald G.] Herzberg from Rutgers, and [Howard R.] Penniman from Georgetown. They were both — they were very good [U.S. observers of South Vietnam's 1967 presidential election].

NIXON: Well, fine. Put them on —

BUNKER: Scammon helped me out on the briefing questions.

NIXON: Scammon?

BUNKER: Yes?

NIXON: Put him on.

BUNKER: Right.

NIXON: But Scammon, of course, is a top Democrat, which helps, too —

BUNKER: Yeah.

NIXON: — if Henry puts him on the thing. Look, those elections are more fair than most elections in most American cities. Now, let's face it.

BUNKER: Yeah.

[unclear exchange]

KISSINGER: Than any of the elections in Southeast Asia.

NIXON: Well, there are no — there are no fair elections in Southeast Asia, and there are no fair elections in Latin America. You know that.

BUNKER: Yeah.

NIXON: Maybe Mexico.

BUNKER: Well, Scammon —

[unclear exchange]

NIXON: Well, they can't — our Democratic critics can't question Scammon because he's their bible on politics.

KISSINGER: Yeah.

NIXON: Well, let's take the offensive on that. Let's get that out right away. That it's — it's to knock off the Stevenson thing. We should see Stevenson, and — but point out that we welcome him. And I'd just disarm him. Say, "There's nothing to hide."

BUNKER: Yeah. Yeah. Yes. Right.

NIXON: The interesting thing is that the, that the — apparently, from what I hear, most everybody who goes to Vietnam comes back [unclear]. Dick Watson is a case in point. He says, "You know, I went there with great skepticism," and he says to me, he says, "I've — anyways, I came back a convert."

BUNKER: Oh, yes. He had a breakdown there. He was —

NIXON: Yeah. But the point is that he'd been exposed to the French.

BUNKER: Yeah.

NIXON: He came out there and saw what was going on. He says, "I came back, said they were all wrong." Our real accomplishment is that, at this time, is that nobody, really, would have predicted that things would be going as well as they are now. Put it — yeah, you can talk all you want about Lam Son, but, how in the world, how in the world would casualties have been averaging twenty, unless we'd done Lam Son, right?

BUNKER: Sure.

NIXON: Nineteen last week, twenty-three this week, right?

KISSINGER: Twenty-five this week.

NIXON: They'd have been seventy-five, I mean —

BUNKER: Oh, absolutely. I — Lam Son, you know, in spite of the press, was a good operation, and some of the Vietnamese units did superb jobs: the First Division; the Marines; the Airborne. They did a tremendous job.

KISSINGER: Well, actually, the Vietnamese units that bothered me are not the ones in Lam Son. I think they fought well. It's the ones that have, that fought in Cambodia.

BUNKER: Well, one division —

NIXON: I think that's Tri's.

KISSINGER: Yeah. The one that fought in Snuol.

BUNKER: Well, that's the Fifth Division. Now — and this — Abrams and I have been a year trying to get that commander changed. And Thieu has agreed and agreed and agreed. Finally, six weeks before Snuol, Abe was off — was away a week in Thailand on a holiday, and Mike Davison sent in a memorandum [unclear] and said they had to really get this fellow out. I went to Thieu, and I said, "This is it. We've been talking about this for nine, ten months. You've got to do it." He said, "Yes, a top priority to finally get the right man." Well, it took Snuol, finally, to get the job done. Now, he's put in a — what Abrams said was the best regimental commander from the Twenty-first Division, in the Delta, which was Minh's old division, before he became [unclear]. But Minh is a good man. He's — he's all right.

NIXON: What is your — of course, when you come back to this country — it must depress you when you see —

BUNKER: Well, it sure does.

NIXON: But, out there, how do you feel?

BUNKER: Oh, out there, I feel fine. Out there, I mean, I think things are going well, except for this damn drug business. But, I think that as far as the Vietnamization goes, I think things are going, going great. And now, the situation is stable, and I think things are moving. The campaign, I think, is going to be rough —

NIXON: Sure.

BUNKER: — and — but, I think it's good. I think [unclear] if Ky and Minh do run, because I think Thieu will win, and I think that they have a chance to play for a big, open competition.

NIXON: Mm-hmm. Hmm.

BUNKER: There's criticism, of course, of this endorsement provision, but the reason for it is entirely fair, in that we had eleven candidates last time.

"Reassure people that those who do come back, like Kerry and the rest, don't speak for all."

June 16, 1971, 4:30 p.m.
Richard Nixon, John O'Neill, Melville Stephens, Charles Colson, and Henry Kissinger
OVAL OFFICE

It is no surprise that Richard Nixon eventually thanked John O'Neill for his work with Vietnam Veterans for a Just Peace. Later that month, on June 30, O'Neill and John Kerry debated on ABC's Dick Cavett Show. Nixon wanted to personally encourage O'Neill to keep up the fight, even when the media coverage of his efforts was not favorable.

• • •

NIXON: It's refreshing to have some guys who are willing to stand up and speak out as you have, particularly in light of the fact that you read polls, and they say, if you ask the individual, "Do you favor getting all Americans out of Vietnam in 1971?" and I'm surprised it isn't a hundred percent! I know that.

• • •

NIXON: So all this adds up to this, it adds up to the fact that a majority of the American people are sick of the war, a majority now think it was a mistake to go in, a majority of the American people want to get out as quick as they can, and many want to get out regardless of the consequences. So that's the public opinion that you run into. Also, other attitudes that have been created by the media are ideological. Most American servicemen serving abroad are brutes, savages. Second, that many others who have served abroad are dope addicts. Third, in any event, the morality is such that Johnson lied, Kennedy before him lied, and naturally you assume that because we were lied into war, that now as we are getting out probably we're lying as we get out.

• • •

NIXON: Having said all that, I know that what really happens is, like when you fellas go on before some audiences, if you go on and debate or, for example, before a live audience, you go on some of these like the Cavett show, and so forth. Inevitably, first the producer will stack it against you. Second, you get the impression the country's all against you and the rest. And it must be terribly discouraging, frustrating. So why do you do it? Well, the answer I have to give you is this. The answer is that, it's not terribly reassuring, unless you can take a very long view. The answer is that you're on the right side.

O'NEILL: Yes, sir.

NIXON: It's hard to say that to people, to say, "Do you believe that we've done the right thing? Do you believe that we'd get out in a respectable manner?" Otherwise that would be disastrous to not only seventeen million South Vietnamese, but to American policy in the Pacific and the world. The answer is that the United States' record in Vietnam is full of heroism and self-sacrifice, and so forth. And that under all these circumstances, it's time for, when Americans look back on this difficult time in their history, that they're going to look back with some pride. It's going to take some time, take some time. It'll take some luck. The South Vietnamese have to survive for a while after we leave, et cetera.

But you know, I just presented a Congressional Medal of Honor yesterday to a few people. [unclear] Most of them, you know, [unclear] military officers, [unclear] enlisted men, they come from middle-class, working families for the most part, from all over America. Not particularly well educated, and the rest. But they're great people.

O'NEILL: Yes, sir.

NIXON: And this is the kind of thing, I really feel, in other words, what you're doing, you'll take [unclear]. When you go on some of these TV shows like the Cavett thing you're going to get banged, and you'll feel terribly discouraged and say that the whole country's against you, and so forth. But I think you've got to remember, we have to remember that, now I would serve your same [fellow servicemen still] in Vietnam, once you get out, that now would you have the added burden of having to get back and reassure people that those who do come back, like Kerry and the rest, don't speak for all.

"July 15, Mr. President. It's the big play."

June 29, 1971, 4:21 p.m.
Richard Nixon and Henry Kissinger
OVAL OFFICE

The clock was ticking until Kissinger departed on his secret trip to China, and the Soviets had not yet responded. Whether the Soviets realized it at the time or not, had they responded before Kissinger's departure they likely would have had a summit with the United States first, before China. But, absent a response from the Soviets before Kissinger's departure, Nixon and Kissinger had to move forward with the Chinese.

• • •

NIXON: The play — I mean the play that we're making — I'm not a damn bit concerned if we — if you were just taking a trip normally, I wouldn't be concerned. But, boy, on this one, I just want to make that big play.

KISSINGER: July 15, Mr. President. It's the big play.

NIXON: Yeah. If we can make the new China on something.

KISSINGER: Yeah.

NIXON: My current thinking is still, if we don't get the answer from Dobrynin — you're going to tell him we've got to have an answer by when?

KISSINGER: Well, my thinking is we should be done by July 4.

NIXON: And he's got to inform Haig of that.

KISSINGER: Yeah. You're leaving here for the West Coast when?

NIXON: On the sixth. I'll be here.

KISSINGER: I'll give him till the evening of July 5.

NIXON: All right.

KISSINGER: So that Haig can get it to me.

NIXON: That's why [I] have him here. Well, can I just say we got to know by, you know, around the evening of July 5? Good. Fair enough.

KISSINGER: And —

NIXON: Then, in the meantime, if he doesn't make a move, then we go.

KISSINGER: Then we go this year. On the whole, Mr. President, I have to — my candid judgment is that the impact on Asia of immediately announcing this, announcing a summit, would really be a price we shouldn't pay lightly, in terms of impression. I think it would help, if we can afford it, it would help your posture best, through '72, if we — you can be seen to have moved deliberately but decisively. We've been talking about a summit so long that we forget how it, big it will [be] even if we had to send a special emissary to Beijing. But if we don't get a Russian summit, we may be —

NIXON: We may have to, Henry.

KISSINGER: If you feel you need it, nothing is more important —

NIXON: I understand. The impact on Asia, I know, is bad — I don't want to complicate it — but we're going to have to make some play [showing] that Nixon's still in the arena.

KISSINGER: I agree, Mr. President.

NIXON: That's it.

KISSINGER: And I'm just putting —

NIXON: I know the impact is going to be enormous.

KISSINGER: The ideal: if we could get the Russian summit and if we could string the Chinese one into April —

NIXON: Mm-hmm.

KISSINGER: — with a Bruce visit before — and Bruce will play it so low-key that he won't skim the cream off.

NIXON: In the meantime, though, you realize that others will go skim the cream off. They won't wait that long.

KISSINGER: But they —

NIXON: I mean, I'm just thinking of what we got to think about, what is possible.

KISSINGER: Yeah. But, you see, I think if we announce that we've had high-level conversations with —

NIXON: I should be the first; I should be the first to go after you do it this time. Other case — unless it's Bruce. Right?

KISSINGER: Well, you'll have been the one that opened it.

NIXON: Yeah, I know —

KISSINGER: You'll have been the first one —

NIXON: — but that's not the same thing. It isn't the same thing. The first time an American politician goes there, that's going to be it. Everything else will be encores.

"You just don't treat the president of the United States this way."
June 29, 1971, 6:30 p.m.
Richard Nixon, Henry Kissinger, and Alexander Haig
OVAL OFFICE

Two hours later, at the end of the workday, Nixon was even more tired of what he saw as Soviet dithering. He consoled himself with imagining the response in Moscow when news of the U.S.-China summit was announced.

• • •

NIXON: We ought to — you think we ought to, we really ought to go for the summit?

KISSINGER: I think, Mr. President, in their brutal, cheap, third-rate way, they're a miserable bunch of bastards. I mean, if you look at —

NIXON: It's terrible.

KISSINGER: — the way the Chinese have done business with us, and the way they do business. You just don't treat the president of the United States this way. Here is

Gromyko sitting in here, inviting you to Moscow, and now they've been stringing it along, maneuvering, dancing around. And basically they've always been forthcoming when we scared them most.

NIXON: Mm-hmm. That's true. [unclear] the truth.

KISSINGER: Absolutely.

NIXON: Boy, if they only knew what the hell was coming up, they'd be in here panting for that summit, wouldn't they? Huh?

KISSINGER: I'm sure.

"Fourteen million against 750 million."
June 30, 1971, 12:18 p.m.
Richard Nixon and Walter McConaughy
OVAL OFFICE

By late June, Nixon was ready to discuss his decision to pursue a two-China policy, at least with select people within the administration. One was Walter McConaughy, the U.S. ambassador to the Republic of China (Taiwan). He and the president discussed the response to the support of the United States for mainland China's entry into the UN.

• • •

McCONAUGHY: Am I authorized, Mr. President, to continue telling them that we do not intend our efforts to lower tensions with the Chinese Communists—?

NIXON: Our intentions—

McCONAUGHY: And to get some context. I mean, we do not intend for those efforts to prejudice the vital interests of the Republic of China. You authorized me to say that about twelve months ago.

NIXON: I think that's fair enough. Just say that we, that our—as far as the Republic of China is concerned that we have—we know who our friends are. And we are continuing to continue our close, friendly relations with them. As for their vital interests, what you really mean by vital interests, what you mean is, are we going to turn them over to the ChiComs, is that it?

McCONAUGHY: Well—

NIXON: Is that what they're afraid of?

McCONAUGHY: I think they, they'd find—of course they know we wouldn't do that. I believe they think of that as just general support for their membership in the UN—general international backing of them.

NIXON: We will—we will certainly in the UN. We're not going to support any proposition that would throw them out.

McCONAUGHY: Yeah. Exactly.

NIXON: Now, whether or not we can do what they want to do, which is of course to support the proposition that they stay in the Security Council, that's really—I think we can support them, but it isn't really going to work.

MCCONAUGHY: Yeah.

NIXON: I mean, if they get in — if they should — and when they — that's why the whole two-China thing is so really rather ridiculous, even if we eventually have to come to that. But our position will basically be that we support the Republic of China and especially in the UN. We will continue to. We will not support any resolution — our China position will not support any propositions that have the Republic of China put out of the UN.

MCCONAUGHY: Yes.

NIXON: We will be strong, steadfast on that point, so that's one. Now when you get into the other areas, we, after all, have a treaty commitment. We won't manage to break our treaties. We are working with them economically, too.

MCCONAUGHY: And they're —

NIXON: But we must have in mind, and they must be prepared for the fact, that there will continue to be a step-by-step, a more normal relationship with the other — the Chinese mainland. Because our interests require it. Not because we love them, but because they're there.

MCCONAUGHY: Yeah. Precisely.

NIXON: And because the world situation has so drastically changed. This has not been a derogation of Taiwan.

MCCONAUGHY: Exactly.

NIXON: And it's done because, as I say, because of very great considerations in other areas.

MCCONAUGHY: Yes. Yeah.

NIXON: It's a hard thing to sell.

MCCONAUGHY: Yes it's a —

NIXON: I know it's terribly difficult.

MCCONAUGHY: Yes. It's tough.

NIXON: They're going to see it in black and white. And they — my personal friendship goes back many years.

MCCONAUGHY: It does indeed.

NIXON: They sent the most beautiful gifts to our daughter's [unclear] wedding and so forth. We just — that's the way we're gonna deal with it. The personal considerations here are — we'll put it this way, we're not about to engage in what the Kennedy administration did with Diem. Because they might think that way. Either physically or philosophically, we don't do that to our friends.

MCCONAUGHY: Yeah, exactly.

NIXON: You remember that?

MCCONAUGHY: Yes. Of course they —

NIXON: The Kennedy administration has Diem's blood upon its hands, unfortunately. That was a bad deal.

MCCONAUGHY: Yeah. The president [Chiang Kai-shek] says repeatedly that you are the president, and your administration is the administration that understands the China issue and really sympathizes with his government, understands its ideals and its aspirations and its role in the world better than any other American president, any preceding administration, and he's unshaken in that view.

NIXON: Yeah. Yeah. That's why, of course, it causes me great concern that we have to move in this other direction. When I say we have to move, we have to because our failure to move would be — would prejudice our interests in other areas that are overwhelming.

McCONAUGHY: Yes. Exactly.

NIXON: Let us suppose, for example, we require some cooperation in Vietnam. Let's suppose that we could affect other relations — see many, there are different guesses on that — all these things are there.

McCONAUGHY: Yeah. The real crunch on the UN issue is the Security Council seat.

NIXON: Of course it is.

McCONAUGHY: I'm convinced we can keep them in if there's no tender of the Security Council seat to the Chinese Communists. If there is — as of now it looks like they would withdraw.

NIXON: Yeah.

McCONAUGHY: That would mean they're giving up on the thing. They've pretty well convinced themselves they could make a go of it without UN membership.

NIXON: Oh, hell yes. To be perfectly frank with you —

McCONAUGHY: And that would be —

NIXON: To be perfectly frank with you, if I were to be, if I were in their position, and the UN, as I say, the UN moves in that direction, I would just say the hell with the UN. What is it anyway? It's a damn debating society. What good does it do?

McCONAUGHY: Yeah.

NIXON: Very little. [unclear] They talk about hijacking, drugs, the challenges of modern society, and the rest just give hell to the United States. That's all they do.

McCONAUGHY: Yeah.

NIXON: No, my views about the UN, I must say, despite publicly I have to go through the usual façade, the act of praising the UN, but it's had it.

McCONAUGHY: Yeah.

NIXON: Every sophisticate knows it.

McCONAUGHY: Yeah.

NIXON: I mean, it does not serve our interests to put anything up to the UN. As you know, none of our vital interests have ever been submitted to the UN and will never be while I'm here.

McCONAUGHY: Yeah.

NIXON: So as far as they're concerned, I think they ought to not give much of a damn what happens in the UN. I don't think it hurts them one bit, but that's for them to decide.

McCONAUGHY: They recognize that it's got a certain psychological importance, I think. They don't want to be isolated —

NIXON: They don't want to be isolated. They don't want to be outside the community of nations.

McCONAUGHY: A sort of a pariah. And they — they're afraid that other countries might use their absence from the UN as sort of a pretext for discriminatory actions against them, even in the trade sector. And there might be some danger of this. For instance, the European Economic Community is rather inclined to exclude Taiwan from the list of preferential countries, the less developed countries that get preferential treatment on import duties. And they're afraid that there'd be an extra argument for the EEC to cut them out if they're not members of the UN. They might say, "Well then, who are they? They don't even have UN status. Why should they go on any sort of a preferential list for concessions?"

NIXON: Uh-huh. Oh, I see.

McCONAUGHY: That sort of thing. They're just afraid that their efforts to keep up their exports might suffer.

NIXON: No, I —

McCONAUGHY: And they've got to export to live, of course.

NIXON: Oh, yes.

McCONAUGHY: And they've been phenomenally successful, as you well know. And that remarkable rate of growth is continuing. Their foreign — total foreign trade last year was greater than that of entire England and China.

NIXON: Yeah. Sure.

McCONAUGHY: Just over three billion dollars, which slightly exceeded the total import and export trade of the Chinese Communists.

NIXON: Just think of that.

McCONAUGHY: Fourteen million [people on Taiwan] against seven hundred fifty million [people on the mainland] — they had a little larger foreign trade.

NIXON: Well, you can just stop and think of what could happen if anybody with a decent system of government got control of that mainland. Good God.

McCONAUGHY: Yeah.

NIXON: There'd be no power in the world that could even — I mean, you put eight hundred million Chinese to work under a decent system —

McCONAUGHY: Yeah.

NIXON: — and they will be the leaders of the world. The Indians — you could put two hundred billion Indians to work, and they wouldn't amount to a goddamn.

McCONAUGHY: Yeah.

NIXON: You know, basically they're different kinds of people.

McCONAUGHY: That's right. Yeah.

NIXON: But the Chinese, they're all over Asia. I know. They've got what it takes.

McCONAUGHY: Yeah, with an elected system of government. The one thing that —

NIXON: [unclear]

McCONAUGHY: I'm just back from New York on some trade conference work for the Businessmen's Council for International Understanding, Mr. President. I've assured them that we are well disposed toward continued American investment there. You know —

NIXON: Absolutely.

McCONAUGHY: — this very loyal American investment. I've encouraged them to continue. I've told them so far as I know the political climate is going to remain favorable if they can make an independent business judgment, which they must make for themselves. It's good business risk. Then as far as we know, the political climate certainly would argue for their going in. We don't foresee any change there. We anticipate it will be, continue to be a good climate. We're continuing to give our export guarantees there, in concurrence the Ex-Im Bank program has done an awful lot there — wonderful job. Also, the AID guarantees on investments apply — the same as in other countries. So I encouraged them to continue their interest in investment.

NIXON: They should.

McCONAUGHY: I got a very good response.

NIXON: I consider [unclear] a stable country and I certainly would not fault any course but that.

McCONAUGHY: Yeah.

NIXON: But it's a delicate line.

McCONAUGHY: It is.

NIXON: And you're going to have to — we're going to depend on you to be as, you know, as effective as you can be under difficult circumstances to keep them from, well, just throwing up their hands. There isn't anything they can do to us, of course. It isn't that so much. But the point is we take no comfort in seeming to hurt our friends.

McCONAUGHY: Yes.

NIXON: No comfort at all.

McCONAUGHY: Right.

NIXON: But the world is — theirs is a very delicate problem.

McCONAUGHY: It's something not to be talked about now, of course, Mr. President, but I conceive of Taiwan as gradually developing its own orbit, separate from that of the mainland.

NIXON: That's what —

McCONAUGHY: And I think this is going to be in our national interest too. We don't need to talk about formal independence now or sovereignty questions. I think we're wise to leave this open.

NIXON: That's right.

McCONAUGHY: In public.

NIXON: That's right. They should go on. I think that's their whole — their whole line of their thinking should be along that line.

MCCONAUGHY: Of course, the Generalissimo couldn't come to that now. But someday I think they are going to accept a separate status, independent of the mainland, in a different orbit and a separate status. But Taiwan is a part of the general equilibrium in the Far East, and I think that'd be seriously disturbed, apart from every humanitarian consideration, if the Chinese Communists took it over. It'd be a disaster.

NIXON: If Chinese Communists took it over [unclear].

MCCONAUGHY: Yeah. Of course, it'd be a bloodbath, the same as Tibet. But from the geopolitical standpoint it would just change the sensitive equipoise in the area, I think. And I know the Japanese would be greatly disturbed, too.

NIXON: Yep.

MCCONAUGHY: The Filipinos would be. And of course with the reversion of Okinawa, the Japanese are all the more sensitive to any change there. I think we've got a real ally in the Japanese. [unclear], they're basically with us.

NIXON: They sign on?

MCCONAUGHY: The LDP [Liberal Democratic Party] is. I don't know how the Japanese Socialists would be, if they came into power. They never do. But the LDP is with us.

NIXON: Sure. Sure. Sure. Sure. The Socialists [unclear]. Well, you don't have — there isn't any more delicate assignment, or I must say, as events unfold here, any one that will be more difficult than yours. And I just wish you the best. It's just one of those things, as I say. I look around the world, and you have to deal sometimes with a bunch of damn bandits. We do. And we're dealing with bandits, thugs, international outlaws, and so forth. But sometimes you have to because our interests are so deeply involved. With the Soviet — they're really a despicable [unclear], but you've got to deal with them.

MCCONAUGHY: That's right.

NIXON: You've got to talk with them.

MCCONAUGHY: Yeah. And we've got a complex interplay here — the Soviets and the Chinese Communists. They've obviously got very mixed feelings about the prospective entry of ChiComs into the UN. They don't really want it, but they think they've got to give lip service.

NIXON: Sure.

MCCONAUGHY: I guess they'll vote for the —

NIXON: Oh, sure.

MCCONAUGHY: — resolution, they don't really want it.

NIXON: Boy, they just love sitting there with them. That'd be the worst thing that [unclear].

MCCONAUGHY: Well, you know that I will use every resource in my power, Mr. President, to keep them confident and reassured.

[unclear exchange]

MCCONAUGHY: You've given me a lot to work with.

NIXON: Well, I can't say much more to be quite — just say as little as you can. Reassure them. But on the other hand, they have a friend, but we have to continue our other thing for other reasons that have nothing to do with our friendship with Taiwan.

"You set it up now that we could go visit China."

July 1, 1971, 9:54 a.m.
Richard Nixon, Henry Kissinger, and Alexander Haig
OVAL OFFICE

Still with no response from the Soviets on their intentions vis-à-vis a summit, Nixon and Kissinger had a final huddle before the latter's departure for China. Unless a Soviet response arrived in time, Kissinger's marching orders were to flip priorities and schedule a Chinese summit first.

• • •

KISSINGER: This was Rogers, who just wanted to talk about it. He's going up to testify —

NIXON: Yeah.

KISSINGER: — and he just wanted to know how to — what the [unclear] —

NIXON: Is this about the Papers? Do you think he's gonna have to testify on the Papers? Is that what he — the Pentagon Papers?

KISSINGER: No, on the —

NIXON: This thing?

KISSINGER: — on the Vietnam proposal. But Sullivan is also thinking that he'll — as long as they've added his political conditions, we're in good shape.

NIXON: Sure, but it's the same offer. I mean, we're not going to overthrow —

KISSINGER: Yeah.

NIXON: — throw our — and the thing is to not to use the word "overthrow" with "Thieu-Ky government." You understand, Al?

HAIG: Yes, sir.

NIXON: We're not going to turn the country over — seventeen million people — over to the Communists against their will. Put that down and get those sons of bitches to say it that way. Do I come through?

HAIG: Yes, sir.

NIXON: We are not going to — what they are saying is to turn seventeen million South Vietnamese over to the Communists against their will.

KISSINGER: Yeah.

NIXON: That's right. With the — and, and to — against their will with the, with the bloodbath that would be sure to follow. Put those words in! Now, I want them to go out and say it. Get out there and tell them to say it right now!

• • •

NIXON: Now, let me say, just a few other odds and ends as I read this thing [Kissinger's briefing book for his secret trip to Beijing]. As I say, it is a brilliant job. You just tell your staff, get them together and tell them that I was enormously impressed; I've been reading the damn thing. Now, you've got to put in, more than you have here, a very real fear. Now, I want to say, "The president has been generous." This general thing comes through as me being too soft and puts — it talks about [how] I'm a very reasonable man; I am not trying to do this; I am trying to have a position where we can have —

KISSINGER: Yeah.

NIXON: — less presence and more permanence, and so forth. That's all nice and so forth and so on. But I want you to put in that this is the man who did Cambodia. This is the man who did Laos. This is the man who will be, who will look to our interests, and who will protect our interests without regard to political considerations.

• • •

NIXON: Now, I think without being obvious about it — I mean, without being, without saying in so many words, but you should put in a little more about the necessity for our moving toward the Soviet. In other words, "With regard to the Soviet, we have to realize" — I mean, "They [the Chinese, have to realize] — we are seeking détente with the Soviets. It is not directed against you. But we have — our interests clash in Europe. Our interests clash in the Mideast. Our interests clash in the Caribbean. We intend to protect our interests. But we are going to seek it. And our interests clash, of course, as we have competition on arms."

• • •

NIXON: And, in the same vein, we got to make it — put in fear with regard to the Soviet. [In his handwritten notation in the briefing book, Nixon expressed this point as follows: "Put in fear R.N. would turn hard on V. Nam. Play up our possible move toward Soviet." "Put in more fears re Japan."]

KISSINGER: Absolutely.

NIXON: We fear — we don't know what they'll do. We know, for example, that — one thing you didn't have in there: we have noted that our intelligence shows that the Soviet has more divisions lined up against China than they have against Europe.

KISSINGER: The one reason, Mr. President, I —

NIXON: You can't put that in? [unclear], but why?

KISSINGER: Well, they're undoubtedly going to tape what I say, and I didn't want them to play that to the Soviet ambassador.

NIXON: Sure.

KISSINGER: But I've got some stuff in there —

NIXON: Well —

KISSINGER: — about exchanging military information.

NIXON: Well, I'd just put it in, that there are reports in the press then. Put it that way. Not that we show what you want. Reports in the press indicate that the Soviet has — that it has this. We were aware of that. Just sort of a low-key way. And we are also

aware of the fact that in the SALT negotiations the Soviet are against zero ABM because they are concerned about China. Put it in. I want to build up their fears against
Chiang. I want to build up their fears against Japan. And I want to build up their
fears of what will happen on Vietnam. Those things are going to move them a hell
of a lot more than all of the gobbledygook about all —

KISSINGER: Oh, no question.

NIXON: — about, you know, our being civilized — which, also, is important.

KISSINGER: Well, that's just —

NIXON: But, Henry, it's excellent.

KISSINGER: Yes.

NIXON: And it's excellent for the historical record. And it might have some effect. I
don't know. But I'm just telling you that I — my own inclination is to feel that you
got to get down pretty crisply to the nut cutting. And, but — in other words, I like all
that, but I would thin it down a bit so that you can get to the stuff that really counts
very soon.

                                    • • •

KISSINGER: Well, I think, Mr. President, we have now positioned the Russians. I
haven't — didn't have a chance to tell you.

NIXON: You had Dobrynin in. Did you tell him?

KISSINGER: Yeah. From Dobrynin. I told him. He said — he said this: he thinks, his
own guess is that the answer is yes. But, he says, Brezhnev was in Berlin until the
twentieth, and now he is afraid that the session they had scheduled today of the
Politburo is going to be canceled because of the cosmonauts. [After twenty-four
days in the *Salyut 1* space station, the *Soyuz 11* spacecraft was destroyed on June 29
upon reentry into the Earth's atmosphere, killing its crew of three cosmonauts.] So
he —

NIXON: Well, you should tell him, "Look, we've got to have an answer —"

KISSINGER: I said, "I've got to have an answer."

NIXON: Or if he doesn't have it, they'll be embarrassed [by] what we do.

KISSINGER: I said, "We've got to have an answer by the close of business on the sixth.
And, if it comes in any later than that, I just want you to know, the president has
already extended it. He may — he's got to make other plans." And so in a way now —

NIXON: Mm-hmm.

KISSINGER: — if they can't — if they — the best way for us to get off the hook with them
is to say, "Anatol, I've told you and told you. I told you June 10 we had to know it on
June 30 —"

NIXON: Right. Right. Right. I know, you said that. You set it up now that we could go
visit China, well, as far as the Russians are concerned.

KISSINGER: If the Russians do not give us a summit, we could go in December or —

NIXON: Yeah.

KISSINGER: — late November, a summit to China —

NIXON: Yeah. Yeah. Yeah. Yeah. Yeah.

KISSINGER: Don't you think, Al?

HAIG: Yes, sir, I do.

KISSINGER: And we can tell the Russians, and Anatol can go home and say, "You crazy sons of bitches, you screwed it up."

NIXON: Yeah. That's right.

KISSINGER: And — actually, technically, if we don't get it by the seventh, it doesn't make any difference what they decide.

NIXON: Yeah.

KISSINGER: Al can't get it to me fast enough.

NIXON: Yeah. The other point, of course, is this: if we don't get it there [by] the seventh of —

KISSINGER: On the other hand —

NIXON: — you have to fear — you've got to figure that the Russians then, if we go to China, there is a chance that they'll blow Berlin — no, they won't blow Berlin —

KISSINGER: Berlin they won't blow, but —

NIXON: — we'll blow that — but that they'll blow SALT. And they'll risk the summit.

KISSINGER: The Russians — the risk we run with the Russians —

NIXON: On the other hand — on the other hand, this or this presents hellish problems for them.

KISSINGER: Well, if they blow SALT — they could blow SALT. They could —

NIXON: Yeah.

KISSINGER: They could jack up the Middle East. And they could start —

NIXON: Definitely.

KISSINGER: — raising hell in the Caribbean.

NIXON: That's correct.

KISSINGER: Now, of course, we can go hard right.

NIXON: They won't do Berlin, because they want to get along with the Germans.

KISSINGER: Yeah. That's right. And, in fact, our major problem in Berlin now is we are coming up with — I know we'll never get credit for it — but we are coming up with a really superb agreement on that —

NIXON: Yeah. I want to —

KISSINGER: — which is actually an improvement —

NIXON: Can we still sink it?

KISSINGER: Yeah, but, you know, they are, the Russians are making so many concessions now that it's getting tough to —

NIXON: Yeah. Fine.

KISSINGER: I've got Rush held until July 20.

NIXON: Yeah.

"Who, but America?"

July 3, 1971, 10:01 a.m.
Richard Nixon and Alexander Haig
OVAL OFFICE

Nixon was meeting with Haig about foreign affairs because Kissinger was on his long-planned trip to North Vietnam. After that, he was to fly to Pakistan, where, as Nixon wrote in his Memoirs, *a "stomachache was scheduled for July 9–11." While Kissinger was supposed to be sick in bed, he would actually be in Beijing, meeting with Chinese officials including Zhou Enlai. The two men discussed the reasons that mainland China needed America, if it wanted to find its way back into the world community.*

• • •

HAIG: Henry came back. He said that — he asked me to get your guidance. If we get an affirmative Soviet response on the summit, and if the Chinese insist on an early summit in December, we'll have these two, and he wanted to know if you would authorize him to —

NIXON: Oh, sure. Oh, absolutely.

HAIG: All right.

NIXON: Don't hold it. I'll see the Soviet then have a return Soviet visit next year. We got to get everything out of the way before July. Nothing can be done after that for this summit, see? You see, anything to do [with] foreign policy, because after the damn guy —

HAIG: Exactly.

NIXON: — the other guy is nominated, the left wing around here will try to say they got to go along. They never said that when I was nominated, I must say. They didn't say the president ought to participate, et cetera.

• • •

NIXON: I was thinking a little about this whole business of Henry will clear it up, whether he really oughtn't to say to them — I just don't know what the hell the Chinese are going to say about what they want to do. I think he's got to tell them, of course, that we're — he's got to be very forthcoming with regard to the fact that we're meeting the Soviet.

HAIG: That's correct.

NIXON: I mean, you can't just slap them, or they'll say, "To hell with you," and they'll get tough.

HAIG: Right.

NIXON: You got to be — but this thing with the Soviet, that son of a bitch Dobrynin comes in, which I won't — Henry thinks he will. I don't. Well, I don't know. I mean, I won't guess on that.

HAIG: I rather think he will. Your —

NIXON: Do you really think he's going to come around? I want to know.

HAIG: Yes, sir. Everything they've done the last six months has been very much in the direction of—

NIXON: Yeah, I know. But whether they want to have a summit, they may be thinking that they can knock me over. I think they're petrified of the thought of my sitting in this place for another four years.

HAIG: Oh, ho! No question about it.

NIXON: Yet, on the other hand, if they don't get along with me now, they figure it'll be worse.

HAIG: Could be. The one thing is that we've got two alternatives, and maybe we can get both of them, which would be the ideal. But either one of them is a very significant achievement. Very significant.

NIXON: Isn't the Chinese—? Now, in terms of what we'd accomplish, in the short term, the Soviet thing is infinitely more important. In other words, we got SALT, we got Berlin, and we got the Mideast that we can talk about.

HAIG: Yeah.

NIXON: In terms of, on the other hand, what we can bring back from the Chinese thing is the biggest—

HAIG: Much, much more imaginative, and much more than that.

NIXON: Well, [unclear] people will be incredulous and that indicates—

HAIG: That's right, sir.

NIXON: —that anything is possible.

HAIG: That's right. But in the realities of the dangers of our position, the Soviet is—

NIXON: The Chinese is a long way off.

HAIG: Long way.

NIXON: Although they should be our natural allies, interestingly enough, shouldn't they?

HAIG: They should.

NIXON: Against the Soviets, they need us. And also they need us against the Japanese.

HAIG: Exactly.

NIXON: You know, we aren't [but] they must be petrified of the Japanese, because the Japanese did it to them once before. And here sit the Japanese over there, needing breathing space. Who's going to keep the Japanese restrained? Who, but America?

HAIG: Who has all the economic power—

NIXON: Mm-hmm.

HAIG: This is very bad.

NIXON: God, they need us. If you really think straight, they need us desperately.

HAIG: Yes, and very much back in the traditional power configuration there, where the United States has got to give them some hope, some kind of threat on Japan's flank, and some kind of a threat on Russia's. Well, I think it's a natural alignment, but [there's] no sense kidding ourselves about the ideological problem. Those bastards are tough.

NIXON: Oh, yeah.

"'What's done, Henry.'"

July 6, 1971, 11:26 a.m.
Richard Nixon and Alexander Haig
OVAL OFFICE

Still with Haig, Nixon began to fear that Kissinger might become part of the problem in the aftermath of the China announcement. It was a dramatic betrayal of Kissinger to his underling. One of the characteristics that made Nixon appear strong in foreign relations was the fact that he really didn't trust anyone. Ultimately, that included his partner, every step of the way, in formulating foreign policy.

• • •

NIXON: I think that the whole business here with regard to the Soviet, on reflection, is the more that he — I've come closer to your view of it. First, it's what I expected, because I just was, as I told Henry, I said, "Henry, what the hell do you think? What's in it for them?" He says, "Well, we got Berlin." He says, "I'll tell them I'll cut off this channel" and all that. But, anyway, he could get it.

HAIG: Yeah.

NIXON: There isn't a Soviet [unclear] — you know what it's like. Well, that's why I'm for getting out of this Paris meeting.

HAIG: Exactly.

NIXON: What's in it for them, they get out anyway.

HAIG: That's exactly right.

NIXON: Do you feel he's going to get out of this Paris meeting?

HAIG: No, sir. I never have.

NIXON: Really?

HAIG: No.

NIXON: Huh?

HAIG: I had not. And I do not.

NIXON: No. I think he's going to get a straight opinion. But the thing we've got to do with Henry on this is be very tough on him.

HAIG: Exactly.

NIXON: "What's done, Henry" — you know what I mean? He just can't keep going over there and diddling around, because he gets too impressed by the, basically, the cosmetics. He really does. I mean, as much as he's — as realist as he is, you know, it does impress him. Cosmetics usually impress him. Now, he'll —

HAIG: His background is a problem. He's cut from that goddamn —

NIXON: That's right.

HAIG: —left wing and he, even though he's a hard-line, tough guy, he's working for the [unclear] class.

NIXON: You see, he wouldn't realize, for example, that when I write a letter to an astronaut, I'm not doing it for the goddamn Russians. Fuck them. I'm doing it because it would look awfully good here, right now. You see what I mean?

HAIG: Yeah.

NIXON: People like to do that. But Henry's just got to get him a little bit, got to be more — you know, he always has these long, goddamn tortuous meetings with Dobrynin, and it seems very interesting, very exciting, and all that sort of thing. Al, they're suckering us along.

HAIG: That's right.

NIXON: And I think you've got to be — now, it may be that their interests require a SALT agreement. Think so? Do they want a SALT agreement?

HAIG: I think they want an improvement in relations because they think they can unravel the NATO alliance —

NIXON: Yeah.

HAIG: — and split Germany up.

NIXON: Mm-hmm.

HAIG: That's what they're after.

NIXON: They want a Berlin agreement? Right?

HAIG: Yes, sir.

NIXON: Oh, we've got to screw that up. Now, that is, I mean, awfully clear to Rush. Is it?

HAIG: Yes, sir. And it's sufficiently complicated —

NIXON: Yeah. Sure.

HAIG: — and still has a long enough way to go that we can do that. And this announcement, when it comes, will hit them right between the eyes. They'll know goddamn well that they're not fooling with people that are going to sit and get raped.

NIXON: Well, I just hope Henry gets in there.

HAIG: Well, I think that — that's what I'm concerned about. I think it will work fine. I —

NIXON: You haven't heard from the Paks yet?

HAIG: No. No.

NIXON: He said he thought there was another message here.

HAIG: Well, I think he said that he had alerted his number two —

NIXON: Yeah.

HAIG: — to convey additional messages because he felt there would be more.

NIXON: Mm-hmm.

HAIG: Because all they did was register their concern.

NIXON: Mm-hmm. Now, well, let me say this: if they — if it's knocked down, if this one goes because of that, it was too tenuous to begin [with] anyway.

HAIG: That's right, sir.

NIXON: You see my point? If this — we better find out right now that if it ends because of some little pipsqueak story, they're going to knock it down as too tenuous. Do you understand?

HAIG: No, I think they want it, sir. They've really made a firm commitment.

NIXON: Well, he sort of thought that, Henry's always felt, the Russians wanted it. You sort of felt so too, didn't you?

HAIG: Well, I did. And I still think they do, but they want to suck us dry.

NIXON: I guess they think, they think they can get more out of us for it. They're going to ass-pick to pay a bigger price, which we have to consider.

HAIG: No, that response was an effort to just suck us dry, not to turn it down.

NIXON: Yeah, that's right—

HAIG: They kept it open.

NIXON: "We hope our relations will improve. We've noted some positive things. What else are you going to do, boys?"

HAIG: Exactly.

NIXON: Well, what we're going to do is kick them right in the teeth.

HAIG: Yeah.

NIXON: But the message to Henry is that no—I want him to be—and this is absolutely categorical—there is to be no intermediary. No Bruce trip.

HAIG: I sent him that this morning, sir.

NIXON: Don't you agree?

HAIG: Yes, sir.

NIXON: And you can see why, Al, that the Bruce trip is now irrelevant. I mean, why do it twice? And we will just announce that, as I already said, that I'm prepared to go. And that's much more frank with them, and they—

HAIG: Well, that's one thing. You're dealing with a more straightforward customer. They're tougher. But I think the Chinese are more direct and honest. When they say something, they mean it. They've made a decision. Oh, I think that's going to go. They never would have sent you the message, if they didn't mean it. Now, they may ask a price that you may—might not be willing to pay.

NIXON: Christ, yeah.

HAIG: That would be the complication on the Chinese. But the Soviets are just playing pussyfoot. They're—

NIXON: Yeah.

"Dobrynin said . . . 'What can you really settle with the Chinese?'"

July 19, 1971, 5:10 p.m.

Richard Nixon and Henry Kissinger

EXECUTIVE OFFICE BUILDING

The news of Kissinger's secret trip to Beijing, which was released on July 15, was a sensa-tion. In the United States, war hawks and doves, Democrats and Republicans, those under thirty and over thirty, all paused to marvel at the thought of a quarter-billion people reaching out to China for the first time in a generation. According to the announcement, Nixon was to visit China sometime before May of 1972.

Very few people, even among Nixon's inner circle, knew about the Kissinger trip in advance. Many had to be brought up-to-date, including the secretary of state, but of prime importance to Nixon and Kissinger was Dobrynin. That was a moment that Nixon had been waiting for, and on July 19, Kissinger briefed him on his first conversation about China with the Soviet ambassador.

. . .

NIXON: Well, Henry, tell me about your meeting with Mr. D.

KISSINGER: Oh, God, he was [unclear] —

NIXON: Who isn't? How was your staff? I bet they were ecstatic.

KISSINGER: Oh, yeah, Mr. President. Their morale is way high.

. . .

NIXON: Well, Henry —

KISSINGER: They have —

NIXON: But I think it's too late.

KISSINGER: Every sophisticate —

NIXON: Well, sophisticate? I want the people.

KISSINGER: Well, the people —

NIXON: I don't give a shit, but the story has now set in.

KISSINGER: Yes.

NIXON: State cannot —

KISSINGER: They can't do it.

NIXON: I'm not going to let them do it.

KISSINGER: State can't do it.

NIXON: On that, we did something that's good. They're not going to come in and pre-empt it.

KISSINGER: Well, they sure as hell —

NIXON: You've given Rogers one hell of a lot more than he pleaded about.

KISSINGER: They sure as hell weren't claiming that they participated in the Cambodia decision, although they did a lot more there.

NIXON: Or Laos.

KISSINGER: Or Laos. Or anything else that was tough. Well, I told Dobrynin that I began to doubt that there is a God, because I lied to him actually. I'm sure that if there were one, I would have been punished. But —

NIXON: [laughs]

KISSINGER: But I started off and then he — first of all, I've never seen him so forthcoming before today.

NIXON: Good. Really?

KISSINGER: Well — oh, yeah. Even the State Department will someday —

NIXON: Ambassadors.

KISSINGER: — know —

NIXON: Rogers.

KISSINGER: But it's best not to talk about it. I've got a lot of details here to show you.

NIXON: Sure.

KISSINGER: Let me —

NIXON: Yeah.

KISSINGER: [I said,] "Let me give you a picture of how the president's mind works. This isn't to pacify you. He just — and he wants me to tell you that, in terms of world leadership, he recognizes only the Soviet Union and the United States will lead. But after June, we're using every stop."

NIXON: Precisely.

KISSINGER: "I want to tell you, under one trivial condition, which, well — which I've heard here as well." I said, "Remember, we gave you until July 1. I can tell you in strictest confidence that, before we left Washington, my instructions to the president — I was going to go to China in June. My instructions to the president — from the president."

NIXON: Which? Your role?

KISSINGER: It's not that kind of relationship.

NIXON: That's right.

KISSINGER: But that — the burden's on them.

NIXON: Him.

KISSINGER: And then I said, "We have no choice. The president has said if anything we conduct will destroy us all, it's the arms race." I think here we could tell Rogers what we're doing.

NIXON: Good. Tell him.

KISSINGER: Again, I told him that, he said I told him that — I said, "Moreover," I said to him, "I told you six months ago that we couldn't do it in November or December. So when you said you wanted it in November or December, well, the president had to assume that this was a nice way to back out." He said, "No, no, no, no. We want it. We very much want it. I can tell you in strictest confidence, off the record." Well, we're both pushing at each other.

NIXON: Yeah, I know.

KISSINGER: You know, pushing this strictest confidence, off the record.

NIXON: I know.

KISSINGER: And they had already made their decision. They were getting ready to pick the date. Well, he said — "But now," he said, "can we pick the date now? What can I report?" Then I said, "Well, in principle, yes, but, of course, now we have a new situation." He said, "Would you be willing to come before going to Beijing?" I said, "Anatol, be classy." I said, "We have to go now in the order in which we announce it." He said, "Would you be willing to announce it before you go to Beijing?" I said,

"Well, I'm not sure what the president's" — but I said, "We may consider it. But I'll talk to the president. The president makes decisions."

NIXON: That's right. I've approved anything —

KISSINGER: He said, "Well, it better go tonight; they're having a meeting on it on Thursday." So, what I think —

NIXON: Right.

KISSINGER: Then I said — then he said, "Well, if you go" — [laughs] the shoe is really on the other foot now — he said, but he said, "If you come after you've gone to Beijing, why won't Beijing hold you up until May?"

NIXON: They can't.

KISSINGER: I thought it was somewhat of a cheesy play. I said, "Sorry, I don't know what Beijing is going to do, but if they try to make conditions —" What reason would they have for treating you, the president —

NIXON: Just one.

KISSINGER: — to such a condition? "But I have no reason to believe that they would make such —" Well, he was just sniffing in a conniption. So what I think is going to happen now, unless they make public the decision to go very tough — which would be but, well, maybe thirty percent — I think they're going to calm down. I think we can announce the Moscow summit before you go to Beijing. And that would actually help —

NIXON: Exactly.

KISSINGER: — with the Chinese because —

NIXON: Yeah.

KISSINGER: — taking effect after we go to Moscow.

NIXON: Before.

KISSINGER: And the sequence that I now see is I might go to Beijing at the end of September, get the damn thing locked up.

NIXON: Then announce it.

KISSINGER: Then announce the summit for Beijing.

NIXON: Yeah.

KISSINGER: Then while I'm in Beijing tell them that you're going to announce the summit for Moscow. And then at the end of October announce the summit for Moscow for the end of March.

NIXON: So, April is too early.

KISSINGER: Is April early for that?

NIXON: We could still do it in April. Work out your — you don't have to worry about, well, going in the order we put ourselves in.

KISSINGER: Well, that's April.

NIXON: April. Yeah. I hope they embrace it, that the Russians will do that time and play over there.

KISSINGER: But I think we could have one spectacular after another.

NIXON: Yeah.

KISSINGER: The other trip to Beijing; the announcement of —

NIXON: Why don't you let him know —?

KISSINGER: But I'm going to phone him tonight.

NIXON: I'd let him know that, well, there really are several — let me put it: I will hold the period around the first of May.

KISSINGER: I won't even give on that.

NIXON: Okay. The spring of next year.

KISSINGER: No, I think what I would do is to say — we tell them in Sep[tember] — as I told them, that we'd do it after Beijing. And they sort of —

NIXON: Yeah.

KISSINGER: — come in with a specific proposal of when to announce it and so forth.

NIXON: We'll ask them —

KISSINGER: We're thinking of roughing [out] our schedule.

NIXON: That's right. And we're seeking accommodation on other things and so forth. But he was certainly not unpleasant.

KISSINGER: Then he asked me, he said, "It would really help," he said, "if you give our people a briefing —"

NIXON: [laughs]

KISSINGER: "— of what went on in Beijing." Well, I gave him a briefing about this *Aviation Week.*

NIXON: Yeah.

KISSINGER: He said, "Did you discuss Soviet air defenses or Soviet bases?" I said, "We avoided it for the first powwow." He said, "Well, are they worried that we'd attack them?" I said, "Anatoly, you seem to be very [more] worried about China than Japan."

. . .

KISSINGER: I think they [the North Vietnamese] have got to settle now, because if we —

NIXON: Yeah.

KISSINGER: Mr. President, if we get a Russian summit, I think — oh, another thing Dobrynin said is — who knows about these things? — "What can you really settle with the Chinese?" He said, "I thought we were your natural partners in Southeast Asia. We're both trying to avoid Chinese expansion in Southeast Asia."

NIXON: Shut up and get out!

[laughter]

KISSINGER: Then he said about India and Pakistan. He asked me what my impression was of, due to the fact there hasn't been any war there for a while, whether it should become international.

NIXON: I agree.

KISSINGER: Exactly. The UN is chained up. He [Dobrynin] talked to me with a respect that I hadn't encountered before.

NIXON: Did you see Harriman? Was he more affected?

KISSINGER: Oh, I saw him with the Indian ambassador.

NIXON: Was he shaken?

KISSINGER: He was shaken.

NIXON: Oh, well. You know, it shows what you've done. You know another thing too that shakes them, Henry. They worry, worry in a different sense: the information, gut issue. I was their fear. This shakes them up completely because people say, they say, "This son of a bitch went into Cambodia; this son of a bitch went into Laos; this son of a bitch may be a disaster; this son of a bitch is unpredictable. We don't know what he's going to do."

KISSINGER: Yeah, but I —

NIXON: You see? That's a good thing.

KISSINGER: "But he has big plays." I mean, here you were, by any reasonable prediction, you were totally on the ropes.

NIXON: Sure.

KISSINGER: And if you, then, by any reasonable prediction, however, save yourself —

NIXON: Who would've dreamed —?

KISSINGER: Oh, absolutely. But that you held it with ice-cold nerves for two months.

NIXON: That's something —

KISSINGER: You took the shellacking.

NIXON: That's something that you could use with the people tonight, you know.

KISSINGER: Now, who, in God's name —

NIXON: Yes.

KISSINGER: — which other American political figure would have just had the effrontery to take the riots, the congressional action for two months —?

NIXON: Without saying, "Gee whiz, fellows."

• • •

NIXON: We're going to be goddamn loose on Vietnam though, Henry.

KISSINGER: I thought I'd be in my manner much, very gentle with them.

NIXON: Exactly.

KISSINGER: Because they — I'd put it right into their heart, for one thing.

NIXON: Yeah.

KISSINGER: They know now I'm not a pushover.

NIXON: I think that we — and I think in general it burns to say, you know, "Here's what we differ on" — that kind of a spirit, Henry. "What do you have to offer?" and so forth; "Well, we'll look it over," then, "Screw you."

KISSINGER: But never — that shouldn't be gloating.

NIXON: No gloating ever. No. No, I agree. I agree. I think that the very cool and strong position that we know what we're doing, we've got the hole card, and we're not going to gloat over you. What do you got to offer? Another settlement.

KISSINGER: I—

NIXON: Now, what in the hell are they [North Vietnamese] going to do? What the Christ is their option now—except, I guess, to fight on?

KISSINGER: Well, but Mr. President, I think—there's one point I made to Dobrynin here today: "You know, he [Nixon] has guts. There never was, to tell the truth, a tougher guy."

NIXON: You told him that too?

KISSINGER: Yeah. I think—the Russians cannot control the Berlin thing. They can try to stir up the North Vietnamese people. And the North Vietnamese have to decide whether they want another series of bloodbaths. The Russians have to decide whether, that, having caused one great play, they might still go into a few other places. I mean, I can tell Dobrynin what I want, but I'm not concerned with the Soviet Union. That doesn't, that's just something for the record. We don't have to discuss it. The mere fact though that those with ties to the Chinese, who have troops on the border—

NIXON: That's fine. You know, they're capable of bringing a freeze, a deep freeze, you know, with the Chinese attacking the Russians for their program—that would be after SALT, you know.

KISSINGER: But when you consider that Kuznetsov has been—

NIXON: Yeah.

KISSINGER: —their deputy foreign minister, has been in Beijing for nearly two years and has yet to see Zhou Enlai.

NIXON: But, what I mean is, with the Chinese fear of the Russians on this, they would be close to us.

KISSINGER: That's right.

NIXON: Now, now that this—this is just a total upheaval.

PART II

The Collapse of the Gold Standard to the India-Pakistan War

August–December 1971

"We get involved in all these screwball causes."
August 2, 1971, 9:20 a.m.
Richard Nixon and Henry Kissinger
OVAL OFFICE

As the humanitarian situation deteriorated between India and Pakistan, foreign aid poured into the region. One prominent fundraiser for the Indian refugees was "The Concert for Bangla Desh," held on August 1 at Madison Square Garden in New York City. Organized by former Beatle George Harrison and Ravi Shankar, the event also headlined Bob Dylan, Eric Clapton, former Beatle Ringo Starr, and former Beatles collaborator Billy Preston. As seen in his comments to Kissinger, Nixon had little consideration for those sympathetic to India.

• • •

KISSINGER: We'll really, next year, have a record. Every problem we came in with will have been solved, except the Middle East. And that will have been improved.

NIXON: Tell me about Pakistan now. I read the, I see now the Beatles are out raising money for them. You know, it's a funny thing, the way we are in this goddamn country. We get involved in all these screwball causes.

KISSINGER: Well, we have a hundred million dollars, it depends, for whom are the Beatles raising money for, the refugees in India?

NIXON: Refugees, yeah.

KISSINGER: Is it India or in Pakistan?

NIXON: The goddamn Indians.

KISSINGER: Well, the Indian side of it is economically in good shape. We've given them seventy million dollars.

NIXON: Mm-hmm.

KISSINGER: More is coming in, and no one knows how they're using the goddamn money, because —

NIXON: You're giving it to the government?

KISSINGER: Yeah.

NIXON: Well that's a terrible mistake.

KISSINGER: Yeah, well, they don't let anyone in there. They permit no foreigners —

NIXON: The Indians don't?

KISSINGER: — into the refugee area. No foreigners at all. Their record is outrageous.

NIXON: Well then, what about Pakistan?

KISSINGER: Well, on the Pakistan side, we have moved in a hundred million dollars' worth of food, which is in the port. We've had a task force working on it, which is either in the ports or on the way to the ports. The big problem now is to get it distributed. The UN has sent in 38 experts. They're prepared to send in 150 more.

"Everything the Chinese have done has been in big style."

August 9, 1971, 8:55 a.m.

Richard Nixon, Bob Haldeman, and Henry Kissinger

OVAL OFFICE

America's status with the Soviets had been altered far less than Nixon anticipated by the developments concerning Beijing. He and Kissinger didn't even bother asking for a schedule for the summit, focusing instead on getting the SALT negotiations, both the public meetings and the secret channels, back on track. At the same time, they discussed the effect of the new Sino-American relationship on other Asian nations. They also hoped to differentiate Americans — Republicans and Democrats — in Chinese eyes, on the assumption that officials in Beijing were still unschooled in U.S. politics.

• • •

KISSINGER: Well, they've [the Chinese] been absolutely meticulous. And we've been meticulous. For example, I keep — every time we send a note to the Russians that concerns them —

NIXON: I know that. That's great.

KISSINGER: — I send a note to them about the content of this. And next Monday, when I'm going to Paris, I will now ask for a meeting with them, and I'm going to tell them about our India policy.

NIXON: Sure.

KISSINGER: Just as the Soviets are making a deal, I thought if I just give them five minutes of what you're doing on India —

NIXON: Oh, I was — I just made a note this morning of that. I saw that Gromyko was down there talking to that damn Indian foreign minister [Swaran Singh]. That little son of a bitch is insufferable.

KISSINGER: Well, they've now signed —

HALDEMAN: Well, they announced a deal [unclear].

KISSINGER: They've signed a Treaty of Friendship and Cooperation [on August 9].

HALDEMAN: Just announced that this morning.

NIXON: Oh, but I didn't see that.

KISSINGER: Yeah.

NIXON: I didn't see it.

KISSINGER: — in which they will consult —

HALDEMAN: It's not in there. It's not in there. It was just on the radio.

KISSINGER: Yes. That's that.

NIXON: [unclear]

KISSINGER: They'll consult with each other in case of aggression — of aggression of other countries against one of the parties. And then, it's not clear —

NIXON: Consult?

KISSINGER: Well, it's not clear whether they promised —

NIXON: I don't think it means a hell of a lot.

KISSINGER: No, it doesn't mean a hell of a lot, Mr. President.

• • •

KISSINGER: I'm going to give that Indian ambassador unshirted hell today.

NIXON: You want me to get him in?

KISSINGER: Well, let me get the text of the — maybe one more turn of the wheel.

NIXON: I know. But the thing is, though, they used to — well, they understand, if they're going to choose to go with the Russians, they're choosing not to go with us. Now, goddamn it, they've got to know this.

KISSINGER: Yeah.

NIXON: Goddamn it, who's given them a billion dollars a year?

KISSINGER: But —

NIXON: Shit, the Russians aren't giving them a billion dollars a year, Henry.

KISSINGER: No. The Russians — really, one has to say, when you compare how Zhou Enlai has behaved towards us — now, ideologically, they're as hostile. And we've understood, they've done some things with North Vietnam, but they've always —

NIXON: Hmm.

KISSINGER: — stayed well short of inflaming the situation.

• • •

NIXON: All the damn Democrat candidates think the Russians are nice guys.

KISSINGER: And the Indians are — what helps us with the Chinese, vis-à-vis the Democrats, is that the Democrats are pro-Indian and pro-Russian.

HALDEMAN: Yeah.

KISSINGER: And we are pro-Pakistani and —

NIXON: In fact, could I suggest one thing? Is there any way that you could, in your conversation [with the Chinese], or otherwise, get it across — is there some way you could plant, some way where Democrats are, Democratic people are? That kind of a story? Or do you think they obviously are going to see it anyway?

KISSINGER: No, that's why I want to see them next week. I want to tell them —

NIXON: Yeah.

KISSINGER: — that the Democratic Congress is putting the squeeze on Pakistan.

NIXON: Now, on the Pakistan — but I also want them to know that —

KISSINGER: On Russia.

NIXON: — the Democratic candidates are pushing us on the Soviet side. I'd like to get that point: that we are —

KISSINGER: I'll get that put in.

NIXON: And also the point that I resisted great pressure to go to the Soviet first.

KISSINGER: Yeah.

NIXON: I think let's get a little — let's make a little mileage out of that. You know we've covered that point. We might as well get the benefit out of it, right?

KISSINGER: Absolutely.

NIXON: Don't you think so?

KISSINGER: Absolutely.

NIXON: We were just — that the president was pressed. The Democratic — say some of his Democratic opponents are putting a lot of heat on the ground. And that's true.

· · ·

KISSINGER: And the Chinese are more worried about the Japs almost than about the Russians.

NIXON: They should be.

KISSINGER: And —

NIXON: You know, the interesting thing is here: what can we do though? What are you going to tell the Pakistan ambassador? What the hell can you tell that son of a gun? I mean, excuse me, the Indian ambassador.

KISSINGER: I'm going to tell him, "I just want you to understand one thing. If you — if there is a war in the subcontinent, we are going to move against you, one way or the other."

NIXON: Right.

KISSINGER: "And you — your development program is down the drain. And if you want — if you think you can afford domestically to throw yourself completely into the Soviet arms, go ahead and do it."

NIXON: That's right. "You're making a conscious choice." Put it — I wanted to say this: "The president wants you to know" — tell him this, use it like this — "the president wants you to know he doesn't want this to happen. The president is a friend of India. He wants India to succeed. He has said that and he means it. But as far as he's concerned, however, the president wants, feels it's his — that it's your obligation" — tell him the president wants him to know that in the event that they decide that they go to war in the subcontinent, and side with the Soviet, that then they have chosen. And that we have — that is their choice. But that we shall have, then have to look in other, in another direction.

KISSINGER: We've —

NIXON: And that we shall look in the other direction. And under the circumstances, much as I will regret it, we will have to take another position — and will. And they have a fit. "The president is" — "Now, Mr. Ambassador" — you can sort of play this — you say, "Now, Mr. Ambassador, you know how I personally feel." Give him a little bullshit about how much you love the Indians. Then say, "Now —"

HALDEMAN: [laughs]

NIXON: "— but I just want you to know that —"

KISSINGER: If there's a God, he'll punish me.

NIXON: Well, then, you go on to say that "I just want you to know that this president is — you must not underestimate him. You know, I had to —" Tell him how hard it was to restrain me on Cambodia. "You know, I tried to restrain him on Laos and China, but he will not — he is — I cannot tell you how strongly he feels on this." Tell him, "I cannot possibly tell you, Mr. Ambassador, how far — strong he feels about the war issue. As far as helping, as far as using our influence to get a political settlement, as far as the refugees, as far as helping India, he's totally generous. But war, no." I'd just lay the goddamn wood to him.

. . .

KISSINGER: And we're giving them [the Chinese] a lot of incentives by being so meticulous.

NIXON: Actually — well, by being meticulous and also by letting them know that we're — the best thing you're doing is letting them know everything the Soviet tell you. I mean that's —

KISSINGER: That's right.

NIXON: — that we're going to deal with them against the Soviet, which is just fine.

KISSINGER: That's right. And also now what the Indians are doing.

NIXON: Yeah. Do they really hate the Indians? They must really —

HALDEMAN: They hate the Indians?

KISSINGER: No, they despise the Indians.

NIXON: Hmm?

KISSINGER: They despise the Indians.

NIXON: Do they?

KISSINGER: Oh, God.

NIXON: What are we going to do about — what about the Soviet? What's the next move there?

KISSINGER: They're coming in to us within the next ten days with something. Actually, we're not in a great hurry about it now.

NIXON: Yeah. But my point is: do you think there is any, that there is a reasonable chance that they may want to have some sort of a meeting?

KISSINGER: I think it's eighty percent right now.

NIXON: Even after the Chinese meeting?

KISSINGER: Yeah. I told them —

NIXON: That's when it has to come, of course.

KISSINGER: I've told them nothing else could even be considered.

NIXON: Why would they do it then, Henry? They don't — they, as distinguished from the Chinese. The Chinese may have mixed emotions about who will be elected. But they damn well want to beat the shit out of us, Henry.

KISSINGER: Except on the Middle East.

NIXON: Yeah, and that's their hubris.

KISSINGER: So —

NIXON: Do they realize on the Middle East —?

KISSINGER: But also —

NIXON: Besides the public sentiment —

KISSINGER: No, I'll tell you why I think —

NIXON: — they can take Israel any day that they want to take an hors d'oeuvre.

KISSINGER: Yeah, but except they're afraid we'll protect Israel.

NIXON: Good. And they know with Democrats in, they have to and I might not. Is that it?

KISSINGER: That's right.

NIXON: Okay.

KISSINGER: Well — but their major reason is they're afraid of what you will do in Beijing if they're in a posture of hostility to you. So they would like to have the visit hanging over Beijing — they would like to have — that you have the visit in the pocket —

NIXON: I see.

KISSINGER: — so that you will not, so that you will be restrained in Beijing. We, in turn, want it because it's helpful to us to have Moscow hanging over Beijing. It re-insures —

NIXON: Right.

KISSINGER: — the Beijing visit. And, after all, when I handed your letter to Dobrynin, I didn't even mention the summit. He said, "Does the fact that there's no summit in there mean the president has lost interest?" He said, "Because I can tell you, unof-ficially, they're considering it now at the highest level in Moscow and there'll be an answer." And he said, "The reason, I'm not" — speaking of himself — "they're not letting me go on vacation is because they want me to transmit that answer, that proposal to you."

NIXON: Mm-hmm. Well, either way, we shall see.

KISSINGER: But — no, I think it's going to come. And for us that would have — then we'd be in great shape. Because if the summit is coming up, say, in the middle of May in Moscow, we know there won't be a Middle East blowup before then, because they'll sit on the Egyptians.

NIXON: Yeah.

KISSINGER: That and India are the two big problems.

NIXON: Yeah.

KISSINGER: And that means we'll be through the better part of next year, and they can't start something up right after the summit either.

NIXON: Mm-hmm.

KISSINGER: And we can keep the two to control each other.

NIXON: That's right.

• • •

NIXON: Getting back to the Russians — I mean, on the Indians, yeah, they're really try-ing to punish the Paks, but they sure as hell don't want a war down there.

KISSINGER: No, but they are such a petty bunch of shits, if you'll forgive me, that they—everything the Chinese have done has been in big style. And they make a deal with you and then they try to make you look good. And look at how they [the Soviets] handled the SALT thing.

NIXON: Yeah, the Russians.

KISSINGER: Grudging, mean, petty.

NIXON: I know.

KISSINGER: And they're just putting—what they're doing in India is putting enough oil on the fire to kick everybody and praying that it won't blow up into a conflagration.

NIXON: It's the same way they did the Middle East.

KISSINGER: Exactly the way they did it in the Middle East.

NIXON: Well, I was—the June war was brought on by [the] Russians.

KISSINGER: And by Russian stupidity.

NIXON: The Russians brought it on. They did.

KISSINGER: Absolutely.

NIXON: They gave the Egyptians—and before the war, and until the final kind of a thing broke loose. Then, after it began, they said, "Let's all get together and try to settle it." But only after they knew the Egyptians were licked. Now, they played a very miserable role in that war.

KISSINGER: That's right. Absolutely. Absolutely. And what they're doing now is, they're getting back at the Pakistanis.

NIXON: Do you really think that's what it's all about?

KISSINGER: Oh, yeah. Well, and at the Chinese.

NIXON: Okay.

KISSINGER: And they're getting themselves some cheap shots in. And I'll bet that when one reads the treaty—we haven't got the text yet—that it has no formal legal obligation that means anything.

NIXON: Hmm.

KISSINGER: But it's enough to make it psychologically tough.

NIXON: We've got to fight like hell against—well, the Congress, thank God, is gone. So we've got at least three to four weeks when we don't have to bother about India/Pakistan and that.

"I don't want to be around to see the Soviet Union ever be in a position of superiority."

August 10, 1971, 10:05 a.m.

Richard Nixon, Spiro Agnew, Melvin Laird, David Packard, the Joint Chiefs of Staff (Thomas Moorer, Elmo Zumwalt, John Ryan, William Westmoreland, and Leonard Chapman), Henry Kissinger, and Alexander Haig

CABINET ROOM

Melvin Laird, in concert with the Joint Chiefs of Staff, kept as strong a hand as he could in the SALT negotiations. His basic concern was that U.S. superiority in ABM systems should not be traded, except in return for Soviet concessions on offensive weapons. In offensive systems, the Soviet Union was very strong and it could, Laird felt, easily emerge from SALT as the more powerful nation, if the United States wasn't careful.

Earlier in the year, Laird had watched in dismay as Kissinger clumsily dropped submarine-launched ABMs from the SALT negotiations; it took a lot of long, hard dealing to reinsert them in the talks. As the one member of the cabinet who was fully aware of Kissinger's ongoing secret negotiations, Laird was determined that both Kissinger and Nixon fully understand the weapons involved in "Strategic Arms," and the problems unique to each, in developing parity between the superpowers.

• • •

ZUMWALT: On chart number five, I show you how I believe we can provide the kind of power that can help you. I'd like to talk about it. There's nuclear standoff, as Admiral Moorer has discussed, and we hope it will continue into the future, preferably through a successful SALT, but if not, then through increased expenditures in strategic weaponry. But the standoff means that nuclear power is not a useful instrument; it's just a necessary umbrella. And assuming the balance holds, the power which resolves issues will be appropriate conventional capability. My —

NIXON: Before we go on at this point, let me interject one thought here. Mel, I noticed something in which Smith, where he's gone off about the zero-ABM thing. Now, I understand, the Chiefs are all opposed.

LAIRD: Mr. President, the Chiefs —

NIXON: Zero ABM, as I — a zero-ABM deal, period. Is that right, Henry? Is that what we're looking at?

KISSINGER: Well, what Smith wants to do is to slide in zero ABM for —

NIXON: For what?

KISSINGER: For the ABM portion of the May 20 agreement.

NIXON: Right.

KISSINGER: And without changing any of the offensive understandings that were reached. And that is what the Chiefs are opposed [unclear] —

LAIRD: We are opposed. And the Chiefs and Defense are opposed, Mr. President. If you go to zero, then you've got to change the offensive —

NIXON: Yeah.

LAIRD: — mix that we've already offered.

NIXON: Spend a second on that. I mean, when I say a second I mean whatever time you need. I didn't mean to interrupt. I just — we started talking about it assuming we have a SALT agreement. Let's see what you're talking about. Why — what is the argument? Why is zero ABM worse than [unclear] the National Command Center, and two Minutemen, and what have you? What's your view on this?

LAIRD: Mr. President —

NIXON: I think I know, but I just wanted to be sure I've heard you.

LAIRD: From a military standpoint, it is difficult to defend the two-site proposal.

NIXON: Right.

LAIRD: The two-site proposal can be defended on the basis that it can be expanded for a twelve-site program.

NIXON: Right.

LAIRD: We have tabled a proposition in SALT, which gives the Soviet certainly an advantage as far as the long term is concerned on the offensive weapons systems. If we were to give up the capability, which we have, to go into a defensive system on down the road, by going to zero at this time, without opening up the offensive proposition that we have put on the table in the SALT talks, I believe it would be — endanger our security planning. And so the position of the Chiefs and the position that I've taken is that: no, do not table the zero at this time, unless you're willing also at the same time to make a reduction as far as the offensive limitations are concerned —

KISSINGER: Then, if you do that, you are — the May 20 thing is down the drain.

NIXON: That's right.

KISSINGER: And we are right back to where we started from last January with the comprehensive negotiations —

LAIRD: It depends. Henry, it depends on what date you attach to the May 20 operation.

KISSINGER: Well —

ZUMWALT: And whether or not in the offensive side you put into it an automatic date by which you have freedom to make it if they happen to come to a problem.

NIXON: Right. But —

KISSINGER: But then, what this will lead us to, if it's a possible way of going, is towards the comprehensive agreement in which all the offensive and defensive weapons are included. What we had attempted to do on May 20 was to make an ABM limitation and a temporary offensive limitation which could act as a bridge to a more comprehensive one. So, what Mel is proposing could be incorporated in the second stage of the negotiation. That is to say, we could then keep the zero ABM for the second stage of the negotiation and couple it with offensive reductions. I agree with the Chiefs and with Mel. I think, however, that if we want a rapid agreement, we've got to stick with the May 20 framework.

NIXON: Do you agree we should stay with the May 20 —?

LAIRD: Yes. But, I had some problems in that —

[unclear exchange]

NIXON: That's all right. Take your time.

LAIRD: I had some problems, Mr. President, with the date that's been used in the — this and seventeenth, and this and twentieth, because it does give the Soviet Union, if this becomes the only agreement we have — and we have to look at it from the standpoint that we might not get anything else — it gives them an opportunity of having a superior force in '74 and '75. And I don't want to be around to see the Soviet Union ever be in a position of superiority. I can accept parity, but I think that this particular proposition, if we don't follow through on something else, gives them the opportunity for superiority. I think that's the position of the Chiefs, too.

MOORER: That's right. And that's what'll happen if the interim agreement turns out to be the final agreement. I don't know, sir—

KISSINGER: But there is a provision, which is that if there is no permanent agreement, the whole thing becomes subject to abrogation after a year—

LAIRD: But, Henry, my problem is this: that I think it's going to be most difficult for the United States to set aside the agreement. I think it's easier for the Soviet Union to set aside an agreement because of the manner of our whole system of government is so much—it's much more difficult for us to set aside the agreement than it is for the Soviet Union.

NIXON: Well, the difficulty with zero ABM—it's just a simple point. Zero ABM, plus a freeze, basically—and that's what it is on their offensive thing—means that we freeze, in terms of ourselves, into an inferior position, both ways.

ZUMWALT: That's correct—

NIXON: That's correct. Right? That's why—

ZUMWALT: In both segments.

NIXON: That's right. So, that is why we can under no circumstance let Smith continue, Henry, on that line.

KISSINGER: I agree.

NIXON: Make that clear to him—

KISSINGER: I'll get a message to him—

NIXON: He must. See that he does. That was never the understanding. We are not gonna freeze ourselves. We can always be: "Well, that's all right. We won't have any ABM." But you look at those charts, we're already inferior, except in numbers, of course, of weapons, and it's because of MIRVing—which we may have, basically, four or five years, if somebody doesn't knock that out. So, we don't want to freeze right now. Right? Is that right?

LAIRD: Mr. President—

[unclear exchange]

KISSINGER: We don't want to have zero ABM.

NIXON: [unclear] Exactly. If you have zero ABM, in the context of the May 20 deal, we are freezing ourselves into a second position, an inferior position. Right?

LAIRD: That's right.

MOORER: And I might add, sir, we are increasing the numbers where we have a lead in technology.

NIXON: Exactly. Go ahead, Admiral.

ZUMWALT: Yes, sir. So, my shorthand term for this appropriate conventional power is "relevant power." On chart six, I show you examples of where I believe—power was held and used successfully, or was relevant. In the left-hand column, and this is—those were successful. Sea power includes the Marines, of course, with their three-division air wing teams. We could add appreciably to the list on the left. The list on the right is shorter because decision makers normally calculate the expected outcome, and hence they find other paths or back down, and these three catch you here. And any president's options will, of course, depend on whether he possesses the relevant power.

Now, on chart number seven, I show you how I think relevant power is shifting. In line one, for example, the term "threat nuclear attack," and the "X" under the column entitled "strategic nuclear forces," shows these forces were exclusively relevant in the fifties and sixties. As discussed, the nuclear balance now makes this threat unlikely, although in ending World War II, and President Truman's threat to Stalin to get him out of Iran, they were relevant.

Lines two to four show Europe. The shift in the threats on the NATO center in the fifties and sixties—line two. To NATO northern and southern flanks—lines three and four. The greater stability in the center is due to the perceived linking of nuclear weapons to conventional forces, to unrest in the Warsaw Pact, to Russia's concern about the Chinese Communist border forces. The instability on the NATO flanks is due to Soviet flanking movements, increased strength of the Soviet fleet. I've just come back from a seven-country trip through central and northern Europe. I found not only the chiefs of navy, but the chiefs of defense staff, of all of those countries had that perception, and in many cases, the ministers of defense. In essence, they see Finland becoming a Latvia, Sweden becoming a Finland, and Norway, within five years, becoming a Sweden.

• • •

ZUMWALT: Now, what is the military situation? In chart ten, I'll compare the U.S. and the Soviet forces, and discuss how we've allocated them. With regard to chart eleven, Admiral Moorer has discussed those, and I'll just point out that in the slide on the right, with the graph on the right, a significant fraction of that MIRV increase is due to the Polaris/Poseidon. On that, those forces, in essence, represent the prestrike lineup. Now, on chart number twelve, I show you the total—

NIXON: Right there, can I just ask one, one question? Are those Titans working well?

RYAN: Yes, sir. The first three have deployed—

NIXON: Yeah?

RYAN: They're highly reliable. The test results looked like it's a real beauty.

NIXON: In fact, the only—the only positive thing on all these charts that Admiral Moorer showed us—which I was surprised, frankly—is the warhead deal. But that's MIRV isn't it? Well, incidentally, the jackasses have been trying to get us to stop MIRV, and that's worse than stopping ABM. Right, Mel?

LAIRD: It is.

[unclear exchange]

NIXON: Interestingly enough, Henry, why in the — why is it that the Soviet isn't interested in stopping MIRV?

UNIDENTIFIED SPEAKER: Because they're going to [unclear] —

UNIDENTIFIED SPEAKER: Well, because of throw-weight —

UNIDENTIFIED SPEAKER: They've got that huge SS-9.

[laughter]

UNIDENTIFIED SPEAKER: It's because of the throw-weight of the SS-9. They could put a hell of a lot of MIRVs up on top of —

KISSINGER: Because they're behind us.

[unclear exchange]

NIXON: And also, it looks like, like they want to develop the capability, too. They figured that we've —

UNIDENTIFIED SPEAKER: They already have the development program.

MOORER: No doubt about it, sir, they're going to —

NIXON: They may be MIRVed already, you think?

MOORER: No, sir.

NIXON: We don't — we don't know for sure?

LAIRD: Well, we think they probably have multiple reentry vehicles —

NIXON: Yeah.

LAIRD: — on a few SS-9s. But I don't like to get into the debate of whether they're independently targeted or not. But they will have that capability, Mr. President, within the 1972–73 time period.

NIXON: Let me ask Dave [Packard] a question. Dave, looking at this from a, you know, the scientists, and all the rest. I mean, you know, we've been around the track on ABM, and MIRV, and so forth. But, you really — it would seem it's rather interesting that there's always these issues that stir the people up. It's hard to realize it. About a year ago, eighteen months ago, it was MIRV; everybody squealing about MIRV, you know, "We got to stop MIRV." What do you think of — MIRV is, wouldn't you say, is almost indispensable in view of — in view of the fact that they have so much of that throw-weight? The advantage that we have, whatever advantage that we have, has got to be maintained by the MIRVing of the system.

PACKARD: Oh, I think it does, Mr. President, unless —

NIXON: And, as I understand, it works. Okay? Well, let's —

PACKARD: Mr. President, let me suggest some agreement to reduce the total number of delivery vehicles, so that they are roughly equal.

NIXON: Yeah.

PACKARD: The MIRV is the one significant advantage we have. Let me just say a word for —

RYAN: Minuteman —

PACKARD: — General Ryan's —

[unclear exchange]

PACKARD: — Minuteman III. I just looked at that program. That's the MIRV program —

NIXON: Right.

PACKARD: — that the air force had. That force has better readiness than the previous Minuteman, and the improved accuracy gives each one of the Minuteman III warheads, of which there are three, each one of these warheads has as much probability to kill a hard target as one of the large Minuteman I warheads.

NIXON: Hmm.

PACKARD: So, we have provided a significant improved capability with that program, and that's the one advantage we have against that numbers imbalance, and I look at this MIRV program as being one of the only balances we have. It was put in originally as a hedge against ABM, but I think it has to be looked at in terms of the balance against their increased capability, and also as giving us more flexibility in terms of targets we can cover with the Chinese — the China situation buildup. So, I would consider that to be a very important program, and we should not give it up under any conditions.

AGNEW: Mr. President, may I ask a question?

NIXON: Ask it. Sure.

AGNEW: The — I raised this question before. I'm not sure I understood the answer. If you've got an offensive limitation on delivery vehicles, based on the megatonnage, throw-weight capability that they have, wouldn't, in time, through their technological improvement and their ability to MIRV, wouldn't they, then, far outstrip us without violating the agreements?

ZUMWALT: It depends on how many MIRVs they can put into the SS-9. We, for example, put ten into the Polaris —

NIXON: You put ten into the Polaris?

ZUMWALT: Yes, sir. We can put fourteen; we're only putting ten —

NIXON: Phew —

ZUMWALT: So that there's ten to fifteen [unclear]. The intelligence estimate says three for the SS-9. I believe they ought to be able to get twenty in, if they get our technology.

AGNEW: Looking ahead to the technological development of, Leonard [Chapman], how proficient we've become, we still have that question of throw-weight, though, and, eventually, as silos become harder, so that throw-weight is going to mean something different than it does. Shouldn't we be thinking more about limiting throw-weights than delivery vehicles, for instance?

CHAPMAN: No, this is why —

NIXON: They won't play.

CHAPMAN: This is one of the reasons why —

LAIRD: But this is one of the reasons that, that we're concerned about this. But, I also think that it should be borne out and kept in mind, that, with our research and de-velopment program, which is so important, I think we can still keep ahead of them. There is a lot more we can even do with the Minuteman at the site as far as getting it even more accurate —

UNIDENTIFIED SPEAKER: At a small price —

LAIRD: — and we can do it at a very small price, because we have the technological capability that far outstrips the Soviet Union. This is important to maintain this leadership.

NIXON: Let me say this, and I think this is the — this is important [unclear] of course, the big budget things won't come up. The one place that, again, those of you with proficiency in this area — that I think we've really got to, got to prepare the forces is in improving our technological capability. Now, within the May 20 deal, that is allowed, right, Henry?

KISSINGER: That's right.

NIXON: Both sides. Now, this is one place where we ought to do better. We have to, I mean, in terms of a higher standard, in terms of computers and all that sort of thing. That's one of the reasons the Soviets are concerned. We are better in this, are we not?

PACKARD: Yes, that's correct, Mr. President.

NIXON: And I feel that's the place where research and development, R&D — not only in R&D, but of application, and so forth, where technological breakthroughs may be the answer.

UNIDENTIFIED SPEAKER: For increased accuracy —

[unclear exchange]

UNIDENTIFIED SPEAKER: Increased accuracy is the —

[unclear exchange]

NIXON: Exactly. One of the things — we talk about these huge weapons, and — but one that is — I mean, after all, the bang of one-tenth — of one-tenth of a Polaris is a hell of a bang. Right?

ZUMWALT: That's right.

NIXON: If it's accurate —

PACKARD: It's as accurate as it can be made —

ZUMWALT: It is — it's easily within —

NIXON: It's like — it's like hitting with a shotgun or a rifle —

PACKARD: That's right.

NIXON: A shotgun may scar a guy up pretty good, but the rifle pierces his heart.

PACKARD: But you run into the people —

NIXON: Yeah?

PACKARD: — who claim, "Look, you're improving the accuracy. It gives you a first-strike capability." And, if that's developed —

[unclear exchange]

PACKARD: — we've got — had got a hell of a lot of flak on that.

NIXON: I know. I know. But you see, the point that I've been — I think we have to, we have to make — there's a real fight to be sure that on the — on that area, we do not, at this time, just talking about any kind of a SALT agreement, and so forth, that we go gung-ho on the accuracy side, because that is unlimited. Right, Henry?

KISSINGER: That's right. And when we were discussing the strategic planning vis-à-vis China, one problem we had is that you can't use the Minuteman against China — because it will have to overfly the Soviet Union. So, if we want to use — and against China, we do have a substantial preemptive capability for the next ten, fifteen years. So, with that, we have to use planes or Polarises. But Poseidons have — therefore, accuracy is absolutely essential.

NIXON: How long do we have a preemptive capability with China, you think?

KISSINGER: We've said about fifteen — ten, fifteen years.

MOORER: [unclear] twenty-five missiles.

KISSINGER: Yeah. Yeah. And that's something that we should —

NIXON: And that preemptive capability depends upon Polarises and planes —

PACKARD: Aircraft, too. See, you can't get it to China without overflying Russia —

NIXON: Yeah.

[unclear exchange]

NIXON: [unclear] This is where your aircraft becomes even more relevant.

ZUMWALT: Flexibility in the air.

NIXON: But, more relevant, really, than they are with the Soviet [unclear] —

KISSINGER: And also, I don't believe — well, most people don't believe — that the Poseidons are going to be very effective, no matter how accurate, against very hard Soviet silos. But they ought to be able to knock out anything the Chinese have —

NIXON: Yeah.

KISSINGER: — for the foreseeable future.

ZUMWALT: Well, if we get stellar-inertial guidance, we can get down under a thousand feet and become highly accurate. So, your, your guidance there will —

NIXON: Well, go ahead, Admiral. We interrupted you.

ZUMWALT: The last thing I want to say about strategic, Mr. President, is chart twelve. This chart shows that using the surface forces [unclear] February of '71. Over on the right, the costs — twenty-two percent of the strategic budget of the years '73 through '77, will provide, in the three ballistic missile forces, the capability to deliver forty-three percent of the equivalent megatonnage and seventy-three percent of the independently targeted weapons, as a result of the very high capability of the Poseidon.

Now, on chart thirteen, I show you just four of ten charts that I showed last year, which depict a continuing change in conventional balance. In the upper left, the two hundred thirty-seven percent shows you that they continue over a five-year period to out-build us at the rate of about two and a half in most categories of ships. In the upper right, their missile platforms have increased fourfold in ten years. In the lower left, they over — they've overtaken us in numbers of merchant ships, and will in deadweight tonnage shortly. And over in the lower right, there, theirs are new and ours are old.

NIXON: This is all U.S., and not — not with the British, and all the rest added in. Right?

ZUMWALT: That is correct, sir —

NIXON: Only U.S. versus USSR.

ZUMWALT: However, I will be showing you outcomes of —

NIXON: Right.

ZUMWALT: — that on the next page. The most worrisome thing of all is their continued submarine force. This shows you their attack boats, without the missile boats, a threefold superiority. They have more nuclear boats than we do, and in 1973, they will have more nuclear boats than the total number of diesel and attack boats that we have. More honest still, the lower graph shows you that their noise levels are rapidly catching up with ours.

NIXON: We're doing better though?

ZUMWALT: Yes, sir. We reckoned we could kill five to one in the sixties. It's down to something like two to one now. If they're building twelve per year, we're building five per year, so they're overtaking us.

• • •

ZUMWALT: The temptation for the Soviets to hold out for a better and better deal on SALT, and the pressures on you to settle for a lesser and lesser deal on SALT, and MBFR, and in the Mideast, are getting great. There is decreasing inclination on the part of Moscow and Beijing, with this '73 budget, to work with us to resolve the conflict in Southeast Asia, or to follow up on any initiatives you take after your trip to Communist China.

"We kick the Russians in the teeth — and they invite us."

August 11, 1971, 9:15 a.m.
Richard Nixon, Bob Haldeman, and Henry Kissinger
OVAL OFFICE

While reviewing 1971's developments in foreign affairs, Nixon discussed Kissinger's contributions with Haldeman, and then all three talked about the shifts they'd already witnessed. Nixon candidly spoke of what he thought were the successes of his bold style. He also lambasted many of the ranking officials of his administration.

• • •

KISSINGER: They're having three-day sessions on Berlin. [The Four Powers met from August 10 through August 23 at the Allied Control Council building in West Berlin to negotiate the final terms of the Quadripartite Agreement.]

NIXON: Who? State?

KISSINGER: No, no. The Four Powers. And it's — the problem is to get the French [laughs] —

NIXON: Hmm?

KISSINGER: — from shutting up long enough so that the Russians can make the concessions which are already agreed to. We have a text. It's all agreed to. But we have to go through a —

NIXON: Yeah.

HALDEMAN: You go through the ritual so the French will keep quiet.

NIXON: Yeah.

KISSINGER: We're going through the ritual. We have a script in which the Russians make extreme demands and then yield.

• • •

NIXON: Henry, how much have you talked to Bob about the other thing? Did you just mention it to him?

KISSINGER: I just hinted — I mentioned it to him in passing. I haven't —

NIXON: Well, did you talk about the meeting?

KISSINGER: On walk — going into the boat yesterday evening. [Nixon and Kissinger had dinner aboard the presidential yacht *Sequoia*.] You mean the Russian thing?

NIXON: Yeah.

KISSINGER: I haven't given him any of the details about it.

NIXON: You mean, about it — but you keep hinting to him about the possibility of a meeting?

KISSINGER: Yeah.

NIXON: A summit or something of that sort?

KISSINGER: Yeah.

NIXON: Yeah. Yeah. The reason I wanted to get you in, Bob, was to emphasize that, probably, ten times as important as keeping the Chinese thing secret, this must be secret. Now, this means Ehrlichman. It means, obviously, Peterson. It, of course, means Scali. It, naturally, means Ziegler. But it particularly means — let me say: I don't want you to break over — the only one that I'm sure you'd even be tempted to ever mention it to would be Ehrlichman, because he's so —

HALDEMAN: I don't mention any of these to anybody.

NIXON: I know. I know. I know. What I meant is, though — incidentally, we got to go further. It means John Mitchell.

HALDEMAN: Right.

NIXON: It means John Connally.

HALDEMAN: Right.

NIXON: Naturally, if we just mention it to either of those, and you haven't told Agnew, he gets pissed off. Now, what is involved here is that, in essence, is that the Soviet have replied — replied in a very positive, simple note. Henry's going to meet with Dobrynin — when?

KISSINGER: Next Tuesday, after I'm back from Paris.

NIXON: The purpose is to — he's got — the purpose is to set the date. And the date of the meeting we've decided upon will be between May — May 20 to June 1.

HALDEMAN: End of May.

NIXON: So the Soviet meeting's set. And they've offered May or June, did they not?

KISSINGER: That's right.

NIXON: So we — that would fit in perfectly then. I wouldn't mind having it — the later in May, the better, in my opinion.

KISSINGER: I agree.

NIXON: The date, May 25, May 27 — something like that. It's just —

KISSINGER: My [unclear] —

NIXON: If you could even start it on May 28 and finish June 3 or something, that would be all right. Do you understand?

KISSINGER: Right.

NIXON: Because then you have — it's a good time. The weather's a little better and all that crap. Now, whatever you want, but if they want it a little sooner, that's fine. Now —

HALDEMAN: Do you care at all about coincidence with primaries? In other words, do you want to look at that in any of that context?

NIXON: I think it's — that's always irrelevant.

HALDEMAN: Well —

KISSINGER: I think California —

HALDEMAN: — except for the way it's going to be played. The California primary is clearly going to be the primary. It's the first Tuesday in June.

NIXON: Yeah, but that's — what day is it?

HALDEMAN: I don't know. I'd have to look — get it now.

NIXON: Yeah. Well, do you think we'll run right into it?

HALDEMAN: Oh, that's the thing. Whether you want it — we ought to at least consider whether you want to run into it or whether —

NIXON: Or not. These are bigger than China in March now — bigger, Henry. They're earlier in March.

KISSINGER: Yeah. First —

HALDEMAN: June 6 [the California primary election].

NIXON: Well, that's fine.

KISSINGER: I think —

NIXON: No, no, that's too late.

KISSINGER: I think it's a mistake, Mr. President. When we've told the Chinese we — the Chinese, after all, first asked us for —

NIXON: It must be in May. All right, fine. We've got to have it in May. So we'll work it out in May. And the other one, you figure March for —

KISSINGER: I thought any time in the first ten days of March.

HALDEMAN: Then you got the other — the other big primaries will be next year in Florida and Wisconsin, which are [in] March and April.

NIXON: Well, you said we were heading in there in April.

HALDEMAN: Afterward.

NIXON: All right.

KISSINGER: Well, if you go from around —

NIXON: March?

KISSINGER: If you go in the first week of March to Beijing, that runs into the campaigning in New Hampshire.

NIXON: Well, the campaigning in New Hampshire itself is really all February and part of March. But we can't say that we're not going to go anyplace until April.

KISSINGER: No, no. That's good. I mean, it blankets the — if the trip —

HALDEMAN: Yeah, but there's some advantage to not blanketing the Democratic campaign for one thing.

NIXON: Well —

HALDEMAN: There's also the question of whether you get charged with the cheap shot of trying to blanket it by taking your trip.

NIXON: No, we should not take it — no, I've deliberately worked it out so we would not take either one on the day of a primary.

HALDEMAN: Right.

• • •

KISSINGER: Now, what date should I give the Chinese? This is important because —

NIXON: When is the date of the [Florida] primary? Fourteenth?

KISSINGER: Oh, I'm sorry.

HALDEMAN: It's another [unclear] —

KISSINGER: Because, now, we have to play it differently. The original idea was not to give them a date until I'd been in Beijing — to have that hanging over their heads. But now that we've got to make the announcement with the Russians in September —

HALDEMAN: You have to announce Russia in September?

KISSINGER: Well, my worry is this: if we tell the Russians we agree now, but we'll announce it in December, which was the original game plan —

NIXON: No, no —

KISSINGER: — and then I go to Beijing before —

NIXON: Well, yeah.

KISSINGER: — it will look like a transparent slap in the face.

HALDEMAN: Yeah.

KISSINGER: That we're running —

NIXON: But when you got something, use it.

HALDEMAN: On television, the Chinese —

NIXON: When you got something, use it.

KISSINGER: So the way to handle the Chinese is to do it — if you agree, Mr. President, what I thought I would do on Monday is say this: we're willing to set the date, whichever we agree on here —

NIXON: Right.

KISSINGER: — and give it to them. But we'd like to announce it only after I've been to Beijing.

NIXON: Don't you think that we should give them a choice?

KISSINGER: Yeah, I'd give them a range of days.

NIXON: Yeah.

KISSINGER: Then, secondly, I'd say, "Now, you remember I told the prime minister —"

NIXON: "I told you it should go in order — the president's the very first to come."

KISSINGER: Yeah. I told him, and I'll tell them that I've —

NIXON: For maybe four days?

KISSINGER: Yeah.

NIXON: For talking, we need a week in China.

KISSINGER: I think you'll need four days in Beijing. And then —

NIXON: To talk.

KISSINGER: Yeah.

NIXON: Yeah, I'd say a week. That we're — a week to one —

KISSINGER: And I think if they, for example —

NIXON: The translation problems. You see, the visits to both Russia and China take twice as much time to accomplish — first of all, there's more to talk about. Second, they take twice as much time because of the enormous translation problem.

KISSINGER: And you don't want to put yourself through what I did.

NIXON: Yeah.

KISSINGER: It was necessary in my case, but it's too dangerous for a president to be talking —

HALDEMAN: Going all night.

KISSINGER: — ten hours a day. I mean, because if you make a slip —

HALDEMAN: Except that's the way they do these things.

NIXON: Well, but —

KISSINGER: Well, but —

HALDEMAN: Well, the point is that the Chinese —

NIXON: Yeah, we'll see.

KISSINGER: But we can break that up.

NIXON: But we won't — it will be better, better handled than that.

KISSINGER: At any rate, what I would propose to tell them, Mr. President, is — give them this date. We'll set the time for my trip to Beijing. But, I'll remind them of the fact that I told Zhou Enlai, and you said in your press conference, that whenever a negotiation reaches a certain point — that we had already accepted before I had been there — that, under those conditions, we'd go to Moscow.

NIXON: Yeah.

KISSINGER: Now, it looks as if Berlin is coming to a point. Thank God, it is.

NIXON: Yeah.

KISSINGER: And I can't tell them [the Chinese] yet whether it will or will not. But, if it does, if they then extend the invitation, we can't refuse it, except that we will do it two or three months after we've been there, and we'll give them a week's warning —

NIXON: But we will have — we will announce it, but we — our trip will be three months after their trip.

KISSINGER: Right. But I won't tell them, yet, that it's set. I'll tell them we'll let them know five days or a week ahead of time if we do announce it. I don't think it — I want to give them a full week.

NIXON: No.

KISSINGER: Besides, I've got to tell them you're going to see the emperor of Japan, too, which they won't like.

NIXON: Yeah. Just a courtesy. They'll understand that.

• • •

NIXON: Put yourself in the position they are in. Bill [Rogers] and his people over there, naturally, are proud men, and they're intelligent men, and the rest. They do like to think they run foreign policy. They don't, and they're just finally learning it. Because in every major decision, they have either been against it or don't know about it. They didn't do SALT. They didn't do Cambodia and Laos. And they were very glad not to do it. They had no influence on our whole — they peed, you know, on all of our programs. Take the Jordan thing. Christ, they didn't do anything but screw that one up.

KISSINGER: And then there's Cienfuegos, for which we've never gotten any credit.

NIXON: As a matter of fact — as a matter of fact — Cienfuegos? Christ, did they do anything about it? Hell no.

KISSINGER: They fought like hell.

NIXON: We have played a very goddamn tough, skillful game here. It'll come out sometime. And I don't mind Bill now and then getting a little of this. But, Bob, we're not going to let State put out any line that they pushed me into something. Now that would be a very bad thing —

HALDEMAN: Yeah.

NIXON: — to be in the press. Do you agree, Henry?

KISSINGER: Oh, yes, and that's what the liberals would like. They need some guy who made you do these things.

NIXON: Yeah.

KISSINGER: We've avoided this on China. There's no one — that hasn't been written at all.

NIXON: Well, this is being said. It will be —

KISSINGER: Yeah, but it hasn't happened yet. And I think this one ought to be positioned as your initiative —

NIXON: Yeah.

KISSINGER: — growing out of —

NIXON: Well, Henry, I can understand —

KISSINGER: I can background it —

NIXON: But let me say that I — you can do the backgrounder as you should, but, in a very curious way, even though it is, on reflection, a little embarrassing at the moment, I backgrounded it a bit when I mentioned that we discussed the matter with Gromyko.

KISSINGER: Hmm.

NIXON: They know damn well —

KISSINGER: But I thought we could tie it back to —

NIXON: And did you know — and we remembered too late — the day we were across the street, and we talked about it a little and so forth, that day we had a long discussion and we decided then that there should be one in principle?

KISSINGER: That's right. That's why we ought to hold the announcement tight. Once it's made, we can background it the way we backgrounded the China thing.

NIXON: Yeah.

KISSINGER: Tying it back to your moves over two years.

NIXON: That's right.

KISSINGER: And I think we can get the same sort of stories again. Not as dramatic, because — but still enough people will write it.

NIXON: Well, but I think when you play down the dramatic, we may be thinking a little too small here. I knew the China thing would be big because of the land of mystery. But the reason this is dramatic is that a trip [to the Soviet Union] would not have occurred to unsophisticated people. The reason this is dramatic is that so many, though, of the smart people have said, "The China thing makes the Russians mad."

KISSINGER: Of course, the —

NIXON: "Now, the Russians, we have a terrible problem in our foreign policy." Here we kick the Russians in the teeth — and they invite us. So it shows enormous hope on the big problems. Now, I don't think the Russian — I mean, the Russian thing is going to be one hell of a story.

KISSINGER: Well, you're changing the whole approach to foreign policy, because all the wise guys, the people who told you, "ABM will kill SALT" — that's been proved wrong. "Go to Beijing, it will drive the Russians crazy." That's been proved wrong. "If you play it tough in Jordan, there will be a war." The opposite was true. It ended the war.

NIXON: Well, they're —

KISSINGER: No, I think the record in foreign policy next year is going to be —

NIXON: Well, hold on. One more. We've got two out of three now.

KISSINGER: I —

NIXON: And we always said there were three. The two is pretty good.

KISSINGER: Well, Mr. President, if I were in Hanoi now, this is not a brilliant position for them. They've got their — I don't think either Brezhnev or Mao wants them to screw it all up.

HALDEMAN: Will they give you a signal on that before you go over this week, do you think?

KISSINGER: No.

HALDEMAN: Will the Russians signal what — not on the trip, but on what their position ought to be?

KISSINGER: No, they may wait till November. But, in my view, they'll accept it either now or — by next spring, I think we'll be — we'll have to meet before we go on these trips.

• • •

[KISSINGER leaves the conversation.]

NIXON: They [the Department of State leaders] do not think big. Henry is, I mean, he's probably a little off the wall, and I know that in these NSC meetings, I am too at times. The earlier ones we've had. Henry and I would take, we both talk about long-range strategy and philosophy and so forth. And Bill gets very impatient with this philosophy. In all honesty, what are we going to do, he says. He doesn't understand that you must not talk about what you're going to do outside of a framework of philosophy. You've got to talk philosophy; you've got to be a great mosaic and you put in the pieces.

And State is not thinking in mosaic terms. The Communists do. The Chinese do, the Russians do. We must. The British used to. They don't anymore, because they aren't a power anymore. And the British are only thinking about how much they're going to get and whether or not whipped cream goes with their strawberries, going to be higher or less and that sort of thing. They're down to the piddling little goddamn things which are not worthy of a parliament. But that's all they've got to talk about. But we've got big things to talk about, and we're going to play it. But on Bill, we'll handle it well.

"All that is needed is to close the gold window. That stops the crisis, right?"
August 12, 1971, 5:30 p.m.
Richard Nixon, John Connally, and George Shultz
EXECUTIVE OFFICE BUILDING

When Vice President Richard Nixon lost his 1960 presidential bid to Senator John F. Kennedy by the narrowest of margins, some encouraged Nixon to challenge the result. While he did not do so, there was plenty of blame to go around for Nixon's loss. There were charges of corruption in Cook County, Illinois, and various South Texas counties that had a history of voting irregularities. Some thought Eisenhower did not do enough to support

Nixon. Some blamed the candidate himself, especially after Nixon looked pale and tired during the televised debates against the tanned and handsome Kennedy.

Nixon believed some of the blame belonged to the Eisenhower-appointed Federal Reserve, which did not do enough to help the nation out of a mild recession that occurred in the run-up to the 1960 election. The recession handed the Kennedy campaign an easy issue: Kennedy critiqued Nixon and the Republican Party as no longer being the party of prosperity. The issue fueled Nixon's resentment of the Fed, which carried into his presidency. Nixon clashed with Chairman of the Federal Reserve Board Arthur Burns on numerous occasions, delayed appointing board replacements, and threatened the Fed's traditional independence.

In the summer of 1971, Nixon was faced with the decision about whether to end the gold standard. Something had to be done. The United States had $30 billion in printed dollars and debt in circulation, yet less than $10 billion in gold reserves to pay for this debt. The one-to-one link had been lost more than a decade earlier, but the system depended on the understanding that while in theory dollars could be exchanged for the gold equivalent, the United States did not have enough gold to pay its debt. It was an unstable system, but it was how the system had always worked. Some economists predicted global depression if the system were ended.

Disconnecting the world's currency—the U.S. dollar—from a stable commodity like gold was a test of our faith in capitalism and the free market. With untethered currency, there would be no limit on growth, but also no limit on losses. Nixon feared making any decision without the consensus of his economic advisors, especially considering that the decision took place little more than a year before the 1972 elections. If this decision went wrong, it could mean losing another election over economic policy. Therefore, what Nixon decided to do was a combination of actions that addressed the problem of gold, but—in case anything went terribly wrong—also contained protectionist elements that could allow the government to intervene and restabilize the economy.

On August 15, 1971, Nixon severed the link between the dollar and gold, a first experiment at "floating," which has been the norm for major world currencies since 1973. He also announced a ten percent tax on imports to appease labor unions, which largely backed Nixon in 1972. For businesses, Nixon included a business tax credit to encourage businesses to expand and invest. For conservatives, some of whom were not in favor of Nixon's opening to China, he announced a system of wage and price controls. Although universally condemned now, the controls were popular among the "heartland" voters in the Farm and Rust Belts then.

In addition, the Sunday night televised announcement that preempted Bonanza came as a shock to the rest of the world. It was largely a unilateral decision, coordinated by Nixon and his two top economic advisors, John Connally and George Shultz, in the meeting that follows. Some have called Nixon's severing of the link between the dollar and gold the beginning of the global financial system. It was one of the most important economic events since the Great Depression. In the long run it made the nation's economic woes *worse in the late 1970s, but in the short run the decision was popular and contributed to Nixon's landslide election victory in 1972.*

. . .

NIXON: Looking at what we, what is needed now, in order to stop the crisis, if we look at the international monetary thing, all that is needed is to close the gold window. That stops the crisis, right?

CONNALLY: That stops the crisis from our losing assets, but in effect it may create a crisis in terms of the international money markets. It'll leave them in a chaotic state until something else happens, in my judgment.

NIXON: You have to say of course, that when you do this, well the way I had it positioned is that, the way it would be done, and I mean just putting it out, was that you would make an announcement to the effect that because of speculation against the dollar, that the United States was taking action to preserve the dollar, to that effect, and that we were temporarily closing the gold window, and that we would be prepared now to discuss with our major, with nations around the world, the setting up of a new, a better, more stable system, or whatever we want to call it, and that we're prepared to do that. Right, George? Is that the way you would say it?

And then, that sets in motion so that you and Arthur [Burns] — could go have your meeting with five nations, or one, or ten, or fifty, or none. You know what I mean? Frankly, at least you can say you're doing it for the purpose of defending the dollar against speculators, and, and incidentally, I would, if we did just this one thing, I would not have you do it — you should do it, not me, and you should not do it at prime time at night. Those people are — there's no use to stir up a lot of people about things they don't understand. You should do it just in a straight, a brief statement, take questions, and that's it. Now that's the way I would position that.

Then also, you would say that, in Burns, I think you could lift the lid, but we can't lift it up on the wage-price freeze unfortunately, but you could say that, we are going to take actions, that we want to take actions this year, the president will present to the Congress when it returns, and we can say on the budgetary front, put 'em off a little, because you see, if you say it's going to have a wage-price freeze, as you know, then, the cat's out of the bag, they'll all raise their prices, and, we're screwed. So you might throw 'em off on that, that we're going to take action, something of that sort. And then three weeks from now there'll be other — now that's one way to plug it.

Now, the other way to plug it, is to do exactly the reverse. And that is, just to announce now, only to announce, only the wage-price freeze. Just that. That's another way to do it. And then, figuring that that, will, sort of stabilize the, that that might, we should say stabilize the situation, and then, then come up with our legislative package on taxes, on, including the border tax and so forth at a later point, and then if necessary, as necessary, work out your international problem on a negotiated basis, rather than on, unilaterally closing the gold window. Now that's another way you can get at the damn thing.

And of course the third way is to, frankly, to go before we're ready, do it now. The difficulty in going before we're ready is that I, I think they're about the same as we talked about before, and, you've probably had a chance to think about it, too, is that, first that we, we won't do it as well, not nearly as well, in terms of everything we do, in terms of our budget action, in terms of our — well, we can put that off I guess, we can really put our budget and tax action off, we could put that off until the seventh in any event, because that is not essential to this. We, all we have to do in relation to the present crisis is to do the wage and price thing, and presumably the gold window. We ought to do both, I mean to be sure that we deal with it most effectively, we ought to do both of those things.

Now, on the other hand, that misses the great advantage of your program, in the way we put it of one, big, bold, play, that you do the whole damn thing at one time.

CONNALLY: Right.

NIXON: Now, the question is, if we do the whole thing at one time, could we do it now, tonight? I don't think so, no, and you would agree with that. And I don't think we could do it even — well, I guess we could start burning the coal and we could get it by tomorrow night. But I don't see any damn advantage of that, I mean. In my view, if we don't do it tonight, John, then if we're thinking of doing the whole package, what I was thinking we would do, is call the whole working group together, and we could whip up to Camp David tomorrow, and spend Friday, Saturday, and Sunday, and then on Monday, we announce the whole program.

CONNALLY: Right.

NIXON: Now that's one thing we could do, go for the whole ball on Sunday, and on Monday. It's like all these [unclear] because we have this one, we know, we have a good idea what the public reaction will be to everything else, but nobody knows what the public reaction will be to the gold window, I mean, because, frankly, good God the people that are the experts don't know what the hell it ought to be! They —

CONNALLY: I'll make a prediction —

SHULTZ: [unclear]

CONNALLY: I don't think —

NIXON: Go ahead.

SHULTZ: I was going to say, I think that the closing of the gold window and the impact of that has already been taken into account in the marketplaces, and is not going to produce any [unclear]. My [unclear] that there will be a big currency devaluation [unclear] be a gyration of the stock market.

NIXON: All right, John, your turn.

CONNALLY: That's basically my judgment. There's been too much this week, too much written —

NIXON: That we're going to do it.

CONNALLY: It has to come, there's not a question of whether, it's a question of when. There were three stories I just picked up, there were three stories on the editorial page in the *Dallas Morning News* this morning on the gold devaluation, three different stories, one with a question-and-answer stockholders' advice, what does this mean, does this mean to me, you know, and so forth, some woman, who writes the stock market —

NIXON: Oh.

CONNALLY: — and basically she said it's not going to affect you —

NIXON: Sylvia Porter?

CONNALLY: No, it's not Sylvia Porter, someone else, and it's not going to affect you. None of the stories were bad, and all — they're all just in effect —

NIXON: Well, even Hobart Rowen called me!

[laughter]

CONNALLY: Well, they're all predicting, all the professionals think it's coming.

NIXON: That may be one of the reasons everybody's so jittery.

CONNALLY: Well, sure it's why.

NIXON: The professionals are all so jittery.

CONNALLY: Sure it's why it's jittery, that's why it's going to remain jittery. I don't really think we ought to be concerned about that. I think we ought to, primarily be concerned about how you can most effectively convince the American people that you, number one, are aware of your economic problems, number two, that you have thoughtfully considered them not as a piecemeal emergency stopgap measure, but that you have analyzed them in depth, and that you have dealt with them in a substantive manner, and of all of them, I think that's the whole point. I wouldn't consider the Congress too much.

NIXON: No.

CONNALLY: And your impact on the Congress, I wouldn't think about what the reaction of the gold window thing is, that's not going to be the big news. The big news is going to be in the, in what else you do, the wage and price, just as you said a moment ago —

NIXON: That's the big news.

CONNALLY: The wage and price, hell, this is the big news.

NIXON: Oh yeah, that's all the folks are going to care about.

CONNALLY: Sure, that's all they're going to care about. Oh, they won't worry about —

NIXON: They aren't going to analyze something about the tax thing.

CONNALLY: Oh, the businesses will eat the tax up, the investment tax credit. And most people will have to say the problem with doing it piecemeal, and this is what worries me —

NIXON: Yeah.

CONNALLY: The problem of doing it piecemeal is number one, everybody's going to be saying, well what's — he's got to do something else, what comes next?

NIXON: Yeah.

CONNALLY: And beyond that, they start speculating. That everybody starts trying to jump the gun on you, you get a bunch of leaks, you get a bunch of congressmen, and they all want to be holding things to show how smart they are. And they've already proposed a lot of these things. This is what, and I just think you're going to get robbed of a hell of a lot of the impact of it, that's what worries me about it. I agree with you completely that if you could wait until the day before, wait until September 7 to do it, no question whether that's the wise thing to do, no question in my mind that if you do the whole package, the impact will be infinitely greater than the sum of its parts.

NIXON: Okay. The main point is —

CONNALLY: I don't think you can wait that long in terms of the international money market. We've lost since August, in the twelve days in August, they, the foreign governments have acquired over three billion dollars.

NIXON: Yeah.

CONNALLY: And when we consider our three billion six hundred and ninety-four million dollars, just since the last twelve days. Today was a billion-dollar day, tomorrow might be three billion. We could ride it out, but when you consider what debts we have and the —

NIXON: Well, let me ask you this, John, just so we can see what our options are, in terms of doing it all in one package, and what you prefer. Let me see if I get your thinking correct. You believe, you would have doubts about closing the gold window, and then doing the rest of it on September 7. That doesn't sound good to you.

CONNALLY: I don't think it's the best solution.

NIXON: Because you think you'd be nibbled to death in between.

CONNALLY: Yes, I think the net effect of that is, that number one, the impression is that you were forced to do it by what's happened in Europe in the last two weeks. And secondly, that you didn't know what to do, it took you from now, from tomorrow, to September 7 to figure out what to do, and that you were merely reacting. That's the thing that worries me about that.

NIXON: Another way you could do it, to get around that is to say when the Congress returns I will propose something. That's the way you could do it.

CONNALLY: Yes, you could do that, that immediately of course, that immediately starts wild speculation —

NIXON: Correct.

CONNALLY: What's he going to propose? What's it going to contain? And then you've got everybody, you got everybody harassing now with them trying to find out, and everybody's going to be speculating, and, I don't think you should butcher it, which may not be bad, but —

NIXON: No.

CONNALLY: But it is bad, I think it's bad, and frankly, you don't have a good situation. Polls indicate you're taking a whipping on this economic issue, so I don't think we ought to think in terms of a crisis. We're lined up here with six billion dollars. What the hell difference does it make whether we've got six or ten billion, in the final analysis. I'm not worried about that, that doesn't worry me in the least, that's the reason I was thinking we [unclear] pay it out, I couldn't care less. We owe thirty billion, so what, so we can't pay it [unclear], if they call us. That isn't the critical point.

It seems to me the critical point is that enough has been written now to trigger a comprehensive action on your part. I think that's the main point. And the main point you want to come out of this, and I'm being repetitive and redundant here, is that none of this is new to you, that you knew what was happening, you picked a time, and you can just say, "I'd hoped that I might wait, but the situation has reached the point where I think I must say to the nation and the world now what my plan is, or I hope not to reveal this until Congress returns on the eighth, but the situation is such that I think damage would be done to the international monetary stability as well as the domestic economy to wait further. I'm telling you now what my plan is going to be and what I'm going to ask the Congress to do."

I just think that overall it makes you a much wiser person. I think it gives you the initiative again. I think it takes away a lot of the criticism that is going to be heaped on you between now and then, which you can always recoup from, but I don't think it helps to have these polls coming out showing that more and more people think the Democrats are the party of prosperity, and they've got less and less faith in your ability to deal with this economic issue. And we are all looking at that going too long, that you [unclear], how long can you stand it, I'm not going to say that you can't stand it until September, but I'm going to say, though, that we can't go tonight, we're not ready for it, we can't go tomorrow, we're not ready for tomorrow night. We don't have the text, we don't have this type of presentation ready.

SHULTZ: [unclear] I think we could have a good thing [unclear] Camp David.

CONNALLY: Well I agree with that.

NIXON: Well why don't we, it seems to me, George, based on what you say, that, let's come back to Arthur's view. Arthur's view is that we should do it all at once.

SHULTZ: Well, if he had his choice, but his program, to do these domestic-type things, including the border tax, and see if that doesn't handle the gold crisis. Don't close the gold window, and carry on these discussions that are essentially aimed at changing the price of gold.

NIXON: In other words, what I had suggested to you over the phone, John, of doing the whole domestic side and letting the gold — you don't buy that?

SHULTZ: And then, to say —

CONNALLY: Well, I buy it, but I just don't see the point. Hell if you're going to do all this domestic stuff, let's close the gold window, so we don't have the rest of these guys just keep nibbling at us. Because if they keep nibbling, if the announcement of the domestic program doesn't work, then next week you got to close the gold window, and I think that's a —

NIXON: I think he has a point there.

CONNALLY: I think that's a risk you don't have to take.

NIXON: As a matter of fact, George, as we look at your analysis, we really, the gold, we really ought to close the gold window, shouldn't we?

SHULTZ: Sure, I believe as a long-run proposition —

NIXON: That's right.

SHULTZ: — that we ought to close it and keep it closed.

CONNALLY: [unclear]

NIXON: That's what I mean. That's why I —

SHULTZ: Arthur does not agree with that.

CONNALLY: No, but you've got to remember now, Arthur gives a standpoint, Mr. President, of a central banker. He doesn't want to close the gold window. He doesn't —

NIXON: But he said he would support whatever we decided.

SHULTZ: Sure he would.

NIXON: Oh, I'm sure he would.

SHULTZ: I told him that I was just coming over to get an official reading, and that I knew that you would want to talk to him personally before you decided anything. He said [unclear] conversation that he wanted to be involved —

NIXON: Oh, sure, he's got to be involved.

SHULTZ: He is critical to putting [unclear]. He'll support whatever you do.

NIXON: And also, Arthur of course is getting something out of this that he dearly wants, the wage and price freeze. Does he buy that?

SHULTZ: Well, he wants that, but he —

NIXON: Refers to the wage-price board.

SHULTZ: He — no, he thinks the idea of the freeze and the board —

NIXON: Following —

SHULTZ: — coming out of it, fine, and he's very agreeable. He has his ideas, but he's very agreeable.

CONNALLY: What was Paul Volcker's reaction? Did you talk to him?

NIXON: He wants to do the whole ball.

SHULTZ: Well, I think Paul feels that this is D-Day, he said, the way he puts it. And then second, I [unclear] of what he said, but I think he feels the domestic problems [unclear].

NIXON: In other words, he feels that the two have to go together, which of course we all feel, but the question is whether or not it can be separated, separated one from the other. I don't think that'll work.

CONNALLY: What did he say the attitude of the market was this afternoon? The last thing I talked to him, he said it looks like panic. Just, [unclear], it looks like panic in the market, and in the international funds [unclear]. Did he say?

SHULTZ: No, just presumably, the [unclear].

CONNALLY: Yeah, we'd already had the figures, but I got an eval[uation] for [the impact] psychologically [it could cause]. It's hard to determine.

SHULTZ: Well, on the other hand, the stock market went up.

CONNALLY: The stock market went up, yeah.

NIXON: Which, of course, has another — has an effect the other way, even on this side of the thing. You just never know, do you?

CONNALLY: No, Mr. President, after all, this international monetary thing, in a way, it's a mystery, and in a way it isn't a mystery. Now the guy who is the best-informed man in the United States on it is down here. And at some point, you ought to, I think you ought to talk to Paul Volcker yourself, and get a direct feel from him. The [unclear] to the Fed down here, and he'll [unclear] run the country. In terms of the mechanics, I must say his judgment [unclear], but, in the final analysis —

NIXON: Oh, look, I'm not going to talk to him tonight. We all know what his views are, we'll just have to, if we have to bite the bullet, we bite it.

CONNALLY: I don't know that it's that big of a deal. I think ultimately, what you have to do, what is really important in this whole thing, is the impact on the American people, and their reaction to you and what you did, and their reaction to your action. That's the important thing. The international thing, hell, it's going to be in turmoil or a state of turmoil or semi-turmoil from now on. And it has been before. The French franc went through the gold, went through the bottom, the British pound has, the German mark has, the Italian lira has, and the dollar will be up and down. And I just don't think you ought to worry too much about that.

NIXON: Yeah. One point where Volcker, previously, where I disagreed with him. He, like all people, is so tied up in the international thing. He thinks that we should make every sacrifice domestically to save the dollar internationally. I do not agree with that.

CONNALLY: Well, I wouldn't say that's his view, but —

NIXON: Well, he leans more — my view is, John, we've got to look mainly, as you have indicated, too, at the domestic problem. The international problem is going to be here regardless of what we do.

CONNALLY: Well, to put it in perspective, we talk about the balance of payments, Mr. President —

NIXON: Yeah.

CONNALLY: — the balance of payments, the exports from this country, represents four percent of your GNP. So we can't let the tail wag the dog.

NIXON: Exactly.

CONNALLY: Now what's happening in the international markets, frankly, is a reflection of what's happening here at home. You're not to cure it. This is what I've said to you since the outset. There's monetary magic, international monetary magic that's going to solve our problems. Our problems are basically, to the extent that we have them, right here at home. And when they're solved, your international problems are solved, your international trade problems to a large extent are solved, because it's merely a reflection. It just mirrors your economic strength at home, that's all.

NIXON: Well that's good. What I meant, John, one thing that you and I, on a political matter, in talking to the Quadriad, have to remember, is this: our primary goal must be a continued upward surge in the domestic economy. And we must not, in order to stabilize the international situation, cut our guts out here. See what I mean?

CONNALLY: I couldn't agree more.

NIXON: In other words, blood, sweat, and tears, hell no. [laughter] Well, I mean, we'll cut the budget, that isn't a problem, but I mean we're going to, we've got to continue to have an expansive policy in terms of — that's why we're going to have a package for this. That's expansion.

CONNALLY: Well, here's, to put it a different way, let me try to approach it a little different way, the reason why the whole package appeals to me so much. At home, if you have a problem with the conservatives because of the China thing, cutting the budget, these budget cuts are going to be manna from heaven for them.

NIXON: That's why Weinberger agreed with us.

SHULTZ: Yes, sir, he's the guy [unclear].

CONNALLY: Fiscal responsibility is just going to be like opening the gates of heaven to them, to the social conservatives who are critical of your China policy. To the American businessmen, who sit around, they really want to be Republican, but they'll support anybody that they think —

NIXON: Times will be better? Right.

CONNALLY: — is better for them. When you start talking about the investment tax credit, and these other tax actions, they're going to jump up and down and shout hallelujah, whether they're Bohemian Grove, or [unclear] Club, wherever they are. Now, to the average person in the country, this wage and price freeze, to him, means you mean business. You're going to stop this inflation, you're going to try to get control of this economy. Now, if you, when you take all of these actions, you're not going to have anybody out, you're not going to have anybody left out to be critical of you. Again, you're going to have, it seems to me, you're going to have your critics and your opponents fenced off to where they can't really latch onto you.

NIXON: The critics will develop, John, we have to realize, on the administration, the administering of the wage and price son of a bitch.

CONNALLY: Sure.

NIXON: We must have no illusions.

CONNALLY: Sure.

NIXON: But on the other hand, we all know that a great majority of the American people want to go down that road at this moment, so you've got to give them a little whack at it. That's why I told him to do it. See what I mean?

CONNALLY: As soon as the problems get insurmountable in the administration, let go of the damn thing, and follow it with something else. No one, none of us —

NIXON: That's why we have to be ready, that's why I think it's good to have people ready for, say, the idea of the selecting of the major industries that'll come up with George's plan, [unclear] and have the board, we can do pretty well that way. Fortunately, we don't have many labor negotiations coming up next year.

SHULTZ: On the wage-price, it seems to me, a freeze of no longer than 120, perhaps shorter, number of days. I lean towards short [unclear].

NIXON: Right. Well, the shorter it is, the simpler it can be. The longer it is, the more you have to have provisions for equity. But for a short freeze, what the hell, anybody can suffer for 60 days, or 90 days, 120 maybe.

[laughter]

SHULTZ: Then I think there has to be some kind of body to deal with these kinds of problems that John mentions, that eventually can deal with these generalities and spin off the problems that they come up with. If a coal man dealt with the coal problem until the coal problem is over and then that disappears. But if you don't have a permanent structure to deal with —

NIXON: If you continue your [unclear] panel indefinitely —

SHULTZ: If you continue the [unclear] panel, and have by design a notion of something going to business and they go out of it, so that you don't get a bigger structure and get [unclear].

NIXON: Yeah.

SHULTZ: Now, in World War II, they had sixty-three thousand full-time federal employees and another two hundred thousand [unclear] people. They had close to three hundred thousand people in jobs.

[laughter]

NIXON: What I think we should do is this. I think that, after hearing all the possibilities of trying to separate it out, waiting and so forth and so on, which is better to have preparation, in view of what you say, George, about the amount of work you've already done, and, you've done a lot of things, all these people have done, what I mean is, George, you've already done —

CONNALLY: Yes, sir.

NIXON: McCracken's people, see, John, we've put all these people working not knowing what the hell they're working on, and so we've got a little work done. I think we ought to go Monday, with the whole ball. Now, I think, George, it just makes sense, for reasons that, first of all, I think — I don't think it's, [unclear], the way I would do it is that, I would suggest that, and this is one way we can keep it closely held, is just have a meeting in Camp David over the weekend, and have everybody locked up up there. Does that sound all right to you?

CONNALLY: Yes, sir.

NIXON: Is that all right to you?

SHULTZ: Yes.

NIXON: Now, we go, I think we would leave, say, tomorrow afternoon. Whether we can get away, I've got a few, McCracken I guess I'll do tomorrow, I think maybe I'll put that in the NSC meeting, I'll slip that in, all right, [unclear] — well anyway, this is more important. I just don't want to [unclear], to get through that at this point. It's on the national, it's on the budget, defense, in fact, I may even have them come to California to do it [unclear].

Now, as I suggested, do either of you have doubts, do either of you have anything? What I would like to do would be to set the whole thing up. The men that I think should participate, and definitely we will need some staffers, the man from your shop should be—

CONNALLY: Volcker.

NIXON: Well, and whoever else you want. I think Arthur obviously should come, and, I don't, as far as people who participate in the meeting, the only ones who should participate in the meeting now are the three of us plus Arthur, and McCracken, and Peterson. I think Peterson has to be in there, too, because he's been all over this, don't you agree?

SHULTZ: I agree.

NIXON: And he's got some good ideas, too. So those are the people that I want, we'll have basically, the quintuplet people. The five of us will be the meeting. Now, as far as staff people, I would not expand it beyond what is needed. But you can take—you, for example, have to have Weinberger up there, don't you? Well, let me say—

SHULTZ: To deal with the budget thing?

NIXON: Yeah.

SHULTZ: Not necessary.

NIXON: Oh no?

SHULTZ: Not necessary.

NIXON: You can, frankly, just get it from him before he comes [unclear]. Let me say that, and also we don't have to get into the nuts and bolts and that sort of thing. We can just say that we are going to cut it by so much money, including these things, da-da-da-da-da-da! And later on that can come. But, if we get Arthur up there, he may want to bring one man with him. I think having—the fewer we bring the better.

SHULTZ: Arthur can handle it.

NIXON: You—all right, you should have Volcker of course. You need him, right?

CONNALLY: Right.

SHULTZ: Volcker would disapprove, I would say. He knows the mechanics of the monetary system, whatever you may think of his judgment. He knows the mechanics of the system.

NIXON: Who? Volcker?

CONNALLY: No question.

NIXON: Oh, hell yes. Sure, well why we've wanted him over there. He's—

CONNALLY: He's the best man in your government.

NIXON: I think that the three of us, I think we should go up there, and I just think, think we ought to bite the bullet. It does appear that, well let's face it, George, answering my own, I raised this question, not wanting to appear to panic, and that, to do this in a deliberate way. We have been meeting for a long time on this subject, so we're up there over a weekend, and we go over this thing, and I don't think, incidentally, John, that the reason for presenting it, that I would say that I was hoping I could delay.

CONNALLY: Okay.

NIXON: I think I wouldn't be a bit defensive. I think we can just go out and say that we are taking these steps because we think it is time now for the United States to do this, that, and the other thing, da-da-da-da-da-da! Just crack it out there. Very simple, not too much explanation. I'll tell you, the wage-price freeze is going to be so — you see, first of all, as far as the tax things are concerned, you don't have to explain anything, the business guys will all get the message. As far as the budget cut is concerned, you don't have to explain anything, people are going to know that goddamn it, he's cutting the budget.

CONNALLY: That's right.

NIXON: As far as the wage-price freeze is concerned, they're going to say thank God, we've got a wage-price freeze. This isn't something where I think that there should be, the more I think about it, well, a great big long presentation, you know, half-hour speech about the economy and so forth. I don't think that's as good. I think this is something where action, it's like the China announcement, where action is so powerful, the words should be very brief. That's my view, or do you disagree?

CONNALLY: No, I don't disagree with that.

NIXON: See what I mean? We're doing things that are so powerful, and so —

SHULTZ: Combine that with some really —

NIXON: Backgrounder.

SHULTZ: — some good, strong materials for background.

NIXON: Well, the background thing —

SHULTZ: In one of our sessions, John mentioned to me the idea of having a chart —

CONNALLY: Right.

SHULTZ: — that shows the buildup of the liabilities and the decline of the gold —

NIXON: Right. Yeah.

SHULTZ: — and shows this goes way, way back to —

NIXON: That is something, on the other hand, that is something I should not do probably —

CONNALLY: Right.

NIXON: — because it is too complicated, but it is something John should do. I mean, there's where you have, where the experts will then see it and write it.

CONNALLY: The reason you want this background, in detail along these lines, is to show that we've been deteriorating for twenty-five years —

NIXON: Right.

CONNALLY: — and that you're the first president that's had the guts —

NIXON: Yeah.

CONNALLY: — to take this comprehensive —

NIXON: Great.

CONNALLY: — action, because out of this whole thing —

NIXON: Yeah.

CONNALLY: — we want to come, hopefully somebody will say that he not only did move in the international field —

NIXON: Right.

CONNALLY: — moved on the domestic front, moved on the —

NIXON: That I would want to get in my own remarks. I would say that for the past twenty-five years we've seen a gradual deterioration of our position, and we've had this situation, we've had these monetary crises and so forth, and it's time now to call it off. What we're going to do is do these things. First, we're going to close the gold window and we'll be prepared to negotiate about this sort of thing and have a more stable situation. Second, we're going to have an import tax, da-da-da-da. Third, we're going to do this thing.

Now, let's wait a minute here. One thing here. The import tax thing is the question, George, is the legal question that you raised. George has got two different ways, John, that we might be able to do the import tax, without asking the Congress. I'd hate to have the Congress go in there, because they'll put in exceptions and screw it up beyond belief. So he thinks that you might use, he doesn't know, the national security [unclear], or you might use, the GATT provision, but this could only cover those items that remain GATT, and could only mean moving up our duties, like on automobiles it would be six percent.

CONNALLY: That's right.

NIXON: Not bad though.

CONNALLY: Well, we've got this divided opinion on that —

NIXON: Yeah.

CONNALLY: — in Treasury. Within Treasury, we've got two legal opinions, one says you can do it, and the other says you can't. One of 'em's Trading with the Enemy Act going all the way back, that's one way you can do it, to 1917. And the other is, that you can use your authority that was granted under the — let me see the precise title of it —

NIXON: Emergency preparedness —

CONNALLY: Trade agreements, your tariffs —

NIXON: Yeah.

CONNALLY: That's what you're —

NIXON: Yeah, that's George's dealing. I don't understand what that is.

SHULTZ: John is, John Mitchell is working on that now. He may know whether or not he is prepared to give an opinion.

NIXON: Yeah. Well now, let's take that out a bit. Are we — let us suppose, John, we go for Monday, that we say that I am going to ask the Congress for a legislation proposal, an import tax?

SHULTZ: Well, could I —

NIXON: Maybe, if, let me say, if we have to get it to the Congress, I don't think I should say it three weeks before. Get my point?

CONNALLY: Understand.

NIXON: I'm afraid of that. Now, the freeze, you don't have to go to the Congress. Other legislative proposals, no problem, you can just send these to the Congress. But this one — go ahead.

SHULTZ: Two points, I think, on the import tax. One is, that it has the same attributes as the wage-price, in that if people think that might be imposed, they'll import as much as they can beforehand —

NIXON: Yeah.

SHULTZ: — and it'll tend to aggravate the balance of payments for a while.

NIXON: Yeah.

SHULTZ: Now, that has the same —

NIXON: Therefore —

SHULTZ: The second point of this thing is, if you go back again to your point about the connection between the devaluation and the tax, in a sense the tax is a form of devaluation, and —

NIXON: [Gives unrelated instruction on the telephone.]

SHULTZ: The devaluation question and the tax question are closely connected, as you pointed out, the tax is a form of devaluation.

NIXON: Sure, sure.

SHULTZ: So you have the gold, and the float, and will anything happen as a result of that, question mark. And as some time elapses you can find out how much. So then you know more about what you want to do on that. Second, there's the question of what kind of creations take place and what can be done on that score. So that it seems to me there's an argument at least for saying do these things not including the border tax, and let the border tax come along a little later, whether or not you decide you can do it unilaterally or have to do it through the Congress.

NIXON: Well, let me put it this way, let me say this, if we decide that it is too close a question from a legal standpoint to do it unilaterally, then we must not announce it. I think you would agree, John, on Monday, or do you?

CONNALLY: Yes, I would.

NIXON: I do think that the idea that they would pour in the imports and then we would aggravate the balance of payments is probably true, but then we hold that in reserve, and smack that later. But how much does that detract from our package, John?

CONNALLY: Well, quite a bit. What I would do, I would simply say that I'm going to ask the Congress to impose the border tax effective as of today. Congress can always backdate things. They do it on a tax bill. They do it on everything else. You have to assume they are going to act favorably on it. And they certainly will, just say I'm going to, I'm going to ask —

NIXON: What about the budget?

SHULTZ: That would take care of this speculating problem, but I think that it still leaves the question of these interrelationships, and whether or not you can get what you want out of the devaluation, because on the whole, that's a preferable way to do it —

CONNALLY: George is right.

SHULTZ: — [unclear] out of the marketplace.

NIXON: What's that?

CONNALLY: George is right. The two are, that they really, reach toward the same objective. And Paul takes the same position, and George does, really if you're going to have the float, this ought to cure your problems.

NIXON: Yeah.

CONNALLY: You don't need the border taxes. You're trying to reach the same objectives. But I want it to get the devaluation. I just think if you don't have something, and just say we want the Congress, if the Congress will put it on there, you can say, then we can say, the Japanese, the Germans, and so forth, if we get it, a proper exchange rate, differential here, we'll repeal the border tax. But, I just think you ought to leave it in strength as long as we're doing it.

Now, I recognize full well that the two, the two are basically incompatible. You shouldn't need both, except that, that we're dealing with all these countries around the world, and hell, they're not going to just let us do what we want to, to the extent that we want to. Now they'll give you a five percent, or they'll give you a seven percent, differential in your exchange rates without too much trouble, but that's not going to solve our problem here. I'd like to have a fifteen percent border tax, and then say we want a ten percent, differential in the exchange rate, or ten percent devaluation, whatever kind of wording you want to use.

NIXON: In other words, your idea would be to impose the border tax, but then have, would you ask for the Congress to impose it?

CONNALLY: Sure, I'd ask them to impose it. To give you the authority to remove it when, in your judgment, the international exchange rates have reached a point where the United States is receiving a fair deal, in effect, in its trade relations. I'd even ask them to impose it. Now, the other way you play it, and I assume it's a part of George['s views] and a certain part of Paul['s views], is, if you're going to float, that this tends to let the currencies seek their level, so you don't need the border tax. But to threaten them with the border tax, say now, we haven't got it, but if we don't get an exchange rate that is satisfactory to us, if you don't in effect reevaluate the yen twenty percent instead of five percent, we're going to ask the Congress for a border tax. So it's just a question, it's a question of which comes first, the chicken or the egg. You can get the tax and agree to remove it if you get what you want, or you can try to get what you want and threaten to impose it. Because I think you have to have something to deal with these countries, other than just a float. I just —

NIXON: Incidentally, George talked to Rogers, and Rogers said that he would not oppose the border tax threat.

SHULTZ: He called me to give me that feeling.

NIXON: Who would have talked to him, Peterson?

SHULTZ: I don't know who talked to him, I mean [unclear] on the Hill.

CONNALLY: Well, how's he talking to him?

SHULTZ: Bill Rogers has been around a lot. He called me to tell me that, and specifically asked me to tell you about it.

NIXON: Well, that's an interesting view.

CONNALLY: It sure is.

NIXON: It sure doesn't represent the views of the State Department bureaucracy! [laughter]

SHULTZ: Well, it represents the fears that we will have a big quota bill and they would rather have [unclear].

CONNALLY: That's correct. That's what I said.

NIXON: We're talking, George, about some other things, here, too. Think about the border tax. It has some appeal to me. I think it gets us away, even though it doesn't solve the textile thing. It gets at it in a way.

CONNALLY: It gets at a lot of these problems. My God, if you can get the Congress in, I can't believe they won't pass it. And you immediately lay in on textiles, and automo — and Japanese automobiles, Japanese steel, and everything else, while you're negotiating. Mr. President, we can be negotiating. George is not going to be in a hurry to stop the float, of the dollar. And a lot of people are not. We may be floating years from now. This exchange rate will be up and down, and, and you have to remember, that we are the least controlled currency, and we are the least controlled economy in the world, among the industrial nations. Isn't that a fair statement?

NIXON: I'll say.

CONNALLY: We certainly are less controlled than Japan, we are certainly less than Germany, we are certainly less than France, or Italy, or Great Britain, or any of these countries. So they've got to be [unclear].

SHULTZ: That's the reason why we've got a good economy.

CONNALLY: Well, that's very true, but they've got the advantage over us in negotiations, because we don't have any tool with which to negotiate with 'em. That's the problem. Now, philosophically, I don't have any argument with George. Not at all. But as a practical matter, I'd damn sure rather have a fifteen percent tax on 'em so that they can't ship in their cars without paying it on their textiles, and then it makes them a little more pliable if we say we'll take it off, fellas, if you all could give us an exchange rate that is acceptable to us.

SHULTZ: This is, I suppose, just the kind of thing we need to take out —

NIXON: Yeah.

SHULTZ: — over the weekend, and the first thing is to have in place, if it's possible, if there's a legal basis for doing something —

NIXON: Right.

SHULTZ: — and research that out, which I'm sure we can.

NIXON: Right.

CONNALLY: Well, I don't think we'll take action for something we don't have a sound basis for.

NIXON: I think that John's point that about the [unclear], that's a good point —

CONNALLY: And again —

NIXON: Get an [unclear] —

SHULTZ: [unclear] if we impose the tax here, I think, on the [unclear], move to impose the tax [unclear].

CONNALLY: Let me point out to you now, George, if you don't, going into a political year, and if we don't get some real relief, if we don't improve, odds are that our balance of payments is not going to improve the rest of this year, because the turnaround time takes so damn long as you well know. Maybe —

SHULTZ: I'll wager —

CONNALLY: All right.

SHULTZ: — a dollar that the third quarter's better than the second quarter.

CONNALLY: Well, it may be anyway. I would anticipate it would be.

NIXON: As bad as?

SHULTZ: Better.

CONNALLY: Better. But, I would anticipate that anyway. But my point is that our actions are not going to result in any great change for several months. Now, during that period of time, you're going to have these guys in Congress holler for more protection, and they're going to go on a quarterly basis in an election year, but if you go with the import tax, you can remove it, and there isn't a person I don't know that wouldn't rather have the tax, the border tax, than to have a quota.

NIXON: Yeah, I must say, George, that argument is quite persuasive to me. The quota thing is, just testing it out, is just desperate. It is totally wrong, and I have come down, John, against the textile thing. I've been wrestling with that, and [unclear]. But I just can't, I've come down against the use of that national security authority. Mitchell is for it, Stans is for it, Hodgson is for it, in fact, all the most political people. I'll tell you what, if we do it there, we are opening Pandora's box, and I'll have to do it for steel, and it's stretching one hell of a lot. I think Lincoln, well, not that he would, he'd probably have to resign. I mean, we really can't, you just can't beat him over the head and say, look, textiles, you know what I mean? I just don't like, I don't think we can stretch it that far, and I think it's a hell of a bad precedent.

Now, on the textile thing, however, this could give you one hell of a — looking at the textile problem, George, here is [unclear], goddamn, look at that paper, would you [slaps paper]? But anyway, this gives you some bargaining position with the Japanese.

CONNALLY: That's right.

NIXON: Even on the textile problem, in my view.

SHULTZ: No, I think we could—

NIXON: Even the quota thing, I mean, the border tax.

SHULTZ: Anyhow, suppose that we get a favorable opinion from John on the GATT thing—

NIXON: Yeah. Right.

SHULTZ: —that would be [unclear]. Everybody knows that you have that, so that you've got that tool there. Then, you can go to border taxes, or you go to closure under that. Closures are more specific, and that involves [unclear], and maybe in addition to the devaluation, you can hit the textiles thing like a ton of bricks on the basis of that, and walk away.

NIXON: What do you mean, how would you do that?

SHULTZ: To, if—

NIXON: On the basis of the GATT thing, how?

SHULTZ: It may be that you could—you wouldn't have to go across the board. That you could just take a particular thing, under the devaluation, take the textile bit, and do something of it [unclear], a special case could be probably made on textiles, that again, is something that you could do.

NIXON: Hmm. In other words, rather than the national security authority, the GATT, under the rules of GATT, you could do this?

CONNALLY: Yes, sir.

SHULTZ: That may be.

NIXON: On textiles? Why in the hell haven't we thought of this before then? What's the matter?

CONNALLY: Well—

NIXON: [unclear] [laughs] Well, I just think, it seems to me that if that were possible somebody should have told me a year ago. Maybe it's not possible.

SHULTZ: This is related to the, to the recognition of a critical point in the balance of payments, in general here, that is the situation.

NIXON: Well, everybody says it's critical.

SHULTZ: There's no doubt about that.

NIXON: That's the one thing you've got agreement on. What's unanimous is we're in a crisis.

SHULTZ: Well, I think there's also an interesting agreement on the basic set of points that you and John have talked about, [unclear] somehow some combination of the gold and the monetary business, and the wage-price, the budget stuff, and the border tax. Some combination of that is the right answer, and those are the pieces that everybody comes up with. And there's a very strong, centrality of view on that, and of course there's a great relationship both politically, as John brings out, and I think, substantively among these things.

It seems to me you have a short-term monetary crisis that has to be dealt with. That's part of that package. There's a long-term monetary, or international balance of payments problem that has to be dealt with that the package deals with. There is a problem of domestic inflation, regardless of the international debacle, that has to be dealt with, that this deals with. And then, beyond that, there are these great underlying points that you emphasize, that there is the problem of continuing domestic expansion—

NIXON: Stimulating the economy.

SHULTZ: —and stimulating the economy.

NIXON: We're speaking to those pressures.

CONNALLY: And creating jobs.

NIXON: We're speaking to all these pressures.

CONNALLY: We're speaking to every single one of them, and that is the beauty of it.

SHULTZ: Then there is the notion of leadership from you, domestically, and I think that this also can be said, depending on how it is structured, as a chance to make a strong international economic leadership pitch here—

NIXON: Yeah.

SHULTZ: —to go alongside the other, and that's very [unclear]—

NIXON: That's a—right, that's a very good point, and would be a good one to say. Now we're—rather than that we are doing this because our backs are against a wall, we're simply saying we're doing this because it's time to change this obsolete system to set up a new system in its place, and these are the steps that we're going to take, and now we're prepared to negotiate with our friends around the world, to tend to solve the problem. Is that the way you would do it?

SHULTZ: Here I think the border tax has a, it's a negotiating point, it is a point of, it's one of these retaliatory things, to a greater extent I think than the monetary is, if you just do it—

NIXON: Yeah.

SHULTZ: —and then negotiate it. And, at the same time, it seems to me, a very good thing to surface if we can say it is in your hands to do, and let everybody know.

NIXON: In other words, rather than doing it, to threaten?

SHULTZ: Just to let people know it's there, and not do it.

NIXON: Well, the thing about doing it that appeals to me, is that, of course you would go either way—

CONNALLY: No, I'd go for imposing it.

NIXON: I prefer to do it, George, for another reason. That I feel we're dealing in the world with some very tough customers, and that I feel that, that we, like with the

Japanese, if we say well, we'll put some quotas on, and that sort of thing. Well Christ, they don't believe it, and naturally we want them to feel it. I'm inclined to think that we'll act first, talk later, after we've shot the gun out of their hands.

But, anyway, that's the way I lean at this point, particularly if we do it all in a context of, of leadership and conciliation. We will say, now look, we're not doing this for the purpose of permanency. We're doing this for the purpose of building a more stable system.

CONNALLY: I'd call—

NIXON: We're prepared to negotiate. See, that's the way I would, prepared to negotiate. We'll deal with this. See my point?

CONNALLY: Yes, sir.

NIXON: I don't think we should—I don't think, John, it would be in our interest, it isn't in the interest of world leadership to step up and say the United States is going to isolate itself with a fifteen percent wall around it—

CONNALLY: No.

NIXON: —because also that's very bad for American industry. A lot of these guys are going to sit on their butts and won't work.

CONNALLY: I couldn't agree more.

NIXON: So, the purpose of this, really, is the use of a temporary nature, to get the—

CONNALLY: In the bill, I would insist that you have the authority to lift the tax at any time, when in your judgment, you no longer need it. And if they didn't give you that, I'd veto it. I don't think they are going to impose a fifteen percent tax, without your having the right—

NIXON: Well, the beauty of not having to do it in a bill, if we could do it in the GATT it would be much easier, just do it and take it away.

CONNALLY: That's correct.

NIXON: Go ahead.

SHULTZ: I was just going to ask. Suppose you could have it either way, unilateral through the president, or through the Congress, would you have a preference?

CONNALLY: Oh, unilateral would be the preference.

NIXON: Yeah.

CONNALLY: I think you need to have flexibility, because I would use it as a trading—

NIXON: I prefer the unilateral thing for another reason, that the Congress is likely to put, hedge it with so many restrictions—

CONNALLY: That's correct.

NIXON: —with regard to, it must, it cannot be imposed without sending it to the Congress, or it cannot be removed, et cetera. It'll just get screwed up, George. It'll just get screwed up.

CONNALLY: One way or the other.

NIXON: I think we have got to bend the law. Let me say, we're not bending the law. So somebody will sue us, so what the hell! We'll be sued for two years. We'll fight that damn thing in the Supreme Court. Right?

CONNALLY: I think you've got enough coverage from Clark [possibly Ed Clark, a Treasury Department attorney] under both the Treasury Act of 1917 and the Treasury Agreements Act to do it, and one of our young lawyers over there thinks so now —

NIXON: Another one doesn't?

CONNALLY: Another one doesn't.

NIXON: What are lawyers for if they disagree?

CONNALLY: Well sure, as long you can get one good lawyer to say you can do it —

SHULTZ: It's one good lawyer that counts —

CONNALLY: That's right, and if he can find a way, why, I just —

NIXON: Well now, John, John Mitchell, let's get the ducks in a row then. I think we can go Monday. And I think that having this meeting, George, to a certain extent, answers my concern about not being orderly. Another thing about this is, putting it in the context of the China thing, I did that with great surprise, and we could, when we brief on Monday, we'll say the president has had this under consideration for, which is actually true. Peterson wrote me a memorandum months ago on border taxes. You wrote me one on, well, you know —

CONNALLY: Mr. President, I think you take the position that we have been actively discussing this since the mark crisis in the spring.

NIXON: That's right.

CONNALLY: Because we did talk about it.

NIXON: This has been discussed, and that now is the time for decision. And we're decided, and we're getting up there, and then we just come on it, when, unexpected, and whack it right to it. And off we go. Now, we've got to remember, that, apart from the fact [unclear] we weren't listening too much and so forth and so on. What the hell [unclear].

SHULTZ: They'll hear this.

CONNALLY: They'll hear this.

NIXON: The businessmen will hear it, and —

CONNALLY: It'll be the shot heard around the world, you can be sure of that. [laughter] It'll be in every town and hamlet.

NIXON: Can we talk again about who goes, because I don't want to get this beyond — John, do you like anybody besides Volcker?

CONNALLY: No, we ought to have one good lawyer knowledgeable in this field. Now, if Justice is going to brief this question, they ought to have a man. Otherwise, we ought to take Roy Englert or somebody from Treasury who has lived with this —

NIXON: Well, another thing you could do, is of course, once you —

CONNALLY: He doesn't have to sit in all of the meetings —

NIXON: Fine.

CONNALLY: — just be available.

NIXON: There is a little problem of how do we get space provided, you see. You would want?

SHULTZ: There is one possibility, Cap [Weinberger] —

NIXON: No, not necessary.

SHULTZ: — one possibility is this fellow named Dan Whitlay, who is a lawyer, he is very, very good, who was brought over —

NIXON: Yeah.

SHULTZ: — I don't know what he's been [unclear].

NIXON: He's good, he's working. Well, bring him along, there's no problem there. Well then, look, you fellows decide. Arthur — alone, right? He is. Arthur just needs his wisdom. Arthur, then Peterson — incidentally, I think Peterson should be alone. Do you agree?

SHULTZ: Yes, [unclear].

CONNALLY: Yes.

NIXON: He should. He's another principal. McCracken? I think we ought to have Mc-Cracken —

CONNALLY: I think he has to be there.

NIXON: — and Stein.

SHULTZ: Stein adds a lot.

NIXON: The reason I'd have Stein, John, now I said, I wouldn't have the new man, because he isn't up with it yet. But Stein has a very, what I would call a very cold, hard, mind. And he's the kind of a guy who will contribute more than McCracken will to this kind of conversation. McCracken will contribute to the discussion, but Stein will contribute to the decision. He's a very cold customer. So I think they ought to come.

How's that sound? Now will you, George, take down the logistical thing and work it out with them? With regard to what we put on, with regard to what we're going to put in that budget cut, and so forth and so on. That's all the domestic field, you should have Ehrlichman there, not to participate in all of our meetings, or maybe we can just have him there.

Well, there are two major things. One is that, putting off the deferring, maybe you can talk to him about it tomorrow, the deferring of the —

SHULTZ: We can go over all of the budget things at the cabinet tomorrow.

NIXON: Yeah. Could you do that? Good. You do that. Now, and arrange for that. Let me, John?

CONNALLY: Yes, sir?

NIXON: I think what we'll do is just helicopter up. We'll go up at noon, well, right after lunch, let's say. Does that sound all right?

CONNALLY: That's fine.

NIXON: Go right up there, and then we'll have a meeting. But if we have a meeting we'll spend a lot of time gassing. What do you fellows visualize as a good way to structure this thing? What do you say, John?

CONNALLY: I would simply say that you ought to have a meeting with everybody. I wouldn't take anybody up there that you couldn't have in this meeting.

NIXON: Yeah.

CONNALLY: And this is Stein, Volcker, and so forth.

NIXON: Oh yeah, all of them.

CONNALLY: And let 'em all sit there, and then discuss this whole problem as if you have not made a decision at all. Don't tell them you've made a decision to do it. Now, let 'em all sit there, let 'em all discuss it, and lead the thing. Then after an hour or so of general discussion, which they all [unclear] —

NIXON: Send it back?

CONNALLY: Ask 'em to do something, and set out, and say all right, you all go and work on this and this and this and this, and come back and we'll have another meeting —

NIXON: Saturday night?

CONNALLY: — Saturday night, and that I'll be thinking about it and make a decision. Let 'em all feel that they're a part of the decision.

NIXON: Oh, sure, I want them to do that, but what I meant is how do we get a lot of them to do their thinking and homework before they get to the meeting. You see my point? Now maybe they've already done it.

CONNALLY: Oh, I think they —

SHULTZ: To some extent, we could work up a little thing for who —

NIXON: All right.

SHULTZ: — would report on what —

NIXON: Well, I think —

SHULTZ: — I wonder if —

NIXON: Yeah.

SHULTZ: — you have a general meeting like that, and the elements are laid out, if you then might want to suggest and say John chair a meeting, that's essentially you task the people up there who is going to be in charge of coming up with what —

NIXON: Right.

SHULTZ: — and then let him —

NIXON: Right.

SHULTZ: — chair another meeting that in a sense develops that material before it's brought to you.

NIXON: Right.

SHULTZ: And then we have a second meeting with you. We have these pieces lined up, and we have this kind of a discussion people always have and kind of ramble around a little bit —

NIXON: Right.

SHULTZ: — without having you to have to sit in —

NIXON: Well, I know — listen, I am perfectly willing to sit in and talk all night, you know, if it's useful. But I do know that when time is of the essence, that you finally get down to the nut cutting, and some guy's just — you've got to go off and I say what the hell is the program? Now let's see what it is, you see what I mean, John?

CONNALLY: Now may I suggest, that you take somebody with you, designate one of these people to start working on the speech?

NIXON: Yeah, yeah.

CONNALLY: I don't know who you like to have do it, but we can start to work on it. I can work on it, [unclear] want your speechwriters [unclear]. But someone should be there and they should get started fairly early on that.

SHULTZ: [unclear] could have Ziegler run the press [unclear]. The marketing for this is through the press. Now that has to be done, and Ziegler [unclear] —

NIXON: No, there's not.

SHULTZ: — or Haldeman, or —

NIXON: Haldeman is the one to do that. I mean, he will supervise it, you know, Ziegler, Ziegler and Klein, and all those people, and he knows how to, we can bring somebody up [unclear].

SHULTZ: [unclear], he's as clever a writer as there is, there's not [unclear] —

NIXON: You know, you're right.

SHULTZ: — he's just written a little piece that I got this morning, I don't know whether you've seen it, called "The Discouraged Employer" —

NIXON: The what?

SHULTZ: "The Discouraged Employer," who is —

NIXON: How fast is Dennison? How fast can Curt write?

SHULTZ: Oh, he writes very fast. He writes like Safire. And —

NIXON: [unclear], Stein, I'd just as soon not to have another speechwriter there. I'm going to do all of the writing myself, of course, but I, that's the reason that I've got to have the damn decisions made fairly soon so that I'll know what's going to go in. But what I'd like is, let me say, that what we need, from your side, John, let's get from your people what they think ought to be said. Let me get, I feel, that what ought to be said should be crisp, reassuring, and brief. I feel very strongly that, incidentally, where you have strong, powerful actions, that it loses by adding a lot of fat and words around it, you know, and I think it's, in a sense that, then if I am not satisfied with the way it's coming around, on say, Sunday, then we have to [unclear] for something like that, well, I'll try to think of one of our people here. Safire has considerable abilities in this field. He's done, he's done one [unclear]. I think I'd like to give St — let's see what, Stein is so sophisticated here.

SHULTZ: [unclear] Stein [unclear] —

NIXON: What's that?

SHULTZ: I said that probably helps Stein —

NIXON: Right.

SHULTZ: — that's one of his roles.

NIXON: Right, well, but on the other hand, John, your people have already done some writing on this.

CONNALLY: Oh yeah, they know. We just give whoever you want —

NIXON: The raw materials.

CONNALLY: — the raw materials, if you'd like —

NIXON: Right.

CONNALLY: — or we can try to prepare a finished draft tomorrow.

NIXON: Well, let's start with this. You might as well give it to them right now. I'd like to see what they come up with in the way of a finished draft. And say, it would be very helpful, because you know I find in this speech business, I dredge out nuggets out of everyone.

CONNALLY: Sure.

NIXON: You get the best of 'em that way. Fine, will you do that?

CONNALLY: Yes, sir.

NIXON: And I would say —

CONNALLY: I agree on Stein. I've seen a bunch of his stuff, and he is quite [unclear]. He really has improved.

NIXON: I would say that we would go, let me say that we would set our meeting for three o'clock tomorrow afternoon. We will be prepared, my thought is in that first meeting, to meet for, basically six o'clock. I think, John, you just take three hours —

SHULTZ: Three to six?

NIXON: Huh? Don't you think so?

SHULTZ: Three to six in the afternoon?

NIXON: Yeah. Don't you think so?

SHULTZ: Okay.

CONNALLY: I hope it wouldn't take that long, but we'll —

NIXON: Well, three to five, maybe.

CONNALLY: That certainly ought to cover it.

NIXON: Well, let me say, I was just thinking that if you wanted to give everybody a chance to say something —

CONNALLY: Fine. That's right. And you see, when we talk about the investment tax credit, Mr. President, we need to talk about is it going to be seven percent, or why not ten percent?

NIXON: Yeah.

CONNALLY: Why not eight percent? I think that after everything that's been said, we had seven, I don't even know how to change it, we've been ordered to change it.

NIXON: Yeah. Okay. At least make it eight!

[laughter]

CONNALLY: Sure, make it eight.

SHULTZ: After the tax thing passes, about [unclear] then we can [unclear] —

NIXON: Maybe five. But that is without the import tax.

SHULTZ: That's without the import tax.

NIXON: We don't want [unclear].

CONNALLY: Yes, sir.

NIXON: Ten percent and fifteen. And also you ought to check it out in terms of GATT things, and the other things, you know. Would you do that?

CONNALLY: Yes, sir.

NIXON: Well, we'll have a lot of fun. We will have, we'll work, then it would be my view that after we have the opening meeting, then we break up, and each group would, you take the budget stuff, you take the tax stuff, right? And, we'll go after it all, on Saturday, we'll get down to some real tough arguments. I think we ought to decide the meeting Friday should be for discussion. I think Saturday afternoon by three o'clock we should begin, we should then get into the purpose of where I say well, this is what we want to do — isn't that a reasonable thing? Incidentally, I've got to be decided —

SHULTZ: You can —

NIXON: — because if you see, the speech then, I then have to know, I've got to let them know by Saturday night, so that I can then use Sunday, and Monday, well, all day Sunday, and part of Monday, to write the damn speech.

SHULTZ: You'll have a meeting on Friday afternoon —

NIXON: Yeah.

SHULTZ: — and then let them dredge up on the basis of discussion —

NIXON: Yeah.

SHULTZ: — and then, you can decide, and then let everybody know that I have to have a meeting about it [unclear], and everybody decides do you want to go on Monday, or do you want to leave it, tighten the thing, and have all of the details, or just what happens —

NIXON: You would say that Friday?

CONNALLY: Saturday?

NIXON: At the end of the meeting?

SHULTZ: Well, maybe Saturday morning, just send word to us —

NIXON: Right.

SHULTZ: — that's what you've decided, and then people are no longer working on the question of whether —

NIXON: Yeah.

SHULTZ: — they're working on a question of what's decided, now how do we do it —

NIXON: Now that's very —

SHULTZ: — because I think that really is what we want to spend our time on.

CONNALLY: Of course, you're not going to have that much time for all the other things. We'll just have to know how we do it.

NIXON: Yeah. Well, the thing is, John, I personally have pretty much decided what I want to do anyway.

CONNALLY: Well, announce it Friday.

NIXON: And, I think that, you know what I mean, there is a difference. It's one of the things where there are no safe choices, and nothing worthwhile is ever safe, and perhaps no difference. But on the other hand, I feel that on this thing that I'm pretty well decided, and I think that [unclear] maybe Friday afternoon, George, I'll just say well, this is what I think we ought to do. That's really the way I tend to operate anyway, and everybody knows it. I usually don't horse around and say, let's take a vote. And so, then I say, now fellows, let's work out who's going to do what. I mean Arthur's pretty good at putting a few words together.

CONNALLY: Oh, yes, he is.

SHULTZ: Very skillful.

NIXON: Very skillful. We could have him help on the press thing. Do you all think we should have a speech? Let me just, just be the devil's advocate for one moment. On the other side of it, rather than going on television, and you know, talking to the American people about, the crisis we've got, and so on, just make up a hell of a good statement, and then background on it—

CONNALLY: That's it.

NIXON: You've got to educate them. The advantages of that are, it's a very, the fact that it is a complicated subject, and no one could judge whether a speech, no matter how carefully written, is going to have the effect of shaping the confidence of the people. The very fact of the speech, you know can take, it may be that these actions are so effective, so effective, that they, that they would be—that rather than asking for it, you see, the speech requires asking for it, John, and a major announcement, et cetera, et cetera, et cetera. And then of course, the other way to do it, is to just put out the thing at, say, four o'clock Sunday afternoon, and give my proposal. Now—

SHULTZ: I think it's good, well we'll know of course on Friday that they'll screw this up at Camp David—

NIXON: Yeah.

SHULTZ: —you'll know who it is—

NIXON: Right.

SHULTZ: —so it'll be clear what it is about—

NIXON: That's right.

SHULTZ: That would, to me, mean, that of course the markets will boil Friday afternoon, and then on Monday they'll know what happened. There'll be a tremendous amount of speculation about what was in those meetings concluded. Perhaps there's an advantage to saying, either making your statement, or issue a statement Sunday night.

NIXON: Well, if you do it Sunday night, it has to be issued by—well, not has to be, but it's a little diff—it's not really quite a diff—if it is to go on Sunday night, you know,

I don't want to preempt time for the purpose of, talking about this kind of subject. This might work. I see your point about Sunday night. Well, if we can get ready, that would be better, then we wouldn't screw around and have Monday to lose another billion dollars. What's your feeling, John, do you think it should be a national speech, or do you —

CONNALLY: Well, I'm inclined to agree it ought to be. I'm inclined to think it ought to be a national speech. It is a national speech, it is a major one. Oh yeah, it is a very major, and rather than viewing it as, again, as a reaction to a crisis, I think you, you've got to posture it as a position, you're speaking from a position of strength, and finding solutions to problems that plague this country, and you've got to, you're going to ensure —

NIXON: Let me —

CONNALLY: — that we have continued expansion and job opportunities —

NIXON: Let me say this. Let me say this. I think Monday is good. I think you're just going to have to take the risk Monday. Monday, so you have another Monday and there'll be a lot of speculation of what you're going to do, but what the hell.

SHULTZ: Well, you're —

NIXON: We'll do a better job.

SHULTZ: And second, our time, beginning about midnight Sunday night, in other words the markets in Brussels, the European markets —

NIXON: Yeah.

SHULTZ: — with the time difference, all this, this kind of speculation is going on beginning about midnight on Sunday.

CONNALLY: No, it would be later —

NIXON: Five o'clock.

CONNALLY: Five hours' difference.

SHULTZ: Well, three in the morning.

NIXON: Yeah.

SHULTZ: That's, that's another point on Sunday.

NIXON: Yeah.

CONNALLY: Oh yeah, well, no question about that. We're not thinking just in our markets. We're doing things about the international markets.

NIXON: Well, those international markets, though, we're going to have to do something, so what can we do, so we take more dollars out?

CONNALLY: Yes, sir. We may know the answer to that, we don't have to make that decision. We may know the answer tomorrow depending on what happens with that market tomorrow. Monday's going to be a very bad day because, and I've got to check, they're going into a big Catholic holiday over in Europe tomorrow, that's why we think tomorrow could be such a donnybrook. Tomorrow will be the last trading day. I don't even think they'll trade.

NIXON: Oh, in Europe, I see.

CONNALLY: Well, they may trade, but in any event, my information is fragmentary, but if they do, it's going to be [unclear], because—

NIXON: Mainly because—

CONNALLY: I think they've got an extended weekend holiday. Tomorrow's the last day before the holiday.

NIXON: You prefer a speech?

CONNALLY: Yes, sir, I do, simply because, I think you can make some real hay out of it. You're talking to the American people, and they get their impression from you, about your concerns for expansion, your concerns for jobs, and you're taking these actions to ensure that they're going to have equal opportunity.

NIXON: I can do it myself, but I'm just trying to raise the whole—

CONNALLY: And now, if it were just going to be a strictly technical move in terms of closing the market or something, no, I wouldn't do it. But my God, you are announcing the import tax, if you can do it, the investment tax credit, and so forth and so on. All of this has a direct impact on these people. Wage and price freeze, why, I'd be sure I think you ought to do it.

NIXON: It ought to be done, but why on that basis?

CONNALLY: Because I just think—

SHULTZ: I think it's the biggest economic policy since the end of World War II.

CONNALLY: I can say in twenty-five years, no question about it.

SHULTZ: And that's—

CONNALLY: I think it's good. I think it gives you an opportunity to make a tremendous [unclear]. I may be wrong. I'll be the first to admit that I'm wrong, but I think this might put your critics so far behind the eight ball that they're not going to know what to do.

NIXON: Well, I'm supposed to take my wife so that we can get out. Wolf. Trap. Farm. Has anybody been to Wolf. Trap. Farm?

CONNALLY: No, sir. I've heard of it.

NIXON: Don't do it.

[laughter]

SHULTZ: It's fantastic.

NIXON: You've been there?

SHULTZ: I've not been there, but I've heard about it. I was going to go tomorrow night, as a matter of fact.

NIXON: Well, I'll tell ya, I'll tell ya, you can have my seat! [laughter] Do you want it?

SHULTZ: The program tonight is supposed to be marvelous.

NIXON: Yeah. Yeah, yeah.

SHULTZ: It's a great place.

NIXON: This is fine. Listen, John, it occurs to me, hell, we don't have to, why screw up the market tomorrow? If it's your thinking about the—you think that our stock market tomorrow, I don't think that's going to make a difference.

CONNALLY: Don't worry, they'll know—

NIXON: In fact, we'll get our helicopters, we don't have to announce we're all going. We won't announce a goddamn thing.

CONNALLY: I think that's—

NIXON: We'll just get on the helicopter at two o'clock. I go to Camp David regularly, and some of you, the rest of you happen to come up, that's all.

CONNALLY: I would low-key it, but I'm not sure where—

NIXON: The main purpose of going to Camp David, I happen to—see, I can take people up there and they don't need to know a hell of a lot about it. The main purpose of going to Camp David, frankly, is to get everybody in there where they're not going to talk to anybody.

CONNALLY: Right.

NIXON: Where everybody keeps his damn mouth shut, and there's no papers. Now, I know there's going to be a story in the *New York Times* Sunday about the fact that within the administration [a select few are] going out [to Camp David]. That is what I don't want. But we meet for three days, get the job done, and come back and slap 'em on Sunday night. And I can keep 'em up there, too, until I get back. You see what I mean? Without any leaks. That's the way I can do it. But we won't say, I think, just say, I would tell everybody who's going. You can tell Paul about this. Everybody, what I'd say, look, the president's inviting you up for the weekend. Inviting you up to Camp David for the weekend, and have all the arrangements. Fair enough?

SHULTZ: It's a very heavy, work-type weekend. People will, look to bring their families along—

NIXON: What's that?

SHULTZ: At least I know that question will be raised.

NIXON: Families? I wouldn't bring 'em. Not on this one. I think, because of the work and everything.

"Who knows about the Kennedys? Shouldn't they be investigated?"
September 8, 1971, 3:26 p.m.
Richard Nixon and John Ehrlichman
EXECUTIVE OFFICE BUILDING

Less than a year before the Democratic National Convention would name a 1972 presidential nominee, Nixon continued to fear that Senator Edward Kennedy would become a surprise candidate in the race. Even while other candidates started to formalize their campaigns, including George McGovern, Edmund Muskie, and Hubert Humphrey, it was Kennedy whom Nixon was most concerned about, despite the fact that he had not declared any intention to run.

• • •

NIXON: I could only hope that we are, frankly, doing a little persecuting.

EHRLICHMAN: Right.

NIXON: We ought to persecute them [Democratic candidates] [unclear] you can.

EHRLICHMAN: That's right.

NIXON: And on the IRS, if you can do it, are we looking into Muskie's returns? Does he have any? Hubert [Humphrey]? Hubert's been in a lot of fine deals.

EHRLICHMAN: Yes he has.

NIXON: Teddy? Who knows about the Kennedys? Shouldn't they be investigated?

EHRLICHMAN: IRS-wise, I don't know the answer. Teddy, we are covering —

NIXON: Are you?

EHRLICHMAN: — personally. When he goes on holidays, when he stopped in Hawaii on his way back from Pakistan.

NIXON: Does he do anything?

EHRLICHMAN: No, no. He's very clean. Very clean.

NIXON: Be careful now.

EHRLICHMAN: Affirmative. He was in Hawaii on his own. He was staying at some guy's villa and we had a guy on him. He was just as nice as he could be the whole time.

NIXON: The thing to do is to watch him, because what happens to fellows like that, who have that kind of problem, is that they go for quite a while —

EHRLICHMAN: Yup.

NIXON: — and they'll break open.

EHRLICHMAN: Yup.

NIXON: Huh?

EHRLICHMAN: That's what I'm hoping for.

• • •

EHRLICHMAN: This time, between now and convention time, anything could happen.

NIXON: You mean that he [Kennedy] will be under great pressure?

EHRLICHMAN: He will be under the pressure, but he will also be out of the limelight somewhat. I mean, he was in Hawaii pretty much incognito. Very little staff, and played tennis, moved around, visited good people, and socialized some. So you would expect at a time like that that you might catch him. And then he went up to Hyannis. And we've got an arrangement.

"It isn't a miserable war. The goddamn war was fought for a great cause."
September 17, 1971, 5:37 p.m.
Richard Nixon, Bob Haldeman, and Henry Kissinger
OVAL OFFICE

On September 16, Nixon met with reporters in a news conference, where three highly controversial questions pertained to the presidential election in South Vietnam. Because Thieu was running unopposed, many U.S. critics of the war wondered about the need to

defend such a dubious democracy. Nixon defended South Vietnam, "where they at least
have some elections, [as opposed to] North Vietnam, where they have none." To that kind
of argument, Senator Henry "Scoop" Jackson (D-WA) suggested that the United States
had enough influence over South Vietnam to ensure a fair election.

In a frank discussion with Kissinger and Haldeman, Nixon expressed his belief in the
Vietnam War, whether or not it had any effect on what he considered the major issue of
foreign policy — Soviet relations. Nixon remained a hawk, even though he successfully
reduced the number of American troops in Vietnam.

. . .

KISSINGER: We're going to go on Monday, Mr. President, with a —

NIXON: Good.

KISSINGER: — maximum effort, everything that flies in a stretch of twenty miles north
of the DMZ —

NIXON: Good. They've been asking for it.

KISSINGER: — and —

NIXON: Because they're building up, and they've been violating the thing. Don't you
think it's the right thing to do?

KISSINGER: Oh, yes. Oh, I — you know the domestic heat we're going to take. But
we're — the way we're going to do it, you know, you can judge it better than I
can. I think the way we're going to do it — see, if we hit Monday — what is Monday morning there, that's Sunday night here — by the time it's Monday morning
here, we will already have announced that the raid is over, and there'll be no other.
We'll just say, "This completes — this is protective action, and violation of the understandings. They've built a road across the DMZ; they've been shooting at our
planes."

NIXON: "And endangering — and endangering our forces as we withdraw."

KISSINGER: That's right.

NIXON: I'd put that point in, rather than protective — "endangering our forces as we
were withdrawing."

KISSINGER: So, we'll have a —

NIXON: I don't think anybody's going to complain about that.

HALDEMAN: They're going to know you did. Really, they [unclear] —

KISSINGER: Well, four hundred airplanes [unclear] —

HALDEMAN: Okay, but they get confused, Henry. But —

NIXON: Yeah.

HALDEMAN: — the people — the paper — the press will know it, but when they write it,
it still comes out as — they think we're bombing all the time there, anyway.

KISSINGER: So it's —

NIXON: But you see, Henry, from the standpoint of our diplomatic move —

KISSINGER: It's essential.

NIXON: — it's indispensable.

KISSINGER: It is essential, because —

NIXON: Yeah.

KISSINGER: — it's — in terms of what you said to the Romanian [Ambassador Corneliu Bogdan] this morning, which I thought was superb, incidentally.

NIXON: Well, Henry —

KISSINGER: Right?

NIXON: — did he get the message?

KISSINGER: Well, if he —

NIXON: [unclear]

KISSINGER: — didn't get the message he ought to be fired.

NIXON: Huh?

KISSINGER: You said — and you said it in this nice, quiet way. You said, "I just want you to know my patience with these people is wearing thin." And — that they — you —

NIXON: And I says, "I don't want you to be surprised by anything that happens." I said, "You — you know what I mean." I mean, after all — I says, "I —"

KISSINGER: Now, with this thing happening —

NIXON: [unclear] we did in Cambodia, and Laos, and China, and so forth. I said, "I — I'm just not gonna — I mean, they have — we've been forthcoming, and they haven't." And I said, "My patience is coming to an end." I said, "They just mustn't press me too far."

KISSINGER: That's right.

HALDEMAN: [laughs]

NIXON: [unclear]

KISSINGER: Well, they've played into our hands in one respect. Yesterday, Xuan Thuy tied the overthrow of Thieu again —

NIXON: To POWs, even.

KISSINGER: To POWs.

NIXON: That was good. That was good.

KISSINGER: So, they're going through a tough phase now, for a few weeks. So this —

NIXON: Well, I feel that — I kind of feel in a way, that with the vote on [extending] the draft today, which I just as — of course, I mean, we were all pleased with: forty-seven to thirty-six.

KISSINGER: Yeah, but it was another example where everyone of — told you, or told me at least — I don't know what they told you —

NIXON: Oh, we were behind seven votes.

KISSINGER: — that it was lost. It was like the Mansfield thing, and when —

NIXON: That's right.

KISSINGER: — you stepped in there —

HALDEMAN: They didn't tell us that; they told us it was forty-five to forty-five.

NIXON: No. No. Seven votes behind, Bob, is one thing.

• • •

KISSINGER: You know, Jackson was stunned by what you said yesterday; he thought it was aimed at him.

HALDEMAN: It was.

NIXON: Jackson did?

KISSINGER: Yeah, and he said that he's releasing a letter —

NIXON: [unclear]

KISSINGER: — he's releasing a letter he wrote to you, which is, in effect, saying the same thing.

NIXON: That it's [unclear]? Well, what do you mean?

KISSINGER: Well, he's releasing a letter saying how you should fix the election: that get another — he said he would never have wanted to suggest overthrowing Thieu.

NIXON: He — oh, he denies that, huh?

KISSINGER: Yeah.

HALDEMAN: Well, you didn't aim that at him. But, you said that he said, specifically, you should withdraw — withhold foreign aid.

NIXON: Mm-hmm.

HALDEMAN: If they don't —

KISSINGER: Oh, yeah.

HALDEMAN: — hold free elections, and you said [unclear] —

KISSINGER: Well, he didn't quite say it. He said he wants to reserve it —

NIXON: Nevertheless, at least it got him to respond.

KISSINGER: Oh, yeah.

NIXON: I think they're all on a —

KISSINGER: And that's one of the great advantages — great advantages, Mr. President. If they are responding to you, that's a hell of a lot better than if we are running around defending ourselves against their nitpicking.

HALDEMAN: That's really kind of the difference we're in now. We're on the offensive, and they're, they're having to swing back, instead of the other way.

KISSINGER: McGovern looks like a horse's ass now.

HALDEMAN: Yes, he does.

NIXON: How?

KISSINGER: Well, he says they're softening their terms the same week that they're hardening it. He says you can get — when I explained to these AP and UP guys this morning the — what, what they mean by a cease-fire when they offered it, they said, "Well, how can McGovern do this?" I said, "Well, I know him. He's a very honest, very honorable man. He just didn't study this thing. We live with it day after day. He doesn't know the strict terminology they use."

NIXON: Cease-fire, yeah.

• • •

NIXON: But, getting back to [Lyndon] Johnson, don't you think he's just terribly — must be terribly frustrated, the poor son of a bitch? You know, you think of this miserable war — and, first of all, Henry, it isn't a miserable war. The goddamn war was fought for a great cause and a good cause —

HALDEMAN: But it's been made —

NIXON: — and we didn't have to get into it, to begin with. We shouldn't have started down the Diem trail. We shouldn't have made the Laotian deal, in my opinion. All right, that's all second-guessing. But once in it, this war could have been ended in a year or two years —

KISSINGER: Mr. President —

NIXON: Using our air power we could have knocked those bastards right off the lot —

KISSINGER: — if you, if you had been in office — if we had done Cambodia in '66 —

NIXON: Yeah.

KISSINGER: If we had done Cambodia in '66, and Laos in '67, the war would be history.

NIXON: And with a victory.

KISSINGER: And with a — they couldn't have taken that, plus the bombing. Impossible.

HALDEMAN: We wouldn't have had to do it if we had done the bombing right, early enough —

KISSINGER: That's right.

NIXON: And [unclear].

KISSINGER: And we might not have had to do the bombing if you had done Cambodia and Laos. So —

NIXON: Now, Moorer — evidently, Laird is clued in on this thing, isn't he?

KISSINGER: On the — Monday? Yeah.

NIXON: Yeah. All right.

KISSINGER: We did it through Laird.

NIXON: Fine. And he knows that, that there were a variety of reasons [unclear]. Good. Good. Okay. Do we —

KISSINGER: Well, you —

NIXON: — tell Rogers, or not?

KISSINGER: No.

NIXON: And he shouldn't. Probably not.

KISSINGER: He's up in New York.

NIXON: Probably not, it's just as well to just let it —

KISSINGER: To let it —

NIXON: — and when it comes, just say, "Well, it's a routine matter." I just — I wouldn't play the whole thing.

KISSINGER: Or, I could call him tomorrow and say that —

NIXON: I'd just say, "Look, you ought to know that we had this —"

KISSINGER: "The president has author —"

NIXON: "— we had this enormous buildup in the DMZ, and it threatened our forces, and because, and so forth. So, we thought — the president just authorized this one —"

KISSINGER: One —

NIXON: "— two-hour strike to take out the stuff so that we aren't going to have some casualties." I'd put it on that deal.

KISSINGER: Right. Right.

NIXON: Would you do that?

KISSINGER: I'll do it tomorrow —

NIXON: And then, we could — and we're not going to comment. We're going to throw all the comment over to Defense —

KISSINGER: Right.

NIXON: — and we're not going to say anything. It's just the one — the few hours.

KISSINGER: I'll do it.

NIXON: But I want him to know.

KISSINGER: Right. I think it's better.

NIXON: Yeah, then we — but, you see, Henry, in terms of your diplomatic game, coming back to [unclear] —

KISSINGER: We must have it. If we're going to —

NIXON: — I feel that, I feel that — now, the little Romanian gnome, he'll wire that tonight, won't he?

KISSINGER: Oh, yeah. That's back already.

NIXON: And then, what you told him — you left that hanging over the son of a bitch, didn't you? You had —

KISSINGER: Oh, and I warned them. Our records show I warned them at every meeting, "Stop this buildup of — north of the DMZ." They've been firing from north of the DMZ.

NIXON: Mm-hmm.

KISSINGER: And we're getting a poop sheet together in case if the public —

NIXON: That's right.

KISSINGER: — reaction gets bigger than we think it will.

NIXON: Good.

KISSINGER: To get it around. And, uh —

HALDEMAN: Can you hang that on violation of the DMZ?

KISSINGER: Yeah.

NIXON: Sure.

KISSINGER: Oh, yeah.

NIXON: It's a violation of the understanding, a clear violation of the understanding. But tomorrow's thing, I — rather than a technical thing — I never get into that.

HALDEMAN: Yeah.

NIXON: I'd simply say, "They had a buildup in —"

HALDEMAN: [unclear]

NIXON: "— violation of the understanding, which endangered our American forces that are withdrawing. It would have increased our casualties, and we've taken it out." Yeah, boy, and then let it fly —

HALDEMAN: And you've said all along if, you know, we're —

NIXON: Sure.

HALDEMAN: — pulling out [unclear].

KISSINGER: No, in terms of the diplomatic game that we are proposing it's essential —

NIXON: Mm-hmm.

KISSINGER: It's highly important because it enables the Russians to say things could get worse.

• • •

KISSINGER: But, for example, you know very well, Mr. President, if they could launch a big offensive, now —

NIXON: Yeah?

KISSINGER: — they'd have us on the ropes. And the fact that they are not launching a big offensive shows that they just haven't got it. Laos used up this year's supplies, one way or the other, because they expended them or because they were destroyed. But, one way or the other, they couldn't launch an attack even in I Corps. Every other year they've had an attack in the highlands in the summer. This year we figured, with elections coming up, they'd certainly have an attack.

NIXON: And they didn't.

KISSINGER: And they haven't had any significant — even —

NIXON: Well, now the argument that could be made that they didn't do that is because they were having talks with you, you know.

KISSINGER: But no one thinks they have the forces there.

NIXON: No, I'm just suggesting that.

KISSINGER: Yeah. You could say that. That's true, you could say that.

NIXON: That's possible, because we have been restrained.

KISSINGER: You could say that.

NIXON: I don't agree. I — but you don't think that's the reason?

KISSINGER: I don't think so. Because —

HALDEMAN: Can they still attack now?

KISSINGER: Because their usual tactic is —

NIXON: Sure.

KISSINGER: But they —

NIXON: [unclear] but, so they don't.

KISSINGER: Well, but their usual tactic is not to do that. Their usual tactic is to hit you while they're talking.

NIXON: That's correct. And so is ours.

KISSINGER: Although, I did warn them that if there were attacks —

NIXON: Well, all right. We're going to do this for — incidentally, this has to be done anyway.

KISSINGER: Yeah.

NIXON: Because, looking down the road, I think it is dangerous to have this buildup. Do you not agree?

KISSINGER: Oh, yes. Well, Abrams urged it on me when I was there in June. He was pleading for it then.

NIXON: Well, here we've given it to him. And, incidentally, won't there be a bigger target now?

KISSINGER: Oh, they'll — that — that's a big one. Oh, yeah.

NIXON: There's plenty of stuff in there to hit.

KISSINGER: Oh, well, he wants to hit it for five days. But that we can't. That —

NIXON: Is there enough to hit?

KISSINGER: Oh, there's more than enough. I — there's five days' worth of attacks in there. He wanted five to ten days, but that would create too much of a furor, don't you think?

NIXON: No, no, no. We're just resuming the bombing in the North.

"I think you ought to take Dobrynin, [and] brace him damn hard."

September 18, 1971, 10:40 a.m.

Richard Nixon, John Mitchell, and Henry Kissinger

OVAL OFFICE

In mid-September the Quadripartite negotiations in Berlin were coming to a close, after eighteen months. The American position in the negotiations was taken by Kenneth Rush, ambassador to West Germany. Meanwhile, the SALT conferences were a source of aggravation for Nixon. The idea of a total ABM ban had been seriously discussed since early July, but Nixon — prompted by Laird — had rejected a total ban in August. Smith continued to believe that a total ban had deterrent strength. Nixon found it easy to believe that his chief negotiator was continuing to maneuver in that direction, as the SALT meetings drew to a close in Helsinki.

• • •

KISSINGER: [There's] some shooting going on along the Suez Canal, which started — in the middle of the week, the Israelis —

NIXON: I saw that.

KISSINGER: — shot down an Egyptian plane that was overflying them for reconnaissance. And they have been firing machine guns at these planes just to show that they weren't —

NIXON: And they hit one?

KISSINGER: When they hit one by, really by accident, more or less —

NIXON: [laughs] Goodness sakes, if you can bring a quick, a modern plane down with a machine gun, it must be a horrible, poor pilot.

KISSINGER: Right, it was —

NIXON: Jesus Christ!

KISSINGER: It was a lucky hit. Thereupon, or maybe for other reasons, the Egyptians shot down an Israeli plane thirty miles inside Israeli territory yesterday: a transport, a combination transport/intelligence plane that was thirty miles inside the Sinai Peninsula. So this morning the Israelis have taken out some [Egyptian] SAM sites. And that's where it is. Now, there were some people who wanted you to appeal to both sides to show restraint. I think it'd be a great mistake at this stage. The thing may stop now. The Israelis have said they'd stop. The Egyptians know we want to preserve the cease-fire. I think we ought to watch it another couple of days.

NIXON: Mm-hmm.

KISSINGER: I don't think we ought to get ourselves drawn into another negotiating round there.

. . .

KISSINGER: The Israelis won't do anything; the Egyptians won't do anything unless the Russians urge them — or unless the Russians tolerate it. For reasons we know, the Russians are unlikely to have a big blowup in the Middle East between now and October 12.

NIXON: Do you think that really reached them?

KISSINGER: Yeah.

NIXON: Do you think you ought to call Dobrynin?

KISSINGER: Dobrynin isn't back yet. He'll be back Monday, which is another reason —

NIXON: Well, you could tell Dobrynin [on] Monday, "Now, look here, [unclear]."

KISSINGER: If it's still going on Monday I think it would — that would not be a bad move to appeal to the Russians — whether we should jointly cool it.

NIXON: I marked, incidentally, Henry, on the letter from Brezhnev. I think you ought to take Dobrynin, [and] brace him damn hard on the fact that Brezhnev did not respond with regard to the offensive weapons thing at SALT.

KISSINGER: Yeah.

NIXON: I don't want that. We have enough of a problem with our hawks here. They, as I understand it, at SALT, all they've talked about, and I assume that Gerry Smith has not pressed them on it, is about defensive — totally. They haven't — have they blocked offensive or [unclear] —?

KISSINGER: No. No. That's Laird. Laird is beginning to try to make a record on that. The major problem has been — there've been two problems. They've been pretty tough on the defensive ones. And they've —

NIXON: Yeah.

KISSINGER: — on the offensive ones, have not gone into great detail, but they've discussed it. But, part of the trouble has been our delegation. John [Mitchell] sits on this committee —

NIXON: Yeah?

KISSINGER: — and it's the goddamnedest thing you've ever seen. They're running this as if it's — if they had gone in there early in July and said, "Here is our understanding of May 20. This is what we want to discuss," then we would've known within three weeks where we stood.

NIXON: What've they done?

KISSINGER: Instead, they — first, they raised zero ABM. Then they raised so many abstruse points that you have to be a theologian to understand them. And finally, last week, John was at the meeting, I just cut them all off.

NIXON: Henry, for Christ's sakes, I wrote a letter to the son of a bitch, Smith, and said, "This is the line." Why didn't he follow the letter?

KISSINGER: Because, he is like —

NIXON: You mean [unclear] everything here?

KISSINGER: Well, he's like a shyster lawyer. You put in that letter that we are willing to have zero ABM —

NIXON: Oh, yeah.

KISSINGER: — eventually. So, the next thing —

NIXON: He started there, at the beginning. I get it. [unclear]

KISSINGER: So, the next thing, he now wants to put it into the preamble of the present treaty. He's wasting time on it when he doesn't even have an agreement yet. And the Russians have put up a whole series of really cynical proposals, which —

NIXON: Mm-hmm. Yeah. Which, of course, they would.

KISSINGER: — which they would, and which we should have disposed of in the first week.

"He doesn't have to do it. We just say he did it."

September 21, 1971, 12:46 p.m.
Richard Nixon, Bob Haldeman, and Henry Kissinger
OVAL OFFICE

The Soviet foreign minister, Andrei Gromyko, scheduled a visit to Washington on September 29. The details of the summit had finally been worked out, after a year of sometimes dizzying negotiations, and Nixon was determined that no aspect of the announcement could go awry. The sides had already decided on a statement, to be released simultaneously in Washington and Moscow, and so the president couldn't be deterred, not even by the possibility that Gromyko would fail to verbalize the invitation. He and Kissinger even had a contingency plan for that.

• • •

NIXON: Well, let me say, your conversation with your friend [Dobrynin] was very interesting, though.

KISSINGER: I thought it was.

NIXON: It's very important.

KISSINGER: And when they start feeding out this stuff through a lot of other channels—

NIXON: I have a—and I particularly liked the idea that you have in mind. And the way I'm going to do it this time, I'm not going to continue in another room. I'm just going to ask Rogers and everybody else to leave—say, "I'd like to speak with the foreign minister for a moment alone."

KISSINGER: Sure.

NIXON: You just leave and I'll talk to him here.

KISSINGER: We go to the Cabinet Room.

NIXON: You get the hell out. That's right.

KISSINGER: Absolutely.

NIXON: No reason for me to take him out. And I'll say, "Now, I want to tell you about this." And then he, at that time, should give me the summit invitation. Right?

KISSINGER: He doesn't have to do it. We just say he did it.

NIXON: Well, I'll just say that, when I speak to him, I'll say, "I appreciate the summit invitation," and so forth, and then we—but that is the basis for telling Rogers.

KISSINGER: And that gives you an explanation of what you spent a half an hour with him on.

NIXON: Sure.

KISSINGER: We'll just tell Rogers that you agreed on the spot to the announcement. That keeps me out of it.

NIXON: That's right.

KISSINGER: His feelings won't be hurt. And it focuses it all on you.

NIXON: That's right.

KISSINGER: And then, as they leave, then they're attacking you.

NIXON: Well, the minute that it's done, I'll just call him [Rogers] in and say, "Well, he [Gromyko] made the summit thing and I just agreed that we'd have the announcement on the twelfth."

KISSINGER: Right.

NIXON: And I've agreed it'll be in May.

KISSINGER: Right. I think that way, you'll get—

NIXON: Right. Very polished.

HALDEMAN: I mean, you then tell Bill not to tell anybody at State?

NIXON: Hell, yes. You're goddamn right. I'll say, "We're going to have the same rule on this we had on China." We'll inform them right before because the Russians are just as sensitive as the Chinese about a leak.

KISSINGER: That's right.

NIXON: Don't you agree?

KISSINGER: Absolutely.

NIXON: Everybody will be informed. Incidentally, anyway there isn't the same problem of informing. People expect us to meet with the Russians.

KISSINGER: Well, we'll have to let NATO know about it.

NIXON: I understand, but it isn't the —

KISSINGER: Well, it's not the bombshell —

NIXON: What?

KISSINGER: It's going to — the funny thing is —

NIXON: It isn't?

KISSINGER: It doesn't got to fit a goddamn, Bob. No one is speculating on it.

HALDEMAN: Not anymore. They used to. They used to talk about a Russian summit, didn't they?

NIXON: Well, they think the Chinese thing knocks it out of the box and so forth.

HALDEMAN: The one thing they're speculating on now is that what's-his-name is coming to the UN and will come down and see you or something.

NIXON: Yeah, Kosygin.

KISSINGER: Gromyko.

HALDEMAN: Kosygin.

NIXON: Kosygin.

KISSINGER: Is he coming to the UN?

HALDEMAN: He's going to Canada and then, or something —

NIXON: Right.

HALDEMAN: And then they're saying he may go to the UN, and then he'll come down and see the president on the SALT thing.

NIXON: That must not fly. [unclear] Damn it, I won't see him here. I'm not going to.

KISSINGER: Oh, no, no, no.

HALDEMAN: The speculation, they're just going wild. They've also got you going to China this weekend too. They say the Alaska trip is just a cover and that you're really going to China.

NIXON: Yeah. [laughs]

KISSINGER: Dobrynin asked me that too. I said, "Listen, Anatol. Do you really believe — can you seriously believe that the president —"

NIXON: [laughs]

KISSINGER: "— would go from a visit with Hirohito to Beijing?"

NIXON: [laughs]

KISSINGER: You should have [seen] my face.

HALDEMAN: But that's the value of your surprise stuff. They now —

NIXON: They're scared to death.

HALDEMAN: — scared to death.

NIXON: I know.

HALDEMAN: They fear probably you're [laughs] — you're capable of anything.

KISSINGER: When we announce it — and that's why I think it'd be best if you didn't go to this accidental war signing [the signing of the Agreement on Measures to Reduce the Risk of Outbreak of Nuclear War Between the United States of America and the Union of Soviet Socialist Republics on September 30, 1971].

NIXON: I don't want to go.

KISSINGER: It makes it too big.

NIXON: Good. Who decided that? Well, I didn't want to go. It builds it up too much.

KISSINGER: Yeah. It builds it up too much and also makes people think something else may be going on.

NIXON: That's right.

KISSINGER: And since it's close enough, the twelfth is —

NIXON: Well, Gromyko's going to be in here. That's enough. We'll give them that.

HALDEMAN: That's enough Russian stuff.

NIXON: And then for me to go on — it's slobbering over the Russians too much.

KISSINGER: That's right.

NIXON: And —

HALDEMAN: Then two weeks later you're announcing the trip.

NIXON: Yeah.

• • •

NIXON: You know, incidentally, one thing that may have helped us a little — I was mentioning it to Bob before — one thing that may help us at the present time with both the Chinese and the Russians is that, as Colson was pointing out here, we have a situation where both Gallup and Harris have reported within the last two weeks that the president has moved ahead of all three Democratic candidates.

KISSINGER: Yeah. Oh, enormously.

NIXON: Yeah, now that — we haven't moved yet enormously.

KISSINGER: No, no. It helps enormously.

HALDEMAN: It helps enormously.

NIXON: Exactly.

HALDEMAN: That's what Henry was talking about. On the floor of the Senate —

KISSINGER: That's what I was talking about, Mr. President.

NIXON: Yeah. Yeah.

HALDEMAN: That figure he had was not that.

NIXON: Yeah. Yeah. I didn't think there was some new Gallup poll.

KISSINGER: No, no. No, I was talking about the fact that in the trial heats you were ahead of them all by —

HALDEMAN: You won the [Senate vote to extend the] draft, fifty-five to thirty.

NIXON: That's great.

KISSINGER: Last week, at this time, everyone felt that we couldn't —

HALDEMAN: The fall-off in votes was due to the fact that many senators thought the debate would go on, so they walked off the floor and missed the final vote.

NIXON: [laughs]

HALDEMAN: So when they held it for a while to give them [some time] but only eighty-five voted out of ninety-one.

KISSINGER: Well, but when the Russians say, Mr. President, that — you know, I've [unclear] seventy percent of the [unclear]. But when Dobrynin says that a lot of his people used to think that you couldn't be dealt with, that they'd be better off with another president, and that this has changed completely, that's a gratuitous comment he doesn't have to make.

NIXON: That's right.

KISSINGER: And since they said essentially the same thing to Brandt, if that word gets around, that's, as it must —

NIXON: That'd be fine.

KISSINGER: Yeah.

NIXON: Thanks, Henry.

KISSINGER: Right, Mr. President.

"Either side . . . has got to play this game with us."
September 21, 1971, 4:04 p.m.
Richard Nixon and Henry Kissinger
OVAL OFFICE

Kissinger, watching Chinese affairs more closely than ever, received word of some unusual developments in Beijing. Nixon speculated that the improving relationship with the United States had caused unrest in government circles among those who did not agree with the Chinese effort to ameliorate relations with their ideological enemy. Naturally, the two wondered what any change in the Chinese regime might do to their master plan for 1972 as a year of summits.

• • •

KISSINGER: Something funny is going on in China, Mr. President. They have — there is a stand-down on civil aviation there for nearly a week now. And today they have canceled the October 1 parade on their national holiday. We've had other reports that they've been taking down pictures of Mao.

• • •

NIXON: — taking it out on Zhou Enlai for his American initiative.

KISSINGER: Conceivable, but those are the guys who are also the most — no, they are the most anti-Russian too. The Cultural Revolutionists were the ones that physically peed on the Russian ambassador.

NIXON: Well, put yourself in their position: either side has got, it would seem to me, has got to play this game with us.

"We've got everything linked together, just as you said."
September 21, 1971, 5:02 p.m.
Richard Nixon and Henry Kissinger
OVAL OFFICE

One of the overarching Nixon foreign policy strategies was known as "linkage," an approach in negotiations of leveraging strengths in order to reduce weaknesses. For example, if one is negotiating both economic and military issues, a compromise in one area may help in the other in such a way that both sides can come away satisfied. This was the basic approach Nixon and Kissinger used in looking for improvements in the American position across the board: with China, the Soviets, and the North Vietnamese — politically, economically, and militarily.

• • •

KISSINGER: We've got everything linked together, just as you said. We've got the Middle East. We've got everything in the game now.

NIXON: Well, if the Chinese should knock this thing off, what does that do to the Russians? They'll still want the visit?

KISSINGER: Oh, yeah. But we've just got a little less pressure on them. With a visit, I think if the visit to China is in the cards, the Russians are going to be most eager to — not most eager. We have a pretty good chance now of bringing off that ploy which I have in my memo to you. If the visit to China is not in the cards, they'll be a little less eager. They'll be a little less under pressure. On the other hand, they might figure, they better use this time to get us lined up. It would be better for us, if there were no turmoil in China.

"The two most likely possibilities are either that Mao is ill, which I don't believe, or that Zhou is purging his opponents."
September 22, 1971, 10:03 a.m.
Richard Nixon and Henry Kissinger
EXECUTIVE OFFICE BUILDING

Even though Lin Biao had been named Mao's official successor during the Chinese Cultural Revolution, beginning in 1970 he had a falling-out with other Chinese leaders. The succession that followed was noticed by Nixon and Kissinger, who could not help but wonder whether it was related to the recent thawing in relations between China and the United States.

• • •

KISSINGER: Well, I've reviewed the thing a little more until I've — and I'm beginning to think — this is a good summary of what we know.

• • •

KISSINGER: The two most likely possibilities are either that Mao is ill, which I don't believe, or that Zhou is purging his opponents.

Afterword: China underwent a brief purge, after Mao's vice chairman, Lin Biao, and his wife, Ye Qun (a Politburo member), were suspected of plotting to assassinate Chairman Mao on September 12. In what was described as a rushed attempt to escape China, they were said to have been killed in a plane crash. The details have always been sketchy, but whether or not there really was a plan for a coup d'état, Mao had approximately one thousand officials executed or arrested. There is no evidence that the situation stemmed from the thaw in relations with the United States.

Preparing for Gromyko

September 29, 1971, 12:00 p.m.
Richard Nixon and Henry Kissinger
OVAL OFFICE

On September 29, Nixon was set to host Gromyko at the White House. It would be his first meeting with a Soviet official in just about a year. In a preconference coaching session, Kissinger meticulously previewed the topics and procedures. One of the surprising concerns involved the fact that the president would be accompanied by both Kissinger and Rogers — and Rogers was not aware of secret communications sure to be mentioned by the Soviets.

• • •

KISSINGER: Well, first, for the procedures [for the meeting with Gromyko]. They'll come in here, pictures and so forth. You have about forty-five minutes —
NIXON: Sure.
KISSINGER: — to an hour with him in here.
NIXON: Sure.
KISSINGER: Then you ask us all to leave, and you'll talk to him privately.
NIXON: Yeah.
KISSINGER: Here, what he expects is that you'll say, "Mr. —" something like, "Mr. Foreign Minister, it's been a year since we've met. Do you want to give us your impression of — where do Soviet-American relations stand now?"
NIXON: That's at the beginning of the formal —
KISSINGER: At the beginning of the formal meeting. Then he'll give you a little speech, which will be very conciliatory, and then he'll turn to European matters. On that, incidentally — well, let me first go a little through it, on European matters.

NIXON: All right.

KISSINGER: He'll probably wind that up by saying, "Now, where do you stand on [the] European Security Conference? How do we move it forward?" I think you ought to preserve as much of that for the private channel as possible, so that we can play it into the summit, and say that, well, the conditions are getting ripe — that with the Berlin, once the Berlin agreement is ratified, and the German treaties are ratified, then you think we can go ahead with some preparatory work on [the] European Security Conference, and that —

NIXON: Except he wants the Berlin. Hmm?

KISSINGER: And that then there should be some informal discussions in the meantime of what the agenda might be, and so forth.

NIXON: Beginning now?

KISSINGER: Beginning once the treaties are —

NIXON: Oh, the informal discussions would begin when?

KISSINGER: I'd say after the German treaties are ratified.

NIXON: Mm-hmm.

KISSINGER: But we could have some informal — you'd always be interested to hear from them what agenda —

NIXON: On an informal basis and on a bilateral basis.

KISSINGER: Right.

NIXON: Okay.

KISSINGER: Then, on the Middle East, he'll give you — he'll do that —

NIXON: At which part — will he raise that in the public meeting?

KISSINGER: The European — Middle East?

NIXON: Yeah.

KISSINGER: He'll do it in two parts. He'll raise it at the public meeting —

NIXON: Right.

KISSINGER: — in the familiar way, and I've written down what our official position is.

NIXON: Sure.

KISSINGER: And if you just stick with what's in the basic memo —

NIXON: Don't worry. I'll follow your instructions right to the letter.

KISSINGER: — on that. Early in the discussion, Mr. President, you should raise SALT.

NIXON: Mm-hmm.

KISSINGER: And on SALT, the issue, briefly, is this. We had told them that — in the private discussions — we had told them: three of our ABM sites for their Moscow system, plus an offensive freeze. They now say it's got to be one for one on the defensive side too. But that means their Moscow system covers forty percent of the population, while one ABM site for us covers only two percent of the population, up in North Dakota. Now, you shouldn't go into all this detail, but —

NIXON: All right.

KISSINGER: — what you might say, though, is, "We have to move it forward at the next session." Our proposal, in effect, is that both sides stay where they are in both categories. We have two ABM sites defensively, but they have more missiles offensively. And therefore the freeze is equiv — that if we freeze now, and on both of them, that is fair. They can't ask us to cut down on our ABM sites but keep an edge in offensive missiles.

NIXON: So, in effect, we just reiterate we want a freeze?

KISSINGER: We reiterate that the — that when they speak of equivalence, they can't say there's going to be the same number of things on the defensive side, but they can stay ahead in the offensive side. So, what you could say: the essence of our proposal is that both sides stay where they are in both categories, defensive and offensive.

NIXON: Mm-hmm. What if he says, "What about MIRV?"

KISSINGER: He won't say that.

NIXON: That changes —

KISSINGER: I'll guarantee you he won't change —

NIXON: That changes the number too. Well, go ahead.

KISSINGER: That's right. I mean, that's our hole card.

NIXON: That's right.

KISSINGER: But we need that with two —

NIXON: You know, you stop to think here. Suppose we'd given in to Percy and, frankly, broken the rest and say, "Why don't we have a ban on MIRV?" You know, we will have — we would have — if a Kennedy, or a Muskie, or a Humphrey had been sitting in this chair, the United States today would have Gromyko looking right down our throat.

KISSINGER: This, Mr. President —

NIXON: It's close as it is.

KISSINGER: This is where these — when these conservatives say, "Well, what difference did it make who was here?" Good God, we would have no ABM, we would have no MIRV.

NIXON: That's right.

KISSINGER: In net, we would have no B-1; we would have no ULMS.

NIXON: Henry, the conservatives, I frankly think they're — then let them squeal. I'm almost inclined to think that a little of their squealiness has got to be, is just par for the course. And if they're going to do it, they're going to do it.

KISSINGER: Yeah. I think so.

NIXON: This time, we'll stick it out anyway.

KISSINGER: Now, on Vietnam — I wouldn't let him — then, on the Middle East, he will go through their formal position, which is that the Israelis are unreasonable —

NIXON: Mm-hmm.

KISSINGER: — and that we have gone ahead on the interim settlement without consulting them. And I would just repeat the position that we want an interim settlement as a first step and we think that this thing can help quiet the situation in the Middle

East — our formal position on that. Then he will mention trade, and he will suggest that you might send either Stans or Peterson to the Soviet Union. Incidentally, I told Dobrynin this morning we have granted — we've approved two hundred million dollars more of the Kama River project; we're now up to over four hundred million dollars on that.

NIXON: Only now, let's be sure it gets some credit in this country.

KISSINGER: Yeah, I've called Scott on it because it's in his area.

NIXON: I know. Good. Well, that's a good national story too.

KISSINGER: Yeah.

NIXON: Okay. Be sure it's highly publicized.

KISSINGER: Well, it will be formally announced on Friday.

NIXON: All right. Would you give that to Scali? Yes, tell him, because he likes to run with those things. And let Stans — and let old Stans run it too.

KISSINGER: Right.

NIXON: It's a chance for Stans to do more East-West trade.

KISSINGER: I'm beginning to think that we'd be better off having Stans go there rather than Peterson. Peterson would be —

NIXON: Do we want Peterson? I think Peterson would be too outgoing. And, well, he might —

KISSINGER: And he'd freewheel too much. There's no telling what —

NIXON: What I mean, when I say "outgoing," I mean he would tend to want to really negotiate. Or another way is to have the two go together. That might be an idea.

KISSINGER: Well, you don't have to react at all. You just have to say it's, you're very sympathetic. You might mention you've already approved over four hundred million dollars for the Kama River project, and over —

NIXON: I can also say that, as we finish Vietnam, more will come.

KISSINGER: Right. That would do it.

NIXON: And I think I'll get right into it.

KISSINGER: You know, altogether, we've approved over six hundred million dollars of —

NIXON: Trade and money, and the rest. I know.

KISSINGER: Right —

NIXON: On the Middle East, if I can come back to it. What he wants — do you want me to say in the public session, you know, [that] we're —?

KISSINGER: I'd just be very vapid in the public session —

NIXON: All right. All right. Now —

KISSINGER: Just say that you're supporting —

NIXON: You're going to take up the Middle East with him in your private session? Is that correct?

KISSINGER: Right. Well now, that's where — what I wanted to ask you. We'll first go through the formal ones.

NIXON: All right. Go ahead.

KISSINGER: Then on — then South Asia, I would urge them that — I would tell them, "Whatever one's views on East Bengal, that a war in that area would have the gravest consequences of international involvement." And that you —

NIXON: If he's going to raise the subject — or am I?

KISSINGER: Well, if he doesn't —

NIXON: I don't want to raise all these things. Do you think I should? Well —

KISSINGER: No, no. He will raise — I'll tell you what you can be sure he'll raise: he'll raise Europe, Middle East —

NIXON: Mm-hmm.

KISSINGER: — trade. You might consider raising SALT —

NIXON: SALT.

KISSINGER: — and South Asia. And maybe they'd only give you first —

NIXON: On SALT, I'd say that it's important to have progress, and this defensive thing is — well, we can't freeze offensive, an offensive superiority and a defensive inferiority. Is that what we've agreed?

KISSINGER: Well, you see, we can't insist on a de — that they can't insist that on the defense things must be equal, but on the offense they can stay ahead.

NIXON: Right. All right. Good.

KISSINGER: And that, therefore, you do not believe we can adjust, that we've gone from — we — that from three to one in our proposals, we've made a concession; we've gone down to two to one. But you might as well say you cannot go any further on the defensive thing.

NIXON: Mm-hmm.

KISSINGER: And you just want them to understand that.

NIXON: Mm-hmm.

KISSINGER: Because then I think we can break it. But they have to hear it from you.

NIXON: Mm-hmm.

KISSINGER: Those are the major topics he's going to raise with you at that session. Then he will, when you see him alone in this office — and I think your instinct is absolutely right. You shouldn't have a system that you always take him into a different —

NIXON: No, no. That's right. It looks no good.

KISSINGER: But I have now told them that you'll take us all to the Map Room, and I'll have —

NIXON: And have the cars there.

KISSINGER: I'll have the cars there —

NIXON: We'll all walk out together.

KISSINGER: Right.

NIXON: And that's not unusual. We'll just walk out that way and say, "I'd like to take you to your car, and on the way, I'd like to show you —"

KISSINGER: Map Room.

NIXON: "— this room." And we'll stop in there.

KISSINGER: I think it has historic significance for them. Now, there, he has — oh, no, I meant, forgot one other thing. He will mention to you Vietnam. He will say that Podgorny is going to Hanoi; that they will have very serious discussions about Southeast Asia: "Do you have any additional ideas that you want to say?"

NIXON: No.

KISSINGER: You want to say no. Now, I would — there I'd be very tough. I would say, "We've been very disappointed. The Soviet Union hasn't done a great deal. All we ever hear from Hanoi is the concessions we want to make — have to make. We've made one concession after another, and it is time for Hanoi, now, to talk to us seriously." That's all I'd say at the formal meeting, because it helps to give, to have them be able to carry this, as having heard from you. Now, then we go to the private meeting. The private meeting, they'll discuss two subjects: one is he will bring you a warm message from Brezhnev. He [Dobrynin] hasn't told me what it is.

NIXON: Does he know that I will suggest a private meeting?

KISSINGER: Yes.

NIXON: And —

KISSINGER: He's asked for it. But he's all programmed —

NIXON: And he doesn't want me to say that we've asked — just to say that I would suggest that I'd like to have some words alone.

KISSINGER: Right.

NIXON: Can you tell Rogers that he's asked for it?

KISSINGER: Right.

NIXON: You tell Rogers in advance that —

KISSINGER: I'll tell Rogers. As soon as I leave here, I'll call him and say Dobrynin has just called me and says that —

NIXON: Just say on this that Gromyko has a private message —

KISSINGER: Right.

NIXON: — he wants to give the president. See, I want the lay of the thing to be on the summit thing —

KISSINGER: Yeah.

NIXON: — that Dobrynin has just called; and that the president has — what we'd like to do is, he'd like to, he'll have us go to the Cabinet Room while he receives them, and then we will walk out and as — and he's going to escort him to the car. And then, afterwards, that the president — that the president will — no, no, don't tell him that we —

KISSINGER: Don't, because we don't know what it is.

NIXON: Just say to him — and he'll be — I'll tell him that afterwards. I'll —

KISSINGER: Well, you don't — I won't say anything. You can tell us after we've said goodbye to Gromyko —

NIXON: I'll tell Gromyko to step in —

KISSINGER: You can just say, "Why don't you step into my office?"

NIXON: "Come on in." Yeah. "Come in and come back into the Map Room." Good.

KISSINGER: Yeah.

NIXON: Okay.

KISSINGER: Well, then you can fold it and put it into your pocket. Then it's natural that you kept it folded —

NIXON: All right. Good. All right. Now, in the private meeting, he will give me a message.

KISSINGER: In the private meeting, he'll give you a private message. Well, it won't be in writing. It will just be a personal message on bilateral —

NIXON: All right.

KISSINGER: Then he will raise the Middle East. And he will say something to the effect that, last year, I had mentioned — he won't mention my name — to them that, if any real progress is to be made in the Middle East, the Soviet Union and the United States have to agree on their basic presence there. You remember? Your press conference —

NIXON: Right.

KISSINGER: — and my backgrounder. And they're ready to talk in that framework to us now, until there's a comprehensive Middle East deal.

NIXON: If there's any progress in the Middle East, they have to agree to our presence there?

KISSINGER: No, no. They are willing, in effect, to limit their presence.

NIXON: Oh. Yeah. All right.

KISSINGER: And they're willing to have some general exchanges.

NIXON: Mm-hmm.

KISSINGER: And I think he's going to say that this should be in the same sort of channel that handled Berlin. My recommendation is, Mr. President, that you say, "This is a very complex subject," that you recommend that Dobrynin and I have some preliminary conversations to find out just how it could be done, after which you'll make a decision. This doesn't commit you to anything —

NIXON: That's right.

KISSINGER: — but keeps the carrot dangling.

NIXON: [unclear]

KISSINGER: You might also, at the private meeting, reaffirm again this channel. It's just good for them to hear.

NIXON: Oh, don't worry.

KISSINGER: Now, then finally, you should say — if you agree — that you understand that I will be talking to him the next day, and I will talk to him more fully about Vietnam —

NIXON: Right. Right.

KISSINGER: — and that you want to say that what you say has had the most — what I'll say has had the most urgent consideration here —

NIXON: That's right.

KISSINGER: — and that you're fully —

NIXON: Yeah.

KISSINGER: — behind it and —

NIXON: Behind it and all the rest.

KISSINGER: Something like that.

NIXON: And I'll say, "He'll be — when you talk to him, you're talking to me."

KISSINGER: Yeah. And on Vietnam — and he —

NIXON: And how do we get the summit in the deal?

KISSINGER: He won't make — they know that —

NIXON: I see.

KISSINGER: They know that — he doesn't have to say it will be — they know that Rogers —

NIXON: Now, on the summit: he isn't going to mention the summit in the public meeting.

KISSINGER: No.

NIXON: Now, he must not do that, because I don't want Rogers to get involved in that.

KISSINGER: No, no, no.

NIXON: Fine. Okay.

KISSINGER: They are fully programmed, Mr. President. They know, however, that before — Gromyko is giving a lunch for Rogers tomorrow at one.

NIXON: And he knows that Rogers will know before the lunch?

KISSINGER: That's right.

NIXON: Fine. But it's not to be talked about here.

KISSINGER: No. Now, another thing he does not know about — that Rogers does not know about — is the exchange of letters between you and Brezhnev, to which they're attaching enormous importance.

NIXON: What exchange is that?

KISSINGER: You wrote a long letter.

NIXON: Doesn't Rogers know about that? He doesn't know about that?

KISSINGER: No.

NIXON: No. Well —

KISSINGER: Because it mentions the summit, Mr. President.

NIXON: Oh, I see. Well, frankly, it was done while I was in San Clemente; I was still out there.

KISSINGER: Yeah. Well, they won't mention it.

NIXON: No.

KISSINGER: You can be sure.

NIXON: Not yet. Well, Bill's — Christ, he can't object to this one. He might say, "Oh, what the hell?" And that's why he's willing to put up — well, that's the date they suggested, and I said, "Fine."

KISSINGER: That's the — and you just felt you wanted to get it done.

NIXON: And also — no, I'm going to say that once this sort of thing is agreed, it's going to leak. And I then — well, even if he's — I said, "Fine, we'll do it. We'll do it."

KISSINGER: But you better pledge him to absolute secrecy.

NIXON: Pledge Bill?

KISSINGER: Yeah.

NIXON: Oh, shit. Don't worry. I'm going to say, "Now, this has got to be absolutely secret."

KISSINGER: This is the easiest way, Mr. President. That way, it makes a lot of sense. Gromyko brought you, technically, the invitation last year.

NIXON: That's right. That's right.

KISSINGER: And he — now, he made it definite, and so —

NIXON: Right. And Bill can think that's what the whole damn meeting was about.

KISSINGER: Yeah. Oh, yeah.

NIXON: Yeah. So that we don't have — so I don't have to go right in — and the other thing is that —

KISSINGER: Bill has such a naive conception of foreign policy that he really will think this is how it happened.

NIXON: Yeah. Well, we'll do it that way. And then —

KISSINGER: And also it keeps them absolutely from leaking that they rammed it down your throat. And it keeps me out of it, so then —

NIXON: Well, Bill knows that I took him over and talked about the summit in the Red Room.

KISSINGER: Well, actually, last year, Mr. President —

NIXON: It was here.

KISSINGER: — he brought the summit up.

NIXON: I know. And Bill said, "Why don't we announce it now?" And I told him —

KISSINGER: Yeah.

NIXON: I said, "Well, they came — he [Gromyko] came back with this summit thing." And he [Rogers] said, "Its time has come." And I said, "This is a good thing." I said, "Fine, we'll go."

KISSINGER: That's right.

NIXON: Yeah. Bill will probably wonder how we agreed on a date so quickly. But —

KISSINGER: Well, you can — if he asks that, you can say that before he went back, Dobrynin said, "In principle, does the Chinese summit rule out —"

NIXON: Yeah.

KISSINGER: "— a Russian summit?" And I said —

NIXON: And then he said, "I'll send you a message."

KISSINGER: And I said, "No —"

NIXON: Sure.

KISSINGER: "— but it has to be after the Russian — the Chinese one."

"I do not take charge of things that don't matter."
September 29, 1971, 4:40 p.m.
Richard Nixon and Andrei Gromyko
OVAL OFFICE

After ninety minutes of general conversations that included Nixon, Gromyko, Dobrynin, Kissinger, Rogers, and interpreters, the president had a private meeting with the Soviet foreign minister. In a talk that both sides later described as cordial, the most noteworthy interchange concerned the Mideast and specifically Egypt.

• • •

NIXON: Well, I thought it would be helpful if we could have a private chat like we did before, and to say that I am pleased that we are now going forward on our meeting, which I think can — will come at a useful time. A meeting at the top level. I have noted with —

GROMYKO: Good.

NIXON: I think it's good —

GROMYKO: Very good.

NIXON: — and it's time. It's time we begin with our list of the — [with] Berlin out of the way, and then if we can move on these other areas, it will be — for example, if we could get the SALT thing ready, that would be a pretty good time. But maybe we can get it ready before that. Who knows? The Mideast and SALT — the main thing at such a meeting is to have some things that we can make progress on.

GROMYKO: It must be done — something good.

NIXON: Yeah. That's right.

GROMYKO: What is possible — what is possible on the —

NIXON: Yeah. Right. You know, or maybe —

GROMYKO: Even before.

NIXON: Yeah.

GROMYKO: For that we —

NIXON: Yeah.

GROMYKO: — which is, it must be done.

NIXON: We have to decide —

GROMYKO: Must be done.

NIXON: Yeah. Then, for example, at such a meeting we can — I would like to, I want to talk to you about the channel to use here. We might be able to make some significant announcement on trade and things of that sort. You see there — we must have some positive things come out.

GROMYKO: Just now? No.

NIXON: No, no. I meant when the meeting takes place, that we should plan it so that some positive —

GROMYKO: Yes, yes.

NIXON: — statements can be made. I thought — basically, I think we would have a new —

GROMYKO: Whatever —

NIXON: I have nothing in mind, but something to do with trade or something to do with, as well as on the political side.

GROMYKO: Before the May meeting?

NIXON: Before — or at the meeting.

GROMYKO: Or at the meeting. Yes.

NIXON: So that when, for them to come, when leaders at the top sit down, they produce something.

GROMYKO: Yes. Yes.

NIXON: You see, the mountain cannot labor and produce a mouse.

GROMYKO: Yes.

[laughter]

NIXON: Right. You know this? It's an American expression.

GROMYKO: This is — this subject, as well, I would say.

NIXON: All right.

GROMYKO: This subject, as well.

NIXON: And I will — I shall look forward very much to meeting the — I do not — I have not met either Mr. Brezhnev or Mr. Kosygin, and I shall look forward to it. And we will be forthcoming, and we hope — and we know you will too.

GROMYKO: Good. Mr. President, I would like to open — broach essentially two questions.

NIXON: Sure.

GROMYKO: Yes?

NIXON: Sure. Sure.

GROMYKO: First, you received letter from our Mr. Brezhnev.

NIXON: Right.

GROMYKO: Mr. Brezhnev attaches importance — I would say major importance — to the letter.

NIXON: The one that he sent?

GROMYKO: Yes.

NIXON: Yeah. Yeah.

GROMYKO: That is right.

NIXON: I have not replied yet. I didn't.

GROMYKO: No. You didn't.

NIXON: I have not yet. No.

GROMYKO: Not yet. Not yet.

NIXON: You see, that correspondence is private. The letter I sent to him —

GROMYKO: Letter.

NIXON: — was private, too.

GROMYKO: Private. Yes.

NIXON: So, let's see, the State Department doesn't know, so —

GROMYKO: I know. But I've got —

NIXON: But I will respond soon.

GROMYKO: Nice idea.

NIXON: I see.

GROMYKO: Good idea.

NIXON: Good. It may be —

GROMYKO: Only for us two.

NIXON: Good.

GROMYKO: Only the ambassador —

NIXON: Good. Us two.

GROMYKO: — who will be —

NIXON: It's best to keep it to us two.

GROMYKO: I think Mr. Brezhnev attaches great importance —

NIXON: Mm-hmm. Mm-hmm.

GROMYKO: — to the letter, and I am sure when you reply, he will study your reply —

NIXON: All right.

GROMYKO: — most thoroughly.

NIXON: Good.

GROMYKO: I wish to also tell you something that I know: [I saw] Mr. Brezhnev twelve days ago —

NIXON: Yeah.

GROMYKO: — and maybe it could be useful to have.

NIXON: Yeah.

GROMYKO: He is not a new man —

NIXON: No.

GROMYKO: — in our leadership. He is not new man. He —

NIXON: A long time.

GROMYKO: — has been in the Politburo a long time. He was one of the secretaries, a state provincial secretary, and an authoritative, I would say, secretary of the Communist Party. Even before, he was chairman of the, even on the Supreme Soviet, our parliament —

NIXON: Hmm.

GROMYKO: — for a long time.

NIXON: Yeah.

GROMYKO: And he followed, he became joint secretary of the Central Committee of the party, and then secretary-general of the Central Committee. He is man of great authority in hands.

NIXON: Hmm. He's in charge.

GROMYKO: Yes. Yes.

NIXON: That's good. That's the man we want to talk to us.

GROMYKO: Absolutely. Absolutely.

NIXON: And also you know that we know —

GROMYKO: You probably know this, but I think it is not, it is not uninteresting now to hear it from me —

NIXON: Yeah. Sure.

GROMYKO: — today. I know Mr. Brezhnev for a long period of time. He spoke with me; we met on the eve of my departure from Moscow to the United States to attend the session of the [United Nations] General Assembly, and then to meet you.

NIXON: Hmm.

GROMYKO: We spoke quite extensively, a great deal, on Soviet-American relations. And he expressed his urgent wishes to see improvement of our relations.

NIXON: Good.

GROMYKO: He said this. And he said that he stands for — whether if you can achieve it or not, we do not know — but he would like to see friendly relations between the United States and the Soviet Union.

NIXON: Mm-hmm.

GROMYKO: And he knows that I'm going to tell you —

NIXON: A couple things.

GROMYKO: Then, after conversation, we went together to — he received [unclear] —

NIXON: Mm-hmm.

GROMYKO: — of that organization. Then next, we continued conversation, left together to the airport, because he was going to meet — to Crimea to meet Brandt.

NIXON: Oh, yeah.

GROMYKO: To meet Brandt.

NIXON: [unclear]

GROMYKO: I needed to do some interview. And we continued to discuss this matter in the car to the airport.

NIXON: Mm-hmm.

GROMYKO: And he especially expressed his hope that it would be good if we can achieve sometimes point of view to say — I stressed the point in my conversation — to say that "all — at last our relations are good, and maybe even friendly."

NIXON: Mm-hmm.

GROMYKO: This is the thing I wish to tell — to tell you personally.

NIXON: Mm-hmm.

GROMYKO: Not in presence of —

NIXON: I understand.

GROMYKO: — interpreters.

NIXON: Translators.

GROMYKO: The second thing, he is not the man, which would like for you to dismantle the NATO.

NIXON: Oh, no, no.

GROMYKO: Test NATO. He does not like. He does not like.

NIXON: Mm-hmm.

GROMYKO: And maybe you sometimes, sometimes read or hear information about the Soviet press, hear your name, well, in connection with the policies sometimes of another correspondent — private correspondent. But this is not the line of the leadership —

NIXON: Right, right. I understand the difference. I understand the difference —

GROMYKO: Not at all. Not at all. Not at all. And he does not like this line they employ.

NIXON: No. Mm-hmm.

GROMYKO: He is against it. He is against it. I wish just to inform you, if you don't know about it. Never he — what still more, I would like to tell you, so he — [laughs] initiative he's asked me to tell you about, this guarantee. But I'm privy because I know him very well.

NIXON: Mm-hmm.

GROMYKO: And I take this responsibility.

NIXON: Sure.

GROMYKO: Responsibility. He is man of strong character, strong character — strong character, strong will. And when he says that something must be done —

NIXON: Mm-hmm.

GROMYKO: — he is going in the direction he outlined.

NIXON: Mm-hmm.

GROMYKO: It relates to all questions. It relates to the question of our relations with the United States.

NIXON: Mm-hmm. Mm-hmm. Good.

GROMYKO: If I did not know you for a long time, maybe I would not go this far.

NIXON: Well, I appreciate that.

GROMYKO: But I think —

NIXON: Let me say that — let me — let me just — let me say that, first, I will continue the private correspondence with him. You tell him that —

GROMYKO: I will tell him.

NIXON: — that I will respond personally, myself. Second, and — I appreciate his sentiments that he's expressed and I have the same sentiment. I am known, I know, as the — it's rather ironical — as really anti-Communist and all that, but I'm a very realistic man, a very practical man.

Also, I am one who has, as I've often said, enormous respect for the Russian people — a great people. I know that looking at the world, even if we — even though our political systems are very different, that the future of peace in the world for twenty-five years — and nobody can look further than that, I think — is in our hands. It's in the hands of the United States and Russia. Nobody else. Someone else can stir it up, but if we put our foot down, we can make a great contribution. I think that the — I think that it would be a great signal to the world if — not only the announcement that we're doing, but also if, at such a meeting, it could be said that the relations that existed between the United States and the Soviet Union during the Great War began — were — are again resuming.

Now, of course, that doesn't mean — we have to be practical — that we're going to agree on systems of government, that we won't be competing here and there. But it does mean that we have a new dialogue, a new relationship where we solve the problems. That's what I want. And I — you can tell the chairman —

GROMYKO: I will —

NIXON: — that I feel exactly the same way. And I also feel that now is the time. I think it's very important. If we let the time slip by, the events may drag us into something, so now is the time to get together if we can.

GROMYKO: That means that both sides must work with patience —

NIXON: That's right.

GROMYKO: — work with will —

NIXON: That's right.

GROMYKO: — and —

NIXON: That's right.

GROMYKO: — with determination.

NIXON: Determination. Bargain hard, but agree.

GROMYKO: This, let me say, it will require time and energy —

NIXON: Let me — let me suggest a couple of things that are very important. Kissinger's meetings with Dobrynin are very important. As you know, they were helpful in —

GROMYKO: In Berlin.

NIXON: Yes. Tomorrow, I have asked Kissinger to meet with you, to call on you, or I guess he's going to meet you. He has a message —

GROMYKO: I know.

NIXON: — that he would like to convey. It's from me —

GROMYKO: Yes.

NIXON: — on a technical matter. It has to do with Vietnam. And we just want to pass it on to you.

GROMYKO: Mm-hmm.

NIXON: The other thing that I didn't want to go into in the circle here is on the Mideast.

GROMYKO: Mm-hmm.

NIXON: Now, it may be that working very, very quietly — Kissinger and Dobrynin, you see — that we can explore something on the Mideast. I don't know.

GROMYKO: Mm-hmm.

NIXON: But you raise that subject with him, with Kissinger, if you like.

GROMYKO: I will tell you —

NIXON: Then the —

GROMYKO: — I will tell you something there though.

NIXON: Yeah. Just — and so, because it may be that the Mideast is too complicated to handle at the —

GROMYKO: With Rogers?

NIXON: — or SALT. Well, at the foreign secretary level. See?

GROMYKO: Mm-hmm.

NIXON: It may be we have to work very privately.

GROMYKO: Mm-hmm.

NIXON: Now, I think that those — but I think — I think that in — and even take a matter like the European Security Conference: I think it's probably better to keep that in this channel, you know, where we're very private. And it will — and, sure, of course, some things will be at the State — ambassador level, and the secretary of state, and the rest — but the more we can have in this channel, then I will personally take charge, which is what is important. And Brezhnev, of course, must do the same.

GROMYKO: Good. Good.

NIXON: Is that fair enough? Good?

GROMYKO: Good. Good. Good. We —

NIXON: Good. You see, I — we're — I do not take charge of things that don't matter, but where they matter, like between our countries, then I make the decisions.

GROMYKO: The channel proved to be effective, in the experience of the Berlin negotiations for us.

NIXON: It couldn't have been done without that channel.

GROMYKO: One thing on the Middle East, I would like, if you had not mentioned it, I would mention it. I wish to tell you privately, strictly privately —

NIXON: Yeah?

GROMYKO: — two key points. Frankly, some time ago, the United States government, and you personally — and I think a sufficient decision was made — expressed concern about how delivery of armaments —

NIXON: To Egypt? Right?

GROMYKO: Right.

NIXON: Fine.

GROMYKO: We think that it would be possible to reach understanding, if some kind of framework is reached, which would provide [for] withdrawal of Israeli troops from all occupied territories. We would agree on the limitation, or, if you wish, even on stoppage — full stoppage of delivery [of armaments] —

NIXON: Hmm.

GROMYKO: — in connection — even in connection with understanding on the first stage —

NIXON: What to do here —

GROMYKO: On the —

NIXON: Exactly. In terms of the —

GROMYKO: — even in connection with the interim [agreement] —

NIXON: — interim. Right.

GROMYKO: You agree.

NIXON: Right.

GROMYKO: Even in connection, provided that this is the — connected with the final, with the withdrawal —

NIXON: Yeah.

GROMYKO: — of — from all territories, within a certain period of time. More than this, I would like to tell you, also frankly, confidentially, both this point and then the third one I discussed with Mr. Brezhnev. So this is not the second point here. The second point is this: some time ago, you expressed interest — oh, I don't know — in Egypt, about our presence there, our military —

NIXON: Yeah, yeah, yeah, yeah.

GROMYKO: — presence in Egypt.

NIXON: Yeah.

GROMYKO: I do not know whether you know precisely our position, or not, on our presence, but, in a sense, we are present there. In a sense —

NIXON: Mm-hmm.

GROMYKO: — north of Cairo, certain personnel, and certain forces —

NIXON: I see.

GROMYKO: — and such presence, the presence is agreed. We are ready, in connection with understanding, full understanding, on the Middle East —

NIXON: Mm-hmm.

GROMYKO: — we are ready to agree not to have our military units there.

NIXON: Mm-hmm.

GROMYKO: Not to have soldiers based there —

NIXON: Not the civilian, I understand.

GROMYKO: Not precisely. Not to have military units, you know, there —

NIXON: Not there.

GROMYKO: We probably — we would leave a limited number, a limited number of advisors for purely advisory —

NIXON: Advisory purposes.

GROMYKO: You know —

NIXON: Technical advisors.

GROMYKO: — like you have in Iran.

NIXON: Like we have in Cambodia and the rest.

GROMYKO: Yes, that is right.

NIXON: That's right.

GROMYKO: I said it's for —

NIXON: I understand.

GROMYKO: — for purely advisory purposes.

NIXON: But not for — I see.

GROMYKO: Hmm.

NIXON: Right. I understand.

GROMYKO: Absolutely right. I know that you —

NIXON: But these are matters that I deal with.

GROMYKO: Okay.

NIXON: Yes.

GROMYKO: I know. You understand very clearly.

NIXON: Yeah.

GROMYKO: I would say limited, and maybe very limited.

NIXON: I understand.

GROMYKO: Maybe very.

NIXON: Well, those are matters that could threaten — be discussed, if — but that has to be very private.

GROMYKO: And it would be very private, very private —

NIXON: Right. Right. Right. The Mideast is so tense — so touchy, politically, in this country —

GROMYKO: All these —

NIXON: — it has to be private here.

GROMYKO: All these —

NIXON: Right.

GROMYKO: — ideas, we did not put into motion —

NIXON: Sure. Right. Right —

GROMYKO: — with anybody. Never. This is —

NIXON: Mm-hmm.

GROMYKO: — new, and this is principle.

NIXON: Mm-hmm.

GROMYKO: And the third point, whether you attach importance or not, but Israel always stresses anything you don't want to stress. It would be — we would be ready, even if this accord is written on this basis, even in connection with the interim agreement, in the third stage.

NIXON: Mm-hmm.

GROMYKO: And we will be ready to deal — to sign, if you wish, together with you, or with U.S. and other powers, or with all other powers who are on the [United Nations] Security Council. This initiative [is] possible in a document, if with additional —

NIXON: Mm-hmm. Mm-hmm.

GROMYKO: — agreement and understanding on security for Israel —

[unclear exchange]

GROMYKO: — that is —

NIXON: Sure.

GROMYKO: — in connection with the interim. With the interim —

NIXON: I see.

GROMYKO: — provided that interim is —

NIXON: All right.

GROMYKO: — connected. [unclear] and our own suggestion was that, well, when vis-à-vis the border or finalization of the agreement, only some kind of decision —

NIXON: True.

GROMYKO: — should be taken on guarantees. But we are ready to discuss this idea in connection — we can sign any agreement with guarantees in connection with the interim, provided that the interim is linked with Israeli [withdrawal]. The limitation of even — limitation, even stoppage [unclear] —

NIXON: Your arms?

GROMYKO: Second —

NIXON: Present?

GROMYKO: — not presence of any Soviet units. Not —

NIXON: Sure.

GROMYKO: — [unclear] heavy units, intermediate military —

NIXON: Right.

GROMYKO: — you could say.

NIXON: Sure.

GROMYKO: Some of the limited — I say this would [be] limited number of advisors for purely, purely, purely advisory purposes.

NIXON: I understand.

[unclear exchange]

GROMYKO: If you —

NIXON: Let us do a little — as I say, we'll do a private talking on this. And then, on this message that Kissinger brings you tomorrow on Vietnam, I think you'll find very interesting. It could be very —

GROMYKO: Good.

NIXON: It could be very important.

GROMYKO: Very good.

NIXON: If we could get that out of the way, you could see — and I don't, we don't want to ask you to do anything that's not in your interest — but if we get that out of the way, it opens other doors. You see?

GROMYKO: Good. I have to say — what I told you about this Middle East, this is —

NIXON: Comes from —

GROMYKO: — result of the conversation personally with Brezhnev. And he wants me to say to you —

NIXON: Yeah.

GROMYKO: So we are taking a position.

NIXON: I understand.

"And then we say that I am going to resume the bombing."
September 30, 1971, 9:22 a.m.
Richard Nixon, George H. W. Bush, and Henry Kissinger
OVAL OFFICE

In the postmortem of the Gromyko meetings, Nixon and Kissinger were enthusiastic about the Soviet offer of a reduced presence in the Mideast. Buoyed by the success of the previous day's talks, Nixon presented a new scenario for the Vietnam War, one that would end it, but on his terms.

• • •

KISSINGER: I was wondering, we were exploring all possibilities, but if the American speech [in the UN General Assembly] could be put after I've left there, since the debate will go on for three or four days after I've left there.

• • •

KISSINGER: You said yesterday I should check with you about that Gromyko conversation.

NIXON: Yeah. He said that — three things that they've agreed to — except I don't think we're going to give on. He said, "First," he said, "we will agree to stop sending arms into the area [Middle East]. Second, we will agree to remove all military units from the UAR — all military units." He said, "Now, these" — I want to be precise. He said, "We will keep advisors, like you have in Iran, but no military units. We will remove them all. And third, we will agree to participate in any kind of a guarantee of Israel's integrity, sovereignty, et cetera, et cetera. Any — with you or anybody else, we will agree to participate." And then he said, "We will do all this at the time of an interim settlement, provided there is an understanding it should go on to a more permanent one" — or I could get something like that.

KISSINGER: That's a tremendous step.

NIXON: Well, it is a — and so I said — through the whole thing, when he said — the last point, I think, is a significant [one]. I, through the whole thing, I said, "Well, Dr. Kissinger's assistant will, first," I said, "will bring you a message that I consider of enormous importance on the Vietnam thing." And I said, "I have discussed it with you. Second, let him discuss this. And third," I said, "as I told you, on any, on European security, and all these other matters," I said, "let's keep to — let's talk about it in this channel." And I said, "So that we can work things out privately." It was about what — that's what he was talking about. Now, it seems to me that on the Vietnam thing, he has to [unclear]. Actually, the idea of getting the damn thing out of the way before the summit is important. But also, the idea that [unclear] make a settlement — I mean, that we're — I don't know how far you're going to go in talking about the Thieu thing. Not far, I trust.

KISSINGER: No. No. I won't even —

NIXON: I haven't [said] I think that you ought to disclose that to him in any way.

KISSINGER: What I thought, with your permission, I would tell him, Mr. President, is that we are going through those eight points.

NIXON: Mm-hmm.

KISSINGER: We are prepared to make a compromise in the political field and in the withdrawal field, but I won't tell him what it is, that we may propose it — we will propose it to Hanoi within the near future, and we want Hanoi to think about it. That's going to be our last offer.

NIXON: Mm-hmm.

KISSINGER: And we want them to use their influence —

NIXON: Well, I wrote down something last night that I just — in view of all the malarkey he was giving me about the desire of Brezhnev to — and it may be that Brezhnev would like, does realize that a Soviet-American pact of friendship is very much in their interest — and also that we may need it too. You know, not a "pact," but, you know, the idea we are friends and so forth.

KISSINGER: Mm-hmm.

NIXON: It occurred to me that the way you could put this is that Brezhnev wants friendship. That, "Look, Mr. Foreign Minister, I myself can't even predict what this president, Mr. Nixon, President Nixon will do. He surprises me. But he is a man, more than anybody that has been in this office in this century, who will make a daring, big play."

KISSINGER: That they've learned now.

NIXON: "A daring, big play. He made it. Now, you people wondered about China." They wondered about the economy; they wondered about this. "He is prepared to make a very big play with you, because he considers your situation infinitely more important than anything else. You know why?" I thought — my little analogy is, when I talk about it, I said, "Now, we always say in these meetings that we want peace, and that it's important." I said, "We want peace with Bolivia, but whether we have peace with Bolivia doesn't make any difference, because the world —"

KISSINGER: I think, Mr. President, your meeting yesterday ranked right up there with the Ceausescu meeting [Nixon's visit to Bucharest in August 1969].

NIXON: Yeah.

KISSINGER: And, in a way, it was more difficult, because you couldn't be quite that tough —

NIXON: Tough.

KISSINGER: [unclear] But you were so firm, and when he started with this malarkey, and you said, "All right, but that we say this — we say this, but what else can we say here? But let's" — in effect, you said, "Let's get concrete."

NIXON: Yeah.

KISSINGER: I think when the history of this is written, it will turn out that you turned around SALT yesterday, as much as you turned around Berlin. You remember — you notice how he said to you what you said last year about Berlin has come true?

NIXON: Yeah.

KISSINGER: And I think these are going to be —

NIXON: At least we got through this — we got through on SALT the very simple point that we couldn't freeze in a superiority for them on offensive weapons, and an inferiority for us on defensive weapons —

KISSINGER: Right.

NIXON: — and that we had to look at the whole bag.

KISSINGER: Well, and he kept — and Dobrynin, while we were waiting for you —

NIXON: Yeah?

KISSINGER: — kept coming back to that two or three times.

NIXON: All right, now, that, in my opinion, and also that I am the only one who can deliver on a big play — I'm the only one that can deliver because I can hold the Right. If Vietnam is the only thing that stands in the way, it will open all doors. Now, just — and that it's time to get it over with. Now, I think we go on just throwing the carrot out there. Put the stick out there. Say, "Now, his patience is running out in Vietnam and he may be very embarrassed in the polls." And I'd throw in a hell of a threat. Because my view on Vietnam, the more I've thought about it, is that toward the end of the year — and I'm going to poll it in advance to see what it is — that I will say, "All right, we'll make an announcement of some sort." And then we — I'm assuming these bastards turn us down — and then we say that I am going to resume the bombing —

KISSINGER: That's what I think.

NIXON: — of military targets in North Vietnam unless and until we get the prisoners back.

KISSINGER: That is what I would say. Absolutely.

NIXON: Just lay it right to them —

KISSINGER: I would say that we —

NIXON: "I will resume the bombing until — when we get the prisoners back." Just put it on that basis.

KISSINGER: I'd say we've offered everything. Go through the whole record.

NIXON: Yeah.

KISSINGER: We've been there. We have gone to the Russians. We've gone to the Chinese. We've gone every avenue. We've offered to replace Thieu. Everything has been offered. All has been rejected. And this is it.

NIXON: Yeah. Ehrlichman [unclear]. But anyway, we have a —

KISSINGER: Incidentally, I think, Mr. President, if we could go back to the China thing for a minute.

NIXON: Yeah, we've got to go —

KISSINGER: We wanted this stuff early in this congressional session.

NIXON: Where's Ehrlichman? He can come in now, if you can find his [unclear].

KISSINGER: We wanted this early in the congressional session. We're having a terrific double play with two successive Tuesdays [the announcement on October 5 of Kissinger's trip to China and on October 12 of Nixon's trip to Moscow].

NIXON: I know.

KISSINGER: And I think it's going to pull the teeth of a lot of opponents. When we planned this in the middle of August, we just couldn't know they —

NIXON: Look, we just got to — don't worry about it, Henry. We've got to — I'll sit there with Bill, and we'll talk about it, and I'm going to talk about the Russian summit a little with him.

KISSINGER: Right.

NIXON: Listen, this is a — the Russian summit is a hell of a thing for Rogers.

KISSINGER: Well, we don't want him, though, to start planning it. He screws up really every —

NIXON: He's not going to plan it, but, I mean, it's a hell of a thing for him to go!

KISSINGER: Oh, yeah.

NIXON: Jesus Christ, I'm going to do it. You know that. By God, I'll tell you one thing: I have decided, with all his faults, I'm not going to let him do anything. I'm going to do it. And do it — Christ, by that, I mean this office is going to plan on the summit matter.

KISSINGER: And he really doesn't understand.

NIXON: He —

KISSINGER: In fact, I don't want to go into detail, but he screwed up something on Germany with Gromyko on the Berlin thing, because he couldn't understand it.

NIXON: When will you see Gromyko?

KISSINGER: At five thirty.

NIXON: Yeah.

KISSINGER: I'll call you — or you'll be on the way? Will you — I'll call over here.

NIXON: I'll be over here at a reception. And then I'm seeing — I ought to have a talk with Haig. Is Haig here?

KISSINGER: Yeah.

NIXON: To get his report. I'll tell you what I might do: I might have — Shultz is going down to get me a report on the domestic thing, and maybe — and then come back the next morning. Maybe I could have Haig do the same thing, and we can go back —

KISSINGER: Sure. Sure.

NIXON: — right away. Because I just want to just hear from him —

KISSINGER: Absolutely, I think it'd be very useful.

NIXON: — hear what the hell the story is. But what do you think of my plan? That, by God, if they turn down everything, we resume the bombing of military [unclear] with the purpose of bringing them home. I'll bet you the American people back it with seventy percent. What do you think?

KISSINGER: I would do it. I think we cannot go out whimpering.

NIXON: Yes, sir. Incidentally, though, I think, speaking of whimpering, that goddamn Teddy [Kennedy] overstepped when he said he would crawl on his hands and knees —

KISSINGER: Mr. President, if we think where we were when we came in here, and at the various stages, to get Gromyko here the way we were — he was yesterday.

NIXON: Jesus.

KISSINGER: To get the Chinese. We've got everything working together. The only thing that's missing — I think with this, we may do something on the Middle East.

NIXON: Well, I don't understand the Middle East problem well enough to know whether we can, but, it seems to me, it's a hell of a concession.

KISSINGER: Oh, it's a —

NIXON: Yeah. If we really focus —

KISSINGER: — if he really means it.

NIXON: But the point is, the way it now ought to be done, frankly, you — and that, of course, means me — I ought to get in Rabin and say, "Now, look here, this is a hell of a deal. And we think we can sell — this is what we're prepared to put, to run down the Russians' throat, if you'll do something." See my point?

KISSINGER: Yeah, but we'd have to —

NIXON: Don't tell him the Russians offered. Tell him we will get it for them. Come on in, John [Ehrlichman].

[EHRLICHMAN enters.]

KISSINGER: But we'd have to find out first what they want in return for the interim settlement.

NIXON: Oh, I know. What — but what by whom? [What] the Russians want?

KISSINGER: I mean, how they define interim settlement, because —

NIXON: No, look. I mean, no, before we get — in order to get the Russians — let me put it this way: the Israelis are the tough ones. They're going to be a hell of a lot tougher than the Russians. Now, in order to get the Israelis to come some way, we've got to say — we've got — we mustn't let them think the Russians are prepared to offer this, until we get a hell of an offer from them.

KISSINGER: No, but we have to find out from the Russians, and I can find out from Gromyko, what he has in mind, how far the Israelis have to go —

NIXON: Oh, yeah.

KISSINGER: — on the interim settlement.

NIXON: Yeah, but don't tell anybody. Never tell the Israelis what the Russians are prepared to do —

KISSINGER: Oh, God.

NIXON: — because then they'll say, "We'll start from there."

KISSINGER: No, no.

NIXON: Okay, I'll see you later.

"I want them to want something from us on the Middle East."

September 30, 1971, 12:20 p.m.

Richard Nixon, William Rogers, and Henry Kissinger

OVAL OFFICE

The follow-up to the Nixon meeting with Gromyko was in Rogers's hands, as he was scheduled to have lunch with the foreign minister at the Soviet embassy on September 30. While there, the two would sign a pact ancillary to SALT; it called for upgrades to the "hot line" between the two superpowers, literally and figuratively keeping the line of communication open in order to reduce the chance of nuclear war. Nixon and Kissinger, however, had become more interested in the Soviet attitude toward the Mideast. They wanted Rogers to keep that topic alive, even while he said nothing that was in the least bit encouraging. It was a diplomatic trick for which they rehearsed just before he left for the Soviet embassy.

• • •

NIXON: You're going to see Dobrynin?

ROGERS: Yeah.

KISSINGER: Gromyko went home.

ROGERS: Gromyko. I have a lunch today at the embassy.

NIXON: Yeah. Yeah. Just keep the Middle East dangled.

ROGERS: Really?

NIXON: They need us — what I meant is: I have a feeling, in my talk with him, that they're at least — the two reasons that they're, two things that they want from us, not only — one is the China thing worries them; and the second is the Middle East. They really are worried about the damn place. I've got — but I've had — in the private conversation, he talked about the Middle East a great deal. You know, that Brezhnev, particularly, was interested and that sort of thing. And I think it's very important that you —

ROGERS: When you say "dangled," what do you mean exactly? In other words —

NIXON: Well, what I meant is that — well, I don't want them to think that we can help solve this problem but that it's terribly difficult, as we emphasized yesterday, working with our Israeli friends; it's terribly difficult, and that it's going to take an awful lot on their part to do it. What do you think, Henry? I don't know. You — you're —

KISSINGER: I think the way it is now —

NIXON: Yeah.

KISSINGER: — they really — I think the way Bill has it now, as between the Israelis and the Egyptians, without tricking them into it —

ROGERS: I think it's perfect now. That's why I already told them that —

NIXON: Well, but after that meeting — but I think we —

ROGERS: I don't have a plan to —

NIXON: By "dangle," I mean leave it right there. I don't want to —

ROGERS: Well, the point I —

NIXON: I don't want you to go any further. Don't be too — what I'm getting at is this: I want them to want something from us on the Middle East. They must want our cooperation, and we must not be in the position of wanting theirs so much.

ROGERS: I don't think they want ours, and I don't think we want theirs, especially.

NIXON: Well, we sure don't want to guarantee or something.

ROGERS: I mean, from the — you see, the way we've been playing, Mr. President — I've been playing is — they don't want anything from us; they like it the way it is. So I kept them out. I haven't asked them for a goddamn thing. We haven't yielded one of the things that concerns them.

KISSINGER: I've been impressed with the —

NIXON: One has to say —

ROGERS: Now, what I've tried to do is, this time, is to give him a little more information, without really telling him anything or without asking anything. I've been telling him, "We're working this for this cause; we think it's a good one; we're the only ones that are doing it; both Egypt and Israel have asked us to do it; and we're going to keep pushing at it; and we don't want you to work with us; we don't ask you to do anything."

NIXON: Hmm.

ROGERS: But we want to keep advised —

NIXON: Good. Good. Because — that's good. That's good. Because I have —

ROGERS: This is the position I take —

NIXON: Listen, I'd say to him — I'm not so sure, Bill, that you are, just based on what he said then, I'm not so sure but what they may get a hell of a lot more worried about the Middle East and their clients.

ROGERS: Sure, their —

NIXON: And for that reason, they may not like things the way they are. They may not. That's my point. So I'd keep them worried.

ROGERS: Yeah.

NIXON: Keep them worried. That's what I mean.

ROGERS: Yeah. On this European [Security] Conference, if it's all right with you, I would like to suggest to him that any discussions on it should be with me. That we don't want any other — that it's such — it's got to be such a private matter, and we can't let our allies know that we're seriously considering a conference —

NIXON: Absolutely.

ROGERS: — until a satisfactory solution to the problem [unclear] —

NIXON: No ambassadorial —

ROGERS: And if there's any contact on it, let Dobrynin talk to me or have him send a message, because I think we should seriously delay any discussion —

NIXON: Yeah.

ROGERS: — of substance for a while.

NIXON: Good. Good.

KISSINGER: I agree.

ROGERS: Then when he has something —

NIXON: I would say that we would do not — well, you noticed how I was trying to dance off of it, because I'd read your briefing paper. I think you should tell him that I said when I used the word "preliminary" and "private," I meant exactly that.

ROGERS: Hmm.

NIXON: And that means preliminary and private — that we do not set up a working group.

ROGERS: Working group.

NIXON: On the first part, we don't have it done in a, you know, in any formalized way, and that you'll just chat about the thing.

ROGERS: Well, what I was going to tell him —

NIXON: Yeah?

ROGERS: — is that you and I had first talked, and that you said —

NIXON: Right.

ROGERS: — "preliminary" and "private," and that you wanted him to understand that it would be with me. If Dobrynin wanted to talk about it, fine, come with me.

NIXON: Fine.

ROGERS: Because, otherwise, he's going to pass the word to everybody that we've agreed to private talks.

NIXON: Exactly.

ROGERS: And I don't want that.

NIXON: Exactly. Exactly. And also, tell him how the meeting would — but you would say — be with you on a completely private basis.

ROGERS: Oh, oh sure. Well, they would understand that.

NIXON: No crapping around.

ROGERS: They've been pretty good about that.

NIXON: Well, that's what I mean — if you tell him that. Good. Good.

ROGERS: They're pretty good when they deal with you privately. But they're not very good when they deal with everybody else in a big —

NIXON: Yeah, well, as you noticed, Gromyko was trying to push us toward, yesterday, into the position of saying —

ROGERS: I know—

NIXON: "Can I say we'll do it before a conference?"

ROGERS: Oh, sure. Sure.

NIXON: But I didn't say that. And I think that's pretty clear.

ROGERS: Yeah, it was.

NIXON: Oh.

ROGERS: No doubt about that.

NIXON: Yeah.

ROGERS: Okay.

NIXON: All right. Bye.

"A non-Communist Asia . . . without the United States is potentially
more dangerous than an Asia with the United States."
　　October 14, 1971, 3:05 p.m.
　　Richard Nixon and Henry Kissinger
　　EXECUTIVE OFFICE BUILDING

As Nixon looked forward to his summit in China in February, he became noticeably nervous. Practically everything about his China was "goddamn," even the schools that Mrs. Nixon was scheduled to visit. Some of the president's discomfort probably related to the approaching conundrum of Taiwan and the UN. The General Assembly was preparing to vote on a single-China resolution later in the month, while the United States tried to enlist support for a delay on the part of the resolution that ejected Taiwan from the UN. If that didn't work, the resolution was expected to reach the Security Council before the end of the year. At that point, the United States could veto it, but Nixon had no plans for doing so.

• • •

NIXON: My idea is that the time for Taiwan to go out is next year, shouldn't be this year, it's not good for the Chinese.

• • •

NIXON: Let me say, there's never been a, no president in my memory has made a state visit longer than four days. That's our standard rule. And I'm just not going over that.

KISSINGER: I have no problem with that, the more serious, the more businesslike—

• • •

NIXON: I just meet them at the airport and then I go in and get closeted for four days. And she [Mrs. Nixon] goes out to the goddamn schools. You know what I mean? So they get the feel of Americans; you see, there's a missionary feel about China. And they just like the idea that we love the goddamn Chinese, that's what I really meant about that.

• • •

NIXON: — get a feel for the goddamn place. That's one thing about the Communist system, the capital is the least, it's like Washington, it's the least representative. It's so tightly controlled. You get to another city, it's an entirely different thing.

• • •

NIXON: We're in a stronger position, particularly in Cambodia, than they are, and a lot stronger than we were in October. I'd be tougher on Cambodia and I'd be tougher on Laos.

But with Japan, I believe that we have got to frankly scare the bejeezus out of them more on Japan. It's just my sense as I read through this [an early U.S. draft of the communiqué]. I can see what they're doing. He's [Zhou Enlai] talking with strong language. But on the other hand, here's the key thing, they have got to become convinced that a Japan and going further, a non-Communist Asia, without the United States is potentially more dangerous than an Asia with the United States. Now, you made that point, but I'd hit it right on the nose, say we're going to stick around.

• • •

NIXON: For example, we'll take the Taiwan thing, we know what has to happen. Korea, we will work that out in an oral way. Except, I'd work that out orally. But also — but I would state very, very firmly, "Now look, the United States is a Pacific power and an Asian power, and we are going to maintain a presence there."

• • •

KISSINGER: One of two things are going to happen. After the election either Beijing is going to get impatient and then there's going to be a blowup in their relations with you because their demands [unclear]. Or Chiang will die and there'll be negotiations. Or Mao and Zhou will die and there's such a goddamn turmoil in Beijing that no one will know anymore what the hell is going on anymore.

NIXON: So the only thing I think is that we have to remember that everything always comes out. I don't think we can have a secret deal, if we sold out Taiwan, you understand? I know what we're doing, but I want to be very careful.

"You can be mighty proud of the Pirates."
October 17, 1971, 4:18 p.m.
Richard Nixon and Danny Murtaugh
WHITE HOUSE TELEPHONE

While it is hard for any president to break away from the daily demands of the office for very long, President Nixon found time for sports as much as he could. He was an intense fan, especially of baseball and football, and can be heard yelling at the television on the Nixon tapes.

Moments after the conclusion of the World Series, he called both team managers. Speaking first to Danny Murtaugh of the Pittsburgh Pirates, Nixon congratulated

him on winning the best-of-seven-game series. The Pirates, led by MVP Roberto Cle-
mente, defeated the Baltimore Orioles four games to three. The final game was a pitch-
ing duel in which Pirates pitcher Steve Blass threw his second complete game win of the
series.

. . .

NIXON: Hello?

OPERATOR: Mr. President —

NIXON: Yeah.

OPERATOR: I have Danny Murtaugh.

NIXON: Hello?

OPERATOR: There you are.

NIXON: Hello?

MURTAUGH: Hello!

NIXON: Danny, I just want you to know that I saw the game on television, and you can be mighty proud of the Pirates. You beat a great team, and yours was a great team.

MURTAUGH: Well, thank you Mr. Pr—

NIXON: And I must say, the way you sat in that dugout without ever being flappable, that's really something.

MURTAUGH: Yeah, but I chewed about four packets of tobacco today.

NIXON: That's right. Well, I know that, of course, Clemente, of course was fantastic, and Blass, but really it was a team effort, the fantastic defense you had, I thought, was really outstanding.

MURTAUGH: Well, I actually—

NIXON: That second baseman, you know, they said he couldn't field, but I didn't see him miss a chance the whole series.

MURTAUGH: He did a tremendous job out there, Mr. Pr—

NIXON: Well, I don't want, I know all the press is there to talk to you, but I just wanted you to know it was a great effort and you can be mighty proud of them.

MURTAUGH: Well, thank you, and I appreciate you taking—

NIXON: Yep.

MURTAUGH: — the time out —

NIXON: Yep.

MURTAUGH: — of your busy schedule to call me.

NIXON: I must say, I was hoping I'd get out there, but I'm a little busy right now, but I caught most of the game on TV.

MURTAUGH: Well, we realize that, and thank you for your interest in our game.

NIXON: Right. I'll bet Pittsburgh tears the town up when you get back! [laughs]

MURTAUGH: We sure intend to, I believe.

NIXON: You bet. Good luck. Bye.

MURTAUGH: Bye, Mr. President.

"I've lost a few, and I know that you don't get many calls when you lose."
October 17, 1971, 4:22 p.m.
Richard Nixon and Earl Weaver
WHITE HOUSE TELEPHONE

Next, Nixon called legendary Baltimore Orioles manager Earl Weaver to congratulate him on a good season, even though the team fell short in the final game of the World Series. Nixon also wished Weaver good luck on his team's visit to Japan, where the Orioles would face off with the Yomiuri Giants.

• • •

NIXON: Hello?

OPERATOR: I have Mr. Weaver for you.

NIXON: Yes.

OPERATOR: There you are.

NIXON: Hello?

WEAVER: Hello, sir.

NIXON: Earl, I know this is a tough time for you, but let me tell you that the Orioles played like champions when they lost, and it's, you, and I also admire your fighting spirit.

WEAVER: Well, Mr. President—

NIXON: Yeah.

WEAVER: I'll tell you, you couldn't have called at a better time, because—

NIXON: Well—

WEAVER: —because it means much more now than it would have meant at another time.

NIXON: Well, let me tell you, you know, I've lost a few, and I know that you don't get many calls when you lose, but boy you fellows were great, and, I saw the game yesterday on TV, and, that was one of the greatest, and the one today was, it could have gone either way. I'm telling you, [Mike] Cuellar and your boys were just fantastic.

WEAVER: Well, thank you very much.

NIXON: And, just tell the boys that, they played like champions, and you'll get a great reception in Japan, too, I'm sure.

WEAVER: Well, we hope to represent the United States as well as we can—

NIXON: Listen, I—

WEAVER: —and we would have liked to have gone as World Champions, but, we're going as American League Champions—

NIXON: American League Champions, and just one run away from the top.

WEAVER: Thank you.

NIXON: So, after all, as you've pointed out, I guess no other team's won a hundred games for three, three straight years in the American League, and there'll be another day. Well, tell all those fellows that, I must say, when I saw, yesterday, when Frank

Robinson went to third, and then, and that one, and then, I said, "My God, if an old man can run like that, he's doing all right!"

WEAVER: Well, thank you very much, Mr. President. I'll go right out and tell him.

NIXON: Fine, and good luck to you, Earl.

WEAVER: Okay, thank you.

NIXON: Fine, bye.

"Well, that was a bad vote, wasn't it?"

October 26, 1971, 11:13 a.m.

Richard Nixon and Ronald Reagan

WHITE HOUSE TELEPHONE

On October 25, the General Assembly of the UN voted to admit the People's Republic of China and expel the Republic of China (Taiwan). A compromise by Ambassador George H. W. Bush to permit membership by both nations was defeated.

California Governor Ronald Reagan called Nixon to express his disgust with the vote. He suggested recalling Bush in protest and announcing that the United States would no longer take part in or be bound by General Assembly votes.

• • •

NIXON: Well, that was a bad vote, wasn't it?

REAGAN: Well, I want to tell you —

NIXON: We worked our tails off, I must say. I think —

REAGAN: I know. I was just sick.

NIXON: Fifty-four to fifty-nine, I'm telling you. I just finished a meeting with Ted Agnew. He's back from Greece and Turkey, both of whom we got, incidentally. We didn't get Iran, though, damn it. You know, you figure there's the shah, we've done all the things for him, but —

REAGAN: Yeah.

NIXON: These African countries, they're the ones that I must say were disappointing.

REAGAN: Well, Mr. President, the reason I called was I know it is not easy to give a suggestion or advice to the president of the United States. But I just feel so strongly that we can't, in view of '72, we can't just sit and take this and continue as if nothing had happened. And I had a suggestion —

NIXON: Mm-hmm.

REAGAN: — for an action that I'd like to be so presumptuous as to suggest. My every instinct says get the hell out of that —

NIXON: [laughs]

REAGAN: — kangaroo court and let it sink. But I know that would be extremely difficult, and not the thing to do. But it has occurred to me that the United States, the people, I just know, first of all, they don't like the UN to begin with.

NIXON: That's right.

REAGAN: And it seemed to me that if you brought Mr. Bush back to Washington to let them sweat for about twenty-four hours as to what you were thinking of, and then if you went on television to the people of the United States and said that Mr. Bush was going back to the UN to participate in debate and discussions, to present our views and so forth, but he would not participate in any votes. That the United States would not vote, and would not be bound by the votes of the UN, because it is a debating society. You don't have to say that —

NIXON: Mm-hmm.

REAGAN: — but it is a debating society. So we'd be there. Our presence would be there, but we would just not participate in their votes. I think it would put those bums in the perspective they belong.

NIXON: Ha! It sure would! [laughs] Yeah.

REAGAN: I think it would make a hell of a campaign issue.

NIXON: Hmm.

REAGAN: Because I am positive that the people of the United States are thoroughly disgusted. And I think that this would put any candidate from the other side, the constant question would come to him —

NIXON: Mm-hmm.

REAGAN: — in the midst of this campaign, "What would you do, now?" And if he was stupid enough to open his mouth and say, "Oh, hell," you know, "we'd go right back to operating as usual [in the UN]," I think he'd be hung out to dry.

NIXON: Mm-hmm, mm-hmm, mm-hmm. Well, we've been trying to think here about what the reaction would be. I must say that the congressional action may be very interesting, on the appropriations side.

REAGAN: Well, you see, Mr. President, then, if they [the Congress] did what they threatened to do, they would simply be confirming your action.

NIXON: Mm-hmm.

REAGAN: They'd be making the budget meet that new position of the United States in the UN.

NIXON: Mm-hmm.

REAGAN: Reducing our importance. If the other way, if we do nothing and they take that action, it's a rebuff.

NIXON: Mm-hmm. Yeah. Well, let me give some thought to the whole thing. It's a tough one, as you're well aware. We've got some fish to fry on India-Pakistan. We're trying to avoid a war there. And the UN may have to play some damn role there, because we don't want to get involved —

REAGAN: No.

NIXON: — let me say, in that miserable place. Let me give some thought to this whole thing. As you know, I have been thinking about it. And I've talked this morning to two or three people about it. What the legal problems are, and so forth.

REAGAN: Well, I just felt I had to make this suggestion.

NIXON: No, I know, I appreciate it.

REAGAN: Last night, after that announcement came on, one commentator called me.

NIXON: Yeah.

REAGAN: He told me that the — and I told him, I said, "Well, I just think it confirms the moral bankruptcy of the organization —"

NIXON: [laughs]

REAGAN: "— of the UN." He told me the phone was ringing off the wall, and he said with people that are just enraged!

NIXON: Mm-hmm.

"It's at their initiative this time."

November 2, 1971, 9:32 a.m.
Richard Nixon, William Rogers, and Henry Kissinger
OVAL OFFICE

The two main negotiators for the North Vietnamese in the peace talks, chief delegate Thuy and special consultant Le Duc Tho (Le Duan's second in command in North Vietnam), requested a meeting with Kissinger in Paris toward the end of November. Tho had already been meeting with Kissinger in secret, but Nixon had directed him to clearly decline further talks unless there was new movement on the part of the North Vietnamese.

• • •

NIXON: We just got word that Le Duc Tho is coming back to Paris on the twentieth to meet with him on Sunday.

KISSINGER: That's [unclear].

NIXON: Huh?

KISSINGER: [unclear]

NIXON: Now, in my view, this is either fish or cut bait. There isn't any more reason to meet again. On the other hand, the — you know, you know the pattern of the previous meetings, and how much we have offered. We've answered the seven points, and they've agreed to some things, and so forth and so on.

KISSINGER: Bill has seen every memo —

NIXON: Yeah.

KISSINGER: — that I've given you.

NIXON: Yeah. What is the situation at the present time? Le Duc Tho —

KISSINGER: Well, [unclear] —

NIXON: — wants this meeting, though. What I'm getting at is this meeting assumes more importance due to the fact. Remember, I said, "No more meetings unless they have a direct expectation to discuss something new."

KISSINGER: Well, they — they sent us a message, which said that. We left it the last time, as you'll remember, Bill, that if I decide there's nothing to say, we'll meet again —

ROGERS: Mm-hmm.

KISSINGER: — but — that if you'll schedule a meeting. Well, we got a message — actually, we got it while I was in China — while in Paris; we didn't hear it in China — which said that Le Duc Tho is coming back to Paris, and Xuan Thuy and Le Duc Tho would like to meet me on November 20. We got it four weeks ahead of time. In other words, we got it the last week of October. They added to it that the reason they're suggesting November 20 is because Xuan Thuy is ill and recuperating. And you remember, they've given us that message also in the official —

NIXON: Hmm.

KISSINGER: Normally, they don't give any explanation for their movement. And —

NIXON: Yeah, that's public knowledge.

KISSINGER: Well —

NIXON: The Xuan Thuy part is [unclear] —

KISSINGER: Yeah, but normally when Xuan Thuy doesn't come to a meeting —

NIXON: Le Duc Tho is not public knowledge?

KISSINGER: That's right. Well, but —

NIXON: Yeah. Then he's coming back.

KISSINGER: That he's coming —

NIXON: He will be —

KISSINGER: He will be coming back. So, now, fifteenth, sixteenth, seventeenth — if he's coming — through the twentieth, he'll be in Paris, and that's [unclear] —

NIXON: The most important point is that this is —

KISSINGER: That he's asked for a meeting in a public venue.

NIXON: Yeah. Now, the most important point is that, then, the — we know, we've always said that there will come a time when the negotiating track is either closed, or it could really mean something. It could mean something this time. It could. I — I don't know. But, it — the point is, it's at their initiative this time; they want to meet. Now, this occurred, of course, before this damn vote. [On October 29, the Senate rejected H.R. 9910, which authorized $3.4 billion in economic and military foreign aid, in part to Vietnam.] I don't know how much effect this will have [unclear]. But, if we can get a continuing resolution through before that meeting, it would be very helpful. You see? Well, as a matter of fact, continuing resolutions have to go through —

[unclear exchange]

NIXON: — the fifteenth.

KISSINGER: It's got to go through with —

[unclear exchange]

NIXON: I think we really need the heat on that [unclear]. Now, this comes back to the point about the, about the troop withdrawal that — which — we got Laird on it; Laird's set up for it, but no idea that I've — here's what I had in mind, and, see if [unclear]. I think that we cannot make a — what I would call, and you know — I felt that there has to come a time when we make a — [unclear] you — we talk about a proposal, we may make an announcement: "Well, this is it. We have finished, and now—and the war is—it's completed, now." I was hoping we could do it now. We can, in the light of this meeting. We can. Before the meeting, you say, "Regardless of what happens, on the negotiating front, we're going to do this, or that, and the other thing."

"While she was a bitch, we got what we wanted too."

November 5, 1971, 7:50 a.m.

Richard Nixon, Bob Haldeman, and Henry Kissinger

OVAL OFFICE

At the beginning of November, Indira Gandhi visited Washington to press India's case and explain the dire nature of the refugee crisis. Nixon and Gandhi had already made up their minds long before they met in the Oval Office. Nixon believed that India wanted to confront Pakistan and underlined the potential consequences: American aid to India would be cut off, and the American people would not understand aggressive action. Gandhi knew that Nixon would not take India's side and had already calculated that the consequences would be short-lived. The American perception that India was going to go to war against Pakistan was fairly well established in the wake of Gandhi's trip to Washington.

• • •

NIXON: This is just the point when she [Gandhi] is a bitch.

KISSINGER: Well, the Indians are bastards anyway. They are starting a war there. It's, to them East Pakistan is no longer the issue. Now, I found it very interesting how she carried on to you yesterday about West Pakistan.

NIXON: I think I'll make the meeting today rather brief, cool. [unclear] I don't mean by that cool in terms of not trying to bring up [unclear]. I'll talk to her a little about Vietnam, and—

KISSINGER: I'd let her talk a little more, maybe today—

NIXON: Yeah?

KISSINGER: —to be a little less forthcoming. But basically, Mr. President—

NIXON: So I was trying to give her no excuses. Now I've talked to her, told her everything we're going to do. Now it's up to her.

KISSINGER: While she was a bitch, we got what we wanted too. You very subtly—I mean, she will not be able to go home and say that the United States didn't give her a warm reception and therefore, in despair, she's got to go to war.

NIXON: Yeah.

KISSINGER: So her objective—she has a right to be a little sore because you thwarted her objective. She would rather have had you give her a cool reception—

NIXON: That's right.

KISSINGER: —so that she could say that she was really put upon.

NIXON: Oh, we really—

KISSINGER: And —

NIXON: We really slobbered over the old witch.

KISSINGER: How you slobbered over her in things that did not matter, but in the things that did matter —

NIXON: Yeah.

KISSINGER: — you didn't give her an inch. So that she's —

NIXON: She knows.

KISSINGER: She knows she isn't coming out of here with any — she can't go home and say, "The president promised to do the following for me," and then when you don't do it —

NIXON: Did you get across with that clown [Sardar Swaran Singh, the Indian minister of foreign affairs] yesterday afternoon at five? You went on the, that as far as the, as she was concerned that she would consider letting him —

KISSINGER: Yep.

NIXON: — consult with regard to the designation. We want to be sure he understood that was the situation.

KISSINGER: Right, and I fixed it in the memorandum of conversation which I'm giving him in such a way that it — just a little. I've made it a little more explicit.

NIXON: Now you've covered Rogers for long enough —

KISSINGER: Oh yeah, Rogers is in good shape.

NIXON: He's prepared to be told this?

KISSINGER: Oh yes. They've apparently treated him personally in a way that he doesn't like, so he's very —

NIXON: Ha!

KISSINGER: No, no. He'll be very tough with them.

NIXON: Yeah, he's likely to be sharper with them than I was, you know. He can do that [unclear].

KISSINGER: Well, he will be personally sharper but he doesn't like her. In substance he won't be as tough as you —

NIXON: He's likely [unclear].

KISSINGER: — because he doesn't know the subject so well. I mean the skill —

NIXON: You should have heard, Bob, the way we worked her around. I dropped stilettos all over her. It's like, you know —

KISSINGER: She didn't know [unclear exchange] about the guerrillas in East Pakistan. [unclear] One thing that really struck me, the blown-up [unclear] and that takes a lot of technical training. I wonder where they got that.

NIXON: She [unclear] so fast.

KISSINGER: She said the East Bengal rifles [unclear — used to?]. That's where it came from.

NIXON: That's right. We also stuck it to her on that book — Henry's book about India-Pakistan.

KISSINGER: She said she studied a lot about the problems — how these conflicts started. Read a book by [Neville] Maxwell, called *India-China War*, which is a book that in effect proves that India started the '62 war. It was done with an enormous politeness and courtesy and warmth.

NIXON: Well I acted as if I didn't know what the hell had happened —

HALDEMAN: Yeah.

NIXON: — so she couldn't say anything. But she knew goddamn well that I knew what happened, don't you think?

KISSINGER: Oh, yeah. You stuck it to her about the press.

NIXON: On that I hit it hard.

KISSINGER: And I told —

NIXON: I raised my voice a little.

KISSINGER: And I told her assistant — I told my opposite number that the thing that is really striking to us is that last year Mrs. Gandhi, during her election campaign, made official protests that we were intervening when we weren't. And she never produced any proof. And yet every opposition candidate gets a royal reception, tremendous publicity, personal meetings. And then after you do all of this you come over here and ask us to solve all your problems.

NIXON: You told him that?

KISSINGER: Oh, yeah.

NIXON: Good for you.

KISSINGER: I said look at the record the last three months. You've had a press campaign against us. You put out the word that our relations are the worst ever. You get Kennedy over. You get that Congressman [Cornelius] Gallagher over. You make a treaty with the Russians. And then you come here and say we have to solve your problems for you.

NIXON: Well if it was any —

KISSINGER: But, Mr. President, even though she was a bitch, we shouldn't overlook the fact that we got what we wanted, which was we kept her from going out of here saying that the United States kicked her in the teeth. We've got the film clip of this; you've got the toast. You've got the general warmth that you generated in the personal meeting.

NIXON: I do think at dinner tonight [unclear].

KISSINGER: You didn't give her a goddamn thing.

NIXON: [unclear]

KISSINGER: If you would have put on a Johnson performance, it would have been emotionally more satisfying but it would have hurt us. Because — I mean if you had been rough with her —

NIXON: Yeah.

KISSINGER: — then she'd be crying, going back crying to India. So I think even though she is a bitch, I'd be a shade cooler today, but —

NIXON: No, no. I mean, "cool" in terms of, like yesterday, as you noted, I tried to carry the conversation —

KISSINGER: No, I'd let her carry it.

NIXON: — and was sort of saying, "Look, we're being as good as we can in dealing with Pakistan. What else can we do?" Today, I'm just going to say [unclear].

KISSINGER: That's what I would do. Except for Vietnam, I'd give her five minutes of the Tito talk because it will go right back to the Russians as well as to the Vietnamese.

NIXON: Will it?

KISSINGER: Oh, yeah. They have the closest diplomatic ties now with Russia. They leak everything right back to them.

"They'll want to know . . . what kind of a man is the president?"
November 15, 1971, 5:21 p.m.
Richard Nixon, William Rogers, Maurice Stans, and Alexander Haig
OVAL OFFICE

Secretary of Commerce Maurice Stans was scheduled to visit Moscow starting November 22 to discuss trade between the United States and the Soviet Union. The importance of the trip escalated in anticipation of the president's planned summit the following May.

• • •

NIXON: Now the other thing is, as Bill will tell you, that anyone who has talked to the Russians, our Russian friends, Gromyko and the rest, they're enormously interested in trade. That's one of the big things we've got for them.

STANS: Yep.

NIXON: It's something that we must not indicate is going to be linked with something else. But they, in their minds, know very well that if you make progress on the political front, that you'll make progress on the trade front. The way I've always described it is this: that you never say trade and political accommodation are linked. But the two are just inevitably intertwined. If you move on one it helps the other. If you move on — and it just moves like that. So — and we know that. Now I think the thing I want to do is to go out and — if you look at the situation and notice that their — I think it's sixteen billion dollars' worth of trade the Soviet Union has at the present time; sixteen billion dollars' worth and we've got two hundred fifty million dollars' worth, approximately.

STANS: That's in both directions.

NIXON: That's right.

STANS: Our exports were less than — are worth about half of that.

NIXON: That's what I mean. And, so we — we've got a hell of a big say in this. On the other hand, we — and frankly we have been fairly careful up to this point. I think more than anything else it's a, it's a — to the extent you can and then, Bill, if you have a different view, you can express it. I think what we want is for Maury to talk to everybody; listen and learn everything you can. But I don't think we want to appear to be panting so much after. I don't think we want to be — I don't think we — I mean I don't — I think we oughta — I think — let me put it this way: there's some things we'd like to get from them. I mean if, for example, we're still screwing around on Vietnam because [unclear] and, the arms control and the rest. Trade is something. Trade from us to them is infinitely more important than it is for us to have trade with them. We'd like — you know what I mean — I read the *Times* story about, you know, how much it would mean if we had all this and the Europeans are going to trade. But this is something that means a hell of a lot more to them than it does to us. Now you, of course, I don't think you should play it that way. That's too crude. But isn't that about what it is? And I don't want hear a blanket [unclear] as a matter of fact. Bill, do you agree?

ROGERS: Mr. President, I agree to everything.

NIXON: [unclear]

ROGERS: It's important to let them know that the climate for trade has improved, that the political climate is better.

NIXON: Exactly.

ROGERS: The political climate will be better when the president goes there, particularly if they cooperate with us on some of these things that we're trying to accomplish — Berlin, Indochina, and other matters.

NIXON: And arms control.

ROGERS: And arms control. Now they need to trade a hell of a lot more than we do. They, they've got a real problem because what they're doing — some of their allies, particularly Hungary, is doing a lot better in the trade field than they are, so they're trying —

NIXON: Hungary is?

ROGERS: Oh yeah. Hungary is doing very well. And, of course, Romania is building up a little trade. So they're concerned about having more trade with us. And I think we should, we should set the prospects for trade —

NIXON: Right.

ROGERS: — and listen and see where we can get some benefit, but not seem overeager. If they think we're overeager for trade, they'll snap at it. Furthermore, they've got a lot of other irons in the fire. They want this conference on European security very much.

NIXON: Yeah.

ROGERS: They want discussion on mutual balance force reduction.

NIXON: Watch all of this.

ROGERS: They want an agreement on Berlin, but they don't want to concede very much. Now, as the president said, the presence of trade is something of a weapon that we have. They need it. Now it will benefit us some, and politically it's always good to talk about it. But if you analyze it in real terms, it doesn't amount to a hell of a lot with us and it won't for some time, little bits and drags once in a while.

STANS: Now I differ a little bit on that, Bill. There's a great interest on the part of American businessmen and quite a number have been over there recently —

ROGERS: Oh, yes.

STANS: There's a group of fifty, of a hundred, including our friend Don Kendall, who's going to be over there the last day or two that I'm there.

NIXON: Let me say, let me say, Maury, I think that you're absolutely right. I know Don Kendall and all this group. But what I'm suggesting that you do, to you is that you play a different game. That's our businessmen, and they're over there panting around over the Soviets so much that they're slobbering away and giving away our bargaining position. You should not go there and say — I want you to take the position, which indicates that we're going to look at this stuff. We're very interested in hearing what they have to offer. We have people, of course, who would like to do this, that, and the other thing. But you see, 'cause I think — I really do believe that on the, this business side of it — Bill, I've talked to some of these guys and, gosh, they'd give away the store.

ROGERS: Yep. But we don't disagree on this thing.

[unclear exchange]

ROGERS: The total impact at the moment, for the next couple of years, isn't going to amount to a lot. We can talk about it.

NIXON: That's right.

ROGERS: We should tell American business we're doing everything we can. We want to increase our trade, but if you look at it in the total, in the overall picture, it's not going to amount to a hell of a lot in the next couple of years.

STANS: Well, I think there's millions of dollars of business there. The big problem is that they have difficulty in paying for it.

NIXON: Yeah.

STANS: And the next thing they're going to ask, and I'm sure they're going to press it with me, is two things: export-import credits so they can buy more, and MFN so they ship more to the United States.

NIXON: Yeah.

STANS: These are the roadblocks. I think that the business is there. I think that we could have four or five billion dollars by 1975 if we —

NIXON: You think so?

ROGERS: But think about what they'll use to give us. What have they got that we want? That's the problem.

STANS: Well, they're — they've taken a new line, which is a very interesting one. And I've spent a lot —

NIXON: You haven't said that before.

STANS: I've spent a lot of time over the last couple of weeks talking to American businessmen. They're talking about joint ventures. Not of the type that we're talking
about in Romania, Yugoslavia, where the American company would have a fifty
percent interest in the business and a fifty percent interest in profits. They're not
willing to give up title to property or define profits. But what they are talking about
is having American companies come over there and develop natural resources — oil,
gas, copper, other minerals, and so forth — under a deal where we put up the technology and part of the money. They put in some labor. We get the product; get our
money back out of the product and then have a share in the product rather than in
the profits.

   Now there's a lot of minerals — oil and natural gas — that would be a great deal
to us. They're already talking with one American company about a deal for natural
gas similar to the Algerian deal where there would be about a billion dollars' worth
of gas moving over the year beginning about 1975. And the American companies
who would go in there and invest wherever they think the natural gas is, freeze it,
and bring it over to the United States. Now they're talking some real big things to
think you know [unclear]. Real big things of that nature. And, of course, the one
thing our American business has to learn is that anything we do in terms of trade is
not going to be small potatoes because the Russian government is the buyer for the
whole economy.

NIXON: That's right.

STANS: They can buy ten thousand lathes at one time if they want to and spread them
around to all their plants. They can buy two thousand drill presses.

NIXON: Oh, I — what we — what — what I look upon this trip as being, which you
have — would you have — tell the photographer I want to get his pictures of this. So
that we could [unclear, pause] I think that it would be very helpful for us to know,
that we just, just before the world [unclear]. What do you have in mind? What do
you think? Don't you think so, Al?

HAIG: Yes, sir. I think [unclear].

NIXON: And incidentally I would say that you have mentioned these other things. If
they raise, and I don't know the extent to which they get it, the European Security
Conference and all the rest. That should stay miles away.

STANS: I thought I would listen and ask them if they have any message for me to bring
back to you. But the message —

ROGERS: But, you know, if they do they're just playing games because they talk to us
all the time.

NIXON: Yeah. Yeah. I would stay away from the political questions because we're
not — we don't want to talk about a European Security Conference. We're not, but —

STANS: I'm not informed on the military —

NIXON: And I would just simply say that that's not your responsibility. That's — you'd
just rather not express any opinions on it, that you're just an expert in the one area.

I think that's very important to play. Why don't you shoot the picture there so that we can [unclear].

STANS: I would—I would like to look at ideas that you could develop for your May visit. I think that maybe some things could come out of this that you could use for May.

ROGERS: [unclear] that they could give us some gold [unclear]?

STANS: Well, they don't have much gold left. They only have about a billion eight.

ROGERS: They've got more [unclear]?

NIXON: What? Is that right?

STANS: In reserves. A billion eight.

ROGERS: No, they've got a lot in the mines.

STANS: They've got it in the ground.

ROGERS: They've got petroleum and aluminum, what, chrome and a few other minerals. [unclear] If they start—if they start exporting petroleum to this country, that's a whole other ball game.

STANS: That's an element of risk according to—for that to be on a minimum basis. But what I propose to do is go over the whole list of possibilities; talk to all of them; see what needs to be done. As I say, they're going to press for export credit. They're going to press for MFN treatment—most favored nation.

NIXON: I think on those things that you can, you can indicate—the thing that we have done and the conversation we've had here with Gromyko is to indicate that there are very great possibilities in this country for improvement in those areas. But obviously they are contingent upon, they're related to improvement in political areas. Now we can't talk about the MFN, the Export-Import Bank as long as they're helping the North Vietnamese.

ROGERS: Or joint ventures for that matter. You know, our large investment for joint ventures has got to be—the political climate has got to be pretty good.

NIXON: Yeah.

STANS: I think the American companies are going to want that.

NIXON: But we have a very—our, our, our attitude toward progress on the political front is very, very open. And our attitude toward progress on the trade front is very open.

ROGERS: How about manufactured goods? We could send them manufactured goods.

STANS: Well, I think they'll buy something. I don't think they'll buy much—

ROGERS: See, that's what we should push for.

STANS: It's machine tools they want—

ROGERS: That's what we should push for. We've got plenty of manufactured goods we can send them.

NIXON: Boy they need [unclear].

STANS: They need it.

NIXON: Exactly. Their economy has been flat for how many years? Four or five years?

ROGERS: Oh, yeah, at least. What they want us to do is teach them how to manufacture them so they don't have to buy them from us—

STANS: Well—

NIXON: They want computers. [unclear] They want technology. They don't want the goods.

ROGERS: Machine tools.

STANS: Right, but the American automobile companies and some of them have been pretty smart about this. Ford and General Motors have told them and told us that they're not interested in going over there and building a plant for them. They're interested in going in there and working with them if there's a longtime relationship of some kind from which they can benefit. They're not going to build a plant and walk away from it. And I, I told a group of American businessmen today that I'm concerned about selling our technology too cheap—

ROGERS: You're damn right.

NIXON: You're so right.

STANS: Three percent patent and license fee and so forth doesn't give us much of anything.

NIXON: No. Oh boy.

STANS: If we can't get more than that out of it. If we can't—

NIXON: It will do absolutely no harm at all for you to be a very shrewd trader—Yankee trader—with the Russians. That's the way they are. They expect it and they'd be very surprised—but, well, you know, as you would, of course, with a very, very—we're very interested in this, but as you know this is the way our guys look at it. It's something we may want to do. If you'd like to help on this sort of situation, but we've got some real problems and what can you do? And they come. They come that way. The Russians are a tough bunch of bastards.

ROGERS: Sell them campers and television sets and radios.

NIXON: Any day, any day.

STANS: They're probably buying those from the Japanese right now.

NIXON: Have you been there before?

STANS: I've never been in Russia before, no.

NIXON: What cities are you going to visit?

STANS: Well, it's still pretty indefinite. We've—we will go to Leningrad the first weekend, on Sunday, and spend a day there. The second weekend I suggested that we go south to Georgia. They're suggesting Baku and Tbilisi and possibly—

NIXON: [unclear]

STANS: —Samarkand and Tashkent. Which is—

NIXON: Samarkand?

STANS: —strictly sightseeing.

NIXON: Go.

STANS: Really?

NIXON: Beautiful place.

STANS: Never been there.

NIXON: Well, Samarkand has—you know that's one of Genghis Khan's residences. It has those magnificent little temples.

STANS: It sounds heavenly.

NIXON: Oh yeah, yeah. Oh you go. Go.

STANS: Well, I'd love to do that. I think—

NIXON: That's worth going [unclear] out there, but I'd go.

STANS: They're making quite a thing of this because—

NIXON: And you'll see Asians out there. That's the interesting thing. You see you'll get out there and you realize that Russia is not a country of Russians. There are all sorts of Asians. You go down the [unclear]—which is right near—

STANS: I'd like to see that—

NIXON: —the Chinese border—

STANS: It looks pretty fun.

NIXON: —you'll see the valley of apples. And, by God, they're all Chinese. They're all slant-eyed. It's a fascinating thing to see this.

STANS: Well, they're putting out the red carpet because they say it is an ordinary expense. They want me to stay even longer. We'll probably stay longer [unclear].

NIXON: Are you going to—how about to one city—for example, I wonder if they'd want you to see it. How about Sverdlovsk? Are they going to have you go there?

STANS: They haven't mentioned it—

NIXON: It's a huge steel complex place. Novosibirsk, in Siberia, how about there?

STANS: They offered to take us to Lake Baikal, but that's so far. It's seven hours outside Moscow on the fastest jet. It's farther than across the United States.

• • •

STANS: Well, Mr. President, I'm going to stop over in Sweden on the way over to rest a day.

NIXON: Oh, for Christ's sake—

STANS: And—

NIXON: —why did you have to stop in Sweden?

STANS: Well, they're a big customer. They buy a lot of goods from us.

NIXON: Fine. All right, fine. Sell them something they don't want. [laughter] All right, that's fine. That's fine. Have you ever been there before?

STANS: No.

NIXON: Neither have I—

STANS: We're going to stop in Warsaw on the way back. We're—I didn't realize Volpe had been there, but the embassy [unclear]—

NIXON: That's all right.

STANS: — the embassy and then a press conference —

NIXON: That's all right.

STANS: Is there any special message in Warsaw?

NIXON: You get your message [unclear]?

ROGERS: Yeah. We — I told them, "Be cool. Be polite but cool."

NIXON: What? Yeah. They've done an awful lot for us —

[unclear exchange]

NIXON: We respect their — we respect their people. They've contributed so much to this country. But basically we, we're not too damn happy about the way they kick us around the world. But that's fine. Let them do it. That's their choice. Warsaw is another matter. I think there, we do want to play the line of — the more — and all the rest. They are —

ROGERS: Yes they are.

NIXON: They are already [unclear] —

ROGERS: But we also have good, good relations with them. And they've improved some in the last year —

STANS: Warsaw, oh, excuse me.

ROGERS: And the people, of course, particularly Poles, very much —

NIXON: They love Americans.

STANS: Warsaw doesn't have [unclear] credit, and they're actually going to press for that. I would guess from all the discussion [unclear] that they'll come after Roma-nia. Possibly fairly soon.

NIXON: Well, what —

STANS: They're —

NIXON: Well, let me say this. I think what the Russians, and all the rest, I'd hold it all out there. Hell, [unclear] hold it all. This is something you'll look into and so forth. Don't you think so, Al?

HAIG: Yes, sir. I think [unclear] sympathetic with us —

NIXON: Yeah.

HAIG: And with that we can —

• • •

NIXON: You have to remember that Khrushchev — incidentally, you can also recall, [he] wrote in his book, he bragged that he helped to defeat Nixon in 1960. And we're quite aware of that. That may come up. You might bring it up. See? And at this time, we're, we — it's just an interesting little point. That just shows how much they care about our politics.

ROGERS: Be a little careful with him, Maury, if you raise this. They'll — they leak things all over, hell. Particularly Dobrynin. So we wouldn't want to be in a position of ask-ing for any help for the president.

NIXON: Oh, God no.

STANS: Oh, no. No.

[unclear exchange]

ROGERS: The thing that we really need to do is convince them that he [Nixon] is going to be the sure thing.

NIXON: Yep.

ROGERS: Because that's what they pay more attention to than anything else. I think they've come around to that point of view. I think that's one of the reasons they're anxious for the president's visit.

NIXON: I think that's probably why they agreed to it. The — I think there might be a, a — basically, they'll want to know what kind of a man is this — another point, Bill, I think you would agree — what kind of a man is the president? And so you tell them [unclear] is like that. But particularly emphasize, though, that he's a man you can make a deal with. But he's a, I mean a — eyes totally open; you know, he's a pragmatic man.

STANS: Analytical.

NIXON: Analytical and far-seeing. You know, give them all that crap. Because they — I think this is the important thing. I noticed that when I talked to Tito he was very interested in telling me what kind of a fellow Brezhnev was. And, and he compared Brezhnev to Kosygin. The Communists are quite interested in men. I mean in the —

ROGERS: In what sense? In how they get along?

NIXON: That's the point. In their personalities. You could say, "Here he is and —" You could say — I must say — I mean I have to be because we deal with a Democratic Congress and I'm naturally conciliatory all the time.

"A hell of a good time to bomb."

November 20, 1971, 8:45 a.m.
Richard Nixon and Henry Kissinger
OVAL OFFICE

Frustrated with the diplomatic process of ending the war with North Vietnam, Nixon spoke emphatically of using a bombing campaign to bring Hanoi into submission. On this occasion he didn't necessarily speak of winning the war anymore. He was interested in a deal that acknowledged the stalemate with a return of all POWs and security for both North and South Vietnam.

• • •

KISSINGER: Then, I gave them a personal note from me to Zhou Enlai, so that you — about events with the North Vietnamese.

NIXON: Mm-hmm.

KISSINGER: As — and I just recounted when we had made a proposal, when they had agreed to it, that then they canceled it. Their ambassador said, "What? They canceled it three days before the meeting?" And he —

NIXON: Is Walters there?

KISSINGER: Yeah, and Walters said, "Yes." He said, "That's impossible," but that's not an official comment. And that's amazing. And—

NIXON: Well, Xuan Thuy's not sick. Do you think he's sick?

KISSINGER: No, no. He's in—he's in Beijing with Pham Van Dong.

NIXON: So he wasn't sick the last time?

KISSINGER: No. Now, Haig believes that the Chinese—that they are up there because the Chinese are going to try to make them settle. I'm not that sure. I'm not sure about that.

NIXON: [unclear] the Chinese even talk to them?

KISSINGER: No, no. The Chinese are talking. They're up there now.

NIXON: It's right there, I know.

• • •

NIXON: What I had in mind, Henry, is—and I think it fits in, in any event—I'd like to get, first, that major—I'm considering summoning Moorer over here—if it doesn't cost too much—that major movement of the fleet, and an alert, and all that sort of thing, that we did at one other previous time—

KISSINGER: Absolutely.

NIXON: —and the mining exercise, having it ready. And now, it'll be useful to have those carriers up there, anyway, for the purpose of this three-day bombing run—

KISSINGER: Yeah.

NIXON: —that we're going to do if these bastards don't do it. But, if we can get those ships moving now, and also get out something with regard to mining or—I don't know whether that's too far, or if it takes too long or not. Second, I want you to get Helms, and get ahold of him with regard to massive CIA harassment during the period of this two- to three-day deal. Now, by that, I mean everything he can. Third, I think we need a propaganda thing, with regard to broadcasts, and all that sort of thing. In other words, build it up like we did Son Tay [the North Vietnamese prison camp where, in 1970, U.S. special forces conducted a covert mission to free POWs].

KISSINGER: Right.

NIXON: Now, if we're going to do this—in other words, if we have to go hard—or what it basically is: being hard, Henry—let's do it in a clever way this time, in a coordinated approach. If you can think of anything else?

KISSINGER: I think this is excellent. I think—

NIXON: How does that sound to you as a plan?

KISSINGER: I think it's outstanding. And I think that we ought to begin the fleet movement. We shouldn't do it while Pham Van Dong is in Beijing. Let's say—

NIXON: No, I think you could move now, because the fleet, the fleet—

KISSINGER: Okay, we'll start it, then—

NIXON: You see, the fleet has to—it takes time for it to move. We know those bastards. The time in Korea we had a hell of a time—

KISSINGER: That— there's a long distance. I think they can be there in four days.

NIXON: Now listen: they can make movements that are not going to be noted. Well, I want them there so that—

KISSINGER: [unclear]

NIXON: You get my point?

KISSINGER: Right.

NIXON: I think it might be well that they—

KISSINGER: Well, they will be—

NIXON: —that they know that they're moving while he's [Pham Van Dong] there [in China].

KISSINGER: All right.

NIXON: If you don't hit 'em, what difference does it make? Maybe, just [unclear]. I don't know. [unclear]

KISSINGER: Well, what I would like to avoid is for Zhou Enlai to be confronted with a request by Pham Van Dong of a new threat. Because I thought— in the message I sent to Zhou—

NIXON: Yeah?

KISSINGER: —I put in a threat, already.

NIXON: Yeah.

KISSINGER: But, we can start immediately on the fleet movement, and then keep building it—

NIXON: Well, yeah. Now, one other thought occurred to me: we have more of a card than we think regarding settlement. We have always assumed— I mean, you've just assumed, and I have, too— that these fellows would not want to risk my being re-elected. I'm sure it must have occurred to you, Henry, that regardless of how the election comes out in November, I will still be president until January 20, and I'll be commander in chief. And, if I should have lost, I would certainly, certainly, not go out with my tail between my legs. Now, if those prisoners are not back by the time of the election, if we should lose the election, the day after that election— win, lose, or draw— we will bomb the bejeezus out of them. Because then, to hell with history. To hell with history—

KISSINGER: History will think well of you, then.

NIXON: You see my point?

KISSINGER: Yes.

NIXON: Then I'll say, "All right, my predecessor— my successor isn't going to be able to do it." But you can order— as commander in chief— say, "Now, in this case"— and then, I would really take it out. I'd take out the railroads; I'd take out the air force; I'd take out the— you know, just, just knock the shit out of 'em for three months. Now—

KISSINGER: That's the best— I had not thought of that—

NIXON: You see what I mean?

KISSINGER: Right.

NIXON: Now, you have to seize it. Put that into a bargaining equation there.

KISSINGER: Yeah.

NIXON: These guys haven't got all that good a — haven't got all that good a thing. Now, I — they're right: to do anything before the election would pose problems, politically. But, do they realize that they have to deal with, here, a man, who if he wins the election will kick the shit out of them, and if he loses the election will do it even more? Now, there's where we are. Did that ever occur to you?

KISSINGER: I — I have to say, honestly, it did not.

NIXON: Now, some would say —

KISSINGER: [unclear]

NIXON: Some would say, "Well, if you lost the election, the editorials will scream: 'He doesn't have a mandate,'" and so forth. Bullshit! I couldn't care less. I could care, then, about seeing that America didn't lose the war. And getting back our prisoners, which is even more important at that time. See? I'm telling you: we've got cards then, and we'd be ready. And they'd have to do what I said — I mean the [Joint] Chiefs — wouldn't they?

KISSINGER: The Chiefs have to, of course. And they'll do it enthusiastically.

NIXON: But out of that intriguing idea — it occurred to me at two thirty in the morning —

KISSINGER: I think that if —

NIXON: — this morning I woke up, and I was thinking a little, and, you know, sometimes the best ideas come in. I thought, "Why do we have to just think in terms of winning the election, or not?" All right, we lose it. I think we're gonna — we have a chance of winning it, and maybe there is a chance of losing it. I said, "By God, these guys are going to be playing — they're playing with a tough situation here. I'm going to be here from November 7 until January 20, come hell or high water, and that's a hell of a good time to bomb, too." That's another thing: it's good in terms of the weather then. Correct?

KISSINGER: Uh —

NIXON: December and January aren't bad?

KISSINGER: With our bloody air force — no, no, they are — they're pretty good. Our damn air force, you never —

NIXON: I know —

KISSINGER: I have yet to find a time when they think it's good —

NIXON: I'd get the navy in. I'd get them in, and I'd say, "Boys, here's your chance to be heroes. I want you to knock out everything. These bastards have got your buddies up there, and they haven't turned them loose. Now punish them." And, incidentally, I wouldn't worry about a little slop-over, and knock off a few villages and hamlets, and the rest. We've just got to do it —

KISSINGER: Oh, under those conditions, I'd —

NIXON: This would be war. I'd take out — I wouldn't worry about a Soviet ship, you know, that was in Haiphong harbor —

KISSINGER: I think, Mr. President —

NIXON: You see my point?

KISSINGER: And if you win the election, we, we should not make the mistake that we did the last time —

NIXON: [unclear]

KISSINGER: — of wasting the first six months.

NIXON: Never. No, if we win the election, the day after, we say, "All right, we give you thirty days."

KISSINGER: Right.

NIXON: And then, if we don't get it in thirty — I think thirty is an ultimatum. I'd lay down an ultimatum, just like it was done in the old days.

KISSINGER: Right.

NIXON: We haven't done an ultimatum, yet, except through these silly little things with Tito and the rest. But I — this, this is an ultimatum. I'm sure you realize, you know, before, before China — before November 3, we laid down some ultimatums. Then the speech came, but we didn't come through on the ultimatums [unclear]. But, I want you to know, Henry: I meant exactly what I said. If those bastards do not come back with something, we are going to hit them for three or four days. [unclear] It isn't as much as I'd like, but we'll do at least that much. The only reason that I can't do more than that is that I don't want to go so far as to jeopardize the Chinese trip. The Russian trip will go on, I don't care what. The Chinese trip might be difficult.

KISSINGER: I think it will go on, too.

. . .

NIXON: But I just thought that idea would intrigue the hell out of you.

KISSINGER: I think —

NIXON: Regardless of the election, we are going to give them a pop. Huh?

KISSINGER: Well, with, with your permission, it's one that I intend to use — that I should use the next time I see the North Vietnamese —

NIXON: Yeah.

KISSINGER: — because I'll guarantee you, they'll — they're coming back to us.

NIXON: [unclear] And, and just say, "Now, gentlemen, regardless of how this election comes out, don't count on that. You remember that he was — this man is going to be president, and I have never seen a man more determined. He's made the decision. We're going to finish it off." And, I mean, I would. I really would. I'd finish off the goddamn place.

KISSINGER: And they'll —

NIXON: Bomb Haiphong. You know, the whole thing. I would put a crippling blow on it. Go on for sixty days of bombing. Just knock the shit out of them—

KISSINGER: That's right.

NIXON: —and then, everybody would say, "Oh, horrible, horrible, horrible." [laughs] That's all right. You agree or not?

KISSINGER: Absolutely. Absolutely!

"'The Indians have been kicking us in the ass for twenty-five years.'"
November 22, 1971, 3:51 p.m.
Richard Nixon and Henry Kissinger
OVAL OFFICE

The Oval Office was shrouded in the fog of war. On the one hand, reports came in that Pakistani President Yayha had commenced an air raid against India. On the other hand, the State Department was receiving contradictory reports from both Pakistan and India. Nixon and Kissinger genuinely believed that India had started the war by supporting Mukti Bahini forces with regular Indian troops on Pakistani territory; Indian regular forces had violated Pakistan's border in support of insurgents who were both trained and supplied by India. As reports of the number and severity of border skirmishes increased, Kissinger convened the interagency WSAG to develop a response.

• • •

KISSINGER: In my view, I have found, and that doesn't prove anything, but when I'm—in Cincinnati, for example, somebody asked me, "Nobody likes the Indians!"

NIXON: I talked to Connally. I asked him about it. He said, "For Christ's sakes," he says, "the Indians have been kicking us in the ass for twenty-five years."

KISSINGER: And I said, I just laid it into them. I say, "On refugees we are helping them. We are giving more than half of the aid. What we do not want is a military aggression by them against their neighbor, in such a way that the whole country disintegrates." What I would recommend, we are meeting again at eight thirty tomorrow morning. First, I'd like to stall out the Security Council resolution till Wednesday so we can find out what the Chinese are planning.

NIXON: The Security Council resolution [unclear]—

KISSINGER: The Security Council meeting.

NIXON: Yeah.

KISSINGER: Because the strong possibility is that the Chi—we'd be caught between the Soviets and the Chinese, between the Indians and the Pakistanis. And there's nothing in that lineup that, they're gonna pass a resolution urging a political accommodation more likely than condemning India.

NIXON: The Chinese would never agree to that.

KISSINGER: Probably not. But we have to take a position. I'm not—

NIXON: Yeah, I'm just trying to think of how, if I agree to a stall, can we get it stalled?

KISSINGER: Well, I've got a back channel to the—to Yahya saying if he could wait till Wednesday it would help us, but he hasn't—

NIXON: Oh, he's asking for a Security Council resolution?

KISSINGER: Not yet. So that they don't ask for one. I've also told their ambassador here who asked my advice what they should do.

NIXON: Mm-hmm. Is Yahya saying it's war or not?

KISSINGER: Yeah, they're saying it's war.

NIXON: And the Indians say it isn't?

KISSINGER: It isn't. That's right. It's a naked case of aggression, Mr. President. There's absolutely no—

NIXON: Goddamn it, maybe we ought to say that.

KISSINGER: They have been back exactly one week. If you cut off arms, you told her [Indira Gandhi] we were going to try to move them politically.

NIXON: That's right.

KISSINGER: She doesn't even know yet what the answers to these various proposals are that you made to them, that we said we were going to take up with Yahya—

NIXON: A unilateral withdrawal.

KISSINGER: Unilateral withdrawal. So, we've done everything that is humanly possible. I think if we, I think if we line up with India and the Soviet Union—

NIXON: We're not going to do it. Don't worry. We aren't going to do it. Never!

KISSINGER: What I think we should do is to send a sharp note—

NIXON: Goddamn it! I told those people over there! They sat in those meetings—

KISSINGER: Well—

NIXON: They know how I feel about India.

• • •

KISSINGER: The thing to do, Mr. President, in my view, is to send a very sharp note to the Indians reminding them of all the things we've done and saying that, repeating what you've said, that it simply will not be understood in this country, without any pledge.

NIXON: That's what I want to do. So—

KISSINGER: Urging at this point, and—

NIXON: And then what—

KISSINGER: Two, we should get a note to the Soviets along the same lines.

NIXON: Right. Right.

KISSINGER: Point three: well, those are the two things we ought to get done immediately.

NIXON: All right.

KISSINGER: The third one is we ought to talk to, which I'll do tomorrow night, to the

Chinese to find out what they'll do at the Security Council. If they take it to the Security Council, but we have to lean, we don't have to go as far as the Chinese, but I would lean —

NIXON: I want to go damn near as far! Now, understand: I don't like the Indians!

KISSINGER: We ought to lean pretty close to the Chinese and make it an international —

NIXON: And, also, let's remember the Pakistanis have been our friends in these late few days and the damn Indians have not been. You know —

KISSINGER: And above all I don't see what we gain by helping out the Indians.

"There's a totally immoral attitude of our critics here."
December 8, 1971, 4:20 p.m.
Richard Nixon, John Mitchell, and Henry Kissinger
OVAL OFFICE

Nixon and Kissinger got together to relieve frustration at the fact that many intellectuals and those in the American media continued to disagree with the Nixon "tilt" toward Pakistan.

. . .

NIXON: You see, this is where the *New York Times* and the rest are wrong, where they said that if aggression is engaged in by a democracy it's all right.

KISSINGER: That's right.

NIXON: But where it's engaged in by a dictatorship, it's wrong. They forget that most of the countries in the world are dictatorships —

KISSINGER: Yeah.

NIXON: — including all these little countries!

. . .

NIXON: There's a totally immoral attitude of our critics here. First, they say, they make the point that because there's six hundred million Indians and only sixty million in West Pakistan, we're on the wrong side. We should be with the six hundred million Indians. I said since when do we determine the morality of our policy on the basis of how many people a country has? I said the second reason that they're wrong, then they say but India is a democratic country, and Pakistan is a totalitarian country, a dictatorship, and therefore India, we shouldn't be on the side of a dictatorship but on the side of the democratic country. I said if aggression is engaged in by any country, it's wrong. And in a sense it's even more wrong for a democratic country to engage in it because democratic countries are held in a higher degree of morality. And I said international morality will be finished — the United Nations will be finished — if you adopt the principle that because a country is democratic and big it can do what the hell it pleases. I really think that puts the issue to these sons of bitches.

"A federal offense of the highest order."

December 21, 1971, 6:07 p.m.
Richard Nixon, John Mitchell, Bob Haldeman, and John Ehrlichman
OVAL OFFICE

During late 1971, investigative journalist Jack Anderson published a series of exposés on Nixon's "tilt" toward Pakistan during the India-Pakistan war then taking place. Anderson's reporting was based on a leak of highly classified National Security Council records pilfered by Charles Radford, a navy yeoman assigned to a liaison role between the National Security Council and the chairman of the Joint Chiefs of Staff, Thomas Moorer. When it was discovered that Radford stole records from Henry Kissinger's and Alexander Haig's offices, briefcases, and burn bags, Nixon called Radford's actions "a federal offense of the highest order."

Nixon ordered John Ehrlichman to launch a rigorous internal investigation into what motivated Radford to steal the material and give it to Anderson. Nixon wondered whether a sexual relationship between Radford and Anderson was a possible motivation. While he weighed criminal prosecution of Radford and the Joint Chiefs, Nixon decided against it. He believed it was more important to avoid a public break between the White House and the military during the Vietnam War. Radford was reassigned to a remote duty station in Oregon, where FBI wiretaps provided further clues to the relationship between Radford and Anderson.

The scandal stayed out of the public eye until 1974, when Congress held hearings and conducted an inquiry into the matter. However, the effort was short-lived: by that time a scandal-weary nation was overwhelmed with Watergate, and the investigation into what became known as the Moorer-Radford affair went nowhere.

• • •

EHRLICHMAN: They were able to pinpoint that there was really only one place in the whole federal government where all of those documents were available.

NIXON: That's here.

EHRLICHMAN: And that was here in the Joint Chiefs of Staff liaison office of the National Security Council.

NIXON: Yeah.

EHRLICHMAN: And—

NIXON: Jesus Christ!

EHRLICHMAN: —there are only two men in that office. One's an admiral [Robert Welander] and one's a yeoman [Radford]. So they began interviewing both of them, and they polygraphed both of them. And the yeoman, obviously, was the guy. He knew Jack Anderson. He had had dinner with Jack Anderson the previous Sunday. His wife and Jack Anderson's wife were Mormons and friends, and were doing things together, and so on and so forth. He had been stationed in India for two years. He felt strongly about the India-Pakistan thing. So there was motive, opportunity, and access. The whole thing.

NIXON: Can I ask how in the name of God do we have a yeoman having access to documents of that type?

EHRLICHMAN: Well, he's the key man. He is the, he's the fellow that types all the memcons, the memoranda of conversations, who files all the —

NIXON: Does Henry know him?

EHRLICHMAN: Everybody knows him.

MITCHELL: He's traveled with Henry.

EHRLICHMAN: He's traveled with Haig.

NIXON: Did he go to China?

EHRLICHMAN: No, but he went to —

NIXON: Indonesia?

EHRLICHMAN: — Indonesia with, I mean Vietnam with Haig. And did all Haig's dealings with [unclear]. So he's been right at the crux of this thing. Now, he works for this Admiral Welander, who is the Joint Chiefs of Staff liaison man. Before him, there was a captain, a navy captain [Rembrandt Robinson] in the office.

NIXON: I remember him.

EHRLICHMAN: This fellow, while being polygraphed, was asked, among other things, if he had ever —

NIXON: You did that with the polygraph?

EHRLICHMAN: Oh, yes. Yes, indeed. And he has refused to admit turning any documents over to Anderson. But he has admitted something else. That he's had access, so on and so forth, all the way through.

NIXON: Yes.

EHRLICHMAN: He realizes he may be the only man in government other than the admiral [Welander] to have access to all these documents. He understands the circumstance. Says, "It's obviously a good, tight circumstantial case. I'll answer any questions that you have."

NIXON: He's trying to be very polite.

EHRLICHMAN: He's very, very polite.

NIXON: Right. Incidentally, is he Jewish?

EHRLICHMAN: No. He's Mormon. [unclear] But, in the course of the polygraph, he was asked whether or not he had ever stolen any documents. And —

NIXON: Stolen? The fact is, he leaks.

EHRLICHMAN: Sure.

NIXON: He had to, to give them to Anderson.

MITCHELL: Taken them out of the security —

EHRLICHMAN: [unclear] They put the question to him, as if they were assuming that he was [unclear]. They got a big flip on the polygraph. So then they doubled back.

• • •

EHRLICHMAN: The interrogator then doubles back. Says, "Now you got a bad reading on your polygraph on this. What other documents?" And the guy [Radford] broke down and cried. And then he said, "I can't answer that question without the permission of Admiral Welander." So David Young called me, and he called the admiral [Welander]. And he said, "Would you talk to this fellow [Radford]? I want you to tell him to tell everything he knows." To the admiral: "Do you have any problem with the guy?" He said, "Hell, no."

So then it all came out. He has, under the express directions of Captain [Rembrandt] Robinson, and under the implied approval of his successor, the admiral [Welander], he has systematically stolen documents out of Henry's briefcase, Haig's briefcase, people's desks, anyplace and everyplace in the NSC apparatus that he can lay his hands on. And has duplicated them and turned them over to the Joint Chiefs, through his boss. This has been going on now for about thirteen months.

NIXON: Well, has that been a Joint Chiefs' practice for a long time?

EHRLICHMAN: Apparently so.

• • •

EHRLICHMAN: It is all written up, in memo form. And he has access to everything out of State, the Pentagon, NSC, everyplace. And he just Xeroxed it and turned it over to Anderson. There's no question. Now, as I say, we started off on Anderson.

NIXON: Right.

EHRLICHMAN: We were slowed down by the fact that this guy is obviously very hot. Then we got this Joint Chiefs angle, and so we've shut the whole thing down. The guy is obviously cooperative. We've had him standing by at home for further interrogation. We then, I think we have him tapped. Do we have him tapped?

MITCHELL: No, we do not.

EHRLICHMAN: We don't have him tapped.

HALDEMAN: Can't you put him under some kind of arrest?

EHRLICHMAN: Well, we could —

MITCHELL: We could, but that's not the point.

EHRLICHMAN: This is a little bit like trying to catch a skunk. And, you may get some on you if you [unclear].

NIXON: You're right. Exactly right about this point.

EHRLICHMAN: The Joint Chiefs' liaison office is over here in the EOB, and it's right in the NSC complex. It's very nice. It's Captain Robinson, who, Dave got to know on the first day Dave came to work, and said: "Now, Dave, we're really your eyes and ears in the Pentagon. You can trust me entirely. My job is to get you fellows information out of the Pentagon." It turned out to be, in effect, a reverse agent. Working for the Pentagon inside here. That office, it seems to me, constitutes a clear and present danger to the, since [unclear] in the NSC. John has suggestions as to how to proceed in this that I think are very sound, and I'll leave him to explain them.

MITCHELL: Well, Mr. President, I'd like to point out that this thing goes right into the Joint Chiefs of Staff. Undoubtedly they'd know if it has participated in this ill-gotten gains they received.

NIXON: Sure.

MITCHELL: The first thing you're —

NIXON: Prosecuting is a possibility for the Joint Chiefs. Now, I have to think about it.

MITCHELL: I agree with you, but we have to take it from there as to what this would lead to if you pursued it by way of prosecution of Moorer, or, even a public confrontation. You would have the Joint Chiefs aligned on that side directly against you. And the, what has been done has been done. I think that the important thing is to paper this thing over.

NIXON: Yeah.

MITCHELL: This way, first of all, get that liaison office the hell out of NSC and put it back at the Pentagon.

NIXON: Correct.

MITCHELL: Secondly, to get a security officer into the NSC.

NIXON: Correct. But what about Henry Kissinger?

MITCHELL: Well, I think that whoever goes in there is going to have to ride herd not only on the rest of the staff, but on Henry. It turns out that one of these most important memorandums here that Henry had was lost, and that somebody just handed him another copy. They shouldn't have even had another copy. This came out in the papers.

Now, with respect to the Joint Chiefs, you have to get, in my opinion, this guy Admiral Welander the hell out of there, by way of a signal. That way you can transfer him to Kokomo or Indiana, or anywhere we want to have him, along, of course, with this yeoman. And I think the best thing to do is for me, and we'll leave Laird aside for a moment, but for me to sit down with Tom Moorer, and point out what this game is that's been going on.

NIXON: Mm-hmm.

MITCHELL: And it's the end of the road. The liaison is going back to the Pentagon. If they want him, they can call him over here. And there's a security quotient going into the NSC, and this ball game's over with.

• • •

NIXON: Let me ask this first. Is Anderson guilty of anything?

MITCHELL: Yes.

NIXON: What?

MITCHELL: He's guilty of possession of these documents.

NIXON: Can you really prosecute, let's say, the person that publishes them?

MITCHELL: You can prosecute 'em not under the publication. But for the possession of them. I don't know if we need to find that. But if you start opening up —

NIXON: [unclear]

MITCHELL: If you start opening up on Anderson, assuming you did make the case, turned this guy [Radford], give him immunity and so forth, then Lord knows where this is going to lead to.

NIXON: Yeah.

MITCHELL: Because he's [Radford] going to come out with a story, "Well, I gave it," this business with Admiral Welander, "and he's had all of this," and the Joint Chiefs and all the rest of it.

NIXON: Well, it blows the Joint Chiefs right out of the Pentagon, through the roof of the Pentagon, right?

EHRLICHMAN: It ruptures your relationship.

• • •

EHRLICHMAN: I lost more sleep than —

NIXON: Yeah.

EHRLICHMAN: [unclear] on what to do with this guy. And I have finally come to the conclusion that you can't touch him.

NIXON: I agree.

EHRLICHMAN: And, you probably can't touch him because it would —

NIXON: Hurt the Joint Chiefs.

EHRLICHMAN: Exactly.

NIXON: And the Joint Chiefs, the military, et cetera, cannot become our enemy. We cannot have it. And also, we can't have this goddamn security problem!

EHRLICHMAN: There's that, too.

• • •

NIXON: There is a federal offense of the highest order here. And you have reported it to the president. The president says you can't discuss it.

"I want a direct question about homosexuality asked."
December 22, 1971, 11:03 a.m.
Richard Nixon, John Mitchell, and John Ehrlichman
OVAL OFFICE

Nixon received the latest update in Ehrlichman's investigation of the Moorer-Radford affair. The president was desperate to learn anything about what could have motivated a navy yeoman to steal and leak classified records to journalist Jack Anderson.

• • •

NIXON: Any verdict at all on this?

EHRLICHMAN: Yes and no. This fellow's undergone a thorough polygraph exam.

NIXON: Good.

MITCHELL: This is the yeoman [Charles Radford]?

EHRLICHMAN: The yeoman.

NIXON: Yeah.

EHRLICHMAN: And I'm going to have [Radford's supervisor, Admiral Robert] Welander up at one o'clock, and tape an interview with him. Henry has signed a letter instructing Welander —

NIXON: Henry, does he know what we're up to yet now?

EHRLICHMAN: I just put the letter under his nose and he signed it. So, we'll know more in the middle of the afternoon than we do right now.

NIXON: The problem that I, after sleeping on it, one thing I — John, when you approach him, I want him to ask. I want a direct question about homosexuality asked. You never know what you're going to find.

EHRLICHMAN: Mm-hmm.

NIXON: Because we got a couple on Hiss and Chambers, you know. Nobody knows that, but that's the background on how that one began. They were both that way. And relationships sometimes poison a lot of these things. Now, if Anderson, I'm just getting, but if there's any possibility of this, John, that could be a key as well. If something, he may be under blackmail.

. . .

EHRLICHMAN: They've got a perfect excuse for reinterrogating him [Radford], because of yesterday's Anderson column. And the question of whether this fellow had access to that. So I'm going to get into that, and then slide into this other thing in passing. Because the interrogator first thing this morning got him all upset.

MITCHELL: This is the polygraph again?

EHRLICHMAN: Yeah.

NIXON: Yeah. The thing that concerns me, John, and I think your strategy is exactly right, except with one thing that I would worry about. This guy is a potential Ellsberg, in terms of, and he knows more. He knows —

EHRLICHMAN: Mm-hmm, mm-hmm.

NIXON: Because he really knows what happens. Now, fortunately, what he knows is not anything that's going to be, in my view, I wouldn't have it all come out, but it's better for it not to. The point is: is there any way that we can keep him scared to death, so that he doesn't get out and think, "Oh, I'm now going to write the book, or I'm going to do this, or that or the other thing"? Can he be told that a criminal, I think he's got to be told that a criminal offense hangs over him, that it's going to hang over him, and that we're going to be, you see what I mean? I'd like to scare the son of a bitch to death!

MITCHELL: I would believe —

NIXON: And if, do you believe that's what you ought to do?

MITCHELL: Yes.

NIXON: Do you agree we should?

MITCHELL: We talked about that yesterday, Mr. President. I think the sign-off on this guy, when he's sent to wherever he's going to be sent, is going to be just that. You can sit down and read the statutes to him, and the background, and the sentences, and so forth, and really give him a good understanding of what is going to be in his background for a long time to come. I think this, if anything will keep this fellow from opening up, will be that.

NIXON: I think it's important just to silence him. Correct? Fine. And also, the important thing is to handle the captain — and the admiral [Welander] — in a way that they do not talk.

EHRLICHMAN: Well, they're career, and I suspect that that's enough leverage —

NIXON: And they're probably loyal fellows.

EHRLICHMAN: I suspect so.

NIXON: They're just doing it for the service. This fellow, I think they'd be shocked to know what this guy did.

EHRLICHMAN: Oh, they know! They're the —

NIXON: They know about the packet?

EHRLICHMAN: Absolutely!

NIXON: Oh.

EHRLICHMAN: Absolutely! See, they — Welander and the captain — used him!

NIXON: And they knew that he was stealing from Kissinger?

EHRLICHMAN: Oh, they had to! They had to.

NIXON: Jesus Christ!

EHRLICHMAN: I just don't see any escape from that.

NIXON: Well, that's the reason they need to be transferred. If they knew he was stealing from Kissinger —

EHRLICHMAN: See, the complicity there —

NIXON: Yeah. If they knew that, they have to be transferred.

MITCHELL: This is the only way you're going to have a deterrent on future such operations.

NIXON: Right. That's why you've got to have Moorer, you're going to do him when?

MITCHELL: Well, your suggestion was to let this fester.

NIXON: Yeah.

EHRLICHMAN: Well, now, I'm going to interrogate Welander today at one.

NIXON: That's fine.

EHRLICHMAN: And then we'll just let it sit for a bit, and regroup, and we can compare notes and see where we go from here, depending on what we get. But I hope from this interrogation comes an admission from him that he has been passing this stuff to the Joint Chiefs, so that we can complete the chain. That's the missing link right now. One thing that concerns me a little bit: I met Hughes's successor this morning, and he is from the Joint Chiefs. Now, I don't know that everybody in the outfit's tainted, but —

NIXON: Mm-hmm.

EHRLICHMAN: It rang a bell just because I'm kind of alert to that these days.

NIXON: Hmm.

MITCHELL: And Welander, Welander's going to have a pretty difficult time not talking to the subject matter.

EHRLICHMAN: That's right. Oh, he's, he's going to have to talk to it.

MITCHELL: Yeah.

EHRLICHMAN: Or that's the end of his career. I think that's his choice.

NIXON: [unclear] This son of a bitch Anderson really knows how to work on us.

EHRLICHMAN: He does. He's a master.

MITCHELL: He has more people around this government than, I guess, anybody has ever had. Far more than Drew Pearson ever had.

EHRLICHMAN: Well, he got them from Pearson. He was Pearson's leg man.

MITCHELL: Yes, I know, but he —

NIXON: He was all over the town!

MITCHELL: He's developed a lot more of them.

NIXON: He developed them all around.

MITCHELL: Yeah.

NIXON: I certainly would say this: I'd watch around. I'd see anybody that's — he was close to Wally Hickel, as I recall. I just think that —

MITCHELL: Does he have —

NIXON: I think we better check everybody that Anderson knows and talks to. I really think we better do that, you know, if we want to find out where it leads, what he believes, if that's gonna help us.

EHRLICHMAN: I'm not so sure. I think his regular sources are not a problem for us. That is, Safire, if he's a source, or something like that —

NIXON: Yeah.

EHRLICHMAN: That's not a problem.

NIXON: Yeah.

EHRLICHMAN: It's the hidden guys like this, who bootleg stuff to him, that we just stumble onto occasionally that we've got to root out. Now, I don't know how you find those people.

MITCHELL: Have you had a report on a check-back of his columns yet?

EHRLICHMAN: No, not yet. David [Young] may have it for me when he comes in.

• • •

NIXON: Well, incidentally, on this, I think you've done a marvelous job of sleuthing. This is a great job of, of detective work —

EHRLICHMAN: Well —

NIXON: — and one day we'll write it. But the point is now, as I say, John, your strategy is correct. We can't blow it. But we ought to get out of this. Keep this guy under wraps by scaring him to death. And something's got to hang over it. And second, use this as a device, of course, to clean out the Joint Chiefs operation. And third, you got to get to Henry. Now, you've got to get to Henry another way. Henry, we all know State leaks, and tries to jive Henry, and vice versa. On the other hand, Henry is paranoia-cal with regard to anything that comes out. He says, "Well, it's somebody at State," you know, "Rogers is doing this," or something. Now you, we've got to get to the point, he's got to have it brought home to him that he's got to look to his own shop, and not always assume that somebody else is doin' it *to* him. Right?

MITCHELL: And there has to be ordered in there that security officer.

NIXON: That's right.

EHRLICHMAN: Yeah, yeah.

NIXON: Mm-hmm.

EHRLICHMAN: And I think we'll get Young to sit down with him, because Young knows that system so well. Sit down with the security officer and give him everything he knows, so the guy starts out ahead of the game a little bit.

NIXON: Yeah.

EHRLICHMAN: Now, Young is writing up a memo for your file on this whole episode.

NIXON: Good.

EHRLICHMAN: And it'll be just the only copy there is, of the whole thing, and we'll just sock that away, so you're in a position to write about it sometime. But then, Young —

NIXON: See, what we're doing here is, in effect, excusing a crime.

EHRLICHMAN: Yeah. Yeah.

NIXON: So it's a hell of a damn thing to do.

EHRLICHMAN: Well, I —

MITCHELL: But this has been the history all through this question of espionage —

NIXON: Has it?

MITCHELL: — all the way through.

NIXON: Yeah. All right.

"In the end, we're still going to be accused that we fucked up something."
December 23, 1971, 12:27 p.m.
Richard Nixon, John Mitchell, Bob Haldeman, and John Ehrlichman
OVAL OFFICE

Nixon continued to weigh whether criminal prosecution was an option he held for those involved in the Moorer-Radford affair. At the same time, he wondered what damage that would do to his relationship with the military, on which he continued to depend as long as the Vietnam War waged on.

• • •

NIXON: Boy, there's something to be said really for prosecuting the yeoman.

HALDEMAN: I hope John is bringing Admiral Robinson back in. Because that —

NIXON: The yeoman really was giving him what amounted to a high crime.

HALDEMAN: Yep.

NIXON: He really ought to be prosecuted for it. I mean, my God! It reflects on us here. But I don't know.

HALDEMAN: Well, it blows up that Joint Chiefs business.

NIXON: That's the problem. It hurts the military. They can't take it. This kid will go in and rat on them. That's for sure. It's a smart motive if he will take it.

HALDEMAN: Sure, it'd get —

NIXON: Put it all on those [unclear].

HALDEMAN: [unclear].

NIXON: Frankly, by the end, it will reflect on us because, in the end, we're still going to be accused that we fucked up something.

HALDEMAN: That's right.

NIXON: It's the whole story. It's like the Pentagon Papers. We didn't have anything to do with it, but in the end hurt us some.

• • •

NIXON: I'm not sure what to do about the news of this fact that Henry is not in here telling us what the hell he's going to do to find out about that leak! You know what I mean? There's something wrong. There's something screwy here. But let him stew. Let them all stew. There's a great tendency, Bob. We all have this fault, but there's certainly a particular tendency in Henry's case, always to find blame in other people but to deny anything in his shop could be anything but perfect. Goddamn it, that's what could be involved here. I mean he said — look, if he thought this was being leaked from State, he'd be in here pounding the table —

HALDEMAN: "If this was true —"

NIXON: — threatening to resign.

HALDEMAN: "— he should be shot!"

NIXON: That's right.

HALDEMAN: He'd go berserk.

[EHRLICHMAN enters.]

EHRLICHMAN: Good day.

NIXON: This is pretty big. It's pretty serious.

EHRLICHMAN: Well, John [Mitchell] talked to the admiral. The admiral said he didn't exactly say what Mel says he said, but Admiral Moorer feels that his admiral should go to jail for all the terrible things he's been doing over here!

HALDEMAN: That's their standard [unclear]. [laughter] Send some guy down the ladder to do it!

NIXON: Everybody else should go to jail!

EHRLICHMAN: That's about it! John says that Moorer admits that he saw stuff, but that he operated on the assumption that his liaison man was working this all out with Henry.

• • •

EHRLICHMAN: David replayed the tape last night and there's something you kind of miss going by, but this yeoman could be sent into the process over in the NSC paper mill to pull out what the staff was recommending to Henry on decision papers that were coming to you in advance of the decision. And this was, he described, too, some names of people that meant nothing to me but that Young recognized. So that in fact the Joint Chiefs were getting advances on where the weaknesses were in their case in a decision that was coming to you, ahead of the word getting to you so that this would be —

NIXON: Yeah. That sort of thing doesn't bother me so much.

EHRLICHMAN: Well, it'll bother the hell out of Henry, and —

NIXON: It will?

EHRLICHMAN: I think that will, in a way, be more important to him than the rifling of the briefcases. So that's the integrity of that whole process that he holds pretty dear.

NIXON: Yeah.

HALDEMAN: Nobody knows what's coming forward.

NIXON: You better talk to him. You talk to him. Understand that it should be kept away from me, don't you agree?

HALDEMAN: Absolutely.

NIXON: I mean, I've decided Henry is like a child in certain — he won't know how handle it, and what to do, and so forth. Just say we're going to handle this this way, and that Mitchell sent it to us. Now, I've put it in the hands of the Justice Department and it's, the blood's going to flow here.

• • •

HALDEMAN: That's the way it goes, though.

NIXON: Intellectuals are that way. They're —

EHRLICHMAN: Bunch of jackals!

HALDEMAN: They back off fast.

NIXON: You must remember, though, you've got to remember this. That's also Henry. Henry's got that intellectual arrogance, too, you know. And, he will justify every goddamn thing he's ever done. He cannot be like we are in terms of saying, well, we all justify it to an extent that he cannot. One thing he cannot bear, believe me, is to be wrong.

HALDEMAN: Yeah.

NIXON: That's the problem, when I said he'd backstab me, Bob. You know —

HALDEMAN: Sure it is.

NIXON: It's like when he, did that backgrounder on the plane. He knew he screwed it up. And, it's like, remember that other one he did out here once? Well, it's hard. It's hard. That's the problem with too much education. People get the feeling that they can do no wrong, and then, well, their defense is always to show, whenever they do make a mistake, they didn't do it. But that, actually, they were right all the time. Whenever you make a mistake, unless you cut your losses and get out, you compound it by trying to prove you're right. That was the trouble with Kennedy and Johnson on Vietnam. Assuming it was a mistake, they compounded it by trying to prove that it wasn't.

EHRLICHMAN: Yeah, yeah.

NIXON: So it got deeper, and deeper, and deeper, and deeper, and deeper.

EHRLICHMAN: They showed that one sequence in a show. McNamara kept going over there and coming back, and they had clips of the things that he said and they compared it with what was really going on.

NIXON: Yeah.

EHRLICHMAN: It was just devastating.

NIXON: I know.

"Have you got any ideas?" "Yeah, but they're all illegal."
December 24, 1971, 12:00 p.m.
Richard Nixon, John Ehrlichman, and Henry Kissinger
EXECUTIVE OFFICE BUILDING

With the Joint Chiefs' liaison office in the National Security Council closed down, Nixon's attention turned to others who might know about the Moorer-Radford affair, as well as monitoring the yeoman for additional clues as to his motive.

• • •

EHRLICHMAN: The admiral was cleaned out last night, lock, stock, and barrel.

NIXON: Who was cleaned out?

EHRLICHMAN: Welander. He closed the office and moved out.

NIXON: Good.

EHRLICHMAN: Al Haig called David [Young] last night and indicated that he is very concerned about the quality of the evidence of the perjury that the admiral was being jobbed on. It's circumstantial evidence. So, I had Henry and Al up this morning and I played the tape for them of the, Welander's interview, and they were both convinced—

NIXON: Of course.

EHRLICHMAN: And they both now are—

NIXON: For Christ's sakes! They're just covering up here. That's what Al wanted to do.

EHRLICHMAN: Well, no, I think Al genuinely was concerned. He at least has now sold me—

NIXON: Well—

EHRLICHMAN: —that he's loyal. He and Henry both agree in very strong terms that Moorer should go. They're both now satisfied that Moorer is heavily implicated in this. They're doubly concerned because they've been using Moorer's back channels for all kinds of communications and they're afraid that they've been compromised. Whatever problems that raises I don't know, but the indications are there, but Henry then treated me to a half-an-hour monologue.

NIXON: On Rogers?

EHRLICHMAN: No, not just Rogers, but just the whole gap, but Rogers is certainly a big part of it. And he then came down very strong and said that he would never mention this to you, and that Al would never mention this to you, but that he wanted me to understand that their very strong feeling was that Goodpaster should replace Moorer at the earliest possible time, that their ability to work with a man like him was impaired, and on and on and on. So —

NIXON: I don't know, it sounds like they're railroading Moorer.

EHRLICHMAN: Well, this whole thing has been that way. The admiral wanted to railroad the yeoman and Moorer is —

NIXON: Moorer is too good a man. Moorer stood with us when it was tough, remember?

EHRLICHMAN: Sure.

NIXON: I don't feel that way at all.

• • •

NIXON: His problem with all these things, is when they don't go quite the way we expect them to. I said, "Now look, it's going to come out all right, Henry. India-Pakistan is going to come out not looking [unclear]. No sweat."

EHRLICHMAN: Well, you cut your losses there.

NIXON: Yeah, he has. And Henry thinks that the whole world thinks that he's failed, and that we've failed, and so forth. That's bullshit, don't you agree?

EHRLICHMAN: That's what's worth working on.

NIXON: Do you think there's that much to be concerned about?

EHRLICHMAN: No, I don't.

NIXON: In his case, put yourself in his position.

EHRLICHMAN: Well, Henry, of course, sees his reputation as sort of a reputation for the ages and —

NIXON: Hmm!

EHRLICHMAN: — as a sort of Metternich of the sixties —

NIXON: Yep.

EHRLICHMAN: — and seventies.

NIXON: We don't want to make any mistakes.

EHRLICHMAN: No mistakes at all.

NIXON: Grip of steel. Perfect man. Yeah.

• • •

[KISSINGER enters.]

KISSINGER: What concerns me is the way the system had leaked at the time, leaked out from within the government.

NIXON: But not by Moorer.

KISSINGER: No, no. Not by Moorer. No, that's —

NIXON: That's the point.

KISSINGER: That's where the major problem is.

NIXON: He seems to be doing the job that — you see the problem is that I don't care if Moorer is guilty [unclear]. We cannot weaken the only part of the government that for philosophical reasons supports us. We can't do anything with the problem that would just weaken the Joint Chiefs. The military would receive a blow from which it'd never recover. It would never recover if we did do it. We can't do it. The military must survive. We'll see that they — this is not the place to do the disciplining. That's the problem. Now get — take care of the yeoman. We better do something with him, but I don't know what the hell. Have you got any ideas?

EHRLICHMAN: Yeah, but they're all illegal.

NIXON: All of them illegal? Hah, hah. That's good.

EHRLICHMAN: Put him in a sack and drop him out of an airplane.

NIXON: That would do it. Yeah.

• • •

NIXON: Keep the yeoman here in Washington. Is anybody talking with him at all? Keeping in touch with him?

EHRLICHMAN: We're keeping in touch with him, but he doesn't know it. He's under surveillance. We're tapping him.

NIXON: Tap him, all right.

EHRLICHMAN: We had a report in yesterday that the yeoman, he's taking his time off. I don't know where.

NIXON: Keep him in Washington. I have a feeling it's better to have him here where we can watch him —

EHRLICHMAN: Mm-hmm.

NIXON: — than to put him out at some post where he'll be thinking about all this, worried to death, carrying out a lot of information. I'd like to have him closer, where we've got the FBI or, you know, our organization that can watch him —

EHRLICHMAN: Well, that's one, that's the —

NIXON: I'd put him over in the Pentagon.

EHRLICHMAN: That's one thing that John [Mitchell] and I have discussed is the possibility of just keeping him here under surveillance in the hope you catch him in bed with Jack Anderson some night.

NIXON: Exactly. Exactly.

Richard Nixon and National Security Advisor Henry Kissinger in the Oval Office.

Kissinger and Secretary of State William Rogers.

White House Chief of Staff Bob Haldeman working at his desk.

All photographs courtesy of the White House Photographic Office Collection, Richard Nixon Presidential Library, except where otherwise noted

Nixon and John Connally in the Oval Office just after the Democratic former Texas governor was appointed Nixon's secretary of the Treasury. Nixon admired Connally more than any other man in his cabinet.

Nixon and Governor Ronald Reagan (center) at Nixon's Western White House, La Casa Pacifica, in San Clemente, California.

The famous handshake with Chairman Mao during Nixon's visit to China in February 1972.

Nixon at the Great Wall. A snowfall that morning nearly canceled the visit, but Zhou Enlai (at Nixon's left) ordered thousands to sweep the streets with rudimentary brooms throughout the night so that Nixon could travel by car from Beijing to the wall. Other faces in the crowd include William Rogers, Bob Haldeman, and advance men Ron Walker and Dwight Chapin.

Nixon and Zhou (and Kissinger and Rogers) at one of the many long negotiating sessions during Nixon's famous trip.

The Nixons and Zhou Enlai share a laugh in the Great Hall of the People.

Following the visit of the American Ping-Pong team to China in 1971 and Nixon's visit to Beijing, the United States invited the Chinese team for a reciprocal visit in the spring of 1972. The visit took place in the White House Rose Garden.

The first two pandas given by the Chinese government to the National Zoo in Washington, following Nixon's visit to China.

Many conversations with Soviet officials were needed to lay the groundwork for Nixon's visit to Moscow and for the summit meeting. Here, Nixon meets at the White House with (left to right) Anatoly Dobrynin, Andrei Gromyko, and William Rogers. Henry Kissinger is off camera.

On May 22, 1972, Nixon became the first U.S. president to visit Moscow. Here, he and Kissinger take a stroll in Red Square.

Inside the Kremlin, Nixon and Kissinger confer between negotiating sessions.

On May 26, Nixon and Soviet Premier Leonid Brezhnev signed the SALT I agreement.

Pat Nixon and Kissinger watch Nixon's live address to the Russian people from an adjacent holding room.

Vietnam was a constant preoccupation during Nixon's first term. The president visited with troops in 1969, his first year in office, and in private spent many hours reviewing military tactics and, with Kissinger, the protracted peace talks.

As antiwar protests grew and Nixon became concerned with John Kerry and Vietnam Veterans Against the War, he met with Charles Colson (right), John O'Neill (center left), and a companion of O'Neill's. O'Neill helped found Vietnam Veterans for a Just Peace. Many years later, he would serve as spokesman for Swift Vets and POWs for Truth, opposing Kerry's presidential campaign.

Kissinger and Le Duc Tho in Paris after agreeing to peace in Vietnam, January 1973. Since their talks were almost always secret, this was a rare photo opportunity.

By day, Henry Kissinger conducted secret negotiations with American enemies from China, the Soviet Union, and North Vietnam. After hours, the media feasted on the image of Kissinger as a ladies' man with a string of celebrity companions, in this case Marlo Thomas. A 1972 poll of Playboy bunnies selected Kissinger as the man with whom they would most like to go out on a date.

Thanks in part to the historic summit meetings in Beijing and Moscow, Richard Nixon cruised to an overwhelming forty-nine-state victory in the 1972 election. In 1973, inquiries into Watergate began, bringing an end to the taping system and, in August of the following year, an end to his presidency.

PART III

Summit Planning and Escalation in Vietnam
January–May 1972

"I'm gonna get this son of a bitch straightened out a little."
January 3, 1972, 9:25 a.m.
Richard Nixon and Henry Kissinger
OVAL OFFICE

The SALT talks, which had recessed December 22, were due to begin again on January 4, but Nixon postponed them by a day. He considered it urgent that he see his chief negotiator, Gerard Smith, at the White House for last-minute instructions. The antagonism Nixon felt for Smith was evident, especially in his suspicion that Smith was angling to take credit for any success resulting from the talks. As they planned the next session of talks — the last before Nixon's summit meeting with Brezhnev during the final week in May — every announcement regarding the proposed arms treaty was regarded as sensitve.

• • •

NIXON: Incidentally, we've got a little problem on Bill [Rogers], because I had him come on over here — I had him come over here [unclear] the damn meetings on the economic thing [unclear]. I — what I'd like to do is review the meetings with Smith, first; to give Smith his marching orders; and I told Bill not to come 'cause he's not coming till ten — till ten thirty, but when he comes in —

KISSINGER: Gets his picture taken.

NIXON: Now, I —

KISSINGER: That wouldn't make any difference —

NIXON: — wouldn't be too concerned about his trying to get credit for SALT, because, as a matter of fact, as it — we're going to screw SALT up. There isn't going to be any goddamn SALT if — unless these people get a little bit better.

KISSINGER: Well, what — to give you the feel for what Smith will want from you —

NIXON: What's that?

KISSINGER: He wants your final position on ABM. I'd never give that to him —

NIXON: [unclear]

KISSINGER: Besides, I don't think you should give much ground on ABM, because we've already gone a long way towards them.

NIXON: Yeah. But, the thing I would encourage is to get him in and —

KISSINGER: It makes no difference if Bill wants to be here.

NIXON: [unclear] No, no, no. I'll — no, no. I would like to, I'd like to get some tough talk with him, first, and say —

KISSINGER: Well —

NIXON: — "Now, look here: there isn't going to be any final position on ABM." There's nothing left, but he —

KISSINGER: It'd just —

NIXON: — he wants the final position on everything so he can negotiate a settlement. Isn't that it?

KISSINGER: That's right.

NIXON: All right. What other things do you want me to say, Henry? [unclear]

KISSINGER: I wouldn't even say there won't be any final position, Mr. President, because he'll just leak it. I would say you're studying the problem very carefully, as you—

NIXON: [unclear] I'll say we've got a hell of a problem with Defense. How about that?

KISSINGER: Well, no. He's already dealing with them, because they've got their own fish to fry. I've got to get Moorer positioned. I would just say you're studying it; it's a tough problem; and you'll let him know—

NIXON: All right. What—what—why don't—

[unclear exchange]

NIXON: Why don't you say what we can give?

KISSINGER: Yes. Well, I think you can tell him that he can tell them that it should be a treaty—

NIXON: Fine.

KISSINGER: —for ABM, and an executive agreement for offensive—

NIXON: All right, all right, all right. Okay.

KISSINGER: That the SLBMs should be in terms of tubes, rather than in terms of boats.

NIXON: Right. Fine.

KISSINGER: These are two major—

NIXON: That's fine. But, but on the other things, I [unclear]—

KISSINGER: On the other things, you want him to go on the present line for a while longer.

NIXON: Until we let him know.

KISSINGER: And then—

NIXON: Henry, the best thing to do is to get him in. Under, under those circumstances, it would be best to get him and let Bill hear that, so that he knows that the treaty entails this move, just to tell him that I made this decision. And just let him ride—and have to ride out the thing. This fellow is—this fellow Smith, how's he thinking, Henry?

KISSINGER: Well, he's greasy and oily.

NIXON: [unclear]

KISSINGER: Now, we—well, you know, we are told that Bill is launching, and I'm—this happens to be one that's so complex that he doesn't understand it, so I'm not that eager to get him into too much of the line of command on it. But, whether he's in on one meeting or not, doesn't make any difference.

NIXON: This meeting is not a big deal.

[pause]

KISSINGER: It's not a major deal.

NIXON: Smith will run right over there afterwards. That's our problem.

KISSINGER: Yeah. And I don't want to come—

NIXON: Did he say he's got Laird under control?

KISSINGER: Well, Laird is playing such a crooked game —

NIXON: Ha!

KISSINGER: — as always. He has a bewildering series of memoranda here.

NIXON: Just don't tell him any more. Don't — I [unclear] —

KISSINGER: And, there are such — one of them is that he wants three ABM sites. Another is that he wants to go for an NCA defense, now, a defense of Washington. Another is —

NIXON: I'll tell you what I'm going to do. I'm going to take a very hard line with Smith, and I know this could get back to State, but, honestly, I've been very concerned about the Soviet buildup. I've been concerned about the fact that they have had — I'm gonna get this son of a bitch straightened out a little, Henry — that they have more tests this year than in any year since the Test Ban Treaty. Under the circumstances, that I have some very grave doubts about what their intentions are, and that I'm just — that we're going to go with these two steps and then take a look. I want to leave 'em in their tracks. How's that sound?

KISSINGER: That's right. And I think I can — the Soviets have already asked for a recess on the twentieth. Now, Smith thinks he can talk them out of it —

NIXON: Bullshit.

KISSINGER: — and I don't think you should show any eagerness for a recess, because I think I can position the Soviets to ask for it, so you're not the villain. Smith's line is — every Verification Panel meeting, Smith says, "I just want to make sure, now, that the president isn't stalling this for the summit." Of course, if [Edward] Kennedy were the president —

NIXON: What the Christ is he talking about?

KISSINGER: He should be stalling. I always say, "No, your instructions are to get it as fast as possible." But, of course, if Kennedy were the president, the whole goddamn bureaucracy would be stalling it for the summit.

NIXON: And that's just the SALT thing, Henry.

KISSINGER: Of course.

NIXON: Goddamn positioning. Why shouldn't we stall for the summit? So that he can get the credit, is that it?

KISSINGER: He isn't running for reelection this year, Mr. President. And he —

NIXON: Well, I, of course, can't give him any indication that I want to stall for the summit. That's not —

KISSINGER: That's the problem.

"I wish we could do something tough in Vietnam."

January 20, 1972, 6:08 p.m.

Richard Nixon and Henry Kissinger

OVAL OFFICE

The Indian subcontinent was roiled in violence during 1971, encompassing Pakistan and India in two related wars. Since 1947, Pakistan had consisted of separate regions to the west and east of India, controlled by the government based in West Pakistan. A strong movement for independence arose in East Pakistan and evolved into a civil war.

India, the giant between its two enemies, backed the fledgling new state of Bangladesh, in order to weaken its rival, leading to the Indo-Pakistani War in December 1971. Mainland China supported Pakistan, while the Soviets backed India. Nixon threw U.S. support to the Pakistanis, who were losing badly. Nixon's move was seen as a continuation of his courtship of Beijing. Controversial on humanitarian grounds, it gave Pakistan the chance to sue for peace with some dignity after only sixteen days of war. Nixon took pleasure in the outcome, looking on it as a sign of his ability to steer world events. That made him all the more frustrated that he couldn't do the same in Vietam.

• • •

KISSINGER: Dobrynin called me.

NIXON: He did?

KISSINGER: Yeah. Through Haig. Said he had a — he needs a long conversation with me. I made some jokes about India-Pakistan. He said, "Let's put it behind us. Let's work positively for the future." And I'm having dinner with him tomorrow night.

NIXON: So he doesn't appear to be negative about it?

KISSINGER: Not at all. No. One massive problem we have is in Vietnam. We had a message from Abrams today. They are putting in every reserve unit they have. Everything. They're stripping North Vietnam.

NIXON: The North Vietnamese are?

KISSINGER: Yeah, they're stripping it bare and —

NIXON: What can we do?

KISSINGER: Well, he wants to bomb the southern part of North Vietnam, where they have their logistic buildup. So we've got to look at it tomorrow. I want to talk to Dobrynin and tell him, "Look, if this offensive" — of course, they want to put it to us.

NIXON: Well, I think they want to put it to us. My view is that we may have to risk the Chinese thing, Henry. I —

KISSINGER: It's my view, too, Mr. President —

NIXON: I just don't believe you can let them knock the shit out of South — I mean China — so if the Chinese — the Chinese aren't going to cancel the trip [Nixon's upcoming visit to China, scheduled to take place in February].

KISSINGER: No.

NIXON: They're not going to cancel the trip because —

KISSINGER: I don't think we should go quite as far north but we should, as we did in the last attacks, I think we should let him do something. I think if —

NIXON: Well, Henry, you — you remember I —

KISSINGER: Particularly after your peace speech. [Nixon planned to make a major nationally televised speech on the status of the Vietnam peace negotiations on January 25.] I don't think you should do it —

NIXON: I wouldn't do it now. I mean, wait till the — after the peace speech.

KISSINGER: Yeah.

NIXON: I think you're right.

KISSINGER: I'd wait until they've —

NIXON: Do you think they'd respond with — to our speech — with an increased buildup?

KISSINGER: Yeah.

NIXON: I think so, too.

KISSINGER: That's my understanding.

NIXON: We could just simply — what does Abrams — does Abrams have a plan? Or —

KISSINGER: Well, he has targets. And I think they probably are going to make an all-out — and then they're going to settle. If they don't tip it then, they're going to settle. They're going to settle either way, because if they win, of course, they're going to have it, and if they don't make it then they're going to —

NIXON: When you speak in terms of the win, what are they doing? What do you envision?

KISSINGER: Well, what they could wind up doing is have a massive attack in II Corps, and come across the DMZ, and across the — and go all out in I Corps. Now, we ought to be able to handle it with massive air. But, if they go across the DMZ, of course, they'd be violating the understandings totally —

NIXON: Yes.

KISSINGER: And, of course it's also conceivable that Dobrynin brings us a message tomorrow. I don't really believe it. Not on Vietnam. He's — but he was very conciliatory and very — somewhat apologetic.

NIXON: About what?

KISSINGER: India-Pakistan.

NIXON: You think so?

KISSINGER: Yeah. I said to him, "You know, Anatoly, every time you leave town I know you're doing something mischievous 'cause every time you're out of town things are in crisis." He said, "Oh, I can tell you some interesting things." He said, "Let's put it behind us. But as a friend, I'll give you a lot of explanations which will —"

NIXON: He'll probably say that Kuznetsov tried —

KISSINGER: Well that I believe. But that, in fact, there's no doubt. Because we have the telegram from the Soviet ambassador to India, Pegov, who told the Indians on Friday, which was the tenth, that they should take Kashmir as quickly as possible. And on Sunday Kuznetsov showed up and everything began to turn. So the signals were clearly changed after your conversations with that [Soviet] agricultural minister [Vladimir Matskevich on December 9, 1971].

NIXON: [unclear]

KISSINGER: There's no question. No question.

NIXON: Let me ask you, is there anything that—there's nothing you can do with Dobrynin on that damn Vietnam thing. Not a damn thing—

KISSINGER: Well, I'm gonna, well, I'll see him tomorrow.

NIXON: You're going to have to see him tomorrow night?

KISSINGER: Tomorrow night. For dinner. I'll call you.

NIXON: Is your present thinking though that we still go ahead Tuesday night? That's what we want to do?

KISSINGER: I think so. Oh, no question about that.

NIXON: [unclear] I mean, in relation to the Dobrynin conversation, will that change anything?

KISSINGER: Well, unless he has a message that they are ready to start talking in which case—but that's inconceivable to me. They wouldn't send it through him.

NIXON: You think that what they're really doing is—what Abrams says is a massive buildup?

KISSINGER: Biggest buildup in four years. Every reserve division they've got. Literally, they've stripped it. If we could land one division up north we could drive to Hanoi.

NIXON: And where are they all? He says—

KISSINGER: Well they're coming down—

NIXON: How'd they get there so fast?

KISSINGER: Well some are on the train and some are just north of the DMZ. And they've built a road across the DMZ, which they don't need for infiltration—

NIXON: Well what the hell. Why aren't we hitting the road?

KISSINGER: Mr. President, this has been one of the—

NIXON: What in the name of God are we doing about the road?

KISSINGER: Well, oh yeah, we are bombing it. But it's one of the worst disgraces, that here the great U.S. Air Force can't keep a road from being built. They still haven't finished it completely so I don't think they'll start the DMZ attack yet. Our judgment is, or the intelligent judgment is, that they'll start their attacks in Vietnam in February, and in the II Corps area in March, and the I Corps area. I think they'll have knocked it off by May 1. They will not—my judgment is that the Russians will not want you to come to Moscow—they'd like you to be in Beijing.

NIXON: Beijing—

KISSINGER: With egg on your face. But, if we set up these negotiations on the Middle East properly, they'll need you to deliver on it. If you're the one that delivers, you need to be strong. If we—that's why we have to set up trade and the Middle East in such a way that you are the one that has to deliver it after the election.

NIXON: Coming back to this immediate problem, I see no choice but to, do what Abrams recommends on that. The—

KISSINGER: We kicked the Russians in the teeth when we had to for the national interest and we'll have to do it to the Chinese.

NIXON: That's right.

KISSINGER: But I'd do it after the peace offensive.

NIXON: Yeah. Yeah, I think you're right. That isn't going to make that much difference, is it?

KISSINGER: I think we should send a note to the Chinese when you give your speech and a note to the Russians. And —

NIXON: If they'll [unclear] escalation we will have to respond in kind?

KISSINGER: Yeah. And we hope —

NIXON: It's not [unclear] against them.

KISSINGER: And we hope that they'll use the affair to help us — to help our settlement.

NIXON: Who will you do that through? Have Walters deliver it in Paris?

KISSINGER: Walters in Paris and I can give it to Dobrynin on Tuesday just before your speech.

NIXON: I'd do it beforehand. That's what I'd do. I really would.

KISSINGER: Well, the warning I can give Dobrynin tomorrow, but I think the speech with the request — we don't want to —

NIXON: Yes, yes, I know.

KISSINGER: Because otherwise —

NIXON: What will you tell him tomorrow?

KISSINGER: Well, I'll tell him —

NIXON: Do we think, for example, that our air strike did any good? We do, don't we?

KISSINGER: Yeah. I'll tell him that what — I'll say, "Now look, you've watched the president. Time and again he's done things which you would have not predicted. Run enormous risks, and I'll tell you now he's going to do it again if this Vietnam offensive comes off at the scale at which we're now seeing it develop."

NIXON: Incidentally, what are the South Vietnamese doing in terms of preparing to meet the offensive? Are they —

KISSINGER: Well, he's changed a commander of the second — of two of the divisions in II Corps.

NIXON: Has he?

KISSINGER: Yeah.

NIXON: Has he — the commander change been — they must be pretty good now, the South Vietnamese.

KISSINGER: Well, in I Corps they're pretty good but that's where they may run into a lot of tanks. This may be a replay of the —

NIXON: We have tanks there now, remember? We've been delivering tanks to [unclear].

KISSINGER: No, no. That should be a gory battle but, you know, it would be a lot of publicity in this country.

NIXON: Look, if it doesn't involve Americans, it's all right. They're going to have publicity on it anyway.

· · ·

KISSINGER: I told Dobrynin — I said, "I saw you applauding the defense program part." He said, "No, you must have been watching this [unclear]."

NIXON: Did he say anything?

KISSINGER: I said it as a joke. I knew he hadn't applauded. But it was a good story.

NIXON: Well, we had one little hooker in there, for the good of the Russians too. We said, "We're for limitation of arms, looking to the future." We want to reduce arms. Dobrynin should know that.

KISSINGER: Oh, yeah.

NIXON: That we're willing to talk about that.

KISSINGER: Mr. President —

NIXON: He didn't object to the speech, did he?

KISSINGER: Oh, no.

NIXON: [unclear]

KISSINGER: Mr. President, I have — one thing is clear to me ever since my meeting with the [Soviet] cultural minister [Yekaterina A. Furtseva]. What we did in India-Pakistan, I don't care what it does here, we've got new respect from the Russians. She's now sent me presents and a note of [unclear].

NIXON: Did she?

KISSINGER: Yeah.

NIXON: Great.

KISSINGER: And Dobrynin. I can tell how he slobbers. He says, "I have some very interesting communications for you and it's terribly important. We have a big agenda. Let's get right to work." And he wanted to come for breakfast, as you know. He said — but he said he needs most of the morning, so I said, no, why don't we do it —

NIXON: At least it's — at least the summit is still on. You know, you hear about these people that — I —

KISSINGER: I told your staff this morning that I thought we would have more results —

NIXON: They kept saying — they kept saying, "Well, because of India-Pakistan Dobrynin will come back and tell you to go to hell." Well if they do then we know where we are.

KISSINGER: Mr. President, there is absolutely no chance —

NIXON: They've got [unclear].

KISSINGER: He told me — I had told his minister, his trade minister [Nikolai Patolichev] — I dropped in at Sam's for drinks with his trade minister and I said, "You know the president is prepared to do things that are beyond the imagination of everybody. On the other hand, if you don't stop these propaganda attacks on us, we can only conclude you — you want — you don't want improved relations and in that case we're not going to trade." So we've got to get Dobrynin back. We've got to get him back. He's the only guy that can straighten it out. And Dobrynin said he really had intended to stay another week, but they made him come back right after that conversation because they are determined to have this thing develop. So —

NIXON: Why don't you talk to him about Vietnam and give, you could give 'em almost anything right now. The trade, of course, you could give them.

KISSINGER: Oh, yeah.

NIXON: But damn it, they don't want to play. I don't know what we can do. We don't have any cards there, Henry, nothing but the damn air force. We'll use it. We've got to use the air force —

KISSINGER: Mr. President, I think the demonstration of impotence, of getting them out of Vietnam physically —

NIXON: What's that? I couldn't hear you.

KISSINGER: I mean —

NIXON: It's a demonstration of what?

KISSINGER: Of being run out physically. It would be too great.

NIXON: Oh, we can't do anything.

KISSINGER: Because I think they will be — after this shot — I think they —

NIXON: They've got to settle.

KISSINGER: Yeah. That's it.

NIXON: Don't you think so?

KISSINGER: They've got to settle this summer. One way or the other, I think, in making your planning, you can pretty well assume, one way or the other it's gonna be done —

NIXON: [unclear] we get number three?

KISSINGER: It's going to be —

NIXON: Remember we always talked in terms of two and three.

KISSINGER: Well, we got the two. I think we'll get number three.

NIXON: You know, it's interesting when you think, when you put down, you read the little foreign policy section in that speech. It's a pretty goddamn good policy, isn't it?

KISSINGER: It was very strong.

NIXON: Yeah.

KISSINGER: And very thoughtful.

NIXON: And you know we've said our commitments will be minimal. We will not enter in militarily, but we will do this and that. And also we've got in — we'll use our military — we've got it all down there. People know exactly what we will do and what we won't do. And it's damn strong. And of course, as you know, the kicker is an interest.

KISSINGER: Yeah.

NIXON: Oh. It's what — that means everybody gets it. I might decide that our interests were threatened in Bolivia, right?

KISSINGER: It was no —

NIXON: See the interest is the thing that they — that the peaceniks will — well, some of them will be smart. But a lot of peaceniks will say, "Ah, thank God we're not going to intervene." Bullshit. We'll intervene in any place —

KISSINGER: [unclear] —

NIXON: If [unclear].

KISSINGER: Well, with you as president, I —

NIXON: They'd be scared to death I might do something foolish.

KISSINGER: Foolish hasn't been your record but something tough.

NIXON: I wish we could do something tough in Vietnam. I don't — well, goddamn it, that air force plus the South Vietnamese should be able to do it. I don't think the North Vietnamese are that strong. I can't believe —

KISSINGER: What we ought to do —

NIXON: — in Laos, in Cambodia they could be that strong.

KISSINGER: What we ought to do is get a series of one- or two-day strikes. I don't think we can do five days at a clip, but we can —

NIXON: No, I — we can't. As I told you before, I really think that the last two days of the last mission [in Cambodia] — it wasn't fatal, but it didn't help us. I don't think it was worth [unclear] just continuing. It looked like we just didn't hit 'em. But hit 'em for a couple of days and then stop. As you noticed that, we stopped the bombing. They quit talking about it after three days —

KISSINGER: Yeah. Yeah. In two days, we can do one week. And then two weeks later, another day. They've just got to, and then —

NIXON: Why do you think that the fact — the reason I asked you about the other one, Henry, I think the fact that we did that five-day —

KISSINGER: Oh, that was very strong —

NIXON: — gave them some pause.

KISSINGER: Oh yeah.

NIXON: Don't you think it would worry them a little? They needed [unclear] —

KISSINGER: Yeah, but I think we may have to hit them early in February. I don't think it's —

NIXON: Well, that means next week maybe, though.

KISSINGER: No, the week after your proposal.

NIXON: Oh, you want to wait that long?

KISSINGER: Oh, maybe at the end of the week. I'd like to give your proposal a little more ride. I think they're going to —

NIXON: Yeah, I think we should let it ride the weekend, if we can.

KISSINGER: Yeah.

NIXON: How about that?

KISSINGER: And then if they hit us, then maybe we hit them for five days. You know, if they respond to your proposal with an all-out offensive.

NIXON: That's right. But we can — in your briefing you could hit that. I don't want to say it. I don't want to threaten in my speech —

KISSINGER: No —

NIXON: Or, do you think I should?

KISSINGER: No, you should not.

NIXON: I don't think I should be threatening at all in the speech.
KISSINGER: No, no, no.

"Play the weaker against the stronger. That's what we're doing with the Chinese."
January 24, 1972, 1:51 p.m.
Richard Nixon and John Ehrlichman
EXECUTIVE OFFICE BUILDING

Since President Nixon's initial overtures to China, first through intermediaries like Romania and Pakistan, then later through direct dialogue, his thinking had matured. What originally was a scheme devised to break a stalemate in U.S.-Soviet relations or result in more favorable treatment at the negotiating table by the North Vietnamese now had greater meaning. Nixon's secret tapes reveal the risk he took in order to raise the global position of China — his standing in the Republican Party, his reelection, and relations with allies and adversaries. In the short run, doing so was a scheme to extract concessions from others, such as the Soviet Union, but in the long run the friendship that Nixon offered to the Chinese had much greater consequences.

• • •

NIXON: You see, in the field of foreign policy, I can remember my direction, you know, but I must say that Henry, once he's got the direction from the beginning followed it to a T. We are playing a game, without being too melodramatic, whatever happens with the election [unclear] is going to change the face of the world. And it just happens that we are the only administration with the willingness, the only country in the world at this time —
EHRLICHMAN: Hmm.
NIXON: Now, the China move I've made not because of any concern about China, because I have none, not for fifteen years. [unclear] the need to do something about the Russians and to have another specter over 'em. The reason the Russians are now playing a very forthcoming thing on their summit, and it is forthcoming as hell —
EHRLICHMAN: Right.
NIXON: Dobrynin came back [unclear] because we had this flop over India-Pakistan, and all that, and the Russians are taking us on, only to find we're going to China. The Russians are going to throw the summit, throw it [unclear]? Not on your life. They've gone exactly the other direction. They want theirs [unclear] the Chinese. The Chinese want theirs because of the Russians. Now, this is a good thing.
EHRLICHMAN: Yeah.
NIXON: As long as you can play it evenhandedly. Now, this, therefore, can put us in a very powerful position. It's the sort of position the British were in in the nineteenth century when among the great powers of Europe, they'd always play the weaker against the stronger. That's what we're doing with the Chinese. You see? [unclear] and that brings the stronger around. Now, we're — if we can survive this, there'll be

ups and downs in this, too. Christ, how many columns have you read that said the Chinese game screws us with the Japanese?

EHRLICHMAN: Yeah.

NIXON: Screws us with the —

EHRLICHMAN: Yeah.

NIXON: — Russians? Right. And, "Was it worth it?" We're gonna hear more and more of that. Those who write are, basically, pro-Russian. That's where [unclear] pro-Russian columnists, and the Russians have figured that out. Now, on the other hand, if we had not played the Chinese game, we'd be in a hell of a spot today with the Russians —

EHRLICHMAN: Looking down our throats.

NIXON: We wouldn't be —

EHRLICHMAN: Yeah.

NIXON: Shit, they wouldn't want them to deal with us. Why would they?

EHRLICHMAN: Yeah.

NIXON: What can we do for them? But we can do something to them.

EHRLICHMAN: Yeah.

NIXON: They know that the Russian — that American-Chinese détente, with the Russians outside, is a hell of a dangerous thing. American power and Chinese manpower gives us the balance of power in the world. Correct? Now, I saw they sent Gromyko to Japan. Naturally. [unclear] You think for one minute any Japanese government is gonna give up its nuclear shield to make some silly deal with the Russians? Never. They'll trade with them and do other things.

EHRLICHMAN: Particularly not before they see how the Chinese summit's going to come out.

NIXON: The Chinese summit is not going to hurt them. They're gonna want to get to China first. That's all right. We don't mind if they do. See, we're playing the Chinese for different reasons than the Japanese.

EHRLICHMAN: Yeah.

NIXON: The Japanese are playing it for themselves. We're playing the Chinese because of the Russians. Well, this is the game. Henry understands, totally. I understand. Rogers will play. I think he is — I didn't tell him about it for [unclear] China thing, and two, because, God only knows, not only State Department finds, you know, [unclear] say, "Oh, Christ, it'll make the Russians mad."

EHRLICHMAN: Yeah. Yeah.

NIXON: So, there's where we are on that. But let's assume for the moment that we get through those two. I don't think it's probably going to help us in terms of public opinion polls and the rest. People rather expect we'll do well on that and the rest on that basis, but when you come right down to the election, I just wonder what the American voters are going to think. Assuming that your economy is not totally [unclear] how could — they're going to think a hell of a lot before they risk the possibility of, shall we say, some so-called generation of peace.

"Take Vietnam. . . . we should have flushed it down the drain three years ago, blamed Johnson and Kennedy."

February 1, 1972, 10:03 a.m.

Richard Nixon, Billy Graham, and Bob Haldeman

OVAL OFFICE

Since its start in 1953, each president since Dwight D. Eisenhower had taken part in the National Prayer Breakfast, a yearly event hosted by members of Congress that typically takes place in February. The audience often includes at least three thousand guests from industry, politics, society, and many foreign countries. Following the 1972 breakfast, Nixon and Reverend Billy Graham returned to the Oval Office for a recap of the morning's discussions. Nixon expanded on his prepared remarks, including his feelings about the media, the Vietnam War, and the role of the United States in the world.

• • •

NIXON: It's a very interesting thing. You really can't talk about it publicly. Do you know Paul Keyes?

GRAHAM: Yeah.

NIXON: He was saying, on his show, he says it's true of every show in Hollywood. Eleven out of the twelve writers are Jewish.

GRAHAM: That's right.

NIXON: Now, *Life* is totally dominated by the Jews. *Newsweek* is totally, is owned by Jews, and dominated by them, their editorials. The *New York Times*, the *Washington Post*, are totally Jewish.

HALDEMAN: [unclear]

NIXON: The ownership of the *Los Angeles Times* is now totally Jewish. Poor Otis Chandler, who sits on the top of the heap. The other thing, though, is that all three networks, except for, they have front men — they have Howard K. Smith, or [David] Brinkley, or a Cronkite may not be of that persuasion — but the writers though, ninety-five percent are Jewish. Now, what does this mean? Does this mean that all the Jews are bad? No. It does mean that most Jews are left-wing, particularly the younger ones like that.

HALDEMAN: [unclear]

NIXON: They're way out. They're radical. They're for peace at any price, except where the support of Israel is concerned. The only way [unclear] that I have on this, and this is the reason: the best Jews, actually, are the Israeli Jews.

GRAHAM: That's right.

NIXON: Because Israel, the reason [Prime Minister of Israel] Mrs. [Golda] Meir sup-

ports me, which she does, is for a very fundamental reason. They know the Democratic candidates will be catering to the domestic Jewish vote, but she supports me.
Because she knows the greatest danger to Israel is Russia. And she knows that in
the [1970] crisis involving Jordan that I faced the Russians down for 'em. She knows
that I am the only one that will do it. She knows that any Democrat will cave to the
Communists, to the Russians. See, that's the point. She's tough. We talked about this.
Rabin is the same way.

GRAHAM: Oh yeah.

NIXON: Rabin, of course, is a Russian Jew, and boy does he know them. Now, however,
in this country we must be under no illusions. You're aware of that, aren't you? You're
aware of the fact that in the media, we confront almost a solid block of people [un-
clear]. And it doesn't have anything to do with anti-Semitism. It happens, though,
insofar as the media is concerned, the power of the media —

GRAHAM: They've got it!

NIXON: They've got it right by —

GRAHAM: And they're the ones putting out the pornographic stuff, and putting out
everything.

NIXON: I don't know why they do.

• • •

GRAHAM: But this stranglehold has got to be broken or this country is going to go
down the drain!

NIXON: Do you believe that?

GRAHAM: Yes, sir.

NIXON: Boy! I can never say it though, but I believe —

GRAHAM: But if you've been elected a second time, you might be able to do something.

• • •

NIXON: The remarks I made this morning were not fit for a column, but there was
much more to it than that if any sophisticated person was listening. And there normally is on that occasion. The point being that we are in a situation at the present
time where, and it will be the last time when the United States, through its power,
can create conditions which can lead to peace for, perhaps, twenty-five years. Nobody can look beyond that. That would be a great deal.

Now, what is important is that the United States use that power, and use it effectively. Now I said something which many people, of course, do not like to hear. Most
people like to think that "if we just get to know each better we'll have no differences."
But the people that have the biggest fights are people that are married! They know
each other too well! The problem, of course, that we have with the Russians and the
Chinese, as I say, and I am sure you get the point. It's not that we do not know each
other, but the fact that we do know each other! They believe in one thing, we believe
in another. They believe in one kind of world, we believe in another.

But if you start talks with that in mind, then there is a chance to find those areas where you live and let live. Which is about the way the world is going to have these, the millennium is going to come someday, we hope, when everybody may want peace for the right reasons. But at the present time, we may want peace for reasons of necessity. They're not necessarily wrong, [unclear] but we do. The only thing I would give to the other side is what I say about the fact that any man, no matter how tough, or savage, or barbaric he is, probably does think of young people, the kids. I mean, the Russians must think of the Russian kids, and the Chinese must think of the Chinese kids, and would hope that they not be incinerated. And they know, as we know, that in the event of war it will be mass incineration. So we can think of that.

Now, but the point I make, however, is that there has never been a time when the United States needed, in this office, somebody who knew the Communists, who knows our strengths. Take Vietnam. Who is more keenly aware than I am, that from a political standpoint, we should have flushed it down the drain three years ago, blamed Johnson and Kennedy. Kennedy got us in, Johnson kept us in. I could have blamed them and been the national hero! As Eisenhower was for ending Korea. And it wouldn't have been too bad. Sure, the North Vietnamese would have probably slaughtered and castrated two million South Vietnamese Catholics, but nobody would have cared. These little brown people, so far away, we don't know them very well, naturally you would say.

But on the other hand, we couldn't do that. Not because of Vietnam, but because of Japan, because of Germany, because of the Mideast. Once the United States ceases to be a great power, acting responsibly, to restrain aggression, which is actually what we did in India-Pakistan. Our problem was no quarrel with India. I can count. I know there are a lot more Indians than there are Pakistanis, and I prefer the Pakistani government. But we could not allow India, with the support of Russia, to gobble up its neighbor. So we said stop, and it was right!

"I don't think anybody else sitting in this chair would have ordered Cambodia or Laos."

February 2, 1972, 10:05 a.m.
Richard Nixon and the National Security Council
CABINET ROOM

Nixon had promised the American people that U.S. troop strength in Vietnam would be reduced dramatically to sixty-nine thousand by May 1. The North Vietnamese and Viet Cong were well aware of his commitment to the withdrawal, and they gradually increased their aggression early in 1972, leading the president to a long discussion with the National Security Council regarding his options. The meeting centered on a series of requests made by the U.S. field commander, General Creighton Abrams. Most controversially, he wanted permission to use increased air power against North Vietnamese targets. While his strat-

egy would compensate for the reduced troop strength, it could be interpreted as an escalation of the war in the midst of Nixon's deescalation policy. Nixon had two good reasons to let the war end without further effort: first, his reelection campaign in 1972, and second, the overtures he was making to Vietnam's erstwhile ally, mainland China. Instead, facing a fork in the road regarding the course of the war, Nixon offered the reasons why he felt compelled to hit back in an effort to win.

• • •

NIXON: We have this meeting for purposes of one subject, which we have discussed individually with several of you here, but never in an official group. I've talked with Bill, Mel, John, and others numbers of times. I have also [unclear] I thought it would be well to pull all together at this time to see where we stand and what we can do in terms of responding to the enemy's actions over the next three months, three months or four, at least through the dry season. The intelligence community has a, I was going to say, not a divergence, but there's a shading of views on this, as there always is, as to what to expect. But they all agree that the enemy wants [unclear] in this period, so I think we would start with the intelligence analysis of how we're going to [unclear], then we'll go to Admiral Moorer for his briefing on ARVN capabilities, our capabilities, enemy capabilities, what we see from the standpoint of the services. And then we'll go to what we want to do.

• • •

NIXON: Could I ask one question there? Perhaps Ambassador Bunker could comment upon it. I indicated a couple months ago that Thieu might consider the possibility, rather than just, you know, just a nitpicking kind of operation, of some major action in the Cambodian area in order to divert the enemy's attention. When you see the fact that the South Vietnamese ground forces are, in terms of numbers, three times as strong as the North Vietnamese, and you see the fact that the South Vietnamese have air support and a navy, and the North Vietnamese have neither, it would seem that they might consider the possibility of blunting the enemy's offensive by some action on their own. Is that — as I understand, the South Vietnamese have rejected that idea due to the fact that they want to be in place for the expected enemy attacks. Is that —

[unclear exchange]

NIXON: Do you think that's the case?

BUNKER: Yes, I think that's true, but they were, as you know, in Cambodia.

NIXON: Yes.

[unclear exchange]

NIXON: What I was referring to, of course, now, here we sit and we see three divisions there, we see this, that, and the other thing. Everybody's worried, well, what are the North Vietnamese going to do? Well, here the North Vietnamese have one-third of the forces, with a long supply trail, with no air force, no navy; and here's the South Vietnamese. I'm just trying to put it in terms of — is that accurate at the moment?

AGNEW: To follow on that, because the same thing was going through my mind, except that between modifications, is it feasible or possible to consider an initiative on the part of the South Vietnamese, possibly on a reserve unit of the North Vietnamese in North Vietnam, instead of in Cambodia? Mainly looking at the propaganda effect of a South Vietnamese initiative in response to all this, where they actually go into North Vietnam, where there's a large concentration of reserve troops or materiel, and maybe another parachute operation will stop them. Just knock the hell out of them eventually. Give the papers something to write about.

NIXON: Have they considered those kinds of actions, commando raids, anything of that kind?

BUNKER: Well, yes, they've considered that. I think that's one thing that Thieu thought that they might be able to do is small raids. But not anything on a large scale like Lam Son, for example, last year. They won't take — their view is, I think, and I think we agree with them, is that the defense against this sort of thing is better on their territory than it is trying to move into, into Laos, which is very difficult territory to fight in.

LAIRD: Well, their military people, though — isn't it true, fair to say, Ellsworth? — are more apt to be willing to do some of these things presently. Now, the president [Thieu], when I discussed this matter with him, this was very firm and as frankly as I could. You remember —

BUNKER: Yes, yeah.

LAIRD: — on this operation, and also on raids to the north, and went into these things in some detail with him. He is a little reluctant. He was reluctant in Lam Son. He didn't personally put the, the hold on Lam Son when [unclear] up there would have done a — would have gone a little further, and Tom might be well to comment on that, because he really feels that his primary responsibility is not to Cambodia. He'll help Cambodia if he thinks it helps him.

BUNKER: Well, I think that's true, and I think he's not willing to risk the destruction of his own forces. That's the main thing, and this is the — this is why he didn't go further in Lam Son.

NIXON: Given Napoleon's biography —

[unclear exchange]

NIXON: — during Napoleon's earlier years, the way in which to avoid the destruction of your own forces is not to sit in place and get your ass beat off. The way to avoid it is to go in with inferior forces and knock the hell out of the opposition. We've seen that. In fact, I just, without getting into the strategy, but I — it seems to me that the long range of communications, no air force, no navy, and here they all say, sit there and say, "Gee whiz, we're going to have an offensive." Well, I wonder. I can understand that, but I understand that you can't do anything that he will not approve. I mean, he's been, he's been fine, and he stands up brilliantly in this political thing and the rest. And I'm not suggesting that our people are [unclear]. We aren't engaged in his activities on the ground, but — and I know Mel didn't raise this because we discussed it before.

LAIRD: You told me to and I had that.

NIXON: The thing that I'm concerned about is that — well, it's probably too late. They're just not going to do it. Isn't that right? They're going to wait and take the blow, is that correct?

MOORER: In this particular [unclear] —

NIXON: As regards the enemy, the enemy's going to take the play and they'll just play the defense.

• • •

MOORER: At the same time, we have moved out on several precautionary actions. The first three I'm going to talk to separately. Additional air authorities have been granted. We have developed plans for a certain amount of air capabilities. We have carefully reviewed our helicopter assets. We have planned for increased CV and naval gun fire support, we have allocated all the CV using munitions that we have. These are the small antipersonnel-type weapons, Mr. President, that have been very effective recently. We've sent over — we've made certain that all we have in inventory is available for this operation. We have developed a plan for strikes against the LOCs in North Vietnam. I mentioned the airlift augmentation. And General Abrams has talked about the security of our forces. He has formed twenty-eight teams. He sent them to examine the defense plans and the alertness of every U.S. unit in South Vietnam. He reports to me that the oral reporting received so far is good, that they are — that all our people are aware of the threat and they are not going to be surprised. And in addition to that, we've developed plans to increase P-3 offshore patrols in the event that the sea infiltration is kept up during this crisis.

Now, I'd like to talk about these first three: the air authorities, the plan to develop the surge of air elements, and the availability of the [unclear]. First, the air authorities, I've listed here with the red dots. This is what General Abrams requested. Next to it, the black square shows the authority he's been granted so far. Now, the first thing he asked for was air support for the Vietnam forces that might be in pursuit across — to conduct cross-border operations. This has been given to him. Across the Laotian and Cambodian borders he can't use U.S. air assets to support the South Vietnamese if they conduct operations across the border. Secondly, he asked for authority to release the sensors north of the DMZL. Heretofore, we had only been supplying the operating sensors south of the DMZL. This will give us a readout on the activity along the northern part of the DMZ, both lateral and vertical activity, and will, I think, provide more warning and permit a better counteraction can be taken.

Next, he asked for authority to strike the GCI radars in North Vietnam that are directing the fighters, the MiG fighters. He was given the authority to fire the antiradar missiles, mainly the Shrike and the Standard ARM, against these GCI sites when they locked on or when there was MiG activity and the GCI site was operating. In addition to that, so far, he was not given authority to attack these radars whenever one was located, but rather we have directed CINCPAC to prepare contingency plans for this purpose. So, if it's directed from here, he can in fact do that.

NIXON: How many? What are we talking about there in terms of numbers of strikes?

MOORER: No, there were five radars, sir. Of course, we were given five of these large [unclear]-type radars. I have them on this other chart —

NIXON: It's all right. I don't need it. I'll explain to you something: what I'm trying to get at is the magnitude of the authority he's requested. He wants authority to go in and hit the five radar sites, and —

MOORER: Yes, sir.

NIXON: — we have said only, basically, hit them only if it is really protective reactions? That's in effect what he asks?

MOORER: No, that isn't what we said there. That's a little different, Mr. President. You have noticed that whenever they're using — directing MiGs up in that particular area, he wouldn't hit them.

NIXON: Look, I understand. But that — but the —

MOORER: They're already in there.

NIXON: Yeah. The authority he wants is to what, to hit —?

MOORER: Once he locates one, he wants to go get it, when the weather permits, regardless of MiG activity. In other words, he does not want to wait for protective reaction situations.

NIXON: How many would it be? What does it require? How many strikes and where to do that?

MOORER: Well, he wants, he asked for authority for those south of twenty degrees —

NIXON: Those?

MOORER: Five, sir. There are five sites, I believe.

NIXON: Okay, I got it.

LAIRD: Well, we asked him to develop a plan, Mr. President, how many strikes it would take to do it and we haven't got that plan back yet.

NIXON: Yes, well [unclear].

KISSINGER: And also, as I understand it, there are three different states that one could talk about that one. One is that if the radar locks on the airplane that then they can fire a strike against that radar, which —

NIXON: Sure —

KISSINGER: The second is that while the radar is locked they can also use other explosives that are not focused on the radar, that do not depend on being — on homing in on the radar. Third, is what he's asked for, namely to attack it outside the engagement, but even while the engagement's going on, he does not now have authority to use anything other than homing beacons.

MOORER: That's right.

KISSINGER: Isn't that correct?

MOORER: Yeah.

KISSINGER: So, then he would—

NIXON: But he would like authority, he has asked for authority, to strike regardless, regardless of engagement.

MOORER: When he finds it. [unclear] You have to understand, Mr. President, that one strike might not necessarily, although he may demolish [unclear] they would bring it—they would put it back in action a week later, so what he was really asking for was the authority to—

NIXON: To keep it up?

MOORER: —anytime he found one, to go knock it out—

NIXON: Yeah. Okay. I was just wondering.

MOORER: Now, the same thing he—was requested with respect to the SAM sites. As you know, he already had authority to fire the antiradar missiles against the SAM sites, and we have been doing this with increasing regularity as the SAM activity increases. He would advise that once the ground offensive starts, that this authority would be considered on a case-by-case basis. And we would go ahead and prepare contingency plans for the one-time strikes against SAM sites. I should point out that we have authority today to strike those four sites in Laos, and we have struck the four sites, parts of them. What they do is they—these are mobile, and they move them around all the time. And consequently, you may know where one is today, and it may not be there tomorrow.

NIXON: Do I understand, that what we have, in effect, said to them that after the enemy launches its massive attack, that he then, on a case-by-case basis, has got to get authority to take out [unclear]?

MOORER: Yes, sir, that's what we're talking about.

LAIRD: Well, what we've asked him—

NIXON: Change that.

LAIRD: —we've asked him, Mr. President, to come in with a plan to do it now. And that plan is to be submitted. [unclear]

NIXON: Well, I just—I'm just trying—I know that there's been some disagreement as to what should be done and so forth.

LAIRD: I don't think there's any disagreement.

NIXON: Well, [unclear] what I meant is that I just want to be sure that there's a clear understanding here as to the two different phases: what do we do now, what do we do when it starts. Now, without, of course, giving commanders in the field the right to start a nuclear war, once their major offensive has begun the situation totally changes, in my opinion. We're not going to go through this crap of saying, well, we have to approve every goddamn thing. It's not going to be done that way and I want to—

LAIRD: I don't think there's any question.

NIXON: No, there is. That's exactly what we've been talking about in both places. If they start an offensive, we're not going to go through this nonsense of saying that we'll wait until a SAM shoots and then we'll knock it out. That's what the real argument's about?

MOORER: Yes, sir.

NIXON: Okay.

MOORER: Well, we will have plans to strike these sites and these radars subject to the authority.

NIXON: Yeah.

MOORER: Also, he requested permission to strike those airfields that I showed you, that—

NIXON: Now, here the argument is also, though, the question—what has been granted here? The authority, that's to be done on a case-by-case basis, right?

MOORER: We have told him to increase his airfield reconnaissance and to make certain these reconnaissance aircraft are heavily supported with bombing aircraft, and if these aircraft are fired upon, which they always are, he was to then attack the airfield, and so we have been doing a series of operations of this type, sir.

NIXON: You've got all the intelligence ready, you know how to hit 'em, and so forth and so on?

MOORER: Yes, sir. Now, we have not attacked the Haiphong airfield, which is the one right up on the edge of the twenty-degree parallel, but we've attacked Dong Hoi, Binh, and Quan Lang. [unclear] And, incidentally, they're very effective. Usually what happens is they have one reconnaissance plane, two fighters protecting against MiGs, and eight attack planes. And when the reconnaissance plane goes over the airfield, and as machine AA fires, they target their weapons on the—openly on the AA or on the support facilities at the airfield. But here again, Mr. President, I'd emphasize that this has be done continually in order to make certain that the airfield is not restored to operation.

NIXON: Go ahead.

MOORER: Well, he's also been told that, again, that once the battle is joined, so to speak, that any aircraft south of eighteen, as Secretary Laird just said, is hostile and they can be attacked at any time in A-1. I should add to this that we have stationed two tail cruisers, with an awful big pulse radar in the vicinity of Binh, and they also have authority to fire at these MiGs that are indicating hostile intent. And we are interpreting hostile intent very broadly.

LAIRD: I guess we've had one firing hit.

MOORER: We had one, one firing so far. Right.

LAIRD: A hit, but they're standing off. They're ready to fight.

NIXON: Right.

CONNALLY: Mr. President, may I ask if the later discussion will bring out the objections to granting these authorities that he's asked for?

NIXON: Let's be particular and we'll see at the next one. The last one is against — go-ahead — logistics.

MOORER: Yes, sir. He asked for authority to strike stockpiles and transshipment points, and conduct all reconnaissance against trucks moving down the LOCs leading into Laos, mainly through the, primarily through the Ban Karai and the Mu Gia passes. I have a chart here. We have —

NIXON: The point here is, the point here at issue, is the authority to hit such logistic places in North Vietnam?

MOORER: Yes, sir. South of eighteen degrees. Again — give him the first chart, Mel. Yeah, that's all right.

NIXON: How close is twenty degrees to Hanoi?

MOORER: Well, it is — twenty degrees, sir, is right here, and it's — that's about —

NIXON: Yeah?

MOORER: — sixty miles, one more degree.

NIXON: Eighteen is —?

MOORER: A little over seventy-five miles, let's say.

NIXON: I don't understand this. What's that? [unclear]

MOORER: [unclear]

NIXON: Now this logistics business, tell us what that's all about.

MOORER: Yes, sir. [unclear] Here, we — I drew up a concept of the plan, have sent it out to the field to get them to flesh it out in terms of the exact numbers of sorties, the exact — some of them — they'll take it apart and so on, and we have the candidate plan available, sir, which would authorize General Abrams to make these attacks on these logistics activities taking place, feeding into Laos.

NIXON: What's the weather situation at this point? Will it be —?

MOORER: Well, during the month of February, sir, of course, is about — in January–February, as we found out last year, is the worst part of the year in the panhandles. Actually, there are six days out of February that have ten thousand feet altitude for a period of three hours, and there are three days that have a period of six hours wherein you have ten thousand feet. So, this is one of the reasons that General Abrams has asked to go when he has the opportunity so that —

NIXON: Whenever there's a window?

MOORER: Whenever there's a window is what we talked about. Yes, sir.

ROGERS: Tom, these are all based on what General Abrams requested. How about the Joint Chiefs? Are there things that we should be doing now that aren't included here? Because it seems to me that because of the importance of this new offensive we ought to take every possible action. I don't think we have anything to lose. The American people don't understand all this stuff. [unclear] The only thing it seems to be, the only question we have, is what can we do that will be effective?

MITCHELL: Well, that kind of brings up the point that the one airfield with the seven

MiGs is above the eighteenth parallel, and the other airfield with the one MiG is the one that below which he has the authority.

LAIRD: Mr. President, I'd just like to make a comment about what we can do. Because I think that's the important question as to what we can do as far as the offensive is concerned. The offensive, I think, if it takes place, will be in the B-3 Front. ["B-3" refers to a North Vietnamese–designated area in the highlands, the B-3 Front, which was located within MR-2, the U.S.-designated Military Region 2.] I think that that's indicated by all of the activities that that's where the attack will be made. Now, we've got to concentrate on limiting that attack, it seems to me, and do everything we possibly can with all the air power we have, because this inasmuch as it gives the South Vietnamese a much greater advantage than any kind of artillery or anything else the other side can have. The activities in the North will not have anything to do with B-3 activities because every bit of logistic support, if the activities that are going to take place in the next three weeks have already gone through these passes and is already in place. Anything that needs to come down to support that operation now won't be available until March or April.

So everything that for this attack that we're concerned about is in place and has been, including the people that are involved, as far as the B-3 Front is concerned. Now, as far as an attack may be in March or April, I think these logistic strikes should be authorized, and I hope that the contingency plan, as finally approved, gives the latitude to General Abrams to go three or four times for letting him pick the particular day that he goes, based upon the weather conditions that exist. I think it's better to give him either twenty-four or forty-eight hours two or three times that he can make the choice, because that's the most effective way to limit a possible offensive in the March–April period, because those would be the supplies that would be used in March and April, not the February offensive. In that way, we can live with it as far as the country is concerned. I think it's understandable in a short period that if we go for five, six, seven, or eight days in a row, there is a certain amount of political pressure that people get over a long period of time. And I am sure that General Abrams would be more effective with the use of his assets if he has the authority himself to go twenty-four or forty-eight hours in the North in these areas to hit logistics. Now, I don't want to mislead anybody at this table. That is not going to have an effect upon the B-3 Front offensive if it comes.

It will have an effect upon a possible future offensive that might come in the April–May period, but it takes at least that long. Now that's not true of Military Region 1, but it is true of Military Region 2 and in the highlands area. That stuff is already in place.

MOORER: I suppose, Mel, you have —

LAIRD: Yeah —?

MOORER: — you have a built-in restraint in terms of the weather. [unclear]

LAIRD: Well it is—the weather is going to be lousy all month, so that this idea that we're going to have great weather out there—it's going to be lousy weather.

NIXON: In February?

LAIRD: Yeah, the weather—the weather in December, January, and February is lousy, and it probably will be lousy into March.

MOORER: Yes, sir. The point I'm making is you're not going to have a seven-day good-weather period.

LAIRD: No.

MOORER: So, we don't have to worry whether you make it seven days or not—

NIXON: What is the situation—let me come back to that DMZ, the possibility of their moving en masse across there, at the sanctuary they have where the line is drawn? The authority—has he asked for authority to hit above that line now to knock those roads out? [unclear]

MOORER: That would be part of this logistics plan.

NIXON: That's—that'd be fine.

MOORER: Yes, sir—

NIXON: That's fine. He's not asked for that authority yet?

MOORER: Yes, sir. He has authority for [unclear]—

LAIRD: One pass area there goes through the upper part of the DMZ, and that he has asked for.

MOORER: And the road runs right parallel to the DMZ—

NIXON: How many—that's one road. How many roads are being built? You said several roads are being built across the DMZ? That they'll come, they thought, potentially might come down those roads.

LAIRD: There are two roads, two roads being built; one major road and the start of another—

NIXON: We bombed part of it, but not the other part now? Is that correct?

LAIRD: Well, the road is not in use now, but we are—it goes into South Vietnam—and we are, presently, are bombing it.

MOORER: We bomb all of it south of the DMZL.

NIXON: I understand.

MOORER: Yep.

LAIRD: But it has not been used and there hasn't been much to hit there. They just reconstructed it.

NIXON: He wants the authority to be sure. Well—

LAIRD: He wants the authority to use that target area if there is a logistic buildup there. He won't go up and just hit it if there isn't a logistic buildup—

NIXON: [unclear]

LAIRD: But if there is a logistic buildup there, and he has a good-weather window, and there are supplies there, he'd like to hit it.

ROGERS: Mr. President, can I ask a question to Tom? It seems to me that in view of the fact that we've only got two weeks before the president leaves for Beijing, and I don't — I think the American people feel the president's gone so far now to try to work out an equal settlement that they'll support it, [unclear]. It seems to me that if this offensive takes place while the president is in Beijing, and even if it's reasonably successful from their standpoint, when we all try to second-guess the plan, then we should, the president should, seriously consider giving the military any authority that it wants — within reason, of course, not nuclear authority, but anything else. Because short of that, it seems to me we will — that this is, this is the key play. It could well be that this could be the turning point of the whole battle for South Vietnam. [unclear]

So, I would — what I was wondering about, in addition to what General Abrams is asking for, are there other things that the military thinks the president should consider and authorities that they should have to prevent this offensive or to deal with it successfully? In other words, is everything being done that can be done? Or are there other things that we should be thinking about, too?

AGNEW: I'd like to expand on that if I might. Listen, what you said really anticipated what I was going to say to some extent and that is this: that it seems that all of the military preparations and the carefully defined limits of what can be done prior to any strike are pretty well — have pretty well been anticipated and explored. Where — the point I'm worried about is what happens to us after this strike? And I'm not talking about, necessarily, actions that are of grave military importance. I'm talking about the psychology of the war and the fact that the North Vietnamese have now responded to, not only to the president's peace initiatives, but to his three-times- or four-times-repeated warning that any escalation of the war on their part that jeopardizes the success of our troops there will be responded to immediately in a very affirmative way.

So, now it seems to me that military considerations aside, we have to look at the psychology of what's going to take place in the United States the minute that they launch these attacks. That there's going to be cries of the failure of Vietnamization, and we should have been out by now, and that it's all lost, and the only thing that'll overcome that, as I see it, is something that should be very carefully planned now that represents a punch action by the United States with the South Vietnamese in an area that we've never gone. And then, let them call it a widening of the war, but someplace where we can go in there and hit 'em in the gut real hard. Maybe — I don't know whether you could think about doing something to Haiphong harbor or anything else? I mean, maybe that's an unmentionable subject, but the point is that they've been warned three or four times not to do this. They're going to do it anyhow. They're going to do it for political reasons more than military reasons, because they think they can drive us out through the pressure of public opinion.

And it seems to me that it's time when they do it, the president having issued these warnings on four occasions, not to make 'em idle, but to move in there and hit 'em a good one in the gut somewhere where they've never been touched before.

CONNALLY: Mr. President, may I add one thought to what the vice president said? I think both from the standpoint a public voter sees it and actions over there that a good part of it ought to precede your departure from the United States. We ought to be preparing our own propaganda offensive now, that you're going to China didn't precipitate all this, 'cause this is the posture which our enemies here are going to play it, "If you hadn't gone to China, they wouldn't have launched this offensive." This — the propaganda offensive that ought to be launched here at home now, is that this is another Tet. Westmoreland's the only man that I know of that's really made a point of it.

Look, we ought to be saying it tomorrow, and the next day, and the next day, long before people are conscious that you're leaving on whatever day it is in February. And so that when you do react, you're reacting to an offensive on their part that parallels what they did in the Tet offensive in '68. It ought to be tied back in [unclear], so they're prepared and they're going to do it and so forth. Otherwise, I think the American press, our enemies in the press, are going to, frankly, lay it to your door and just say, "Well, if you hadn't, prior to this Beijing trip, this wouldn't have happened."

LAIRD: Mr. President, can I add something to that? I want to make a point here that I think is overlooked, and that is that I am confident that this will be a success as far as the South Vietnamese are concerned, and I am confident that our program will hold. Now, they're going to lose the battle or two, but they're doing nothing differently than they did last year or the year before. The numbers are the — about the same.

Now, they're going into a different area. They're going into the B-3 Front and they will conduct a battle there, but let's not forget that we have done certain things for the last three years to build up the South Vietnamese, to build up their capabilities. And I don't believe that we're going to be in a position where the South Vietnamese are going to get such a bad, bloody nose that it's going to be any kind of a defeat, interpreted in that way here in the United States.

AGNEW: But, no, if it looks like a failure —

LAIRD: It doesn't help —

AGNEW: — it doesn't make a damn bit of difference how successful it is —

LAIRD: It's very important, this one, but as far as the B-3 Front battle is concerned, we've got all the authorities we need for the B-3 Front battle. I'm concerned about the next battle, maybe on down the road in two or three months after you get back. We've got everything in place to handle the B-3. When I got back in November, I made the report to the president that, in that report, I anticipated the B-3 Front as the battle site, and at that time I went to the Joint Chiefs and asked them to prepare the plans to defend on the B-3 Front. And we've been planning for this since November. Now, we — everything that we have on the B-3 Front is in place right now. You can't do a hell of a lot more on the B-3 Front. We've got a surge capability on our '52s, we have a surge capability on our tactical air, we have a surge capability as far as our naval air is concerned. And if the president's — while the president is in China that could be the major area of concern. Now, as far as the next offensive is concerned, that's a different problem, and that's why I believe that some standby authorities given to General Abrams in the area of logistics support, knocking out these particular areas. I would limit those authorities to him to go for a twenty-four- to forty-eight-hour period, but three or four times that he can do it, because then you can start the attack and you can announce when it is over. He should choose the times when there are logistic buildups up there so we can actually hit something, and you do have to have good weather. I think that is needed and necessary.

That isn't going to help the problem while you're in China, necessarily, Mr. President. I think that should be understood around the table. Because the — that battle is pretty well drawn, and if it comes —

NIXON: Well, you have a week then. That's only a week that we're there, so the point is that —

LAIRD: But I just don't want people to get too panicky about the period of time that you're gone in China because those particular supplies and the combat personnel — I think Dick would have to agree with that — that they're in place on that front —

CONNALLY: Look, Mel, I can't understand, if all the supplies are in place, all the personnel are in place, we obviously know that, we have to know where they are —

LAIRD: And we're hitting 'em —

CONNALLY: — are we hitting 'em now?

LAIRD: All right. [unclear] what we're doing there with the B-52s and with the TacAir right now. We've got the best all-source intelligence operation going on in the B-3 Front that we've ever had in the whole history of this war. And I think it would be well to explain to you exactly what we're doing as far as hitting in there right now to — you've got some —

MOORER: Here, take these —

ROGERS: While they're getting the charts out, though, Mel, your comment doesn't — is not inconsistent [with] what John said —

CONNALLY: No. Not at all —

ROGERS: We can make this, if we do what John suggested, and I think we should, then if it doesn't come off or is not successful we can say, "Well, hell, we anticipated it and we guarded against it and that's why it was unsuccessful."

LAIRD: But I don't want anyone around this table to think that by hitting those places — [unclear exchange]

LAIRD: — something to do with that fact, because it will not.

ROGERS: Everybody [unclear] —

LAIRD: And the problem that you have here is, you know, there are a lot of people who seem kind of panicky around here each time that you roll for four or five days. I happen to know. I sit down and I, I, I love to take the heat for this stuff; it doesn't bother me a bit. I've always said, Mr. President, publicly and all over, that I would recommend — that never committed you — but I would recommend that we blast hell out of them if they come across the DMZ.

NIXON: Oh, well, we've said that, too. The point that I make is that you have that period when we're back from China, the twenty-eighth of the month or something like, that's plenty of time to get that March and April buildup. Don't you think?

LAIRD: Oh, yes, sir.

MOORER: If I may make a point, sir? They're always hard sell. The problem of hitting these fleeting targets is nothing more than weather. And so, it won't be a matter of General Abrams discovering a supply buildup or something of this kind. Anytime during the next three months there will be targets, and if he has the visibility — if TacAir has the visibility, so they can strike these trucks, these moving trucks, these temporary stockpiles, and so on — they will find productive targets anytime that the weather was suitable.

CONNALLY: And they have authority to strike?

MOORER: And they have authority. Yes, sir. If they have the authorities.

CONNALLY: I'm asking, do they have the authority to strike?

NIXON: They have it. They have it outside of North Vietnam. The authority we're arguing a bit, we're discussing now, is the authority to go into North Vietnam —

LAIRD: The authority —

MOORER: That's correct, sir —

LAIRD: The authority we are discussing is an authority which would grant him, below the eighteenth or maybe up to the twentieth in those pass areas, to go after any logistic buildups. We've gone after them before.

NIXON: In the period, for example, in the five-day period after Christmas, between Christmas and New Year's [Operation Proud Deep Alpha, during which U.S. aircraft flew 1,025 sorties against targets north of the DMZ but south of the twentieth parallel]. That was originally authorized as a, basically, a two-day operation. Weather was lousy, so they took it for two days and we extended it finally — well actually, it was four days in turn, it was in total, but we extended it for two more days. The — what we're really talking about here is rather than having the — rather than having these authorities in which you hit four days at a time, which each day escalates the news story, is to have the authority.

If we give the authority, it might be extended over, say, what as I understand it, is they want the authorities over a thirty-day period to hit for twenty-four hours, whenever the weather is good. In other words crack 'em, crack 'em, crack 'em.

LAIRD: And that's what I'd like —

MOORER: That would be more effective, sir —

NIXON: That's a different — rather than — rather than attempting on an ad hoc basis, to say, "Well, now you can go for five days." Well, those five days may be the lousiest damn weather there is, so you wouldn't want to do it. And also the difficulty is that, again, when it's continued over a period of time, unless there is enormous provocation, you see, that's more of a problem. On the other hand, if you follow your intelligence reports, we're having correct protective reaction strikes every damn day right now, so you're hitting things. Incidentally, and I understand, and I just want to be sure, that that's being interpreted very, very broadly.

LAIRD: I don't know if they can, because they can't interpret it any — I've gone out and talked to Tom. Haven't we given them the broadest interpretation?

NIXON: You see, the thing is they, they — there was a story here in the *New York Times* to the effect, first, that after the period after Christmas that we ordered these strikes for no military reason, which was not true, because as you remember, Mel, you came over, and some of the Joint Chiefs said, "We've got to hit 'em now." Right?

LAIRD: Right.

NIXON: And because you were anticipating the B-3 buildup, right?

LAIRD: Right.

NIXON: Right. And that's what we were trying to hit. And the second point was that it was extended beyond the time that it was useful, for no good reason. Well, the reason it was extended was because you said the weather was bad, right?

MOORER: Yes, sir. [unclear]

NIXON: The story was totally inaccurate.

MOORER: Those strikes were effective —

NIXON: It shows you the problems you've got. Huh?

MOORER: Those strikes were effective. We —

NIXON: Well, of course they were —

MOORER: We made the equivalent of 750 truckloads of supplies were destroyed —

NIXON: That's very —

MOORER: — and —

NIXON: That's very worthwhile —

• • •

NIXON: When people ask, "What should we do to bear out the indication of a practical use of a five-day strike?" We got through to 'em pretty tough and all of our intercepts indicate that. They've arranged to hit 'em. We should put in some more, too. You have to see to it some more —

MOORER: Yes, sir. I'll tell you, sir, what we have laid on an effort here, not only against trucks coming down, but also against the infiltration by foot and bicycle, et cetera, that have been taking place, the several thousand that I indicated. And the B-52s near the An Khe area, in the base areas that they are going to use, would use against the highlands, have been laid on quite heavily using these CBUs, which I mentioned to you is equivalent — I think that one B-52 strike would be about 130 hand grenades — 130,000 hand grenades going off at one time. And we do have indications, I believe, that everything's effective against the forces that are moving into the B-3 Front. So we've — we've been, been working on those all right. I think an answer to add to the vice president's question, the authorities that General Abrams has requested would give him the latitude, certainly south of eighteen, to do something that we haven't done before. Of course, they think it would require some action north of the twentieth.

NIXON: How many — how many B-52s do we have at the present time operating in this area?

MOORER: Forty-seven, sir.

NIXON: Forty-seven? How many — how many do we have in the world?

MOORER: Four hundred fifty.

NIXON: How far away?

MOORER: They aren't all equipped. Some of them are renewed, silent.

[unclear exchange]

NIXON: Well, I know that they're silent [unclear] anyway. What is the situation with regard to the — where the rest of those are? How far away are some of them? How many of them in Europe and other places?

MOORER: Well, sir, the aircraft like this are currently operating in Laos — in Thailand.

NIXON: [unclear] No, what I mean, is if we wanted to supplement the forces.

LAIRD: We have additional in [unclear] now.

MOORER: And, additionally, it would be the bombing and [unclear].

LAIRD: Right now, we're not flying as many B-52 sorties as we could. Now, General Abrams has the authority to surge now. He has chosen not to surge at this particular time. But he can surge now, and he could surge from three to thirty days.

NIXON: Yeah. Yeah. To a certain extent, Mel, to a certain extent, though, I just want to be sure I understand where the real danger is. Is it the SIOP? Not now? The other danger is here —

LAIRD: You go there —

NIXON: We already have forty regiments against four hundred, and I want to see something on that. I know you're looking into it, but [unclear]. Because you talk about saturation up there, you have to hit everything that moves out there. You might, you might, you might get another four or five hundred. When we really come down to it, I think we have to make sure that the South Vietnamese are taking some casualties, but their casualties are down this year as compared to last also. But, when you really come down to it, when you look at the North Vietnamese — I know we can't agree on them, but they're at least — when you look at the North Vietnamese casualties, their numbers are probably exaggerated, but a great, great number of those are due to our military — our air operations this spring.

ROGERS: Tom, what if we operated our B-52 strikes from Thailand? Would that be helpful in deterring this offensive?

MOORER: Well, that would certainly broaden the capabilities, particularly if we have problems here with — up in Long Tieng. The problem is it would push a couple of people to put in Thailand, for one thing. But we'd have to increase the numbers, [unclear]. And, in addition, we have been —

NIXON: Put it in temporary duty?

[unclear exchange]

MOORER: And we could run the number of sorties up. We could do twelve hundred a month now for one month, and then when the month runs out then he's — he can go back to his previous [unclear] —

ROGERS: What I was thinking about is getting — getting a signal to the enemy: we're getting ready, if you start something we will, we will really move massively.

LAIRD: We can move, Bill — and I looked at this — we can move '52s off of Guam into Thailand to carry on the surge now, and he can't surge now, but we're not at that point yet. But we have the capability to take some of those aircraft and retrofit them in Guam. You see, we have to retrofit the aircraft and change them from nuclear weapons into this type of bombing, which can be done. But we have aircraft in Guam now that could be used at this particular moment.

NIXON: What about your carrier aircraft, Admiral? How many — I mean, could you bring some down from the Sea of Japan to supplement them? I mean, how many carriers do you have now operating with TacAir?

MOORER: Three, sir. Let me run through this, if I may. Currently, as this chart indicates, we have available more operating — 5,000 South Vietnamese sorties a month. The U.S. Air Force is programmed for 6,700 and the Navy for 3,300. That gives us a total of 15,000 TacAir sorties and 1,000 B-52s, 33 a day. Now, in country we have the capability to assume we take certain actions for sixty to ninety days to stay, by increasing the numbers this much, up to 17,540, and surging the B-52s to 1,200.

Now, this 540 is the result of a plan I made, which would move aircraft from Clark Air Force Base in the Philippines down to Thailand. It would give us 18 additional —

NIXON: Are they A-1s? A-1s?

MOORER: No, sir. They're F-4s. F-4s —

NIXON: Oh, F-4s, that's okay. Right. Right. You mean the small planes?

MOORER: Yes, sir. Now, for thirty days where you would make an all-out effort, but of course subsequent to those thirty days you'd have to drop down considerably —

NIXON: Yeah.

MOORER: Now, we have the capability of about this many with the three carriers that are there. Now, I've issued instructions for none of those carriers to go north of Hong Kong.

NIXON: Where are those? You've got three carriers there in the area now [the USS *Con-*

stellation, the USS *Coral Sea,* and the USS *Hancock*]. How many other carriers do you have? How many are over in Hawaii and others [unclear]? Could you get three more carriers out there, for example? I'm just thinking.

MOORER: Yes, sir. Well, we've got the next one we've had on standby is the *Kitty Hawk.* And she could—and we're giving her ten days to get out. She could move out and be out there in—by the end of the month, sir.

NIXON: We're into this month. The end of which month?

MOORER: The end of this month, sir. Yes.

NIXON: The *Kitty Hawk?* Where's the *Kitty Hawk* now?

MOORER: The *Kitty Hawk* is stationed on the West Coast.

NIXON: That'd give you four?

MOORER: That would give us four, and that would—

NIXON: What about the one that's up there around Korea?

MOORER: No, sir, we have all three of them down south.

LAIRD: All three, yes—

MOORER: Three of them on—

NIXON: So, if you had—you could—you couldn't do—I'm just trying to—

MOORER: Yes, sir. We could send one more. We could send one more carrier, and—

NIXON: And have this, particularly the *Kitty Hawk.* I'd like to see a, see a contingency on that one.

LAIRD: Yes, sir.

MOORER: Yes, sir. And then of course the next step would be, if we needed more tactical air, would be to take the F-4s from either Okinawa or South Korea and move them down. And, so those are the alternatives we have. But we have right now, subject to making this call to deployment from the Philippines, a surge capability of 21,500 for thirty days. At that point, we would put all three carriers in the Tonkin Gulf and run them up to 5,300. The *Kitty Hawk* will add another 1,600 sorties to this number.

LAIRD: We probably wouldn't ever use that many sorties, Mr. President, but we do have the capability. I think it's—

NIXON: You'd have to get a real break on the weather.

LAIRD: We could double.

NIXON: Or—let me put it this way: when we think in terms of twenty-four-hour strikes, you get just as much heat for fifty as you do for five thousand, if it's for twenty-four hours. If you expand it to five days, then the heat is enormous.

In other words, the point that I would like, what I think we need a contingency plan after all, because I—remember we once talked about this before, the contingency plan, I remember, Henry, we talked about earlier—I said, "Be ready that when there's a window you can give them a hell of a sock. Then get in, get out, and then say it's over." Remember, we talked about this? Mel, you've got to have it there ready to give 'em the hell of a sock, rather than just dribbling it out, you know, and running over and dropping it on the combat troops, if the weather's bad. That happens, too.

LAIRD: We can do that —

NIXON: More Air Medals are made that way.

LAIRD: We can do that, Mr. President. [unclear] And I just — I don't think we'll ever go as many sorties even on a good day as we can find on a surge basis. But we can do it. The B-52s are the ones that are limited as far as their surge to thirty days. The others can surge up to sixty to ninety days.

MOORER: Incidentally, [unclear] —

NIXON: The '52s can move from what, from forty-two?

LAIRD: Well, we can go up to about forty sorties a day.

NIXON: Right now, the number of '52s?

KISSINGER: Unless you increase the total number of planes there, you cannot reach the point that the president is making for twenty-four to forty-eight hours.

LAIRD: We can with three carriers there. We've never had three carriers there before —

KISSINGER: The way you get the surge capability is to increase the daily average and then that gives you a higher total at the end of the month. But if you want to put everything into one day or two days you need more airplanes there, because there's no way you can [unclear] —

[unclear exchange]

NIXON: The possibility of a one-day mission. If we think about the real problems of this war, public-relations-wise and the rest, I suppose many books will be written about it in the future, I hope that perhaps maybe — maybe it will come out all right. But, if you look at the problems we must remember that — and I don't think it's a criticism of people who have to take care of all of the decisions, but it was the gradual escalation, day after day, failing to use maximum force at a maximum point in time, that gradual escalation takes away all the strength that we had. It didn't have the effect. It — it had, like water dropping on a rock, it destroyed the American support for the damn war. Now, as far as the American people were concerned, if we do something and do it not gradually — to them the theory of gradualism in war has always been wrong, totally wrong. It's this tit-for-tat crap.

The only — the only thing to do if the other guy gives you a, you know, a slap on the wrist, is you kick him in the groin. That's, that's one theory. You know, that's what we've got to do here —

AGNEW: Mr. President, Henry, you're talking now — you were talking about flexibility, but you're limiting your flexibility [unclear]. But the point I was trying to make before is that the flexibility that is really going to be valuable is the flexibility —

NIXON: That's a plus —

AGNEW: — [unclear] something new that's going to shock these people.

NIXON: Well we have a few places [unclear] and yet they were surprised. But I know exactly what you mean there. We — we wanted —

MOORER: Incidentally, it's the first time we've been up to twenty degrees since the November '68 stand-down —

. . .

NIXON: The point that you should make, of course, that everyone should make out there, is that putting it in its coldest terms: South Vietnam should get demoralized if they concluded that the peacenik portions in this country led to not just an American withdrawal, but led to withdrawal of our aid programs —

BUNKER: Oh, yes.

NIXON: — military and economic, in the future, which is their real objective.

BUNKER: Yes.

ROGERS: Yeah.

NIXON: Now, the revelation of our peace initiative has bought a little time in that respect. The Congress, I mean the jackasses who are ready to go off on another one of their kicks, not just a withdrawal date, but to cut aid, cut sorties, and cut everything else. I think if the point could be strongly made, that public support at the moment, which is reflected in congressional support, support which is in turn reflected in the appropriations, is more solid than it has been for a long time —

BUNKER: Yeah. Yes.

NIXON: — and therefore they can have confidence that they're going to continue to have economic and military aid so that they will be able to fight the enemy. That's the key point —

BUNKER: Yes. Yes.

NIXON: — if they take the long view.

BUNKER: Yeah.

NIXON: Then, of course, you have the short problem, the short-view problem. That's what you're addressing [unclear]. There you say they think they're ready for it.

BUNKER: Yes, sir.

NIXON: They're not frightened to death of them, huh?

BUNKER: No.

NIXON: I don't think they would feel ready if, as I say, if I had an air force and a navy, and short communication lines up against an enemy with a long communication line, no air force, and no navy. Good God, if they aren't building morale now, what can? They never, they can't make it alone, can they, if they cannot at this time? Do you agree, Admiral?

MOORER: Yes, sir. I think this is a critical test of leadership —

NIXON: Good. It's pretty good, pretty good odds on their side.

LAIRD: They've gone from two — a little under, about two hundred attack aircraft to over a thousand that they're operating, in a period of twenty-four months.

NIXON: Who? The South Vietnamese?

LAIRD: The South Vietnamese.

NIXON: On their own? On their own. That's right —

LAIRD: No, I — I, I just feel that, Mr. President, that we have accomplished something here in giving these people this capability, and I don't want them to get into a panic situation. I want to do everything we can to protect them, but I don't want to give the impression, as far as this country is concerned, particularly in view of the — I've got to testify before the Congress. Maybe everything is all right, but I'll tell you it's not going to be easy to get that economic aid through for Vietnam.

NIXON: Sure.

LAIRD: It's a tough damn problem right now. We're three hundred million dollars light right at the present time. Maybe others think that the atmosphere has changed and that we can get these — this money through easily, but it hasn't changed as far as the damn gut questions in those committees.

Look at this last action of the Senate, just this last week. Those people are in there and sometimes I think our people aren't being tough enough on this thing, but by God, they'd gut us. On the — they really gave us a gut shot this week on economic aid on Vietnamization. We've got to get that money back somehow, and it's not easy.

NIXON: That's right.

LAIRD: It's going to be a tough, hard, rough fight, and they're trying to take everything out of my budget and put it over in the AID administration, now, up there on the Hill, the Fulbrights, the Mansfields, and the rest of them. I'll tell you, if it gets out of this defense budget, the Vietnamization program is down the drain in '73 and '74, because the only thing that keeps us going is that it's in the defense budget, not over there in the AID budget. That's the only thing that keeps it going. You know that, don't you?

ROGERS: Yeah, for sure. Yeah. We all agree. You bet.

• • •

NIXON: The thing we have to bear in mind is that, the point that was made earlier, that if this offensive is one that was as far as the North Vietnamese is concerned, it isn't about China and it isn't about Russia. It's about South Vietnam.

MOORER: Absolutely.

NIXON: It was going to come, it was inevitable, and they're going to try to get on top. From the standpoint of the offensive, it will have — if it's a failure — it will have a massive effect on them. It will have a massive effect on them because they will have failed not against the United States, although we will, of course, have helped a great deal in the air, but they will have failed against the ARVN, for whom they claim to have great contempt. Under these circumstances then, they then have to look at their hole card. And, so, as we see this offensive, the one that will come in February, or at least that's anticipated, then the one that will come later in March and in April, we must realize that this — must know the North Vietnamese will come if they feel, after we're out, they can make it. And, if they fail they're going to have to look very, very closely to what their options are. If they succeed, [unclear] — the other point that should be made is this: that we don't want to do anything that is stupid. We don't want to do anything that unnecessarily exacerbates our public in this country, the ugly youth. We must realize that as support for what we're doing — or, shall we put it, as the level of criticism of what we do escalates, it encourages the enemy. And therefore we don't want that to happen, to the extent that we can mitigate it. On the other hand, we must also realize that in terms of a — of getting ourselves into a position where we can react very strongly to enemy offensive action, we have not been in a better position to do so for a long time. The American people will understand for two reasons: one, because American ground forces are not involved, and therefore we won't have all that on television; and, second, because of the peace proposal having been made, and having been rather generally supported, and having been reacted to by a step-up in the military. So under these circumstances, we're now in a position for a period of time which could pass. It might pass in sixty days, it might pass in thirty days. It will last for a period of time where the action we've taken, we can take, or the level of activity, is in the air. That's what we're talking about.

MOORER: Right, sir.

NIXON: It would be much greater than it otherwise would be. Now, we'll look — do you want to look at the contingency plan in terms — because it is well to give enormous discretion, because there may be a day or a time when something very sensitive may be discussed on the diplomatic front. It might be, for example, one of the reasons you don't give them just a blank [unclear] in this thing is that who knows? Maybe not too good a chance, but it could be. But who knows whether or not, perhaps, there can be some nibble in the negotiating. If there is — I'm just using that as an example — you have to be in a position to know whether you want to do it at that time or at another time. That's what we have to do; we can't go flat-footed. On the other hand, when we see other contingency plans, let's see not only what the North, but the South Vietnamese we've got, who have been trained, but they're still somewhat ignorant in terms of modern warfare is concerned, what they have asked for, what General Abrams asked for, but also what the CINCPAC, the Joint Chiefs, and the rest have come up with as to what we can do that we are not doing. That's why I want to see the *Kitty Hawk,* we want to see more B-52s, we want to see A-1s, anything that you think.

[unclear exchange]

NIXON: Just a minute. Maybe, maybe, maybe we won't do any of them, but maybe we'll do all of them. And, also, in terms of the targeting thing, we've gone over this before. I think we've got two or three plans I know on that issue. I think we've got a pretty good range of targets, including the ones you mentioned, but we'll take another look at the targets, too. Because [unclear] those — if the level of enemy activity is such, and the timing is right, and the weather is dry, we can do quite a bit.

MOORER: Yes, sir, and the most —

NIXON: And we thoroughly intend to do so. The main thing we all have to understand here, is that the greatest miscalculation the North Vietnamese make is that we will pay, on our part, an exorbitant price because of the political situation in the United States. That's not true.

Because there's one determination I've made: we're not going to lose out there. I determined that long ago. We wouldn't have gone into Cambodia; we wouldn't have gone into Laos, if we had not made that determination. If politics is what was motivating what we were doing, I would have declared, immediately after I took office in January of 1969, that the whole damn thing was the fault of Johnson and Kennedy, it was the "Democrats' War," and we're ending it like Eisenhower ended Korea, and we're getting the hell out, and let it go down the tube. We didn't do that. We didn't do it, because politically, whatever, it would have been wrong for the country, wrong for the world, and so forth and so on, but having come this long way and come to this point, the United States is not going to lose. And that means we will do what is necessary. But we can't do it in terms of pusillanimous planning and options that are inadequate. So, we want to see what you have. [unclear]

AGNEW: Don't just write it for the record.

NIXON: No, I know we're going to write all of this stuff out. We'll ask for all this, you know, turn down this story that appeared in the *New York Times*. [unclear] I don't think anybody else sitting in this chair would have ordered Cambodia or Laos. If we hadn't had Cambodia or Laos our casualties would be a hundred a week today rather than —

HELMS: At least.

NIXON: — five. So my point is, even with the election facing us, even with the diplomatic initiatives we have, we, we have to win it. We have to be sure we don't lose here for reasons that affect China. They affect Russia. They affect the Mideast. They affect Europe. That's what this is all about. Now, having said all that, we — we don't want to be dumb about it; that's really what it gets down to, because we have a very delicate public opinion situation in this country. And the — at the moment, it's a little quieter, but they'll stir up again.

ROGERS: Mr. President, I'd like, on that score, also, I think if you could impress on President Thieu — he probably knows it, but, as Tom says, this is a critical test. And even if it looks, after this is over with, that we had to come to his rescue, it's going to cause us trouble getting him additional economic and military aid for him. If he comes out of this looking as if Vietnamization is working, if he is successful, that's going to help us in our future.

LAIRD: That's going to help us a lot.

ROGERS: It's damn important for him to fully understand that —

BUNKER: He understands that. There's no question —

NIXON: He's got to win this on his own.

BUNKER: That's right —

NIXON: That's right. And, incidentally, as far as our own activities are concerned, do everything. But, fire every goddamn PRO officer in the Defense Department. Don't talk about it, just do it. You know? Let them in there, but don't say we had so many sorties and all this thing.

Let the ARVN — if the ARVN pulls this off, let them have the credit. It's very important that they get the credit. Not our B-52s, not our A-1s, not directly. Let's do it, but let's be sure that the ARVN in this instance gets the credit. We'll get the blame if it fails, but we want them to get the credit. That, also, is very important in terms of your getting the dough for [unclear].

LAIRD: Yes.

MOORER: At the same time I think we ought to be prepared for Ron Ziegler and the others to —

NIXON: Yeah.

MOORER: — straighten out the record, because —

NIXON: Oh, I know —

MOORER: — I can already see the press is going to try to frame this, you know, pose this as a North Vietnamese victory, no matter how it comes out.

NIXON: I know.

ROGERS: Yeah.

NIXON: Yes. Every, every, every yard of ground that is lost, every hamlet that is captured, every provincial town that may fall will be — that's part of it. That's true. And you have the situation, the rather ironic situation — you think of World War I and World War II, and even Korea — remember the Inchon landing — whenever our side won, good God, it was front page and everybody was cheering. It was great. Now, whenever our side wins it's with the corset ads, and whenever — anytime the enemy does anything good, big, "Wow that's great." [unclear] We, we have that situation, you know. We all know. You're absolutely right about that. But that's all right. Let me say, the important thing in the long run, though, is to win. The important thing — I'm not going to — the propaganda will hurt for a while and, sure, there'll be — what Mel has described as spectaculars and the rest, and we don't want to be Pollyanna-ish about it. Say, "Yeah. This is a hell of a battle. Many battles have been lost." And just to leave it in the proper context, the — all of you students of military history, I mentioned it before here, remember March 21 [the second battle of the Somme], the period of World War I was the greatest [unclear]. Let's talk about it. It was supposed to be an enormous defeat. General Joffre was disgraced as a result of it and retired, and, yet, historically, when you look at the fact that in the week, in the two weeks of that battle, they lost four hundred thousand and the Germans lost four hundred thousand. It was the first time they lost so many to the other side. The Germans lost the war because of that battle, because he put everything he had in there and it didn't break. And so — and so the most important thing here is to remember the headlines may be bad but we will have lost — to hell.

How many times have we lost Cambodia? Good God, I mean, if you look at CBS over the past year — I was looking at it — there have been at least thirty broadcasts that said Phnom Penh's going to fall. It hasn't fallen. Maybe it will, but the point is we, we've got to face the propaganda. But, we're talking about just being sure that we're doing everything we can to see that the ARVN comes through.

"I am simply saying that we expand the definition of protective reaction to mean preventive reaction."

February 2, 1972, 10:53 a.m.

Richard Nixon, Ellsworth Bunker, and Henry Kissinger

OVAL OFFICE

Nixon's resolve to renew a strong air attack in Vietnam included using the B-52 bomber there for the first time since 1967. America's brute in the air, a single B-52 could carry over a hundred bombs. The concern, however, was the ability of North Vietnam's surface-to-air-missile (SAM) installations to shoot down American planes. Before the full force of America's bombers was exposed, it was crucial to identify the SAM sites and reduce their number, a job that the air force began with dangerous missions to tease out missile launches and then destroy the sites before they could be dismantled and moved. This action, however, and the entire planned air offensive stretched Nixon's policy of "protective reaction," which had promised that air strikes would be defensive in nature.

• • •

NIXON: One thing we're hitting on, I think you should know, the — this — don't say this to anybody —

BUNKER: No.

NIXON: — beyond this meeting.

BUNKER: No.

NIXON: But, we've ordered the extra carrier in.

BUNKER: Oh, good.

NIXON: In our briefing. We've ordered more B-52s in.

BUNKER: No, I was going to —

NIXON: We've ordered A-1 — A-1s, and everything. Now, incidentally, I just want to — I think you've got to put it toughly. Well, I'll see Moorer today. I would just double the number of '52s if necessary, whatever is necessary, so there's one hell of a show. We've got four hundred. I know a lot of them have to be refitted, or whatever we have to do, but get them the hell over there, right now. Let's have an awesome show of strength. Now, between now and the time we return from China, we cannot hit the North.

BUNKER: No —

NIXON: Nor will I. On the other hand, we can dump everything we've got on the South.

BUNKER: Yeah.

NIXON: And I think that—that it seemed to me [unclear] when Moorer came in, from a military standpoint, if they hit in there, our [MR-]3 area, or whatever it's called, that this saturation bombing over there is bound to kill a hell of a lot of people.

KISSINGER: Well, Mr. President, a lot of this argument about targets is phony, because when they know they have X number of sorties, they gear the targets to the sorties. When they have more planes, they'll find—they'll waste a few bombs. If they—

NIXON: Yeah?

KISSINGER: There's got to be somewhere in a definable area they're going to attack.

BUNKER: Yes. Sure.

NIXON: You mean, in other words, having them be—I'd like to see—

KISSINGER: If you have more B-52s—

NIXON: I'd like to see Moorer and Abrams concentrate on just bombing. [unclear] If they're going to have a battle in a certain area, and they know where the North Vietnamese are, saturate it. Just saturate it. Remember that personnel bomb? Don't you think so?

KISSINGER: I think so.

NIXON: Instead of screwing around trying to hit a milk truck one time, or, oh, a buffalo the next time, or—you know, some of this bombing is silly. Utterly silly.

BUNKER: Yes, sir. Yes. And the—this B-52 bombing, you know, affects the enemy morale tremendously.

NIXON: Yeah, that's what I understand.

BUNKER: Yeah, oh yes. And also, Mr. President, as I said yesterday, they've done an increasingly good job on this interdiction.

NIXON: Mm-hmm.

BUNKER: The trucks they get in, the input—the throughput, it's a small proportion of the input. They've done a fine job on this. This—on this question of bombing with more B-52s, the bombing of these SAM sites becomes important. And one thing that both General Abrams and I—

NIXON: Mm-hmm?

BUNKER: [unclear]

NIXON: Mm-hmm?

BUNKER: —we could get authority to bomb these SAM sites. Now, the authority is for—to bomb them when they fire at aircraft—

NIXON: I saw that.

BUNKER: —when the radar's locked on. But, the problem is that's, that's late to start attacking them.

NIXON: Right.

BUNKER: And the other problem is weather. You've got to see them. Now, you'll sometimes only get an hour a day—

NIXON: Well, my point is, Henry, I think protection and reaction should include the right of the — and Abrams is not going to do something, do something utterly stupid — the right to hit the SAM sites.

BUNKER: Clearly —

NIXON: Nothing — protective — reaction should include preventive reaction.

KISSINGER: I think —

NIXON: [unclear]

KISSINGER: I think the way to handle it, Mr. President — I haven't had a chance to talk to Ellsworth, yet — is that, one, is to give them a blanket authority. That has the disadvantage —

NIXON: It'll get out.

BUNKER: Definitely.

KISSINGER: — of getting out and also —

NIXON: Yeah.

KISSINGER: — of — it's doing that, something when we are in China. The other is, right now they can only hit when the radar is locked on —

NIXON: Yeah.

KISSINGER: — and that's very restrictive because that means that the plane which is in trouble also has to fire. The third possibility is to say that Abrams can hit any SAM site that has locked on, even if it is no longer locked on. In other words, if a — and —

[unclear exchange]

NIXON: Would that broaden it up?

KISSINGER: — and use high explosives, too. Right now they can use only Shrikes.

BUNKER: It — this is one thing we would like to do.

[unclear exchange]

BUNKER: Here are these locations of the SAM sites here.

NIXON: Have all of these fired at some time on our planes?

BUNKER: No. Now, but they've — but we've located it.

NIXON: Yeah?

BUNKER: That mean is their range. So, the B-52s have got to keep out of this.

NIXON: Yeah, I see.

BUNKER: And what, what Abrams would like to have is authority to bomb these SAM sites within the nineteen nautical miles of the border.

NIXON: Hmm.

BUNKER: You see? [unclear]

NIXON: [unclear]

KISSINGER: Could he knock it off while we're in China? And not to hit [unclear] —

BUNKER: Oh, yes. Yes.

NIXON: Could he do it now, though?

BUNKER: He could do it now, and he can stop.

NIXON: I don't think they should be doing it while we're in China.

BUNKER: No, no.

NIXON: The only thing in China, it should only be protective reaction —

KISSINGER: But couldn't —?

NIXON: — in the technical sense, but right now, counteractions are to be stopped —

KISSINGER: But couldn't we stage it, as long as we in this room agree, and on the grounds that they have fired, rather than —

NIXON: I want him to say — no. No. What he [unclear] —

KISSINGER: Or that they have —

NIXON: He is to say, we — he is to call all of these things "protective reaction."

KISSINGER: Right.

BUNKER: Yeah.

NIXON: Just call it "protective reaction."

BUNKER: That's what it is, really.

NIXON: Tell that to him, because preventive reaction —

BUNKER: [unclear]

NIXON: I am simply saying that we expand the definition of protective reaction to mean preventive reaction, where a SAM site is concerned. And I think that, but let's be sure that anything that is done there it's best to call an ordinary protective reaction. Who the hell's going to say that they didn't fire?

KISSINGER: No, but could they stop from blabbing it at every bloody briefing?

BUNKER: Yes, absolutely —

NIXON: Yeah. Why do we have to put —? You tell him I don't want it put out anymore.

BUNKER: Right.

NIXON: Tell him — I want you to tell Abrams when you get back, he is to tell the military not to put out extensive briefings with regard to our military activities from now till we get back from China. Do it, but don't say it.

BUNKER: Yeah.

NIXON: Goddamn it, he can do that.

BUNKER: Yeah.

NIXON: Because, goddamn it, these PRO officers blab.

[unclear exchange]

BUNKER: Yeah, sure, and, you see, Mr. President, there are about — the enemy has about 168 SAM sites. They've got some in southern Laos, 3 in southern Laos, now. Now, they've got about 28 of them manned, but they can move these anywhere within six hours from one site to another, and that's what they do.

NIXON: Mm-hmm.

BUNKER: [unclear]

NIXON: Henry, we need —

BUNKER: The B-52s are very vulnerable.

NIXON: If we lose a '52, I'll never forgive myself for not knocking those sites out. [unclear]

KISSINGER: I have no problem with it.

NIXON: All right. Your problem is you don't want it done while we're in China? Is that it?

KISSINGER: I don't want it done —

NIXON: [unclear]

KISSINGER: — from the seventeenth, from the time you leave —

NIXON: Yeah.

BUNKER: Yup, until you get back.

KISSINGER: — until you get back.

NIXON: All right, between now and the seventeenth —

·KISSINGER: Yeah.

NIXON: — you work out the authority.

KISSINGER: Yeah.

NIXON: He can hit SAM sites, period. Okay?

KISSINGER: Right.

NIXON: But he is not to build it up publicly for the duration [unclear]. And, if it does get out, to the extent it does, he says it's a protective reaction strike.

BUNKER: Yeah.

NIXON: He is to describe it as protective reaction, and he doesn't have to spell out that they've struck. After all, it is a SAM site, a protective reaction strike against a SAM site. As you know, when we were hitting the [Mu] Gia Pass and the rest, we'd call that protective reaction —

BUNKER: Yeah.

NIXON: — and then bomb the hell out of a lot of other stuff.

BUNKER: Sure.

NIXON: Okay?

BUNKER: Sure.

NIXON: So what we want is protective reaction. Fair enough?

KISSINGER: Fair enough.

NIXON: So he's got about two weeks — about ten days, now —

BUNKER: Yes.

NIXON: — to [unclear]. From the seventeenth until the first of March, he's dead —

BUNKER: Yeah.

NIXON: — as far as North Vietnam is concerned. But then tell him to get those damn bombers and start hitting something in South Vietnam, and hit it good. Yeah?

BUNKER: Yeah, sure. In the B-3 Front, and, of course, in Laos, too.

NIXON: Yeah. In the B-3 Front, and Laos, and don't forget Cambodia. There's something to hit there —

BUNKER: Yeah. Yeah.

NIXON: Knock the bejeezus out of it.

BUNKER: Yeah. Right.

NIXON: Now, the other thing, Henry, that we have to remember when we talk to Moorer about the DMZ: we are not going to hit across the DMZ until after we get back from China.

KISSINGER: Oh—

NIXON: [unclear]

KISSINGER: —no.

NIXON: That's a silly thing to have—

KISSINGER: No, I think—

NIXON: —we bomb the road [unclear]—

KISSINGER: I have no problem with hitting on the northern side of the DMZ.

NIXON: Will you—

KISSINGER: I mean—

NIXON: Yeah?

KISSINGER: —short of the border.

NIXON: That's what I meant. I think we should cover the whole DMZ. Now, would you make that in our—in the talk with Moorer this afternoon?

KISSINGER: Yeah.

NIXON: And, at least, let's blunt that offensive a bit. You know? They've said, "Well, we can hit the road, but [unclear]." It's a lot—I agree they can fix the road up quickly, but it's more difficult if you hit it all the time.

KISSINGER: Well, yeah. It's—that's—

NIXON: Also, if the enemy knows you're only going to hit south of that dividing line, they can all be in a perfect sanctuary north of it. So hit it.

KISSINGER: I don't think—I don't know what Ellsworth believes—that they will attack in I Corps before the middle of March.

BUNKER: I think, I think that's about it, yes. Maybe the first of March on. The weather gets better then.

NIXON: Well, we're going to be back—

BUNKER: Sometime in March. No, I think that's—oh, sure. Yeah. Sure. Well, that'll be fine, I think. It's great.

NIXON: We will see that the authorities are adequate. I can assure you that the authorities will be adequate. We will see that more planes are put in there, and carriers. Goddamn it, they should have asked for more planes and carriers. Henry, I don't understand the military.

KISSINGER: Mr. President, if you hadn't been at the briefing yesterday, that thing was sort of fixed to lead you to the opposite conclusion, but—

NIXON: Oh, I know that we were doing everything we could.

BUNKER: Now, I thought it was great. I got tremendously encouraged from—when you moved in on it, I must say.

NIXON: Well, they have to do it. Now we—but I'm just concerned that we haven't— well, the one carrier, it's got to be on its way now, you know. [unclear]

KISSINGER: It will be there before the end of the month.

NIXON: Okay.

BUNKER: Mm-hmm.

KISSINGER: Which is about as fast as they can get it there —

NIXON: Full speed.

KISSINGER: Yeah.

NIXON: Because they go out there and get ready, then boy. And those little naval pilots can hit better than the air force pilots, too, you know. They really know how to target —

BUNKER: They're good. Yes.

NIXON: They're fantastic.

KISSINGER: And they discover targets once you — once they've got the plane. That's the question of priorities.

BUNKER: Yeah.

NIXON: Explain that again.

KISSINGER: Right now, they'll always tell you they're hitting every target they get. But, they also know that they have certain limitations.

NIXON: Oh, I see.

KISSINGER: So —

NIXON: So, if they've got more planes, they'll find more targets?

KISSINGER: That's my guess —

BUNKER: Yeah.

KISSINGER: — what do you think?

BUNKER: Yeah, that's for sure.

KISSINGER: And for the next three months, we are better off wasting bombs —

NIXON: Yeah.

KISSINGER: — than we —

NIXON: Well, I would very much like to have in the B-3 Front — if that's what it's called — I'd really like to have some saturation bombing now. I mean, just take — take it off of everything else, and for a couple of nights, just bomb the bejeezus out of where they'd invade. There are two or three divisions there.

BUNKER: Yeah.

NIXON: They've pinned them. We ought to be able to just frighten the hell out of them —

"It's going to be psychologically damn impressive."

February 9, 1972, 11:00 a.m.

Richard Nixon and Alexander Haig

WHITE HOUSE TELEPHONE

For twenty-four hours, starting at 6:00 a.m. on February 9, American pilots conducted a

massive assault in eighty-four sorties, most of them against enemy targets in the hotly con-
tested central highlands of South Vietnam. It was the biggest show of American air power
in six months, but as Nixon knew, it was only the precursor to a far bigger air campaign.
For that reason, he was especially nervous about it.

• • •

NIXON: Al, I wanted to ask you, how about that, the B-3 strike. Is it going to get off? Or
do we hear yet, or what?

HAIG: Yes, sir. As of now, it's on schedule and the weather is favorable, and that would
be the only thing that would —

NIXON: Stop it. Right.

HAIG: — cause it to be postponed.

NIXON: And that'd be starting tonight then, or —

HAIG: Yes, sir —

NIXON: Or today?

HAIG: At six o'clock our time.

NIXON: Good. Good. Good. And you're convinced now that they're gonna carry that
out and do — and, at least, do their —

HAIG: They're delighted with it —

NIXON: — do their best to concentrate, will they?

HAIG: Yes. They want to do it because they want to first exercise the system completely
to a max surge.

NIXON: Yeah.

HAIG: And to enhance their responsiveness.

NIXON: Are they —?

HAIG: They're in total agreement with it; they just think it's great —

NIXON: Have they — Al, have they been, do you think they have really now looked
around to see if they've got any targets in the damn area?

HAIG: Yes, sir, they do —

NIXON: I mean —

HAIG: — they have fixes —

NIXON: — being there must be if — there must be with all the infiltration. And if they're
expecting a thing, aren't there — there must be troops, that's what I mean. I realize those are secondary targets, but goddamn it if you hit enough of 'em they're
not.

HAIG: No, sir. I think they've got some good targets. General — I talked to Admiral
Moorer last evening. He said they're very pleased. They have communications fixes
on regimental and division headquarters, and they're just gonna pour it in there for
forty-eight hours.

NIXON: Yeah. What is the advantage of doing forty-eight? You know, if you hit them,
you mean that they will then try to — wouldn't they, wouldn't they move out? I'm
just — I'm just figuring, trying to figure out how does it work.

HAIG: Well, what they hope to do, sir, is to put this concentrated load in at max effort.

NIXON: Mm-hmm.

HAIG: They are going to have to, to recycle a little bit —

NIXON: Sure —

HAIG: — and if they wanted to get a read from the communications —

NIXON: Mm-hmm.

HAIG: — it'll give them a sharp new communications [unclear] —

NIXON: Yeah, the intelligence. I see —

HAIG: That's right. And then they can do it again. And then, you know, I think General Abrams —

NIXON: Yeah?

HAIG: — wants to do this.

NIXON: Yeah. Well, that's good —

HAIG: I think it's going to be a very effective psychological — if not even, if they miss, it's going to be psychologically damn impressive.

NIXON: Because why? Because —?

HAIG: Well, the enemy has not seen — they've been deceived, because as we've drawn down we have held down our sortie levels.

NIXON: Mm-hmm.

HAIG: Laird's done that for economic reasons, but —

NIXON: Yeah.

HAIG: — Abrams has actually gone along with it.

NIXON: Yeah.

HAIG: So, I think they have the impression that perhaps we're a lot weaker than we are. And when they get hit with this kind of a massive firepower demonstration, they're gonna know —

NIXON: Yeah.

HAIG: — at the outset what price they're going to have to pay.

NIXON: When they start. I get it.

HAIG: And they have picked up already that there's a third carrier in the Tonkin Gulf, and a fourth on the way.

NIXON: Hmm.

HAIG: Now, this is — this is a hell of a [laughs] —

NIXON: The North Vietnamese know this?

HAIG: Yes, sir. I'm sure they do —

NIXON: That's good.

HAIG: The press has picked it up.

NIXON: The press has? Good.

HAIG: Yes, sir.

NIXON: That's good. That's good. That's more of that psychological bull.

HAIG: That's right —

"The Beijing move did it."
February 14, 1972, 1:04 p.m.
Richard Nixon and Henry Kissinger
OVAL OFFICE

One week before Nixon was scheduled to travel to Beijing for his much-anticipated summit, he and Kissinger discussed new overtures that unexpectedly came to the White House from the North Vietnamese and Viet Cong negotiators at the Paris Peace Talks. One apparently came from the Viet Cong's chief negotiator, Mrs. Nguyen Thi Binh, possibly out of concern that the United States and China would strike their own bargain. The president also thought that the increased air war in Vietnam had made a difference in the attitude of the negotiators.

• • •

KISSINGER: Well, you remember, Mr. President, before this — before this move, I said that I figured that they would make a move between the Beijing, and the Moscow summit, that they didn't want to settle this before the Beijing summit, which would have given the impression that the Beijing, that the Beijing move did it for her.

NIXON: Yeah.

KISSINGER: And they probably don't want to be in the position at Moscow — in the Moscow summit where you and Brezhnev conceivably pressure them. That Brezhnev letter to you last week was extraordinarily mild.

NIXON: Mm-hmm.

KISSINGER: In fact, it didn't give them any support. It just quoted what the North Vietnamese were saying but it didn't say that the Soviets endorsed it. You remember, I said that before this. And therefore my calculation has always been: one, that they'd make a move between the two summits. Secondly, that there was something like a fifty–fifty chance that they'd settle before the election. In fact the way I put it to myself was if it looked as if you would probably win or possibly win, they'll settle before November. If it looked as if the other side would probably or possibly win, they'd certainly not settle before November. If it was a stalemate, then I would guess they'd still try to settle before November because it's too risky to have you back in office unconstrained. But what you've done in the last few weeks is strip away the secret negotiations, to attack your domestic problems. In this respect, what Bob [Haldeman] did was tremendously helpful with Hanoi because it showed that we are going for broke at home. That we are not just going to sit there and let ourselves be chopped —

NIXON: [unclear]

KISSINGER: — and this massive movement of air power.

NIXON: Yes, and that helped. I know.

KISSINGER: We've moved thirty-five B-52s to Guam. We've taken —

NIXON: [unclear]

KISSINGER: Yep. Yep, we've put two more aircraft carriers on station. We only moved one out there, but they've always had one on leave. We've canceled all leave. That's how the news hit about the one coming back from Hong Kong.

NIXON: We've only had one out there?

KISSINGER: Well we had — actually, we had one on stage, one being repaired, and one on leave.

NIXON: [unclear]

KISSINGER: And there will be another one in San Diego. Now we have four on station.

NIXON: Well not yet.

KISSINGER: Well we will have on March 1. But we have three on station within another week. So I think this whole combination of events — their fear of the pressure. It isn't just that for the first time our dealings with them, in two administrations, that they have asked for a meeting. All previous meetings we've asked for. But also that they have asked for lunch. I mean, I know, Mr. President — I'm not saying they're going to settle. I'm saying if nothing else happens except that they've invited me to lunch, it means we have a month of no offensive, almost certainly. It means that they —

NIXON: You'll get a hell of a tip against —

KISSINGER: The probability is, Mr. President, that this is not going to be the only meeting. We have never had just one meeting with them.

NIXON: But the thing I'm thinking, though, Henry, is that they may be willing for other reasons —

[unclear exchange]

NIXON: — with the hope that we will lay off our preemptive air strikes.

KISSINGER: They think you are getting ready to club the North Vietnamese. There's no question about that.

NIXON: That's right. But now I'm not sure we want to wait.

KISSINGER: Oh, I wouldn't — we can wait till the eighth.

NIXON: Well I — you can't wait too late because then you'll have it just before the Russian [unclear] —

KISSINGER: Mr. President, you're coming back on March 1. Presumably you'll report to the nation on the second or third.

NIXON: Is that right? I don't know.

KISSINGER: I don't know what the date is. But you wouldn't want to divert everybody that week anyway.

NIXON: No.

KISSINGER: So we're talking about a week or two.

NIXON: Right.

KISSINGER: That is —

NIXON: All right. Understand, I'm just trying to see what would go through their minds if they're trying to screw us.

KISSINGER: Well I think, Mr. President —

NIXON: [unclear] The second thing it made me think of was that — they must, in other words, you've got to assume that their purpose is not to invite you to talk. Their purpose is to keep us from doing something else. One is that they're afraid that we're going to hit the North. Fine, they've accomplished that purpose.

KISSINGER: Yeah, but we won't do more than twenty-four or forty-eight hours anyway.

NIXON: What? I know that. But what I mean is, what I mean is if that occurs — now that's interesting. The other thing is, if you put it to them on this offensive thing — I can't believe that they would tell you on the other side of the coin, now I might be wrong, but they would have you for a private meeting and then proceed to kick the hell out of us.

KISSINGER: It's almost inconceivable.

NIXON: How could they? Because that's why [unclear].

KISSINGER: Absolutely.

NIXON: Because if, for example, let's put it another way. If you accepted the meeting and then they kicked the hell out of us and then we canceled we're in a [unclear] if you warn them in advance. Right?

KISSINGER: That's right. Mr. President, you've been very tough with them. You know, we canceled this Thursday's meeting because of the Versailles conference. I mean, we're just — we have to look at it through their eyes. They must think we are looking for an excuse to kill them in the North.

NIXON: You think so?

KISSINGER: Oh, yeah. The last few times we canceled meetings we've then hit them for five days. I believe that our December strikes did a hell of a lot more damage to them than our idiotic air force will admit.

NIXON: [laughs]

KISSINGER: Because if they hadn't they would have had people there looking at their holes.

NIXON: Yeah. That they didn't amount to anything?

KISSINGER: That they didn't amount to anything. That they hit the open fields. That they hit peasant houses. That they wanted the French to protect them and the French said let's look at where the damage is, they refused to show them. And we've had another report that has been particularly — they inflicted enormous casualties on some troop barracks. Now, I wouldn't place this report in the absolute context that it is, I didn't put it in here —

NIXON: Sure.

KISSINGER: — because you don't want to bother with these things.

NIXON: I know.

KISSINGER: So they are worried that you may go for broke against them in the North.

NIXON: Mm-hmm.

KISSINGER: And that they want to stop. On the other hand, you and I know that you were going to go for broke against the North. So that what they're going to stop is not something we wanted to do.

NIXON: That's right.

KISSINGER: Secondly, they are terrified that when all is said and done, Beijing and Moscow are not going to let them screw up the whole détente.

NIXON: You think so?

KISSINGER: Yeah. After all —

NIXON: I must say, when you read though, totally all the records of Zhou Enlai's comments and so forth [unclear], it's a hard-line goddamn thing.

KISSINGER: Well it's hard-line. But in practice —

NIXON: On the other hand, they show that they are susceptible to [unclear]. They always show that we make big promises that we can't keep, and we never do this. And yet, their behavior in the India-Pakistan thing was goddamn timid.

KISSINGER: That's right.

NIXON: They talked about the Russians being timid. They were timid. Zhou Enlai told you in July that they would not stand idly by. And then he went on and [unclear]. And then afterwards admitted Bhutto let you down. Now they know what the hell they did.

KISSINGER: Oh, exactly. So — but also the North, actually with respect to the North Vietnamese, you'd have to read the whole record. What they do is they're asking for [unclear] the things we are going to do anyway. Like troop withdrawal.

NIXON: Yeah.

KISSINGER: They've never done much about the political conditions.

NIXON: Yeah, I noticed that. I noticed that.

KISSINGER: So the Chinese are building up a fierce record on those issues, which are not contested, and they have been no help to the North Vietnamese. They killed their seven points by having the announcement of your July — of your visit of July 15. So that the North Vietnamese will not forgive. I believe that they did make an effort to get them to negotiate because for about six weeks after you were there — after your announcement of July 15, the North Vietnamese press were beside themselves. Then in November after I was there for another six weeks the North Vietnamese press was yelling at them.

Then Pham Van Dong went to Beijing and in public speeches never declared complete identity of interest between the two countries. It's only in the last few weeks as we are going there that Beijing has been making some noises. But even so when I proposed that if Le Duc Tho was in Beijing that I was prepared to meet with him there, they sent back a very mild reply saying we are not going to meddle in the Vietnamese war but you could read it both ways. And the reason I sent that message was so that if the Russians came through with an invitation to meet in Moscow, we could then go to Beijing and say we offered it to you first. On the other hand, I believe the more we can get the Russians to press for a meeting in Moscow, which they want for their reasons, the more eager Hanoi will be to have the meeting in Paris because Hanoi will under no circumstances in my view settle in either of the other Communist capitals.

NIXON: I see.

KISSINGER: So the reason I'm going — I'm going to see Dobrynin tomorrow and I'm going to put it to him again that I'm eager to meet them in Moscow. And I'll bet it's a poker game. It's a way of — I already know they proposed a meeting in Paris.

NIXON: Yeah.

KISSINGER: There isn't a chance of a snowball in hell that they will accept a meeting in Moscow. They've already objected in October so they —

NIXON: Did it work?

KISSINGER: But if Moscow proposes a meeting, it's to them a sign that Moscow is eager to settle. I'm certain that Moscow is playing such a big game that they are not going to let Hanoi screw it up in May. So they're up against a whole series of deadlines. Then they see you — if you look at the press, say look at *Time* and *Newsweek* this week, it's a little play on the State of the World report, which is on the whole positive. But above all it's China. So they know for the next three weeks.

The American role in Asia
February 14, 1972, 4:09 p.m.
Richard Nixon and Henry Kissinger
OVAL OFFICE

In preparation for the trip to China on February 21, Nixon and Kissinger discussed aspects of the diplomacy, from major issues to strategic details to basic agreements on wording. It was a seminal conversation in which they described the interlocking policies related to nations across Asia. Nixon had just finished a meeting with André Malraux, a French writer who had served as the French minister of culture during the 1960s. Known as much for mendacity as for eloquence, Malraux had a checkered reputation.

• • •

NIXON: When he [Malraux] said, you know, he said, "You will meet a colossus, but he's [Mao] a colossus facing death." And then he said, "You know what will impress him most about you? That you are so young!" [laughter] Isn't that something! God almighty, that's a commentary on the leadership of the world these days. It's all too damn old. But —

KISSINGER: You will find, Mr. President, that these people are the —

NIXON: What would he think if he could see Kennedy?

KISSINGER: He would have thought Kennedy was a lightweight.

NIXON: You think so?

KISSINGER: Mao would have had total disdain for Kennedy. He would have felt about him the way De Gaulle did. De Gaulle had absolutely no use for Kennedy.

NIXON: Oh, I found him very interesting.

KISSINGER: These historical figures can't be bluffed, and they won't fall for pretty phrases. And these Chinese, I mean the only security they have at this moment is our understanding of the international situation. The tactical details are relatively unimportant. And you will find that even Zhou, of course, I've never met Mao, will always begin with a general discussion —

NIXON: You know, it's a very strong speech —

KISSINGER: And, but not —

NIXON: One thing to note that is very important, though I even felt that Malraux who is basically, you know, has raised hell about Vietnam and not to mention anything else, and I know all that. But also, everybody is ready to say the United States should get the hell out here, and everybody says — but I think you've got to always try to stand very firmly on the point, do you want the United States as an island with no —

KISSINGER: No foreigner wanted us to get out anywhere. It's our domestic —

NIXON: He didn't want us to get out of Japan. He didn't want us to get out of Europe. He wants the United States to play a role, a role in the world. He only says let it be an intelligent role.

KISSINGER: It's our domestic critics who don't understand anything, who want us to get out —

NIXON: I don't believe it; it's a matter of fact. I believe, I believe, well, the Chinese I noticed there throughout the thing, the United States should withdraw from all nations. They don't really believe that. They can't really believe that.

KISSINGER: Well you — Zhou said to me, we need a general principle, but the troops we are worried about are the million troops on our northern frontier. While we're there, Mr. President, I should seek an occasion to give them some information about the disposition of Soviet forces on their frontier.

NIXON: They're worried; I should say so.

KISSINGER: You shouldn't do it. But I'm going to get from Helms —

NIXON: I think that what I would like to do though, the way I would do it, is to say —

KISSINGER: You ordered it.

NIXON: I ordered this for our trip and I would like for Dr. Kissinger to give it to [unclear] or whoever you want.

KISSINGER: Yes, but only at a private meeting.

NIXON: Oh yes, at a private, well, I'll say it.

KISSINGER: No, you should say it at a private meeting, not in a plenary session.

NIXON: Well, I hope it wasn't too painful for you. It is hard when a man has a — I mean, you feel for the poor guy, he's got such a [unclear] fighting it all the time.

KISSINGER: I found it —

NIXON: I admire a guy who goes over physical disability. You know, it's painful for him to talk?

KISSINGER: I found it fascinating; I didn't find it at all painful. First of all, I completely agree with him in his analysis of these people. Now, you have a tendency, if I may say so, Mr. President, to lump them and the Russians. They're a different phenomenon—

NIXON: No, I know.

KISSINGER: They're just as dangerous. In fact, they're more dangerous over a historical period. But the Russians don't think they're lovable, and the Russians don't have inward security. The Russians are physical, and they want to dominate physically. What they can't dominate, they don't really know how to handle. The Chinese are much surer of themselves, because they've been a great power all their history. And, being Confucians, they really believe that virtue is power.

NIXON: [unclear]

KISSINGER: Now, their present philosophy is different from Confucianism, but the basic principles, that if you have the correct principles, you can dominate the world. It's still inbred in their civilization.

NIXON: I realize that. I think—

KISSINGER: No, as far as he's concerned, that's correct, but I just, I'm just taking the liberty of saying this for the action when you deal with them. I think, in a historical period, they are more formidable than the Russians. And I think in twenty years your successor, if he's as wise as you, will wind up leaning towards the Russians against the Chinese. For the next fifteen years we have to lean towards the Chinese against the Russians. We have to play this balance-of-power game totally unemotionally. Right now, we need the Chinese to correct the Russians and to discipline the Russians.

NIXON: You know, looking at the situation in Vietnam, I suppose if we had only known the way the war would've, was going to be conducted, that we would have to say that it was a mistake to get into it. The way—

KISSINGER: Yeah. Oh, yeah—

NIXON: The way it was conducted, correct?

KISSINGER: That's right.

NIXON: Because the way it's been conducted has cost us too much, compared to what it would cost to let it go. However, having taken it where we found it, we had no other choice. You know, you wonder, after you read Malraux and, of course, you remember De Gaulle saying, and we were there at the palace—

KISSINGER: Mr. President—

NIXON: —he said you should get out; you should wipe your hands of it and so forth.

KISSINGER: I am sure that historians—you wouldn't have had the China initiative without it. It's the demonstration of strength. The Chinese are torn about us. The reason we had to be so tough in India-Pakistan, for example, is to prove to them that we could be relevant in Asia. On the one hand, they want us out of Asia as a threat. On the other, they need us close enough so that they know we can do something. They don't want us back on the West Coast, because if we're back on the West Coast we're just a nice, fat, rich country of no concern to them. And I am convinced that the history books, if we don't collapse now this year, if the whole thing doesn't fall apart, is going to record the U.S. withdrawal from Vietnam on the same caliber, at least, of De Gaulle's behavior in Algeria. It took him five years to get out of there. And after all, I think that game isn't, isn't over. I think we've, they've come to us now, that's a fact. That's a significant fact —

NIXON: Damn right. Well, whatever it is you said this morning, you saw much more through it than I did, and Bob [Haldeman] saw it too, that regardless of how it comes out, it gives us a two-edged sword for our enemies at home. My God, the fact that they asked for this meeting —

KISSINGER: And it won't break up right away. They cannot possibly want me at a meeting, unless they have something to say. It's not their style. So, what we're going to get out of this is another series of meetings.

NIXON: Of course, you say another series of meetings. We have to remember that now time is running out. There isn't a hell of a lot we can do about it, is there?

KISSINGER: Well, but they must know that, too. I mean, we're coming now to the —

NIXON: Yeah.

KISSINGER: We're going to get it to a point where you'll have to say yes or no to some difficult [unclear] —

NIXON: Yeah, that's right. We do want to remember that the meetings are enormously important to us in terms of the POWs. And they've got to know that.

KISSINGER: Well, we, Mr. President, you always correctly express concern, are they stringing us along? If we have to draw up a balance sheet of the meeting, I think we gained a hell of a lot more from the secret meetings than they did. In fact, I don't see what they gained out of the secret meetings. They didn't prevent Cambodia. They didn't prevent Laos. They didn't prevent anything we really wanted to do. They gave us a tremendous coup in public opinion, which is an important weapon in this war. And they settled six of eight points. I think we're not too far [apart]. If they are willing to maintain a non-Communist structure in the South for a while, I think we can find a solution.

NIXON: He [Malraux] obviously feels that China is inevitably going to dominate Southeast Asia. Do you agree?

KISSINGER: I think that's true.

NIXON: You think so? Maybe they're just going to gobble them up?

KISSINGER: No, but I think eight hundred million people confronting thirty million people —

NIXON: No, but I meant how? By subversion?

KISSINGER: By subversion, by cultural example.

NIXON: So they'll go Communist? You also ought to remember that there's a strong pull the other way. One system works a little bit better than the other one [laughs].

KISSINGER: Yeah, but it's a —

NIXON: That, of course, is the big argument.

KISSINGER: But we'll be so weak—

NIXON: The reason Japan will not go the other way is the Japanese are going to like their living too damn well to turn toward the Communist system. Don't you agree?

KISSINGER: I think the Japanese could do surprising things. I don't think they'll do it. They'll begin competing with the Chinese. But I think our immediate problem is we can get out of it with an interim period where we are not the ones that have thrown our friends to the wolves.

NIXON: I agree.

KISSINGER: There is a possibility—I don't think the Chinese are in a condition for five years to put real pressure on Southeast Asia, and even then—

NIXON: What do you think of his argument to the effect that the Chinese foreign policy is all posture?

KISSINGER: There's a lot to that, but—

NIXON: I brought up, you know, that deal of his, which I thought was a nice little point. Where he said they had two thousand dancers and three hundred thousand people in the street for the king, for the president of Somalia. [During their conversation, Nixon and Malraux discussed a passage in the latter's book that concerned a visit by the prime minister of Somalia to the People's Republic of China. Malraux observed that this was "nothing but speeches and receptions for small chiefs of state."]

KISSINGER: Our concern with China right now, in my view, Mr. President, is to use it as a counterweight to Russia, not for its local policy.

NIXON: I agree.

KISSINGER: As a counterweight, to keep it in play in the subcontinent for the time being. But above all as a counterweight to Russia. And, the fact that it doesn't have a global policy is an asset to us, that it doesn't have global strength yet. And to prevent Russia from gobbling it up. If Russia dominates China, that would be a fact of such tremendous significance.

NIXON: Well, quite frankly, Henry, if Russia or China dominated Japan that would have to be a factor and have enormous significance to us.

KISSINGER: That's right. I think, Mr. President—

NIXON: It would be in our interests; it is important to us to maintain the Japanese alliance.

KISSINGER: The decision you made that Sunday morning, when we asked you what you would do in case China came in, and you in effect said we'd back it. That is the decision some future president may have to make, or it may be you in your second term. And I think it's gonna be a tough one, but we may be able to bring it off without the decision having to be made.

NIXON: Yeah. Malraux, of course, has seen every top leader in the world. I suppose going over back to 1918. He's seventy years old. He started to write, when he was twenty, in 19[unclear]. You know he spent three years in prison in Cambodia for stealing sacred art, trying to take a sacred art object out of the country when he was twenty-two years old. But you know it's really a nice thing, in a way, for this old man. Any — I say "old man," but this man who has seen so much, who is out, you know, on the shelf, to be invited over here, to —

KISSINGER: I thought your questions were very intelligent.

NIXON: I was trying to keep him going, because —

KISSINGER: Well, you did it very beautifully.

NIXON: — I know he was having a hard time talking.

KISSINGER: That, incidentally, is a good method to use with Zhou too, because that's not too strong, understated.

NIXON: We'll try to be a little more subtle about it.

KISSINGER: No, no, well, maybe a little more —

NIXON: Except that we cannot, we cannot be too apologetic about America's world role. We cannot, either in the past, or in the present, or in the future. We cannot be too forthcoming in terms of what America will do. Well, in other words, beat our breasts, wear a hair shirt, and well, we'll withdraw, and we'll do this, and that, and the other thing. Because I think we have to say that, well, "who does America threaten? Who would you rather have playing this role?" I mean there's a lot of people that could look at their hole cards here. There's a lot of things they've got to consider about the American role that they —

• • •

KISSINGER: No. I don't think he [Connally] can even deal well with the Europeans. I think he's the best man in your cabinet, and I like him personally, but foreign relations is not, quite honestly, in my judgment —

NIXON: He picks it up as he goes along.

KISSINGER: He's very pugnacious. It, uh, the phrase we have in there is that the United States retains its abiding interest in a peaceful settlement.

NIXON: Yes, that's fine.

KISSINGER: Uh —

NIXON: Then, tell me — could I ask you one other thing? What have you done with regards to Rogers in terms of the communiqué?

KISSINGER: I've just shown him the Formosa section.

NIXON: What's he say he wants to do with it? Is he trying to rewrite it?

KISSINGER: Yeah.

NIXON: Has he offered you anything?

KISSINGER: Yeah, but it's totally, I mean, it's ridiculous. They'll never accept it. We can take part of it.

NIXON: What, I'm sorry you offered it to him. I was going to, I should have gotten it sooner. I would not have shown him the sections that you have. You've shown him the ones that Haig has worked on?

KISSINGER: No, no, that I haven't shown him. I've shown him the first draft of theirs [the PRC's]. So, if they accept the Haig, the one we've sent through Haig [in his early January trip to the PRC], that will be a big improvement over what he's seen. And he [Rogers] hasn't seen that.

NIXON: Well, what's he want to put in, has he said?

KISSINGER: Well, what he wants to put in is to get a Chinese commitment that they will not use force in the settlement of the dispute, and that's almost inconceivable. I mean it's not that they—

NIXON: On the other hand, after it's over, and after we get out of there, we could certainly agree to the effect that, well, if they do use force, then we have a treaty with Formosa.

KISSINGER: Oh yes.

NIXON: I mean, we're not giving up on our treaty.

A visit from the Taiwanese ambassador

March 6, 1972, 4:00 p.m.
Richard Nixon, James Shen, and Henry Kissinger
OVAL OFFICE

James Shen, the Taiwanese ambassador, had received a degree in journalism at the University of Missouri in 1936. He understood both the United States and the tenuous position that his own nation occupied in the new era of rapprochement between the United States and China. In his first visit to the White House since Nixon's trip to Beijing, Shen was looking for assurances of continued U.S. loyalty. Nixon and Kissinger responded nervously, knowing that they had said things in private during the trip which gave Zhou Enlai reason to believe that the loyalties of the United States were already tilting away from Taiwan. Shen, for his part, was always polite but rarely fooled. He subtitled his memoir How the U.S. Sold Out Its Ally.

• • •

KISSINGER: Before you see him [Shen], I didn't want to bother you, but I should tell you that the Chinese [PRC] have called us, that they have an urgent message to give us, which can only be delivered by their ambassador [to the UN, Huang Hua]. So I have to send somebody else up there [to New York]. And the North Vietnamese have asked to see us, almost concurrently. I'm really very worried that this public linking of Taiwan to Vietnam, which we promised them we wouldn't do, which State did on Thursday [March 2].

NIXON: Which what? State did?

KISSINGER: You know, the State Department spokesman said that the six thousand troops [on Taiwan] would be unrelated. You hinted at it.

NIXON: Yeah, I hinted at it, I did. I take some responsibility on it. Yeah.

KISSINGER: But they didn't — yours wasn't picked up. Yours was repeated by Hugh Scott in sort of a mushy way. But — well, we'll have to see, but it makes it important now that we don't add salt to the wounds and let — I think you should just say to him [Shen] what I've repeated. You know what I've said to him, you repeat that assurance. But I wouldn't say another quote he can give.

NIXON: Well, that's why I wondered whether we should see him.

KISSINGER: Well, the way things were at noon — well, whatever damage has been done has been done, and we'll find out in the message. It may simply be that they'll tell us it's a funny coincidence. But they [PRC leaders] told us, they told me that when I put in [into the Shanghai Communiqué] the phrase "as tensions diminish" that it couldn't be linked to Vietnam, and it may be — I also sent them a message, as you requested, that we wanted to announce the Paris contact; it may simply be funny coincidence, it may be their answer. It's highly subjective.

NIXON: Well, let me say you can't worry about every meeting.

KISSINGER: No, no. The level at which they want to deliver it concerns me.

NIXON: Yeah. When do you have to get it?

KISSINGER: We'll get it at seven.

NIXON: Tonight?

KISSINGER: Yeah. And the others, we were going to deliver theirs at eight, their time, eight thirty, and when we got there, they said it isn't eight thirty, it's ten thirty. But the North Vietnamese message, we'll have in another hour and a half. There's no sense worrying about it now. And I wasn't going to tell you if you hadn't seen this fellow until after we had the message.

NIXON: [unclear]

KISSINGER: I think that would be too [unclear]. I think it's important.

NIXON: Why not just not sit down when he's here?

KISSINGER: No, I'd sit down for ten minutes. He put off his departure, he tells me. Just give him your regards and say we have — it may be something perfectly technical.

NIXON: I hope so.

KISSINGER: But if even if it isn't —

NIXON: Of course, we're trying our damn level best, as you know.

KISSINGER: Oh God, I mean —

NIXON: We're, I haven't said one word except that, of course, unfortunate thing that got picked up. But State then puts it out on the record, their statement was made publicly.

KISSINGER: Their statement was on the record. Yours was a quotation from Scott in a sort of vapid way. But, I don't want to do them an injustice. It might not be that.

NIXON: Well, let me say this: let's keep our balance on these things, Henry. After coming this long road with us and our going down a long road with them —

KISSINGER: I'm not so worried.

NIXON: They're not going to, say, discontinue relations.

KISSINGER: Oh, no. That's true.

NIXON: At this point, I mean they —

KISSINGER: No, but what they may do is to — it may be another delay in the Vietnam talks. That's the thing that worries me more. So that it doesn't —

NIXON: The Chinese wouldn't be doing that. I mean, what you're hearing from them, that's — hell, I don't care what we're hearing from the goddamn Vietnamese. They're — I've never felt they were going to do anything anyway. But I mean, we hope for the best. But what I meant is, if you don't, we're not getting —

KISSINGER: No, I think what the Chinese may do is to send us a blast to the effect that they had always said Taiwan and Vietnam were not related and that they want to officially state that our interpretation of something or other —

NIXON: Well, that wouldn't —

KISSINGER: Well, it depends on how far they carry it.

NIXON: Yeah. We can confirm that we —

KISSINGER: As long as they keep it in a secret channel, we can live with it.

NIXON: We can confirm that that is our understanding too, and that this public statement that was made was not authorized.

KISSINGER: Right.

NIXON: That was an interpretation by a senator and the other —

KISSINGER: Yeah.

NIXON: Of course, Scott's going there.

KISSINGER: Well, Scott we can handle. It's important that —

NIXON: No, the fact that he said it though, that's what I mean.

KISSINGER: Well, if we get a note, that's one reason, they said we could pick it up anytime before five tomorrow evening. As long as we get — if we get it, I'll just tell Rogers and send him the note if it's a blast, so that he can guide himself at his press conference. That wouldn't hurt.

• • •

[AMBASSADOR SHEN joins the conversation.]

SHEN: Well, Mr. President, I'm going back to Taiwan tomorrow —

NIXON: Yeah.

SHEN: — and I just want to know if there's any message you have for my president — a very great old friend of yours. Also, if there's anything you want to say to him for his ear only. I'll mention your trip to the mainland and anything concerning Taiwan that you may or may not have discussed with Zhou Enlai and the others.

NIXON: Well, I think that the important thing to first tell him is that, I know that when Green was there — Ambassador Green was there — that he indicated that he did not want to see him, that he wanted to see Kissinger. I think that you should know that when we came back I told Dr. Kissinger to talk to you.

SHEN: Yes.

NIXON: And he has talked to you. Of course, I have a record of the conversation. I knew what he was going to say before he talked to you. And I want you to tell the president that Dr. Kissinger's conversation with you represents my view. I mean to say it's an accurate description of what we talked about, and that the — and also, of course, my public statement when I returned.

SHEN: Yes.

NIXON: Which is the public statement that I made. But I think that the more important thing is that he naturally — and I can understand this, knowing that Dr. Kissinger sat in on all the talks, and also that Dr. Kissinger had conversations before I got there, where no commitments were made. As a matter of fact, none were made this time, except indicating expressions of [unclear]. That you — he now, through you, and through my authorizing Kissinger, because he can't fly out there, of course, that you are able to convey to him the facts of the matter. I think that's the thing. Don't you agree, Henry, with that? Because you see, it's important that he not feel that we sent [went?] to see him on a matter, which is very important to him because somebody that he didn't feel had the information. Naturally, Green we had filled in on the basic facts. But Green sat in on the secretary's talks, and not mine. And Kissinger was in on every minute. There was no conversation that took place with Zhou Enlai or Mao, of course, where Henry was not present. And I authorized Henry to tell you the substance of the whole thing.

So, I think that we could have that, that you could convey to him the, in addition, of course, to my personal regards, that you could convey to him, say that Dr. Kissinger has briefed you and that these are the facts of the matter. Now, of course, all this, you hear all sorts of talk about secret deals and so forth. You know I covered that in my remarks when I came home. What Dr. Kissinger told you are the facts; that's the fact of the matter. And you should rely on that statement. If he were to go to Taiwan, he would tell [unclear] exactly what he told you. Is that correct, Henry?

KISSINGER: Absolutely. I told the ambassador that what we have on the public record the facts [unclear] we've now said it through every organ of our government.

SHEN: Mr. President, we're grateful to you for your government's continued interest in a peaceful settlement. Now, did Zhou Enlai say anything on the steps he planned to renounce force or propose what he intended to do and how he could tackle the problems of — any indication of anything? [unclear]

NIXON: [unclear] On the subject of Taiwan, I think that there is no other subject that is more thoroughly covered by the communiqué, and what Henry said in his backgrounder in Shanghai. What I indicated, when we talk about peaceful settlement, that is something which we're — well, for example, I think it can be said that despite great disagreements, the two things in which President Chiang and Zhou Enlai agree on is the fact there's one China, that's one thing they can agree on. And the second thing is that therefore settling the problem [unclear] between the two. But in terms of how to do it and so forth, I would say that there was no discussion on that; that is something they don't think is our business frankly.

KISSINGER: Well, except that we put in the communiqué two things, which are very clear. One is we reaffirmed our interest in a peaceful settlement—

NIXON: That's right.

KISSINGER: — in this case, which is after all saving our commitments. Then secondly we put in the phrase "with the prospect of a peaceful settlement in mind." So if the words — if you know your compatriots, the word "prospect" was not idly chosen.

NIXON: The Chinese, they're very careful about words.

SHEN: [laughs]

KISSINGER: They were not given a *carte blanche* to launch a military attack on Taiwan, quite the contrary.

SHEN: What kind of time frame does this thing have, I mean —

NIXON: None set, as a matter of fact. None set. That was not discussed. That would be — in other words — when you say do it now, do it next year, I mean it's a question of — and in fact, what we're trying to do now is put everything in that was there. We knew, on their part they knew too, that's a highly sensitive issue and felt it should be covered. But there was no discussion of should we do this now, next year, two years from now, three years from now, four years from now, five years from now, no kind of time frame.

SHEN: Now, Mr. President, you're familiar with our history and our relationship with the Communists over the last forty years.

NIXON: Oh, yes.

SHEN: And you know the situation that exists there better than anybody else in the world.

NIXON: Yeah. Yeah.

SHEN: If you were in my president's shoes what would you do, and what would your advice to my president be about how to handle this thing? I mean, I hope it's not too much of a—

NIXON: Well, I know. Let me say I think along the following lines.

SHEN: Yes.

NIXON: What would you do? And, I would say in the first instance, I would say that I would not raise the question of whether there is a U.S. commitment. I would accept that. Because if you raise the question, and force a vote, to do that is to create in this country, and also create in the PRC, the necessity [unclear]. We have stated the situation, and Kissinger on Chinese soil stated there wasn't [unclear]. Now the moment that you raise the question you hurt your own cause. I have to say that quite candidly. I understand your concern, you understand, but if you raise the question it will only hurt your own cause.

The second point is that in terms of what he does, what you do with regard to the mainland, I frankly do not have an answer, a view on that. In fact, Henry and I talked about that on the way back, and I said Henry, I meant we were asking ourselves the same question, how can this thing be worked out? And do you have any thoughts on it, Henry, since you and I have talked about it?

KISSINGER: First of all—

NIXON: Because the ambassador is certain to raise exactly the question I raised. You understand this. We're in a delicate position because both governments consider this to be an internal problem. So what—and I know there's some that say, well the United States should step in and set up some [unclear]. Some say that.

KISSINGER: I told the ambassador, first of all, we made it clear to the people in Beijing, we called their attention to a phrase in the [State of the] World report, we're not urging either side to do something.

NIXON: That's right.

KISSINGER: So that means in effect they cannot count on us for, they can't expect us to exercise any pressure to negotiate. Secondly—

NIXON: Or to find a formula.

KISSINGER: Or to find a formula. Secondly, I think we have to be realistic about the prospects. First, if you ask yourself what would have happened if the Chinese had done to us what the North Vietnamese do? Some of the people who now support you in the Democratic Party would be the first to start organizing peace conferences about our being tied up with another old-aged military dictator. I'm just telling you the scenario.

NIXON: Yeah.

KISSINGER: And really undermining the commitment, they would have done to us what they're doing on Vietnam.

NIXON: And with no deadline at all.

KISSINGER: And with no deadlines. Supposedly they had played a deadline game with us and used Quemoy and Matsu and other things as a lever. Thirdly, in the period ahead, say four to five years, as I told you when we met, many things can happen. You are under no pressure to settle. Mao could disappear. Zhou could disappear. Or both could disappear. So that this is not an issue that we have the impression will be very urgent in any intermediate [immediate?] time frame. And therefore it would be a mistake for you to panic or do anything rash.

NIXON: Well, I would not be belligerent. And second, I would not quarrel with our statement to the effect that there is a commitment. We've made it. And when you keep raising it, all you do is cause us to answer and we say, well, we've covered that. But if you keep raising it, you're going to force an eventual failure, which would not be in anybody's interests.

You see, there's, as you know, Mr. Ambassador, there's a tremendous isolationist movement developing in this country. And I'm having a hell of a time ending Vietnam in the right way. As you know, ending it in the right way is important because if we don't end it in the right way America will withdraw from the Pacific. Period. Because of enormous frustration. Now, so it is in other things. If the new isolationists in this country get the impression that we're going to become involved in a great conflict because of the defense commitment anyplace — it could be Japan, Philippines, even Thailand, Korea, Taiwan — you can have, you can set in motion forces that you and I, that none of us want to set in motion. It's for that reason that I think that your foreign minister made a very good statement when he said that he accepted the proposition and that the United States keeps [unclear] its commitment will be kept. And if I were to come — so I would start with that process.

The second problem, with regard to how would we resolve it. Believe me, it would be — I just don't know. I have no answer to that problem. And incidentally, they didn't ask us. Right?

KISSINGER: That's right.

NIXON: They didn't ask us how to resolve it. They must be — you must be thinking about it. What ideas you might have as I would say would be certainly extremely interesting. But we are not going to try to intervene and force it either way. I think that's the proposition. I think that's a pretty clear assessment.

KISSINGER: Except for the statement that we are opposed to the use of force.

NIXON: Oh, well, that's a different matter.

KISSINGER: That we will resist it.

NIXON: No, but I meant intervene to force a peaceful settlement.

KISSINGER: That's correct.

NIXON: You see, that's the difference. This isn't like the Israeli-Arab thing, where we are attempting to try to broker it. You know? Here we are not trying to broker anything. That's the difference that I think you should have in mind. Now, where it goes from here, I think has to develop over a period of time. I wouldn't be panicking. I wouldn't be in too much of a hurry to produce an agreement.

KISSINGER: [unclear] There's no obligation to do anything. And there's no obligation — I mean first of all everything we said we stated unilaterally, not as an undertaking to the PRC.

NIXON: There's no treaty.

KISSINGER: Secondly, it's very carefully drafted, if you read it carefully.

SHEN: Yes.

KISSINGER: And thirdly, we are under no obligation whatever to —

NIXON: It's unilateral on their part too, you see? Both sides — there's a Taiwan section as well as a Korea section, a Japanese section, a South Vietnamese section. It's all unilaterally stated; we agreed to disagree, you see? Because their position on Taiwan, you know, is stated hard-line.

SHEN: We know that. [laughs]

NIXON: Oh, not as hard as it has been, because they didn't use the force line in it. Very significant.

KISSINGER: They didn't attack the defense treaty. And also there's a slight nuance, they said Taiwan is a province of China, and we didn't say that. We said a part of China.

NIXON: I wrote that in. I used the word "part" instead of "province."

[unclear exchange]

NIXON: They say they agreed to it; they do not object to it. Of course, it depends on where you are as to whether you say "province" or "part," isn't it?

KISSINGER: It's slightly less, we just wanted to—

NIXON: Province indicates downgrading to Americans, and it would not indicate that to the Chinese because you think of the whole country being province, province, province, you know? But in our country, the word "province," and in most, it means a lower level, you see? Not an equal level.

SHEN: Any personal word for my president?

NIXON: By all means, to him and to Madame Chiang my best wishes for their health. I'm amazed when I get reports from the vice president and other friends who go out there, they say he's just as sharp as a tack, and I've always been impressed with that. And I wish him good health, and we know this is a painful time, and we know that this trip was a very difficult thing for him. We had to take a long view of what the great forces are that are operating here, also recognizing that we're looking at the long view—a peaceful resolution of these problems. We may be able to be more effective if we're talking to the PRC than if we're not talking to them.

That's really the philosophy. The peaceful resolution is important. In the event that we have the use of force in any part of the world, in any part of Asia, in view of the Vietnam experience, it may be, we know what I would do if I were here, but I'm a little bit tougher than some, but I would have serious doubts about what other presidents might do. That's the real problem, you see? So a peaceful resolution we think is very, very important, and that's what this trip is about. But—

KISSINGER: [unclear]

NIXON: Many times. But in terms of both, my very best wishes.

SHEN: Your continued friendship?

NIXON: Oh, absolutely. Our friendship, personal, without question, as well as the [unclear]. We have a treaty, but we also have personal friendship. They know that and they will continue to have it. You've got a long journey ahead of you.

"What do the Russians want? We've got to look at the world from the way they look at it."

March 9, 1972, 9:28 a.m.

Richard Nixon, Henry Kissinger, and Bob Haldeman

OVAL OFFICE

Nixon's summit in Moscow was scheduled for May, and Nixon was counting on bringing home a signed SALT treaty. Two months before, though, the SALT talks stalled over the issue of submarine-launched ballistic missiles (SLBMs). The Soviets weren't interested in close discussions of their submarine programs, but Smith and the SALT negotiators had long attempted to reach agreement on an acceptable number of such missiles. One of the questions was whether the treaty would cover present or future capability, including new technology. As Kissinger explained, there was an ocean of gray area in such topics.

• • •

NIXON: But, be honest: are you — did you tell him [Laird] that we're going to have to get the Joint Chiefs lined up on this?

KISSINGER: Yeah.

NIXON: Does he agree, or not? Well, he's got to agree.

KISSINGER: On the SALT thing?

NIXON: Yeah.

KISSINGER: I told him. You probably — I didn't — you can disavow me, but I said if Moorer can't line up the Chiefs, then maybe we shouldn't reappoint him, because his term is up at the end of [unclear]. And I think it's too early —

NIXON: [unclear] the only problem is — I don't care whether the Chiefs believe it — they cannot go out and leak to the likes of Buckley and Tower, and the rest, that we have sold out to the Russians.

KISSINGER: Look, and they're so insane. They say if we exclude the submarines, the Soviets are going to have seventy submarines, all — in total, before we can build a new one. That's true. But, if we don't have an agreement, that same condition exists. So, in order — so, in — and, in addition, they will then be building land-based missiles, too, which at least we'd be stopping.

NIXON: The point is that we, at least are — without an agreement, they're going to build submarines.

KISSINGER: That's right.

NIXON: With an agreement, they're going to build submarines.

KISSINGER: That's right.

NIXON: But with an agreement —

KISSINGER: We're giving up nothing.

NIXON: — which would mean we're not going to give them land-based submarines [missiles]. So what do they want [unclear]?

KISSINGER: Mr. President, that's right. So, we are not giving them —

NIXON: Well, we're going to try. We're going to try to get submarines in, yes.

KISSINGER: That's right.

NIXON: But, if we can't, we're better off with an agreement on land-based rather than no agreement at all.

KISSINGER: That's exactly my view. Exactly my view —

NIXON: But remember, we're gonna have a hell of a time selling it to everybody.

KISSINGER: Well, what we'll have to do —

NIXON: How about waiting? This is one bloody gig we'd get Rogers lined up on pretty quickly —

KISSINGER: Oh, no question. But, we ought to get a crash program then, which accelerates some of the submarines. Build some new ones for the interim period.

NIXON: Our own?

KISSINGER: That's right. If they won't include submarines, there's a new — before the ULMS comes into being, there is — we could build something called "6-40 submarines." That's —

NIXON: Good.

KISSINGER: — a submarine with the present hull, but with new missiles.

NIXON: Can we order those, now?

KISSINGER: We could go to those now. We wouldn't get any before '75, but at any rate, we could do it —

NIXON: All right. How about — how about putting it out right now, in between?

KISSINGER: And —

NIXON: Is that all right with you?

KISSINGER: Well, I think we should do it after. I think if we put out another program, the Russians may use it as an excuse.

NIXON: Not to make a deal?

KISSINGER: Not to make a deal. But, if we can't get a deal, we should, then, go to the Congress and say, "Since we tried for a deal, they wouldn't give it to us. We've got to go —"

NIXON: Let's start building up the idea on the submarines, now, if submarines are not included, and that, therefore, that we're going to Trident. But, that — what I'm getting at is: let's don't have a situation where we get them to communicate out and then say, "Aha."

KISSINGER: Oh, no.

NIXON: We'll get screwed. See what I mean?

KISSINGER: No —

NIXON: You know, Henry, in China, we knew we would be screwed, but in Russia, they think — they might have something to say.

KISSINGER: Well, what we'd be able to do is — I don't think you should be the one who finally makes that deal. I think we should get Gerry Smith to recommend it and put it through the Verification Panel. I mean that part of the deal.

NIXON: Yeah.

· · ·

NIXON: Here's what I want to keep for myself, and that is, basically, here in this house: SALT —

KISSINGER: Yes.

NIXON: —the Middle East, and the decision with regard to the European Security Conference.

• • •

NIXON: But, if we'd left SALT with Rogers, first of all, he would have—there would have been a flat-out battle with the Joint Chiefs.

KISSINGER: That's right.

NIXON: [unclear] we'd have just given away our goddamn balls.

KISSINGER: That's right.

NIXON: Right?

KISSINGER: I don't think he can explain the issues to you today on SALT.

NIXON: SALT. Christ. [laughs] I must say, on that, you've got to hand it to old Laird. He knows the issues on SALT.

KISSINGER: He knows them.

NIXON: You're goddamn right.

KISSINGER: He plays this politically, but he knows it.

NIXON: But, but, but he knows—

KISSINGER: Oh, no—

NIXON: He also knows what the hell it's about. Bill doesn't know. [unclear] I don't know 'em too well, but at least I know what the Christ—now, but Bill will, Bill will not indulge himself in the luxury—what he considers to be a waste of time—on the philosophical [unclear]. In other words, whenever I raise the question, "What do the Russians really want out of SALT?" [Rogers replies:] "Well, that's [unclear]. It's not important." He says, "The important thing is what can we get?" Unless you know what the other guy wants, you just—you don't know how to screw 'em.

KISSINGER: Exactly.

NIXON: That's basically—remember how every time I've raised that subject with him, Bill won't listen?

KISSINGER: He will not listen.

NIXON: You remember?

KISSINGER: No, he doesn't bother to study it, either.

NIXON: And this is the most important thing that we've got to do. What do the Russians want? We've got to look at the world from the way they look at it.

• • •

NIXON: Henry, you remember the first time we went around on this? What was it, Henry, one of the early SALT meetings? And I raised the subject just like—because I thought he was such a liar on the subject [unclear]. I says, "Well, look, before we get into all this business about counting how many, and throw-weights, and so forth," I said, "well, look, what do the Russians—what are their motivations? What do they want?" And Bill—Bill constantly comes back, "Oh," he says, "we can't guess about that sort of thing. There's no use to speculate about that sort of thing. The thing to do is to really negotiate," and this and that. [unclear]

KISSINGER: But he never knows what to negotiate.

NIXON: Well, my point is: unless you've got the framework, and know what the other guy wants and what you want, and know deep down what you're going to do, you're going to make a deal, but the deal may be a bad one.

"Have you ever heard of the Taiwan Independence Movement?"
March 13, 1972, 10:15 a.m.
Richard Nixon, Henry Kissinger, and Bob Haldeman
OVAL OFFICE

The Taiwan Independence Movement was an effort to separate the Republic of China from its historical relationship to mainland China. Since the ROC (Taiwan) seemed in all practical respects to function as an independent nation, the spirit of the movement was a matter of nuance to many outsiders. Yet it was critically important to the two Chinas. Despite the fact that the mainland and the island of Taiwan had gone in very different directions, each considered China to be essentially united and that it was indeed the rightful leader of the other. The Independence Movement sought to sweep all of that aside. The government of Taiwan didn't approve of it and yet bristled at the disapproval of mainland China for the same movement. For that reason, the U.S. position on the Taiwan Independence Movement was a closely watched barometer of American loyalties. Remarkably, Nixon had to ask Kissinger to explain the Taiwan Independence Movement in the aftermath of his trip to China. More remarkably, Kissinger claimed ignorance about it in their conversation. And yet, the second point on the five-point agenda that Kissinger prepared and that Nixon himself had presented to Zhou Enlai on February 22 stated, "We have not and will not support any Taiwan Independence Movement."

• • •

NIXON: I noticed in the *Washington Daily News* summary, the editorial, they made it to be critical of the fact that there was no mention of the Taiwan Independence Movement [in the Shanghai Communiqué]. Let me ask, is the Taiwan — that source is interesting because that's a more conservative paper. But is the Taiwan Independence Movement, is violently opposed to Chiang Kai-shek, violently opposed by the Chinese, and violently opposed to the Japanese, isn't it? Am I wrong? Or the Japanese —

KISSINGER: Well the Japanese haven't taken a position on it, but it's —

NIXON: What in the hell is the Taiwanese Independence Movement all about?

KISSINGER: It's not a significant movement now. It's violently opposed by both the Chinese governments. Chiang Kai-shek had locked up the leader of the Taiwanese Independence Movement, and he's now in this country as an exile.

NIXON: I know.

KISSINGER: And we had major problems with Chiang Kai-shek when we let him in here.

NIXON: That's right.

KISSINGER: So—

NIXON: And with the Chinese in the PRC.

KISSINGER: And with the PRC. But I noticed somebody must be feeding that because the *New York Times*, which never used to give a damn about Taiwan, had an editorial about that last week too.

NIXON: On the independence movement—

KISSINGER: Yeah.

NIXON: Do you think it's out of State? Or could there be somebody pushing the Taiwan Independence Movement? That's so goddamn—have you ever heard of the Taiwan Independence Movement?

KISSINGER: No.

HALDEMAN: No. Not enough to matter.

KISSINGER: I can't speculate.

NIXON: But we haven't, the other thing, I didn't see anything in the State Department papers indicating that we ought to support the Taiwan Independence Movement.

KISSINGER: Absolutely not.

NIXON: Did we?

KISSINGER: No.

NIXON: There's some kind of flap on it. Did Rogers raise that in his—

KISSINGER: No. Well, they raised it at—

NIXON: At the end?

KISSINGER: Well, they raised it at the end. At the end he raised it.

NIXON: He raised it at the end? What did he say—you ought to take note of this?

KISSINGER: But he never raised it in the preparatory papers they gave us, never. At the end he did raise it among five hundred other nitpicks.

NIXON: What five hundred?

KISSINGER: Well, eighteen, fifteen. But in this catalog of nitpicks there was the Taiwan Independence Movement. But our formulation doesn't even preclude, it states it has to be settled by the Chinese themselves. Naturally the Taiwanese are Chinese.

NIXON: Are Chinese.

KISSINGER: If they want to secede, that's their business.

NIXON: Well—

KISSINGER: Well, except—

NIXON: Our private understanding is that—

KISSINGER: That we won't encourage it.

NIXON: We won't encourage it, that's all.

KISSINGER: We didn't say we will oppose it either.

NIXON: We didn't say we will discourage it either.

KISSINGER: We didn't say we'd oppose it. We said we will give it no support. And that's been our position. We have never given it any support.

The pandas

March 13, 1972, 11:16 a.m.
Richard Nixon and Crosby Noyes
WHITE HOUSE TELEPHONE

When First Lady Pat Nixon accompanied her husband to Beijing, she toured the zoo there and was much taken with the giant pandas that she saw. The species lives in the wild only in China and was rarely seen in captivity outside of that nation. In conversation with Zhou Enlai at a state dinner that evening, Mrs. Nixon enthused about the pandas. An engaging man, he immediately offered to make a gift of two pandas to the United States. Only two months later, Ling-Ling and Hsing-Hsing arrived, and as Mrs. Nixon commented, the result was "Panda-monium." The gentle and irresistible pandas brought home the concept of rapprochement to Americans, who couldn't get enough of the pair.

• • •

NIXON: Hello?

NOYES: Mr. President.

NIXON: Hi, how are you?

NOYES: Fine, thank you, sir.

NIXON: I don't have anything of earth-shaking importance enough for your column, but I thought you'd be interested to know that most of your readers would be more interested in this, I'm afraid, than what I say on international affairs or you say in your column, but I noticed the [*Washington*] *Star* had an editorial about our pandas —

NOYES: Yes!

NIXON: — and I think you'd be interested to know that I just told Ziegler at the morning briefing, so that it could make the afternoon edition of the *Star,* that Mrs. Nixon and I decided that the pandas should go to the National Zoo.

NOYES: Oh, that's very good —

NIXON: Now, I —

NOYES: — news indeed —

NIXON: — I think you should know, too, we've — as you can imagine, the requests from over the country — San Diego has a splendid zoo, St. Louis —

NOYES: Yes.

NIXON: — New York, Chicago, and the rest, but we, basically, this is the place for them from the standpoint, first, it's a national —

NOYES: Sure.

NIXON: — zoo rather than a local one. Second, and this was the key thing, the reason we were waiting on it: the key thing is climate. The panda, of course, we want to be sure they don't come over here and die and we find that the Washington climate is somewhat more mild than their usual habitat, but nevertheless cold enough, we think, for what they are, so —

NOYES: Yeah.

NIXON: — so, in any event you're going to get the pandas.

NOYES: We're going to get both of them?

NIXON: Yeah. Oh, yes! Now, as a matter of fact, let me tell you an interesting thing about — that you must know, you can only use on your own if you want, but not on comment. I was just talking to Bob Haldeman who talked to his Chinese hosts, and this question of mating is very interesting. These are — this is a male and a female.

NOYES: Uh-huh.

NIXON: The problem with, uh — the problem, however, with pandas is that they don't know how to mate. The only way they learn how is to watch other pandas mate. You see?

NOYES: [laughs]

NIXON: And, so they're keeping them there a little while — these are younger ones —

NOYES: I see.

NIXON: — to sort of learn, you know, how it's done.

NOYES: Sure, learn the ropes —

NIXON: Now, if they don't learn it they'll get over here and nothing will happen, so I just thought you should just have your best reporter out there to see whether these pandas —

NOYES: Well, we certainly will —

NIXON: — have learned. So, now that I've given you the story of pandas let me let you get back to your more serious questions. [laughs]

NOYES: How soon are they arriving, sir?

NIXON: April 1.

NOYES: Uh-huh.

NIXON: But when we, uh — we think about April 1. I just asked Ziegler and, you know, it's been shrouded in mystery when the —

NOYES: I knew that.

NIXON: — pandas arrive. And of course, as you know, the head of the National Zoo took the musk oxen over and we're trying to work it out, although I don't know whether he's bringing them back or if somebody else is, but so there they are. But I can imagine that that zoo will get the biggest play in history —

NOYES: It certainly will.

NIXON: Everybody will want to see those.

NOYES: It's a big deal.

NIXON: Yes, sir. Okay!

NOYES: Thank you, Mr. President —

NIXON: I just want you to know that we do pay attention to the editorials in the *Star* —

NOYES: [laughs]

NIXON: — now and then.

NOYES: I'm glad to learn that.

NIXON: Okay.

NOYES: Thank you, sir.

"Don't give the antiwar people an issue, Henry. That's all we're saying."
March 14, 1972, 9:03 a.m.
Richard Nixon and Henry Kissinger
OVAL OFFICE

Just as the presidential campaign swung into gear, Nixon's major thrust, the air war in Vietnam, was gaining momentum. He had no intention of turning back from the new initiative in the war, yet he had to consider the political effects of remaining in Vietnam, let alone of expanding the combat there. Nixon discussed with Kissinger ways to balance the war news with the progress made in troop withdrawal and the reduction of casualties. More cynically, they explored ways to tie the continuation of the war to the popular concern over prisoners of war.

• • •

NIXON: At a certain point, we must make a dramatic announcement that — which in effect will say something like, "Well, we've got to keep our people there until we get our prisoners," or something like that —

KISSINGER: I couldn't agree more —

NIXON: Now, as a matter of fact, let me be quite candid, [unclear] at this point, having stuck with Thieu as long as we have, if they can't make it, then it's a bad bargain, and we just can't stick around on the ground. It's going to affect ourselves all over the world. You know what I mean? I think they can make it. That's my view, but if we stick around — I'm not speaking about getting out now, but I'm speaking about saying we'll stay another five years with air power and all the rest, it just doesn't go. It won't wash. It won't wash as a, as a use of American strength.

KISSINGER: No, but I think that five years is ridiculous. But —

NIXON: That's what [unclear] —

KISSINGER: — I think at this stage, though, we have to balance — well, first of all, in my judgment, I think the April announcement [the next announcement of U.S. troop withdrawals from South Vietnam] ought to be a nothing announcement.

NIXON: I agree. Just say nothing. We may not even make one.

KISSINGER: Or just a few thousand, and just do it —

NIXON: Well, obviously, we'll then just say the withdrawals will continue, we'll have another announcement in May, if everything —

KISSINGER: Right.

NIXON: The withdrawal has —

KISSINGER: Or June.

NIXON: — already begun. Don't even give a number. Just say, "Withdrawals will be continuing. We'll have another announcement [unclear]."

KISSINGER: Right.

NIXON: I won't say anything this time.

KISSINGER: Because we are — I think that should be a nothing one. By the middle of June, off the Moscow trip, or even later than June, depending on how you need it.

NIXON: It isn't a question of whether we need it. It's a question — it has to be then, do you see? You know how the political conventions work. Two weeks before the Democratic convention begins, they start hearings on the platform.

KISSINGER: Well —

NIXON: It is there they will make the issue on Vietnam. Now the issue isn't worth a damn, but they can make it worth a damn. You know what I mean? They'll say, "All the rushing in there, well, now we still have fifty thousand in Vietnam, and we're still bombing," et cetera, et cetera. And they'll be running over each other to say, "After four years Nixon has still got us in Vietnam and hasn't ended the war." We mustn't give them that issue. We've got to defuse it to the point where it's a nothing issue politically, but you see? And that's a very different thing from being a nothing issue with [unclear] you talked to the other day. See?

KISSINGER: Well —

NIXON: I urge you to think, I have no illusions about what they'll do with it.

KISSINGER: Yeah, but I think — I think this — my own view is, well, first of all we get an all-volunteer army, we can set a figure which can be almost arbitrary — thirty-five thousand, thirty thousand — of a residual force. I think we ought to announce going to that in the middle of June rather than now.

NIXON: Sure.

KISSINGER: And say we'll have reached that by the middle of July or something like that. Or the first of August and have it all-volunteer. It doesn't make a hell of a lot of difference whether it's forty or thirty thousand at that point.

NIXON: I saw something in the news summary where, obviously, we thought they would exploit us for it, it said our real problem now is: how we are going to defend the remaining Americans. Now, that's bullshit. Look here, we can't defend them now as you well know. Okay, if they get hit with less than a hundred thousand there, we don't have any combat forces to defend people there.

KISSINGER: So —

NIXON: Ten thousand.

KISSINGER: So, that is —

NIXON: Right?

KISSINGER: So that can be done. Also, we can then see — I share your judgment, almost certainly the negotiations aren't going to bring any, aren't going to bring anything. But there's just a slight chance —

NIXON: [unclear] If this happens soon it could get worse.

KISSINGER: Absolutely. If they don't produce anything then the only thing we have to balance is not to let the thing unravel before November because then —

NIXON: Let — then South Vietnam unravels.

KISSINGER: That's right. Then —

NIXON: [unclear]

KISSINGER: Then we'd really be vulnerable. That, I think, would make us more vulnerable than a small, residual force of volunteers.

NIXON: I agree.

KISSINGER: Who the hell can —?

NIXON: You understand, nothing is to be done at the cost of unraveling. On the other hand, we mustn't — we mustn't go overboard in terms of every time Thieu sneezes then we get a cold. And we've got to talk the talk tough —

KISSINGER: Well, but Thieu has been pretty good.

NIXON: I know. But we must have — he must have —

KISSINGER: But if we can't get —

[unclear exchange]

KISSINGER: Mr. President, I think that would —

NIXON: He'd expect too much.

KISSINGER: Also it will — it will draw attention to Vietnam. I'd rather take a trip out there.

NIXON: The best way to do that is to just [unclear] —

KISSINGER: Have Haig go out there.

NIXON: Huh? Yeah.

KISSINGER: I think that's better. If I go there —

NIXON: [unclear] I know. Haig can go.

KISSINGER: It will make —

NIXON: You see what I'm getting at here? Thieu has got to stand firm on any kind of an announcement we make, having in mind the fact: don't give the Democrats an issue.

KISSINGER: That's right.

NIXON: Don't give the antiwar people an issue, Henry. That's all we're saying.

KISSINGER: I couldn't agree more. But if we can, I think you'll —

NIXON: And we might get — we might get a negotiation out of it —

KISSINGER: Right —

NIXON: [unclear]

KISSINGER: We'll come out — if things break right, we'll come out of Moscow in a very strong position. It isn't just —

NIXON: It's not Moscow, as you know. The underlying goal is not whether we're right on Moscow or China, that helps us a great deal, but in terms of a political issue, Henry, it's like a — well, [unclear] it's like the ITT thing, nothing to the damn thing at all. ITT stock went down twelve points, and it's never recovered as a result of the trust settlement we imposed upon them. But they're making it an issue. Now, that's what this is. See, in the campaign there'll be made issues, not real issues. So we must not look at the merits. We must look to the politics of it.

"Is the United States in an inferior position to the Soviet Union?"

March 21, 1972, 5:10 p.m.

Richard Nixon, Gerry Smith, and Alexander Haig

OVAL OFFICE

Nixon had a long and unusually frank conversation with Smith, in company with Haig. Without Kissinger in attendance, both Smith and Nixon seemed to speak freely, exploring the options for an agreement with the Soviets regarding SLBMs in advance of the president's May summit in Moscow. They agreed on a rather radical turn away from tying a SALT agreement to the summit, even though that was inevitably the goal. While Smith wanted to use the tactic to bolster his own upcoming talks in Helsinki on March 28, the president angled to leave the clinching negotiations for Moscow.

• • •

NIXON: Let me begin by saying that — speaking of hard work, you're all working awfully hard, and I know that we're now coming down to the real tough decisions. When I say "decisions," I mean, I have to put some down. And the thing that I think I need you — that we've all got to realize that — and I told them this, and I'm going to tell you the same thing — is that if we get an agreement, the great danger that that agreement will pose to us, it's not going to be on the side of those who want arms control, because they're for any agreement. They'd prefer one that goes further, and so forth. But there will be a potentially very significant danger from those who say, "Who got took?"

Needless to say, as you recall, after our China trip, they took a communiqué, which had very little to do with substance, but the whole — but many said, "Who won? Who lost?" Well, in a way because that was a good deal for both sides. But, in this instance, this is a highly substantive matter, as you know. And everybody is going to be watching the darn thing. Who won? Who lost? Is the United States in an inferior position to the Soviet Union? Did we get, you know, suckered here by these people and the rest? What we have to do, therefore, is to be in a position, Gerry, where we've heard everybody.

That's why I gave the Defense Department plenty of time to present their case, you know, at one of the last meetings, and where I told them I have to consider it. You've not only got to hear 'em, but we've got to be in a position that, if we make an agreement with these fellows, that we will not be open, particularly in this political year, to a resounding attack. And it's — and in a political year, never underestimate from which side it will come. You may find some of the most, what you thought were all-out peace-at-any-price crowd, if they think they could take us on for making an agreement in which we got taken by the Russians, they would do it.

Now, an example of that, if you think I'm overestimating, it is the very amusing thing that some of those who, at first blush, when they didn't understand it, criticized, and wooed, and had wept buckets of crocodile tears about Taiwan, are people that would have sunk Taiwan without a trace twenty-five years ago — twenty years ago. What they saw was the political [unclear]. See my point?

SMITH: Sure.

NIXON: So what we have to do is to build a record. First, build a record that we considered the thing. And second, there ought to be an agreement, which is some — in other words, it's — which we can thoroughly defend from a national security standpoint. The attack, in other words, is going to be from the Right. It will not be from the Left. And if it is from the Left, to hell with it. We'll just have to fend it off, because it's better than anybody else was going to be able to do.

But the attack from the Right could be — by the "Right," I'm referring to not the nut Right. I think that they'll attack anyway. *Human Events, National Review,* and the rest will knock the hell out of us, saying, "Why do you even meet with the Russians? Why do you have a toast with them?" And all that. We understand that. But, what we want to remember is the responsible Right. What I mean by that, you know, after all, the fellows like Laird, and Moorer, and Henry Jackson, and others. I mean, the responsible Right will start raising hell — Stennis. We've got to be — if they do, we've got to be in the position to say, "Well, now, we considered all these views, and we rejected them for these reasons." Or, "We accepted these positions," and then be able to defend them.

So, if you, when you go back, in talking to the delegation, as you get down to the, you know, the hard, hard ground, that last five yards to the goal line, which we hope that's where it is, this is just scoring a damn touchdown, but it's one that's going to — maybe, we'll be able to hold and still win the game in the public opinion field. There's also another very substantial danger that's tied to that, in my view. If there is a great hue and cry, an outcry in this country, a lot of it politically inspired, coming as it does just three weeks before the Democratic convention, if we don't get the agreement until Moscow, for example, or two — or a month before if you get it in May. I mean, on that sort of thing [unclear] the Democratic thing in July, there's this great hue and outcry on this issue, joined in by some Republicans, as well. I don't mean, I don't mean all the Democrats; it'll split them down the middle. But some of them will, will see it as a political opportunity if they — not only — not because they're really against it but because they'll want to say that we are stupid.

But, this could create grave doubts in the world among our friends, because they'll say, "My God, if the Americans are divided on this, maybe the Americans did make a deal which was not in the American interest, which was in the Soviet interest." So, what I'm saying here is that let's try to get an agreement, of course, above everything else, that we can live with, that is sound. But we also have to remember that about half of this battle — maybe a little more than half — it's got to appear that way. It's got to appear that way. You know, and I know, it's got to appear that way, because if it doesn't appear that way, it could, it could raise a lot of hell, and particularly in this kind of year.

It's unfortunate that it's coming in this year. It'd be better if it came last year or next year. But it does come this year. We can't choose. Coming as it does, just before the conventions, it will be a lively, lively subject. And, based on what I've heard, I think, I think we're going to get this agreement, if we get it, if we get a package we can defend. But, it's those considerations that I think we have to have in mind at this point, and rather than simply considerations of — I mean, which would be more obvious: well, does Smith feel that, you know, you don't need to be concerned about the critics? Because, it isn't a case where, normally — which would be normal. I wish it was where everybody could be — breathe a sigh of relief and say, "Thank God. It's a good thing. It's a good step. It's a step toward peace. It's a step toward limitation of armaments." That would be the normal reaction, overwhelmingly, in this country. But, we can't count on it now. It's got to be solid, strong, and tough, so that we can debate it, stand up for it, kick hell out of the critics who are criticizing it for the wrong reason. You see what I mean? So that's a — that's a little of the thinking that I felt. Would you agree, Al?

HAIG: Absolutely —

NIXON: You, you're talking to all these conservatives who come in, and they're violent. Hell, you've been — you've been talking to 'em —

HAIG: Yes, sir.

NIXON: — Tower and that bunch, huh?

HAIG: [unclear]

SMITH: Mr. President, can I just on that —

NIXON: Yeah.

[unclear exchange]

SMITH: — report.

NIXON: Sure.

SMITH: I have talked to congressional committees, I think, thirty-five times —

NIXON: I know.

SMITH: — since we have been back.

NIXON: Uh-huh.

SMITH: And I don't detect except in Tower, and perhaps Byrd and Scoop —

NIXON: Yeah.

SMITH: — any —

NIXON: How about Stennis?

SMITH: Stennis said — and this is all on the basis — I mean, we're trying to get IC — SLs included — he said, "Look, I'm for you."

NIXON: He wants SLs in?

SMITH: But he wasn't biding his time —

NIXON: You see, he called me today and took a very hard position. But I — I — frankly, I think, took him off of it a little, because I said, "Now, look, you're really coming down to the point of saying that we shouldn't have agreement if we can't get SLBMs in?" He said, "Well, that's where my position is, but on the rest of the committee —" I said, "Well, suppose the price is too high?" Now, understand: I think — I think we've got to try. And, you know, Defense wants it in. Defense agrees. Defense wants it in. State wants it in. Everybody else, but I don't know. [unclear]

SMITH: But, State will back off from that position, I'm sure. I want it in at the present time, but I want to be perfectly clear now with you, Mr. President, that I think —

NIXON: You don't think we can get it, do you?

SMITH: I think it — I think it would be a good deal without it, a first-class deal. I think what you need —

NIXON: Well that's — Al, isn't that your feeling? That it would be a good deal, Al? As a military man?

HAIG: Yes, sir. That's my general —

NIXON: [unclear] I understand is that the Defense Department can't figure out on SLBMs. Let me — look, let me be quite candid with you on it. I got apprised of that at this meeting and also at the other meeting. Looking at it from the standpoint of what the United States really can do in terms of more defense in the event that the other side goes for more, we have a much better chance to go for submarines than land-based stuff. There's no way you could get any more land-based stuff! No way. Right?

HAIG: That's right.

NIXON: Hell, we've been down in there with ABM, the defensive weapon system, it was close. But, of course, this country for years — well, ever since the turn of the century — has gone for navy, right? And that's one view. On the other hand, if we get SLs in, you could make a — it's certainly going to look a lot like that. Let's have in mind the fact that — I don't know. Unless it's a good deal on SLs, I'm not for it. [unclear] But what is your — but, I've interrupted. What do you think? Your feelings are somewhat similar?

SMITH: Well, I think [unclear] we ought to try, and there's some chance that we can get the SLs included. Now, in this clause —

NIXON: You think there is a chance?

SMITH: Yes. Bill Rogers asked me about it, to mention to you. He's going to send you a memo suggesting you write Kosygin stressing the importance of this. Now, I feel —

NIXON: If I wrote anybody, I wouldn't write Kosygin; I'd write Brezhnev. But the second point is: I don't think at this point that I should write — well, it's just my reaction, I don't know if you agree, but I don't think I should be writing — using that chip with that fellow at this point. Do you agree? Do you want it done?

SMITH: Well, I think that there is a real chance that the Soviets are interpreting May 20 as —

NIXON: Excluding them —

SMITH: — not requiring them to go into SLBMs.

NIXON: Mm-hmm.

SMITH: And, as long as they have that interpretation —

NIXON: Yeah.

SMITH: — our chances —

NIXON: Yeah. Yeah. Yeah.

SMITH: — they are —

NIXON: Impossible.

SMITH: Now, whether this is the right time for you to weigh in, or later, I don't know.

NIXON: I don't like to weigh in, Gerry, on something that we're going to get turned down on.

SMITH: I agree.

NIXON: I think that when I weigh in, we've got to have a pretty good idea that, that we're going to get the deal, you know what I mean?

SMITH: Yeah.

NIXON: And, and then, we'll go in with everything. You can say, "Now, this is the president." These guys are tough, as you know. And, of course, the other way will be tough, too, but — well, anyway, I've got the message, and I'll consider it.

SMITH: My —

NIXON: [unclear]

SMITH: My read, Mr. President —

NIXON: The intuition is not to do it.

SMITH: We're — we're trying to stop —

NIXON: Why don't you tell them?

SMITH: Well, I've told them many a time. [laughs] Again, I think —

NIXON: Well, you can tell them you and I have talked, and you're working on it. Well, we'll put it in the — and we're going to have it in the instructions, isn't that right, Al?

HAIG: Yes, sir. We'll have the instructions —

NIXON: Yeah.

SMITH: But when we started Vienna last November, Mr. President, I communicated a personal message from you —

NIXON: Right.

SMITH: — to Semenov on this buildup. And I think the least we should do is something like that —

NIXON: Yeah.

SMITH: — or else, they'll think that we're [unclear] —

NIXON: 'Cause there's something else you could do. Is there any way you could, as a fallback position, say that that would be the next phase, or something to that effect? That's another way to get at it, you see?

SMITH: Oh, they'll agree to that in a minute —

NIXON: They've already agreed to that?

SMITH: They'll — they say we immediately should sit down after this and negotiate [unclear] like the summit.

NIXON: Also, I suppose other things that are — well —

SMITH: But you have all sorts of arguments that I haven't heard surface. I didn't want to get in a donnybrook —

NIXON: I know.

SMITH: — in the NSC.

NIXON: No use for 'em, did you? No, I [unclear] but I hear them all, so that nobody can say I didn't listen, you see? Hmm.

SMITH: For instance, one of the things we don't often hear is that the French and the British are going to have nine votes, which is over twenty percent of ours, and the Soviets flatly say to me those votes are not going to be on our side; they're going to be on your side. And this is a little bit of an insurance policy we've got to have. We're trying to stop three Soviet programs to just one of ours.

NIXON: Three?

SMITH: IC, SL, and ABM. Now, if you only stop two of the Soviets' to one of ours, it still seems to me a pretty good deal because our, our programs are not going to be stopped at all — the intensity. And they're big. They're much bigger than we like to make out. Poseidon and the Minuteman are tremendous.

NIXON: Poseidon and —

SMITH: And the Minuteman III, which is a MIRV —

NIXON: Yeah.

SMITH: — that can be a land-based missile.

NIXON: Yeah, yeah. I know.

SMITH: So that it —

NIXON: And that won't be stopped?

SMITH: That won't be stopped. Now, there's a tactical point that I hesitate to raise now —

NIXON: That's all right. Raise it if you want.

SMITH: [unclear] You mentioned Scoop Jackson. Scoop is the oldest friend I have, and —

NIXON: Great guy.

SMITH: — and I think [unclear] —

NIXON: If the Democratic Party had any damn brains they'd nominate him, but they won't.

SMITH: I have worked with him for twenty-five years, I think. Last year, on the twenty-ninth of May — March, he made a proposal for an interim freeze, and it did not include SLBMs. See the *Congressional Record*. He wanted also to stop the American Minuteman III program, and the Soviets were just going to stop their ICBMs. Now, in addition to that, he proposed —

NIXON: Mm-hmm?

SMITH: — this hard-site defense thing, but he —

NIXON: He's on the hard-site defense?

SMITH: But the inclusion or exclusion of SLs, logically, has nothing to do with the type of defense you can [unclear] that for, so that if Scoop starts to — acting up —

NIXON: Hell, I know [unclear] —

SMITH: — it might be a little slower.

NIXON: Well, on the other hand, let me say I don't like to take him on for other reasons, because he's such a damn decent, responsible guy, you know what I mean? It isn't that. I don't think that he's the one to be concerned about. The ones that are going to surprise you, da-da-da-da-da. To me, the Taiwan thing was a hell of an eye-opener. Good God, when I, when I read about some of these clowns that I know, that I mean, attacked Eisenhower for Quemoy/Matsu; who were always kicking Foster Dulles in the ass because of that, the China Lobby, and the rest. And here, they're all crying tears over Taiwan. And I thought, "What the hell gives here?" And I realized it's all politics. [laughs] They knew there was no problem, you know? So, that's what I think we've got to watch. In other words, just be sure the record is one — we've got to be sure the record is a darn good one, and we can go out and sell this deal and sell it strongly as one that is in the interests of the United States, and this is going to be in our interest; it isn't going to make us second best. You know, let's put it in the vernacular. That's what I'm trying to get at.

SMITH: Well, I'm completely persuaded by this. If I were a Soviet planner, and I've told this to a lot of people, I would be concerned about the way the balance is going. Because —

NIXON: You would?

SMITH: When you came into office, we had 1,710 independently targetable warheads. Now we've got double that. In two and a half years, we're going to double our present figures.

NIXON: Because of MIRV?

SMITH: And that, I think, is the important thing: the number of warheads you can deliver. Not the fact that they have some more submarines [unclear] —

NIXON: That's in power-weight?

SMITH: That's the thing. Now, each one of these is three times the size of the Hiroshima explosion.

NIXON: [unclear]

SMITH: And the Minuteman MIRVs are, I don't know, ten times the size of Hiroshima. Now, if we want more to do the job, if you make a deal without the boats, we'll just build boats. I don't think you need more, but you — your hands aren't tied at all.

"We must have the world's worst air force."

March 30, 1972, 9:38 a.m.

Richard Nixon and Henry Kissinger

OVAL OFFICE

On March 30, the North Vietnamese launched a blistering attack on South Vietnamese bases near the demilitarized zone that separated the two nations. Known as the Easter Offensive, it was the most extensive assault in four years. Nixon and Kissinger didn't yet know how long it would last, but Kissinger expressed frustration that the U.S. Air Force couldn't immediately retaliate. It did undertake missions against SAMs in other regions and succeeded in destroying one.

• • •

KISSINGER: It looks as if they are attacking in Vietnam.

NIXON: The battle has begun?

KISSINGER: Yeah, right at the DMZ. And the sons of bitches again, I made them check whether the — of course, the weather is too bad for us to bomb.

NIXON: Hmm.

KISSINGER: We must have the world's worst air force.

NIXON: What's the situation? They — is this the — this is an attack on a broad front?

KISSINGER: It looks that way. It's — they have attacked eight fire support bases, which is usually the way these things start. And —

NIXON: How —?

KISSINGER: And they are attacking within range of the SAMs in North —

NIXON: How are they doing?

KISSINGER: It says they're doing fairly well, but, you know, the first six hours of an attack, you know, who can tell?

NIXON: How's the ARVN doing? It's done fairly well?

KISSINGER: Yeah. That's what they say. It says they're reacting well, but —

NIXON: Yeah.

KISSINGER: — but you can't really believe them. I think if this is a real attack, we should hit the SAMs in North Vietnam —

NIXON: Sure.

KISSINGER: — that are protecting — and we told them we were going to do it.

NIXON: That's right.

KISSINGER: And —

NIXON: Well, I don't see why we don't do it right now. Is it — it's weather?

KISSINGER: Well, let's wait until the end of the day to see whether it's a real attack or just a blip.

• • •

NIXON: Well, now, let me ask — what the hell is the situation here?

KISSINGER: Well, I, Mr. President, before I —

NIXON: Should we start bombing right now? I mean, [unclear] —

KISSINGER: I think it is infinitely better for us that the attack is coming now. My nightmare —

NIXON: I understand that.

KISSINGER: My nightmare was —

NIXON: September —

KISSINGER: — that they'd do it in September and October.

NIXON: That's right.

KISSINGER: If — we'll either win or lose. And I don't think we'll lose because, as I watched them in Laos, for example, there's no reason why they haven't been able to take Long Tieng yet.

NIXON: They haven't done that?

KISSINGER: And — except for the fact that they're a lot weaker than they used to be. And if we — they'll use up their supplies this way and we know when this is over there isn't going to be anything the rest of the year. I think it's a hell of a lot better —

NIXON: I agree. Oh, I'm not concerned about the attack, but I am concerned about the counterattack. By God, you've got the air force there. Now, get them off their ass and get them up there and hit everything that moves —

KISSINGER: Well, I think if this attack continues twenty-four hours, then we should hit them by Sunday or Monday [April 2 or 3] —

NIXON: I want you to call Moorer and tell him that I want a plan ready, and they are to meet and agree —

KISSINGER: I think a forty-eight-hour attack.

NIXON: Forty-eight-hour attack? Great.

KISSINGER: And that —

NIXON: Fine, but, but don't scatter it around. Hit — hit in ways that are going to affect this thing.

KISSINGER: That's right. Well, just north of the DMZ is the place to do it —

NIXON: Is that where it is?

KISSINGER: Yeah.

NIXON: Like within — like the B-3 strike there? [Nixon ordered an air strike in the highlands B-3 Front in early February.] Is that what you think?

KISSINGER: Yes, sir. And that would get rid of the — we could take out the SAMs there, plus the supplies. And then they can go in with gunships against this attack.

NIXON: Is that right?

• • •

KISSINGER: Brezhnev wrote you a letter this week which is very, very conciliatory.

NIXON: First of all, do your best to cut the deal on Poland.

KISSINGER: I think I can handle that.

NIXON: But the second thing — and then say, and you can point out that, he can have, he need to not be concerned about what I say on Poland. He can be very sure. There's no problem on that. That we'll be totally discreet. But that I think we're going to be in a terrible position if we turn it down. Second point is, I think you should tell Dobrynin that, we're rather surprised by this attack. I'd tell him [unclear], and you can say, "Look, you don't know what — the president has said he wants to make the best possible arrangement with Brezhnev. We're all on — we're on the same track. But an attack on North Vietnam may make it impossible. It may spoil it."

KISSINGER: Well —

NIXON: I'd play it very hard.

KISSINGER: In fact, at the end of his letter, he had a rather mild expression of hope that we wouldn't bomb North Vietnam. And I can just take off from that and say —

NIXON: Sure.

KISSINGER: — we have showed great restraint.

NIXON: Great restraint since this. Now, instead we're going to have to do it. And it's only because they're attacking. And you've just got to keep, have them knock off this attack or we're going to bomb them. But I'd tell him, "Now look, Mr. Ambassador, I cannot vouch for what he won't do. I mean don't think that it's going to be limited to what we have done before." Throw that in again. "If these attacks continue, I believe I owe it to you to say that don't assume that it will not be — that it will be limited to the kind of a bombing we've done before."

An unofficial Soviet deal on Vietnam

March 30, 1972, 3:17 p.m.
Richard Nixon and Henry Kissinger
OVAL OFFICE

According to Kissinger, Ambassador Dobrynin was so pleased to be consulted on a Polish proposal to hold peace talks that he posed a simplified, let's-let-our-hair-down solution to the war in Vietnam.

• • •

KISSINGER: Well, I had a long talk with Dobrynin. And I put the Polish proposition to him. And I said, "You know, the basic departure that we are doing here is that we want to build policy on the recognition of we're two superpowers and that we don't want to interfere in each other's basic concerns." And I took — I showed him the cable we had from Warsaw and the reply we gave. I said, "This is the spirit in which we would like to deal with you. We don't need to ask you whether we want to go there but we want to show you the president is particularly concerned in what your reaction is." So he was practically in tears. He said, "This is the most generous thing I've heard. You will — I cannot tell you, Henry, how much this will impress Mr. Brezhnev."

NIXON: That we asked because he knew what we did on Romania.

KISSINGER: Yeah. I said, "I want you to know, when we went to Romania, we knew it would annoy you. We're going to Warsaw because, and if it raises any problems for you, we'll look [unclear]." And he was practically in tears. He said, "Speaking informally and as a member of the Central Committee, I am certain that they will say yes.

But if you can wait till Monday," he said — so that he is formally — "so that you get a formal reply from us, it would mean a great deal to us. But I can tell you now that it will be yes. It will almost certainly be yes." But he was practically in tears.

NIXON: You see, they, we have to realize we've got some chips to play too here.

KISSINGER: Oh yeah.

NIXON: And they, they know we can just, that, but it does show we're trying to cooperate.

KISSINGER: Exactly.

NIXON: And you told him that I would not embarrass them and that I —

KISSINGER: I said you will say nothing that would embarrass, and I said it [unclear] to our support in domestic considerations.

NIXON: He understood that?

KISSINGER: Oh yeah. And I said, "We are not doing this for the same reason as we did Romania, which wasn't done to annoy you, but in which we were willing to pay the price."

NIXON: Mm-hmm.

KISSINGER: "In this case, we frankly want to stay the same."

NIXON: You told him that — did you reiterate that I felt that the importance of the summit was utmost on my mind?

KISSINGER: Oh, well, that's how I started.

NIXON: He liked that, didn't he?

KISSINGER: Oh God, yes. And then on Vietnam I said, "You know, you've been mentioning now two or three times that Vietnam may be discussed." And I said, "First of all I want you to know what the president just said to me." And I mentioned —

NIXON: That's why I called you.

KISSINGER: That's what —

NIXON: I didn't know you were there. I called him here to talk about it. And then when I found you, I thought, what the hell, I'll just call. That impresses the son of a gun. He knows that we are in contact.

KISSINGER: Secondly, he said, "Now let me make a proposal to you which just occurred to me." He said, "It's got no official standing; it's just my own idea. But how would this be." He said, "Why don't you offer a withdrawal for a deadline?" I said, "Well, if we do that then they'll say you have to stop military aid too and we can't do that." He said, "But maybe we can help there." He said, "Supposing you made, this were the proposal: that you withdraw in return for a deadline: you give a deadline for withdrawal in return for prisoners, and you and we agree not to give any more military aid — we to North Vietnam and you to South Vietnam." That wouldn't be a bad deal.

NIXON: Ha. I'll say.

KISSINGER: So I said, "You know," I said, "frankly the president thinks he's got this war won. You know I —" I played it very tough. I said, "We feel that if we can last till November, which I'm sure we can, that we have four years to settle accounts. So your, we don't feel any pressure. You stage an offensive, I'll tell you right now we're not going to have any secret or other meetings." [unclear]

NIXON: Yeah.

• • •

KISSINGER: [I told Dobrynin] "that if you want to find out how Moscow reacts to this proposition, the president has always said that he'd be open-minded and I'll explore it in the meantime with the president." I frankly think if we could get that sort of a deal, it would be —

NIXON: What, you mean that they would stop their aid, we'd stop ours, we could agree to that?

KISSINGER: Military aid. We can continue to give economic aid.

NIXON: Why the hell shouldn't we give military aid if the North —

KISSINGER: I think if the North doesn't get military equipment, why should the South then get military equipment?

"To have the president in the Kremlin."

March 30, 1972, 5:07 p.m.
Richard Nixon and Henry Kissinger
OVAL OFFICE

As the Soviet summit neared, Nixon began to worry that maybe the Soviets would consider canceling it. His trip to China had caught them by surprise and caused no small loss of face. That was supposed to be their summit, but instead, not only did Nixon make peace with the Chinese, but he did so in a way that subordinated the Soviet Union to China. Before the China trip, the United States needed the Soviet summit more than the Soviets did. After the China trip, the Soviets were the ones put on the defensive. Kissinger, however, reassured Nixon that the Soviets would not cancel. Hosting an American president in the Kremlin was no small achievement, and they did not plan to throw it away.

• • •

NIXON: I was thinking more about your conversation with Dobrynin. Trying to look at it pragmatically, Henry, what the hell is in it for them pulling us off over in Vietnam?

KISSINGER: Well —

NIXON: I'm just being the devil's advocate. I don't know.

KISSINGER: Well, I'm not sure they're going to do it. But —

NIXON: No, no. I'm just — that's what I mean. That's why we don't know whether it's worth exploring unless you think it's —

KISSINGER: What's in it for them is as long as Vietnam goes on we have an additional incentive to play with the Chinese. Secondly, we —

NIXON: Also it avoids most favored nation and other little things.

KISSINGER: We are setting up a lot of things now in the economic field. They're really moving massively with us, and I have every intention of let — and, well, at any rate it's so set up that we can control the delivery. And —

NIXON: I see.

KISSINGER: — and I don't think we should deliver unless they do something.

NIXON: Right.

KISSINGER: Then they're really panting after the Middle East. Now —

NIXON: Right.

KISSINGER: I — I haven't —

NIXON: [unclear] with respect to the Middle East —

KISSINGER: I haven't bothered with all the details, but I've made some propositions to them on the Middle East, which they won't accept, but they have promised me a reaction, which is the first time they have moved off the position of just blanket endorsement of the Egyptian position. In turn — what I have to do with the Israelis, it's got to be very tricky. I told them they were such double-crossers that I was disengaging from the negotiations. That I did —

NIXON: And you told Mr. Dobrynin that?

KISSINGER: I told Rabin that.

NIXON: Ha.

KISSINGER: And I told the Israelis this only in order to be able to stay in the negotiations, because if they think we're talking, we've got to be a little — I want to see first a little bit more of what's going on.

• • •

KISSINGER: You'll have a tremendous one in Tehran. You'll have a big one in Warsaw. [Kissinger is referring to the receptions Nixon was likely to receive on these stopovers before continuing to Moscow.] And my instinct tells me the Russians somewhere along the line are going to —

NIXON: Will let people out? If they do, they'll react. The Russian people are an emotional, strong people.

KISSINGER: One thing he told me was that, you know, we're having a little problem of our space in the Kremlin. And he said, "For God's sakes, don't turn the Kremlin down. It's the biggest honor that Brezhnev could pay you."

NIXON: I won't turn it down. Space for what? For staff?

KISSINGER: Yeah. And he said, "Above all, the Russian people, that's for the Russian people that means that there's a solid basis for our relationship, and it's a tremendous signal to our people —"

NIXON: Mmm.

KISSINGER: "— to have the president in the Kremlin."

NIXON: Mm-hmm.

KISSINGER: And I think that's right.

NIXON: [unclear]

KISSINGER: But I think, if I may make a suggestion, I don't — I think we should play it very cool about the summit. We should give the impression that not much is going to happen at the summit.

NIXON: Yeah.

KISSINGER: [unclear] Right now no one really expects much out of the Moscow summit and that's great. We've got the thing split up over the bureaucracy in such a way—

NIXON: That's good. Well, I think we can play the line that there are a number [of] things we're going to discuss, but some things that we're pretty far apart on too.

KISSINGER: That's right.

NIXON: That we're pretty far apart.

KISSINGER: Yeah. They're going beautifully now on SALT.

NIXON: Is it?

KISSINGER: Yeah. That's moving.

NIXON: Don't get—but Smith's not going to settle now?

KISSINGER: Oh, no.

NIXON: Well, the Russians aren't, right?

KISSINGER: No. I told Dobrynin again today.

NIXON: You did?

KISSINGER: On the Middle East, if we could get an interim settlement—

NIXON: That's already—

KISSINGER: —and defer the final settlement until, say, September. They are sort of counting on my going out, over there in September, because it's—

NIXON: It's done. We've got to do China too.

KISSINGER: I've got to go there at the end of June.

NIXON: Incidentally, it's good to go to China and good to go to Russia, because we're going to have to use everybody in the campaign that can be used and you can come back from China and garble around a bit. Then, you see, you can do a television thing, and then after you go to Russia you can do the same thing. You see, I want to be—we've got to really throw the big guns in.

KISSINGER: [unclear]

NIXON: We need foreign policy up front and center in that period too.

KISSINGER: China, we now have scheduled for the end of June, just before the June [July] Democratic convention.

"I am commander in chief, and not secretary of defense."

April 3, 1972, 10:06 a.m.
Richard Nixon, Thomas Moorer, and Henry Kissinger
OVAL OFFICE

Nixon still considered the air response to the North Vietnamese Easter Offensive to be woefully inadequate. He was only barely able to control his temper as he summoned Ad-

miral Moorer, chairman of the Joint Chiefs, for a tense meeting. He reviewed the American air war, which not only was a reaction to North Vietnamese incursions but was carefully timed from his point of view not to coincide with diplomatic efforts with Beijing and Moscow. One of the central topics of the meeting was Nixon's disappointment with Laird. Rather than confronting Laird, though, the president gave Moorer a series of personal and military messages to deliver to the secretary.

• • •

NIXON: Let me come, maybe, directly to the point, because I want — Admiral Moorer has heard me speak in this vein before. I want you to hear it, too, because Packard, of course, was quite familiar because he was at the WSAG meeting and so forth and you're not. And, first, I think there has to be a very clear understanding that — of a matter which I have discussed with the admiral on occasion before, and that is that I am commander in chief, and not secretary of defense. Is that clear? Do you understand that?

MOORER: I do indeed.

NIXON: Now, I ordered a briefing on Vietnam this morning, yesterday, and to be over here by about seven o'clock. It didn't come until nine — eight thirty. That's a direct violation of orders, and I want somebody who was supposed to be here to be demoted or reprimanded. That's to go in his file. Is that clear? I ordered that, and I was told he would be here at seven fifteen, and I understand well the secretary of defense said he couldn't come until eight thirty. Now, I'm not going to have that kind of crap anymore. From now on, that man is to have his ass over here in this office at seven o'clock every morning. Is that clear?

MOORER: Yes, sir. He'll be here.

NIXON: All right, no more crap. The second point is I ordered the use of strikes, you know, in this zone above the DMZ. There were five hundred sorties that could have been flown; they flew a hundred yesterday — one hundred twenty-five —

MOORER: One hundred thirty-eight, sir.

NIXON: One hundred thirty-eight. Yeah. The excuse is weather. I understand.

MOORER: No, sir. In all fairness, you see, we got that directive, Mr. President, at midday and they, as they will tell you, they had their schedules laid on, their LORAN laid on —

NIXON: That's right.

MOORER: I asked Abrams last night and we started right way.

NIXON: I understand. Now, let's come to Abrams. Why didn't he think of that? What is — what is his job out there? Just to do it in the numbers or is it his job to try to see that this kind of offensive is stopped? Now, I want you to understand, there's some talk of Abrams going to chief of staff of the army. I want you to know that I don't intend him to have to go to chief of staff of the army because of his conduct in this business. He's shown no imagination. He's drinking too much. I want you to get an order to him that he's to go on the wagon throughout the balance of this offensive. Is that clear?

MOORER: Yes, sir.

NIXON: Totally. The other thing that's going to happen is that he is going to start coming up with some ideas as to the use of the air force and so forth and as to the planning here, rather than just sitting back on his ass waiting for things to happen. Now, I have read the reports that came from Defense on this thing, on Friday, on Saturday, they've — that's from out there. They did not — they were not accurate. They did not explain what the facts were adequately. And what is happening here is that Defense, in its usual way, is temporizing with the situation which is serious, but which can be turned to our advantage. But it can only be turned to our advantage with the massive use of all of our assets, and also in terms of our air power by not waiting until it's ceiling unlimited before we get out there and clobber them where they are. Now, from the moment you leave this office, I want somebody to get out there, and I want everything that can fly, flying in that area. And good God! In the Battle of the Bulge they were able to fly even in a snowstorm. Now what in the hell is the matter with the air force that they are unable to, to, to conduct offensive operations in this area? So they're going to fly down and drop it over a cane field in Cambodia? Sure, they'd get another Purple Heart — I mean an Air Medal for that. But I want this air force, and I — that includes the navy — you've only got, as I understand it, that instead of having the four carriers we ordered in, we got two. Is that right?

MOORER: No, sir. There are three there. The fourth one will be there very shortly, sir.

NIXON: How shortly?

MOORER: About — I would say they have fifty hours.

NIXON: All right. That's too long. Too long. We shouldn't have left it. When those four carriers are there — now, we have got to use this air power in a way that will be as effective as possible. The other thing is an immediate study is to be made of the use of B-52s in the — a study and I need the recommendation within eight hours, and I don't want to go through the — I'm not going to crap around with the secretary of defense on this either — I need the use of B-52s if it will be helpful in that forty-mile — five —

MOORER: Forty-five miles.

NIXON: That's right. If it will be helpful. Understand? The idea that if, if we don't have the assets that can do it otherwise, we'll use '52s. Now, if the reason for not using the '52s is because they are vulnerable, I understand that. If, on the other hand, the use of B-52s, after you've taken out the SAMs, would be helpful, we'd better use them. Because the thing that I am concerned about here is that — well, first, I don't like this business of not getting information when I ask for it. I was on the phone all day yesterday and couldn't get a goddamn thing out of the Department of Defense. I got one half-assed memorandum, which was so disgraceful in terms of it being inadequate, that I really don't, I'm really ashamed to have it in my file. I have it in my file, but I'm going to keep it personal and I hope I don't have to write a book. But from now on, we're to have the truth and that guy is going to be over here. Incidentally, not just in the morning; he should be here at seven o'clock at night. Let him work a little overtime over there. Is that clear?

MOORER: Yes, sir.

NIXON: Get him over here. And I want the plans — I want what he's done and I want what has been done to carry out these orders. Now as far as this, as the — and then Abrams and that MACV staff and all the rest, they're to knock off all the parties. Is that clear?

MOORER: Very much, sir —

NIXON: There isn't to be anything out there. And from — until they get this thing contained, they have got to have what we need from them. What we need from them are some ideas on their part as to what they're going to do, rather than we'll run the same numbers, you know, we'll hit same targets here, here, here, here, here, here, and here. The idea that we could have been surprised by this, the idea that we didn't — I mean, we thought the B-3 thing was coming and so forth. Well, they had more tanks there than we expected, and they had more forces there than we expected, and all that sort of thing. I don't buy that.

MOORER: Our reason —

NIXON: Now, it isn't we being surprised. I mean it's — this is ARVN being surprised. That's what they said, that MACV was pissing on the ARVN. We're the ones that are supposed to have the intelligence. The ARVN doesn't have much in terms of intelligence. But my point is that, I know we don't have many assets out there in terms of ground forces. And we're not going to have any. This is not going to be said, but we've got some very considerable assets in terms of air power. But those assets have to be, they have to be concentrated, concentrated in areas that will provide shock treatment now as we did in the B-3 area. Remember? We had a couple-day strike; it did a little good. Now, we've got to concentrate in these areas and give it some shock treatment. And, incidentally, rather than twenty-five miles, you've got to go up to thirty miles in order to do the job.

KISSINGER: We have that Dong Hoi area.

NIXON: Take out the Dong Hoi area right now. Now, the forty-eight-hour strike is not going to wait till Friday; it's got to go Wednesday. Is that clear?

MOORER: Yes, sir.

NIXON: Yeah. Unless — is the purpose of waiting till Friday weather?

MOORER: Well it's not — it's not too bad —

NIXON: You can't get it ready?

MOORER: No, sir. It'll go —

NIXON: [unclear]

MOORER: Nothing, no problem if the weather is satisfactory it can go —

NIXON: Well, don't go if it isn't; the weather —

MOORER: There's no restriction on it till Friday, sir. There's no order to go Friday —

NIXON: What's the problem you said about Friday?

KISSINGER: Laird told me last night it wouldn't go till Friday —

MOORER: Well, he was just guessing at the weather.

KISSINGER: Oh.

NIXON: All right —

MOORER: There's no, no —

NIXON: Weather is one thing. But let me say the decision has been made. We need it Wednesday. We need it Wednesday for a number of reasons, not the least of which is military. There are other reasons, too, that are supplemental, but the military is the most important one. And we may not get a chance to whack some of those supplies up now, and they might be coming in September and October. So, let's get that damn strike off, I mean, if the weather is reasonable. I don't want to go off in bad weather.

KISSINGER: It shouldn't go if they can't do a good job.

NIXON: No, no, no, no. I don't —

MOORER: We'll deal with it —

NIXON: There's absolutely nothing. If they can't do an adequate job there's no reason to go over North Vietnam. It's got to be an effective job in the North. But right now, right now when the ARVN is under a very serious attack the air force has got to take some goddamn risks, just like the air force took some risks in World War II in the Battle of the Bulge because we were under serious attack. If the air force hadn't taken some risks, we'd have lost the battle. Now, that's really what it boils down to —

MOORER: Yes, sir. Well, the air force is not reluctant in any sense to take risks, Mr. President. The problem is that north of the DMZ in these — with these missile sites, they're moving them around all the time and you need some kind of visibility in order to get the —

NIXON: Yeah.

MOORER: — sites themselves. Now, in all fairness to General Abrams you should know that he and CINCPAC, Admiral McCain, have repeatedly asked for authority to, to attack these missile sites north. And we hadn't been given the authority, because you just gave it to us here yesterday. But we knew that they were accumulating these forces in tanks and mobile artillery and so on north of the DMZ. And with — the way the weather is this time of year, the only way to do that right is for the man on the scene to be — to have the authority to go make it. You might get four hours a day, or two hours all of a sudden. It's just the —

NIXON: That's right.

MOORER: The flow shifts back and forth. And it's very difficult, almost impossible, to run that from Washington. And so far as the reports to you are concerned, let me tell you right now, that if I am directed to give the reports you will get them precisely when you ask. But I am not running this reporting business. And I am passing the information up to the secretary of defense and it's being run from up there, but it's —

NIXON: Right. I am directing you —

MOORER: If you want me to do it, I can do it —

NIXON: I am directing you, and if the secretary of defense raises the question, I am directing you. I have to have them directly, and they must be unsanitized. And also when an order goes, it's got to go from me. The secretary of defense is not commander in chief. The secretary of defense does not make decisions on these kinds of things —

MOORER: I understand that, Mr. President —

NIXON: He's a procurement officer. That's what he is and not another goddamn thing. And from now on this has got to be done this way. So under these circumstances we can go. Now, getting back to this thing, let's see what kind of an excuse is being developed here. You say that —

MOORER: I'm not giving excuses —

NIXON: No, no, no. What Abrams was dropping. You — I thought I asked you about this earlier, Henry, about this authority with regard to hitting. You said they had it already in the DMZ area?

KISSINGER: Well, you gave — well, they — you gave the authority in February. Then it was stopped during the —

NIXON: China thing.

KISSINGER: — during the China thing.

NIXON: That it hit North Vietnam, no?

MOORER: Yes, sir —

KISSINGER: That's right. In the DMZ — they have had authority to hit in the DMZ, but then the authority was never implemented after you came back from China for this nineteen-mile area that we had agreed to because the offensive didn't come. Then when they asked for it again, we gave it and you actually ordered a wider belt than the one they asked for —

NIXON: When was that?

KISSINGER: This weekend.

NIXON: Yeah.

MOORER: But we asked, sir, on the eighth of March for this authority to go north of the DMZ and it was turned down and —

KISSINGER: It was never really discussed in here —

MOORER: — then we asked again, and we finally got the authority yesterday. But we cannot handle a threat, such has accumulated north of the DMZ, unless you really work on it —

NIXON: That's right.

MOORER: — when you have the weather.

NIXON: Fine.

MOORER: When you have the weather that's the way that works —

NIXON: All right. I understand —

MOORER: You've got to see the target —

NIXON: I understand. Now, the situation, though, is, now is that as far as sorties and so forth are concerned, they'll go to five hundred a day. Will they at least? You can — you can at least do something in this area at this time, can you not?

MOORER: Yes, sir.

NIXON: All right.

MOORER: Now we are, Mr. President, putting all of the B-52s, every one we have, up there.

NIXON: Good. Where? Where? In the DMZ area?

MOORER: In the DMZ area. Yes, sir.

NIXON: They can — they can go above that stuff, can't they [unclear]?

MOORER: Well, we're going up to the DMZ. Now, we've got to get up there and get out to some of those missile sites to make it viable —

NIXON: Is it possible?

MOORER: — to make it feasible so we won't —

NIXON: Yeah. I understand that we can't lose B-52s.

MOORER: Yes, sir. Now, we're working on that —

NIXON: I'll tell you what I want now. From now on, you get those reports in to me. And the second thing is, I want Abrams braced hard. His promotion depends upon how he conducts himself. Now — just — you weren't here at the time. He screwed up Laos [Operation Lam Son 719]. He's not going to screw this one up. Is that clear?

MOORER: Yes, sir.

NIXON: All right.

"For us to be run out of Vietnam would undermine our foreign policy."

April 4, 1972, 9:24 a.m.

Richard Nixon and Thomas Moorer

WHITE HOUSE TELEPHONE

Nixon had decided that the time was right to expand the war and win it. The North Vietnamese had started a new chapter in the war with their Easter Offensive, and the president was determined to take advantage of it. Even while building the air power to a level not seen since the mid-1960s, he wanted to marshal U.S. naval forces as well. Calling upon Moorer in a more positive mood than he'd been in the day before, Nixon instigated the preparation for the mining of Haiphong harbor, North Vietnam's only major naval base. Soon afterward, he and Kissinger met to discuss the military confrontation and the timing of the victory they felt was at hand. From their point of view, it needed to come after the Moscow summit and preferably, but not necessarily, before the election.

• • •

MOORER: Good morning, Mr. President.

NIXON: Hi, how are you? I noticed that you only got off 126 missions yesterday, which I understand because of weather. Now I ask—

MOORER: No, we actually, that's—

NIXON: Oh, you got six more, huh? One hundred thirty-two, is that right?

MOORER: It's over two hundred, sir.

NIXON: Yeah. Well, let me ask you a question. I don't want them to fly in bad weather, but what, where is that report that I was supposed to have here at nine fifteen with regard to whether or not you could not, and without having those planes just sit on the deck, hit in the B-3 area, where they have that immense concentration? What about that?

MOORER: Well, they have been hitting, sir, in the B-3 area, and—

NIXON: Well, how about—how about taking everything that flies, while this weather is bad, and socking it in there for a while again, giving them a massive punch? Is there—is—you see, you've got the planes sitting on the deck now.

MOORER: No, sir. The planes are operating. I think we had about five hundred sorties over the last twenty-four hours, sir. They're operating in the, along the Ho Chi Minh Trail, in the B-3 Front, and along the—down in Military Region 3. And we actually had over two hundred in Military Region 1 and just across the DMZ.

NIXON: Yeah.

MOORER: As you know, some of them got through a hole and destroyed the bridge over the Ben Hai River, and then came down the road and knocked out three tanks.

NIXON: I saw that. Uh-huh—

MOORER: By visible, but I think—

NIXON: That's good. Good.

MOORER: I think that he's made—the report that they made, sir, over there of one hundred and—that was cut off at a certain time.

NIXON: Yeah.

MOORER: And I telephoned out there.

NIXON: Yeah.

MOORER: I sent your instructions yesterday.

NIXON: Yeah. Right. Right. Right—

MOORER: That you wanted a maximum effort.

NIXON: Yeah. Understand, I don't want anybody to fly in bad weather and just to drop it out in the boondocks. But my point is, if you can't hit there then hit—you know, from reading the morning report, you say that you expect that the next blow is going to come in the B-3 area. Is that not correct?

MOORER: That's right. Yes, sir. And they are working hard there—

NIXON: Are we working that as hard as we can?

MOORER: Yes, sir.

NIXON: There's nothing more we can do?

MOORER: Yes, sir. We don't have any aircraft on the deck —

NIXON: Mm-hmm. Yeah —

MOORER: Let me assure you.

NIXON: Now, point two. Have you carried out the order that I gave last night — twelve hours ago — with regard to using naval gunfire on the road above the DMZ in North Vietnam?

MOORER: Yes, sir. I did that right away —

NIXON: Now, is there — does that, can the naval gunfire reach that road?

MOORER: Yes, sir.

NIXON: It can?

MOORER: Yes, sir.

NIXON: All right. Have you — and — and that's — that will be done? Now —

MOORER: Yes, sir.

NIXON: Now, what additional ships are available to get out there? I mean, do you have a few that you could —

MOORER: Yes, sir —

NIXON: — send from Singapore and other places?

MOORER: Yes, sir. We, we've sent four additional destroyers and I've sent in a cruiser —

NIXON: Mm-hmm. Well, have you got any? How long would it take anything to get from Pearl? Is that where most of them are?

MOORER: What I think we can use are the ones in the western Pacific, sir. In fact, they're already there. I had, I started this action as soon as I —

NIXON: How many? How many could you get there, Tom? How many? I mean, could you get a significant number? Because I have a more important assignment that I'll have Henry give to you orally.

MOORER: Yes, sir. We could get, certainly get more there from the Seventh Fleet. It would take, you know —

NIXON: Great.

MOORER: — about eight days or so to get them —

NIXON: Eight days?

MOORER: — from Pearl. But from the Seventh Fleet, we can get them within —

NIXON: Yeah.

MOORER: — anywhere from four hours —

NIXON: Mm-hmm.

MOORER: — to four days.

NIXON: Yeah. Yeah. And that includes what? Cruisers? Destroyers?

MOORER: Yes, sir.

NIXON: Mm-hmm. Mm-hmm. Mm-hmm —

MOORER: But right as of this moment, there are eight —

NIXON: Yeah.

MOORER: — on the line, sir.

NIXON: Yeah —

MOORER: I told them to put four south of the DMZ and four north.

NIXON: And they are, but you can't get — couldn't you get more than that?

MOORER: Yes, sir. We can get [unclear] a few —

NIXON: Well, order every, every — order everything that is used. Incidentally, forget the SIOP and all that crap —

MOORER: We have, sir —

NIXON: That doesn't mean anything anyway. And get all the cruisers and destroyers in the Seventh Fleet in that area. We have another purpose for 'em. And get 'em there as fast as you can. And give me — give Henry a report by ten o'clock, because I have a reason I have to have them there. Okay? And he'll let you know. Okay?

MOORER: Yes, sir. Thank you.

"That's a hell of a lot of firepower."
April 4, 1972, 12:13 p.m.
Richard Nixon and Henry Kissinger
OVAL OFFICE

Nixon and Kissinger continued to press the military for a major buildup in Vietnam. Nixon had a plan for this massive show of force, although he was not ready to reveal it yet.

• • •

NIXON: Hi, Henry.

KISSINGER: Hi. We had just a good WSAG meeting. You've really charged these guys up now.

NIXON: Did we get some weather, did you say?

KISSINGER: Well, we're getting some weather, but they are really pouring in naval ships now.

NIXON: Did he [Moorer] get the point with it?

KISSINGER: Oh.

NIXON: Did you tell him about the — is he ready for a mining exercise?

KISSINGER: He'll have a plan first thing in the morning. He said thank — tell the president —

NIXON: Leak it.

KISSINGER: "Not since '64" — no, I'm — we're doing it even better. I've told him to start loading mines in the Philippines —

NIXON: Good.

KISSINGER: — on ships.

NIXON: How about —?

KISSINGER: That will leak it.

NIXON: How about having — telling Helms. Did you tell him that?

KISSINGER: Yep, that's good.

NIXON: Would you mind giving Helms the word that I —?

KISSINGER: Helms, of course he's a bit of a whore, but he's thrilled. Now, Rush asked to see me yesterday, asking me to see me after the meeting. He said he reviewed the whole record. And, he said whatever you said yesterday was an understatement; Laird has been playing games with us. And —

NIXON: And about giving the reports of —

KISSINGER: Yeah.

NIXON: — both sides.

KISSINGER: And also the request for authorities. You see, one reason I was so leery is they wanted to hit logistics and SAMs. Laird didn't approve it; he just wanted to hit SAMs. And to me the price just was too high for that.

NIXON: Mm-hmm.

KISSINGER: Well, I just want you to know that. This thing —

NIXON: What is it? Have they got — they've gotten a little charged up then?

KISSINGER: Oh, God. We — they're now. We have one question, I don't really —

NIXON: Yeah?

KISSINGER: — know whether I need to bother you with it. I think we ought to put in some more aircraft.

NIXON: Well, where the hell is it?

KISSINGER: Well, the choice is to move thirty-six Marine planes out of Japan or fifty-four from the United States Air Force. The Marines would have to —

NIXON: Bring them —

KISSINGER: — bring in five hundred more people with them because they don't have their ground support —

NIXON: They are to be stationed in — in this country?

KISSINGER: — in Da Nang —

NIXON: In country? If we can do it —

KISSINGER: — in order to move the air force out.

NIXON: Yeah. The air force thing is not considered to be an increase in our complement there, is it?

KISSINGER: Not — no. Maybe a hundred people, but that would be —

NIXON: Yeah?

KISSINGER: — absorbed by the withdrawal.

NIXON: The Marines are better. The Marines will do a better job. Let's do whatever does a better job. What do you think?

KISSINGER: All right.

NIXON: First you're going to raise more aircraft. Oh, the air force isn't that bad. Let's not [unclear]. We shouldn't blame those pilots; they're brave. The poor sons of bitches are all POWs and this and that. You know? They fought well. It's these goddamn airplanes that are no good.

KISSINGER: Well, they're both using the same planes. Let me check with Haig who he thinks will do the better job.

NIXON: But would you give me it quickly? Would you say that—

KISSINGER: Well—

NIXON: —would you say, first, that Moorer is charged up now? Huh?

KISSINGER: Absolutely. And the whole admiralty. I said, I repeated what you had said this morning. I said, "The president said he doesn't want to be told about political campaigns or anything else. He has the responsibility for the security of this country. He has concluded that for us to be run out of Vietnam would undermine our foreign policy. And he has an obligation to do the right thing. So all you people are obliged to do is to tell him what the right thing is." And—

NIXON: Except pouring them in.

KISSINGER: Except pouring them in. I said, "Anything short of ground combat we want to do."

NIXON: So what'd they say?

KISSINGER: "There's not—you are responsible for telling all your subordinate commanders—"

NIXON: Mm-hmm.

KISSINGER: "—that they should think of things to do." He said, "God, I haven't heard"—Moorer said, "I haven't heard this since '63."

NIXON: Oh, yes. He's heard it from me.

KISSINGER: Well—

NIXON: He forgets it.

KISSINGER: Yeah. And—

NIXON: Very well.

KISSINGER: Well, they are now, they—they're moving twenty B-52s out there.

NIXON: Good.

KISSINGER: They've already moved eighteen F-4s.

NIXON: Good.

KISSINGER: They are moving—

NIXON: Are they moving another carrier?

KISSINGER: Well, the other carrier they think would take too long.

NIXON: All right, fine.

KISSINGER: And they'd have to move it—

NIXON: These four would be enough, probably.

KISSINGER: These four would be enough—

NIXON: And how about the fleet? Can they get some more of them? Get some more than four destroyers? Let's put in—

KISSINGER: No, no. They've already—

NIXON: — put in one hundred destroyers.

KISSINGER: They've already got ten destroyers there; they're moving eight more down, plus three cruisers. And —

NIXON: Well, that's a hell of a lot of firepower.

KISSINGER: That is. And you remember these have five-inch guns. And, I told him to start hitting logistics installations in Dong Hoi, to start hitting the airfield in Dong Hoi. [Located in southern North Vietnam, Dong Hoi contained military barracks, an airfield, and an important bridge and was a major logistics center with a railway terminal just south of the city.]

NIXON: That's right.

KISSINGER: He said, "Do you mean it?" I said, "Of course we mean it."

NIXON: Right.

KISSINGER: And —

NIXON: Is Dong Hoi an airfield? Can it be reached by, by this —?

KISSINGER: Yes.

NIXON: Have we done it before?

KISSINGER: Never.

NIXON: We haven't? Why not?

KISSINGER: Because of the bombing understanding.

NIXON: Oh, you mean we haven't. But it was done by Johnson, I presume?

KISSINGER: Right, but never by naval gunfire, because —

NIXON: The naval gunfire, it seems to me, would be better than bombing.

KISSINGER: Yeah. Oh, yeah. We should really pour it in there now.

NIXON: Geez.

KISSINGER: They'll scream like crazy. But I think — my view is this, Mr. President, this is not going to break open the war.

NIXON: Your view also is, I think, correct, that we ought to delay a forty-eight-hour strike because the weather has been bad.

KISSINGER: I —

NIXON: Has there been any improvement in the weather? You say they got two hundred strikes off. I hope that Moorer didn't go drop 'em over the boondocks —

KISSINGER: No, no —

NIXON: — because of the number of strikes.

KISSINGER: No, no —

NIXON: Goddamn it, that isn't what I was telling him.

KISSINGER: I've talked to — I've talked to Moorer, incidentally. He thinks if we give him unlimited authority to hit up to the eighteenth parallel —

NIXON: Yeah?

KISSINGER: — in other words, just extend it five more miles —

NIXON: Do it!

KISSINGER: — he'd prefer that to the forty-eight-hour strike all over South Vietnam.

NIXON: All right, fine.

KISSINGER: And it gives us a better position because we can then say we're just supporting the immediate combat zone.

NIXON: That's right. We're supporting the combat zone and that's all.

KISSINGER: And we can then, as we—

NIXON: And then we can do more in a smaller—

KISSINGER: That's right.

NIXON: —place.

KISSINGER: That's right. And—

NIXON: And then also it's a signal to them we might do more later. Now, you see, the mining, though, will really be the—will really be the thing that'll tick them off. We've got to—I think that one has got to come—

KISSINGER: But we should wait at least a week—

NIXON: —quite soon. Quite soon. I'm not so sure we have to even wait. I'm not so sure [unclear]—

KISSINGER: But it wouldn't take effect, Mr. President, for a month or two.

NIXON: I know, but you know we're in a position now where—

KISSINGER: Well—

NIXON: —a bold play is going to make the difference.

KISSINGER: But I think, Mr. President, they've given us a chance. They threw down the gauntlet and if we now break them, if the South Vietnamese can form a line, this is beyond contention—

NIXON: Did you tell Moorer about my theory about retreating?

KISSINGER: Right.

NIXON: You see, I read again last night. I went back to, deliberately, and read Churchill's chapter about March 21 [the spring offensive by Germany in World War I, in 1918]. And as you know, [Lieutenant General Sir Hubert de la Poer] Gough, a great one of the British military commanders, the hero of '16, was cashiered as a result of the damn thing. And then—and Churchill finally said it, it was a—and then he pointed out why it was a German defeat and a Brit—and an Allied victory. He said for the first time in the war since Ypres, he said that the Germans lost two to one on the offensive in casualties to the British, and three to two in terms of officers. But look, but look—but look what it looked like, I mean what it looked like in terms of the battle. The Germans captured, Henry, in the first four days of that battle, they captured sixty thousand British. Captured sixty thousand. Captured over a thousand heavy guns. They killed and wounded two hundred thousand British in the course of the day. And everybody said, "a great German victory." Ludendorff was whining. He [unclear] and it was a hell—and, as Churchill said, it was a defeat.

KISSINGER: Well—

NIXON: And we've got to—

KISSINGER: Mr. President, I agree—

NIXON: But how—let me tell you, the other point that I, which I particularly noted, Churchill made the point of retreat. And he said, they kept going back, and they kept going back, and they gave up ground, but they won [laughs] the war. The hell with the ground! Unless it's—unless it's Hue, or—you know what I mean?

KISSINGER: Hue and Da Nang you can't lose—

NIXON: Did you—did you tell—did you tell him that? Has he—have they been figuring about a strategic retreat?

KISSINGER: Yeah, I've told him, and of course, Thieu's interest, he doesn't want to lose any cities.

NIXON: All right.

KISSINGER: But—

NIXON: We're trying to win the war—

KISSINGER: I believe, Mr. President, if we can hold the line, as long as it doesn't mean the loss of Hue and Da Nang, if we can hold the line then we've got them out in the open where they are concentrated; there's no jungle there. And we are going to grind them down. And if they then have to withdraw north of the DMZ, Mr. President, we will be able to do to them politically what they did to us after Laos.

NIXON: They invaded and retreated?

KISSINGER: They invaded and retreated. No one will care how many casualties.

NIXON: The North Vietnamese—the South Vietnamese have got to attack—

KISSINGER: And—

NIXON: —to drive them out.

KISSINGER: And if we get that done, then we must offer a negotiation fairly quickly after that. And then we may be out of the war before the end of the year.

NIXON: That's irrelevant. [unclear] Henry, getting out of the war before the end of the year doesn't make any difference from a political standpoint. If we're not out before the election, then I'll have [unclear]—

KISSINGER: That's what I mean—

NIXON: —can go on four years [unclear]—

KISSINGER: No, no. What I mean is before the election—

NIXON: —we can do the right thing—

KISSINGER: I mean before—

NIXON: We've got to. We've got to, in terms of before the election, the only thing that is going to do us any good is to do it in June, before the Democratic convention. That's when we have to have our big announcement, you know. That's why I say it. That's what we're talking about it here. So as to—it's the—the war is not the problem; it is the issue that is the problem. You see my point?

KISSINGER: Right.

NIXON: And the main thing is to have this battle now in B-1 [Front], where we kick the stuffing out of the bastards.

KISSINGER: So, that they can't come—

NIXON: And win one.

KISSINGER: And, so that they can't come back before the end of the year.

NIXON: That's right.

KISSINGER: But before the election —

NIXON: But I think that in terms of the — but I think that in terms of the negotiation, if this battle moves fairly fast, if there's any chance for it to move, if the weather breaks, my guess is that you'll have your negotiation quite soon.

KISSINGER: That's what I think.

NIXON: [unclear]

KISSINGER: That's what I think. That's exactly my opinion.

NIXON: When will the Warsaw thing be announced? [Nixon planned a stopover in Poland after the summit meeting with Brezhnev.]

KISSINGER: Well, that will take us a week to announce — five days. We've notified them today. We've notified State to notify Warsaw. Of course, it came in through Warsaw channels, not through State channels.

NIXON: Hang on.

KISSINGER: But the major thing is not to tell Laird he did right. Well, not to tell him he did wrong, either. Just have him forget about the past. The major thing is to get this battle won.

NIXON: Yeah.

"We just cannot play these games with the supremacy of the field commander."
April 4, 1972, 3:45 p.m.
Richard Nixon and Henry Kissinger
OVAL OFFICE

Nixon continued the theme of his earlier conversation with Kissinger in a late-afternoon meeting. The two doggedly tried to find a way to accelerate the massive show of force they'd planned. In many ways, they were typical civilians, quarterbacking from the sidelines, but the conversation ended with a dramatic first, as they voiced the opinion that Abrams would have to be removed as field commander in Vietnam.

• • •

NIXON: I have a feeling the weather is going to break. It's beginning to break here. [laughs] Not that that means anything halfway around the world, but in some ways it's bound to start to break, Henry.

KISSINGER: It's got to break.

NIXON: Huh?

KISSINGER: It's got to break —

NIXON: It's going to break —

KISSINGER: — and at any rate —

NIXON: — and then all hell will break loose out there.

KISSINGER: If we can get — I — I was talking to Haig. It really is unbelievable, Mr. President. Every single idea has come out of this office here or out of my office; I mean out of the White House —

NIXON: I know that.

KISSINGER: Nothing from Abrams, not one thought on what to do. He does this by the numbers. We have a computer out there.

NIXON: Who? Who? Who?

KISSINGER: Abrams.

NIXON: Oh! Yes, yes, yes. That's what I said to —

KISSINGER: Haig says, correctly, if he were out there he'd be flying over the battlefield and throw[ing] monkey wrenches out of the plane, on the theory that it would hit somebody.

NIXON: Yeah, that's what I mean. Why don't we just drop personnel bombs and figure that it's [unclear]? And I — well, coming back to my — the proposition I wanted to talk to you about, to be sure we understand that they are — the proposition that we — that our call should figure out where a line can be drawn.

KISSINGER: Yeah.

NIXON: And plan to get back to them. Now, incidentally, I noticed from the news summary that indicated that we have withdrawn from what they call sixteen bases [South Vietnamese forward support bases just south of the DMZ]. That's good. That's what they should do. They should get out of those sixteen bases, whatever it is.

KISSINGER: That's right.

NIXON: Now, if they feel that Quang Tri, or whatever it is, is significant and it's worth holding, hold it, but that I'd be in a position of giving up [unclear] — it's, it's — I'd rather them give up territory, win the battle. That is the way to fight battles.

KISSINGER: That's right.

NIXON: The Russians have won wars that way. The Germans have won 'em —

KISSINGER: That's right —

NIXON: The Brit — French. Christ, Napoleon didn't always attack. Huh? Not always.

KISSINGER: He almost always attacked.

NIXON: Well, he believed in the theory of attack, because he usually had smaller forces.

KISSINGER: Yeah.

NIXON: But on the other hand —

KISSINGER: Well, he was sometimes on the defensive —

NIXON: He'd do the sleight of hand now and then.

KISSINGER: Well, actually, his best campaign, which he lost, but it was a miracle that he fought it so long, was when he had sixty thousand against four hundred thousand, and he withdrew into France, and he threw his sixty thousand back and forth and was really defeating them. The trouble was, every time he defeated one of them, if he lost even five thousand men he was weakened to a point where he couldn't —

NIXON: And finally at Waterloo —

KISSINGER: — sustain it. But that was before Waterloo —

NIXON: Or the Battle of the Nations?

KISSINGER: No, he — at the Battle of the Nations they were still fairly even, but he had no cavalry left, so he lost that. Then, after he lost the Battle of the Nations he withdrew into France. The Austrians came in from the south, the Prussians and English came in from the north. He stood in the center and first defeated the Austrians, then he threw the whole army north against the Prussians. He beat the Prussians, then he moved back against the Austrians. And he was holding them off for six months with these lightning strikes.

NIXON: Yeah.

KISSINGER: But then the Austrians decided to hell with it and just formed a line and ground ahead. And so he — they didn't have their forces divided.

NIXON: Yeah.

KISSINGER: At Waterloo, well that was just screwed up. He nearly — he should have won Waterloo —

NIXON: He should have won. Well, anyway, that's a war of a different time, but basically it's like football. Strategy never changes with football or — you know what I mean? You — you give ground in the middle of the field, hold the line at the goal line, and then score a touchdown.

KISSINGER: Right.

NIXON: That's the way it's done.

KISSINGER: Yeah. I think if we can really get to work on them, Mr. President —

NIXON: I think that will —

KISSINGER: — if we —

NIXON: The point is, you see, Henry, this gives us one hell of an opportunity, an opportunity to really clobber them, something we've been wanting to do —

KISSINGER: Right.

NIXON: — and now, by God, they have walked into it.

KISSINGER: Right —

NIXON: They've just been hitting in the B-3 Front. We couldn't do it, but we can clobber them up and down over that DMZ —

KISSINGER: That's right.

NIXON: — like nobody's business.

KISSINGER: That is right. And I think we can just level that area south of the eighteenth parallel.

NIXON: Do you have any, any thoughts with regard to, to anything more? Now, just think a minute. We don't want to force anything. Anything more? If you — let me, let me suggest one thing that I had in mind that you might get. Rogers isn't going to have a press conference —

KISSINGER: No —

NIXON: — is he?

KISSINGER: No, no.

NIXON: Christ. He should. He should step up to the damn plate —

KISSINGER: Well, except he'd just —

NIXON: Yeah?

KISSINGER: — make it [unclear] —

NIXON: Right. One thing I would like for you to work out, to get out, maybe through State in their briefing tomorrow, is this: how much of the population is under the control, still, of Saigon? Do you know what I mean? Now, you know, when we talk about the losses and so forth and so on, I think it's just as well to keep the perspective a little clear. Would you — do you agree?

KISSINGER: Exactly. Actually —

NIXON: It must be eighty-five to ninety percent.

KISSINGER: Nelson [Rockefeller], incidentally, thinks that the public is on our side.

NIXON: Is it? [unclear] It doesn't make any difference. I wouldn't care if was ten percent on our side, because I don't know if they want to be doing it, and I know that at this point we cannot top this. You think of — I mean, I — as we said earlier, Henry, that we would weaken.

You wouldn't have a viable foreign policy for a reason when an asshole like Muskie, who knows better — McGovern, who doesn't know any better — but when Muskie says, in effect, "Don't react here. I hope we don't do anything precipitate." Henry, he's a guy that might be sitting in this chair. You realize —

KISSINGER: Mr. President —

NIXON: — that if we should lose here, that the United States will never again have a foreign policy? We don't go fight anyplace.

KISSINGER: Mr. President, if McGovern — if Muskie sat here — the worst is if Humphrey sat here. Let's take somebody who acts tougher. He wouldn't do anything. He would find excuses —

NIXON: Terrible.

KISSINGER: — to do nothing, and the whole thing would come apart. All it would take for you is to take a laissez-faire attitude and the Pentagon would be, in effect, doing what they did in Tet; just be paralyzed, not hit back.

NIXON: Is that what they did? Paralyzed?

KISSINGER: Absolutely. We are the ones that are energizing it out of here.

NIXON: I don't think they would have been hitting back or thinking. How — what would they have done had we not called them in and said get off your ass?

KISSINGER: If we had not called them in, they would have hit the SAMs in a belt of fifteen miles [a string of surface-to-air missile emplacements fifteen nautical miles north of the DMZ] —

NIXON: Right.

KISSINGER: — instead of forty-five. They would not have hit logistics installations. They would have limited it to three or four days. They would have kept a ceiling on sorties. They wouldn't — certainly not have sent additional planes out. They would have said publicly —

NIXON: They would not have sent them out —

KISSINGER: — that we are not going to reinforce, that the withdrawals continue. They would have done just enough to make us look impotent and not enough to do anything successful.

NIXON: One of the things about it, Henry, what we are doing has got to make us look — this point, as I'm sure you get out of that banged-up territory that we have, is that the South Vietnamese government isn't gone. Is it? But the point is —

KISSINGER: From this point it's not even under severe pressure yet.

NIXON: Right.

KISSINGER: I mean all the — [unclear] is in the northernmost province, the one that's closest — and Joe Alsop says, correctly, when a government puts its whole army on foreign soil and if it then doesn't win, this is an act of desperation. This is not — no longer an act of policy. And I tend to agree with him —

NIXON: I agree with him. I agree. I think this is one of those things that if [it] isn't the last gasp, they are supermen. They are not supermen.

KISSINGER: This is the last gasp, Mr. President. If we hold firm and if we scare the Russians enough, but for that we have to act ferociously, and I even wonder whether we shouldn't give a pop to Haiphong.

NIXON: Well again, where do you put it?

KISSINGER: Well, just bomb the goddamn town.

NIXON: All right.

KISSINGER: For twenty-four hours —

NIXON: We could do that. We could really do it. I'm perfectly willing.

KISSINGER: Let me look into that.

NIXON: All right. If there's anything you could hit in the Haiphong area, now let me say, anything that we could hit.

KISSINGER: Just level the goddamn docks.

NIXON: Well the point is, it depends whether ships are there, Henry, civilians and all that sort of thing.

KISSINGER: Yeah.

NIXON: Yeah. Understand, I'm for it. I'm — would you prefer to do that to mining?

KISSINGER: No. Mining would be better, but also that would get us —

NIXON: It would last longer —

KISSINGER: — a first-class crisis.

[pause]

NIXON: Well, let's think. Let's think. What will the pop to Haiphong do, Henry? Just think about it. I'm all for it. But understand, I, I thought that all through, though —

KISSINGER: Well, Mr. President —

NIXON: We're going to do the — we'll — I'm prepared to blockade —

KISSINGER: We have —

NIXON: — we're prepared to mine. I'm prepared to take out that railway to China —

KISSINGER: We have to nav — we have to navigate, Mr. President, if we're doing something that's spectacular and scares them —

NIXON: Yeah.

KISSINGER: — and something we can sustain.

NIXON: Yeah.

KISSINGER: If we bomb day after day — I've checked the military. They prefer to bomb day after day south of the eighteenth parallel than to make one massive effort and have to knock it off. And I think that makes sense, because that way they can work on the whole system —

NIXON: That's right.

KISSINGER: — and grind it down. And I think we — on the whole, I lean toward systematically grinding them down, and then giving them a big pop, and then knocking the whole thing off. By the end of the month — what I think is, by the end of the month, if we have broken their back in the eighteenth parallel, we could give them a big pop up north and then knock the whole thing off and say, "Now we've done it," if the mil[itary] — if the offensive has stopped by then.

[pause]

NIXON: I think the pop shouldn't come now. Think of it. What — what would it do? Let's just think if we did it now. What's it going to do to put the hellish pressure on the Russians? [pause] What do you think?

KISSINGER: Well, let me find out. Let me get some reconnaissance.

NIXON: Fine. Is there anything short of it? I mean is there anything in the Haiphong area you could hit? Something, understand, that'd be a shot across the bow? You know what I mean? That's what I'm thinking.

KISSINGER: Yeah.

NIXON: Just let 'em have one. More will be coming. In other words, with the bombing they inflicted, they have violated the so-called understanding.

KISSINGER: Right.

NIXON: Totally. They've done it other times, but this time it's for real. They came across the DMZ. Correct?

KISSINGER: Absolutely.

NIXON: Does anybody say that there was not an understanding about not violating the DMZ? Nobody. That's one thing. They may chat — they chatter about other understandings but this one there was. Correct?

KISSINGER: Yes, sir.

NIXON: All right. They violated it. All right, since the understanding is violated we ought to hit something in the North we haven't hit before. That's the thing I'm concerned about. That's why, you know, I felt hit the nineteenth parallel or whatever it is. But let's come again. Maybe the idea of hitting something in Haiphong is better. What would you do just with one shot? One —

KISSINGER: I think you could do it —

NIXON: — with one run?

KISSINGER: — with one, one shot. Just take out some docks because there the symbolism is more important than anything else.

NIXON: Let's see, you take out the docks, then you have great squeals from people here saying, "Don't bomb Haiphong." Right?

KISSINGER: That's right. And you'd certainly get a violent Chinese response. You'd certainly get a violent Russian response.

NIXON: Hmm. People respond when a friend hurts.

KISSINGER: That's right. But let me see what ships are in there.

[pause]

NIXON: Well, let's just let State do it at secretary level tomorrow, huh? I figure Bill [Rogers] wouldn't, wouldn't go on the damn thing. You know, goddamn it, though, it's really not fair. It's really not fair. You know, here we — here we are, Henry. Somebody ought to step up and say, "What can we do to help?" At least Mel is willing to do that.

• • •

KISSINGER: One thing we must do, Mr. President, just symbolically, is go in with B-52s north of the DMZ.

NIXON: Oh, I ordered it. Was there any — was there any question about that?

KISSINGER: Because that will be a signal to them —

NIXON: Well, that's what I mean. Let me say that, that's at least one shot across the bow that's cheap as hell.

KISSINGER: Right.

NIXON: Now, would you please put that down in —?

KISSINGER: Right.

NIXON: Can't we do that even tomorrow?

KISSINGER: Well, we have to suppress the SAMs first. We need a day of this, of working on the SAMs, and then we go in with the B-52s.

NIXON: All right. Can you find some of the extra targets up there?

KISSINGER: Yeah.

NIXON: Why not take Vinh out for example? Can we do that?

KISSINGER: [unclear] beyond that.

NIXON: Well, but boy, I mean, this is music to my ears. I've been pressing for it for a long time. Let's put some B-52s north of that, north of the DMZ.

KISSINGER: Correct.

NIXON: That tells them what's going to be coming. Doesn't it?

KISSINGER: Absolutely.

NIXON: It's a warning: "Look here, you knock this off or we're going to continue to move."

KISSINGER: Absolutely.

NIXON: We're also in a very good position. You realize all this bombing can be justified as being solely for military purposes?

KISSINGER: But this is the beauty of it. This is where they made their mistake. If they had struck in Kontum, all we could have done is two or three days. Now they've hit on the demilitarized zone and we're just not going to let go for a few weeks. And they — this is an act of desperation on their part. Now, Alsop told me that John Vann thinks, he's in correspondence with him, that, you know who he is —

NIXON: I know John Vann, yeah.

KISSINGER: — who's in charge of the Second of the B-3 area. He says our air attacks have so demoralized the North Vietnamese that they haven't been able to launch a concerted attack.

• • •

NIXON: Now that's a problem. It's supposed to rain tonight, but maybe it will rain and clear it up or make it worse.

KISSINGER: Oh, I think it's got to turn, Mr. President, because this is the time of the [unclear] —

NIXON: Goddamn it, it's got to turn. It's the same thing. You know, when it does turn what's going to happen?

KISSINGER: Well, when it does turn, you know, get out everything that flies —

NIXON: Huh?

KISSINGER: — then we're going to shore up what they got on the battlefield and we're going to hit north of the DMZ, and we're just going to clobber them.

[pause]

NIXON: Look, if it rains, if you get any — once you get another report on the weather, is there any point where we can keep hitting them?

KISSINGER: About eight o'clock tonight.

• • •

KISSINGER: At eight o'clock tonight.

NIXON: Do you get a report on the weather?

KISSINGER: Right.

NIXON: Who sends it to you?

KISSINGER: I check with the — Moorer calls Abrams. If — if this isn't fought more aggressively in another, by early next week, you might want to consider relieving Abrams. We just cannot play these games with the supremacy of the field commander. I know it's rough and brutal, but that guy just does it too much by the numbers.

NIXON: He's had it. Look, he's fat, he's drinking too much, and he's not able to do the job. I [unclear].

KISSINGER: He shouldn't be the one who said they've come up with all the ideas. There's one idea that's come that we've — that's been carried out this week that didn't —

NIXON: Can you call Moorer today saying I'm just waiting for those ideas he's supposed to get? Has he got some more? Incidentally, would you also ask Helms if he's got any with regard to any activities? Then I want you to tell Helms about the mining exercise.

KISSINGER: [unclear]

NIXON: Well, tell me about that and look into the Haiphong thing [unclear] —

KISSINGER: I'll have that looked at immediately.

• • •

NIXON: I've been trying to figure as to — we're sort of busy these days. Try and get the weather. Goddamn it, if any of you — if you know any prayers, say it for weather out there. Just get that weather cleared up over there. The bastards have never been bombed. [chuckles] They're going to be bombed this time. Of course, we've got to have weather.

"If . . . a Communist country . . . is allowed to take over a neighboring country . . . and is not stopped, then that tactic will be used all over the world."
April 10, 1972, 8:57 a.m.
Richard Nixon and Henry Kissinger
OVAL OFFICE

The fact that the North Vietnamese offensive was being strongly supported by Soviet arms placed Nixon's military response on potentially dangerous ground. It was a face-off that had been avoided throughout the war, because of fear of inciting war between the super-powers. Suddenly, the May summit and all other diplomatic initiatives were in jeopardy. Nixon didn't shrink from the line, though, or the implication that part of the reason the U.S. counteroffensive was building up so strongly was to send a message to the Soviets. The president discussed the situation with Kissinger, acknowledging that his strategy carried risks that could be global, as well as national. Later in the day, Nixon was with Dobrynin at a Washington function. The president made a short speech that included a pointed warning for the Soviet ambassador: "Every great power must follow the principle that it should not encourage directly or indirectly any other nation to use force or armed aggres-sion against one of its neighbors." Dobrynin was said to have been stone-faced throughout.

• • •

NIXON: You understand that we're going to have to face something else. As a result of this we'll get attacks. And, you know, one of the things that helped us in China was that we had good polls before we went. We'll get attacks. We will suffer in public opinion. And that will hurt us on our Russian thing.

KISSINGER: No it won't.

NIXON: I know it's just a small thing. On the other hand, we — It doesn't make a hell of a lot of difference due to the fact that, as far as I am concerned, by the time the Russian summit comes off, we will know how this thing has come off one way or another. And if we've lost, the hell with it. If we win in Vietnam, I don't give a damn what the polls show.

KISSINGER: Mr. President.

NIXON: The Russian summit [unclear] —

KISSINGER: We are facing —

NIXON: I'm just pointing out what, that's the argument that Haldeman made to you.

KISSINGER: I know. But polls won't help you in Russia; only geopolitics will. The fact is, if this succeeds, that Soviet arms will have overturned the balance on the Indian subcontinent and will have run us out of Southeast Asia; I don't care what your polls show.

• • •

NIXON: If, for example, a Communist country with the support, or any country with the support of Soviet arms is allowed to take over a neighboring country, to conquer a neighboring country, and is not stopped, then that tactic will be used all over the world. It will be used in the Mideast. It will be used in the Americas. It could even be used in Europe. Therefore, what we are talking about is the critical time, you know, to stop. Now that's what this game is about. You see the crap that Safire and all the rest of these people write, it's all too, it doesn't go to the heart; the State stuff has never gone to the heart of it. As Haig was saying to me yesterday, when I was talking to him along these lines. He said, "The difficulty is you're the first one that's been president since this goddamn war started, who has seen it in the correct sense of its being, of the Russian role. You see," he said, "they all took the Harriman line, that the Russians —" I remember Lodge. Henry, I was in Vietnam seven different times, since — more than you were, as a matter of fact.

KISSINGER: I know. Much more.

NIXON: Lodge was there five of those different times and on five different occasions. And on the other case, the other occasion, Taylor told me; and on the other occasion, this fellow Porter told me because it was the line. He told me, "Now the Russians really don't want this. The Russians really want peace out here. The Russians don't want the Chinese to move Vietnam." I think that's all bullshit. I think the Russians — it isn't a question that the Russians aren't thinking that much. The Russians just want to win. They are supporting them and they'll go as far as they can go.

The difficult — and that's what the Indian thing showed us. I mean, the reason that Rogers and all those State Department people made the mistake on India, Henry, was that they did not see, properly estimate what the Russians want to do. The Russians were willing to take great risks to knock over Pakistan and support India because it [unclear] around the world. The Russians are doing that everyplace. That's what was involved in Jordan. It was a Russian move, not a Syrian move.

You knew that; I knew it. And this is a Russian move. Now what I'm really getting down, I've talked around a lot. If that point were to be made, you're goddamn right. It would shake them to their eyeteeth. And that might mobilize American public opinion.

KISSINGER: Mr. President.

NIXON: You see my point?

KISSINGER: I believe it's premature to do this now.

NIXON: You agree with my analysis?

KISSINGER: I agree completely with your analysis.

"We always run the risk of blowing the whole thing."
April 13, 1972, 2:16 p.m.
Richard Nixon and Henry Kissinger
EXECUTIVE OFFICE BUILDING

The renewed air war over North Vietnam undoubtedly caught the attention of Brezhnev and the Soviet leadership. The question for Nixon and Kissinger was how to maintain that interest without allowing the situation to backfire. Kissinger did most of the talking as the two considered possibilities, one of which was to try to exploit Soviet self-interest in finding an end to the Vietnam War. That vein of negotiation had been suggested first by Averell Harriman, ambassador at large during the Johnson administration, on his return from meetings in Moscow in 1965. The seminal point, which Harriman gleaned and Nixon remembered, was that "the Russians did not think the war would be in their best interests in the long run," according to an account in the New York Times.

• • •

KISSINGER: I had another talk —

NIXON: Right.

KISSINGER: — with Dobrynin.

NIXON: Another talk?

KISSINGER: He came in and said he's already got a message back from Moscow saying that it's very important I should come.

NIXON: Right.

KISSINGER: They want me to come.

NIXON: Did you give him the answer then today and say it was okay?

KISSINGER: I said you were not yet back, but I would give him the final answer. I just thought that we should —

NIXON: Right.

KISSINGER: — wait for —

NIXON: Right. I'm waiting. Right.

KISSINGER: Vietnam will be agenda item number one. And therefore they request that I get there a day earlier than I had suggested. And also they said the Vietnamese delegation for their talk with me is coming through Moscow on Sunday [April 23]. And they want to have completed their talks on Vietnam with me before Sunday.

• • •

KISSINGER: Now, one thing Dobrynin told me is that as of Tuesday night [April 11] the North Vietnamese were still coming on the twenty-fourth. And —

NIXON: Yeah. Well —

KISSINGER: Well, but that's, they made three conditions: that we come on the thirteenth; the twentieth, the plenary session; and that we stop the bombing of the North. We have not met any of these conditions. If they come under those circumstances, that in itself is an unbelievable confession of weakness.

NIXON: I agree.

KISSINGER: Secondly, if they come after I've been in Moscow — and he told me that Moscow [unclear] my going there — which is fine. They won't leak it; they have no interest.

NIXON: We don't care about the leak.

KISSINGER: But after that visit, now what Dobrynin said to me — you know, it's a very different cycle now. None of this —

NIXON: I know he gets to the cold points. I know.

KISSINGER: It's now as cold — now, it's like your conversation —

NIXON: [unclear]

KISSINGER: — at the time you were building up the [unclear]. None of this baloney about what are we doing to us, how does this —

NIXON: Well he comes in and says, "My government [unclear] that." And then he talks just like it's straight out of the horse's mouth.

KISSINGER: He says, "Look, we have this problem. Our national interest is against what's going on in Vietnam now." He also —

NIXON: Yeah, they've been saying that. That's the Harriman line.

KISSINGER: Well, yeah, but not — no, there's been no reply like this.

NIXON: I know, I know. But, you know, that's, that is the Harriman line. Go ahead.

KISSINGER: No, but —

NIXON: [unclear]

KISSINGER: No, their line used to be that we were ruining the possibility of good relations with them.

NIXON: Oh, I get it. Go ahead. But whatever it is —

KISSINGER: He was saying their national interests. On the other hand, he said we shouldn't push them in a position where they seem to be selling out.

NIXON: Right.

KISSINGER: But, he said, "Let's be realists. What do you want?" I said, "We want an end of military operations. That's the minimum. We are not going to sit there and talk and get ourselves chopped up over a period of months. We've now got our forces together out there and we're going to use them." He said, "Can you, is that an irrevocable decision against us?" I said, "We will do what is necessary but the war in Vietnam must stop." He said, "If we give, get you a guarantee that military action stops for a year, is that satisfactory?" Mr. President, frankly —

NIXON: If he needs it. Did you tell him that?

KISSINGER: If these guys after this attack —

NIXON: Well, the point is that you could have a truce for the purpose of talks. That's what I have in mind. But go ahead.

KISSINGER: Well but we may even get peace, that's why I don't want to —

NIXON: Yeah, but don't give it away. Oh I know.

KISSINGER: Don't give it away yet. But, if after cranking up this operation, they stop — I said, "Now the first thing, you have to remember, Anatol, is we don't believe a word Hanoi says. So Hanoi can offer us anything but you, you've got to guarantee it publicly before we can even con — before I can even take it to the president. Because the president is in such a mood now that if I come to him and say Hanoi promises something he will throw me out of the room."

NIXON: Good. What'd he say? Does he believe you?

KISSINGER: Oh, yes.

· · ·

KISSINGER: So he said, "Are you prepared to do this?" He said, "If we get military operations stopped, are you prepared to say to the North Vietnamese you have proposed a coalition government, we've proposed an election; we're willing to talk whether a compromise is possible between these two positions?" Talk about a compromise we can do, Mr. President.

NIXON: Sure.

KISSINGER: If they stop military operations for a year, they're finished.

NIXON: [unclear]

KISSINGER: Because that would be interpreted all over Vietnam as a massive defeat for Hanoi.

NIXON: Right.

KISSINGER: Then he said, "Well, what about this limitation of military aid if both of us agree?" I said, "All of your allies would have to agree too. We can't let you send stuff in through Czechoslovakia."

NIXON: And your allies, the Chinese, have to agree too.

KISSINGER: Well —

NIXON: [laughs]

KISSINGER: All I'm trying to say, Mr. President, is — you remember how many years we tried and they wouldn't even communicate our messages —

NIXON: I know.

KISSINGER: — to Hanoi.

NIXON: I know.

KISSINGER: He tells me they're in active daily contact. He says, Vietnam is agenda item number one when I get there. He says —

NIXON: When you get there?

KISSINGER: When I get there —

NIXON: Oh yeah. Hell yes.

KISSINGER: But they're trying to get the goddamn thing — they're not saying, "If you blockade, you'll be in a confrontation with us."

NIXON: Well, I hope that he doesn't feel, though, that he doesn't come out with a coalition government concession from you.

KISSINGER: There's no chance of it, Mr. President. What he's looking for, as I understand it, is some face-saving formula that enables them to stop the war for a time —

NIXON: Yeah.

KISSINGER: — in which we are committed to talk about something and they are committed to stop fighting. We will have achieved — if they stop fighting, Mr. President, it will be a bigger victory by far than the Cuban Missile Crisis. The Russians will believe that if Hanoi wins that's good for us, for them because it weakens us; and if Hanoi loses, it's good for them because it increases Hanoi's dependence on them. So the southern battle they don't mind. What's panicking the Russians is that we will blockade or that we will so tear up North Vietnam that they will be forced to put in something in an area in which they have nothing to gain. And, therefore, risky as it is, we've got them to where we are in this game by running enormous risks.

NIXON: The Chinese raise hell about it. That's what I would do.

KISSINGER: Well they'll all raise hell about it. I've already told Dobrynin we're going to do something intensified. And he said, "Well, must you do it?" I said, "Yeah." He said, "Well, as long as [unclear] but it won't be a good [unclear]."

NIXON: [unclear]

KISSINGER: The point is, Mr. President, the extent of the damage.

NIXON: Yeah.

KISSINGER: We don't have to do it. But I think showing that we keep coming, that this thing is going to get worse and worse is helpful.

NIXON: [unclear] in my view — and of course we always run the risk of blowing the whole thing. [unclear]

KISSINGER: Mr. President, I cannot believe that. I believe that the only thing that can blow this is if we blink now.

• • •

KISSINGER: What we have to show the Russians is that they are jeopardizing this sort of cooperation by horsing around in Vietnam. Christ, we didn't lose any Americans. The Cuban Missile [Crisis] didn't involve Americans; it involved a bunch of damn Cubans. Let's look at it another way. Supposing tomorrow morning Hanoi publicly said to you, "We are willing to make a compromise on the political thing, are you willing to talk about a compromise without making a proposal?" We've got to say, "Yes, we'll talk about it."

NIXON: Basically what we'll have here is a bombing halt with, with action on their side rather than an understanding.

KISSINGER: But the ball is on their side.

NIXON: On both sides.

"And then I could bow out."

April 15, 1972, 1:00 p.m.
Richard Nixon and Henry Kissinger
EXECUTIVE OFFICE BUILDING

Secret peace talks regarding Vietnam had been scheduled for April 24, involving only Kissinger for the United States and Le Duc Tho for the North Vietnamese. On the afternoon of the fifteenth, however, North Vietnam withdrew from the scheduled meeting. After that, the two couldn't even agree on who was to blame for the cancellation of the meeting, let alone on a path to peace. The combination of military and diplomatic battles made Nixon wobble on the advisability of sending Kissinger to Moscow in advance of the summit. As he continued his conjecture, the president explored the possibility of bowing out of the presidential election.

• • •

NIXON: Now, let's talk about the blockade a moment because that fits into what you say here.

KISSINGER: Right.

NIXON: It might provide another way to go [unclear]. Let me tell you about the blockade. In my view, if we're going to do it, we got to do it very soon or we will not have the support for it.

KISSINGER: I agree.

NIXON: And that support runs out as time goes on. In fact, we probably should have done it this week, you know. I'm just saying, I'm just saying, I'm speaking in terms of having public support in the United States.

KISSINGER: Right.

NIXON: The support can run out. If the blockade comes at a time that disaster is impending in the South, and people know it, or when riots are going on here, then it looks like an act of desperation. But if we can move before either of those things happen, then we might have a great deal of public support for it — for a while. You see that's my reasoning for doing it sooner rather than later.

KISSINGER: Right. I agree.

NIXON: The second point is that that could be an argument for your going to the Soviet even though there's no meeting on the twenty-fourth. The idea being that you go [unclear] with the condition that the primary subject for discussion is Vietnam.

Unless there's something positive, tangible to offer that the president is going to take action. And at that time, you would tell them —

KISSINGER: I wouldn't tell them what action is planned [unclear] —

NIXON: [There will] be strong action. It will not be directed against you.

KISSINGER: The way to do that if I play out that scenario.

NIXON: All right, let's play that out.

KISSINGER: As I thought of it — it was one of the things I had in mind.

NIXON: Yeah.

KISSINGER: What I would say then is, "Vietnam is, must be the first agenda item. There must be concrete progress on this."

NIXON: Yeah.

KISSINGER: If there is no concrete progress on it, I would refuse to go on to summit agenda items.

NIXON: Right. Right.

KISSINGER: If there is concrete progress on it, I would be entitled — empowered to discuss summit agenda items.

NIXON: Yeah. Right.

KISSINGER: But the progress cannot be an agreement to talk.

NIXON: Yeah. [unclear]

KISSINGER: And it must be a precise description of how the war will come to an end.

NIXON: How the war will come to an end. Yeah. Yeah. Not just an agreement that they will deliver the South Viet — the North Vietnamese to a meeting. That isn't going to work.

KISSINGER: Right, that's not going to work.

NIXON: Second point.

KISSINGER: It will slightly affect the message we send to them [the Soviets] this afternoon, Mr. President.

NIXON: That's what I'm thinking. The second point is —

KISSINGER: It also has the advantage vis-à-vis our domestic opinion. That we have gone absolutely the extra mile.

NIXON: Sure. Yeah. Well, that brings me to the second point: the reason for your going. Put on that basis, then you go. [unclear] have to figure that you've got to look at the hard place, which would be that if we don't get anything on Vietnam, except, you know, discussion or something of that sort and the South Vietnamese fold whether we really can still go to the summit. We're going to have to make, we're going to have to make an evaluation. It may be, it may be, that we may still go. In other words, let me put it this way. As I look at going to the summit, Henry, we cannot go — there are two extremes — we cannot go if the South Vietnamese are on the rocks.

KISSINGER: Impossible.

NIXON: We could go, we could go, and I'll make this concession, if the situation is still in flux, with the understanding that we will discuss it at the summit and something is going to come out of it at the summit. But there's our problem there. Now, the point that I make is that you're going — they want the summit. They want it badly. And you're going to of course hold over their heads the — I don't know if the blockade is going to worry them, but the German thing is. And it's been a [unclear] thing but I'll sink that without any question. We'll just tell Barzel and the Russians now we're against it. Do you agree?

KISSINGER: Right.

NIXON: Now —

KISSINGER: But that means we have to get across it soon.

NIXON: That's right.

KISSINGER: [unclear] I told them May 4.

NIXON: [That's] another reason for going. [unclear] So as distinguished from this morning [unclear] I'm inclined to think that probably [our] message to them should be that, in view of this, the president has now changed [his] opinion. The directions are corrected as follows. That —

KISSINGER: I should say this. [unclear]

NIXON: Yeah.

KISSINGER: [unclear] they have turned us down now for the twenty-fourth.

NIXON: Right.

KISSINGER: The —

NIXON: Would you tell them about this rigmarole with Porter?

KISSINGER: Well, then there's the point that, look, they've turned us down for April 24, which means they absolutely cannot deliver them — which raises then serious questions about the utility of my trip to Moscow. I should be very tough. Secondly, the president had turned down originally a meeting in Moscow simply to prepare the summit for reasons that he has explained to Dobrynin. [The reason that I'm] now going to Moscow is [unclear] to discuss Vietnam and in connection with that [I] also would be authorized to discuss the summit. Now we have offered the South Vietnamese, the North Vietnamese a meeting again [unclear] for the twenty-fourth, with a promise of coming on the twenty-seventh.

NIXON: And an announcement.

KISSINGER: And we are prepared to make that announcement before the twenty-fourth. Secondly, we have to have a clear understanding before I come to Moscow that some concrete progress will be made towards a rapid end of the Vietnam War. And before the president can give his final approval to my trip, he would like to hear the Soviet response to this [message].

NIXON: Right. [And we need a] response immediately [because you've got to make your plans].

KISSINGER: That's right.

• • •

After discussing the details on the ground, the two men considered the global implications of their military options in Vietnam.

KISSINGER: And another problem, Mr. President. The Russians have two reasons why they don't want this. One is it would drive, it would force them into a confrontation with us.

NIXON: Yeah.

KISSINGER: Second is, it would force Hanoi towards Beijing. Because the only way that Hanoi could possibly be supplied is for Beijing to supply the —

NIXON: Yeah. Yeah. And of course, well then that brings me to the point, the effect. The effect would be for Beijing to have to get more deeply involved in the war, or get the hell out of the blockade.

KISSINGER: Right.

NIXON: The effect also is it will brake our China initiative. The effect — huh?

KISSINGER: [It will] be tough on our China initiative.

NIXON: Yeah. What would it do to the Russian initiative? If the Russians call off the summit, we blockade, [unclear] here you would, you would have — what we're doing is we're making ourselves hostage, putting it quite brutally, to the Soviet on Vietnam. On the other hand, the alternative is that the Soviet initiative and the China initiative [unclear] all that hangs on, isn't going to be worth a hell of a lot if Vietnam goes down the tubes. So —

KISSINGER: If it doesn't go —

NIXON: We have no other choice.

KISSINGER: If it doesn't it would be the result of strength. You see what the Soviets want from us on the summit is in effect to screw us. Now, I know we're doing it because of long-term interests and all of that.

NIXON: I know.

KISSINGER: But after what we've done to Taiwan, Israel, Vietnam [unclear] it's just not — then this policy that Trudeau described of throwing our weight to one side or the other. It doesn't work because we won't have any weight to throw.

NIXON: If the Russians don't come up with anything here, we have no choice but to blockade. I really have no doubt about it.

KISSINGER: [unclear] recognition, Mr. President, that [unclear].

NIXON: Unless the battle in South Vietnam just goes a hell of lot better than we think it will. [unclear]

KISSINGER: That's right.

NIXON: It could.

KISSINGER: It could.

NIXON: [unclear] could be wrong, do you see what I mean? The forces of opposition in this country and around the world will begin to build next week. If they build too great, the blockade then comes at the wrong time. The blockade could come right

now. We could do it tomorrow. If we, you know, if we see, you know, action, we
always say, stops the [unclear] debate — for a while. That's why I'm just wondering
whether or not maybe our option isn't to blockade now.

KISSINGER: Well, Mr. President, with that people are just not — first of all we have to
play the Russian string out here a bit.

NIXON: Fine.

KISSINGER: I'll say this for the Russians. They are bloody-minded sons of bitches. But
Hanoi hasn't fought for thirty-five years in order to be pushed around by the Russians either. So we have the problem that we must let Soviet pressure on Hanoi begin
to operate, and we must bring home to the Soviet Union that you are really deadly
serious about this. [unclear] And then we've got to give them some time. But not a
hell of a lot of time.

NIXON: Well, I'm just saying, the blockade option is going to run out, Henry.

KISSINGER: Two weeks.

NIXON: I'm afraid —

KISSINGER: We have to do it, if we do it, by the middle of —

NIXON: I'm afraid because I, I'm afraid basically our domestic support for a blockade,
which is — I don't give a shit about the foreign support — but our domestic support
for a blockade might erode in two weeks.

KISSINGER: Incidentally, I'm strongly in favor — I didn't want to leave, leave the wrong
impression — any group that calls for [unclear] I'd be strongly in favor of.

NIXON: Well, we're going to try. [unclear]

KISSINGER: You see if I go to Moscow, it's a hell of a — that's one of these confusing
moves again.

NIXON: I know.

KISSINGER: [unclear] the Communist groups would start screaming at us while I'm
in Moscow.

NIXON: I know the [unclear] will know you're in Moscow.

KISSINGER: Well, if the Communists [unclear], the Germans won't get their peace
treaty.

NIXON: We may have to reveal the Moscow trip, though, if you go. [unclear] I'd just
reveal it, and say, "Now, Dr. Kissinger went to Moscow at their suggestion and it
didn't do a damn thing. Under the circumstances, I'm calling off the Russian summit and I'm blockading." I wouldn't let them call off the summit. That's my point.
Do you agree or not?

KISSINGER: I agree completely. I would list all the sins.

NIXON: Right. They're furnishing arms, they're doing this, they didn't help. We're not
going to have it. A hell of a lot of people would support calling off that summit. We're
ready to talk tough.

KISSINGER: [unclear] give them all the initiative. I don't think they'll let it get to that
point.

NIXON: Well, based on your conversations this past week —

KISSINGER: And Dobrynin is not [unclear].

NIXON: Not on this.

KISSINGER: Not on anything. I mean, he may say things that aren't true but they never said [unclear].

NIXON: Did you lie, [unclear]?

KISSINGER: No.

NIXON: I'm inclined to think, Henry, you ought to take the trip to Moscow. Couch the message in a way that you go.

KISSINGER: Okay.

NIXON: I'm changing my view on that.

KISSINGER: If you are inclined [unclear] that I would go to Moscow, then I have to couch the message somewhat less aggressively, because then I don't want to put ourselves in the position — I'd still have to say —

NIXON: Say that you're coming to Moscow on the condition the president has the clear understanding — what I would say, a clear understanding that Vietnam will be the first thing, first item of the agenda and unless progress is made on that you're not prepared to discuss the other items. I think you can say that.

KISSINGER: That's right. And I'd have to say that [unclear] understanding that this is one last effort.

NIXON: That's right. You see what I mean? I'm sure that you could go to Moscow on that basis. Then they know they've got to fish or cut bait on Vietnam or you're not going to discuss the summit. They aren't going to — they're going to want you to come.

KISSINGER: Oh, yeah. That I can do. But the question is do I tell them you must come back with an answer by Monday that tells us how we're going to make progress? Or is it enough to say [unclear]?

NIXON: They won't be ready.

KISSINGER: That's my concern.

NIXON: They won't be ready — I wouldn't tell them that. I mean, I — look —

KISSINGER: I would say do you agree with this understanding. This I can say.

NIXON: Yeah. There must be an understanding, and that there's not just to be a discussion, but they are to have a proposal at that time, which we can — a solid proposal — to discuss. That is our understanding; that's the basis. That lacking such a proposal you will return to Washington immediately without any further discussion as far as summit matters are concerned. [unclear] Well, in other words, you are giving them the fact that they don't have to tell you that something on Monday, they presented to you on Thursday. You're there. And if you don't get it, you get the hell out of there.

KISSINGER: Let me write something out.

NIXON: Does that sound like a good deal to you?

KISSINGER: Right. It sounds fine. And I should — I think ought to write it out because this is an important message, Mr. President.

NIXON: Oh, I know.

KISSINGER: [unclear] — I myself, my first instinct was that, playing it cold-bloodedly, what we get out of the trip is more than they get out of it.

NIXON: Right. I agree. That's right.

KISSINGER: I mean the worst is they're suckering me along.

NIXON: That's right.

KISSINGER: And telling me nothing. But they have —

NIXON: We have then gone the extra mile.

KISSINGER: Then we've gone to Moscow.

NIXON: We've gone the extra mile.

KISSINGER: And then all the little shitheads here —

NIXON: Yeah.

KISSINGER: — who say, "The man doesn't want to negotiate."

NIXON: Yeah.

KISSINGER: Hell, you have me in Moscow.

NIXON: That's right.

KISSINGER: Then you surface my talk with Gromyko last September. All the overtures we've made through Moscow, because then we don't give a damn.

NIXON: Right.

KISSINGER: And —

NIXON: Surface the Moscow overtures.

KISSINGER: And —

NIXON: And then on the basis of that —

KISSINGER: If we lose, we —

NIXON: On the basis of that — we then have the basis for a very strong case for the blockade.

KISSINGER: That's right. And if we don't want a blockade then just use the Moscow trip for —

NIXON: For the purpose of flushing the summit?

KISSINGER: Well, for the purpose —

NIXON: Of what?

KISSINGER: I mean, supposing you then, supposing —

NIXON: You see, here is the question. Is there any way that we can — we just got to look at all of our cards here. Let me say, you have to realize, we have to realize that there's a lot more on the line here than simply a trip to Moscow, I mean, the war in Vietnam and so forth. Because then I've got to do some heavy, a lot of heavy thinking as to how we can do something about trying to get a candidate in this presidential race. [unclear]

KISSINGER: [You mean] who can be a candidate?

NIXON: [unclear] You get somebody else.

KISSINGER: Why?

NIXON: Because, you have to realize, you have to realize that the position that we have, if we fail, which we could well fail on all fronts, you know, the summit is canceled and the blockade does not succeed — you understand that we're putting everything on the line. That's my point.

KISSINGER: But, there's one other possibility, Mr. President. And this is another reason for going to Moscow. If I don't go to Moscow, then your time is foreshortened. If I do go to Moscow, we have the excuse that I'm going to Moscow and that is why we're not doing more right away.

NIXON: Doing more what? You mean bombing?

KISSINGER: Like blockade. If we don't start blockading by the end of the week —

NIXON: Yeah.

KISSINGER: — without my going to Moscow, the question is why the hell not?

NIXON: Yeah. In other words —

KISSINGER: I'm now looking at all things —

NIXON: Yeah, from the standpoint of the Russians.

KISSINGER: From the standpoint —

NIXON: It means we're not ferocious. If you're in Moscow, it buys time, I agree. Now understand that doesn't help us on this domestic front. This domestic —

KISSINGER: No, no, but I'm back then [unclear]. We've talked about the possibility of canceling the trip and going to a blockade.

NIXON: Yeah.

KISSINGER: Now, there are other variations on this. There is the variation that having been in Moscow, if the South Vietnamese fold, then we might still decide to bomb the shit out of them in the North and go to Moscow. Because if we can break —

NIXON: And not blockade.

KISSINGER: And not blockade.

NIXON: My — on reconsideration I think the Moscow trip ought to be on. It helps the message in a way that, you agree to go and they'll figure that they can sucker us in one way or another. But we're going to be awfully hard to sucker.

• • •

NIXON: If there is a way really, Henry, to not allow Vietnam to sink the Soviet summit — that's what I'm thinking about. If we can, we ought not to do it, having in mind the fact that the Soviet — let's face it. And here we look at the other side of it. If we can find a graceful way to let Thieu down the tubes, then maybe we'll just have to die and live to fight another day — if we fight like hell before it happens. My point is — you see my point? But, on the other hand, if there is no graceful way then the summit goes out the window. That's the problem here we're confronted with.

KISSINGER: It's our long-term position as a people. It's —

NIXON: That's why I — well, understand, I'm only putting it up as what to me is a totally rhetorical matter. In my view, there is no graceful way you can let him go. Remember, you always say, let him go or something. How the Christ can you do it?

KISSINGER: Exactly. It never was good. It never was —

NIXON: It would never work. It was never right.

KISSINGER: Well some of it was a fleeting chance.

NIXON: Yeah. But now, I think what we have to do is this. I think what I have to do is to say in effect that we're going to, everything is on the line. Let them cancel the summit — we have to realize that if the Russians cancel the summit or, as a matter of fact, if we cancel the summit because of the blockade, we are virtually assuring the certainty of a Democratic win unless I can find a way to — and I have been thinking about this too — of trying to move one of the other Republicans and there's only — well when you come down to it, you've got Rockefeller, who probably couldn't get the nomination. You've got Reagan, who could.

KISSINGER: Yeah.

NIXON: He couldn't do — another possibility, which never would have occurred to you, would be [Warren] Burger, who has been suggested. And the other one, and this is really the only long shot that just might pull the plug on the whole bunch, and help you get the whole South, is that I could have a talk with Connally before all this began. You know, and I'd say, "Now look here, you've got to change your party." And then I could bow out —

KISSINGER: There's no way —

NIXON: — and endorse Connally. And then Connally — I mean with what I had to go through — Connally without the scars could go on and win it.

KISSINGER: Mr. President —

NIXON: You see, there's your problem. But the point is, we have to realize that, we have to realize that if we lose Vietnam and the summit, there's no way that the election can be saved.

KISSINGER: Mr. President, they are —

NIXON: That's the problem.

KISSINGER: Mr. President, there's no way we can permit the Vietnamese to destroy two presidents. That can't be permitted. Secondly —

NIXON: I don't know how you can avoid it. Maybe, you see, the blockade might work. That's my point.

KISSINGER: Secondly, there is no realistic alternative to you. Thirdly —

NIXON: Except Connally.

KISSINGER: No. In foreign policy —

NIXON: Well I know.

KISSINGER: That's the main thing.

NIXON: Well, not really, Henry.

KISSINGER: In all humility, Mr. —

NIXON: You see it's something that you could be around with any of these people.

KISSINGER: I think—

NIXON: The only one you couldn't handle would be Reagan. I think he's too much of a lightweight.

KISSINGER: Mr. President—

NIXON: You could handle Rockefeller. You could handle Burger.

KISSINGER: Mr. President—

NIXON: You could—

KISSINGER: It's very hard policy if one has worked as closely with a president as I have with you, to work in a similar position with his successor. That I would never do, under no circumstances. And after—

NIXON: Well, then you realize what we look at. We're looking at Muskie, Humphrey, or Teddy. It's as cold as that. As president. That you see is, that's why so much rides on this damn thing. Now you come around to this proposition that—

KISSINGER: Absolutely.

NIXON: — maybe the Soviets — well look, my point is if we can we've got to handle this way to save the Soviet summit and mitigate Vietnam. What I'm getting at is that, I don't mean to sink Thieu. But I, if you get — do you see what I'm getting at?

KISSINGER: You see I don't think there's a way anymore of mitigating Vietnam, Mr. President, because we'll either win or lose. I think your first analysis was right.

NIXON: Yeah.

KISSINGER: If we lose, it doesn't matter how softly we've played it.

NIXON: Yeah. If we lose then we're out.

KISSINGER: Well then you'd be under such violent domestic opposition.

NIXON: Right.

KISSINGER: And you'd be under murderous pressure at the summit.

NIXON: That's right.

KISSINGER: If you win, now if — I think a blockade ought to be —

NIXON: You think the blockade is going to help?

KISSINGER: No. I think, Mr. President, we, as far as anybody else is concerned, you must give the impression of being on the verge of going crazy.

NIXON: Oh, absolutely. I've got everybody so scared then. Go berserk. Worry them. Why not [unclear]?

KISSINGER: With all respect, you must forget any doubts of anyone — between you and me I think a blockade should be very, very carefully considered.

NIXON: I agree. And after you [unclear] —

KISSINGER: But very prayerfully considered — I mean we shouldn't do it lightly. But I would like in Russia to act as if you just did not give a damn.

NIXON: That's true. That's the way I feel.

KISSINGER: I would like to leave the impression —

NIXON: Yeah.

KISSINGER: — that the hell with the summit; you'll go to, you're impressed by the Wallace vote.

NIXON: That's right.

KISSINGER: You're going to go to the solid South. You're going to go on an anti-Communist kick and by God you've had enough. That's what I've been telling Dobrynin.

NIXON: That's right.

KISSINGER: Now, I — in all of history, the Russians have always backed off when we've [unclear].

NIXON: Yeah, but I know. The Russians can back off but there's nothing — the North Vietnamese might not.

KISSINGER: Well, that is true. But if we can get the Russians to back off, then the question is can we buy the [unclear].

NIXON: Right.

KISSINGER: Even for my own selfish reasons. I'm not eager — we'd both be [unclear] in an unbelievable way.

NIXON: Yeah.

KISSINGER: And all the reputation that has been achieved for great foreign policy would be —

NIXON: Sure. Down the drain, we know that.

KISSINGER: So I have not as much of a stake but also —

NIXON: I know.

KISSINGER: — a stake in not having what I've worked on [unclear] —

NIXON: To go to Russia. I know. I know that. I know that. But we've got to play the Russian card out. I think that's why you have to go, Henry. So write your message that way.

KISSINGER: Let me write the message and bring it back.

NIXON: [unclear] but I think that what I want — what I'm really trying to tell you is that I am prepared to go all the way. And that I am prepared to take all the consequences. But, and that means that you have the blockade as a card to play over there. You may not play it there. But I mean, you see if you know that's going to come, you could be a hell of lot tougher than if you know it isn't going to come.

KISSINGER: Right.

NIXON: If they think we've turned the last screw, there ain't much more to be done.

KISSINGER: You see we may not want to do a blockade; we may just bomb Haiphong [unclear]. In that case —

NIXON: Why would we do that?

KISSINGER: Block every port. We just start bombing every port. So that it's unusable. And then —

NIXON: Why is it better to bomb them?

KISSINGER: Because then the Russian ships will come in.

NIXON: Now, they just hide them outside?

KISSINGER: And we're not challenging the Russians directly.

NIXON: You mean, bomb on the ship front and the harbor? Is that what you mean?

KISSINGER: No, just bomb the bridges. They had it pretty well cut off. [unclear]

NIXON: All right.

KISSINGER: Well, and it takes longer to do that.

"The foreign policy of the United States will not be viable if we're run out of Vietnam. That's all there is to it."

April 17, 1972, 8:58 a.m.

Richard Nixon and Henry Kissinger

OVAL OFFICE

The stakes in Nixon's escalating war effort soared on April 17, when American bombers attacked greater Hanoi and Haiphong harbor for the first time since the Johnson administration. Meanwhile, navy ships — including five aircraft carriers — congregated at Yankee Station, an area in the Bay of Tonkin that was close enough to North Vietnam for action by air or water. Nixon's aggressive show of strength was a challenge to both the North Vietnamese and the Soviets. In the attack on Haiphong harbor, a Soviet ship was damaged, giving Moscow a reason to retaliate. It didn't, but the pressure on Nixon was enormous. Feeling as though he was further and further out on a very dangerous limb, he once again talked about leaving office.

• • •

KISSINGER: Good morning, Mr. President.

NIXON: Hi.

KISSINGER: We had another cable from Haig. It says, "Obviously the fat is on the fire at your end. We will need the coolest of nerves from here on in. From my perspective it is essential that we continue to play our hand with the utmost calm and confidence. As you know several occasions in the past have involved similar risk taking although there has been less opportunity for events to be influenced by spasms of uncertainty on the domestic scene. On balance the military situation here is now well under control. As I reported yesterday, in the near term the enemy will only suffer severe setbacks." And then the rest is all technical stuff. And he's discussed with Abrams this idea of a troop withdrawal of twenty thousand, of an announcement, which would get us down to five [thousand] by July 3, which would get us down to, to where we could say that we've withdrawn five hundred thousand troops. And he thinks it can be done but he wants to let me know tomorrow. And that I would recommend you announce at your press conference, if you have one next week.

NIXON: Yeah. [unclear]

KISSINGER: Now, last night, after you had retired, Dobrynin came in with a Russian message —

NIXON: Mm-hmm.

KISSINGER: —which he said, since they don't want to say too much publicly—it's rather tough; it doesn't have any concrete things. But after five pages of tough talk, which is standard tough talk, he said they'd transmitted our considerations to Hanoi and they'll give us a reply as soon as—which is amazing because in the past they always took the position that they weren't. Now my recommendation is that we say to this there will be no answer. They know what our policy is and we are just going to pursue it. And if that's going to be their attitude, I think, I can tell them now, nothing will come out of the discussion.

NIXON: He seems to understand. Dobrynin. Dobrynin must be certain that we'll go.

KISSINGER: I think, I think it puts us domestically—the reasons you had for deciding to go: I don't agree that it's two for them and one for us; it's two for us and almost nothing for them.

NIXON: Mm-hmm.

KISSINGER: And what do they get out of it? They receive me three days after we bomb Hanoi and Haiphong.

NIXON: Yeah. In any event, the, as far as, when Dobrynin came, comes in, your trip is still on?

KISSINGER: Yeah. Oh, yeah. They didn't cancel it.

NIXON: Fine.

KISSINGER: They didn't do anything. It's just—what I think they did, Mr. President, is to send this first part—

NIXON: —to Hanoi.

KISSINGER: —to Hanoi to say, to show, because publicly they've been rather mild. The CIA has—

NIXON: The Chinese have been mild as well. Zhou Enlai [unclear].

KISSINGER: Very mild.

NIXON: Compared to what we're used to getting.

KISSINGER: Now, let me read you this CIA analysis—and the CIA is always alarmist. "Moscow has given its population only [unclear] of the U.S. air strikes on Hanoi and Haiphong. Publicly the Soviets have not acknowledged damage to their ships at Haiphong."

NIXON: How many were there? Were there forty?

KISSINGER: Yeah. Soviet—

NIXON: They were—

KISSINGER: Poor things.

NIXON: That's not too damn bad.

KISSINGER: That's good.

NIXON: I think it's good.

KISSINGER: Yeah. The protest failed to mention the strikes on Hanoi or anywhere else in North Vietnam. Its concentration on the damage to Soviet shipping, its failure to mention any injury to Soviet personnel, and its delivery at the low level of deputy foreign minister indicate that the Soviets did not want to overstress the implications of the air strike on U.S.-Soviet relations. Maintaining Moscow's recent public reticence about aid commitments to North Vietnam, the TASS statement merely noted that the USSR met its international duties. The analysis of Zhou's remarks is: "Zhou's remarks add little more than a compendium of clichés used by the Chinese over the past year to describe the war. It makes no mention of Chinese assistance, of President Nixon, or of damage to the Soviet ships." Then Hanoi has made a public statement saying that their friends in the world would in time condemn the United States. In time. And the CIA says, "[unclear] appears to be another call for greater support from the USSR and China. In this connection, the North Vietnamese have been playing the Soviet aspect of the raid." And so forth. Now one problem we have, I hope Rogers goes in there determined and tough. [Secretary of State William Rogers was planning to testify before the Senate Foreign Relations Committee that morning.] This is the one —

NIXON: Huh. God only knows what he could do.

. . .

NIXON: When I say I'm for a blockade, you don't, you think I'm just gassing. But I —

KISSINGER: Mr. President —

NIXON: But I'm totally committed to a blockade —

KISSINGER: Mr. President, I don't think you're gassing.

NIXON: — at the end of this week.

KISSINGER: You've done — well, we have to wait until I get back from Moscow but —

NIXON: That's what I meant. That's the end of this week.

KISSINGER: No, I'll be back Sunday night.

NIXON: That's the end of this week. Oh, the first of next week.

KISSINGER: The first of next week.

NIXON: I mean, as soon as you get back from Moscow, if it's a hard-line, rigid attitude, blockade them.

KISSINGER: Mr. President, I think you've always done what you said you would do. And I have every — no, I think that's what you will do —

NIXON: Look, Henry —

KISSINGER: — and I think that's what you should do.

NIXON: Look, Henry, you see, if you — when you really carry out, Henry, to your, to the extreme, your analysis, that you can't have the North Vietnamese destroy two presidents, and in that it isn't really quite on all fours because Johnson destroyed himself, and in my case I will not do it that way. I will do it, frankly, for the good of the country. But nevertheless —

KISSINGER: No, no, but that is for the good of the country. That's why I'm saying it, Mr. President, with all my —

NIXON: Yeah?

KISSINGER: —loyalty I think we cannot have these miserable little bastards destroy confidence in our government.

NIXON: Sure. Well, anyway, I was going to tell you that I'm convinced that the country—you see, for me, let me be quite—Kennedy, even leading a nation that was infinitely stronger than any potential enemy, was unable to conduct a very successful foreign policy because he lacked iron nerves—

KISSINGER: That's right.

NIXON: —and lacked good advisors.

KISSINGER: Right.

NIXON: All right. Johnson was in the same position for other reasons, because he didn't have any experience. Now, I am quite aware of the fact that because of the—what is happening here and the rest, I mean that, that there is a limit, a very good chance—I mean I don't, and it doesn't bother me one damn bit from a personal standpoint—there's a very good chance that sitting in this chair could be somebody else. It could be a Muskie; it could be a Humphrey; it could be a Teddy [Kennedy]; one of those three on the Democratic side. And on the Republican side it won't be Agnew or Reagan, but it—Rockefeller probably couldn't get the nomination, I don't know who, who they would nominate, but nevertheless, but here's the point: I have to, I know that, I have to leave this office in a position as strong as I possibly can because whoever succeeds me, either because of lack of experience or because of lack of character or guts, heading a weaker United States would surrender the whole thing. You understand?

KISSINGER: No question. I know—

NIXON: So that is why, that is why what I have to do, I have to do it not only to assure that if I am here we can conduct a successful foreign policy, I have to do it—and this is even more important—so that some poor, weak son of a bitch sitting here, with the best of intentions can conduct it. It will be hard enough for Hubert Humphrey in this chair, it will be hard enough for him to conduct a foreign policy of the United States that's knocked the hell out of South Vietnam. It'll be very hard because he is a gibbering idiot at times; well intentioned but gibbering. Muskie has proved that he has no, no character. And Teddy is a—well, unbelievable, I mean. It's his up and down. Now, what the—what the hell can you do? So, you cannot leave—you just can't leave the thing. Now, under these circumstances, as I've often said, that it may be that I'm the last person in this office for some time, until somebody else is developing along the same lines, I mean, who's tough and experienced, who will be able to conduct a strong, responsible foreign policy. So goddamn it, we're going to do it. And that means—that means take every risk, lose every election. That's the way I look at it, just as cold as that. Now people say, "Oh well, if you win you're going to lose your path." I'm not sure, but the main point is, we have no choice, you see?

KISSINGER: That's my view —

NIXON: The foreign policy of the United States will not be viable if we're run out of Vietnam. That's all there is to it.

KISSINGER: Mr. President, that is exactly my point of view, selfish, shortsighted, personal point of view.

NIXON: We shouldn't, we shouldn't —

KISSINGER: Your incentive is not to do it.

NIXON: We shouldn't make a deal.

KISSINGER: And my incentive is — I have less at stake but —

NIXON: I know. Your incentive is to not have all these great foreign policy initiatives flushed down the tubes.

KISSINGER: Exactly.

NIXON: Which is exactly what's on the line.

KISSINGER: And is what we're concerned about. Public position, one would say —

NIXON: Right.

KISSINGER: — one could remain —

NIXON: The Man of Peace, the Generation of Peace, all that stuff.

KISSINGER: Although, Mr. President, I must say one thing. You are taking less heat this week than you would if Hue had fallen. The first week, the worst heat we took, it began to build up, was when all these little pipsqueaks were saying Vietnamization was a failure.

• • •

NIXON: I think you ought to tell Rabin you heard the president say it. I want you to get Rabin in and say you heard the president say it. To the leaders, he said, if he's said it a dozen times, he said it once, and I always start with Israel and then I go to Europe. But I say if the United States fails in Vietnam, if a Soviet-supported invasion succeeds there, it will inevitably be next tried in the Mideast and the United States will not stand there either. That's what's on the line. And they should know that. And I think we should get some of our Israeli friends to start to support us.

KISSINGER: Right.

NIXON: What do you think?

KISSINGER: I think so.

NIXON: Don't you believe this is true?

KISSINGER: I'll call Rabin. Now to go through —

NIXON: Right.

KISSINGER: — immediate tactical issues.

NIXON: Right.

KISSINGER: Do you agree, Mr. President, that I call in Dobrynin and say there is not going to be any reply to this?

NIXON: Yeah.

KISSINGER: "The president is determined. You know his course. There is no sense in engaging in rhetoric."

NIXON: That's right.

KISSINGER: "And we will not reply to this. And I must tell you informally if this is what you are going to say to, in Moscow, my trip is going to be a waste of time."

NIXON: Yeah.

KISSINGER: "Because we will not be able to make progress—"

NIXON: The point is, it's just the usual thing that we should stop the bombing of Hanoi.

KISSINGER: Oh yeah. Yeah. It's—they had to do it, Mr. President, because—

NIXON: And just say, just say we did it. Why don't you put it more like I talked to Zhou Enlai: "Look, the president read this and rather smiled." Look, just say, "He smiled and said, he said, 'They have to say this,' he said, 'but,' and then he turned cold and said, 'there will be no reply to this. If the Russians want to talk settlement, fine. But if they want talk to this way, there isn't going to be a summit.'"

KISSINGER: That's right.

NIXON: I'd be very tough. 'Cause I'd very much like to see [former West German Finance Minister] Johann [Franz Josef] Strauss. I like the old fart.

KISSINGER: Right, right.

NIXON: You understand?

KISSINGER: [laughs]

NIXON: Don't you think that's the way we play it?

KISSINGER: Absolutely.

NIXON: I think Dobrynin expects you to play that way, doesn't he?

KISSINGER: Oh, Dobrynin. When he said, "I'll bring you this," he went on to say, "We have to do this in confidential channels because they're not saying much in public channels."

NIXON: Well, Bill [Rogers] asked me whether Humphrey responded. We have responded to the Russian note, haven't we?

KISSINGER: No. He had sent over a cable for clearance. I held it last night because it was just too anxious, saying you had retired, which was true. And that you would clear it in the morning. And what you said was yes.

NIXON: Hmm.

KISSINGER: I mean what you said was exactly that. You cleared it in the morning, this morning.

NIXON: Let me tell you about your trip. I realize it's not two for them and one for us in terms of cosmetics. It may be two for them and one for us in other terms. But, nevertheless. Basically because looking at their big game, the China game, what they want is Henry Kissinger in Moscow because you went to China.

KISSINGER: Oh yes.

NIXON: You see? That's what's in it for them. And you've got to realize. Don't undersell what the hell we're giving those sons of bitches. Now, the other point I make, Henry, is, however, we're doing it for our own reasons. Our own reasons are, you're going to go and then we'll blow it.

KISSINGER: Of course.

NIXON: And I'll blow it. Hell, maybe the day you come back; I might do it in the press conference.

• • •

NIXON: I think that with the Russians, there's one weakness in our game plan with Hanoi. We haven't got a goddamn thing we can do this week.

KISSINGER: Oh, no. Well, first of all, we are holding in the South, Mr. President.

NIXON: You think we are holding?

KISSINGER: Oh yeah. And that is the worst for them. And —

NIXON: But that's only temporary, you know, holding.

KISSINGER: I don't know. I think it's, I think it isn't temporary.

NIXON: [unclear]

KISSINGER: But secondly, we are bombing the southern part of North Vietnam intensively.

NIXON: Is there any bombing that you could do, changing even the pattern this week, so it looks like it's a different kind of strike? Is that something that could be done? Could we have another B-3-type strike? Just so it's —

KISSINGER: In the South or in the North?

NIXON: In the South.

KISSINGER: Oh, in the South. Easily.

NIXON: Yeah. I would like, I think what I meant is, I want something that can be described as a massive, different kind of a strike. Is there anyplace where you think we could do it?

KISSINGER: I'll get off a message right away.

NIXON: Put it this way. That this week — you see what I mean?

KISSINGER: Right.

NIXON: I don't want you to go over there — well, frankly people won't know you're there. I don't want the people here to get the impression — you see what we're up against.

KISSINGER: But next week they'll know why you did it.

NIXON: I know. But this week they'll be writing, because of Russian and Chinese protests, the United States didn't do it again. You see my point? We can't be in that position. Now, we can ride a week of it, I guess.

KISSINGER: We can ride a week of it. If they accuse you of being both too tough and too soft at the same time — and then next week, I think if we can avoid — I mean, we've really put it brutally to them. It isn't — we haven't shown any softness. And they know, I mean, they know you now, Mr. President. They know when I come back without anything to show for it, we're going to blow the lid off, particularly having proved that we've made every effort.

NIXON: Mm-hmm. Now, the last thing to consider before we try to do a Wednesday thing. You see the deep-down decision you've got to make is whether, do you want to conduct the Moscow talk in a way that will enable us to have a Moscow summit or in a way that will make it, leave us no choice but to blockade and flush the summit? Now there's one point that's very important. If the summit is canceled, I want to cancel it. I don't want them to.

KISSINGER: Well, what I would like —

NIXON: That's got to be like the U-2. You understand?

KISSINGER: What I would like to suggest, Mr. President, is this. I think we should conduct the summit part of the talks in a very conciliatory and forthcoming manner in such a way that they get a maximum panting after the —

NIXON: That, that I understand.

KISSINGER: — after the summit.

NIXON: I understand all that. All of that.

KISSINGER: On the Vietnam thing, on the other hand, we should be tough as nails, because the middle position, we will not impress these guys with conciliatoriness. They were not passing messages while Johnson was drooling all over them.

NIXON: Mm-hmm.

KISSINGER: So I think we should do both simultaneously. On Vietnam, we should be very tough. What I'm playing with now —

NIXON: What do we get out — what do get out — what are we — sorry.

KISSINGER: Well, what I think, if we are —

NIXON: We certainly have got to have a cease-fire while we're in Moscow. That's my point.

KISSINGER: Oh, one outcome, Mr. President, that I think we might get is to say, to offer to the Russians, we'll go back to the conditions of May, of March 29. That is to say, the North Vietnamese withdraw the three divisions they put across the DMZ, north of the DMZ; they scale down their military actions to the levels they were on March 29; this is guaranteed by the Soviets; we in turn stop the bombing of the North; and we resume plenary sessions in Paris.

NIXON: That's a good deal.

KISSINGER: That would be a damn good deal, Mr. President.

NIXON: That's right.

KISSINGER: It would be such a defeat for the North Vietnamese, if they are to stop their offensive.

NIXON: That's right.

KISSINGER: And it makes us look damn good in domestic opinion.

NIXON: Withdraw —

KISSINGER: If we say —

NIXON: Withdraw across the DMZ, those forces across the DMZ. After all, we can't tell them to get out of everything.

KISSINGER: That's right.

NIXON: And we'll stop the bombing of the North in return. Because we will have —

KISSINGER: But they have to scale down military actions —

NIXON: We will have shellacked the North by that time anyway.

KISSINGER: That's right.

"We'll blockade those sons of bitches and starve them out."
April 17, 1972, 12:15 p.m.
Richard Nixon and Henry Kissinger
OVAL OFFICE

Nixon was practicing with the Soviet Union what John Foster Dulles called "the necessary art" — "the ability to get to the verge without getting into the war." Throughout America, observers were growing nervous that Nixon's toughness was indeed crossing over the brink. "Nixon's decision to force a major confrontation with the Soviet Union," warned the Washington Post, *"defies sense." By midday on April 17, Nixon was ready to order the implementation of a blockade, which would inevitably put the United States in the position of directly confronting Soviet ships. Kissinger worked to pull the president back several steps.*

• • •

KISSINGER: I was talking with Dobrynin. Bill has done very well, Mr. President [in testimony before the Senate Foreign Relations Committee that morning].

NIXON: That's the report we get. I've been thinking that I don't — what's your, what's the purpose of your conversation with Dobrynin? Just to go about getting this message?

KISSINGER: Yes. And just to keep the —

NIXON: And you've done that —

KISSINGER: I'm not finished yet because he —

NIXON: Well, I don't want you to offer this or even suggest that there is a chance that we might go on this interim idea —

KISSINGER: Oh, no.

NIXON: — that an exchange for a — let me tell you the weakness in that. I've written it out here. The weakness in that, in view of Haig's report, is that it sees it tactically in the short run, but does not adequately look, in my opinion, at the long run, the risks. In the short run, it would be a great gesture and we could punish our critics very, very heavily, if we could get them to withdraw from I Corps across the DMZ. Then we would give up the bombing of North Vietnam and there would be some reduction in fighting and we would go back to the conference tables. All right. The difficulty is that the enemy's capability still to launch significant offensive action is there. That, you know, it doesn't much matter how much time you've got. The difficulty is too that the pressure on the Russians is enormously lifted as far as this confrontation is concerned. Oh sure, we can go to Moscow and we can agree on SALT and a lot of other things. But the point that I make is that having taken the heat that we have already taken for escalation, I think what we have to do is to escalate all the way.

KISSINGER: Well, Mr. —

NIXON: Unless, what I'm saying is, that I think the position that you're going to have to be in in Moscow is not the one being willing to back down. In other words, let us sell them, let us sell — let them sell to us talks for halting the bombing, which is what this really gets down to.

KISSINGER: Yeah.

NIXON: After all — now wait a minute. They invaded; that's true. We bombed them; that's true. But when you finally get down to it, we're giving up the bombing and we go back to talks; and pressuring the Russians is not going to be very great. And my view is, what I really want, you know, I want to caution you with Dobrynin: it's going to be, it's going to have to be tougher than that, Henry. At least, right now, the time, you can't let the time flee by, Henry. We have to have the blockade. I don't give a goddamn about the election. We'll blockade those sons of bitches and starve them out. And that's what we're going to do.

KISSINGER: Well —

NIXON: I'd rather do that than have any talks going on this summer. Talks this summer are not going to help us.

KISSINGER: Well, you have to make this judgment, Mr. President. If — first of all, I agree with you that nothing should be said about this interim solution to the Russians now. That should be the result of a stalemate.

NIXON: That's right.

KISSINGER: And I'm not going to make any proposition to the Russians now.

NIXON: Sure. I understand. But I just don't think that —

KISSINGER: But that should be said in Moscow if it's said anywhere. But, if I may make this suggestion, Mr. President: if we convince the Russians that they, that we are asking something that they cannot in the best will in the world deliver, then we may force them into brutal preemptive action to bring you down this year. That may be their only hope.

NIXON: I know that.

KISSINGER: No, no, but —

NIXON: Meanwhile, we've lost the war.

KISSINGER: Well, if they think they can bring you down — I'm just giving you the case for the other side — then all they have to do is endure six months of a blockade. That they can probably do.

NIXON: Mm-hmm.

KISSINGER: So, what, that interim solution has this advantage, Mr. President. First, it will be seen as a clear defeat for them.

NIXON: You see, that's temporary. Go ahead.

KISSINGER: I know it's temporary. Secondly, it gets us through the Russian summit. After all, the reason you can do this now is because of the China summit. And it's just awfully hard to paint you into the position of a warmonger. It gets us through the Russian summit with some notable successes. We can build into the Russian summit a lot of things, like a Middle East settlement, that we have to deliver next year, which they'll be just as reluctant to break next year.

NIXON: Mm-hmm.

KISSINGER: Then, Mr. President, after your election, I'd go all out with the North Vietnamese.

NIXON: Yeah, but the point is, we'd still have the war on our hands all summer long. As Haig says, which is the disturbing thing in his memorandum; you read it to me yesterday and I quite agree with him. He says, well, after, we'll hold now; and then we've got to get ready for another offensive in July. We're not going to take any offensive in July.

KISSINGER: No, no. No, no, no, no.

NIXON: [unclear] no offensive in July.

KISSINGER: No, no. Part of this deal would have to be a reduction in Soviet deliveries and a guarantee that there would be no offensives this year. All of this year. We're not talking about now.

NIXON: If we get that, fine.

KISSINGER: We're talking about the rest of —

NIXON: [unclear] I don't mind having a little [unclear] out there [unclear] —

KISSINGER: No, no.

NIXON: [unclear]

KISSINGER: Oh, Mr. President, if we can only get this offensive called off with no promise about July. Nor can we accept — I'd go a step further. We cannot accept a Hanoi comment either; we have to get a Soviet public assurance. Now then this would also change the negotiating position. Because then I believe, Mr. President, Hanoi would feel that by its own actions — maybe you'll be brought down, but you cannot be brought down by Hanoi's actions. Therefore it is probable that you'll be president after November; that having acted this violently now, there is no telling what you will do in November. And —

NIXON: You know, their gamble is that they can have the war going on and they'll still have the POWs up until November. And that under those circumstances the possibility of our surviving the election is very, very low. You see my point?

KISSINGER: I think if they are pulled off this attack now, they, particularly if they get ground down more as they do every day — I mean this deal couldn't happen before

May 5 to 10 anyway, in which case much of their offensive would have broken its back anyhow. So I, so I think that for you to do — the reason a blockade will work is if you can endure it. If they think they need only to wait six months, they might just stick it out until November. This is what worries me about the blockade, Mr. President. And, you remember, I had some dealing toward it in '69. You weren't postured well diplomatically to do it in '69. And I strongly supported your not doing it. But this is the reason why I think an interim solution in which — but we should throw in the prisoners anyway.

• • •

KISSINGER: But I frankly believe, Mr. President, that your enormous skill has been that you have been extraordinarily tough. That if — you walked up to all the tough ones but at the same time maintained a peace posture so that they couldn't put you into the position of just chopping away at you. The reason that people trust you is because they know that you have done everything. And therefore, all things considered, I think it is in our interest not to get the Russian summit knocked off as long as we can do it while preserving our essential integrity in Vietnam. That is the major thing.

NIXON: Yeah. I agree.

KISSINGER: And if this Moscow meeting does not work at all —

NIXON: Or maybe we'll blockade in September, you mean?

KISSINGER: No. I would think if the Moscow meeting doesn't work then I think we — no, I mean, [if] mining doesn't work, then you might want to go to a blockade.

NIXON: We might have to, you see.

KISSINGER: That's right.

NIXON: You can't hold the card.

KISSINGER: That's right. I'm not — we certainly should keep the posture that you will go to a blockade. I think we've really got their attention.

NIXON: That's for sure.

KISSINGER: But I —

NIXON: Maybe that's all I want you to get back from Dobrynin. And —

KISSINGER: We've brought this thing a hell of a long way —

NIXON: I had a very nice visit with the Polish ambassador. [Nixon met Polish ambassador Trampczynski in the Oval Office earlier that morning and received an official invitation to visit Warsaw following Nixon's planned visit to Moscow at the end of May.] And I appreciate what he's worked out in that respect, but we —

KISSINGER: Mr. President.

NIXON: To bring that fucking, for that little asshole to come in here, this Polish ambassador, not that he's a strong man, but for him to come in here this day is fine. Now they may knock it off, but I don't want to let them.

KISSINGER: They won't knock it off.

NIXON: Yeah.

KISSINGER: The Russians may knock it off but the Poles will do it only if the Russians do. And I don't think the Russians will right away. I think we've got the Russians concerned.

NIXON: Yeah.

KISSINGER: I can tell him, Dobrynin —

NIXON: Is Dobrynin talking about knocking it off now?

KISSINGER: No, no.

NIXON: Better not.

KISSINGER: No, no.

NIXON: Because if he could get any deal with this, remember I'll move first.

KISSINGER: Yeah, but, Mr. President, for me to be received in Moscow three days —

NIXON: I agree but —

KISSINGER: — after the bombing of Haiphong is unbelievable.

NIXON: Yeah, well, of course, some of the papers this morning were saying that the Russian leaders were out of town over the weekend and that's why they didn't react to the bombing. So, they don't —

KISSINGER: Baloney.

NIXON: They know.

KISSINGER: We've got this Brezhnev message. They just don't know anything in our papers.

NIXON: Thank God. I'll see you later.

KISSINGER: Right.

The priority of Vietnam in Moscow

April 18, 1972, 11:00 a.m.
Richard Nixon and Henry Kissinger
OVAL OFFICE

Kissinger was preparing to leave on a secret mission to Moscow on April 19, ostensibly to prepare an agenda for the president's summit there in late May. Nixon had long since recognized that the European aspects of the summit — arms control and Berlin — were the highest priorities of the Soviets. In view of the Easter Offensive in Vietnam, though, he was adamant that Kissinger engage Brezhnev in a discussion of his nation's influence over North Vietnam in the effort to bring about an end to the war.

• • •

NIXON: What I am concerned about is something you talked about on your schedule. I thought that when you talked to Dobrynin, you only gave him assurance that we would not hit the Hanoi-Haiphong area —

KISSINGER: That is correct.

NIXON: — while you're there. Well, the feeling that we're going to sort of keep the level relatively —

KISSINGER: No, no —

NIXON: — down. Let me tell you that we have a desperately difficult problem with our domestic situation if there is any indication —

KISSINGER: Right —

NIXON: — that we aren't bombing the hell out of them now.

KISSINGER: No, no.

NIXON: It would be just — you see, what ruined Johnson was to start and stop; he — you remember how many bombing halts he had.

Now, we cannot be in that position, even though you're going, because you don't know what you're going to — what we'll be doing here. I'd — what I'd like to see is, in this next week, I mean this week while you're gone, I think on the battlefront, I think everything that can fly should be hitting the whole battlefront, including the stuff up to the nineteenth parallel.

KISSINGER: Of course.

NIXON: Just be sure they understand that.

KISSINGER: Oh, no. When —

NIXON: But you see I don't [unclear] —

KISSINGER: The point is, Mr. President, if you say —

NIXON: You see, the story out of Saigon indicated two things: one, we would not hit Haiphong-Hanoi; and that we would cut the number of sorties in the South. Now, we must not do the latter.

KISSINGER: I — I have had a talk with Moorer, and I've had a talk with Rush this morning, with exactly this theme. My concern was, Mr. President, that when you say "maximum effort," they will interpret this to mean that they should go slow in the South and put it all into the North. Then we are going to have stories to the effect —

NIXON: Yeah —

KISSINGER: — that you are detracting from the battle. They have — they are flying —

NIXON: I don't mind that. I just want them to hit there. I have to get it, to say drop it all in III Corps, if necessary. All of it. But I want — I want what appears to be a maximum effort someplace.

KISSINGER: All over the country.

NIXON: Let's hope —

KISSINGER: Yeah.

NIXON: Let me put it this way: a concentrated effort. So they say the biggest strike, concentrated strike — so we get a story or two out like that in the South. I don't care. I —

KISSINGER: Yes —

NIXON: — just want it definitely to be in the North.

KISSINGER: Actually, Mr. — they have — are — what they are doing in the North now, they haven't done it the last two days but they are starting again tonight, and they haven't done it because of some monkey business that Laird must have been engaged in.

NIXON: What's this?

KISSINGER: They are flying about one hundred fifty sorties, Mr. President, in the North. That's more than we ever flew on any protect —

NIXON: Yeah.

KISSINGER: — protective reaction strike —

NIXON: Yeah.

KISSINGER: — that you ordered. So this is pretty massive.

NIXON: Yeah.

KISSINGER: That's —

NIXON: That's right.

KISSINGER: That's in the area south of the nineteenth. On top of it, they're flying about six hundred in the South and the distribution now is they're making massive — the biggest effort is in Military Area Region 3.

NIXON: All right.

KISSINGER: I genuinely believe they — that —

NIXON: You mean [unclear] —

KISSINGER: — the battle is going so well all over the country that we ought not to give them bombing targets. I think —

NIXON: No, I, we — I think we never do.

KISSINGER: I think they're doing really — I get a detailed briefing of every B-52 strike —

NIXON: Let me tell you one point that I emphasized to Moorer which we have never done in this war to date, is that if the — when the enemy starts to break off, instead of reducing the bombing, increase it.

KISSINGER: And, of course —

NIXON: You understand, that is when you really can punish an enemy. When an enemy is in retreat, you can kill him.

• • •

NIXON: The timing basically was: we didn't pick the time. Son of a bitch. They attacked. That is the provocation.

KISSINGER: Mr. President, I must tell you I know no president who would have had the guts to do it now.

NIXON: That's what Laird thinks.

KISSINGER: To do it with a —

NIXON: They think it's wrong to do it politically. Or isn't that really what they're —?

KISSINGER: To do it with an invitation to Moscow for you in the pocket, and a secret invitation to me, it really shows a lot of gall. They invite us on Thursday — I mean on Thursday they make it definite and on Saturday we clobber Haiphong to tell them, "All right, you bastards."

NIXON: That's right.

KISSINGER: "This is the game that's going to be played in Moscow." But it so strengthens my hand in Moscow. That it was a risk that had to be taken.

NIXON: You couldn't have gone.

KISSINGER: I could've gone but in a very weak position.

NIXON: Well, in a position of only talking about the summit.

KISSINGER: Right.

NIXON: Now we're in the position of talking about Vietnam. Oh, the only other thing I wanted to tell you. It seems to me, Henry, that the least you should get out of your game with the Russians is that when we return, that the president should be able to announce that Vietnam would be first on the agenda at the Moscow summit. You get my point? That would put it to them hard. Why not? Just — understand, I'm not, I'm not concluding this. Let's discuss this tomorrow. But, you see, anything like that that would come out of your trip —

KISSINGER: Right.

NIXON: — that even if you would get only that, even though you don't get a settlement, if we could say, "Vietnam would be on the agenda of our discussion." Now that, of course, makes it necessary for us to get something out of Vietnam in the summit.

KISSINGER: It would be — the only hesitation I have, Mr. President —

NIXON: Yeah.

KISSINGER: — is we, they are now scared. They have to be.

NIXON: Yeah.

KISSINGER: You've got a massive armada there. We have to make sure they're not just playing for time.

NIXON: Yeah. So maybe they would agree to that.

KISSINGER: Well no, this is playing for time; this gives them five weeks.

NIXON: Yeah, yeah. Oh, no, no. I'm just thinking though —

KISSINGER: No, no. We —

NIXON: I think, I'm thinking that when you return, if you've got nothing, we've got to bomb the hell out of them.

KISSINGER: No question.

NIXON: Or blockade.

KISSINGER: No question.

NIXON: One of the two.

KISSINGER: No question.

NIXON: If we blockade them, do you think there'll be a summit?

KISSINGER: No.

NIXON: Well, then do you think we should take that risk? That's the real danger.

KISSINGER: Mr. President —

NIXON: We may have to.

KISSINGER: You and I should act towards everybody —

NIXON: That's right.

KISSINGER: — as if we were going right off the cliff.

NIXON: That's right.

KISSINGER: That's the only way we can make it work.

"Even the nuclear weapon if necessary."

April 19, 1972, 3:27 p.m.

Richard Nixon and Henry Kissinger

OVAL OFFICE

In a talk that lasted much longer than most in the Oval Office, Nixon and Kissinger spoke for more than an hour and a half in the final preparation for Kissinger's secret trip to Moscow. Their diverging points of view were apparent. Kissinger was intent on salvaging the president's Moscow summit in May; to do that, it was clear that he needed to bring home a breakthrough in reestablishing the Paris Peace Talks — both the official ones and his secret ones. Nixon was ambivalent about the survival of his summit, but he was absolutely determined to steer negotiations toward an end to the war.

• • •

NIXON: We have got to play it out. We must not now disappoint —

KISSINGER: I could not —

NIXON: You see. That is why if you come back and we say we've agreed to resume our talks and stop the bombing —

KISSINGER: Oh no. No, no.

NIXON: That's why I —

KISSINGER: No, no, no. But, Mr. President, the point is the talks resume while the bombing goes on. Oh no, we won't stop the bombing. Absolutely not.

NIXON: We indicated that we might.

KISSINGER: Oh —

NIXON: Retrogressively, but —

KISSINGER: No, no. We will retrogressive, if they pull their troops out of South Vietnam.

NIXON: Well —

KISSINGER: That's the proposition —

NIXON: Yeah.

KISSINGER: First let me make one other —

NIXON: Understand, I'm not criticizing. I'm just trying to state, when you come back, I'd like to be able to say something in my press conference about — oh, did you talk to him about the time of the announcement?

KISSINGER: No. I'll do that there, but I've told him that we — because I don't want —

NIXON: Yeah.

KISSINGER: — to get them thinking that there will be an announcement till —

NIXON: That's right.

KISSINGER: —till my last day there.

NIXON: That's right. Now look, presently though, Henry, for my own planning, you will be back Sunday night.

KISSINGER: Yes.

NIXON: Because you're going to see the son of a bitch [Brezhnev] Friday.

KISSINGER: And then Gromyko wants to spend all of Saturday with me.

NIXON: On the details of other things?

KISSINGER: Well, I don't know, he—

NIXON: Well, we'll see.

KISSINGER: I have to admit, Mr. President, I would never say to anyone who comes into your office, "Don't spring any surprises on him, because he may not be able to handle it," which is in effect what they told me.

NIXON: Uh-huh.

KISSINGER: Now—

NIXON: Oh, I see. That's what you mean.

KISSINGER: That's what—

NIXON: Do you think you might see Brezhnev alone?

KISSINGER: Yeah.

NIXON: Or do you think you'll have Gromyko there?

KISSINGER: They said—

NIXON: Or whatever they want.

KISSINGER: I have to be there. I don't know.

NIXON: The point is, if, if—let me say this. There's one, there's another way this could be played. I'm trying to think of the minimum we need. Let me, let me figure out a way, and then we'll come back to your, to what you were saying. As we were saying over there early this morning, earlier this morning, what we must not assume, which is what we have been assuming to an extent, and I'm willing to do this in the event they, in the event they cancel the summit or we have to cancel the summit, you know, which we of course are prepared to do. Totally—

KISSINGER: Not going to happen.

NIXON: They're not going to do that. We know that. Hell, they wouldn't be having you, if they—look—

KISSINGER: May I—

NIXON: These guys would be crazy to have you over there—

KISSINGER: May I make two—

NIXON: Yeah.

KISSINGER: —other points, because you need that for your own thinking—

NIXON: Yeah.

KISSINGER: —before you [unclear]. One is, I told him again, I said, "Anatol, I want you to know this. We will continue to bomb while I am in Moscow. I don't want

Mr. Brezhnev to feel that while he's seeing me and his ally's being bombed that you didn't know that."

NIXON: That's right.

KISSINGER: "Don't consider that a surprise." He said, "I understand." He said, "But you promised me no escalation." I said, "No, I promised you no attacks on Hanoi-Haiphong."

NIXON: Right.

KISSINGER: He said, "That's no escalation."

NIXON: Right.

KISSINGER: So now, Mr. — you know that's not a sign of strength.

NIXON: Ha!

KISSINGER: The second point I'd like to make to you, Mr. President, is there is this port [Thanh Hoa] about sixty miles south of Haiphong —

NIXON: Yeah.

KISSINGER: — which is just snuggling up on the twentieth parallel.

NIXON: Yeah.

KISSINGER: Now, our bombing line is the nineteenth for this week.

NIXON: So you might take that out this week?

KISSINGER: But, if I might suggest, Mr. President —

NIXON: Yeah.

KISSINGER: — we ought to try to take that port tomorrow night.

NIXON: All right.

KISSINGER: Because (a) it's a good signal to the Russians.

NIXON: Yeah.

KISSINGER: As long, as I've said, no Hanoi-Haiphong. Secondly, they've given us another holding reply out of Hanoi. Every time they give us an unfavorable reply, they get another back.

NIXON: That's right.

KISSINGER: And —

NIXON: Good, take it tomorrow night.

• • •

KISSINGER: And, you see, next week the mere fact, Mr. President —

NIXON: Mm-hmm?

KISSINGER: — that the Soviets discuss Vietnam with me —

NIXON: Mm-hmm?

KISSINGER: — in the week that we bombed Hanoi and Haiphong, which these sons of bitches are condemning —

NIXON: Now they will ask, "At whose initiative is this meeting taking place?" I think we've — that I've got to make this another thing. We've got to say that it was at their initiative. I don't want it to appear that we went hat in hand to Moscow.

KISSINGER: No. Well, Mr. President, I —

NIXON: Or we can just say mutually.

KISSINGER: I'd say it was, was mutual. These things always are mutual. We have, it's important — what they are doing is really screwing Hanoi.

NIXON: That's right.

KISSINGER: I mean, imagine if they were bombing Iran —

NIXON: Mm-hmm?

KISSINGER: — and then you received Gromyko here at the White House the same week that they're bombing one of our allies, what impression that would make on the shah. There's no possible —

NIXON: Yeah, and if the Chinese ignore it. Let me go over a few of the items now —

KISSINGER: [unclear]

NIXON: Take some notes. One thing, that on the very limit of what we want to get out of these bastards, we've got to get something symbolic on the POW thing. Now, what I would say is if we could get the POWs that have been there five years, or something like that, or sick POWs. In other words, we'll release so many if they release, and something along that [line]. The second point is that we've got to, and, and, and —

KISSINGER: That I must include in the proposal.

NIXON: Huh? Just include that in the proposal.

KISSINGER: Yes.

NIXON: Yeah. We just need something. It's a human — it's a humanitarian gesture. You understand?

KISSINGER: Right.

NIXON: Don't you think we can include it?

KISSINGER: It's essential.

NIXON: I don't think you're going to get it.

KISSINGER: No, I'll — no, no. I think we must hold out —

NIXON: Yeah.

KISSINGER: Mr. President, we've got some sweating on our —

NIXON: Well, we'll — we'll, we'll — we will do this.

KISSINGER: I must — the risk, with your permission —

NIXON: Yeah?

KISSINGER: — but because it's your risk —

NIXON: Yeah? Yeah.

KISSINGER: — if I fail there, it may be because I'm turning the screw too much, rather than not enough. Now —

NIXON: No, no. If you turn it too much — there's no greater pleasure, frankly, that I would have than to leave this office to anybody after having destroyed North Vietnam's capability. Now, let me tell you, I feel exactly that way, and I'll go out with a clean conscience. But if I, if I leave this office without any use of power, I'm the last president — frankly I'm the only president, the only man with the exception of Connally, believe me, who'd have the guts to do what we're doing. And you know it and I know it. The only man who'd have the possibility to be president, and Connally's the only other one who could do what I'm doing. Reagan never could make president to begin with and he couldn't handle it —

KISSINGER: Connally would do it without your finesse, though.

NIXON: Well, Agnew, Agnew would —

KISSINGER: Agnew. Well, Agnew would have [unclear] — Agnew would be in a worse position than Johnson was —

NIXON: Yeah, but you know what I mean. The point is, as you know, as considering electability, I'm the only person who can do it. Now, Henry, we must not miss this chance. We're going to do it, and I'll destroy the goddamn country, believe me. I mean destroy it, if necessary.

And let me say, even the nuclear weapon if necessary. It isn't necessary, but you know what I mean. What I mean is that shows you the extent to which I'm willing to go. By — by a nuclear weapon, I mean that we will bomb the living bejeezus out of North Vietnam, and then if anybody interferes we will threaten the nuclear weapon.

• • •

KISSINGER: What I thought I would do, Mr. President, to take care of the problem, is when I arrive I'll chopper up to Camp David —

NIXON: Mm-hmm.

KISSINGER: — then come back with you.

NIXON: Good. Sunday night. What time will you arrive back?

KISSINGER: Well, I'll have to let you know. I won't know my schedule till I get there.

NIXON: Well, right. But you'll arrive sometime during Sunday afternoon, won't you?

KISSINGER: On present plans, yes. By six o'clock, I think.

NIXON: Sure.

KISSINGER: If I leave Moscow by two I'll be there at six. And so — I think, I think that the North Vietnamese will settle this summer if we can get them to call off their offensive now. That's the main thing.

NIXON: Call it off. I'd punish them a hell of a lot more before [unclear]. But we'll get a lot of [unclear], won't we?

KISSINGER: Well, this thing won't end — you see, if out of this meeting, just to war-game it. The best we can get out of this meeting is your announcement on Monday night that I was in Moscow, the strong indication on Vietnam, and announcing that we are going back to a plenary on Thursday. It won't fool anybody.

NIXON: Right.

KISSINGER: Then they will say about secret talks, say we never comment on secret talks.

NIXON: Right. That's right.

KISSINGER: But once we have already — we can finesse that so that everyone will —

NIXON: — know there're secret talks. That's right.

KISSINGER: You could just say Le Duc Tho will come back, as you know. Besides the less you say the better —

NIXON: Or I can say so damn little that it doesn't mean much. You know I —

KISSINGER: All right.

NIXON: I have no problem with that.

KISSINGER: So that's what will happen on Monday if we're lucky. On — then there's a private meeting with Le Duc Tho on Friday. We bomb the living bejeezus out of them all week long if everything goes well.

NIXON: Including this one tomorrow night, right?

KISSINGER: Including that one tomorrow night. Then shortly after that we get the deescalation thing done. So that would give us two more weeks of military action, it would, and then if that happens I would guarantee a settlement this summer because they have literally no place to go. Especially —

NIXON: The bombing tomorrow night, do you think, will help [unclear] to understand how we started the diplomatic line?

KISSINGER: Yes. Mr. President, I'll bet —

NIXON: I think it will. But what do you think?

KISSINGER: Right. What I think is that it's, we'll have some anxious moments. It's a gamble, one of these wild things. No other man in this country would have bombed Hanoi and Haiphong having an invitation to Moscow in his pocket — or in the pocket of his assistant. Now here we're bombing a port while I'm in Moscow. What we are saying —

NIXON: But we, but we're not breaking the deal with Dobrynin.

KISSINGER: No, it's right up at the — it will be just what I told him.

NIXON: Right. Not in the Hanoi-Haiphong area.

KISSINGER: That's right. And I'll tell Gromyko, you say, tomorrow night, I'll say that, listen, that this is — the more we do now the better. The more reckless we appear, because after all, Mr. President, what we're trying to convince them of is that we are ready to go all the way. The only way we are able to convince them is to do reckless things. For example, all Soviet ships on the way to Haiphong have been stopped — I don't know whether I've had a chance to tell you this — not just the ones from Vladivostok, from everywhere. And they are backing off, or at least they want to avoid them.

NIXON: Well, they don't want to be in the harbor while it's mined.

KISSINGER: So, I must tell you, maybe they'll tell me Friday morning, "You son of a bitch. You've just bombed Dong Ha while you are here. There is a limit. Go back on the next plane." That's the risk we are running. But it's precisely, I don't think, that isn't the way Dobrynin talks to me.

NIXON: Well, we're just, we're just going — you told him today that we would continue bombing.

KISSINGER: I told him that the only things we will not bomb is Hanoi and Haiphong. My instinct is —

NIXON: That's enough to give them.

KISSINGER: My instinct is the more we — after we've taken out Dong Ha then I'd go back to the nineteenth parallel and stay there. That still gives us 140 miles to bomb.

NIXON: That's pretty good. With regard to your points here —

KISSINGER: Excuse me.

NIXON: I think I would say that, in talking about our relations, I think you could say that you've often heard the president discuss this matter, and he's aware that there are a number of important countries in the world these days, but he says there are only two countries that really matter in terms of power, as of now — the U.S. and the Soviet Union. Others, for example the PRC and Japan, could matter very much in the future. And we have to therefore make our plans accordingly. But today the Soviet Union and everything depends on us.

Secondly, that this summit, as distinguished from other summits, comes at a time when the president agrees that we are equal. I would say that. When neither can push the other around. And also at a time when neither can or will allow the other to get an edge militarily. In other words, that is one of the reasons why they are [unclear] arms negotiations with us and the whole purpose of that is to tell them I am not going to allow them to get an advantage. See? That is they're escalating. So we're, this is how it differs from '59, '61, and '67. The other thing, in terms of cosmetics, is to say the president, as a student of history, knows that there have been spirits that have been raised and then dashed. We had the spirit of Vienna. We had the spirit of Camp David. We had the spirit of Glassboro. He does not want this to be that kind of a spirit. He thinks we should think incidentally of a place to meet outside of Moscow or find a different name than Moscow. In other words, that's why I think where we might have a meeting and then we could have the spirit of Dacha or Yasnaya Polyana or something like that. And that this, however, will be the real thing. Because Brezhnev has talked about the spirit of Yalta, you know, remember when the agricultural minister said it would be better to go back to that. Well, we're not going to go back to the goddamn spirit of Yalta. But nevertheless it shows that he's thinking in those terms. So this is in your soft sell in the beginning.

KISSINGER: Right.

NIXON: The president says let's don't have the spirit of Camp David; that failed. Let's don't have the spirit of Vienna; that was a failure. Let's don't have the spirit of Glassboro; that was a failure. I mean you're reflecting of course on, you're conceding that but it was a goddamn foolish thing. But this is the real thing. Here we're not only going to have the spirit, we're going to have the substance. And that's why this summit is by far the most important meeting in this century. Right? Lay it right out there, you know, in those terms. The president considered the Chinese meeting enormously important because of the future. But we're talking now about the present here in Russia. And he's aware of power. He's aware that China is potentially a great future power. He's also aware of the fact that the Soviet Union is a great present power. And for that reason we have things that bring us together. So — now, one thing I want you to be extremely hard on is, they have a single standard. We can't have this crap in effect that they can support liberation in the non-Communist world but that we, the Brezhnev Doctrine must apply in their world.

KISSINGER: That's a strong —

NIXON: Let me put it this way. Tell them the president doesn't know the particulars of the Brezhnev Doctrine. Now, and the president realizes that the world has changed since 1959 when all over Russia he was harassed by directors of Khrushchev about the Captive Nations resolution. [This was the resolution passed by Congress annually during the 1950s requiring the president to proclaim a week of prayer for the "captive nations" of Eastern Europe. President Eisenhower issued the proclamation several days before Vice President Nixon left on his trip to the Soviet Union in July 1959.] The president has no illusions about what we can do about liberating Eastern European countries. I'd just put it that way — by arms, force of arms. But the Soviet Union should have no illusions that it can directly or indirectly use force of arms to liberate non-Communist countries. I think you've got to say there's got to be a single standard on that. Now what we're really saying to them in effect, look, we'll divide up the world, but by God you're going to respect our side or we won't respect your side. Don't you think that point should be made?

KISSINGER: Absolutely. I'll — the one thing, Mr. President. They'll undoubtedly tape what I say.

NIXON: Yeah.

KISSINGER: I shouldn't say this is the most important meeting of this century because if they play it for the Chinese —

NIXON: I know.

KISSINGER: But I — the thought —

NIXON: In terms of substance, you can say —

KISSINGER: Oh, oh, oh. Its immediate impact or something.

NIXON: In terms of its immediate impact on substantive matters it could be, it could be you say, the most important, depending upon what we agree upon in terms of substance. The other was enormously important in terms of changing the whole world, because, you know — all we mean about that is the president thinks his China initiative is the most important thing he's done so far. I'd say that. Because we have to look to the future.

KISSINGER: Right.

NIXON: Have to look to the future. But we're talking now about the present. And, we might say, it's very different from when Mr. Kosygin and Mr. Johnson talked about their grandchildren [unclear] at Glassboro. Say that President Nixon wants to talk to Chairman Brezhnev about ourselves and our children. Right now. It's not grandchildren. Children. They like that. The Russians like to use that kind of business [unclear]. Point out, give them a little bullshit to the effect that the president has great respect for Mr. Brezhnev — he's a strong man, a determined man.

KISSINGER: I should start with it.

NIXON: He is not, the president is a, the president is a deeply believing ideologue just as Brezhnev is. He has no respect for weak men. He thinks, he thinks Brezhnev's strong. As a matter of fact, and I'd throw in, that's one of the reasons the president respects Mr. Zhou Enlai and Mr. Mao Zedong, because they are strong men. If you want. Just stick in a little needle there. He respects them. He totally disagreed with them, but we found mutual respect. And the president, however, he sees Mr. Brezhnev, he believes he's a strong man, he deeply believes in his system, but that, and he's not going to do anything that will be detrimental to the security of the Soviet Union, he doesn't expect him to, but the president isn't going to do anything detrimental to the security of the United States. There can't be any winner. No winner in this contest. We both have to win or it will not be successful. In other words, unless the agreement is one that both have a vested interest in preserving, the agreement isn't going to be worth the paper it's written on. And he believes, that this, that you believe, having met, knowing the president, studied Mr. Brezhnev, that they will, that they are the kind of, they are two men who despite their differences in backgrounds and the rest, could make very great progress, because they're direct men, they're strong men, but they're honest men. I'd put that crack in there. You see? Hey look, you might as well use flattery. You know the Russians use flattery. They're horrible that way. And also they're susceptible to it.

KISSINGER: Okay.

NIXON: Now, say, on the other hand, that you're not using flattery. You know, you've got all that [unclear]. The other point is that you ought to get in a very strong line that you've heard, the president is very fatalistic about his position. You know he differs, tell them, you knew and respected President Johnson, you did some missions for him, and President Kennedy, you did some missions for him. But this president, each of them had his strong points, this president differs from them in one important fact. All three were politicians or otherwise they never would have been elected president. But President Nixon is one that you have heard say to the top officials when he decided to go forward on the Haiphong-Hanoi, he said politics be damned. That every one of his advisors have said to you, you can say, Mr. President, Mr. Chairman, the secretary of state, the secretary of defense were not suggesting, every one of them, Rogers — well you would say didn't oppose it, but point out the political risks. Say it that way. That the president said politics be damned, we're going to do what's right. And the president is going to take that line right down to the election. I don't want them to have any impression that I was affected one iota by public opinion, by polls, by anything of that sort. Don't you think that's a good point to make?

KISSINGER: I think it's crucial.

NIXON: The other point that you've often made to the Chinese. The president is in a rather unique position. He can deliver what the so-called liberals promise because he has the confidence of the Right in our country. And there's no president who could go to Moscow at this time, at a time Moscow is fueling a war that has cost fifty thousand Americans. No president could go at this time and come back with an arms control agreement and so forth and sell it to the American people except this president. He would have a riot in the streets of the right wing. Now, tell them, now there are still a lot of McCarthyites in this country, Mr. Chairman. You know, tell them that. You know, Mr. Wallace. Scare them with Wallace. You see my point? But this president can deliver. He'll never promise a thing that he doesn't deliver on and he will deliver. In other words, what we have here is two hard-edged, strong men who can, can make this deal. [unclear] But to have a successful summit it's indispensable, not just necessary, but indispensable, to have some progress in Vietnam. That's all.

KISSINGER: But some significant progress.

NIXON: Oh yeah. Fine. You know what I mean. You're going to sell them on it. I would point out on the trade. I don't think they care much about trade any more than the others.

KISSINGER: Oh yeah. Oh, no, no, no, no.

NIXON: They do? But on the trade, you could say the president has looked this over. You could say, "Do you realize, Mr. Chairman, that there isn't a chance that the Congress would approve favored nation treatment, which has to be passed by our Congress, with the present state of Soviet-American relations, particularly in view of the Soviet support of North Vietnam? Not a chance. Now the president can get it through and he will. But that's why a cooling in Vietnam is essential. And then if we do that more is to come, favored nation, credits," all as I told Gromyko, a whole new world opens up. And I'll sell it to the Congress and I can do it. I think you need a little of that in the talks. Don't you agree?

KISSINGER: Absolutely.

NIXON: Congress won't approve credits, won't approve favored nation treatment, if political tensions exist at the present level.

KISSINGER: On SALT, Mr. President.

NIXON: Yeah, let's go through some of those.

KISSINGER: You don't have to make a decision on these various options except, are you prepared —

NIXON: I might with these things. I didn't mean that.

KISSINGER: — are you prepared to give up on the submarines?

NIXON: Am I? Of course. I'm prepared to give up on it — I think we can sell it, can we?

KISSINGER: Well, I think I'm going to tell that son of a — I'm going to tell Moorer the president has just said, your bloody honor, that you are going to do it.

NIXON: But on that, let's give it up provided we have a hard line that we immediately send our negotiators back to work on the SLBMs, you know, [unclear].

KISSINGER: Right.

NIXON: But on that, I don't know, get what you can, but I must say that, you know — let me put it — that we get everything we can, recognizing that we cannot have an arms control agreement that looks as if we got took. They're going to analyze that son of a bitch right down to the wire teeth. So do the best you can. That's all I can say. And the same is true about whether we have a Washington and a Malmstrom [Air Force Base, one of the proposed Safeguard sites], and all the rest. You know. Do the best you can.

KISSINGER: All right.

NIXON: You're a hard worker. Do the best you can.

KISSINGER: All right.

NIXON: Fair enough?

KISSINGER: All right.

NIXON: I've looked at all these things. But if I were to start to say well take this, don't take that and so forth, this is a matter that will have to be determined —

KISSINGER: Frankly, Mr. President, whether we get a hundred and fifty more interceptors or not is just of no consequence.

NIXON: Yeah. Listen, I don't think it makes a hell of a lot of difference. On the SLBMs, actually I think, I think it's to our advantage, if they don't settle, to continue to build some. Maybe not. Maybe we — you know we've got a hell of a budget problem. We've got to cut it down, we've got to cut five billion dollars off next year's defense budget. So, I don't want to [unclear] unless we've got some settlement with the Russians on that —

KISSINGER: I have to talk to you about that.

• • •

KISSINGER: Mr. President, you've played this with a nerve that's [unclear].

NIXON: Well —

KISSINGER: The safe thing for you would be to let — well, the seemingly safe thing — [unclear exchange]

NIXON: You mean, to let South Vietnam fall?

KISSINGER: Yeah. Already we've done our best [unclear].

NIXON: Yeah and that we've done our best, you know, to get the Americans out, as hard as we can, and Thieu has to face that. Huh?

KISSINGER: That's right. That point you made —

NIXON: [unclear]

KISSINGER: That's right.

NIXON: I think the—I think that's quite true, quite true. Well, I know, but the thing is that Laird is so totally wrong. I think based on what I've—with what we've seen, South Vietnam, it might have survived, who knows?

KISSINGER: Yeah.

NIXON: But I just don't think it would have survived, not if we hadn't moved that stuff out there—

KISSINGER: Not a chance. You've talked to Haig. I've talked to him. That situation in Military Region 3 was touch-and-go.

NIXON: Touch-and-go, but he thinks that our power may have tipped the balance.

KISSINGER: Yep.

NIXON: Does he?

KISSINGER: Absolutely, and our reinforcements, and—

NIXON: And, of course that stuff pouring out there now must just scare the living —don't you think, but it must give 'em pause?

KISSINGER: Right. From the point of view, also, of this exercise, Mr. President, it's happening perfectly, because I was wrong about the *Midway*. It's only coming out there next Monday. So we don't—right now, we haven't pulled back from anything yet.

NIXON: Mm-hmm.

KISSINGER: So, they must think you are just getting into the blockade [unclear].

NIXON: Mm-hmm.

"Go back? From where?"

April 20, 1972, 12:30 p.m.
Richard Nixon and Alexander Haig
OVAL OFFICE

While Kissinger was en route to Moscow in an air force plane, Nixon was understandably apprehensive and even edgy. He summoned Haldeman and Connally for separate conversations about the prospects of Kissinger's mission. He also asked Haig to the Oval Office for much the same reason. Their discussion turned to Vietnam, and in answering a direct question, Haig told the president that Kissinger's prime concession in Moscow was to be that the United States would allow one hundred thousand North Vietnamese troops to remain in South Vietnam. Remarkably enough, after all of the endless conversations that Nixon had with Kissinger, it was left to Haig to tell him what Kissinger intended—nothing less than the most significant reduction in American expectations since the start of peace talks four years before.

• • •

NIXON: Well, I woke up last night, and I read Henry's thing yesterday. And I didn't want to disturb him when he was getting ready to go. I think it's so vitally important for him to know, to trust—you know Henry. We have to face the fact that he wanted to take this trip purely for the summit and would have taken it purely for the summit if we hadn't vetoed. That wouldn't have worked. Now Henry, of course, [unclear] priority, but on the other hand, he would consider it to be a success, if he just comes back and says well we worked out the agenda for the summit and the communiqué. No, no, no. It will not be. And — did you read the memorandum?

HAIG: I did. And it's —

NIXON: What did you think?

HAIG: — precisely what I told him when I saw him last night. I said my greatest fear, and I think it will be the president's, is that we've done this now —

NIXON: That's right.

HAIG: — and it cannot appear to be a backing away. And I said that was Thieu's concern. And somehow we've got to be sure that Vietnam is the purpose of this trip and is portrayed as that.

NIXON: What did he say?

HAIG: He said he agreed completely. And he said that what we have to do is, hopefully, if they agree, to come out on Tuesday, announce that, announce the plenary, and we will defuse these bastards totally.

NIXON: Well, if, for example, on Tuesday, you saw a very little simple line, I would continue to think I couldn't agree with that.

HAIG: I don't either.

NIXON: [unclear] So you would agree that they would work toward a negotiated settlement of the conflict. Now that, that is a hell of a — they should say that.

HAIG: That's right. What worried me was that we would announce the plenary, you see, without having referred to Moscow and then it would look like we backed down —

NIXON: The plenary? No, I thought we turned that down today.

HAIG: Yes, sir. But in order to meet secretly, you see, now we're going to have to announce the twenty-seventh.

NIXON: Yeah. When is the secret meeting? When is that? Did you read the message?

HAIG: May 2. May 2.

NIXON: Well, that's all right. That's the bottom line —

HAIG: And it would be ideal if we can have the Soviets —

NIXON: But on the other hand, on the other hand, does this mean that the moment we make the announcement we have to deescalate the bombing?

HAIG: No, sir. He's not going to do that. And of course we might drop down from the Hanoi area and keep it down low as a sign of goodwill till we have our meeting. But we'll keep, we're going to bang tonight.

• • •

NIXON: What is the situation? I was reading a story in the paper this morning about town falls and all that bullshit.

HAIG: Right, sir.

NIXON: What is that out there? That's a [unclear] much expected, et cetera, et cetera.

HAIG: This is — this is the area in southern I Corps and northern II Corps, Binh Dinh.

NIXON: Is it anything like Hue? Is that what's involved?

HAIG: No, sir. It's an area that the Viet Minh hold — a Viet Minh stronghold, in Binh Dinh province. It's an area that we know. It's always been pacified the least. It's the toughest area —

• • •

HAIG: It's the toughest area. Well, that outpost, it's [unclear] —

NIXON: You can't bomb there?

HAIG: Oh, yes, they have close air support in there. They have a hell of a lot going in there now.

NIXON: I see.

HAIG: And that thing is not overrun. As of this morning they're still fighting, but they're badly outnumbered. And it's, it's going to be a tough one. It's not as severe —

NIXON: How many North Vietnamese are in South Vietnam at the present time would you say?

HAIG: I'd say about one hundred twenty thousand, sir. I'll have to get you precise figures.

NIXON: Nobody else will give it a look. Oh, we will. We will. In the end we've got to with all the air and the rest. It really depends on their arms. For Christ's sakes, you can stop one hundred twenty thousand.

HAIG: Yes, sir. You know they — we have that fighting there. The Koreans, who are trying to open up the road on that Route 19, and got a bloody nose at the An Khe Pass.

NIXON: They failed then?

HAIG: Well, they had to reinforce. They got there and they're in a tough fight there. And that's not bad. I'd like to see the Koreans —

NIXON: It's about time. Have they had any casualties at all since the war began?

HAIG: Well, yes, they did in the early days. They had quite a few. [unclear] fighting. Now, they're into it and they've got to reinforce. The other place where it's very active today is in III Corps again, the area that's dangerous —

NIXON: An Loc?

HAIG: An Loc. There's fighting in the town again. They sent an ARVN battalion of Marines down, an airborne battalion south of the town got badly hit. And they've come back into the town. And also the enemy is attacking at Dau Tieng as I indicated they would. They slipped by and they hit it this morning. And that's a tough fight going on right now. We're — we can expect this for another couple of weeks, sir.

NIXON: Yeah, but I mean, I just want to know whether or not the South Vietnamese are fighting well.

HAIG: They're fighting, yes, sir. They're fighting well. And the Twenty-first Division is fighting well. This Minh, who's the corps commander, is just a sorry son of a bitch.

NIXON: I understand.

HAIG: And he's developing —

NIXON: But, basically, in the An Loc area and the rest, they're — they are — you say they're — you say the battalion got a bloody nose, which means what? That they were — just was it put out of action?

HAIG: No. No, sir. But it got — it got mauled. They had a lot of casualties and had to come back in. They were —

NIXON: Did it give any casualties?

HAIG: Pardon, sir?

NIXON: Did they dish out any casualties?

HAIG: Oh, yes. We had 190 air sorties in there last night alone in that one area. So, they've just been banging the hell out of it. And there were eighteen B-52 strikes in support of that action. So, we — we've just got to be clobbering them.

NIXON: Mm-hmm.

HAIG: But they fell back and used those four days to regroup and now they're trying to take it again.

NIXON: In — in III Corps?

HAIG: Exactly.

NIXON: But your point is that each time that — when this happens they don't have as much punch the second time, do they, Al?

HAIG: No, they don't, sir.

NIXON: First of all, their morale goes down some, doesn't it? After you've taken a hell of a mauling?

HAIG: Their morale goes down. The —

NIXON: They don't have much equipment, do they?

HAIG: Equipment is down. They're still knocking out tanks there. They knocked down, I think, thirteen last night. But this is going to be a tough fight and it's going to stay tough. But I think we're going to do it.

NIXON: We will with all the power we've got there in the air —

HAIG: That's right.

NIXON: It's got to just, just pulverize those bastards.

HAIG: That's, that's an incredible number of sorties to put in there. Eighteen B-52 sorties. Geez.

NIXON: On top of the —

HAIG: One hundred ninety fighter-bombers —

NIXON: Yeah.

HAIG: — and gunships that are always on station.

NIXON: Yeah. That's in that III Corps area?

HAIG: Yes, sir.

NIXON: Is it true that the South Vietnamese are flying with their — are flying about half of the tactical air sorties?

HAIG: Yes, sir. They have been.

NIXON: Are they flying pretty well?

HAIG: Well, it's forty-two percent. It's not quite half of it —

NIXON: Are they fighting pretty well?

HAIG: They're —

NIXON: Do they fly pretty well?

HAIG: They're flying very well and their support has been better than ours because they've been able to come in lower.

NIXON: But their planes are not as good as ours [unclear].

HAIG: Hell, they've had some planes shot down because of it. They —

NIXON: But they go in there, do they?

HAIG: They're going in and the ARVN troops are very high on them, [unclear] the ones — the commanders I talked to, very high on them. Now, they're getting a little tired, and we — that's why it was good we reinforced, because they've been going at full bore. In I Corps everything's there, except for that southern province there, which we knew was going to be tough. That — that's a guerrilla stronghold, and always has been, and it'll stay tough.

• • •

HAIG: It's hard not to, but these are all infinitesimal things. Those fire bases that were overrun in the first days that they reported? They weren't fire bases. They were god-damn OPs that were put up there to watch infiltration and to keep the eyes and ears open, and, Jesus, they just weren't intended to be held. They were not defensive positions.

NIXON: In the meantime, when you talk about a town falling it's probably not worth saving.

HAIG: [unclear]

NIXON: [unclear] I actually believe in the strategy at An Loc. Do you think they should try to keep An Loc? I wonder if it isn't — if it makes sense to back out of the town and bomb it to smithereens.

HAIG: In a military sense —

NIXON: Right. It's psychological —

HAIG: — it doesn't make sense —

NIXON: It's psychological. It's like Verdun.

HAIG: For Thieu, he can't. He just — Thieu is the man who has put out these orders, and for him it's psychologically essential that he hold. We could give up some stuff in II Corps. Hell, that place is — if they lost Kontum or Dak To City it would be a very minor incident.

NIXON: On the other hand, I suppose trying to hold them has its points. In one sense, in that we certainly are punishing the enemy if he's willing to take the heat.

HAIG: [unclear]

NIXON: The only thing is that — what I was thinking, Al, our purpose here is not to hold territory; it's to destroy the enemy. If you could retreat and get the enemy in a more exposed position for bombing, then I'd retreat and then destroy it and go back in. Doesn't that make sense?

HAIG: That's the way — that's the way the book says to do it, and that's the way I would do it.

NIXON: Well, you think they won't do it?

HAIG: They won't because of the psychology of it.

NIXON: Well —

HAIG: And on the other hand, it's not so bad because they still have to concentrate around these.

NIXON: And, maybe, too [unclear] from here. Their guys will fight and —

HAIG: It takes a good, disciplined army to be able to withdraw and fight. Once you start moving back, and I think that's another problem Thieu's confronted with —

NIXON: Hmm.

HAIG: — these little guys are good in defense if they have good, strong positions, and they dig in and hold. And they — you'd need a very sophisticated army to be able to withdraw —

NIXON: Mm-hmm. Mm-hmm.

HAIG: — and fight well.

NIXON: I know. You know — of course, there are reasons in it for Thieu, but beyond that, the Germans did it fantastically well against the Russians, you know, in World War I.

HAIG: They were so professional. That's right.

NIXON: But Jesus Christ, I mean they would draw back, you know, and then just clobber the shit out of them. The Russians would come marching in and they'd just kill 'em, just kill 'em.

HAIG: Well, they —

NIXON: The Russians' armies would go, in World War I, in both on the Northern Front, the Eastern Front, and also even the [unclear]. They'd have an enormous victory and number of something, and the Germans would reinforce and just knock the bejeezus out of them. In other words, remembering the maxim of war is not to hold territory but destroy the enemy.

HAIG: Exactly.

NIXON: That's something we have to do out there?

HAIG: That's the way, they're fighting that way in I Corps —

NIXON: Huh?

HAIG: They're fighting that way in I Corps. This, this division commander in the First Division [South Vietnamese Major General Pham Van Phu], he's crazy. He said, "Hell, I don't care about these fire bases." He said, "As long as I can kill them if they are concentrating on it, then I'll keep it up, but when it gets too hairy I'll pull back and we'll hold it at the next one." He hasn't pulled back from one yet, and they've killed about twenty-five hundred in [Fire Base] Bastogne. And they, incidentally, opened the road to them yesterday and completely resupplied and put reinforcements in. So, that's a good strong position, still.

NIXON: This town down in III Corps, it's — well, we can't worry about it. Now, Abrams has got it all, certainly, charted out, and they'll fight —

HAIG: They'll fight —

NIXON: — and lose some, win some.

HAIG: [unclear]

NIXON: What — what good do you think this strategy does? It's more psychological than anything else, is that correct? Do you consider it psychological or what?

HAIG: Yes, but I think —

NIXON: Psychology is important, is it not?

HAIG: Psychology's important, especially now where Henry is [in Moscow]. The news will get to them while Henry's there and that's, that's good. The other thing is this thing is going to get more of a logistics exercise —

NIXON: Yeah. And every time we can reduce their logistics thing —

HAIG: And what's going to happen is — and I think they're in there to hold. That's their strategy, isn't it? They're sitting at a high point and then go on —

NIXON: Can we? Hell, yes. You mean to hold — stay in South Vietnam? To hold the line?

HAIG: Stay there this time and to get their infrastructure built back and to destroy pacification and Vietnamization. And that's why their logistics are going to become a more —

NIXON: What the hell have the Russians agreed to on it? Seriously, what in the hell did they agree to?

HAIG: Well, here's what I would hope, sir.

NIXON: Yeah?

HAIG: If we could get them to agree [unclear], the Vietnamese would go back, the North Vietnamese.

NIXON: Go back? From where? Just from I Corps, you mean?

HAIG: No, status quo ante before the attacks started, which would mean III Corps and I Corps. II Corps, they were in there and, hell, that's worthless country anyhow. And it's going to be mucked down in rain here very shortly. Then we would stop bombing. And hold — and everyone would negotiate; hopefully get some prisoners back —

NIXON: That's good —

HAIG: — as a token exchange.

NIXON: Well, that's good [unclear] —

HAIG: And hold this for a year, with a Soviet firm guarantee in writing. God, I think you — then they would have had the course, because you would get absolutely swept into office on the head of something like that. Kennedy and the doves would be licked. And then they'd be faced with a four-year president who they know god-damn well won't put up with a second round.

NIXON: Well, there's one other course of action we may have to handle and that is if we can get this, through this point —

HAIG: That's right. That's right —

NIXON: If I can keep this, as you know, as support for [unclear], but in my view, then you're faced with the blockade problem. My own feeling is that a blockade, that public support for it now will probably be higher than at a later time. But on the other hand, it may be the best time to throw the blockade is about three weeks before the election.

HAIG: I —

NIXON: You see the point? [unclear] then nobody can find out. And on the basis, now we're doing this till we get our prisoners back. You see? Then you've got something very, very tough. Before that we can't say we're going to blockade and lift it when we get our prisoners, but you destroy South Vietnam. But at that point, you could — if they make an issue out of prisoners, we blockade and say, all right, we're going to keep to it until we get our prisoners back.

HAIG: That would be all right if — I don't think a blockade would, would solve this thing in the short run.

NIXON: No?

HAIG: In a military sense or in a political sense. In a military sense, we've had several studies made now. An awful lot of this stuff can come through China, even the —

NIXON: Sure —

HAIG: — Soviet stuff.

NIXON: By air, too.

HAIG: And by air. So we, we shouldn't fool ourselves about that. It's great now to get the Soviets' attention. They have to —

NIXON: Yeah, but we've got their attention. I think we've got their attention. Correct?

HAIG: Totally. Totally.

NIXON: And we'll find out.

HAIG: And the thing in the long run, that is going to discourage everyone, is to kill those bastards down there. Just wipe 'em out.

NIXON: A hundred thousand is a lot to wipe out, Al.

HAIG: Yes.

NIXON: Well then, they could do it to them, couldn't they?

HAIG: Well, if they lose —

NIXON: They're just sitting there — pound away.

HAIG: When you hear these prisoners, there's nothing left in the villages but wounded veterans. The wounded veterans are telling the few kids that are left to go and hide.

NIXON: They say that?

HAIG: Yes. The young girls have no men, so they have a social problem. The young girls are consorting with older, married men and having illegitimate children. The society is very disrupted by that—

NIXON: This is in the VC country you mean?

HAIG: It's in North Vietnam.

NIXON: Oh.

HAIG: In the North. One prisoner just, he said, it's an incredible situation.

NIXON: The men are gone?

HAIG: No, no young men.

NIXON: Of course not. [pause] It drives me to think they've had, at least, to have five hundred thousand in there.

HAIG: That's right. And they claim that when they came down they all knew they were going to die. They do have deserters up there and the training centers are deserting. They have short training. They're not ready for it. They get down on the battlefields, some of them are wandering around; that's how these RF and PF are killing them. They don't know what they're doing.

NIXON: What is the situation with regard to the bombing of Hanoi and Haiphong? Do you buy the proposition that actually it stiffens their resolve on absolute victory?

HAIG: I think it has that effect in the short term. But this country has been through it before. They've had it. I think at this point in time it's not so much so. They're just sick of it, too. And when the 1968 bombing halt came, we had run it through so long initially it did anneal them, and made them fight harder. But by 1968, when we stopped bombing, they were, they were on their knees. And that was showing, too—

NIXON: Well, as a matter of fact, too, the type of bombing that we intend to do, that we're doing now is really more effective than the '68 bombing, isn't it?

HAIG: Oh, yeah—

NIXON: Right? What I'm getting at is [unclear] the 1968 bombing was picking out of targets and all that sort of thing.

HAIG: It's entirely different.

NIXON: Because this strike was an enormously effective strike compared to most of those. Or was it? Am I wrong?

HAIG: Hell, it was. First place, our techniques are better. Secondly, instead of Robert McNamara, as he used to do, sitting at the desk picking the targets, you've allowed the field commanders—

NIXON: Commanders—

HAIG: —to do this and they're doing it more effectively without, what I call, are debilitating these strikes. And that's what they had all during the '68 period. They just constantly shifted the targets, and they were all run from here where the people didn't know what the hell they were doing in a close [unclear] were oriented on restraint. I think we've done an awful lot in these few strikes that we've put in there, especially when you put B-52s in. That's just—

NIXON: That was not done?

HAIG: Never done.

NIXON: I take it that's an enormously potent ordeal, isn't it?

HAIG: Yes, sir.

NIXON: And that hits even up there.

HAIG: It was a — it's just a frightening weapon. It's a frightening weapon when you're on the ground. I've used it close in to our troops, and I'll tell you it's —

NIXON: It's really something?

HAIG: God, you know, you just see these shock waves. The whole ground trembles and you get no warning because they're up higher and you can't see them when they're coming. You just hear all of a sudden this whistling, an eerie whistle.

NIXON: And the ground shakes?

HAIG: And the whole ground shakes. It does get your attention.

"The crudeness of these guys is not to be believed."

April 25, 1972, 8:53 a.m.
Richard Nixon, Rose Mary Woods, and Henry Kissinger
OVAL OFFICE

Immediately following Kissinger's return from Moscow, he went straight to the Oval Office to brief the president. However, rather than discussing the plans for the upcoming summit, Kissinger described the special hospitality extended to him while visiting the Soviet capital.

• • •

NIXON: Where the hell do you think Kissinger was over the weekend when I was trying to call him?

WOODS: Probably out with some babe.

KISSINGER: That's it —

NIXON: Well, I'd hope so. I hope so.

WOODS: He probably was.

KISSINGER: It wasn't [unclear]. I'll tell you one thing, Mr. President, it wasn't through lack of offers.

NIXON: Is that right?

WOODS: Oh, my word. Aren't you modest, Henry?

KISSINGER: No. No, there it's got nothing to do with modesty. The head of their state security, General Antonov, greeted me at the airport and said he had a whole bunch of girls, all twenty-five years and younger —

WOODS: You ought to remember, that's how they got Joe Alsop. [Woods is referring to a KGB sting of Alsop during a visit in 1957.]

KISSINGER: There isn't —

NIXON: With who, the girls?

WOODS: Not the girls, but the [unclear].

KISSINGER: The crudeness of these guys is not to be believed.

NIXON: I know. [unclear]

KISSINGER: When I said I want to take a swim — and that's also under the state security — so, again, they said — they asked, "Do I want masseuses?" You know —

NIXON: Nurse?

KISSINGER: Masseuses.

NIXON: Masseuse?

KISSINGER: And they said —

NIXON: Masseuse? They use those for that purpose?

KISSINGER: Yeah. Oh, God, and they said any hair color I wanted. But they did it —

NIXON: Jesus Christ! Oh!

KISSINGER: So revolting. You know —

NIXON: It takes all the fun out of it.

KISSINGER: You know, it's — it was just absolutely revolting, and they brought it up on
every occasion. General Antonov was riding shotgun in the car I was in. He's [un-
clear] security too [unclear]. [laughter] We went past the Moscow film studio and I
said I know a lot of actresses in Hollywood. He said, "Try my girls. They've got a lot
more experience."

"You can't put your arms around the Russians at a time when they're kicking the hell out of us in Vietnam."

May 1, 1972, 4:11 p.m.
Richard Nixon, William Rogers, and Henry Kissinger
OVAL OFFICE

*In Moscow, Kissinger found that Brezhnev was not interested in discussing U.S.-Viet-
namese relations. Neither was Kissinger, at least not to the extent that the president had
expected. Kissinger did present his framework for a renewal of peace talks, though, and
the Soviets did pass it on to officials in Hanoi. The North Vietnamese responded on their
own, without appearing to be coordinating with the Soviets. As a result, Kissinger's secret
meetings in Moscow were soon followed by secret meetings in Paris, in the form of a new
round of talks with North Vietnamese diplomat Le Duc Tho. The day before the talks,
Kissinger met with the president and William Rogers, who was leaving within a day for
London and a tour of Western European capitals. Nixon was ready to cancel the Moscow
summit scheduled for the end of the month, in the name of maintaining a clear priority
on Vietnam.*

• • •

NIXON: On this thing too, I would take every opportunity to level them hard on Vietnam. I'd hit the Vietnam issue extremely hard, and say that we're prepared — that for

emphasis this is actually true — as far as I'm concerned, we'll do what's necessary to carry it out, that their interests are deeply involved. And if they say well it risks the summit, say that we're prepared to risk it. I think there should be no — our best bet, particularly when you talk to Brandt, it'll get right back to them.

ROGERS: What's your — do you have your positions made on the next week or so? Are you going to play — I'm assuming —

NIXON: Oh, while you're gone?

ROGERS: Yeah.

NIXON: Well, as you know, Henry's going tomorrow, and I suppose that —

KISSINGER: I'll get word to Berlin.

NIXON: He'll get word to you. My inclination — my — well, who's going to get what. My feeling is that we're going to get nothing out of it. And unless it's very substantial, very substantial, we'll go with what we have in mind, is to hit, is to hit the Haiphong-Hanoi complex on Thursday and Friday — a forty-eight-hour strike — in lieu of their offensive, not because of the failure of this. So that's where it stands. Now, actually where will you be those days? You see, it'll be Thursday or Friday, or Saturday or Sunday, dependent upon weather —

ROGERS: I'll be —

NIXON: But of course it won't be over. It's not going to be longer than forty-eight hours. But it'll be big. It'll be the biggest we've had. It'll be — Abrams has got it at a hundred minimum B-52s, and of course all of the naval gunfire we've got up there. The *Newport News* will be up there by the time with eight-inch guns. And, in addition to that, of course, about four hundred TacAir. So, it'll be by far the biggest strike on the Hanoi-Haiphong area. It will be limited to military targets, of course, to the extent we can. It will hit some new things, like there's a big troop training area that Moorer and Abrams have selected; we'll try to clean it out. That's about where it stands. Now, that whole regime could change in the event — but only in the event there is something really done on this occasion. Henry's prepared to talk very directly. Is that right, Henry?

ROGERS: Will you stay more than one day, Henry, or will you —

NIXON: Oh, no.

KISSINGER: Well, you know, if they come with this spectacular proposal, conceivably —

NIXON: Oh sure.

[unclear exchange]

NIXON: I think you might remember raising your earlier — I think this meeting will blow quickly. And I think, therefore, that upon his return, it should be announced that it has been held.

ROGERS: Oh, sure. [unclear] Nobody knows about it.

NIXON: Well, the [unclear] would know. I don't think we should announce it in advance, because then all the press will be there and want comments by the two. But if you could meet without having to go out and face the television cameras. But I think immediately upon your return we announce, so have it in mind. And I think you need to cable to Bill, of course—

KISSINGER: Tomorrow night—

NIXON: Tomorrow night at ten o'clock. Well, wait a minute, he'll be there. He's going to be in Europe the same time you are.

KISSINGER: Yeah, but he'll be in England and—

ROGERS: I'll be in England.

KISSINGER: England. So I'll back-channel him tomorrow night.

NIXON: All right. So we will announce the meeting. And—

ROGERS: I think the real question that I'm going to be faced with is, is the summit—

NIXON: Yeah, of course, they'll be—what'll they want to know?

ROGERS: Well, they'll want to know what we think the chances are for a summit meeting. And the president said while you were out, Henry, that it was all right for me to say that it's possible the summit meeting might be canceled and he was prepared for that.

NIXON: But we don't think so.

ROGERS: We don't think so?

NIXON: I'd play it in the terms that the plans for the summit are going on on schedule; that nothing we have done so far has affected it detrimentally. And that is totally true. As a matter of fact, it's affected it positively. But on the other hand, that we cannot anticipate what the Soviet reaction will be in the event that the North Vietnamese continue their offensive and we react, as we will react with strong attacks on the North. And if strong attacks on the North bring a reaction from the Soviets, then it will happen that way. It is our judgment, I might say, it is my judgment, and you can say—and you can very well say that it is my judgment that the summit will move forward because I think that they—that they aren't going to like it—but I think they're going to go forward. But I don't want the Europeans to get the feeling any more than the American people to have the feeling that we will pay any price in order to sit down with the Russians. And, I would say also that if the situation in Vietnam is seriously deteriorating with no—nothing by the time we get closer to the summit, there isn't going to be any—we aren't going to go to the summit there. Because you can't put your arms around the Russians at a time when they're kicking the hell out of us in Vietnam. I don't think it's going to happen, from all—did we get Abrams's report today?

KISSINGER: We haven't gotten that yet, but he, of course, he probably is—

ROGERS: I think, Mr. President, the best thing for me to do is to stick with the position that I talked to you and you feel the summit will go ahead—

NIXON: Right.

ROGERS: —that there's always [unclear exchange]. You know it's a possibility, but you feel confident that it will go ahead on schedule.

NIXON: Well, I think so. What do you think, Henry?

KISSINGER: I think, yes, of course —

NIXON: It depends on various people. Certainly the British, with Pompidou — Brandt is the key one, don't you think? Is there any difference there?

KISSINGER: No. I think Brandt has to take advantage and he'll go right back to the Soviets.

NIXON: Yeah. That we expect it to go forward. And I think you might say this: we believe, and we think the Soviets also believe, based on things that have happened up to this point, that there are major concerns at the summit that completely override the Vietnam issue, and that Vietnam should not be an issue that should stop the summit. But that on the other hand, that as far as we're concerned, we have to take the actions necessary to defend our interests in Vietnam, and we'll do so with the thought that the Soviets will go forward with the summit. And we're prepared to if they don't react to it. With Brandt you can't talk nearly as frankly as you can with Heath, naturally.

• • •

ROGERS: Mr. President, I'd like to say just a word about the conversation we had. I think that if you could work out a paper that you can give Gerry to give to Semenov, so that if we work out an agreement, we can say that it was based on your paper.

NIXON: Mm-hmm.

ROGERS: I never liked the Brezhnev paper. I think it'll [unclear] —

NIXON: Let me see it.

ROGERS: In other words —

NIXON: Right —

ROGERS: — if we can — if you can state our position and have a Nixon paper.

NIXON: Hmm.

ROGERS: And then when we are questioned about it we can say that —

NIXON: This is our position.

ROGERS: — this is our position. I just think if we could do that it'd be a big help, because some of those things in there will be —

NIXON: Well, his instructions, I think, will be an equivalent to that because you can have him hand them a paper —

ROGERS: Yeah, and say this is —

NIXON: Yeah. I know.

ROGERS: And then — and then, he can negotiate from that paper —

NIXON: I bet if we could work on it now —

ROGERS: It will help, too.

NIXON: Yeah.

• • •

NIXON: Well, I'll give him [Smith] a letter, like we always have done before. How would that be?

KISSINGER: Yeah, we could send him a letter —

ROGERS: I think that would be good, yeah—

NIXON: How about—how about preparing a letter? When does he leave? Tonight?

KISSINGER: Well, we can wire him the letter.

NIXON: I'll prepare a letter, which I've done before.

ROGERS: That'd be good—

NIXON: I'll say after our meeting that if these are the considerations that—

KISSINGER: Yeah.

NIXON: —he should have in mind, then he has that for the record—

KISSINGER: That's right—

[unclear exchange]

NIXON: —as to what we want—

ROGERS: And then, we can say we've negotiated from your—

NIXON: Yeah. Yeah. The best thing that we could get, yeah. It's a curious situ—proposition. We are—we don't have anything to negotiate [unclear]. We have to face the fact that on the defense—in the defense field that we have a very weak hand in terms of what we can get—

ROGERS: Well, I think we got—I think—

NIXON: A very weak hand. We have to—we have to remember the Russians are moving forward like crazy on submarines and offensive weapons—

KISSINGER: And they've just built a new ship—

NIXON: —and we're not doing a damn thing. And so, we're in a—and, with all the peaceniks, we have one hell of a time getting it. So, I think—I don't know, I—it'll accomplish something to get them slowed down, and yet, in terms of selling it to the country, well, I guess all we can talk about are MIRVs.

ROGERS: I think we can sell it to the country—

NIXON: The MIRVs thing, I think, is a powerful thing to them. Don't you agree?

KISSINGER: Yeah. It is a fact, which isn't our fault, that every missile we are now working with was designed in the Eisenhower administration—

NIXON: That's right. [unclear]

KISSINGER: —that we've wasted eight years of McNamara's tenure.

NIXON: We haven't done, we have—we are at a disadvantage. That's the problem.

KISSINGER: And when you see this damn thing, that new missile they tested—I don't know whether you've seen this—

NIXON: Do you think it's—do you think it's a real one?

KISSINGER: Yeah. And—

NIXON: I thought you said they weren't sure if they had them—

KISSINGER: Well, they popped something out of a hole, which they are applying a submarine-launch principle to land-based missiles. That is, just get it out of the ground, and then give it an additional thrust—

NIXON: Yeah, well—

KISSINGER: That way they can double the payload of the SS-9, and they could give it as many as —

NIXON: Yeah?

KISSINGER: — twelve five-megaton warheads. And it's really a scary thing.

• • •

NIXON: I told Ron [Ziegler] I was really, probably, too hard on Smith, but once he —

KISSINGER: Mr. President —

NIXON: — just pulled out a piece of paper like that. But that's gobbledygook to say that. What difference is it's —

KISSINGER: Well —

NIXON: — State's fucking position. What the [unclear] —

KISSINGER: Mr. President, the problem is this —

NIXON: I don't know what the hell he's talking about.

KISSINGER: Brezhnev — Brezhnev accepted your propositions. Every point in that Brezhnev paper we gave him.

NIXON: Mm-hmm. What the Christ is Rogers talking about?

KISSINGER: We are cutting it down from eight-five to sixty-two, and we're giving up nothing in return. We can't get another goddamn submarine out of them —

NIXON: Why is Rogers so strong, so strong on this?

KISSINGER: So that, so that I'll guarantee you one thing: by Friday of this week, if you don't do this —

NIXON: Mm-hmm?

KISSINGER: — you're going to get stories out of Helsinki —

NIXON: Yeah —

KISSINGER: — that they broke the logjam.

• • •

NIXON: I seldom lose my temper and everything, but I just thought, "Oh, shit," when he handed the little shit-ass piece of paper over to you —

[unclear exchange]

KISSINGER: I didn't need to bother you. I handed Dobrynin this paper, which he had drafted, which said, "While we can't agree with all these considerations." Dobrynin said, "I'll transmit it." But, his reaction was the same as yours.

• • •

KISSINGER: He said, "If Brezhnev reads this, he'll think that we're playing games with him." So, I said, "All right, why don't you give this to Brezhnev [unclear] the other one has been accepted by Smith."

NIXON: Well, the point is, while we cannot agree with that this — with the lawyers, it's like writing a letter for the record or some damn thing.

KISSINGER: Well, in effect, it says —

NIXON: "Shame on you," doesn't it?

**"What you'll find out more from your meeting
tomorrow is just how strong they are."**

May 1, 1972, 6:01 p.m.
Richard Nixon, Henry Kissinger, and Bob Haldeman
OVAL OFFICE

*Nixon and Kissinger had one last huddle before the latter departed for Paris. Neither
knew exactly how the Soviets would respond the more they learned about the American
military buildup in Vietnam, let alone what Nixon intended to do with that buildup.
Kissinger's task was to set up a summit that was anything but guaranteed to come
off.*

• • •

KISSINGER: Got a letter from Brezhnev.

NIXON: Another one? What is it this time? Is he raising hell?

KISSINGER: Oh, he's thanking you for sending me, and as a result of these conversations —

NIXON: That's probably in response to my letter.

KISSINGER: Yeah. And taking into account all of the other negotiations under way, it
can be definitely said that quite a bit has been done [to] ensure the success of the
meeting.

• • •

NIXON: Who did they say will undertake the military action? That we were?

KISSINGER: Yeah.

NIXON: Well, they're going to get it — they're going to find out. That's why we pop
them. And Haiphong's going to be made.

KISSINGER: Exactly.

NIXON: There's not going to be any of this business of who the hell is attacking.

KISSINGER: On — and also, what Dobrynin told me, they're willing to agree to everything on the technical arrangements —

NIXON: Except the plane?

KISSINGER: Except the plane.

[unclear exchange]

KISSINGER: They'll let you go on Saturday to Leningrad. They'll let you go live on
television, although they've never done that before. The only thing they ask is if you
go on live is to give them the text an hour in advance so that their interpreter can
do a good job.

NIXON: Oh, we'll do it more than that.

HALDEMAN: We told them we'd give them the text well in advance.

KISSINGER: All right. Well, I'm just telling you what their reply was. And, every other
technical issue, I forget now what it was, I told him to get in touch with Chapin.

NIXON: He told you about church?

KISSINGER: Church is okay. So Brezhnev —

NIXON: Really?

KISSINGER: Yeah.

NIXON: Well, don't tell anybody, though. I don't want — now, that's one thing I don't want Scali or any of those people to know a thing about. I want to go low-key — much the better way. I'll just go that day to church, not with a great big hullabaloo, because after all, I am a — I mean that's what I do on Sunday, not if I can help it.

HALDEMAN: [laughs]

NIXON: But that's what I'm going to do in Moscow. So, I go to church. And they'll be one hell of a play, right?

KISSINGER: Absolutely.

NIXON: And it will help us here with, you know, with the Billy Graham types.

KISSINGER: It will be great symbolism. But — so they gave you a favorable answer on all of that.

NIXON: Yeah.

KISSINGER: But on the [use in Soviet domestic airspace of an American] plane, they say —

NIXON: I understand —

KISSINGER: — the humiliation to them that we —

NIXON: Yeah. I told Bob we're going to do it, so we're going to do it. Let me ask you something else.

KISSINGER: So, if I may call him tonight and say the [Soviet] plane is okay.

NIXON: Yes. Yes.

KISSINGER: Then they will call Chapin tomorrow and confirm it.

HALDEMAN: Is the plane for Leningrad and Kiev, or just Leningrad?

NIXON: That's right.

KISSINGER: Leningrad and Kiev.

HALDEMAN: You sure? Because they said Kiev would —

KISSINGER: No. That's what he mentioned to me.

NIXON: I don't really give a damn. It's perfectly all right. Go ahead. So then, on the other one, it's done now. I don't want to argue about the plane. This is a small thing. There are other things — I've ridden their planes many times before. If you could get the — they don't want to cancel this summit, Henry?

KISSINGER: No.

NIXON: I think that's why the Hanoi-Haiphong thing's just got to be —

KISSINGER: But they may have no choice.

NIXON: All right. Fine. So we —

KISSINGER: But neither do we.

NIXON: I'd sure as hell rather cancel ourselves.

KISSINGER: But you can't go to Moscow anyway if you've just been run out of Vietnam.

NIXON: That's right.

KISSINGER: So, it's —

NIXON: Well, get the point that if we're run out of Vietnam, we will then blockade North Vietnam to get our prisoners back. Let's face it. We're not going to run out on anything. That's further down the road. Hell, this battle has taken four weeks to get Quang Tri.

• • •

NIXON: What you'll find out more from your meeting tomorrow is just how strong they are.

KISSINGER: What I'll find out tomorrow —

NIXON: [unclear]

KISSINGER: They will certainly not make an acceptable proposition.

NIXON: Oh, I know that. But you're going to find out — if they think they've got the South Vietnamese by the balls. You know damn well they've got them heavily infiltrated. If they think they've got them by the balls — they're probably getting everything from a lot of our Americans over there as well — then, they'll just be as tough as hell, and tell us to go to hell. That is why we'll have to bomb Hanoi and Haiphong. If they are taking that attitude, you've got to get right to the heart of it. Right [unclear]. If, on the other hand, they're taking the attitude, which I have [unclear] of trying to buy time, bomb anyway, because we can't accept it.

KISSINGER: Well, I think we can give them time as long as we bomb them.

NIXON: Oh, give them time. I meant that they must not by promising to discuss things, keep us from bombing.

KISSINGER: Exactly.

NIXON: Now, the other thing is that I think that the only bombing that really seems to affect these sons of bitches is the bombing of Hanoi and Haiphong.

KISSINGER: That's correct.

NIXON: You think that's true?

KISSINGER: The only thing that will —

NIXON: Don't you think that's true? They don't think they're going to win the battle anyway.

KISSINGER: The thing that I must warn you, in all fairness, is that it is very conceivable to me that the Russians will cancel the summit after your next bombing of Hanoi and Haiphong. I'm still in favor of doing it. And then you will unleash — right now we are in the position — the reason we are doing not as badly in the press as we might is because the pro-Soviet guys are buffaloed by this, by the Moscow maneuver, and that will be then unleashed. I am still strongly in favor of bombing Hanoi and Haiphong, and really wrapping it up.

NIXON: If they cancel it, I only hope we can get a little advance information so we can cancel it first. Is there any way we can? How will they cancel?

KISSINGER: I can say under these conditions.

NIXON: How will they cancel? I mean is there any way we can [find out]? Yeah, we can find out. You've got to keep in very close session with Dobrynin so you can sense one word, and if he ever raises the subject of cancellation, we'll just have to go out and say that the president has canceled the summit. Not let those sons of bitches say that they did.

KISSINGER: Yeah.

NIXON: See my point?

KISSINGER: Yeah.

NIXON: We're not going to let them cancel first if we can possibly have helped it.

KISSINGER: Well, if they — you know — they might start a press campaign, and if they do, we can cancel it. That would be a pretty good tip-off. And —

NIXON: We have a little problem [unclear].

KISSINGER: Ah, we may bring it all off, Mr. President. We've gone through other periods before. We've sat in this office —

NIXON: Well this is [unclear], in a sense, because all the chips are on the line; they weren't in Cambodia, and they weren't in Laos.

KISSINGER: And we are winning

NIXON: Now, it's win or lose. And frankly, it's better that way. It's better to get the son-of-a-bitch war over with.

KISSINGER: In Cambodia, we were winning —

NIXON: [unclear]

KISSINGER: In Cambodia we were winning, and then Laos, we weren't losing.

NIXON: Well —

KISSINGER: This time, it's got to be over now by summer.

NIXON: The war will be over?

KISSINGER: By July–August. It's going to be one way or the other now. I mean, clearly, the South Vietnamese can't keep this up for another three months.

NIXON: And the North?

KISSINGER: Well that's the question. I doubt it.

NIXON: Oh, I don't think they can at all.

"I am very sorry he's gone. It'll be a big loss to our country."
May 2, 1972, 11:16 a.m.
Richard Nixon and Lyndon Johnson
WHITE HOUSE TELEPHONE

On the morning of May 2, 1972, J. Edgar Hoover was discovered dead on his bedroom floor by a household attendant. His forty-eight-year presence at the helm of the FBI had come to a close. Both Presidents Johnson and Nixon stood by Hoover loyally when he faced criticism. When Hoover died, Nixon insisted on announcing his death personally, and Hoover was treated to a state funeral where Nixon eulogized him.

· · ·

NIXON: Hello?

JOHNSON: Hello?

NIXON: I was trying to reach you. I just announced the death of J. Edgar Hoover.

JOHNSON: Yes, I just heard you.

NIXON: Right. I know how much you thought of him. I tried to reach you before, but you were out someplace.

JOHNSON: It's nice to talk to you. I'm very grateful. I am very sorry he's gone. It'll be a big loss to our country.

NIXON: Well, one thing about it, you know. They were after him, and a lot of people were trying to get me to fire him. And I told him earlier this year, I said, "Look," I said, "this is no time to change directors because we'd have a hell of a fight in the Senate," you know, political fight. At least he outlived his detractors. I hope! [laughs]

JOHNSON: I hope so, too. He was a good man. I'm awfully sorry he's gone. He was my neighbor a long time.

NIXON: I know that. Yeah.

JOHNSON: Thank you so much for calling.

NIXON: Fine. Fine. Okay.

"On this whole business of negotiating with North Vietnam, Henry has never been right."

May 2, 1972, 12:08 p.m.
Richard Nixon and Bob Haldeman
OVAL OFFICE

On May 2, Kissinger arrived in Paris, full of anticipation for his talks with Le Duc Tho. The two men were together for three hours, which proved to be more than enough time. Tho took no interest in Kissinger's various proposals. "What difference is all this talk going to make?" Tho asked. "The end is in sight." Kissinger had no choice but to report to the president that the negotiations were over for the time being.

· · ·

NIXON: Well, Henry got nothing out of them over there as he expected. I expected it. I understand he's terribly disappointed.

HALDEMAN: I'm not surprised —

NIXON: Why would he —

HALDEMAN: — but I think poor old Henry, I think he really thought he was going to get something.

NIXON: Well, he found —

[unclear exchange]

NIXON: — and this and that. I'm going to talk with Haig this afternoon. He's quite —

HALDEMAN: It really did do nothing?

NIXON: He said it was the most unproductive of all meetings he's had. I demanded we overthrow Thieu.

HALDEMAN: They didn't even serve warm tea.

NIXON: No. But the point is, Bob, we have got to realize that on this whole business of negotiating with North Vietnam, Henry has never been right. Now, I just can't help it, but just have to say that, just a straight-out flat conclusion.

HALDEMAN: Well, Al never thought he was going to get anything.

NIXON: Well, I didn't either.

HALDEMAN: Al told me before Henry left, he said, "It's probably a good exercise, but I don't think he's —"

NIXON: And he's not going to put it out this time, naturally, he — because it would raise hopes that things were going on. We don't want to raise any hopes. You know, that's the line, as I said, that the PR types around here. Thank God I talked to Al about it, but I didn't take that line in Dallas. I mean, in San Antonio.

HALDEMAN: Yeah.

NIXON: Because we have, we have to take the hard line now [unclear]. That's all we can do. We have no other choice. And if you start indicating anything about cease-fire or coalition government or anything like that, we're not going to go down that course. Good God almighty, you realize what happens to your negotiating position, the peaceniks and all the rest. They'll be in there harder than anyone. But we'll just keep crackin' in there.

HALDEMAN: Go ahead with your big ones now?

NIXON: We'll have to. What the hell else do you do?

HALDEMAN: You've got to.

NIXON: What the hell else do you do? You've got to do it for American public opinion. You've got to do it for the South Vietnamese, keep their morale from dropping. And you've got to do it in order to have some bargaining position with the enemy. And also, the thing [unclear] feel strongly about it, I think we better cancel the Russian summit. Now this is the one that just breaks Henry's heart, because —

HALDEMAN: What about postponing?

NIXON: Well, then they'd cancel.

HALDEMAN: You could make it look like you were — if you postpone indefinitely, just announce that you will not go to the summit under these conditions.

NIXON: Yeah, yeah.

HALDEMAN: Don't say, "I'm canceling it." Don't say, "I'll never go." But say, "Under the present conditions I will not go, and therefore I have canceled my plans for the May

27 departure," or whatever it is, May 20 departure, "and what becomes of the summit depends on what happens in other places." Then they can come back and say, "We cancel the summit," but you've still taken the initiative.

NIXON: Oh, I have. You see, all of this is very painful, I know, to all of our people around here. It's terribly painful to Henry, because he sees basically our whole foreign thing in great jeopardy; I mean, all of our seeds, and this and that. But, on the other hand, we've got to look at what else we should do. And what else do you do is to, you know, continue to just to whack them out there and have the Russians cancel the summit — that's the worst of both worlds.

HALDEMAN: If you cancel the summit, you gain something from them. If they cancel it, it hurts you.

NIXON: If they cancel it, it looks like we — peace has suffered a great blow because of our failure in Vietnam, the president's stubbornness and smallness. If, on the other hand, I say I will not go to the summit so long as there is any — so long as we have a massive offensive being supported by the Soviet Union.

HALDEMAN: And the shah [of Iran] and all of those other folks too.

NIXON: Well, that's [unclear] —

HALDEMAN: Yeah.

NIXON: Well, Henry has a point — and Al thinks there's something to this point, he sees more to it than I do — that maybe he's right that to a certain extent you keep the critics off balance as long as they think we may be up to something in the negotiating realm.

HALDEMAN: Right.

NIXON: He may be right.

HALDEMAN: Well, I think that's right. But I don't — it keeps that narrow fringe of critics off balance, and it's important to keep them off balance.

NIXON: Yeah.

HALDEMAN: But that doesn't buy you public support. Your general —

NIXON: I don't think so either.

HALDEMAN: Your general public support is so — of course, the public wants peace. And that's one problem you've got with canceling the summit —

NIXON: Yeah.

HALDEMAN: — is that they —

NIXON: Is that they want the Soviet summit.

HALDEMAN: Because they think that's a peace — not just Vietnam, but other areas. [unclear exchange]

NIXON: They want — they're mixed, they're ambivalent about it, they want peace on the one hand —

HALDEMAN: That's why postponing it rather than canceling it might put you in a better posture too. If they cancel it, it's they who've destroyed it as part of the peace thing. But you've taken a strong position in saying, "I won't sit down with them under the present conditions." Well, the other side of that is what's happening on the military side.

NIXON: Well, I got [unclear]. It's, as usual, it's not — it's hairy, but not nearly as frightening as the press indicates. You get the whole thing under Al's — Al, whose great business [unclear], he says just keep it up, that's all. Thieu's going to stand. See, the point of the military thing is this. What the hell else do you do? Get out? Overthrow Thieu? Jesus Christ, you can't do that.

HALDEMAN: We can't. He can.

NIXON: Oh, yes, as part of the South. But, you know if he just runs out now, suppose he goes off and says I resign, perhaps the whole thing collapses. Your men are in great, great danger to the remaining Americans. No, we'll just hold tight, don't get panicked, you know what I mean?

HALDEMAN: Yeah.

NIXON: Our people shouldn't be so panicky. These are the way wars are. They go up and down. It's tough; damn hard. And you can't make good news, whatever it is, on the other hand. But there's one thing I'm sure of we need: that strike on the Hanoi-Haiphong area. I think that just adds up on all scores. They don't negotiate now, Christ, how are you going to improve your negotiating position? How are you going to get the — so, we'll work on it.

HALDEMAN: [unclear]

NIXON: Well, it's my job. But look, we have to face it. Henry's judgment has not been good on this. His judgment has been terrific on most things. He thought he was going to get something out of the Russians when he went over, you know that.

HALDEMAN: And he didn't get a drop.

NIXON: You remember? And I kept — that's why I sent those goddamn cables. I knew he wasn't getting anything. I said, "For Christ's sakes, don't give them what they want unless you get something that we want." Well, it was all right. So, second point, he's — and I told Al this morning, I said, "Al, aren't you glad I didn't make that SALT announcement?" And I sure am. Never wanted to anyway — making the SALT announcement.

HALDEMAN: Did Henry want you to make it — was he the one that was —

NIXON: Oh, yes.

HALDEMAN: — wanted you to go on —

NIXON: [unclear] he finally agreed yesterday morning.

HALDEMAN: [unclear]

NIXON: Yes. Oh, I hit him on the ground that —

HALDEMAN: Keep it away from Gerry Smith?

NIXON: Oh, also, yeah. I think here he was very personally involved because he wants to be sure that the White House gets the credit and so forth. My point is, Bob, that

I don't think there's a hell of a lot of credit in it. I don't think people give much of a shit about SALT. Do you?

HALDEMAN: Well, it's a plus, but it isn't a —

NIXON: It didn't get any play last [unclear] —

HALDEMAN: Ron calls it a [unclear]. Nobody's going to change their votes because of it.

NIXON: Yeah, it didn't get much. Particularly when the enemy's not knocking ground over there. No, the press is a big deal here, they're just trying the usual thing, to divide the president from, you know, his hard-line soft-line. And also, they're trying another one to build Henry as the peacemaker if we get it, you see? [unclear] At any rate, it isn't going to come. And the reason they're selecting Henry to beat Bill now is that they've given up on Rogers. That's really what it gets down to. They know that they can't go to him. They know that Henry isn't going to be able to come. They know that Henry's spoken. That's why —

HALDEMAN: Henry's so visible.

NIXON: Henry's got to be able to understand this, that when he was — he didn't I must say, to his credit, he didn't talk to the press, he wasn't inciting them. But the purpose of raising Kissinger isn't to help us, it's to screw us. Right?

HALDEMAN: Absolutely.

NIXON: I'd keep Scali going on the other line — that the president's in charge.

• • •

NIXON: I can't see, I just can't see — it's just been hard for me to get this through to Henry — I just can't see myself being in Moscow toasting the goddamn Russians, signing the SALT treaty in the Hall of St. Peter, when Vietnam is under serious attack. Do you agree or not?

HALDEMAN: I think I do. My basic — I very, totally do.

[unclear exchange]

HALDEMAN: I'm just trying to raise the other side of this. I don't know how you argue the other side. I don't see how you can argue —

NIXON: Well, can you compose the question, or a quick five-hundred-word — five-hundred-sample — that we can run with immediately? You can do that, can't you?

HALDEMAN: Yeah.

NIXON: What I'd like to do is to say is that "in view of the continued Communist invasion of South Vietnam, which is supported by massive Soviet aid and military equipment, some," and I'm not thinking how to word it, some, or do you believe "the president should" — no, "as you know, the president is scheduled to go to the Soviet Union for a summit meeting." So, did you get that — but "should he postpone the — his — meeting with the Soviet leaders until after the offensive — unless the offensive is discontinued." In other words, try to get it in the way, "unless the offensive is discontinued, there are some that say that unless the offensive is discontinued, the president should refuse — should cancel" — don't say postpone or postponed, don't give them several, don't give them eighteen questions, in other words make it one — "his visit to the Soviet Union," or "should not go forward with" or "should delay" — to "postpone his visit to the Soviet Union until the summit is" — you're going to word those things — will you try to get some wording out like that? Let's just get a feeling of what kind of public opinion we're faced with on that, see? I have a feeling myself that despite their great interest in having a summit, the people still don't want their president to go there when we're under a hell of an assault from Soviet guns and tanks. See my point?

HALDEMAN: Yup.

NIXON: Now, you just put it very succinctly. Do you believe the president should cancel his — postpone — his meeting with the Soviets, cancel it until —

HALDEMAN: That's it. Cancel until the offensive —

NIXON: Cancel it until the offensive is discontinued. The summit meeting with the Soviet leaders — until the offensive in Vietnam is stopped or discontinued or something like that. Or, do you believe he should go forward with his meeting with the Soviet leaders, regardless of the fact that even as the offensive in Vietnam continues. We're going to be in the position, in my view — this is the second week, we don't get there until the twenty-second — in other words, we've got three weeks; we're going to be in a position then when the offensive will have frankly run its course, and they will not have succeeded. I still think that's the case. When I say not succeeded, they will have succeeded in the public's mind in many ways, and part of the II Corps. But any person that knows a goddamn thing about the country knows that all that matters in Vietnam are III and IV Corps. That's where the people are. Anyway, that's the way it is. You did get your poll off, didn't you — the poll up to the Congress, and so forth?

HALDEMAN: Yes, sure did. With a lot of background.

NIXON: [unclear]

HALDEMAN: I didn't see any. Well that's what I wanted. We got it out yesterday. [unclear] I did that.

NIXON: [unclear] The purpose of this is really to affect our own people's morale, and so forth. You see? I certainly would like to have some public record but I don't think we're going to get it. But everyone — Colson's group knows the importance of it. Now that's something that should be played, you understand? That's not Pollyanna-ish.

HALDEMAN: That's right. That's public opinion. That's what people —

NIXON: That's right. You see, putting out the polls, it's not taking the Pollyanna-ish line. It's should we kick these bastards or not.

HALDEMAN: That's right.

NIXON: So that's a pretty good one.

"In the long run, what we've got to look at is what happens."
May 3, 1972, 10:02 a.m.
Richard Nixon and Bob Haldeman
OVAL OFFICE

As Kissinger headed home, he received a memo from Haig, which included the statement that "the president asked me to convey to you that the political question at this point is his growing conviction that we should move to cancel the summit now." As soon as Kissinger arrived in Washington, he was whisked off to the presidential yacht to discuss the wisdom of canceling the summit before the Soviets could do so, causing possible embarrassment. By the next morning, when Nixon went over the scenarios with Haldeman, he was start-ing to lean away from cancellation.

• • •

NIXON: In the long run, what we've got to look at is what happens. Now, if canceling the summit, and nothing's sure, would substantially increase the chances of bringing the Vietnam thing to a successful conclusion, I would do it in a minute. If, on the other hand, canceling the summit is only marginal in terms of bringing it to a successful conclusion, then —

HALDEMAN: Then you're losing a lot of long-range pluses.

NIXON: What?

HALDEMAN: Then you're losing a lot of long-range pluses.

NIXON: Well, not too big pluses, except you're buying a lot of long-range negatives.

HALDEMAN: Okay.

NIXON: The long-range negatives being that —

HALDEMAN: A collapse of the Nixon foreign policy.

NIXON: A collapse in foreign policy, but also, a massive, when you cancel the sum-mit, upgrading of some [unclear] and all those — the Soviet propaganda force. I'm not referring to the shit-asses that Henry talks to, but I'm referring to all over the world, demonstrations and so forth and so forth — would unleash enormous ten-sions. You'd have embassies and, well you know what I mean, they'd really start raising holy hell with us because they'd figure, "What the Christ? Nixon has drawn the sword; we have no interest in whatever." So we'd have meetings. That's the point that I think we have to have in mind.

HALDEMAN: Is a postponement of the summit not a possibility?

NIXON: A postponement or if you cancel it you fundamentally postpone it too. You can postpone the agreement.

HALDEMAN: Postpone it to June?

NIXON: You see? No. You could say I'm postponing the trip until after the offensive is over. So what would the Russians say — you don't want to come now, screw you. Do you see my point? Either you do it or — you can only postpone it to a degree.

HALDEMAN: So they say screw you. There's a chance that they don't.

NIXON: No. I think that if we cancel the summit or postpone the summit, which I think any way you call it, it's a dodge, it's going to lead to —

HALDEMAN: Massive Soviet propaganda.

NIXON: Massive propaganda. It also bears on the failure or success of our Nixon foreign policy. Now the whole policy comes down through channels as a result of his insistence on fighting this terrible war in Vietnam. Now —

HALDEMAN: That's the line.

NIXON: In a sense, that cost is too high to pay, in a sense. It's too high to pay, because you can confuse the Vietnam thing to an extent.

• • •

NIXON: At first blush you make the announcement, you're going to have a hell of a lot of hawkish sentiment in this country. Say —

HALDEMAN: It won't last — that won't hold very long. That'll give you a blip.

NIXON: What the hell has happened to the Nixon foreign policy?

HALDEMAN: But you then get the erosion. The press will just, they're already trying to set it up that you gambled, all the neat pieces that you were putting together are in grave danger of coming apart. The cancellation of the summit would be the maximum signal that they have come apart, and they, to them, that would give them a rallying point to build that case on. And they are so — you know, they leap on anything they get, anything they can get their foot in at all.

NIXON: Sure.

HALDEMAN: That — so it would erode over — you'd get a good blip. I think you would get a hell of a bounce at first — a strong move by the president —

NIXON: Courageous.

HALDEMAN: Not going to kick us around and that kind of stuff. But then, you have to do that in early May.

NIXON: Second thoughts would be very, very difficult.

HALDEMAN: Would build up, and then the Democrats at the convention in July would say, "Here we are, a president who was going to go to Moscow and bring us a generation of peace has now bogged us down in an unwinnable, desperate war in Vietnam."

NIXON: See, Henry is, if I can analyze it correctly, he doesn't even know this, but put yourself in his position. He feels, and he says as well, and I've tried to explain this to Henry, that it's U.S. policy too; I think that he's, because he failed, I mean because they did not come true as he had hoped they would in both Moscow and Vietnam, he wants to say in effect, "Goddamn you, you can't do this to us," get my point? So it's a bravado act basically. So we say we're going to cancel the summit.

HALDEMAN: It's a good, short-term bravado act.

NIXON: Now, on the other hand, let's look at it this way. Assuming the situation in Vietnam, assuming if we don't go to the summit, we've got to hit the Hanoi-Haiphong area as sure as hell, then goddamn Laird is playing his usual games, saying we can't find targets and so forth. He is a miserable bastard, really.

"I'm the strongest proponent of not making the summit hostage to Vietnam or Vietnam to the summit."
May 3, 1972, 10:59 a.m.
Richard Nixon and Henry Kissinger
OVAL OFFICE

William Porter, the chief delegate to the Paris Peace Talks, had reopened the most recent round in late April by scoffing at the attitude of the North Vietnamese representatives. He announced that it was impractical to go on if they had no intention of moving forward on any issues. The peace talks continued, but a week later, Nixon was again considering another, even *stronger message of American impatience: canceling the summit. For Nixon, it was a decision that impacted nearly everything of importance to him, as he and Kissinger would carefully discuss.*

•   •   •

NIXON: Now, let's come to the other point. At the heart of the matter is what effect the cancellation of the summit would have on the outcome of the war itself. If the cancellation of the summit very substantially improves a chance for a favorable outcome in Vietnam, that is a decisive factor. If, on the other hand, the cancellation of the summit has only a marginal effect in that respect, and would of course [mean] the bombing has a marginal effect, then we have to look at it another way, and that way would be along this line. If we are looking at a situation here where over a period of three years we have built in a masterful way a new foreign policy. The China game, the Soviet game, it's a very big game. You and I both know that it's a very difficult operation. The Soviets have been liars and bastards and thugs, and so forth and so on.

We also know that at the present time we've got some American public opinion developing along that line. However, if we put it in perspective, I think we have to realize that if we're looking at the effect, the effect on the Democratic convention coming up in July, and we're looking at the election coming up in November, at the effect on the election, I think that cold-bloodedly we have to say this. First, the heart of the matter is Vietnam and how it comes out. If Vietnam comes out badly, the election is very seriously jeopardized anyway. However, if Vietnam comes out badly, then we also cancel the summit. In other words, if we cancel the summit and if it still comes out badly, the election would certainly be down the tube, something which Haig and yourself would say would be a very tragic thing. Because it would mean we would not live to fight another day.

God knows it, we need to, there's so much that needs to be done. You hear this military briefing and you realize that our military has let us down — and that's just one. But you need a new foreign policy, and you need a new military policy, and so forth, and it's not going to be done by any successor, but so much for that. If, on the other hand, canceling the summit is the only and critical factor, which may save the situation in Vietnam [unclear], because if the situation in Vietnam is saved, then canceling the summit will look good. I mean, [unclear] even though we will after our first [unclear] and then our erosion will come back up again. Now, there's one other equation to throw into this. If canceling of the summit, now if we see that the South Vietnamese situation is — if our cold-blooded analysis is, and we cannot make that now, I realize that you use the term "fifty–fifty," that's my guess. I mean it's half and half, maybe a little better than that, that they'll survive, because I think they're suffering a hell of a lot more than we have any reason to believe, but we shall see. If the South Vietnamese survive, then — I mean do not survive — then having the summit, even under very difficult circumstances, but having it where we say Vietnam will be at the top of the agenda, will have a bad effect.

KISSINGER: That is not a possibility to put Vietnam on the top of the agenda. I mean, there'll be many issues we'll have to juggle.

NIXON: All right. But having a summit without Vietnam at least as a marginal, is a marginal plus, instead of being a very substantial thing in the long run. That's what we'll have to face — I'm speaking now of the domestic side. So that brings me back to the other option. The other option is to react as we had originally planned, with our two-day strike, and see whether the Russians go forward, whether they stress — they may move to cancel, which they might. The two-day-strike thing certainly would have at first great support in this country.

Again, it would give some encouragement to the South Vietnamese, give some pause to the Russians, and some pause to Hanoi. The argument you made last night is a very strong one, to the effect that, well, it would look like an act of desperation, to the effect that Hue is being threatened, and so forth and so on. Well, maybe so, maybe the first strike will look that way too. But we all know at the present time the public temper will support that kind of a strike we want to look at. So we have to weigh that.

So it really comes down to this. Whether we really honestly feel that canceling the summit could have — could be — a decisive factor or even a substantial factor in resolving the situation in Vietnam. On that point, I have grave doubts. And if that is true, then the case for it isn't as strong as we thought it was last night. As far as the strike in the North is concerned, I have serious doubts whether that will have great effect on the situation in Vietnam. It will have some. But we all know that we know it's a choice between one of two things: either we hit the North for two days or we cancel the summit. We have no other options.

[unclear exchange]

KISSINGER: And hitting the [unclear] of the North for two days may cancel the summit.

NIXON: Oh, I understand that.

KISSINGER: And they may cancel it.

NIXON: I know, I know.

KISSINGER: And then all of the crap that you mentioned, maybe even more —

NIXON: Right.

KISSINGER: — coming against you. I mean every argument that you made on cancel-ing the summit wouldn't fly then even more because it would tie Vietnam even more intricately to it, and you wouldn't be able to get your story out.

NIXON: It's a risk, it's a risk.

KISSINGER: That's right. And I think there'd be a slightly better than fifty–fifty chance that they would cancel the summit, which is why I moved to the point that we should postpone it now. Nobody can present any of these positions to you with the argument that they will save the situation in South Vietnam, because I can't say that they will. Nothing may. Canceling the summit may not, certainly may not. But in this situation, I'm thinking of the presidency, thinking of your position in history, and of the position of the country in the long term. If you go to Moscow without having done anything, it will be a total disaster. We can make it look good, we can put on an act, but all the things that will be needed to be put on, that the Russians will then despise us. We will have lost all credibility.

NIXON: Not doing anything. Will [unclear] —

KISSINGER: No, I know. I just keep going up the ladder.

NIXON: Yeah. Fine. So that's out of the question?

KISSINGER: That I don't see how we can do. And the cramming of all that machinery, after reading them your dispatches. But even without it — secondly, for the United States, I mean, what the Russians have done systematically since last October is put it to us. And they've said you can have your summit, and at the same time we're go-ing to screw you. Now we go in on great principles of coexistence. And I think the feeling of uneasiness among — I'm not even worried now about Vietnam, the fact that Russian arms have run us out of Vietnam and the president goes to Moscow and signs principles of coexistence, gives them credit, and agrees with them to screw one of his allies in the Middle East. Now, you know that I'm in favor, hell, we've got the principles all negotiated, and the trade is all done, and the Middle East one we can do, and in fact we're prepared to do that too. But suppose you do all these three things after India-Pakistan and Southeast Asia, and the fact that the bastards have not done one goddamn thing for us ever.

NIXON: They have not.

KISSINGER: And I must say objectively that this is a sign of great weakness, which will encourage them. Your great strength in foreign policy is your toughness. And your great standing abroad is due to the fact that you've gone your way. Now you could say you could go to the summit, go through with it, don't sign these principles, don't give them credit, and don't make a deal on the Middle East. Well, then, we'll have a pretty lousy summit. Now to get out of the summit what you want, you have to come back and be able to talk about peace. And about having made tremendous strides towards peace, in other words, you give the Soviets a certificate of good conduct. Now, if we can limit South Vietnam while doing all of this that would be great. That'd be the best of all the worlds.

NIXON: But that you can't unfortunately know in time.

KISSINGER: Well if you are in Russia miles away and everything is integrated, there's just no way of making it look good.

NIXON: Correct. Our problem, of course. I just wanted to be sure you considered all those.

KISSINGER: I, Mr. President, I — God, we suffered and anguished to get to this point. So they may give us an answer that enables us to do it.

NIXON: Are you going to get an answer?

KISSINGER: Oh, yeah, there'll be an answer. But they may give us a very threatening answer because in a way they're cornered too. This letter is couched in terms that suggest we're going to attack North Vietnam but there's no threat to the Soviet summit involved here. But they may figure that since that's what we may do they may preempt us and cancel it.

NIXON: Okay. If we cancel the summit, then follow with massive attacks on the North occur.

KISSINGER: Yeah.

NIXON: Am I right?

KISSINGER: That would be my view. And we'd have to go right to the country and we'd have to put it to the press.

• • •

NIXON: You go to Russia then, what the hell can you agree on? That's the point. You can't agree to give credits; you can't agree to —

KISSINGER: See, the whole idea, see, of agreeing, of having you sign health agreements, science agreements — what do the Russians want at the summit? They want to show that you and Brezhnev are ordering the world. Now, when you do it as equals, it's risky enough because it's going to hurt us enormously in Europe, it's going to hurt us with the Chinese. But the risk is worth taking under the assumption that you can recover from it in the next election — after the next election.

NIXON: By turning hard.

KISSINGER: By turning hard. And that's how I'd justify it. But basically Shakespeare isn't wrong in his assessment of what this détente is doing to our allies. Now, there's strong sentiment that somebody to whom you can say look how you stood in all these crises. But it's somebody who's been humiliated or at least can be challenged in South Asia by the Russians, and then the most vital area where we have fifty thousand — I mean vital from the point of view of national sensitivities, not about strategic interest — and he still does it.

NIXON: That's right. That's it.

KISSINGER: That's something I think, Mr. President, that's going to be hard to recover from.

NIXON: That's right.

KISSINGER: And who is then going to be left to respect you? I mean, I shouldn't talk this way, but I mean, the hawks?

NIXON: Not likely.

KISSINGER: The doves?

NIXON: Nah.

KISSINGER: A strong president — the reason —

NIXON: The real heart of the question, and it's good to talk it out this way, the real heart of the question is what I'm getting at really isn't about Vietnam, because if it were, we'd have to realize —

KISSINGER: It's about what you said at the end. It's about the presidency.

NIXON: That's right. The real point here is that the canceling of the summit or the bombing — neither may prove to have too much of an effect on the outcome of Vietnam. So scrub both of those things. The real reason we have to cancel the summit, if we do cancel the summit, is that we cannot go to the summit while Russian tanks and guns are kicking the shit out of us in Vietnam.

KISSINGER: That's right.

NIXON: We cannot make an agreement with people that are doing that. We don't meet with a bunch of outlaws. It's like Rockefeller going to the prison at Attica to meet with those goddamn people. [New York Governor Rockefeller intervened during a riot and hostage standoff at Attica State Prison in New York State in 1969.] Right?

KISSINGER: That's my sense, Mr. President, with great reluctance, and knowing how we may get a turn in the situation; we may get an answer from Brezhnev that we can live with. I doubt it.

NIXON: Well, our answer — our decision on the speech, and so forth, should be made, it seems to me.

KISSINGER: You don't have to make it before Friday or Saturday.

NIXON: The decision to go on — let's get the speech ready.

KISSINGER: I'll get the speech done.

NIXON: You get the speech ready, and I'll work on it, and I can make a decision as to whether to give it or not Monday, and then give it Monday night or Tuesday night.

KISSINGER: Yeah. There's no —

NIXON: And have in mind the fact — and then we can have the strike, in the case I don't make the speech, we can have the strike go Tuesday or Wednesday or Thursday of next week.

KISSINGER: That's right.

NIXON: See my point?

KISSINGER: There's no incentive.

NIXON: I think in any event that we should tell Abrams — see this fits into the other point, that you can have these assets.

KISSINGER: Don't worry about this Abrams baloney. I talked to Moorer. We can wait for that till tomorrow morning. He has got his execute order.

NIXON: Okay. What I'm getting at is this. I don't think we should do it over the weekend. Let's make the final decision with regard to canceling the summit really Monday. I want the speech, however. I'm going to prepare the speech, because getting the speech and writing it will help me get my own thinking and the right kind of thing. So I want the speech, a copy of it by — well, can they — when can they have it, Henry?

KISSINGER: Tomorrow noon.

"The China thing was important from one standpoint only — hope."

May 4, 1972, 9:06 a.m.
Richard Nixon, Henry Kissinger, and Bob Haldeman
OVAL OFFICE

After a day of intense discussion, the immediate course was still uncertain on the morning of May 4. Once again, Nixon couldn't find a straight line through the many overlapping demands on his foreign policy. Thinking clearly at times, he fell into one of his darker moods toward the end of the conversation, calling Americans "suckers." By then, Kissinger was deft at steering him back from that brink. They finally reached a decision about the summit.

• • •

KISSINGER: Oh, yes, Mr. President, we have come back from every crisis stronger, and I think we're going to become stronger because of this one.

NIXON: Well, we have to be quite aware of the fact, Henry, that there's one difference. In the other crises, there was always beneath the surface a majority would be for us. This time, if they're canceling the Russian summit, there isn't any way that I can do it. I could make the greatest goddamn speech that has ever been made in the history of this office, and the people are going to be terribly, terribly put down because of this. So, let's face that. That is all right with me. I mean, I think in the long run what counts is what happens. I think we have to realize though in canceling that people are going to be disappointed, a few hawks will [unclear] that'll be hawk [unclear], which is not a majority. In the meantime, it will unleash our political enemies on the Hill, who will have — will then pass probably resolutions that will just knock the hell out of us and make fund cutoffs and everything else. Got to figure that will happen. You've got to figure — this is what I mean, when you figure consequences, you've got to figure that the Russians, of course, will unleash their worldwide propaganda. They'll go all out in their propaganda here. If you think Joe Kraft has been bad to this point, if he gets orders from the Russian embassy to beat Nixon, he will plant things, lie, steal, anything. I remember this in '60, you see? Perhaps you may not remember.

KISSINGER: I remember that.

NIXON: Khrushchev very deliberately helped Kennedy. He did it the last two weeks. And he helped him all the way. It's all right. And the Russians will do the same on me.

KISSINGER: Well, they may or may not. It depends on —

NIXON: Well, they will for the reason that we will take a bad offing public-opinion-wise. We're going to get squeals, and this and that and the other thing. And as they see then the possibility of a Democrat winning, they'll say, no, we'll push this son of a bitch right down the tubes. I mean, I'm just looking at the worst of both worlds.

KISSINGER: That's one of the things, in my judgment.

NIXON: And let's not have any illusions about that. I — you see, you and I talk — we talk about those things — the government — Hoover today, patriotism, loyalty, principle, and the rest, and that we say we hope to God that there's enough of that in the country. Well, there certainly is enough to support the bombing in the North in order to avoid a disaster. Whether there is enough to support bombing of the North and then give up all hope of peace. You see, it's the hope thing.

KISSINGER: Yeah, but I'm not sure —

NIXON: The hope thing. The China thing was important from one standpoint only — hope. The American people are suckers. Getting to know you — all that bullshit. They're for people-to-people.

KISSINGER: Yeah, but it's for precisely that reason to go there under these circumstances and to cater to that group, it's just —

NIXON: It's not — it isn't that group — I don't mean [unclear]. The gray, middle America — they're suckers.

"I'm going to announce it Monday night [May 8] on television."

May 4, 1972, 3:04 p.m.

Richard Nixon, John Connally, Thomas Moorer, and Henry Kissinger

EXECUTIVE OFFICE BUILDING

Nixon was finally at the point of waging the strongest war campaign of his tenure as president. While ships and warplanes had been directed to Vietnam over the previous month, they had yet to be used in full force. Within four days, they would be. Nixon told Moorer to put the offensive in place on the water in the form of a blockade of Haiphong harbor and in the air with a massive bombing campaign. Called Operation Linebacker, the offensive was intended to protect the Army of the Republic of Vietnam (ARVN), even as it pounded SAMs, railroads, bridges, camps, and other North Vietnamese targets.

• • •

NIXON: That strike should have gone off last week. It didn't go. But it's got to go. Now I want to tell you what I have in mind; it is to go. I don't care what the Russian answer is, it is to go. Then it is to go for two days, but not for two days and then wait to see if they negotiate. It is to go for two days, and then we will wait a little, but we've got to get back to the battle [Hue]. I realize that. And then, if the Russians cancel, we'll blockade. We will blockade and continue to bomb. But we are now going to win the war, and that's my position — if it costs the election, I don't give a shit. But we are going to win the war.

• • •

NIXON: I'm putting it quite bluntly now; I'm being quite precise. South Vietnam may lose, but the United States cannot lose. Which means that basically I have made the decision that whatever happens in South Vietnam, we are going to cream North Vietnam.

• • •

NIXON: We know that we can lose the summit, and still not lose the country. But we cannot lose this war without losing the country. Now, I'm not thinking of myself but I'm thinking of the country. So I return, we cannot lose the war. Having started on that proposition, what do you have to do? For once, we've got to use the maximum power of this country against a shit-ass little country to win the war. We can't use the word "win" though, though others can, but we're going to use it for the purpose.

• • •

NIXON: Now you see the problem is, it is true we're risking the summit for a blockade. But, on the other hand, on balance, I think if we have the blockade, we have a plan which we know militarily will accomplish our goal which is not losing this damn war.

KISSINGER: Mr. President, I am not even sure — my Soviet expert thinks that a blockade is somewhat less risky than bombing because the Soviets don't have to challenge it. But probably it risks certain — I would agree with my Soviet guys — that the trouble with the bombing and that sort of thing is that the North Vietnamese are practically asking us to bomb.

[unclear exchange]

NIXON: The trouble's with the bombing first and the blockade second, because you're for bombing if we blockade.

KISSINGER: Oh, yeah.

NIXON: The trouble's with the bombing first, go ahead.

KISSINGER: The trouble with the bombing first is that the North Vietnamese are practically asking us to bomb them. There must be some collusion between them and the Soviets at this — at this point, even if there wasn't any earlier. They must have the whole propaganda machine revved up. But leaving that aside, you bomb for two days and then stop, or bomb for three days and then stop, then the North Vietnamese — then the Russians say all right, we've got the word and will discuss it with you at the summit. Then we're again, if they don't cancel, then we're in the same box we were at the beginning.

NIXON: [unclear]

KISSINGER: You can't bomb again until after the summit if they launch another series of offensives. That's the box I was in, in Moscow. What else? They say nothing, and then you keep bombing, and they'll cancel the summit because of the bombing, which is the most neuralgic form of behavior. And on top of that —

NIXON: See, it was the bombing, you'll recall, that brought Johnson down.

KISSINGER: So, I think that if you blockade first — I think the basic decision you have to make, which is also the one John Connally mentioned to us, is are you going to win this war and are you going to do whatever is necessary not to lose the war? Once you've made that decision, the rest is tactics, which works better. I think the blockade gives you a chance to state your case. It gives the Soviets a minor opportunity to back off it, if they want to. After all, they did back off in Cuba when challenged with a blockade. It — and then you start bombing systematically, just running down their supplies; you don't have to do a horrendous strike because you can operate like a surgeon.

We just put one aircraft carrier out there with no other job but to take out the POL first. If we mine the harbor and, say, arm the mines in such a way that they are set for four days from now, that forces the ships out of there, because if they are not they are going to be bottled up in the harbor now. Then we go after the docks. And — so we can reduce Haiphong to a shell and we can systematically destroy their war manufacturing capacity. The thing that killed Johnson was that they were pumping in stuff faster than he could destroy it, and that they were fighting a guerrilla war, so they didn't have to keep large amounts of supplies flowing south, and because Sihanoukville was open, so they didn't have to —

NIXON: We've cut a lot of that out.

KISSINGER: With Sihanoukville closed, with all of their stuff having to come down the rails, or the roads, and with Haiphong closed, and with their reserves being systematically destroyed, something's got to give. Now, that's the argument for the blockade. And I think if we go tough, we've got to give the maximum shock effect and get it over with.

NIXON: Now, just one question. What do the Chinese do?

KISSINGER: Well, the blockade incidentally has the additional advantage that it forces Hanoi closer to the Chinese. And therefore, what will happen? The Chinese will scream. The Chinese may even open up their southern ports as a replacement for Haiphong and permit stuff to come in at that port. That will take months, however, to bring [unclear]. But there's a good chance that they would —

NIXON: You don't see the Chinese moving manpower in there? I didn't think so either.

KISSINGER: No, besides it wouldn't make any difference. They wouldn't get enough of them down. But I don't think they'd do manpower. They would open, in my judgment, one of their southern ports as a replacement for Haiphong.

• • •

NIXON: Admiral, what I am going to say to you now is in total confidence of the relationship with the commander in chief and the chairman of the Chiefs of Staff. Nothing is to go to the secretary. Nothing is to go to Vietnam. Is that clear?

MOORER: Yes, sir.

NIXON: What I'm about to say.

MOORER: Yes, sir.

NIXON: I've decided that we've got to go on a blockade. It must — I'm going to announce it Monday night [May 8] on television. I want you to put a working group together. Start immediately with absolutely the best people that you've got. I think you've done a lot of work on it already.

MOORER: Oh, that's right. We're all set —

NIXON: And, if I announce it Monday night, if I tell you now, which I am now doing, can you be ready so that it can be in place Tuesday?

MOORER: Oh, yes, sir.

NIXON: All right. Now, what we have in mind, in addition to the blockade, is that I want as much use of our air assets as we can spare from the battle group. I don't want to take Abrams's word on it, clearly, but I — it's our air assets so that we can at the very least take out the railroad units — that has to go out — and then the POL, the power plants, et cetera, et cetera. After the ships get out, we'll take out the docks. Now, the — the [unclear] as you can imagine, momentous [unclear]. I'll do that on Monday. [unclear] Now, what — what — can you tell me what, what you can do? What — can you do this in secrecy and the rest and bring this thing off? Or, how? I — I'm just asking the question. I don't want you to tell Abrams. He can't know. Nobody is to be told out there. What can you do?

MOORER: Well, sir, as you know, we've done quite a bit of thinking about this already.

NIXON: Yes, sir.

MOORER: And it would simply be a matter of diverting some of the ships and combining air surveillance on the approaches to Haiphong with the positioning of the ships, making the necessary announcements, and giving the ships their rules of engagement as to what they'll do, and I think they're prepared to do that. I would use the destroyers for this purpose.

KISSINGER: Could even more ships help there?

MOORER: Well, I think that — oh, I think we —

NIXON: You've got quite a gang up there —

MOORER: We've got quite a few ships, and we've got some more arriving. I think we've probably got enough ships to start, sir.

KISSINGER: And, if you could, by tomorrow, give us a rough outline of the plan, then we can meet.

MOORER: Yeah.

NIXON: And, also, I need a rough outline of the air assets that can be spared for strikes. Now, understand, I am not ordering the two-day strike. [unclear]

MOORER: Yes, sir. [unclear]

NIXON: We're gonna let Abrams use those, but I want, as I've already told you, I want for once — for once — I want a massive [strike]. I want fifty B-52s on the Hue perimeter for just one night. Can you do that?

MOORER: Yes, sir. A twenty-four-hour strike.

NIXON: That's fine. Would you do that just one time?

MOORER: Yes, sir.

NIXON: Anything that moves on the Hue front. You've got to remember, Hue is like Verdun. The Germans made a mistake. The French probably made a mistake trying to defend it, but it was — it had to be defended, and with the Germans' psychology it had to be attacked because of its symbolism. Hue is exactly the same thing. You can lose Kontum, and you can lose a hell of a lot of other things, but you can't lose Hue. Now, we've gotta get, gotta get, those '52s in there and we've gotta take one damn, good whack at them if there's enough to hit 'em.

MOORER: Yes, sir. Well, they've been, as you know, working heavily on the —

NIXON: Yeah.

MOORER: — A Shau Valley, the most important thing. Some of the [unclear]. Again, I talked to General Vogt on the phone, and he said that during the daylight hours, which is the last time we really hit 'em, we hit 'em really quite well. We can put them —

NIXON: [unclear]?

MOORER: Yes, sir.

NIXON: I'd like to have one massive B-52 strike in that area [unclear].

KISSINGER: Mr. President, I'll excuse myself.

NIXON: Yeah. Okay.

MOORER: Yes, sir.

[KISSINGER leaves.]

NIXON: So, you get ready for [unclear]. But, it will not work, you understand. Of course, you know, over a period of time it won't work; it will not work without very extensive air support. I mean, there's no sense in blockading without taking out the POL, the railroad lines, and the other routes in —

MOORER: Well, we can get to those docks once [unclear], Mr. President, at the end of that op.

NIXON: Yeah. That is from the sea. But I mean there are other ways they can come in. Why don't you go ahead and send the materials — the materiel. Don't you think they're on the docks, unloading them on the docks?

MOORER: Yes, sir. Quite a bit on the docks. What I meant, though, is we can destroy the docks —

NIXON: Yeah.

MOORER: — once the ships get split up in a big way —

NIXON: Right. Yeah. Now my point is what about — about the POL, what is left there? See, well, what I mean is that the purpose of the blockade is not to just keep it on for eighteen months. The purpose is to put it on, and then systematically destroy everything that you possibly can that's already there. They've got a hell of a lot of stuff stored up.

MOORER: Oh, yes, sir.

NIXON: So what I am thinking of, what I am directing, is bombing, all out in that area. In fact, if we weren't involved in the South [unclear] all of our assets there [unclear]. You are to hit, in terms of your bombing, North Vietnam in this period in the Haiphong area. You are to aim for military targets. You are not to be too concerned about whether it slops over [unclear]. The most important thing is to get those military targets. If it slops over, that's too bad. That's the way it's going to be, because we — I've made the decision and we now have no choice but to: we will avoid the defeat of the South. I think we can. We could, but we sure as hell are gonna be making a large effort.

MOORER: We'll do that.

NIXON: And, that's the way it's going to be. Now, can you do that?

MOORER: Yes, sir. Now I think what we really need at some point is for the South to defend itself, for the South Vietnamese to take some kind of initiative. In other words, to either use their own aircraft to attack Dong Hoi, or to use their ships to shell another North Vietnamese area, or to use their aircraft to mine the channel, or to do something; for them to do something in retaliation, which they haven't done yet. What they've done is just simply falling back on these strong points. And, they haven't moved out against the enemy.

NIXON: Well, find a way that they can play a role in the blockade then. Can they do that?

MOORER: Well, they —

NIXON: You talk about the channel [unclear]. Couldn't they do something?

MOORER: To — to some degree, yes, sir.

"We must do something drastic. There's no question about it."

May 5, 1972, 8:55 a.m.

Richard Nixon and Henry Kissinger

OVAL OFFICE

Operation Linebacker was due to begin on Monday, May 8, though Nixon had not yet made it official. On the Friday before, he and Kissinger discussed the diplomatic aspects

of the mining blockade and then the air war. Kissinger argued the downsides of each. A
blockade that relied on thousands of underwater mines would be impossible to stop or
lift, should the course of the war change. The escalated bombing, which would inevitably
cause civilian casualties, would remind Americans of the failed strategies that tore the
home front apart in the late 1960s. While Kissinger was still questioning the right course,
though, Nixon was, by then, certain.

· · ·

NIXON: I was going to ask you to do something today that is very important. I want you
   to be rather cool, particularly outgoing with Dobrynin. I want you to play them like
   they play us, and be very, very nice. Act as if everything was going ahead on schedule. But act very, very nice. Say how gracious we are — how pleased Mrs. Nixon is
   with the graciousness of Mrs. Dobrynin, and all that. Because now that the die is
   cast, we are going to play this in the most vicious way that we can with those bastards.

· · ·

KISSINGER: Now, I feel I must put before you this consideration, Mr. President. We
   must do something drastic. There's no question about it.
NIXON: Hmm.
KISSINGER: The advantage of a blockade is that it commits us irrevocably, that after
   that we've struck, and there's no turning back. That's a great advantage. And the
   other side must then do something. The disadvantage is that it confronts the Soviets
   most directly.
NIXON: That's the thing I said the other day.
KISSINGER: They can hardly step back from that. They may, but my Soviet expert
   thinks that it is more likely that they'll step back from a blockade than from a bomb-
   ing, but —
NIXON: The disadvantage of bombing is, as you put it so effectively yesterday, is that
   they expect it —
KISSINGER: But —
NIXON: — and in their thought it's already been discounted.
KISSINGER: The disadvantage of the bombing is that it will trigger every goddamn
   peace group in this country.
NIXON: So will a blockade.
KISSINGER: And —
NIXON: Either does that, Henry. It's the line — "major escalation" — that they're all talk-
   ing about.
KISSINGER: Yeah.
NIXON: And either the blockade or the bombing will — they're going to trigger the
   peace groups, so have no doubts about that.
KISSINGER: But it's hard to turn off a blockade.
NIXON: That's right.

KISSINGER: I mean, for you to turn off—you can always stop bombing for a day or two, or a week, or—

NIXON: That's right.

KISSINGER: —or two weeks, and therefore—

NIXON: So, and then it would be ineffective.

KISSINGER: The bombing?

NIXON: We cannot have a stop—a stop-and-start thing again. We've been around it—

KISSINGER: That's right.

NIXON: —and around it and around. I understand the problems with the blockade.

KISSINGER: No, I just wanted to put it—

NIXON: Not only—not only—there's that problem. It confronts a lot other than the Soviet Union—the Indians, and the Chinese—

KISSINGER: Those are no problem. But, the Chinese are a problem, too.

NIXON: Yeah.

KISSINGER: But in a way, of course, it's always been a question of degree. A prolonged bombing of Hanoi and Haiphong—

NIXON: They have to react.

KISSINGER: —will do the same thing. It will send the question—

NIXON: The other thing is that the bombing has been done before. It's the same old routine: "He's back to bombing, bombing, bombing, bombing, stop the bombing, stop the bombing." So, they're going to say, "Lift the blockade, lift the blockade." On that point, it isn't as strong of a case for it. The blockade is not as—is not as good a target as the bombing in terms of the riots.

KISSINGER: You can, well, of course, say there's got to be bombing, too, with a blockade.

NIXON: Oh, I understand, but the people are going to look at the blockade. The blockade is going to be so overwhelming in terms of its—

KISSINGER: And you—

NIXON: —public relations.

KISSINGER: And you—

NIXON: I can understand. Look, Henry, the main point is that we ought to raise these points, which you've got to raise. There are no good choices.

KISSINGER: No.

NIXON: There are no good choices. Sure, there's a choice of a two-day pop, and then, then, then go back and then hope to Christ that they'll then negotiate about something. And it isn't going to happen. Hmm?

KISSINGER: That's right.

NIXON: You have no other evaluation of the war situation, do you, that's any more encouraging?

KISSINGER: No.

NIXON: What is it this morning? Anything new?

KISSINGER: Well, it's quiet again —

NIXON: Well, then they're building up again. That's —

KISSINGER: In terms of —

NIXON: — what always happens when it's quiet —

KISSINGER: That's — oh, yeah. That's —

NIXON: It's ominous.

KISSINGER: Well, what it is proves two things. One is, they're weaker than we think. I mean, take Kontum. It shouldn't have taken them two weeks to go from Dak To to Kontum. If they had really a lot of stuff they would have just rolled into it. But they're sort of inching up to it again and taking a lot of casualties. On the other hand, they're doing it methodically, and they'll certainly attack again. And it's a, a tragedy. Of course, they wouldn't do it. If we had one American division to go into the panhandles, they'd be finished. That's — the problem is we can't do it —

NIXON: Hell, if we had an American regiment to land, for Christ's sakes, and then it would finish this damn thing. It'd frighten them to death.

KISSINGER: Yeah.

NIXON: You know? They — they'd call two divisions off the attack, and the South Vietnamese then might inch forward, even.

KISSINGER: Yeah.

NIXON: Oh, I know. I know. I know.

KISSINGER: But —

NIXON: I know — I've got that, about that the — Henry, the, the, the arguments. I mean, you can — we've been around this track about eighteen times. But I must say it's very compelling to me when you say that if we go the bombing route, we're going the same way. It's expected, and, frankly, there's — it's almost a certainty it isn't going to work. The blockade may not work either.

KISSINGER: Well, the blockade has got to work.

NIXON: It'll work in the end —

KISSINGER: It may not work fast enough. I mean, there's no way the blockade cannot work. It's already — even that one bombing of Haiphong, incidentally, they've got such congestion in the port now, that there's one Polish freighter that has to wait a month in Hainan to be able to get into the port. I, in fact, have to say, Mr. President — you keep talking about your instinct — I think your instinct was right. We should have hit soon after that first strike began. And, on the other hand, we have positioned what we have to do now.

NIXON: [laughs] We sure have.

• • •

KISSINGER: No, I'm strongly for the bombing, too.

NIXON: Yeah? No, no, no. Do you know what I mean? Do you favor the bombing, followed by a blockade, which is the other line? That's it.

KISSINGER: Another advantage of the blockade is that you can go to the American people, while you can't go to the American people —

NIXON: About bombing.

KISSINGER: — about bombing —

NIXON: I've already — I've already presented that to the American people on April 26.

KISSINGER: And you can rally the American people for a blockade, while you cannot rally them —

NIXON: That's right. That's right.

KISSINGER: And that's not an inconsiderable —

NIXON: It's a hell of a considerable thing.

KISSINGER: — factor.

NIXON: The bomb — the blockade has the advantage that it's — first, it's a total commitment; it's decisive. I mean, in the end, let's face it — in the end, we've got to figure, Henry, that probably we may lose the election, and so forth, and so on, but in the end, with a blockade we'll win the war.

KISSINGER: Yep.

NIXON: And, by golly that's —

KISSINGER: Well, if you win the war you won't lose the election —

NIXON: Yeah. If you win it soon enough and — you see, that's the problem. The blockade, we know damn well that in eight months we'll have them at their knees.

KISSINGER: Oh, I think that with bombing we'll have them quicker — with bombing, before they can get alternative routes organized.

NIXON: So, my view is that the blockade rallies the people; it puts it to the Russians. I mean, the only advantage, as I told you earlier, as I said to you earlier, about the — which is the line that Connally came up with — is to start bombing again, and then, if the Russians still do not break off the summit, we'll have it. You see, the bombing-blockade thing has this possible advantage, which I ran by you yesterday: you bomb, and after bombing, the Russians bitch, but they do not break off the summit. Then we continue to bomb them. Then, I suppose, we can go to the summit.

KISSINGER: Well, if you bomb enough, they'll break off the summit. There's no question about it.

NIXON: Well then, that perhaps is the convincing reason, because we can't bomb unless we bomb enough. We can't bomb and then have — but you can't bomb them and then have them kicking us around while we're in Moscow. You see? That's the point that you made which is tremendously compelling. I cannot be in Moscow at a time when the North Vietnamese are rampaging through the streets of Hue or, for that matter, through the streets of Kontum.

KISSINGER: That's right.

NIXON: So — [pause]. Well, let's go by it again and give the case its best hearing that we can. If we bomb [unclear]. He'll be gone [unclear] rather than Monday. With the bombing, we'd have to do it on Sunday. [unclear] we could Saturday night.

KISSINGER: Sunday—

NIXON: Or on Sunday. [unclear]

KISSINGER: That makes an overwhelming difference—

NIXON: Well, the main thing is to get it done, to get it going—

KISSINGER: Yeah.

NIXON: —so that it's going to affect the battle and so forth. Hit 'em.

KISSINGER: We've heard from Abrams, incidentally. I've had a—I wrote a cable—I wrote Bunker. I sent a cable to Bunker, saying that I thought that you were—we were beginning to lose patience with Abrams, that every time we want to do something we just want to make sure there are no confusing signals being given to Abrams, and therefore I want him to know that any authentic words from the president come from me to Bunker to Abrams. There are no other authentic words. If anyone tells him that there are—that you want something, it is not true unless it comes from me to Bunker. That doesn't mean they shouldn't carry out military orders. It's that when they psychoanalyze you.

NIXON: Yeah?

KISSINGER: Now, it turns out that he did get crossed signals. So Laird, that bastard, has been talking to him.

NIXON: Crossed signals of what? About bombing?

KISSINGER: No, that you probably—I would not—I believe, and Moorer believes, that Moorer told Abrams that you would welcome a request from Abrams—that Laird told Abrams that you would welcome a request from Abrams that gave you an excuse not to bomb Hanoi and Haiphong.

NIXON: You think he did that?

KISSINGER: Yeah. Moorer thinks it. Rush thinks it. And Bunker two-thirds confirms it.

NIXON: See, Laird is so tricky that he's capable of that.

KISSINGER: Oh, yes. Someone who's clearly capable of that.

NIXON: But why does Laird want to say that? Because if Laird—why doesn't Laird want to bomb Haiphong?

KISSINGER: I think Laird—why? Because Laird has got political ambitions, and he's positioning himself on the peace side of this.

NIXON: He's got about as much chance for a political future—

KISSINGER: But that he doesn't believe.

NIXON: —of being murdered.

KISSINGER: He doesn't believe it. Now, I don't want to drive you off what you've decided because I think we ought to keep on this course now. I just want you—

NIXON: To consider it?

KISSINGER: —to consider—we should go on this as if we were going all out on it, and I'm saying this to you—I'm not saying it to Haig, or to Moorer, or to Connally, or to anyone else. I mean, we still have a few pieces that have got to come in. We still have to get the Russians' reply.

NIXON: That's right —

KISSINGER: So, if it doesn't come by the end of the day, it's too late. But I — I'm sure it will come today.

NIXON: Yes?

KISSINGER: See, another problem you face is you bomb Hanoi and Haiphong, and then the Russians do to you what they did to me, say, "Come, and we'll talk about it." And then you've got to stop again. Of course, you could say, "Fine, but I won't stop now until —"

NIXON: You couldn't — well, putting that case at its best, we bomb Hanoi and Haiphong and then the Russians say, "Look — look, you come, and we'll have sort of a pause while we have the summit," as we did at the Chinese summit. And, you remember, I said that it is a possibility. That's one thing that could happen.

KISSINGER: Of course, we shouldn't look back to the Chinese summit. I suppose we weren't bombing the North then, Mr. President —

NIXON: I know. Let's suppose — let's look at this and leave that out of it —

• • •

NIXON: Because I — I remembered what Eisenhower did, but I had really forgotten that, well, it didn't hurt Eisenhower when the Russians canceled the summit. It didn't hurt him. Goddamn it, the American people don't like to be kicked around. It didn't hurt Eisenhower when the goddamn Japanese canceled his trip. Remember?

KISSINGER: Absolutely.

NIXON: All right, now, it didn't hurt me as vice president. I'll never forget when I got stoned in Caracas. It helped me.

KISSINGER: It helped you.

NIXON: People thought it was great.

KISSINGER: Yeah.

NIXON: Now, it depends on how you react to it. Here's the problem. Looking at the long view, bombing might turn it around. It runs a better chance of keeping the summit alive. The Russians can live with bombing, where they might not be able to live with a blockade. All right, that's the advantage of that. But, we constantly come back to the, basically, Henry, to the fundamental problem. And Connally, with his, you know, with his animal-like decisiveness, and which I also have, except I have through —

KISSINGER: You're much more subtle —

NIXON: — through many years, I've put much more layers of subtlety on it. But any-how, but Connally comes quickly to the point. He says, "Look, the summit is great; I hope you don't knock it off. I think you could do both, and I hope you can do both. I think you will do both." "But," he says, "even if you don't, if you're going to put first things first, you've got to remember: you can do without the summit, but you cannot live with defeat in Vietnam. You must win the war in Vietnam. Or, putting it another way, you must not lose in Vietnam."

That's crystal clear. So, everything's got to be measured against what wins or loses in Vietnam, and here is the weakness of bombing. Bombing might turn the war in Vietnam around. The blockade certainly will turn it around. Now, here, the blockade plus the bombing—you understand? What I'm really saying here is that I think that's what convinced me—

KISSINGER: And the blockade—

NIXON: —like I say: win the war.

KISSINGER: The blockade gets you across the Rubicon. There's no way it can't be ended without the blockade—

NIXON: Well, everybody knows then, that I've thrown down the goddamn gauntlet, and there it is. And they want to pick it up? And, you see, that I'm going to live with the blockade as I've said. Well, it's an ultimatum.

KISSINGER: Yeah.

NIXON: Bombing is not an ultimatum.

KISSINGER: Bombing, they cannot do it. This is the argument for the blockade, now: it heightens the chance of a confrontation with the Russians.

NIXON: That's right.

KISSINGER: It will start the Chinese screaming.

NIXON: That's right.

KISSINGER: And you'll be accused of having blown up everything of your foreign policy—

NIXON: I know—

KISSINGER: —which is, on the other hand, a disadvantage—

NIXON: Now that brings sadness to me. It brings sadness to me. We've had a damn good foreign policy.

KISSINGER: You haven't been wrong, Mr. President—

NIXON: Even if it all goes down the tubes, we'll just—we will be remembered, as Clare Booth Luce says, as the ones who went to China. And in the future, that'll work out.

KISSINGER: Mr. President, you—it would—actually, if you get reelected, it will make your foreign policy. It's the same as the Laos operation. Everyone said that you've now, well, broken it with the Chinese, and three months later we were there. And a year later, you were there. So, I think it won't—

NIXON: Henry, if you come back to the fundamental point, I mean, as I took you up to that map yesterday and I showed you that little place, and we looked at it, and we think of this whole great, big, wide world, everything rides on it. If there were a way, believe me, if there were a way we could flush Vietnam now, flush it, get out of it in any way possible, and conduct a sensible foreign policy with the Russians and with the Chinese—

KISSINGER: We'd do it.

NIXON: —we ought to do it. We ought to do it, because—because there's so much at stake. There's nobody else in this country at the present time, with the exception of Connally, in the next four years, that can handle the Russians and the Chinese and the big game in Europe and the big game in Southeast Asia. You know it, and I know it.

And the big game with the Japanese five years from now. Who could help? Who else could do it? All right, so that's at stake. I mean that's why I — the only reason that I had doubts earlier in the week was that I had to face up to the fact because I saw the inevitability of McGovern, or Humphrey, or if they'd have him, the only other possibility is Teddy, who might be the worst of the three.

KISSINGER: Certainly the worst —

NIXON: But any — in any event —

KISSINGER: Well, McGovern is —

NIXON: — because I saw that — well, McGovern would be the worst for sure if he gets in, but Teddy would be so stop-and-start that he might get us into even worse trouble. Anyway, if you're going to go for peace, you might as well surrender right off the bat, rather than the cost of it all in slaughter. So, my point is, Henry, that I had to put that into the, into the equation. And therefore, I had to go down the line of saying how in the hell can we save — how the hell can we save the, you know, the presidency, and that meant, frankly, the present occupant.

And that meant saving the summit. All right, I have considered it all, and I don't think there's any way you can do it. I don't think there's any way you can do it, and at the same time temporize in Vietnam. I have reached the conclusion that we're in a situation where Vietnam is here and, and I assured Rogers and Laird, [unclear] let's make another offer, and have we agreed to offer this. I don't know whether we have. You know, and they're whining and bitching about it. But, Henry, you know and I know it that it's not true.

KISSINGER: No. Mr. President, you and I know, perhaps as the only ones, if they had given us a face-saving way out —

NIXON: [unclear]

KISSINGER: — I was prepared to take it.

NIXON: Well, I told you before you left —

KISSINGER: You told me — because you told me that. They want us out in a humiliating way. They want us to put a Communist government into power. Goddamn it, let's face it, if they had accepted our May 31 proposal last year, they would have taken over Vietnam within a year or two.

NIXON: [laughs] I'll say. Thank God that I know. I still wish they had, but nevertheless.

KISSINGER: Of course. But it isn't that we've been intransigent in our offers. Not at all.

NIXON: You see, if we could survive past the election, Henry, [unclear] and then Vietnam goes down the tubes, it really doesn't make any difference.

KISSINGER: I agree with you. That's been the whole —

NIXON: But we have no way to survive past the election.

KISSINGER: Well, I think —

NIXON: You see what I mean — before we can go, given their — there's the other, other argument for bombing. Maybe we could bomb, not blockade, and still have the summit —

KISSINGER: No, I think they'll —

NIXON: — we might survive past the election.

KISSINGER: Mr. President, I think they're going to kill you. They're going to put you into the Johnson position. This is the other argument for the blockade.

NIXON: That's right.

KISSINGER: They're going to have you as the bomber. The guy — when I looked at that DRV statement, they wanted you to break off the peace talks, Mr. President —

NIXON: That's right. That's right.

KISSINGER: So you're the guy who doesn't talk.

NIXON: Well, I hope they know, but got across that they helped to break them off — did Porter make that [unclear]?

KISSINGER: Oh, yes, it got across. But all of this is minor because the — these peace groups are going to keep backing —

NIXON: Yeah. The headlines are that we broke off the talks.

KISSINGER: So that six months from now — three months from now —

NIXON: Yeah.

KISSINGER: — it's forgotten that there was an invasion, and therefore —

NIXON: Well, Henry, let me put it this way: I know that you've been thinking about this during the night as I have, but I've never — I come back to the fundamental point, leaving the president out and so forth. And who knows? Something could happen. Maybe the Democrats could get smart and draft Connally, so I could be defeated.

KISSINGER: That's impossible; inconceivable.

NIXON: Well, if they did, it would save the country.

The intensified war

May 5, 1972, 12:44 p.m.
Richard Nixon, Henry Kissinger, and Bob Haldeman
OVAL OFFICE

Kissinger was still probing and questioning the military action in a later conversation on Friday with the president. He didn't like irreversible actions, and the president was about to embark on the greatest one of the administration. Finally, Nixon had to tell Kissinger bluntly that the time for weighing the decision was over, at least within his inner circle. For Nixon, May 8 was to be his D-Day, and he expected the weekend to be crowded with preparation for everyone involved. In an administration of secrecy and even subterfuge, one of the chores Nixon dreaded was simply telling various members of his cabinet about the decision. The secretary of state, William Rogers, for example, was to be among the very last to know. Nixon also had to tell the American public; he, Haldeman, and Kissinger turned to crafting the speech that would present the case for war on the large scale.

• • •

NIXON: It was really quite an exercise for the navy, isn't it? Just think what it must mean to those navy guys, the poor sons of bitches that — who'd love to do something, you know? They get to blockade somebody.

HALDEMAN: These new mines they use are fascinating. They can set those to become active whenever they want them and to become inactive whenever they want them. I mean, they have an "on" and an "off" switch that they can set it on an automatic timing mode.

NIXON: Well, but — but they can't — they're not operated from a distance?

HALDEMAN: No, no. Once they've set it, it's set, as I understand it. And let's hope they're not going to put any "off" switch on it, and they're going to leave them "on." And Moorer is a guy — he just, just practically chortles, you know. He's so — he just loves the mining part, especially.

NIXON: Does he?

HALDEMAN: Yeah, because it's, it's damn effective. These mines, I guess, are much more sophisticated than the stuff we knew about in World War II. They're all — they go down to the bottom. They go down and just lie on the bottom until something comes over them and then it magnetically shoots up and hits it.

NIXON: Hmm. Let's hope one of our own boats isn't sunk by one.

HALDEMAN: There probably will be.

NIXON: This is war.

HALDEMAN: Somebody will sail into 'em. Mining is a beautiful thing, though, really, because that — you lay the mines down, and you tell the people they're there. If somebody sails into it, you didn't do anything to them, they did it to themselves.

NIXON: Hmm. Well, let me tell you, for a few days after we announce this blockade, it's going to be goddamn hard. If I were a member of the House or Senate I'd take this on — or a candidate, particularly when you put it on the basis of POWs, and our sixty thousand Americans who are in Vietnam, and preventing the imposition of Communist government after we've offered everything but that to the North. Correct?

HALDEMAN: Yep.

NIXON: It'll be goddamn hard, particularly when a blockade is aimed not at destroying North Vietnam, but preventing the delivery of lethal weapons which are going to be used to kill people in South Vietnam.

HALDEMAN: Who could possibly — I mean, even — you know, how can McGovern, even, argue that? Nobody can rationally argue the right of North Vietnam to get more arms.

The National Security Council on the subject of bringing the war to North Vietnam

May 8, 1972, 12:13 p.m.

Richard Nixon, John Connally, and Henry Kissinger

OVAL OFFICE

On Monday morning, Nixon presided over a rancorous three-hour meeting of the National Security Council to discuss the expansion of the war. Nixon started by warning those present not to argue about the risk of jeopardizing the Moscow summit. As far as he was concerned, that was a lesser concern. Amid heated discussions, the council failed to reach a common view. Among those speaking vehemently against the military plans were Rogers, Laird, and Richard Helms, director of the CIA. Each raised reasonable questions, such as the cost and the effect on the South Vietnamese. Connally, according to a reporter, didn't hover over such details. He "practically jumped out of his chair, pointing his finger at Nixon and saying that, in effect, he would not be a real president if he failed to act." That was the kind of straight talk that made Connally a favorite with Nixon. Although no votes were taken, the council seemed to be largely in favor of the mining of Haiphong harbor, but against the full-scale bombing of North Vietnam. About an hour and a half later, after the following conversation, the president issued the command to begin the large-scale bombing and the mining.

. . .

KISSINGER: The Russians want it to keep you from acting, clearly, or to put the maximum obstacles against you. Now, we can easily handle the Security Council today. The only marginal utility of delaying twenty-four hours is to pull the teeth of your cabinet members who were going against our plan. You know, the way your position is now that Rogers is saying he was for it if it succeeds and against it if it fails.

. . .

NIXON: I think if we do it — I mean, I think the decision is to either do it today or to not do it at all. Well, or at least not do it this week. [chuckles] And that probably means we're not going to hit at all. But let's, say, let's get your evaluation, John. After listening to the whole thing [the NSC meeting], you just be as cold and deliberate as you can. Tell me what you think.

. . .

CONNALLY: The safest thing is always to, basically, let the status quo remain the status quo. Whatever the ultimate result, that's the safest thing. That's the basic bureaucratic approach, that you never want to disturb things. That, somewhat, is reflected in both Mel and Bill's attitude. Secondly, I think you have to assume that Bill really would not like to see the summit come off, the Russian summit. He would like to see it postponed —

NIXON: [laughs]

CONNALLY: — for whatever reason, but he'd just like to see it go by the boards. Third, I think there's — I think there's some argument there to be made, on behalf of Mel's argument, that, well, you know, it's costing us a hell of a lot, but, dear God —

NIXON: [unclear]

CONNALLY: This doesn't — this doesn't make a lot of sense to me.

NIXON: No, no. That, that, that argument —

[unclear exchange]

KISSINGER: That has nothing to do with the operation, because if you follow that argument, you have to stop the air —

CONNALLY: Sure.

KISSINGER: — because we —

CONNALLY: We'd have to get out completely.

• • •

CONNALLY: There's another advantage. This way, if Russia wants to help, and I really believe they want to help, I just believe that, this gives them an argument to say to Hanoi, now, we told you, we knew you, we just say you've got to come to grips with us now. And it seems to me it gives them a powerful argument to use with Hanoi.

NIXON: It's a possibility. Now, let me put it this way. As far as the Russians helping, we know that given the course — the present course of events they aren't going to help.

CONNALLY: Of course they're not.

NIXON: Now, our doing this may make them more difficult. But that's almost impossible for them to be much more difficult. If there's at least a chance that it does allow them to do something, would you agree, Henry?

KISSINGER: That's right — what — they will cancel the summit, in my judgment, although it's not totally excluded.

NIXON: That's forty–sixty, thirty–seventy?

KISSINGER: I would rate it higher — I'd rate it eighty–twenty. But they may then say that now they've done their duty, that that's the only thing they're going to do to us, and continue bilateral relations with Hanoi.

NIXON: You have here — you should have the contingency plan ready for what we say when they cancel the summit.

KISSINGER: I've got a statement already.

NIXON: You should have a statement ready, and so forth.

KISSINGER: It's ready.

NIXON: I should not have to make it.

KISSINGER: No. These literally are statements I can brief on it.

NIXON: You should read from it, exactly. Exactly. Because I think John's smelled a rat pretty clearly, and Bill, he's not interested in that Soviet summit.

KISSINGER: Well, because he knows we've got it all settled and he doesn't want to be in the position of Beijing. Because actually the fact is we've got —

NIXON: We've got a hell of a summit.

KISSINGER: We can announce two agreements every night.

• • •

CONNALLY: Mel said, "Now, there's a real problem on these finances." And I said, "Mel, I know that," but I said, "Hell, if you're going to take that argument, you ought to pull out all your air forces and all your, all your navy ships. Save some money. Or, you've got to go for broke, get it over with." And then, Bill said, "Well," he says, "as a matter of fact, I would probably go for just complete devastation of Hanoi and Haiphong. Just bomb them." He said, "I just think we ought to raze them." He said, "I'd probably support the option of razing them to the ground." And Mel then said, he said, "Well, the thing that kills us, are pinpointing these damn targets. That if we didn't have these restrictive targets placed on us," he said, "that's why we have to make so many sorties trying to just pinpoint particular targets."

KISSINGER: That's a lie, too.

CONNALLY: And he said — I said, "Well," I said, "I might support, strongly support, razing Haiphong and Hanoi and just devastating them." I said, "I might do that. On the other hand," I said, "I might well support a move by the president, right now, to go and undertake this action and then, at the same time, withdraw the sixty-nine thousand troops. But," I said, "the thing I cannot support is just the continual degradation of our position and the position of the South Vietnamese, and leaving in the hands of the South Vietnamese the viability of the whole foreign policy of the United States." And, I said, "That, that I just can't, I can't go for." He said, "Well, we'll support —"

[unclear exchange]

CONNALLY: I'm sorry.

NIXON: Excuse me. Then they said what?

CONNALLY: They said, "Well, we'll, we'll sure support whatever decision is made." And I said, "Well, that's the important thing, that we all support it." And I said, "I don't care what." I said, "I have strong feelings, but whatever the president's decision is, I'm going to be for it." And that's the way we broke up. Now, I —

NIXON: What is your — how do you balance that [unclear] question that was raised? And I'd like to get Henry's judgment on that, too. I mean, let us assume that South Vietnam is gonna — all right, then the question is: are we better off for having done this, or worse off?

And it's, frankly, I think if South Vietnam goes down, we ought to go down, the U.S. and our foreign policy has suffered a shattering blow in any event. But, is our foreign policy — is our position better, if we have tried — done this, or worse? Rogers says it's worse if we've done this and it goes down. And you think maybe it's better if we've —

CONNALLY: Yes.

NIXON: — done this and it goes down.

CONNALLY: Yes, sir.

NIXON: What's your argument for that?

CONNALLY: Well, the argument is that, at least, we, we have sent a message to other aggressor nations that they're going to suffer some damage. And this is one of the great weaknesses that we have in the American position, always, that we have constantly been on the defensive. We bomb North Vietnam, yes, but it's been targets of—highly selective targets, and so forth. There's been no devastation. People in Viet—in North Vietnam have been relatively free of these fears of retribution.

NIXON: [unclear] civilians, that's right.

CONNALLY: Civilians. And fear of retribution is a powerful motivating force. And we've let them go ten years without it. And at the same time, these poor bastards, the South Vietnamese, everybody says that they stay there, that they've got to stay so many rounds, just to make it—

[unclear exchange]

CONNALLY: —and then, they may break, it's just the sheer—the fear that they're going to get killed. And I don't blame them for evacuating civilians. But, you see, at least, you would accomplish that much by sending a message to other countries around the world that you just can't be an aggressor with complete impunity.

NIXON: Mm-hmm. Mm-hmm.

CONNALLY: That you're going to suffer some damage.

NIXON: Also, I think—and I'd like to get Henry's view on that—but on that critical question, alone, you know, let's assume it goes. Let's—let's assume. Are we better off from having done this, or worse off? What's your view, Henry?

KISSINGER: My view is that we're, we're better off.

NIXON: Why?

KISSINGER: Because, if this thing—

NIXON: The reason he mentions, and what else?

KISSINGER: Well, because if this thing goes without our having done something, we'll have sixty thousand Americans in their hands without any card to play at all.

NIXON: You mean, you really think there's a chance they could be captured?

KISSINGER: I think if—when this thing goes, if it goes—

NIXON: It's gonna go bad—

KISSINGER: —there'll be a massive disintegration—

NIXON: [unclear] You think—you agree with the Agnew theory, rather than the Laird theory? Do you—

KISSINGER: Absolutely.

NIXON: Do you agree with Laird's evaluation of the military situation?

KISSINGER: No. I—remember, Mr. President, when I came back from the Soviet Union, up in Camp David I told you the whole thing is misconceived in terms of the North Vietnamese objective. I do not believe they were after provincial capitals. I believed they were after the disintegration of ARVN, and that they're going to chew up one division at a time, until the remaining divisions are so demoralized that you get a massive collapse.

NIXON: Mm-hmm.

KISSINGER: Or an upheaval in Saigon.

NIXON: And then?

KISSINGER: And then you can get all kinds of situations. You could get some of these ARVN commanders turning on Americans —

NIXON: Yeah.

KISSINGER: — in order to prove to the Communists that they're really nationalists.

NIXON: Yeah. Yup. Yup.

KISSINGER: What you can then get is quite unpredictable. You might get a guy in, in Saigon forming a coalition government, and —

NIXON: Well, not to mention, but, I still get back to the point that, if I may — I still — I do think that this POW issue is a terribly moving, emotional issue among the Americans. At the present time, we've got no card to get the POWs. The problem —

KISSINGER: You —

NIXON: — is getting a card.

KISSINGER: You'll —

NIXON: Do you feel that?

KISSINGER: You'll be in the position, then, if the thing disintegrates in the South, of having Americans — that you have to go, practically on your knees, to this bastardly little country. And if you then do a blockade, it looks like total —

NIXON: Yup.

KISSINGER: — peevishness, and then, then they might really stick a blockade, because they don't have any drain on their supplies, anymore.

NIXON: Yeah. Well, let's wait this thing through. Let's look down the road. If we do the bombing, and the ARVN contingent still collapses, then where are we? That's what I'm getting at —

KISSINGER: Well, Mr. President, if you do the blockade, and the ARVN still collapses, then you trade the blockade for the prisoners. And, at least, you've got a halfway reasonable negotiation. What you also have to consider is the degree to which this reduces the possibility that ARVN collapses, because —

NIXON: Oh, yes. I know.

KISSINGER: — what will happen, at least in the short term, as a result of the blockade in Saigon, is that the opponents of Thieu will be discredited, because, after all, Thieu did deliver the Americans. I'm just looking at it cold-bloodedly.

NIXON: Yeah. I know.

KISSINGER: And — and for a month or so, at least, they're going to get a big shot in the arm. Now, I also believe — I — that the fact that all these measures will do nothing is absurd. That is just insane —

NIXON: That's the funny thing. Mel's point is that they don't accomplish anything.

KISSINGER: That just isn't rational. Now, whether they'll do as much as Moorer says is questionable. But, if you were a prudent leader in Hanoi, and you have four months of POL supplies, and for you to get them overland from the Soviet Union, you'd have — or China — you'd have to get an agreement between those two countries. You'd have to see how this thing works. You'd have to know how your railway system can handle the bombing attack that's going on. You don't just go balls out for four months and wait till you get to, to zero.

NIXON: Of course you don't —

KISSINGER: That just is insane.

NIXON: Of course you don't —

KISSINGER: You'd have to be irrational to do this. Now, what decision they make, whether they'll say we go balls out for a month and then settle — that is — that's a conceivable strategy, that they'll just chew their words for a month and then settle. But, it will have an impact.

It's got to have an impact. My expert thinks that they were pretty closely divided before they went into this operation. Now, you also have to look at that leadership problem. They've got fifteen divisions in the South. They've got to keep that southern front supplied. That's a major undertaking all by itself. Now, you close the port, tonight, or whenever, that means ninety percent of their supplies have to be redirected, their whole logistics system has to be changed, new depots have to be created, new, new storage facilities. Even assuming that it's possible to do all of this, that's a massive undertaking. Have they got the manpower? Have they got the command and control facilities? Can they do all of that and still plan an unlimited operation in the South? It's hard to believe.

• • •

NIXON: Well, let me say this, if I could go into it, the thing that I — the thing that I just, on the military side, I think there's now — I would — I don't know how much — I think there's a forty to fifty percent chance that the South Vietnamese will go down the tube if we do nothing. On the military side, I believe that doing something gives us a bargaining position for the POWs, and a bargaining position for the balance of the Americans there; where we would have none, if they went down the tube the other way. Also on the military side — that's the diplomatic side — but on the military side, I believe there is a chance that it will discourage the North Vietnamese, hamper their military operations. I said in there for their benefit, four or five months from now, we could hammer them within a month or two —

CONNALLY: That's right.

NIXON: — if they start thinking, and that, from a military side, it will give some immediate encouragement to the South Vietnamese —

KISSINGER: I — I would think if it hampers them at all, it will begin within two months. They're not going to the end of their POL supplies. They'd —

NIXON: Well —

KISSINGER: They'd be insane to do that.

CONNALLY: Not only that, but if our bombing is at all effective, if we start knocking out their utilities, it begins to affect them within twenty-four hours, because when you —

NIXON: Those power plants gotta go now —

CONNALLY: You knock out utilities, and knock out the communications, and it has to affect them adversely. Now, I don't care how they fight a war, but you just have to affect them.

The importance of the reaction from Moscow

May 8, 1972, 5:57 p.m.
Richard Nixon, Henry Kissinger, and Bob Haldeman
OVAL OFFICE

Having given the order to launch Operation Linebacker, Nixon was left waiting for the Soviet response, which could have plausibly ranged from nothing at all to a declaration of war in support of North Vietnam. Somewhere in the middle were the cancellation of the Moscow summit and other possibilities. Just three hours before the president addressed America, he was focused on the Soviet Union. In the short term, its opinion of Operation Linebacker mattered most of all.

• • •

KISSINGER: The Russians apparently have ordered their ships to stay in port.

NIXON: In Hanoi?

KISSINGER: In Haiphong.

NIXON: Why do you think they've done that?

HALDEMAN: So we can't blow up the docks.

KISSINGER: So we can't blow up the docks. Well I've never been all that sure that we should blow up the docks, because if we do, we are really taking away an asset. As long as the harbor is mined, they can't go in anyway. So it doesn't make any difference.

NIXON: They're not going to have anything to do — that's the main thing. I wouldn't blow up their docks when their ships are there anyway.

KISSINGER: No, I'd leave it alone. We're going tonight after that railway bridge in Hanoi and after the — tonight we're taking out the POL around Hanoi and the railway bridge and the marshaling yards. They think they got about a thousand trucks in the strike the other day. And they're just going to grind them down now. Tomorrow they go after the Haiphong POL and other railways and marshaling yards.

• • •

KISSINGER: I think the Soviet Union has one problem only, which is how can they maintain their Communist virginity in the face of this challenge. That's — they'd like to get out of it. They don't want to confront us over this.

"'You didn't ask us the question, so we saw no reason to give you the answer.'"
May 11, 1972, 3:51 p.m.
Richard Nixon, William Rogers, Henry Kissinger, and Bob Haldeman
OVAL OFFICE

Three days after the launch of Operation Linebacker, the Soviet Union finally delivered an official response. For all of the criticism that it contained of the U.S. action, it didn't announce any action in response. The communiqué did tacitly invite the international community to join the Soviet Union in disapproving of the U.S. action, especially the mining of sea lanes. "No one has given the United States the right to restrict anyone's freedom of navigation on the high seas," the statement read, as it described as unacceptable "the actions of the United States threatening the freedom of navigation and the safety of Soviet and other ships."

• • •

KISSINGER: He [Patolichev] came in for what was supposed to be a courtesy visit and he literally talked for forty-five minutes.

NIXON: Forty-five minutes about every little thing, that you know, he'd talked about, this fellow, with Peterson and Stans.

• • •

NIXON: The Russian response was not an official response yet, as I understand they have delivered through Patolichev.

KISSINGER: It was an official response.

ROGERS: It was a government —

[unclear exchange]

NIXON: I think we should say, see, they took three days to respond to us, and I think we will take three days.

ROGERS: I think really the question is whether we should give them a quick and sort of noncommittal response, which we can do. [unclear] Or just delay. I think maybe a delay will make it look as if we are thinking of something. There isn't a hell of a lot to say, because their statement was fairly mild.

NIXON: Well, didn't you think it was?

ROGERS: Yeah.

NIXON: As did all the people around here — Helms thought it was mild, too — the whole bunch.

ROGERS: Well, I think what we ought to do, Mr. President, I'll have Atherton send over to you a response, which is quite appropriate, and decide that issue. And then just have Ron [Ziegler] hand it out, and Bob McCloskey hand it out, or wait till later.

NIXON: Your feeling is that it should not be —

KISSINGER: It's the right level —

NIXON: Henry had the feeling that you should because [unclear] —

ROGERS: I don't —

NIXON: They didn't do it at their high level. [unclear]

ROGERS: Oh, they just made an announcement — a government announcement, that's all, and that appeared in TASS.

NIXON: I think that maybe you and Henry can work out the drill there as to what level and when.

KISSINGER: I think we could wait until they hand it to us officially and then in a low-key way reply to that.

ROGERS: Yeah. I don't understand why didn't they hand it to us before they published it. That's sort of interesting.

KISSINGER: I think, frankly, they're not eager for a reply. I don't think they want a long debate with us on it.

ROGERS: I don't know.

KISSINGER: That's my impression.

NIXON: You think they may —

ROGERS: I really just don't know. It's mild enough in one way. On the other hand, it would be a perfectly good way to delay if they're going to take some other action. In other words, they can play it both ways, so —

KISSINGER: It's a holding action.

NIXON: They can't. We'll soon know. They have a — I will say this, my guess is they would consider it a rather risky business, I mean, in terms of their own interest, to wait until, say Tuesday or Wednesday of next week to cancel the summit. I think they're going to do it. I think they have to do it tomorrow or Saturday.

ROGERS: Well, they could provoke something. They could send minesweepers down, and challenge us. And I suppose, we challenge them. And they could call it off, or if they're committed to go ahead with the minesweepers, then we'll look as if we backed down. I think one of the things that we've got to be sure about — and I spoke to Henry about it earlier — if we're not going to answer, then I think we've got to get all our people to keep quiet because there's going to be a hell of a temptation to say, "They blinked, this is the winner," or something like that.

NIXON: We won't comment on it at all.

• • •

KISSINGER: It is not inconceivable, Mr. President, that next Friday they're going to cancel the summit. But it would be such a mean, petty move. So inconsistent. Another thing Dobrynin says, he says, "Of course you didn't ask us the question, so we saw no reason to give you the answer." So I said, "Well, Anatoly, we'll be glad to ask the question." He said, "No, why make us make a formal decision in response? You have said publicly you are continuing your preparation for the summit. Our leaders know you have said this, our leaders haven't canceled it — why raise the issue?" And I think that's right.

HALDEMAN: And their guys, for sure at the bureaucratic level, are going ahead, because our advance — we have an advance team in Moscow. They've been there for a week now. And they're going over every kind of minute [detail]. They're arguing over where the car can drive, going through what rooms are going to be assigned to who, and where the security can set up. We can set up — we've got complete — we got a hot line right now in the White House boardroom to Moscow — I can get them faster than I can get my office.

KISSINGER: It's conceivable that they will cancel you on Monday. I would say, after Monday, the chances go from seventy percent by five to ten percent every day.

NIXON: Anyway, we're not going to worry about it. In the meantime, the strategy over the weekend will be for everybody to pipe down if they can.

HALDEMAN: Yeah.

NIXON: And you, incidentally, you can go over and — you've got to have your talk with Connally. But other than that —

HALDEMAN: Sure.

NIXON: Just so you can have my analysis. And, I think in the meantime, both you and Henry keep the lid on everybody here. I'd also suggest that with congressional people, that Henry spend some time tomorrow with Stennis.

KISSINGER: I'll call Stennis. I'll talk to him. I'll meet him.

NIXON: And just say, say, "Senator, let me just tell you right now that there's a lot going on and it would be terribly helpful if you would just pipe down."

"Mr. President, don't say they won't give an inch because I think they're beginning to give an inch."

May 18, 1972, 12:25 p.m.
Richard Nixon and Henry Kissinger
CAMP DAVID TELEPHONE

The relations between the United States and the Soviet Union relaxed during the weeks between the launch of Operation Linebacker and the Moscow summit. Confident for the first time since the planning stages that the meeting wouldn't be canceled, Nixon and Kissinger focused on the agenda. Nixon was to arrive in Moscow on May 22 and stay for eight days. The Wall Street Journal *was guardedly in favor of the summit, predicting that "it could be the most productive Soviet-American meeting since the World War II alliance days." Some conservatives, however, were far more wary of Nixon's trip to Moscow than they'd been of his summit in Beijing, earlier in the year. Representative John Ashcroft (R-OH) condemned the SALT treaty, a hallmark of the new détente, saying that it would "lock the Soviet Union into unchallengeable superiority." U.S. foreign policy had been delineated for twenty-five years by distrust and disdain for the Soviet Union. Whether that could change or even should change was still a matter of opinion. On the subject of improving U.S.-Soviet relations, Nixon and Kissinger discussed the new phenomenon of*

being popular with liberals and the serious challenge of retaining those right-wingers who
rejected détente.

• • •

KISSINGER: Mr. President.

NIXON: Hi, Henry.

KISSINGER: I just wanted quickly to —

NIXON: Right [unclear].

KISSINGER: They were sending up another book today.

NIXON: That's all right. I've got enough books.

KISSINGER: It's on bilateral things —

NIXON: I've got that.

KISSINGER: — and I've got something coming on SALT and that nuclear agreement. Well, I spent the morning now going over the communications and it's fifteen pages. And they threw in a few curve balls, of course. But it's in better shape than we were in China. I think in a day or two, we're there. We can settle it. It'll be a very significant communiqué, in addition to the principles. But it's been a tremendous leap. And for the first time, people are going to see in one document everything that's been done.

NIXON: Yeah. I was looking at the — I mean I was looking here at the schedule that you laid out and you suggested that I sign the space cooperation agreement which I have is good. I noticed that Train thinks I should also sign the environmental agreement. I see no reason — I think —

KISSINGER: I think space and SALT and the principles —

NIXON: Space, SALT, principles, though — and I have plenty of signings.

KISSINGER: You want — anything you want to sign we can —

NIXON: I see no damn reason why I shouldn't be up front and center. Now they'll say that the environment thing was worked up before we got here. The hell with it, though.

KISSINGER: Well, Mr. President, the fact of the matter is that — I mean, for example, on the science agreement — I don't bother you with these things because I know what you want.

NIXON: I —

KISSINGER: No, but I just want to give you an example. That thing has been kicking around for years. I got [Edward] David and I said, "Let's go over these points and you're going to settle it in three days," so he did. Then — then — we gave it to State to do some drafting. The total deadlock developed immediately because they came up with thirty nitpicks, so we settled that yesterday afternoon. On the incidents —

NIXON: State doesn't know that we settled it.

KISSINGER: No. On the incidents at sea, for example, you remember the issue about the draft that came to you, six distances and so forth. I knew this would drive the military up the wall. We didn't want the military yelling at it since we need them on SALT. So I went to Dobrynin and I said — and I suggested a formula to him by which they accept our terms this year and we agreed to review it at the end of next year. We all agreed then that so on — and I had breakfast with Laird on Monday morning and with Moorer and told him we'd do what we could. And that evening at nine o'clock the Russians yielded and accepted our position. Laird called me up and said he couldn't believe it. He said in eighteen hours we'd settled something that they had negotiated four months over. So your influence, whether you physically have done it all, and —

NIXON: Yeah.

KISSINGER: We can demonstrate that of these agreements not one could have been done without your personal channel to Brezhnev.

NIXON: Now we will have some of the requirements. Peterson will try to claim that he did —

KISSINGER: He can't. He can't argue that.

NIXON: Naturally Smith will say he did SALT. And —

KISSINGER: Mr. President, I think what I ought to do when we get back —

NIXON: You gotta have a —

KISSINGER: I ought to get in some of the leading journalists and maybe go on television.

NIXON: You may have to do more than that. [unclear] It just can't be in three or four columns. Get my point? It's got to be something that has national impact where they know —

KISSINGER: Well, I have no great desire to do it but the way I'm doing it would be —

NIXON: We're not going to let the State's boys get away with everything this time.

KISSINGER: Because the way to do it would be instead of arguing who did what, would be just to have somebody ask me on the biggest forum that you consider as suitable.

NIXON: How will it be done?

KISSINGER: You could say the president has been exchanging correspondence with Brezhnev. This is how their replies came back. This is how we handled it. This is how we — at that point, we don't give a damn because they're all done. I mean to bring these agreements all to a head all at the same time —

NIXON: Now with regard to the signing, there are two different ways. Maybe it's not as well for us, but to be in on all sorts of signing things. It's as well to hold back and do SALT and principles.

KISSINGER: Oh, you should do it with the space because that's got so much imagination to it — and I —

NIXON: Also in my 1959 speech, remember I said, "Let us go to the moon together." And, that's a good point —

KISSINGER: He told me that that evening — your first evening — there'll be a very positive speech and the toast. It will be a short speech, they said, so —

NIXON: I told Haldeman that mine had to be two hundred words.

KISSINGER: Not the first evening, Mr. President. You have to give a substantive speech — about fifteen to ten minutes.

NIXON: Ten minutes of copy or ten minutes translated?

KISSINGER: Ten minutes' copy because they're going to give at least fifteen.

NIXON: Fifteen to thirty minutes? You see what we're talking about is the translation.

KISSINGER: At Spaso House, you can wing it.

NIXON: I'm not going to wing anything. I'm going to —

KISSINGER: No, no, I mean at Spaso House, you could read —

NIXON: Yeah, yeah. My point is I want to find out what the length of their speech is —

KISSINGER: I just found out.

NIXON: — in words. Well, if it's fifteen minutes in Russian, that's thirty minutes.

KISSINGER: They told us fifteen minutes. They said a short speech. Now I asked him what does that mean and he said that means between ten and fifteen minutes in Russian. And it will close with a toast to you. But it will —

NIXON: Who the hell's working on that?

KISSINGER: I've got Andrews and Safire working on it with one of my people.

NIXON: And we have Price working on the television?

KISSINGER: And Price is working on the television one. We spent an hour and a half together yesterday in the light of your [unclear]. We spent some in the morning but then after you called me, I got them all together again. And —

NIXON: They'll come around.

KISSINGER: I think the television speech, actually, we have plenty of time for.

NIXON: Yeah. But the first speech —

KISSINGER: The first speech is very important.

NIXON: I've got to have the damn thing on the plane.

KISSINGER: That is very important. That's got to — that should be rather sober. And —

NIXON: And rather meaty.

KISSINGER: And rather meaty.

NIXON: All right. And on the signing of agreements, what is your view? Should we be up there signing agreements over there? Does that take too much away — well, the space one. The environment I don't have to sign. I don't care much about the environment — do you want Rogers to sign the environment?

KISSINGER: The goddamn [unclear] doesn't know anything about it.

NIXON: The point is there's no reason for him to.

KISSINGER: Is it put in the schedule?

NIXON: Yeah, it's on the second page. Here, I'll get it for you.

KISSINGER: Well, if you did environment and space, then you'd do one each day. Except Thursday or Friday.

NIXON: Might as well start out with a bang. Environment's a big thing in this country.

Might as well do it, environment and space. And then you get the feeling that's another way to get it across that a lot is being done — environment and space, SALT. On the statement of principles I noticed that you had — well, we can talk about this later — some doubts as to whether I should sign it because —

[unclear exchange]

KISSINGER: I've changed my mind. You should sign it.

NIXON: What the hell, why not? It isn't a treaty.

KISSINGER: Yeah, I've changed my mind.

NIXON: If it is a treaty. If they want it, let's do it. Big deal.

KISSINGER: I think you should sign it. It should be jointly signed by Brezhnev and you. And the combination of this really —

NIXON: It's a hell of a thing.

KISSINGER: — a meaty communiqué, which is really —

NIXON: A communiqué, a statement of principles, and these agreements. Kennedy, Kennedy could never get even that, that space thing, something people have been talking about for years —

KISSINGER: Now, what I would recommend though, Mr. President, is that you're very low-key with the congressional people. I wouldn't say that this is going to be the most significant —

NIXON: No, sir. No, sir.

KISSINGER: I'd just say there're a number of things we're going to try to advance or —

NIXON: Or you give us some talking points as to what number, what they say are. I've got to say all these people have been working on SALT.

KISSINGER: I think that is — I think the lower-key we are, the more impressive — I mean nobody has any idea. They all think it's — I mean the newsmen that I see all think it's going to be like Beijing — nothing. And then at the end a communiqué.

NIXON: Each one of these — well, space is a major story. Environment is a major story. Health is not. Science and technology's not. Maritime is not. Incidents at sea is not. The joint commercial commission is and SALT is. So you got — you got four major stories.

KISSINGER: The joint commercial agreement might be good. But, also, incidentally there is a good chance that we'll get an agricultural agreement for three years worth a billion dollars. I haven't put that on there yet. The [unclear].

NIXON: Well, I think we've got Dobrynin — I — well positioned —

KISSINGER: Oh, that was beautiful.

[unclear exchange]

NIXON: — Rogers thing —

KISSINGER: And the way you handled Vietnam was beautiful. And the way you put the Middle East after. And then another thing I did with him, I went over his paper with him on the Middle East and we — for the first time, the Soviets are willing to talk sense now. In addition to the withdrawal of their forces — well you said there're some things you can't ask Israel to do. He said, all right now. Just put down con-cretely—I think the best position for you is to come out of this meeting without an agreement on the Middle East because it sure as hell that, with a—with a plan by which to move it ahead.

NIXON: What do we say about the Middle East, that we discussed it?

KISSINGER: [unclear] that Jarring should redouble his efforts or something like that. Maybe—the trouble with pressing too hard on the interim agreement, which we may get, is that it may raise more questions about the final agreement than it's worth. Because we don't need any more agreements after this, I don't think.

NIXON: Except there's going to be great interest in the Mideast. I don't give a damn about it except—well, we can do that later.

KISSINGER: Well, we can get that before November.

NIXON: We might do it in September.

KISSINGER: Right.

NIXON: Now Vietnam, though—but I think it's well we now agree we bring Vietnam up. No use to bring it up at an early point 'cause we're not going to give a goddamn inch and neither are they.

KISSINGER: No.

NIXON: This idea that we're going to—

KISSINGER: Well, I wouldn't say to them—the one thing I'd—can I perhaps suggest, Mr. President, don't say they won't give an inch because I think they're beginning to give an inch.

NIXON: No, I mean I'm telling you that. I'm not going to tell them that.

• • •

KISSINGER: You're going to kill them next week, Mr. President. No one has any idea what you're—

NIXON: The main problem we've got, Henry, I think, as you're quite aware, is not with the Left but with the Right. This is great with the Left. It's terribly difficult for the Right. Particularly SALT and the statement of principles and that's—we've just got to be sure that on SALT that we're not freaked. They'll do two [three] things: one, that we let down our allies; two, that we put our arms around our enemies; and three, that we froze ourselves into inferiority. Those are the things we've got to an-swer—

KISSINGER: That last one they just can't make. I'm going to get—MacGregor's getting them together for me tomorrow morning—

NIXON: Wonderful. Good.

KISSINGER: —and I'm going to brief them, together with Moorer.

NIXON: Moorer?

KISSINGER: Yeah, and—

NIXON: That'll pull the rug out before Rogers and his people get a chance to piss on it. How can Rogers's people piss on it now though? I mean, Smith is going to be for it.

KISSINGER: Of course, oh, yeah. He's giving us more trouble than the Russians right now. Every day—again if it weren't for your channel, this thing would never have—well, every breakthrough that was done by you—the May 20, the submarines, every solution was worked out in the Brezhnev channel. And every detail this last week—I just don't bother you because I don't believe you give a damn whether it's eighteen radars or sixteen radars but—

NIXON: I haven't got the time to look at them.

KISSINGER: Well—

NIXON: Experts have to determine.

KISSINGER: But there's—

The effort to maintain a full-scale air war

May 19, 1972, 12:55 p.m.
Richard Nixon, Henry Kissinger, and William Porter
OVAL OFFICE

On the eve of the summit, Nixon met with his two negotiators in the Vietnam peace process, Kissinger and Porter. They discussed the intensification of the war, in which the bombing had recently grown lighter than the president wanted. When Admiral John Mc-Cain Jr. explained the missed sorties by suggesting that the Nixon administration's directives were constraining the air war, the president was infuriated. McCain, whose namesake son was then imprisoned as a POW in Hanoi, had been commander in chief of the Pacific command since 1968. Stationed in Honolulu, he was actively involved with the waging of the war in Vietnam. According to Senator McCain, his father did indeed disagree with Nixon's war strategy, but as he wrote, so did "the entire senior command of the armed forces."

• • •

NIXON: Well, I don't think you have anything to do in Paris for a while. You might as well stay here for three or four months.

PORTER: Well, I'll stay wherever you want me to, sir, but we'll have things to do. This place is extremely interesting, and I can at least contribute something to the scene. I think that there they are trying to position themselves to do something quickly, and that's why Le Duc Tho is kept in Paris. It's not an easy matter for them to move a man from Hanoi—especially a Politburo man—from Hanoi into Paris, because the protocol requires that he stop two days in Beijing, and then stop in Moscow, also, to balance things out. And, there's at least two or three days' travel involved. So, I think they just made up their minds that he's going to have something to say sooner or later, and I don't think that what he will say eventually will perhaps resemble what they'd hoped he'd have to say. [unclear]

KISSINGER: Bill thinks that their offensive is way out of kilter now.

PORTER: Oh, I have, what else, my own—

NIXON: They're getting killed.

PORTER: They're getting — they're getting killed, and —

NIXON: Wait till — wait till next week.

PORTER: Well —

NIXON: Of course, because I've just decided [unclear] I mean, I'm — the biggest error we've made was to fail to bomb them before China, and during China, and after China, and it's not going to be made again. These sons of bitches are going to get it.

KISSINGER: Well, we didn't have the excuse then [unclear] —

PORTER: I — I —

NIXON: It's decided. They're going to get it now, because this — the die is cast. We cannot have a situation, cannot have a situation having cast this die, where we worry about somebody saying, "Well, then, maybe we shouldn't hit them this way or that." There're no limits — except nuclear.

PORTER: I think they're going for cease-fire sooner or later, but a cease-fire not involving South Vietnam only. I think to cease the activity in the North. They'll do it to create a diversion, if nothing else. They haven't got their — they haven't reached their objectives in the South by any means, and that will not be the main motivation. But, if you keep up this, giving them this kind of punishment, then what we're doing in the North will become even more important than what they haven't achieved in the South.

NIXON: But then there's no leverage —

PORTER: I think —

NIXON: — there's no leverage to get a cease-fire, or a return of our POWs, unless you're doing something to them that hurts them.

PORTER: Exactly.

NIXON: And they're going to get a little more hurt. We're not doing enough, actually, now —

PORTER: Well [unclear] —

NIXON: — except for the pusillanimous —

PORTER: Yes.

NIXON: — activity, they —

PORTER: Yes, sir.

NIXON: — we haven't done enough in the North [unclear]. We'll need a hell of a lot more shocks on your little —

PORTER: Yeah.

NIXON: — little scaredy cats in the State Department, as usual. But that's all right, they've been shocked before.

PORTER: Well, I'm very pleased to hear —

NIXON: You ought to tell them to develop a little more backbone in the Foreign Service. And, incidentally —

PORTER: I think it's [unclear] —

NIXON: — in the Foreign Service — in the Foreign Service, it isn't just —

PORTER: Sir —

NIXON: It isn't just the Foreign Service. The Pentagon is as bad —

PORTER: Hmm.

NIXON: — a bunch of spineless bastards. [unclear]

KISSINGER: Well, I just gave hell to McCain.

PORTER: Yes?

NIXON: Well, what the hell — what did he say? What —

KISSINGER: Well, I said —

NIXON: — in the name of God? You know Agnew. Now, Agnew is a — you see, talking to him and Church here, Agnew is a wonderful guy, a super hawk, and very simple because he can't really understand these things. So, he goes out there and McCain says, "Oh, gee whiz. We'd do a lot better, but they — our orders restrict us in bombing the North." That's just bullshit, absolute bullshit! They have restricted themselves. They won't bomb. They haven't bombed for four days, because they say that the ceiling isn't high enough, five thousand feet. Now, for Christ's sakes, how in the name of God — I mean we should be hitting the North before this trip [to the Soviet summit] every goddamn day! Right?

PORTER: Yes, sir.

NIXON: [unclear] those books. I wish to God — what'd McCain say?

KISSINGER: Well, he said he'd have to check into it. I said I'd never seen the president so angry.

NIXON: You're right.

KISSINGER: I said —

NIXON: And he's going to see me a lot more angry, because he's supposed to be our guy.

KISSINGER: I said that —

NIXON: He is, and if he wants to stay on the job — and I want him to stay on; I like him, but, damn, not this way — he's going to start taking his orders from here, or else! Now, I'm not going to have this crap anymore.

KISSINGER: Well, and you know, I looked at the pictures. I never look at bomb pictures, but the only restriction we've put on them until tomorrow morning is the twenty-mile zone near the Chinese border.

NIXON: Which we should have. We shouldn't bomb near China because if they head over the Chinese border it's an unnecessary irritant. And, of course, it's not necessary. They're not even hitting anything —

KISSINGER: There are only three targets in that area. One is two bridges. One of those bridges is right on the border and connects China —

NIXON: Have we hit it?

KISSINGER: — and Vietnam. We cannot hit this. We've taken out the other bridge, and the third target is railroad marshaling yards, where they switch from one track to the other. And we have — of course, if that picture is halfway accurate — we've destroyed those marshaling yards one hundred percent, which you never get. I mean they got some lucky hits and they seem to have leveled those completely. So, I don't know what these guys are talking about.

NIXON: Yeah.

KISSINGER: There's no train moving right now in between Hanoi and the border —

NIXON: I'm going to deal with the North —

PORTER: Hmm.

NIXON: We've got to be in the North. There's no limits there, there's no more.

KISSINGER: And —

NIXON: And no trucks.

KISSINGER: Trucks they haven't ever used before. They haven't started it —

NIXON: Well, basically, you're going to — we can — you can take out. Believe me, with rivers to cross they've got a problem —

KISSINGER: Well —

NIXON: Those pontoon bridges are easy to hit —

KISSINGER: It's not a doable proposition anyway to put two hundr — two million, two hundred thousand tons of supplies on trucks. They've never done that before —

NIXON: Well, seriously, I know that you have to go back to Paris, and I know you've got to continue the charade and all the rest, but do it. And — but one day it may, the thing's going to come. When it does, then you —

PORTER: It'll come.

NIXON: — then you'll earn your money.

PORTER: It'll come —

KISSINGER: He agrees that we shouldn't have a plenary session until we've had a private session that had real progress.

NIXON: Absolutely.

PORTER: Oh, yeah —

NIXON: Otherwise you'll have a plenary, you see — well, you've got — you have a plenary session and everybody here in this country will say, "Well, let's stop the bombing when we have the plenary session." Oh, no! We — they sold us that once; they're not going to sell it again.

PORTER: Our position, as I've gone over it with Henry this morning, [is] you've made your offer. You've got them at a disadvantage right from the moment you put the offer through, regardless of which channel you use —

KISSINGER: That's right.

PORTER: — and that's the way to go at it, and also the last time the public is quite convinced of that, they came and said nothing, and that we tried to follow through with a plenary and they said more of nothing.

NIXON: That's right.

PORTER: And we've now got them in a position where they're —

NIXON: They're next with it. It's their move. It's their move —

PORTER: It's their move. Exactly —

KISSINGER: And we will say that we offered through the Russians to meet with them on the twenty-first. They never even answered up till now.

NIXON: Yes. Do you think they might offer that clever plan which, of course, I suppose which in desperation they might now say, "POWs for withdrawal? We will never accept it." But if they do?

KISSINGER: No.

PORTER: I don't think they're going to do it.

NIXON: No?

KISSINGER: Because —

PORTER: They have too many other things. POWs for withdrawal is so contrary to everything that they've said, and are still saying that —

NIXON: Good.

PORTER: — a turnover of that nature is very improbable —

KISSINGER: I don't know what Bill thinks, but I think their actions prove that the *New York Times* and *Washington Post* aren't right that they have won in the South. If they thought they had won in the South they would offer it, because then they'd get us out and knock over the ARVN. But what they're asking of us is that we should knock over Thieu.

PORTER: Because they still have to ask it. They haven't achieved their objectives.

KISSINGER: If they had achieved —

NIXON: They can't knock him over and they're asking us to knock him over —

PORTER: Oh, yeah —

[unclear exchange]

KISSINGER: Don't you think, Bill, that if they thought they could do it, they would get us the hell out of there?

PORTER: That's right. If they had managed to break out of our large pocket there, they'd be proceeding with us separately figuring it's just a question of getting down towards Saigon —

NIXON: The *New York Times*, the *Washington Post, Time, Newsweek,* the networks all are doing wishful writing and wishful talking.

PORTER: Yes.

NIXON: That the — that they won in the South. Hell no; they haven't won in the South. They're not going to. Let me say — no more. Well, we appreciate what you're doing —

PORTER: Mr. President, I admire what you do [unclear] —

NIXON: Well, there're lots, lots of good, lots of good things in the Foreign Service, despite when I bitch now and then. Let me say it's bureaucrats. That's the problem.

PORTER: I know.

NIXON: I mean that's the trouble with the goddamn Russians: they've got too many bureaucrats. But don't ever become a bureaucrat.

PORTER: I haven't yet, and I've been there too long. Now, I think I'm set in my ways—
NIXON: Right. Bye. Good. All right. Bye. Bye—
PORTER: Bye, bye, sir.

"The only problem is how we're going to do the selling back here."
May 19, 1972, 5:25 p.m.
Richard Nixon and Henry Kissinger
OVAL OFFICE

Convincing the Soviets to come to an agreement on the SALT treaty was one challenge for the Nixon White House. Talking the Senate into voting for it was another. One of the most influential senators of the era, especially in matters of defense and aeronautics, was Henry "Scoop" Jackson (D-WA), who balked at the ABM section of the proposed SALT treaty. A longtime detractor of the Soviet Union, he disagreed with the section of the treaty that allowed the Soviets to retain as many as three hundred of their largest missiles. He didn't consider that prudent arms reduction. Since Nixon had a good chance of gathering enough votes to pass the treaty, though, Jackson chose not to fight it publicly — at least not head-on and not immediately.

• • •

KISSINGER: I had to do a little missionary work with Stennis, who didn't understand the substance. That's what he was referring to. [unclear] They're willing to keep the offensive weapons out of the deal.
NIXON: Well, we can't do that.
KISSINGER: Look, the first impact of this — Scoop Jackson went through the roof because he said [unclear]. He's more worried about the ABM. He doesn't care about the offensive ones. What is your take on the individual initial talks I've made with these guys? I have Scoop in my office. Down there, he went through the roof. He said, "I'm through with you all." When I was in my office, he said—
NIXON: He doesn't want ABM?
KISSINGER: No. He thinks we've screwed it. But I explained to him how it came about. I showed him the military recommendations. So he said, "All right, I won't — of course I won't oppose you." But before I handle the bill again, I wanted to talk to you.
NIXON: Goddamn, get Moorer down there.
KISSINGER: I had Moorer with me.
NIXON: Okay.
KISSINGER: Then Stennis — I've gotten aboard now. But it will take some selling. You're quite right. Your instinct was right; we'll have problems with the hawks on this. Partly because they're so dumb, most of them, that they don't understand what we're doing.
NIXON: Goddamn it. If Smith and Rogers would understand it.

KISSINGER: Well, Smith and Rogers don't want to understand it. Smith understands — doesn't want to understand —

NIXON: [unclear] Of course he understands it. Rogers [unclear].

KISSINGER: Now with the press, Mr. President, I'd be very careful about saying something that can be quoted. That we, two great powers have a special responsibility
because —

NIXON: Oh, yes.

KISSINGER: That will drive the Chinese crazy.

NIXON: I won't change it.

KISSINGER: And I wouldn't give them quite as much as you gave the Congress. What
you did with Congress was very skillful, but I wouldn't —

NIXON: We have to give them —

KISSINGER: Oh, no, no. Because you can —

NIXON: Congress is going to be just pissed off as hell if we don't know.

KISSINGER: Oh, no.

NIXON: What part would you want to leave out to the press?

KISSINGER: I would go a little easier on space, environment, and so forth.

NIXON: Don't even mention it?

KISSINGER: Just — I'd make one or two statements. For example —

NIXON: Which is the best one, space or environment?

KISSINGER: I imagine one or the other. But —

NIXON: Yeah.

KISSINGER: I'd mention maybe space and then I'd say you already know about the
commercial —

NIXON: Well they all know about commercial, they all know about SALT. How about
space, those three?

KISSINGER: Yeah, I'd mention those three.

NIXON: Fine. Of course I've put these guys to the point where they don't think much
is going to come out.

KISSINGER: Oh, I thought this meeting was handled masterfully.

NIXON: They know it's going to be tough.

KISSINGER: But we had a piece. One thing we've done is we've got Stennis all steamed
up now about putting Helms through.

NIXON: Do we need him? Well, on the other hand, did you — well, it was good that you
had your meeting now, wasn't it?

KISSINGER: Essential.

NIXON: Yeah. You don't think there's any more you have to do before you leave?

KISSINGER: No. I'm booked up through the evening. I mean with meetings here. I have
to work with Price on this speech. The toast for the first evening is coming along in
pretty good shape.

NIXON: Who's doing that?

KISSINGER: Safire. But really, I'm beginning to think more and more that these big-shot writers aren't worth it. Andrews is, you know, it's just too much of a struggle with Safire. He's got too many ideas of his own.

NIXON: That's right.

KISSINGER: You were absolutely right. It's just—

NIXON: Price is a man who really senses what you want and he writes it.

KISSINGER: That's right.

NIXON: Safire comes in with something that's totally different from what you ever came up with.

KISSINGER: That's right. And then he gets committed to it and then he finally changes it after fifteen minutes of argument but it's terribly time-consuming.

NIXON: We'll get it out of the way and from there on the big speech.

KISSINGER: Price has done a pretty good job.

NIXON: Price has done a great—look, that should be one that has sort of a good feel to it.

KISSINGER: And that has a good feel to it.

NIXON: Toasts, I don't know. Do you want to put Andrews to work on the toast?

KISSINGER: Well, I think—

NIXON: [unclear]

KISSINGER: It's coming along—it's coming along fine. But I think except for being too specific about the various areas, I think you're in very good shape.

NIXON: You would say SALT.

KISSINGER: I'd say we're hopeful about SALT because—

NIXON: I'll say there's an awful lot still left to be worked out.

KISSINGER: Exactly.

NIXON: And there's some—and then the commercial side—

KISSINGER: Actually, the way it stands now, unintentionally, you will have to break some deadlocks in Moscow on SALT, the way it's working now.

NIXON: All right. We are certainly going to have—we just can't have a situation of coming back and having the hawks as enemies, screw the country.

KISSINGER: Well—

NIXON: Maybe we don't want a deal?

KISSINGER: No, Mr. President, I really think, the one we really screwed ourselves is on the ABM because we just gave over a period of years because we got driven back too much. I told Scoop goddamn it—

NIXON: How were we going to get it through the Senate?

KISSINGER: That was the problem. Every year we had a bigger fight in the Senate. So that part of it is—I think the ABM is going to give more heartburn. The offensive one, once it is explained John Tower is aboard now. I talked to him. Stennis is aboard and—

NIXON: And you emphasized, of course, we've still got MIRV, we've still got ULMS, they're giving up the old ICBMs —

KISSINGER: Oh, yeah.

NIXON: — we've still got our aircraft, you know. That's the thing to do.

KISSINGER: Mr. President, we'll go through a couple of days in my judgment, very similar to what we did in the China communiqué and then we'll pull it around and it doesn't hurt to have a little screaming. It will help us with the Russians.

NIXON: Yeah, I don't know. I don't want, though, having taken a strong stand in Vietnam, to throw it all, to piss it all down simply by —

KISSINGER: The only problem is how we're going to do the selling back here.

NIXON: When you're there?

KISSINGER: When I'm there.

NIXON: Well, I'll tell you what's going to happen. I think Laird and Moorer are going to [unclear]. That's what I think. I don't know but they —

KISSINGER: Yeah.

NIXON: You can't come back and [unclear].

KISSINGER: Of course, I'll be working on the communiqué and five principles and —

NIXON: Of course, I don't agree with Scoop on the ABM. He never got a goddamn thing that we could do for him. We couldn't get any more ABM sites if it were flying. And we still are keeping the system. Right?

KISSINGER: Right. No, I think it's a good treaty, Mr. President. You also are going to get very widespread acclaim so that's not — no, you have idiots like [Senator Peter] Dominick [R-CO] who went up like a rocket but he's so dumb that it's almost a —

NIXON: What'd he go off on, ABM? He doesn't understand ABM.

KISSINGER: No, no, he said that you won't get any money out of Congress if you make any SALT agreement because he said therefore when we freeze ourselves, we ruin ourselves. But that has nothing to do with the specific provisions. That's just among the ones there. The argument they were making — that [Senator James] Buckley [R-NY] and Dominick were making — was once you freeze — they all agreed that it's a good deal if we are pushing ULMS. But they —

NIXON: Are we?

KISSINGER: Yeah, but what they were saying was Congress wouldn't vote money for ULMS.

NIXON: Oh, we'll insist on it.

KISSINGER: Well, that's right. So I think we are in a tolerable shape about it. And the alternative was not to have the SALT agreement. There was no other alternative. If you didn't have the submarines in there, you would face the other argument — that their continuing to build nine a year — that was the one the Chiefs were making. And at the end of the freeze, they'd have ninety. This is, this is why the Chiefs — the Chiefs are delighted with it. And they will resound their arguments for it, and Moorer supported us very strongly down there.

NIXON: Interesting they didn't press us on Vietnam.

KISSINGER: Fulbright was very positive.

NIXON: Shit.

KISSINGER: I think, Mr. President, that this summit is going to be an enormous success.

PART IV

The Road to Reelection and the End of the War

June 1972–January 1973

After the Moscow summit

June 2, 1972, 9:45 a.m.
Richard Nixon, Henry Kissinger, and Bob Haldeman
OVAL OFFICE

On the first day back in Washington after the Moscow summit, Nixon and Kissinger had a chance to look back over the crowded events of the previous ten days. In the relatively short span of about three months, in fact, they had opened workable relationships with America's two most powerful adversaries, China and the Soviet Unon.

• • •

NIXON: Well, how are you feeling, how are you doing this morning, Henry?

KISSINGER: Well, it's beginning to catch up with me. I think by this evening I'll—

HALDEMAN: Well, stay up for another hour and a half, will you?

KISSINGER: Oh, no, I'll be all right. [laughs] You know, you must feel it, too.

NIXON: Yeah, well—

KISSINGER: I'm just beginning to—

NIXON: You need to relax after all the things that we've been through pell-mell. You know, the—I know everybody is tired that went over there. Good God, those advance men and others worked their butts off. But, you and I are tired for different reasons.

KISSINGER: Well, the nervous tension of being up for—

NIXON: [unclear] one hell of an emotional fight from having to fight with—the Rogers thing the first day, and then the SALT thing on Wednesday night. Goddamn, you know, you just—Bob, it's hard enough to go to one of these things without going through that, but it's really awful.

KISSINGER: Well, then, the SALT thing Wednesday night, afterward, was probably the single most emotional meeting that I've attended since I've been in the White House.

HALDEMAN: The dacha meeting?

KISSINGER: Oh, yeah.

NIXON: [unclear]

KISSINGER: You've got these three tough guys [the Soviet negotiators] working the president over.

NIXON: It was a rough one. But it was good and interesting, and it was—

KISSINGER: Well, I think it was the turning point of the discussion.

NIXON: I think, probably, what I am trying to do today, Henry, is to say, look confident. The substance is all going to be presented. I'm not going to go into that, but I want to give you—I want to put it in a larger framework. I want to tell you about the men, I want to tell you about—and I'm going to bring both China and Russia into it.

KISSINGER: Right.

NIXON: The China thing only in terms of why do the Chinese want a relationship with us? Because they're pragmatic. Why does the Soviet Union want this relationship with us?

KISSINGER: Right. We just have to be sure they don't go out and blab it. That's [unclear] —

NIXON: I'm not going to say that. I'm not going to say, "The Soviet wanted it because they're against China."

KISSINGER: Right.

NIXON: Or any — or, not for that reason, though, but — but that the Soviet wanted it for other reasons.

KISSINGER: Right. Right. Right.

NIXON: What do you want to cover?

KISSINGER: Well, it's entirely up to you, Mr. President.

NIXON: Well, how do you feel with all the things this ought to cover? What [unclear] —?

KISSINGER: Well, I could cover the sort of thing about the meetings that you can't. I mean, you can't very well cover how the meetings were conducted the way I can.

HALDEMAN: I think you should, too.

KISSINGER: And —

HALDEMAN: I mean, this one is one —

NIXON: What else should I do? Should I start with Henry? Or should I —?

KISSINGER: No, I think you should start.

HALDEMAN: No, you should let out the context and the big picture that you're talking about. But then, Henry should start with a, "Let me give you a little background on how these meetings were conducted, how your president represented you."

NIXON: Without going [unclear].

KISSINGER: And, uh —

HALDEMAN: But this is billed, and they understand it, and the press has billed it as a monumental, personal thing, which is the very interesting thing that comes out of all this. It's — they're not —

KISSINGER: The first time the press has done that since we have been in —

HALDEMAN: And they're talking more about the importance of the personal —

NIXON: Component? No —

HALDEMAN: The promise of what you did, the way you worked, and how you did it —

KISSINGER: You see —

HALDEMAN: — than they are about the substance of the, the whole thing.

KISSINGER: You see, the way I could do this is to say, "Why the summit?" I mean, why could it work at the — could certain, certain things work at the summit that couldn't work anywhere else?

NIXON: Yeah, good. Now, how would you say that?

KISSINGER: And, and that way —

NIXON: Well, tell me —

KISSINGER: Well —

NIXON: — what do we say, so that I don't cover that.

KISSINGER: Well, I would say it two ways: first of all, the imminence of the summit —

NIXON: Yeah?

KISSINGER: — enabled the president to take a personal hand —

NIXON: Yeah.

KISSINGER: — on a number of issues. And I'll give them that incidents-at-sea example, which is —

NIXON: Yeah, I know.

KISSINGER: — a very trivial example of an agreement —

NIXON: Also, if — then again, if you could go on and say how we broke the impasse on — say on such [unclear] —

KISSINGER: Then secondly —

NIXON: — things on SALT.

KISSINGER: — how you broke the impasse. That's exactly what I was going to say: how you broke the impasse on SALT —

NIXON: And how you think — and then, you might say, for example, in a field where we did not reach our goal — and then I think this may not be bad on Lend-Lease. I'd say, "We — the president narrowed the difference. We got it down, but we wouldn't give on the matter of the interest rate —"

KISSINGER: That's right.

NIXON: "— and we're going to have to negotiate it." I think they'd love to hear that.

KISSINGER: So that was point one. Then, point two was that a number of issues were left that, literally, were unresolvable, except at the highest level. And then, thirdly, the whole statement of principles problem, for example.

NIXON: Yeah.

KISSINGER: You wouldn't even have known how to start except at the highest level.

NIXON: And I have. You couldn't say, "Well, let's let our ambassadors work it out." Can you imagine Beam sitting down with Gromyko?

KISSINGER: Inconceivable. Well, the point which I've made to the press, which all of them, or all of the — Max Frankel, I know, used it, and a number of others — I said, "Look, under the best of circumstances, you have to consider one diplomatic note is twenty minutes of presidential talk. Now, you add up forty-three hours that the president spent with these people, and that means —"

NIXON: Was it forty-three hours?

KISSINGER: Yeah. I mean altogether. That's what Ron [Ziegler] figured out.

NIXON: Phew.

KISSINGER: But whatever it is, it would be sixty to a hundred diplomatic notes, each of which taking two to three weeks to get a reply to it. This is without the first-personal impact.

HALDEMAN: It's much easier. You never get the reading from the notes —

KISSINGER: That's right.

HALDEMAN: — that you get from the face-to-face.

KISSINGER: So, that's what I said what you have to consider: it's a four-year proposition. And then, so many other things happen in the interval that you never get it done. I said — on the other hand, I drew a distinction between summit meetings that are not well prepared, where, then, the principals get together, create a deadlock, and make the situation worse, compared to some which had been narrowed to a point where the principals could act with maximum effectiveness.

NIXON: Mm-hmm. Mm-hmm. Mm-hmm.

KISSINGER: And that's sort of the theme. And then, I thought I could hit a few of the high points of the agreements. But the Russians are on an all-out propaganda campaign at home saying what a terrific achievement this was.

• • •

KISSINGER: Brezhnev complains to Grechko saying, "Goddamn it these Americans. You remember that afternoon session, the president and Kissinger hit me about exactly the thing they're worried about." You know —

NIXON: On these ULMS?

KISSINGER: No, with the missile diameter.

NIXON: Yeah. Yeah.

KISSINGER: And Grechko makes all the arguments to him that Jackson is making to us, saying, "How do we know the Americans won't put modern missiles on diesel submarines?" And Brezhnev saying, "You idiot. Why would they scream about our putting missiles on diesel submarines if they wanted to do it?" And Grechko said, "Well you know, Brezhnev, that we're going to scrap the diesel submarines," which is true.

NIXON: Incidentally, what do you want me to get across to him now? What do you want me to say to him, because I —

KISSINGER: On SALT?

NIXON: About anything. Well, SALT, I'm just going to say, I'm going to say, "Look, when I left office and da-da-da-da-da, we had — there was a ten-to-one advantage for the United States. When we came in the advantage had been wiped out. We hadn't done a thing —"

KISSINGER: And they take ten —

NIXON: "— and if we hadn't done something, we were — had to go — we either had two choices: to go for a crash program of building, which I think the American people would have had great concern about, or have a limitation."

KISSINGER: I wouldn't even give them that. I would say, "There was no crash program of building we could have done."

NIXON: That's right.

KISSINGER: You can say, "We had the Joint Chiefs of Staff in. We said, 'Can you do a crash program on submarines?'" I had three meetings with them, Mr. President.

NIXON: Oh, I know, 'cause I asked Moorer in that meeting, too.

KISSINGER: And they said, "No, we cannot do a crash program —"

NIXON: Well, do you think — do you want me to zero in on that or [unclear] —

KISSINGER: But I can do that task better than you.

NIXON: All right.

KISSINGER: If you want to.

NIXON: Oh, yeah, yeah.

KISSINGER: It's up to you.

NIXON: You take up all the things that I —

KISSINGER: I mean you can just say, "When we came in, this was the situation. It worsened every year. I've started a number of programs: ABM, ULMS, B-1. Each of which had enormous congressional opposition. All of you gentlemen know it takes ten years from the time you start a program until it is operational."

NIXON: You've got to remember, we've got doves there as well as hawks. [unclear]

KISSINGER: And then I'd say we had two choices then. We had only one choice. We — what we have done is broken the momentum of their agreement.

HALDEMAN: You don't have any problems with the doves, though. They're so —

KISSINGER: No. You won't have any problems with the hawks after two weeks. I guarantee you, I'll work them over.

HALDEMAN: Except Scoop [Jackson]. He's gotten himself out on a limb.

KISSINGER: Yeah, but Scoop, I think, is being partisan on this.

NIXON: Sure he is.

KISSINGER: I mean, the things Scoop is saying — why the hell didn't he say them two years ago? Or one year ago? They were equally true. They have nothing to do with the agreement.

NIXON: Well, the whole secret deal has gotten, of course — he says, "That's an old point —"

KISSINGER: Well, the secret deal, Mr. President, the way to hit that is this: you can say, "There are a number of interpretive, if they're agreed, statements," which I will be glad to explain to them, "all of which will be submitted by agreement with the Soviets to the Senate." You, just for your information, you have written a letter to Brezhnev —

NIXON: Saying we wouldn't build three subs — saying all that?

KISSINGER: — in which you're saying, "I want you to know we have no plans —"

NIXON: No plans.

KISSINGER: "— to build those three extra submarines to which we are entitled during the period of the freeze." This is nothing but the literal truth. We have no such plans —

NIXON: I mean, we're simply informing him of something. That's all.

KISSINGER: That's not an agreement. You can change your plans anyway. But, the fact of the matter is, you have no such plans. The navy doesn't want them, and nothing in the agreement forces you to exercise your option. That's only an option. That's not something that you're supposed to do. But I must say — incidentally, I talked to some people who heard your speech. Apparently, on television, it came over extremely well.

HALDEMAN: Yes.

KISSINGER: I'm not — I thought he was speaking a little too fast, quite honestly, sitting in the, in the chamber. But, on television, people told me it sounded very effective.

Stennis and arms control

June 13, 1972, 9:52 a.m.
Richard Nixon, John Stennis, Bob Haldeman, Henry Kissinger, and Tom Korologos
OVAL OFFICE

John Stennis (D-MS) was the chairman of the Senate Armed Services Committee and a key figure in promoting any arms bill in the Senate. He met with the president for over an hour, picking apart the treaties. Nixon had to make sure not only that Stennis would support the treaties, but that he would not delay them into oblivion in committee. The most pointed comment, however, came before the meeting, when only Haldeman was in the Oval Office, and Nixon made a frank assessment of Kissinger's future.

• • •

NIXON: We have to realize, Bob, that we cannot continue for four more years the Henry situation. You cannot have a situation where he, basically, is a de facto secretary of state and secretary of defense, particularly with his personality thing. You know what I mean? We could do it now, and that's a vital thing. We couldn't have China, we couldn't have Russia, we couldn't have SALT, without this.

• • •

[STENNIS and KISSINGER join the conversation.]

NIXON: Well, it's very important to do what you've been talking about. The goal is to get that darn Defense Department to, you know, tighten its procedures and the rest. The main thing is that when you're talking about the new weapon system —

STENNIS: Yeah.

NIXON: — it has ULMS —

STENNIS: Yeah.

NIXON: — B-1, and the rest. That's essential, because if we don't have something to give, there isn't anything they can give us. That's just the way it looks. So, I think you should know that all those tortured hours you spend in fighting for an adequate defense budget, fighting for an adequate foreign assistance program, fighting for ABM, of course, that if you hadn't done it, we wouldn't be here — or we wouldn't be, I mean, in this position. So, that's what's coming.

STENNIS: But if you —

NIXON: And, and our peace fellows — our peaceniks, you know, are —

STENNIS: Yeah.

NIXON: — are saying that — I mean, I think it's just really ironic that the people that say that they're for peace, because they voted against ABM and vote — and want to vote to cut the defense budget ten, fifteen, twenty, thirty billion dollars, that proves they're for peace. That's what leads to war. Don't you agree?

STENNIS: Oh [unclear] —

NIXON: We'd have never got an agreement without this. But — but, you really carried a terrible load there, and here.

· · ·

STENNIS: But, now, I want to ask you a question: I've got the problem here —

NIXON: Yeah?

STENNIS: — too, of getting together this military procurement bill, that is —

NIXON: Yes, sir —

STENNIS: — one-tenth axing missiles and planes. That's something we've come down on —

NIXON: Right. Right —

STENNIS: You're familiar with that. Now, I want to know if you — as I understand —

NIXON: Mm-hmm?

STENNIS: — you've put this B-1; you feel like that's a must.

NIXON: Yeah.

STENNIS: That's doctrine.

NIXON: Right —

STENNIS: What about this command post, here?

NIXON: It's a bargaining chip.

STENNIS: Yeah?

NIXON: Yeah.

STENNIS: What about this command post, here? You know, the —

KISSINGER: The ABM?

NIXON: The ABM?

STENNIS: — the ABM [unclear] —

NIXON: A must.

KISSINGER: A must.

NIXON: A must. I know that a lot of people have said, "He's not going to build it." Like Ellender, you know, raised that point the other day, but —

STENNIS: Yeah, but that would be a good bargaining chip, here. I'm not against it. [unclear] —

NIXON: I understand.

STENNIS: — but, if something like that would be a good bargaining chip, legislative-wise here —

NIXON: Mm-hmm. Mm-hmm.

STENNIS: But, if you say you've got to have it, why that's all right. That's just, [unclear] —

NIXON: Well, I think you've got this specific — this problem, John, if we get it. If — let me say, the Russians are going to build everything that they're allowed to build.

STENNIS: Mm-hmm.

NIXON: And if we decide that, even with — after we make an agreement for two sites or two bases, that we're going to build only one, and they build two, you see what it does to your balance?

STENNIS: Yeah.

NIXON: It's all very, very sensitive here. So, I think we've got to have it. Right, Henry?

KISSINGER: Absolutely.

NIXON: It would be misread in Moscow, very much, if the Senate said, "Oh no, we're not going to even build one."

STENNIS: Mm-hmm.

NIXON: And we're only going to build the one that we've got, and we're not going to — and dismantle one, and keep one, and not build the one around the other.

KOROLOGOS: That's going to be a tough fight.

STENNIS: Yes, it will —

KISSINGER: But is it this week?

KOROLOGOS: No, it's on procurement —

STENNIS: No, no. That's the procurement bill, military procurement bill. The tanks and missiles, all of that's in here. Now, number three — but, by the way —

NIXON: B-1s, ULMS — all are necessary. All are necessary.

STENNIS: All right. I just want to say, now, that ULMS — you want that, the alternate, the advanced procurement —

NIXON: Yeah.

STENNIS: — the — it's a crash program, as I look over it.

NIXON: Yes.

STENNIS: You don't want any slowdowns at all.

NIXON: No.

STENNIS: You want it to go all the way.

NIXON: No, no. We've got to do that in order to have a bargaining position, John, for the next round of SALT. See, the next round will be — because they're going to be building. They're going to be — they're — they've got —

STENNIS: Mm-hmm.

NIXON: — they've obviously got good engineers and scientists, and all the rest —

STENNIS: Oh, yes.

NIXON: — and this is about the one thing — place where we can stay ahead.

KISSINGER: There is one other thing, Mr. Chairman. It's highly probable that they're going to be putting new missiles into their old holes. Not — not bigger in size, but greater in power, as you know. You've had that briefing, haven't you?

STENNIS: Yes. Yes, I have.

KISSINGER: There's a pop-out device they've now got.

STENNIS: Well, here's what you're going to have out there, now, as I see it: we're going to have one group argue that, that you don't have to do these positive things we've just been talking about.

NIXON: Mm-hmm.

STENNIS: We have this agreement, now. It's going to be approved — the treaty. And, we don't have to go all out. They want to play it down. Now, Senator Jackson — with all deference to him, and his train of thought — he'll be telling people, "Well, we've given it away. We're taking a second position," and so forth.

NIXON: Hmm.

STENNIS: Now, he's going to get people awfully confused.

NIXON: Mm-hmm. Mm-hmm.

STENNIS: You see, they're a little, they're a little skittish on this thing, now. And, I told him — I was actually standing in there, pounding for this very thing that you —

NIXON: Mm-hmm?

STENNIS: — that you mentioned, as I see it, that you've got to have this strength, there. That is to assure the people of America, [unclear] about the Soviets, yet.

NIXON: Yeah.

STENNIS: I think if they can stir things up, working from the different end to make the people upset.

NIXON: Mm-hmm.

STENNIS: Our people.

NIXON: Mm-hmm!

STENNIS: So, this is an answer to that. I was — I've been in favor of SALT before you came back with this agreement to slow down on this ULMS —

NIXON: Oh, yeah.

STENNIS: — on a crash basis. In fact, Packard recommended that last October, and they've gotten —

NIXON: Mm-hmm, mm-hmm.

STENNIS: — they've gotten his statement on it, you see —

NIXON: Oh, I see.

STENNIS: [unclear]

NIXON: Yeah.

STENNIS: But you came back, and we met at the White House, and —

NIXON: Mm-hmm.

STENNIS: — pieced this thing right off with this positive step.

NIXON: Yeah.

STENNIS: Now [unclear]. I mean, I was willing to —

NIXON: Well, you're right, but, basically, if you want to slow it down, or anything, let's negotiate a slowdown.

STENNIS: Yeah, yeah —

NIXON: Let's — don't give it away. That's my point.

STENNIS: So, now, you've got to have something that assures the American people.

NIXON: Yeah.

. . .

NIXON: Yeah. The argument — the way I — the way John has looked at it, and I will generalize, because you know the specifics and I don't, but if you could simply say this: that the president has demonstrated that this country — by his Moscow trip — that this country is for limitation of arms. The president has talked to you, personally, and has told you that, that the only way we got the limitation of arms was to have a clear position, where we had something to negotiate it with. There is no question that the Soviet Union is going to continue its own arms programs. They may — they — there's — the only thing that is limited is what is on that piece of paper. Nothing else is limited. Under these circumstances, you are convinced that the president wants to go forward, and that the Soviet leaders may want to go forward, with the second round of arms limitation agreement. But, until we get agreement, we must not discontinue any of our programs. We've got to go forward with our programs. Let's settle them by agreement — agreement; settle them by mutuality, rather than unilaterally. That's really what it comes down to. And, if I didn't believe in it — believe me, I'd rather not ask for the money, because we're all under tight budgets, you know.

STENNIS: Well, I've told you what's on my mind. I'm going to support the B-1 and the ULMS, now, for the full amount, if we can spare some of this R&D, 'cause, you see, we've picked up [unclear] having the hearings on all this R&D, and that helps us a lot on the floor. So, we'd have to go back and start hearings again. If that could come later?

KISSINGER: Let me talk to Laird about that. That's one that I think is easier to handle —

STENNIS: But, I don't mean that the idea is I came to you, asking you to —

NIXON: Don't worry. No, no, no —

STENNIS: — do that, you know —

NIXON: All right.

STENNIS: — 'cause I just talked to him yesterday.

NIXON: No, we'll protect you.

STENNIS: Well, I have a [unclear] —

NIXON: No, no, no. What, I mean, we're not going to —

STENNIS: [unclear]

NIXON: — we'll talk to him on our own. Just say that we've had some questions raised on this, and we want to know what the box score is.

KISSINGER: Well, but if he could — if there is anything at all we could knock off, just to show that we're willing to. Because, our problem, really — when we were — when the president was negotiating with the Soviets, it's miraculous what we got this time, when we had next to no chips. They're building submarines; they're building missiles.

STENNIS: Yeah, yeah.

KISSINGER: We don't have a program in either. And, we need the ULMS to have any —

STENNIS: Yeah.

KISSINGER: — something to bargain with in the second round. Without Safeguard, we would have been dead.

STENNIS: Dead?

KISSINGER: We would have had no negotiation at all.

STENNIS: We wouldn't have gotten very far [unclear] —

NIXON: They — we had to be doing something that they wanted to stop —

STENNIS: Yeah.

NIXON: — in order for us to get them to stop something.

STENNIS: Yeah.

NIXON: Now, that's why we need ULMS and B-1. Then, we got to stop — they want to stop. And then, we'll want to stop something they're going to build. They're building these big missiles, and all these other things.

STENNIS: Well, now, you think that this will pave the way, not perfectly, but this will open the door to a second summit?

NIXON: Well, let me say this —

STENNIS: How do you —?

NIXON: You have — you have this: you can say that I — that I am firmly committed to the goal of a second negotiation, with the Soviet with regard to arms limitation, and that — and that it, and that — but that it is indispensable — not only to pave the way — it is indispensable — if such negotiation is to take place, and to be concluded in a way that will not be detrimental to the security of the United States, it's indispensable that the United States go forward with some of its own programs, because the Soviet Union is going forward with its programs.

STENNIS: Yes.

The unwanted link between arms reduction and defense spending

June 14, 1972, 10:04 a.m.
Richard Nixon, William Rogers, and Henry Kissinger
OVAL OFFICE

The White House effort to secure ratification of the arms treaties required negotiations not only with the Soviets and with the Senate, but also with members of Nixon's own cabinet. On June 6, Laird had testified before a closed-door session of the House Armed Services

Committee and then freely commented to the press afterward, insisting that ratification of the treaty would jeopardize national security unless Congress simultaneously authorized funding for the Trident submarine and B-1 bomber. Moorer made similar comments on behalf of the Joint Chiefs. None of it quite jibed with the priorities coming from the White House.

Three days after the meeting, in the midst of Nixon's afterglow from the Moscow summit, five intruders were arrested at the Watergate building in Washington, DC, "in what authorities described as an elaborate plot to bug the offices of the Democratic National Committee," as the Washington Post described it in its first article on the massive story that became known as Watergate.

• • •

ROGERS: On the testimony on the SALT agreement [Rogers was scheduled to testify before the Senate Foreign Relations Committee on June 19], the — I assume that on the question of reservations we want to do everything we can to prevent any reservations from being attached?

NIXON: [unclear]

ROGERS: There has been some discussion at lower levels that maybe we ought to be lenient toward the reservations —

NIXON: Mm-hmm.

ROGERS: — but my attitude is we ought to oppose them like hell. I think it would —

NIXON: Mm-hmm.

ROGERS: — be very dangerous to have reservations.

NIXON: Well, if you do, I think you'd have a hell of a time having to go back and renegotiate with them. [unclear]

KISSINGER: I don't know about reser — but, I would say, in principle, every — any reservation would require a renegotiation. And, some of them might be nonnegotiable; all of it would be damaging.

NIXON: That's right.

ROGERS: So, I think we should just be against the reservations. Okay, well, I'm glad I asked. Now, on the timing of it, because of Mel Laird's testimony —

NIXON: What's — what day is he going?

ROGERS: Well, he's going after me. But, I mean, he — I've talked about the testimony where he will link the defense expenditures to —

NIXON: Yeah.

ROGERS: — ratification.

NIXON: Yeah.

ROGERS: I talked to Fulbright yesterday, and he said that's one of the things he's going to ask about.

NIXON: Mm-hmm.

ROGERS: So, it really gets down to how we do it. Mel linked it very directly. He said he couldn't support ratification unless he got what he wanted on B-1 and on Trident. And, I guess he also referred to the —

NIXON: Hmm.

ROGERS: — to the Washington ABM site.

NIXON: I think he — well, I think that the way I would, the way I would feel about it, just offhand, is this: I saw what Mel was trying to do, and I know the way the question would come to you. I think the — I think our position should be that we favor the B-1; we favor that, and we favor — we think we would be out of our minds not to do the two sites, because of the equilibrium, and the rest. But, I don't think that it makes sense to — and Henry, they'll probably ask you that question. So, what is your view, too? I don't think if you link it, I don't — if you link it like Mel has, you might run into — you might just start a hell of a fight among the Fulbright types, which we don't need.

ROGERS: Or, you'll have a Jackson saying, "Well, hell, let's not ratify until we see what's going to happen to the defense budget."

NIXON: Oh, we can't do that. We need ratification as fast as we can get it —

ROGERS: [unclear]

KISSINGER: Well, now, Jackson was in this morning.

NIXON: Was he?

KISSINGER: And, I think, well, that he is weakening. And, he makes a good point that over the next term, when you get reelected — which he says he hopes if McGovern gets the nomination —

NIXON: He really does?

KISSINGER: That's what he said. He said McGovern would be an unalloyed disaster for the country.

NIXON: Good.

KISSINGER: He said you —

NIXON: He is. You see what the son of a bitch said this morning?

• • •

NIXON: Well, let's get to agree on an announcement, what Bill should say. Now, Bill, would — what are you going to say?

[unclear exchange]

KISSINGER: What I would propose to say, subject to —

NIXON: Yeah?

KISSINGER: — the discussion here, is not to establish a direct linkage, but to say, "We think the treaties are justified in their own right. We believe that the other things are equally justified. That we — that the administration strongly supports both. But —"

[unclear exchange]

NIXON: "Each should stand on their own feet."

ROGERS: Yeah. I think that's the way to do it.

NIXON: But, I would say this, that I think it's very important, Bill, for you to come down. I mean Mel, by the linkage thing, I mean, he was basically too belligerent, too threatening. But, on the other hand, the — he was talking to his constituency. The thing is that if you could — I think that the [unclear] that this is a — the point I made to the Republican leaders yesterday: I said, "Look, this is a deal where we both negotiated very hard." I said, "Neither — and, and neither side got everything it wanted." I said, "That's — and that's why it's a deal which both sides, therefore, can and should accept." That, I said, "On the other hand, we have to realize that it's only the beginning of a long process. It's a total limitation on defensive missiles. It's only a partial on offensive missiles. And, it — we must now set the stage for the next development."

And, I told, incidentally, Stennis yesterday that we would have the next round begin in October, if this thing began. But, I said, "In order to set the stage for the next development, we should pass this in — but after —" Oh, then, I said to the Republicans, "We welcome, we welcome from you a thorough, thorough questioning, a thorough examination of this, because we believe that after — that such examination would clearly demonstrate that these agreements are in the interest of the United States."

ROGERS: Mm-hmm.

NIXON: I think we have to — I think we have to avoid — I mean, and this will hurt us to an extent here, but it's the right thing, and it's the — if it's not the right thing it's responsible. We really can't say this is a better deal for us than it is for them.

[unclear exchange]

NIXON: It isn't. And, it isn't. And, they on their part, have got to avoid that, too. The deal is not a better deal for us than it is for them. Frankly, what — if you really get down to it — is — and this is where Jackson understands it, and I suppose you made this point to him as I made to the [committee] leader, Strom [Thurmond]. I said, "Look, what you really get down to it here is that we in the field of offensive weapons didn't have any cards to play with." I said, "We have — because we're not going to build any, either. The Joint Chiefs are flatly against a crash program for new submarines, so we have no cards to play with. We've got to build ULMS with the fifty-nine billion dollars. We have no land-based missile program. We have no new weapons systems, except those that were started in the Eisenhower administration." I said, "Under these circumstances, therefore, we are not limiting ourselves in any way that we would not have been limited by what the Congress refused to do." I said, "Now, you fellows know ABM only passed by one vote." You can't talk this way in testimony, but you can to our — the other fellows, the realists. I said, "You also know that as far as the defense budget is concerned, it's totally unrealistic to say that we're going to have a twenty-billion-dollar increase in the defense budget in order to catch the Soviet."

ROGERS: [unclear]

NIXON: So, the offensive limitation one, I think — which is the tougher one —

ROGERS: Yeah.

NIXON: Everybody wants to hold the defense down. They say, "Well, isn't that great?" But, the offensive one, really — well, looking at the defensive one, you know there wouldn't be a prayer to get through another ABM if we didn't have this agreement. So, we're not really giving anything away over there. That's the practical thing. The Russians may be just a little worried that there is. On the offensive side, you and I know there isn't a prayer to get a crash program increasing the defense budget —

ROGERS: That's right.

NIXON: — that the pull is all in the other direction. So, we're not giving away anything there. So, looking to the future, yes, we should be for ULMS, we should be for the B-1, we should be for all these other things —

ROGERS: What about NCA?

NIXON: — but I wouldn't link it.

ROGERS: What about NCA? That's, that's a — oh, that's a tough one —

NIXON: You mean, whether we're going to build it?

KISSINGER: As I look back on it, that was one major mistake we made in this bloody negotiation.

NIXON: Well, that's [unclear].

KISSINGER: And, we did it because the Joint Chiefs and Laird — and Laird gave us a written letter saying that in the context of SALT he, as a congressional expert, would guarantee that it would go through.

NIXON: Yeah.

ROGERS: I don't think it could get through.

KISSINGER: And —

NIXON: Well, I'm not too worried, to be perfectly candid —

KISSINGER: Well, but if we weren't going to get it, there was no sense for our going for it.

ROGERS: Yeah, because that gave them a — an extra —

KISSINGER: It gave them the —

ROGERS: [unclear]

KISSINGER: Then, we would have been better off. We could've kept Malmstrom [Air Force Base, one of the proposed Safeguard sites] if we had stuck with it. They would have kicked and screamed, but at the last minute, they would have yielded. They were dying to get the agreement. But, you were in no position to overrule the secretary of defense, the Joint Chiefs of Staff, and all your other advisors. State didn't take a position, as it shouldn't have. I mean, it's not a State problem.

NIXON: No, but I didn't — as you know, I never did feel we ought to build that, then. Do you remember the meeting?

ROGERS: Yeah.

NIXON: Do you remember I didn't? I said, "Why — who in the hell wants to build it?"

KISSINGER: But you had, well, Allison on the delegation. You had Moorer —

NIXON: Yeah.

KISSINGER: You had a unanimous recommendation —

NIXON: Nitze?

KISSINGER: You had Nitze. All of them pressing plans —

ROGERS: It never made any sense to me, because I didn't think we could get it through. Well, in any event, we can [unclear] that.

NIXON: While we're thinking about it, let's just understand, period, the thing about it is to say, "Well, of course, we should build them."

• • •

NIXON: Now, Bill, so that you'll know, I told the congressional leaders. They said, "Now, do you want this?" I said, "We certainly do. Because," I said, "it'd be the wrong signal to the Russians, after we've negotiated it, that we didn't build it." And so, I think we should just take the position: we need it, we should have it, and it provides — and it's essential to the strategic balance. And Laird should say that, goddamn it —

KISSINGER: Laird will say it.

ROGERS: We don't have a budget this year, do we?

NIXON: No, we had the other.

KISSINGER: Not yet.

ROGERS: I'll have to check —

KISSINGER: You know, I think we have it in. Yeah —

ROGERS: Or, beginning — maybe it was —

KISSINGER: Beginning —

ROGERS: — getting seed money to somebody.

KISSINGER: Under their site —

ROGERS: Site selection?

KISSINGER: We have in the budget, we have advanced — whatever the word is — preparation, but not actual construction.

ROGERS: Mm-hmm.

NIXON: Well, it was in the original plan.

KISSINGER: Yeah, but then it was dropped out and confined to advanced preparation. And now it's back in. Speaking in this room, it was a mistake. We should have just told the military to go to hell.

ROGERS: Yeah.

KISSINGER: And that we weren't going to do it.

NIXON: Yeah.

ROGERS: I suppose, though, that even — well, even though it's a waste of money, it might have some psychological advantage for the country.

NIXON: Let me tell you something: it's — it's not all [unclear]. I mean, let's look at it from the standpoint of the Russians. Why do they protect Moscow [unclear]? Because, there's a hell of a lot of important population there. And this —

KISSINGER: And with China.

NIXON: Yes, that's right, Henry; against China. But, there is a very important — let's face it — population complex around here.

ROGERS: Yeah.

NIXON: Right, Henry? It isn't just Washington.

KISSINGER: Hell, we'd cover [unclear] you'll cover as far north as Philadelphia, which would have — it is — against third-country attacks, there's a certain utility in it, and it forces a larger attack on us.

ROGERS: It also gives us an opportunity to develop our technology [unclear] —

KISSINGER: In our population —

ROGERS: In other words, if you don't have something going, you're not going to have any interest in the, the program.

NIXON: But, also, it's a — the technology for the defense of civilian areas [unclear] —

ROGERS: Of course, you know, that's what I mean.

NIXON: — which they've been developing.

ROGERS: Sure.

NIXON: The technological developments will go forward here.

ROGERS: I think that's the best argument for it. It really is that —

NIXON: [unclear]

ROGERS: — they're going to go ahead with theirs, and if we're out of the business, entirely, we'll fall behind. Goddamn, I thought it was amazing how the expenses go up. Already the estimates were way above what they were when we made them, initially.

NIXON: On, on this thing?

ROGERS: [unclear] Yeah —

NIXON: Oh, God. Well, on this, the — I think just, just be —

ROGERS: I think I've got it.

NIXON: Does Mel testify after you do?

ROGERS: Yeah.

KISSINGER: I think he testifies Wednesday; Bill testifies Monday, isn't it?

[unclear exchange]

NIXON: Well, I think, I've covered it, I've covered it with the — with Republicans, and I'll cover it in my remarks. [unclear] I'm not going to talk long, just —

ROGERS: You know, Mr. President, thinking about the renewed negotiations in October, I think, probably, Gerry's going to resign pretty soon, so we have to give some thought to who —

NIXON: Mm-hmm.

ROGERS: — who we'd put in that spot. Maybe you have someone in mind. But it's going to be a long —

NIXON: [unclear]

ROGERS: —tedious job.

NIXON: Get somebody who's gonna give five years of his life to it.

ROGERS: That's right. What do you—what did you say the other night at the dinner? You know, what were you called at the—at the Duke law school? What did your professors call you there? Hell, "Iron Butt"?

NIXON: An iron butt.

ROGERS: [laughs]

NIXON: That's all one needs to learn the law.

"There's no question there's a double standard here."

June 20, 1972, 11:26 a.m.

Richard Nixon and Bob Haldeman

EXECUTIVE OFFICE BUILDING

In this brief excerpt, Nixon and Haldeman discuss Watergate on the taping system for the first time. The five burglars, arrested at the offices of the Democratic National Committee during the predawn hours of June 17, were quickly found to have connections with Nixon's Committee to Re-elect the President. They also wiretapped the DNC for a period in advance of the break-in.

Nixon was at his home in Key Biscayne when the break-in took place and did not return to the White House until the evening of June 19. An earlier portion of this conversation includes the "18½-minute gap," an erasure that Nixon's personal secretary, Rose Mary Woods, contributed to but has still not been fully explained in the face of evidence that the gap contains numerous erasures. Various attempts to recover the erased portion have been unsuccessful. The way that Nixon starts the conversation suggests that perhaps the erased portion included a discussion of wiretapping.

• • •

NIXON: Back in connection with wiretapping, I think it's very, very serious.

HALDEMAN: Right.

NIXON: There's no question there's a double standard here.

HALDEMAN: No.

NIXON: With regard to [unclear] do it—

HALDEMAN: Yes.

NIXON: —[unclear] prior authorizations to have it done. They're all doing it! That's a standard thing. Why the Christ do we have to hire people to sweep our rooms?

HALDEMAN: We know they're—

NIXON: Yeah.

HALDEMAN: —bugged.

NIXON: We have been bugged in the past.

HALDEMAN: Right.

"The real question is whether . . . we settle at a cost of destroying the South Vietnamese."

August 2, 1972, 10:34 a.m.

Richard Nixon and Henry Kissinger

OVAL OFFICE

For the first time, Kissinger came back from the Vietnam peace talks encouraged that a solution was entirely possible. In a morning meeting with Nixon, he reviewed the high and low points of his session with Le Duc Tho, which had taken place in Paris the day before. As a negotiator, Kissinger liked nothing more than having room to maneuver, which he finally had in the form of proposal points that were acceptable to Tho, who had previously stonewalled every proposal. The remaining problem was finding common ground on a government and a set of guarantees that would protect South Vietnam. Kissinger was confident that they could be arranged, even before the election. Nixon was sly enough to know that in truth, it might not be possible to arrange any real guarantees — ever. That wasn't something he cared to admit, not before the election.

• • •

KISSINGER: Well, first, it was the longest meeting we've ever had. It was the most complex.

NIXON: Yeah, I noticed that in your report.

KISSINGER: And — do you want me to run through it?

NIXON: Sure. Sure. Sure. Anything. Anytime.

KISSINGER: Well, but —

NIXON: All I have is Haig's report —

KISSINGER: Right. Well, Haig didn't have much —

NIXON: It was just indicating it was a long meeting and they made some concrete proposals.

KISSINGER: Yeah.

NIXON: You made some concrete proposals, which I assumed.

KISSINGER: Well, the proposals I made you know. They were the ones that Brezhnev and you worked out.

NIXON: Yeah.

• • •

KISSINGER: All right, so we spent an hour on that, which was very acrimonious. As I said, "The president has proved that he does not have goodwill and serious intent?" I said, "Mr. Le Duc Tho, I waited for two weeks to tell you this. The next time you say anything about the president's intentions, motives, or anything else, I will pick up my papers and walk out of this room. We are here to negotiate. The fact that I'm here shows our goodwill. I'm not going to discuss our motives. You discuss our proposals. We'll discuss your proposals. I'm not sitting here to listen to one more word about the president. If you can't take this, I'll walk out now." I figured they were never going to let me walk out.

NIXON: It was a good move, though. You had to test him.

KISSINGER: Yeah, so he pedaled right back. He said, "I'm not attacking you." I said, "I'm not saying you're attacking me. Attack me, that's your privilege. I'm here. I won't let you attack the president. I represent the president." So — so he started dancing away from me. Well, at any rate, after about forty-five minutes of this, I presented in effect what you and Brezhnev had discussed, which I had held back last time, with a few extra frills, which I had mentioned to you, such as a —

NIXON: Yeah, sure.

KISSINGER: — constitutional convention, made a very long speech for publication, in which I showed that we had —

NIXON: Good.

KISSINGER: — that we had —

NIXON: That'll be good for this record.

KISSINGER: That's right. That we had taken every one of their seven points into account, just so that they had to shut up that we had never responded to their seven points —

NIXON: Yeah. Yeah.

KISSINGER: — and — and how we had that evidence, and so on, and so forth. I — he asked a few questions and asked for a recess. There was an hour and fifteen minutes' recess where, for the first time, they served us a hot meal and offered us whiskey, and wine, and tea.

NIXON: Hmm.

KISSINGER: That never happened before.

NIXON: Hmm.

KISSINGER: Then he came back, asked a few more questions, then made a fifteen-minute violent attack on the bombing —

NIXON: Yeah.

KISSINGER: — and what you have said about bombing, and —

NIXON: So, then what'd you say to them?

KISSINGER: And what did I say to them? I was just cold. I said, "We've offered you a cease-fire. You can accept your power to stop the bombing." I said, "It's up to you, it's not up to us. You can stop the bombing." Then he went on again. I said, "Mr. Special Advisor, on May 2, when I saw you, you said, 'Offensives are the result of long wars.' End the war and we'll end the bombing in the next minute." And then I offered him a cease-fire — a three-month cease-fire, a mutual deescalation. I said, "Why don't you tell us, privately, you're going to reduce the intensity of your fighting. I promise you we'll reduce the intensity of our bombing."

NIXON: Good. That's good —

KISSINGER: Frankly, it's cynical. I just made it for the record.

NIXON: Sure, I know. It was good —

KISSINGER: Then he pulled out a long statement, which is the most comprehensive proposal they've ever made. The first, I would say, negotiating proposal they've made. In the past, they've just given us nine brief points. This time it's about an eight-page document, ten points, and then four procedural points. Now, I can get them, if you want them point by point —

NIXON: No, no, no. I think —

KISSINGER: — or I can give the main —

NIXON: — the gist — what's the heart of the matter?

KISSINGER: The heart of the matter is that in the past they had always said that we must set a deadline, which we then will keep regardless of what else happens. In other words, December 1 or whatever. They've given that up. Now, they agree with our formulation that the deadline will be a specified period of time after the signature of the agreement. So they accept our formulation on that. They say one month, we say four months, but I'm sure we can find a point in between. They say one month after the signature of the agreement. That, for them, is a tremendous change because in the past they have always said we must set a fixed date. And only after that phase, and only after we've agreed with [unclear].

NIXON: Which comes first?

KISSINGER: Well, they now agree the agreement has to come —

NIXON: That's right. That's right. Which is our position.

KISSINGER: Which is exact — they've accepted our position. The only thing we give them now is the length of time, but that's unavoidable. Secondly, they propose a Government of National Concord, but they have changed that somewhat. But, quite significantly in the past, their Government of National Concord was composed, as they said, of three elements: peace-loving elements of the Saigon administration, neutralists, and themselves.

NIXON: Jesus —

KISSINGER: And the peace-loving elements of the Saigon administration had to change their policies: disband the army, let people out of concentration camps, and so forth. So, they were paranoid. Now, they say the Government of National Concord should be composed in the following way: the Saigon government, including Thieu, appoints people to the Government of National Concord, anybody they want. Except, they can't appoint Thieu to the Government of National Concord.

But they can appoint anybody else. They, the PRG, will appoint another third. And then the Saigon people — it's not acceptable, but it's a tremendous change for them — the Saigon people and the PRG, between them, select the other third. So, in other words, it's fifty–fifty. That's what it really amounts to. In the past, it was at least two to one for them, and, probably, completely them, because who is a peace-loving element of the Saigon administration? Again, I repeat: this is not acceptable, but it's the biggest shift they've ever made.

NIXON: It's still a coalition Communist government?

KISSINGER: It's still a coalition — fifty–fifty — government. Third, they said they are willing — if we agree to some of these principles — they are willing to set up two new forums in Paris. One, direct talks between the PRG and the Saigon government, including Thieu, which they've never been willing to do. Second, direct talks between themselves, the PRG, and Thieu. The first forum would discuss the implementation of the political program. The second forum would discuss the military things that do not involve America. And then — and they have a lot of other clauses which we can hammer out. The big, enormous change they have made is the willingness to talk to Saigon, plus Thieu, about anything. In the past, they've always said Thieu has to resign before — and the government has to change its policies — before anything happens. That was the condition for negotiation, not the condition for settling. Now they say they're willing to talk to Thieu about a political settlement. They still insist that it should be a coalition government, and this is why I say it's still unacceptable. Now, I asked him, "What happened in the provinces? How are they governed?" And then they said something that was quite interesting. He said, "In the provinces, the provinces governed by Saigon remain governed by Saigon. The governed — provinces governed by the PRG remain governed by the PRG. The contested provinces get a Provincial Administration of National Concord." Now, I didn't press him too hard because I didn't want him to get a negative answer. But if he means that, then what you really have is a standstill cease-fire, which brings this about. Oh, and they agreed to a cease-fire. [unclear] That's the fourth point. And they agreed that all prisoners would be released within one month, and we agreed to withdraw within one month. At any rate, they agreed to a total release of prisoners.

NIXON: Contemporaneous withdrawal?

KISSINGER: Right. Now, there are two — the first question is this: if they mean that each administration continues and some sort of super thing is set up, that we could li — conceivably live with. In other words, if we said — if we reversed the process — if we said, "First, there's a standstill cease-fire," the standstill cease-fire de facto will produce Saigon areas and PRG areas. That's what it's got to do. And then you could say you have some commission over those. That we could live with. If they say, "The Saigon government has to disappear, and only a coalition government can exist," then, we're in trouble. Now, he said one other thing. He said, "You don't have to put this into an agreement. We're willing to write the agreement in a neutral way, provided you tell us privately you will use your influence in the negotiations that will go on between Thieu and us to bring about that Government of National Concord." Now, this gives us a number — first of all, it gives us massive problems, because, if they publish this, this is harder to turn down than their other stuff.

NIXON: Yes. It's harder to say they're imposing a Communist government.

KISSINGER: It's harder to say they're imposing a Communist government. It's harder to say they're loading the process because they want it to abandon its army, police, and so forth, because they've dropped all of those demands. Secondly, you have to say that, for them, they have made a tremendous step. It's not — in the past, we used to say they've made a step because of the mood. But this time — we used to say that when they're willing to talk to Thieu, we are halfway home.

I think we are halfway home, myself. Third, and this I will say only in this room, if you told me to sell out I could make it look brilliant. I mean — I'm not ask — I'm not recommending it, Mr. President, but I'm saying —

NIXON: Yeah.

KISSINGER: — that if we got up against a hard place — I do feel this, that a McGovern victory would be worse than a sellout in Vietnam.

NIXON: Oh, Christ. Of course, of course. We know that for sure —

KISSINGER: But I also think we shouldn't do it.

NIXON: Why?

KISSINGER: We shouldn't sell out, I mean, and fourth —

NIXON: We can survive without it.

KISSINGER: Fourthly, Mr. President, I don't believe —

NIXON: It depends upon how much of a price we have to pay.

KISSINGER: Fourthly, this is not their last word. It can't be their last word. I mean, they — when they start, they're not going to nail themselves to the blackboard. [What] they have done, in my judgment, is this: they have decided — you see, the easy thing to do is to say that they'll wait till October, and then, if you're way ahead, they'll settle with you. I've always said they can't do that, because if they — supposing they had floated this plan in October, we could just — they'd never finish it.

NIXON: That's right.

KISSINGER: If you are ten points ahead in November — in October, we'll accept elements in principle, and it gets to be November 7, and they haven't got an agreement. So, if they want to have the option of settling it early in October, they must start talking about it now. As they talk about it, now, they're helping you, because no one — because these meetings — I don't know what they do to public opinion, but I've seen when I talk to senators — they confuse them. They confuse McGovern —

NIXON: Yeah.

KISSINGER: — and even with this proposal, we're in a position to say, "Hell, we were negotiating seriously, and this son of a bitch makes any negotiation —

NIXON: Mm-hmm.

KISSINGER: — impossible."

NIXON: Hmm. Yeah.

KISSINGER: So —

NIXON: That's fine.

KISSINGER: So I think — and certainly what they have done, now, they've given us a piece of paper which makes it impossible for these talks to break up quickly, because I can now drive them crazy.

• • •

KISSINGER: Now, to get back to this Vietnam thing, Mr. President, I think now, for the first time, we can settle it. And I think — I'm not saying we can settle it on their plan. This is too complex, too detailed, and they're too eager. If you stay ten points ahead, I would say now the chances are two out of three that they'll settle in October.

NIXON: Should we?

KISSINGER: Well, that's a different question, but I'm just telling you what I think.

NIXON: Yeah, what I mean — I guess that my question is then another one. Suddenly, we're ten points ahead and we are — and then, will we settle in October? The real question is whether, whether we settle at a cost of destroying the South Vietnamese.

KISSINGER: Well, we cannot accept this —

NIXON: Yes, we cannot [unclear] —

KISSINGER: — present proposal.

NIXON: We have to have something that would —

KISSINGER: Uh-huh.

NIXON: I would like — frankly, I'd like to trick them. I'd like to do it in a way that we make a settlement, and then screw them in the implementation, to be quite candid.

KISSINGER: Well, that we can do, too. See, they've given us —

NIXON: We could promise something, and then, right after the election, say Thieu wouldn't do it. Just keep the pressure on.

KISSINGER: Well, they can give us a lot of — they've given us a lot of options now. We could —

NIXON: See, we can't — one problem we've got, you've got to remember, we can't — it's very difficult to lift the mining and stop the bombing and then, then restart it again. We could after the election, but — and will — but — yeah. If — you see, here's the advantage. The advantage, Henry, of trying to settle now, even if you're ten points ahead, is that, then, you assure a hell of a landslide. And you might win the House and get increased strength in the Senate.

KISSINGER: And you'd have —

NIXON: You'd have a mandate in the country.

KISSINGER: And you have the goddamn nightmare off your back, I mean —

NIXON: Yeah.

KISSINGER: It's —

NIXON: It's very important. Because, you know, it is a nightmare. It's a nightmare being there, but — and so therefore, I think we, I think our goal should be that. I just, I just don't know how far we can go —

KISSINGER: No, I've never been —

NIXON: — with the Communists. I don't see how far we can go in good conscience, not only — not because of South Vietnam, but because of the effect on other countries in the world —

KISSINGER: Mr. President —

NIXON: — without screwing up [unclear] —

KISSINGER: — we cannot possibly accept what they're proposing.

NIXON: Oh, I know, but —

KISSINGER: That is clear. Then, the question is what —

NIXON: What, if anything, has Henry — has Thieu offered? He [unclear] —

KISSINGER: Well —

NIXON: He's never talked about a Government of National Concord, has he?

KISSINGER: No. I think what we ought to do is this —

NIXON: Yeah?

KISSINGER: — simply to get some procedural things. On the fourteenth, I ought to accept, or nearly accept, every point in their proposal, except the political one.

NIXON: Yeah.

KISSINGER: Because —

NIXON: Oh, I see no problem with that.

KISSINGER: There's no problem with that, but that shows major progress.

NIXON: Mm-hmm.

KISSINGER: Then, we ought to send Haig out to Saigon, or, conceivably, even I should go out to Saigon.

• • •

KISSINGER: And then, I could tell them, frankly, at the next meeting, "Let's make as much progress as we can today, and let's narrow the differences on the political." We can't accept their proposal. Then, the question is: how do we get into alternatives, and I'm really —

NIXON: Yeah.

KISSINGER: I'd like to spend today thinking it through to see —

NIXON: Sure.

KISSINGER: — what we can do to [unclear] —

NIXON: We'll have tomorrow and the next day. Don't press yourself too hard on that [unclear] —

KISSINGER: But, for the first time —

NIXON: — keep yourself available for other, bigger shows.

KISSINGER: But, for the first time, we have a, we have a real — I mean they've given us so many elements to play with, that, for example, we can accept the procedure immediately. We've been trying for three years, Mr. President, to get them to talk to the Thieu government.

NIXON: Yeah. Let me say this — one thing I — they are thinking you don't have to spell out: they are under no illusions that this offer is not open-ended. They are under no illusions that on November 7, there ain't no offers, believe me. None.

KISSINGER: Well —

NIXON: Not even a cease-fire.

KISSINGER: Well, I'm not saying it explicitly because I'm afraid—

NIXON: No, because you don't want to use that premise—

KISSINGER: No, I don't want to be—no, I don't want to be threatening. I don't want it to be published, but—

NIXON: That's what I mean. You don't want to become threatening in the public, I know. I know, but, you see, that's the way it's going to be. November 7, and these sons of bitches have strung us along, then we just continue to step it up—

KISSINGER: They are not stringing us along—

NIXON: This war is over by the end of this year [unclear]—

KISSINGER: Mr. President, the reason I'm convinced they're not stringing us along is that if this proposal gets published, it will be very embarrassing to us. It gives us a tough problem domestically.

NIXON: Yeah.

KISSINGER: But it will be more than murder for them, for them to have offered to us that they will talk to Thieu, which they have said for eight years they would never do under any circumstances. This will have a shattering effect on their guerrillas. I mean, every intelligence document we get holds firm on the proposition that Thieu can't be talked to, so they have made—for what is for them, you know, they are bastards—

NIXON: Yeah. Yeah.

KISSINGER: —they are—they would love it best if you got defeated.

NIXON: Oh, sure. Or shot.

KISSINGER: Or shot, or anything. You could disappear from the scene. They hate you, and they hate me. I mean, they know who did this.

NIXON: Sure.

KISSINGER: But, the question is, now: how can we maneuver it so that we can have a process, so that it can look like a settlement by Election Day, but if the process is still open? If we can get that done, then we can screw them after Election Day, if necessary, and we can get—I mean, if you pull off—these sons of bitches are going to say you're not going to succeed. I mean, that's for sure. They're going to say you lie, and you're not going to succeed.

NIXON: That's right.

KISSINGER: And, I think this could finish the destruction of McGovern.

NIXON: Oh, yes. And it does.

KISSINGER: And it does.

NIXON: Which is just as important—

KISSINGER: And I think—

NIXON: —[unclear] the whole damn bunch—

KISSINGER: And I think we have two problems here. It isn't just that you win, which is crucial.

NIXON: We've got to win big. I mean, you can't —

KISSINGER: And that you win big, but also that, ideologically, if they see — if it is that you knew all along what you were doing — no one is hassling you anymore on Russia and China.

NIXON: Yeah.

KISSINGER: But you said you had a plan. You said you'd do it with Russia and China. You did it with Russia.

NIXON: Yeah, and even with Japan, now.

KISSINGER: Yeah, we'll come out all right.

NIXON: See, I think with this that the — look, there's no question that — I don't know. I don't know. The real problem, which I guess you've got here on Vietnam — Vietnam poisons our relations with the Soviet, and it poisons our relations with the Chinese. We have suffered long and hard, and God knows how do we get out of it. All it is, is a question of getting out in a way that to other countries — not the Chinese or the Russians so much, they don't give a damn how it's settled, just that we're out — but to other countries, it does not appear that we, after four years, bugged out. That's all we have to do —

[unclear exchange]

NIXON: I'm not — I'm just not sure that South Vietnam can survive in any event, you know? I just don't think that I —

KISSINGER: And the South —

NIXON: — the Northerners seem to be — have the more stamina. How the hell they've taken what they have, I don't know. I'll never know.

KISSINGER: And the doves should not be able to say —

NIXON: To have a veto on us.

KISSINGER: Well the doves should not be able to say —

NIXON: Oh, the doves. I thought you said the South.

KISSINGER: No, I said the doves should not be able to say in October that what you did, they would have done in February of '69 and saved —

NIXON: Yeah.

KISSINGER: — twenty thousand lives.

NIXON: Yeah.

KISSINGER: So we've got to have something to show for them. We've got to be able to prove that we had honor and a settlement.

NIXON: That's right.

KISSINGER: And, therefore, even if we go very far, the settlement has to look as if we haven't done a hell of a lot.

NIXON: Of course, what you're going to have here, basically, is a secret deal. Let's face it. That's — that's the only chance of a settlement, a secret deal where we say, in effect, "All right, we agree to a cease-fire, et cetera. And we agree that we will then use our influence strongly on the side of the kind of a political settlement that we have agreed to [unclear]." Right?

KISSINGER: Well, you see I have—

NIXON: And then you don't [unclear]—

KISSINGER: I have a number of, a number of things I've thought of I think we should do. One is, we've asked for a general cease-fire. I think, now, one way of handling it—the reason they're opposed to that is that they're afraid if they break it, we have a right to come back in. Now, if we made a dual cease-fire in which every party makes a separate cease-fire with every other party, then if they don't break it with us, they'll break it with the GVN. We may go back in, but we also may not.

NIXON: Mm-hmm.

KISSINGER: And after January, if we beat them up enough, Mr. President, I don't think they can win against the South.

NIXON: I agree. No, I've—from what I've read, you know, and everybody else in here, they're kicking also. Let's face it, Henry, we didn't do the mining for fun. That mining and that bombing has got to be hurting these bastards.

KISSINGER: That's right. I have an [unclear] feeling about the bombing, Mr. President, that somebody—

NIXON: Is screwing it up?

KISSINGER: —is screwing it up. They're not bombing, and if I—

NIXON: Well, I know that the weather's always—

KISSINGER: Well, but this is the dry season, Mr. President.

NIXON: I know the point. That's my point. I'm thinking Laird—I'm just wondering [unclear] on this weather crap.

KISSINGER: I'm wondering—

NIXON: [unclear]

KISSINGER: —would you would be willing to let me bring Moorer in after some WSAG meeting and tell him now, by God, you want them to go full bore until there's a settlement?

NIXON: Now, if he's willing, I'll—I will order him. Who do you think it is? Laird?

KISSINGER: I think Laird—Moorer, basically, is a tricky son of a bitch. After his present term is over, Mr. President—

NIXON: That's right.

KISSINGER: —in two years—in a year and a half into your new term—but four years is plenty for him. He won't care. My—my recommendation is too far down. It would be somebody like Haig, who is your man—

NIXON: Of course.

KISSINGER: —who understands—

NIXON: [unclear]

KISSINGER: And, in fact, you don't have to fight back with him—

NIXON: Moorer—Moorer—

KISSINGER: Moorer is — anytime you give him an order, he's all right for four weeks, then Laird gets to him, again, and Laird is just —

NIXON: The bureaucracy.

KISSINGER: And Laird is pretty disaffected. Right now, you know, he took you on yesterday on that debt ceiling.

NIXON: On the, the —

KISSINGER: The spending limit.

NIXON: Well, he's wrong on this, and let me — the spending limit does not entail any cut, any limit on defense.

KISSINGER: Right.

NIXON: It's only a limit on the other things. He knows that. But that's all right. Laird's doing all right kicking the hell out of them on these various bases. He's sort of scaring —

KISSINGER: Oh, yeah —

NIXON: — the shit out of people —

KISSINGER: Oh, yeah.

NIXON: That's always a job. That's the kind of a thing he's good at.

KISSINGER: Oh, yeah. Politically, incidentally, he thinks that McGovern has just about killed himself. He told me this morning.

NIXON: I think having Moorer in is an excellent idea. I should talk to him anyway, and, your suggestion, I'll wring him out good. I'll say, "Now, we've got to do it." I'll tell him that we need it from the standpoint of the negotiations —

KISSINGER: Now, Mr. President, I don't exclude — I'm looking at this thing totally cynically, now. I don't exclude that you might want to consider when I come back from Moscow, that you — that we stop bombing north of the twentieth parallel for the six weeks of — if there's to be major progress in Paris.

NIXON: I agree.

KISSINGER: You see, what we need —

NIXON: Oh, I agree.

KISSINGER: — is to have something at home that shows constant progress and could —

NIXON: While that's happening we'll stop bombing, but, also, they're to reduce their level of fighting, too.

KISSINGER: Right, well that will happen automatically, but my point is, if we stop on September — between September 15 and November 8 they can't do much.

NIXON: No.

KISSINGER: After November 7, if you get — there's no question you'll get reelected —

NIXON: If we win —

KISSINGER: We —

NIXON: — after November 7, school's out.

KISSINGER: That's right —

NIXON: No foolin' around, because you say —

KISSINGER: We can't go through another two years—

NIXON: —[unclear] we're going to take out the heart of, the heart of the installations in Hanoi.

KISSINGER: Right.

NIXON: We're going to take out the whole goddamn dock area, ships or no ships. Tell them, "Clear out of there." We'll stay away from the Chinese border. And frankly, Henry, we may have to take the dikes out, not for the purpose of killing people—

KISSINGER: Mr. President—

NIXON: Warn the people. Tell them to get the hell out of there.

KISSINGER: It's the dry season. I would take the dikes out.

NIXON: Sure.

KISSINGER: Right now, you have [unclear]—

NIXON: Sure, but in the dry season, we take them out, and then they have to move, that's all. Isn't that right?

KISSINGER: I'll tell them, "Let our prisoners go," I'll make them an offer again, and then I'd [unclear].

NIXON: [unclear]

KISSINGER: But, when all is said and done, Mr. President, if they want to take—assuming they have decided they're going to accept your May 8 offer—they couldn't go further than they did yesterday. This was, in all the years of the negotiations put together, this is the biggest concession. Well, that doesn't prove anything, because they've never made a concession.

NIXON: I know. I know.

KISSINGER: But they've accepted two of our—I said—we've always said there are three acceptable points. That the deadline has to be conditional on an agreement. They've accepted that. That they have to talk to Thieu. They've accepted that. The only thing they haven't accepted, yet, is the structure of the government. But it was another thing they did which will help us with the record. I read them a long statement last time of, really, garbage, of basic principles. I took it from some of the things you had said to Zhou Enlai about how we can coexist with Communist countries.

NIXON: [unclear]

KISSINGER: I said, "I just want you to know what the president is thinking"—

NIXON: Yeah.

KISSINGER: —and they said they were very impressed by that. It's—

NIXON: Yeah.

KISSINGER: —half baloney, but the fact is they've said it, and we can publish it—

NIXON: Sure. Sure. Sure.

KISSINGER: —and—and what—they really are serious. They say from now on, after every meeting, let's write down what we've agreed to, and then let's shift it into another forum. I don't think they will make a final thing before the second half of—

NIXON: How about getting Bunker over and letting him do the, the brutalizing of Thieu.

KISSINGER: Well —

NIXON: That's one other way to get at it —

KISSINGER: We can also — well, first of all, we have to know what we want you to do.

NIXON: Yeah, I know.

KISSINGER: Which we haven't decided. If we could do two things, we could have, first, Bunker come here. I think either Haig or I have to go out there, at some point. First of all, it will look — if after the next meeting —

NIXON: [unclear] if you wanted to go, because if you go, then that'll have an enormous impact here. I mean, it also doesn't buy time. You have to realize that the more time we buy, the better.

KISSINGER: Well, if after the meeting on the fourteenth, I go to, to Saigon — I mean, I'm looking at it partly now as PR.

NIXON: Oh, I know. That's all it is then.

KISSINGER: Everybody will figure, "Jesus Christ, something has —"

NIXON: That's right.

KISSINGER: "— to be going on."

NIXON: My own view is that you really, probably ought to go to Saigon after the meeting on the fourteenth.

• • •

KISSINGER: Now that they've offered a standstill cease-fire, I know they're going to start a big offensive. I mean, they're going to try to grab every square inch of territory —

NIXON: Oh, yes [unclear] that we may agree to a standstill cease-fire.

KISSINGER: Well, they've objected —

NIXON: But I must say, I think, as I read these reports, and I'm reading them quite carefully these days, the ARVN may be doing a little better on the ground than we had — than they have. They — they seem to be having a hell of a lot of spoiling operations, and I say that not because of the casualties they claim they're inflicting, but because of the ones they're taking themselves.

KISSINGER: Right.

NIXON: In other words, whenever I see low ARVN casualties, I know they're sitting in their foxholes, but when I see them high, they must be out killing somebody.

KISSINGER: They're taking almost as many as the North Vietnamese.

NIXON: They are, are they?

KISSINGER: Yeah.

NIXON: Well, they should be, because they're on the offensive. Now, those spoiling operations, Henry, are pretty hard on these bastards.

KISSINGER: Oh, and then, they pick up — yesterday, they picked up six [unclear] of mortar action —

NIXON: I saw that.

KISSINGER: — in one place [unclear] —

NIXON: I also saw that in one area, in another province, that, where they came into an area of training, they found about 180 dead bodies. Just dead bodies from bombing.

KISSINGER: Yeah.

NIXON: Now there are — that must not be an isolated incident. You know, damn well, these bombs have got to be hitting something.

KISSINGER: Well, we think we've killed about seventy thousand people. That's not even counting B-52s. Now, if that's true, that means we've wounded another seventy thousand. I've talked with [Sir Robert] Thompson, who's going around the world for us, around Southeast Asia for us, and he thinks —

NIXON: Yeah?

KISSINGER: — we've — we — he thinks they're through till '75.

NIXON: Well then, ARVN — ARVN can survive, then.

KISSINGER: And I think, Mr. President, we have a — I'm going to get these terms improved. I mean, we've never yet accepted a first offer anybody made to us.

NIXON: No.

KISSINGER: But I will make specific recommendations to you before the end of [unclear] —

NIXON: Of course, you know, you know that you have a very tough partner in Thieu here. He may not be willing even to go along with this, that he won't run again.

KISSINGER: That isn't — that is not — that's no longer an issue. Actually, their proposal —

NIXON: Says that he will not?

KISSINGER: Their proposal is easier for, for him to handle —

NIXON: Mm-hmm.

KISSINGER: — because it requires a direct negotiation with him. Strangely enough, their proposal is better attuned to Vietnamese psychology than ours is. Their proposal requires that he, that he can participate in the negotiations. Then, he's supposed not to participate in a Government of National Concord —

NIXON: Good. Good —

KISSINGER: — but I'm not yet absolutely sure what that Government of National Concord is. Whether that's a super, sort of, structure, or — and Saigon continues, you see? Or whether Saigon disappears? But he's always said, when there is permanent peace, he won't run. So, he has the face-saving — he will resign. So, he could put it into that context.

NIXON: Well, the Government of National Concord could just be a temporary government until new elections are held. That's —

KISSINGER: Oh, well, that's what they want.

NIXON: And then new elections will determine the government?

KISSINGER: Yeah.

NIXON: You're sure?

KISSINGER: Oh, positive.

. . .

Later, the conversation turned to a very different subject: Ted Kennedy. Even after it was clear that Edward Kennedy would not be the 1972 Democratic Party presidential nominee, he remained a topic of Oval Office conversation. While much has been written about the rivalry between Nixon and the Kennedys, it remains unclear whether Nixon admired or detested them more.

. . .

NIXON: What the hell is the matter with Teddy? It isn't a question, I mean, I don't think it's a sex business. I think his problem, meaning his lack of discretion, don't you think it's the booze? He can't resist the booze?

KISSINGER: Well, these can't — first of all, he drinks.

NIXON: No, no. But, Bobby and Teddy — Bobby and Jack, everybody knows it, had their own way. But they were a hell of a lot more discreet!

KISSINGER: Well —

NIXON: I —

KISSINGER: I've had Cristina Ford tell me, for example, that Teddy's unbelievable. He invited her to the opening of the Kennedy Center, to his house. He had two tables. One upstairs and one downstairs. He took her upstairs. All during the dinner she had to fight him off because under the table he was grabbing her by the legs, and —

NIXON: Oh Christ! And there were other people present?

KISSINGER: That's right, at his own house. With his wife heading the table downstairs. You know, Cristina's past, she's not exactly an innocent.

NIXON: I didn't think so.

KISSINGER: And —

NIXON: She doesn't look like an innocent. I don't know.

KISSINGER: Then, she said, he followed her to New York. They [Mr. and Mrs. Henry Ford II] have an apartment there, in the Carlyle Hotel. He [Kennedy] rented one ten floors down. Walked up the stairs, practically beat her door down.

NIXON: Uh-huh.

KISSINGER: And she said she's been pursued by many men in her life, but Teddy, just, is impossible! She finally told him, "What if the newspapers get this?" He said, "No newspapers are going to print anything about me. I've got that covered."

NIXON: Jesus Christ! That's pretty arrogant.

"If he gets shot, it's too damn bad."

September 7, 1972, 10:32 a.m.

Richard Nixon, Bob Haldeman, and John Ehrlichman

OVAL OFFICE

Following the shooting of controversial presidential candidate George Wallace on May 15, 1972, prominent politicians — whether they were candidates for the presidency or not — were offered temporary Secret Service protection. While Senator Edward Kennedy was not a candidate in 1972, he received more threatening mail than any candidate. Because of this, Nixon debated whether Kennedy should be given permanent Secret Service protection. On the one hand, Nixon did not want to give favors to Kennedy that no one else had. On the other hand, Nixon did not want to be blamed if a threat to Kennedy were acted upon.

• • •

HALDEMAN: You've got one United States senator [Kennedy] who is a secondary factor in the campaign. You give him [Secret Service] coverage through the campaign —

EHRLICHMAN: Understand, I don't like to give him something, but at the same time —

HALDEMAN: And then if he gets shot, it's our fault.

EHRLICHMAN: Sure.

NIXON: You understand what the problem is. If the son of a bitch gets shot they'll say we didn't furnish it. So you just buy his insurance. Then after the election, he doesn't get a goddamn thing. If he gets shot, it's too damn bad.

EHRLICHMAN: All right.

NIXON: Do it on the basis, though, that we pick the Secret Service men. Not that son of a bitch [Secret Service Chief James] Rowley. Understand what I'm talking about? Do you have anybody in the Secret Service that you can get to?

EHRLICHMAN: Yeah.

NIXON: Do you have anybody that we can rely on?

EHRLICHMAN: Yeah. We've got several.

NIXON: Plant one. Plant two guys on him. This would be very useful.

"I think that I can say that fifty-four days from now that not a thing will come crashing down to our surprise."
September 15, 1972, 5:27 p.m.
Richard Nixon, John Dean, and Bob Haldeman
OVAL OFFICE

In late summer, Nixon was focused on the presidential campaign, in which he led the Democratic nominee, Senator George McGovern (D-SD), by a comfortable margin in the polls. He was also struggling to contain the controversy growing out of the break-in at the Watergate office building, an effort that received a blow on September 15, when the five Watergate burglars were indicted on criminal charges, as were G. Gordon Liddy and E. Howard Hunt, two men associated with both the break-in and with the Nixon White House. Counsel to the President John Dean assuaged Nixon's concerns, promising that the cover-up would hold through Nixon's reelection.

• • •

NIXON: Well, you had quite a day today, didn't you?

DEAN: I did.

NIXON: You got Watergate on the way, huh?

DEAN: Quite a three months.

HALDEMAN: How does it all add up?

DEAN: I think we can say "well" at this point. The press is playing it just as we expect.

HALDEMAN: Whitewash? [Reference is to the criticism by some that the FBI investigation into Watergate was expected to not be rigorous.]

DEAN: No, not yet. The, the story right now —

NIXON: It's a big story.

DEAN: Yeah.

NIXON: [unclear]

HALDEMAN: It's five indicted —

DEAN: Plus —

HALDEMAN: Plus they're building up the fact that Watergate —

DEAN: Plus the White House aides.

HALDEMAN: Plus the White House former guy and all that. That's good. That takes the edge off whitewash really.

NIXON: Yeah. [unclear]

HALDEMAN: That was the thing Mitchell kept saying that —

NIXON: Yeah.

HALDEMAN: — that to those in the country, Liddy and Hunt are big men.

DEAN: That's right.

NIXON: Yeah. They're White House aides.

HALDEMAN: And maybe that's good.

• • •

DEAN: The resources that have been put against this whole investigation to date are really incredible. It's truly a larger investigation than was conducted against the after-inquiry of the JFK assassination.

NIXON: Oh.

DEAN: And good statistics supporting that Kleindienst is going to have a —

HALDEMAN: Isn't that ridiculous though?

DEAN: What is?

HALDEMAN: This silly-ass damn thing.

NIXON: Yeah.

HALDEMAN: That kind of resources against —

NIXON: Yeah, for Christ's sake. [unclear]

HALDEMAN: Who the hell cares?

NIXON: Goldwater put it in context: "Well, for Christ's sake, everybody bugs everybody else. We know that."

DEAN: That was priceless.

HALDEMAN: Yeah. I bugged —

NIXON: Well, it's true! It happens to be totally true!

DEAN: [unclear]

NIXON: We were bugged in '68 on the plane and bugged in '62, even running for governor. Goddamnedest thing you ever saw.

DEAN: Well, the shame of that is that evidence of the fact that that happened in '68 was never preserved around. I understand that only the former director had that information.

HALDEMAN: No, that's not true.

DEAN: There was direct evidence of it?

NIXON: Yeah.

HALDEMAN: There's others who have that information.

NIXON: Others know it.

DEAN: DeLoach?

NIXON: DeLoach, right.

HALDEMAN: I've got some stuff on it, too, in the bombing halt study. Because it's all, that's why, the stuff I've got we don't —

NIXON: The difficulty with using it, of course, is that it reflects on Johnson.

DEAN: Right.

NIXON: He ordered it. If it weren't for that, I'd use it. Is there any way we could use it without reflecting on Johnson? Now, could we say the Democratic National Committee did it? No, the FBI did the bugging though.

HALDEMAN: That's the problem.

DEAN: Is it going to reflect on Johnson or Humphrey?

HALDEMAN: Johnson. Humphrey didn't do it.

DEAN: Humphrey didn't do it?

NIXON: Oh, hell no.

HALDEMAN: He was bugging Humphrey, too. [laughs]

DEAN: [laughs]

NIXON: Oh, goddamn.

. . .

DEAN: Three months ago I would have had trouble predicting where we'd be today. I think that I can say that fifty-four days from now that not a thing will come crashing down to our surprise.

NIXON: Say what?

DEAN: Nothing is going to come crashing down to our surprise, either.

NIXON: Well, the whole thing is a can of worms, as you know. A lot of this stuff went on. And, the people who worked [unclear] awfully embarrassing. But the way you've handled it, it seems to me, has been very skillful, because you put your fingers in the dike every time that leaks have sprung here and sprung there. [unclear] having people straighten the [unclear]. The grand jury is dismissed now?

DEAN: That is correct. They'll, they will have completed and they will let them go, so there will be no continued investigation prompted by the grand jury's inquiry. The GAO report that was referred over to Justice is on a shelf right now because they have hundreds of violations. They've got violations of McGovern's. They've got violations of Humphrey's. They've got Jackson violations, and several hundred congressional violations. They don't want to start prosecuting one any more than they want the other. So that's, uh —

NIXON: They damn well better not prosecute us unless they prosecute all the others.

DEAN: I know.

"All I'm saying is that they're moving step by step."

September 15, 1972, 11:43 p.m.
Richard Nixon and Henry Kissinger
OVAL OFFICE

Very late that night, Kissinger arrived at the Oval Office to talk to the president about the Vietnam peace process. It had seen noteworthy progress. Among other signs of movement, the North Vietnamese were within a day or two of implementing a POW release, something they had not done for three years. At the time, they claimed to hold 383 Americans. As a gesture of goodwill, they planned to release three downed fliers, in cooperation with a group called the Committee of Liaison with Families of Servicemen Detained in North Vietnam. It was a group of humanitarian purpose, run by ardent antiwar activists. When Kissinger met with Nixon, he was just back from Paris, where Tho was making so many positive comments that Kissinger was tempted to accept his invitation to extend the talks for another day. Kissinger, however, was wary and came home as scheduled.

• • •

KISSINGER: "You [Le Duc Tho] just don't understand America." I said, "If you had released those three prisoners to us, you would have put us under some pressure to reciprocate. Releasing them to a peace group that's better known in Hanoi than in America," I said, "hurts you."

NIXON: Yeah.

KISSINGER: I said, "I've got trouble enough advising in Washington. I don't want to advise in Hanoi. But I just want to tell you, whatever little advantage you get from releasing three prisoners, you've destroyed by giving it to, I think, giving these prisoners to these people."

Well, [unclear] he said, "'Peace group?' We don't know any peace groups. This is a social welfare organization. It's the first time I hear that it's a 'peace group.'"

NIXON: Jesus Christ.

KISSINGER: [laughs] And, about the announcement, he said, "Why do you think we would object to it? Of course make the announcement." And — so, this, this set the mood. Then I presented our proposal.

But then, he said — then I told him I had to go to Pompidou. He said, "Well, if we don't finish, maybe we can meet tomorrow."

NIXON: Hmm.

KISSINGER: I said, at first, "All right we'll meet tomorrow." And I was thinking of staying over. That would have given us a tremendous press play, but then, the more I thought about it, without preparing Saigon, if I stayed over —

NIXON: Yeah.

KISSINGER: — Saigon, on top of that peace plan, would have thought we had sold them out.

NIXON: Sure.

KISSINGER: So, then —

NIXON: That's true.

KISSINGER: Then he presented maybe thirty pages of documents of — and when you consider that, in the past, they've never presented more than one — now, their new peace plan is still not acceptable, and I'm not arguing that one. But, they're moving stuff out. It's already amazing that every meeting they propose a new plan. Formerly, they made one plan, then stuck with it for a year —

NIXON: Mm-hmm.

KISSINGER: When we started, they said Thieu had to go and a provisional government had to be set up. Then they said Thieu could stay as long as we promised to set up a provisional government, later. Now they say, "The administration in Saigon can stay even after the provisional government is set up, to administer the part of the territory it controls." That also — that's also not acceptable. All I'm saying is that they're moving step by step. But, I don't want to go into the details now, but I can do it tomorrow.

NIXON: Well, sure.

KISSINGER: When he was through all of this, I said, "I've thought about it, Mr. Special Advisor, there isn't enough here to meet tomorrow, and this is so much we've got to study." He said, "Well, when can you meet again?" I said, "Well, I propose the twenty-ninth." And I have a State Department interpreter, a reliable guy, who was apparently — he said he'd never seen anything like that. He said Le Duc Tho went to pieces. He said, "I must know one thing from you, but you must tell me now: do you want to settle it?" I said, "Yes, we want to settle it, but I want to say, simply, we don't have to settle it before the election. Actually, settling it is a liability for the election." And I read him the Harris poll.

NIXON: Mm-hmm.

KISSINGER: And I read him the other one. So, I said, "If you really want other concessions from us because of the election, frankly, we'd really a little bit prefer not to settle it before the election for political reasons, but, because this is so important for the sake of mankind, we'll settle it before the election, if you let us. But don't count on any more concessions."

NIXON: That's right.

KISSINGER: He — he said, "You have to tell us if you want to settle it. All our plans could be made to settle it. If you tell us you don't want to settle, it's childish." I said, "Yes, we want to settle it." He said, "Give me a day." I said, "Well, October 15." He took my hand and said, "Our first agreement. We'll settle it October 15." Then he said, "October 15, between you and us, or between everybody?" I said, "I think we'll be doing, probably doing, between you and us. The others, I will see." He said, "Oh, no, no, no. We ought to get them all done by the end of October, anyway, with Saigon and everybody else." So, I then, I said, "All right." I said, "I'll have to check with the president. Let's — we'll aim for next Friday or early the following week." He said, "Can you come for two days?" So, I said, "I'll try." And I pretty well promised it to him, because I figure if I go for a day, they announce we'd meet in the morning. Then, in the evening, we announce that I've extended it for a day, which we have prepositioned Saigon, so that they don't get nervous —

NIXON: Mm-hmm. Mm-hmm.

KISSINGER: After that, our domestic opposition has to shut up. I mean, something has to be going on —

NIXON: Well, yeah.

KISSINGER: — if we are meeting for two days.

NIXON: Yeah.

KISSINGER: And Hanoi has to shut up. Now, frankly, I don't see how it can be settled —

NIXON: No.

KISSINGER: — with all these issues unresolved. But, he said, "Let's do it this way." He said, "Let's agree on all the things we agree on and draft language on it." He said, "Let's agree on the International Control Commission, and let's spend a whole day on the political settlement."

I, frankly, don't see how it's going to get solved. But I — he was absolutely — I cannot overemphasize how candid he was. Now, you can say he's stringing us along, but if he's stringing us along he would delay the meeting.

NIXON: Yeah.

KISSINGER: He — what does he get out of a two-day meeting? A two-day meeting enables us to say [unclear] that there must be something going on.

NIXON: Mm-hmm.

KISSINGER: It takes care of us for three weeks after that. By that time, we will be so close to the election, that if they go public we'll just say they're trying to affect the election.

NIXON: Sure.

KISSINGER: Then, we won't even have to go public anymore.

NIXON: [unclear]

KISSINGER: I think he's out — he's, he's been totally outmaneuvered.

NIXON: [clears throat] What do you think his reason is?

KISSINGER: I think they are terrified of you getting reelected.

NIXON: Hmm.

KISSINGER: Not one word—

NIXON: [unclear]

KISSINGER: Not one word about bombing.

NIXON: Mm-hmm.

KISSINGER: Not one word about inhuman acts. Not one word about how they're winning. Not one word about how they're going to fight for all eternity.

NIXON: Never.

KISSINGER: I said, "You know, one thing I want you to remember, Mr. Special Advisor," I said, "you and your friends have turned this election into a plebiscite on Vietnam. And after November the president is going to have a majority for continuing the war."

NIXON: Because of them.

KISSINGER: "Therefore," I said, "you'd better think about what the negotiating position will be in November."

NIXON: Good. Good.

KISSINGER: And he didn't say—if I had said this to him a year ago, I would have heard an hour speech about how the Vietnamese people have fought everybody.

NIXON: Right.

KISSINGER: And—but, I don't want to mislead you. If he were Zhou Enlai, I would now say, "We'll settle it."

NIXON: Yeah.

KISSINGER: But surely—

NIXON: They just may not have the capability of doing it.

KISSINGER: They, they are in a panic. They would like to settle. They don't know how to do it. They keep making moves. For them, they have made huge concessions.

NIXON: Mm-hmm.

KISSINGER: I mean, considering where they started, that in three months they have moved—

NIXON: Sure.

KISSINGER: —from disbanding everything in South Vietnam, to keeping Saigon in charge of the admin—of the area it controls. That's an unbelievable move for them, but it's not enough, and whether they can go the rest of the way, I would doubt. But, in order to go the rest of the way—but, in order to find that out, they have to do so many things to help you.

NIXON: Mm-hmm. That's right.

KISSINGER: Then—and—

NIXON: [unclear]

KISSINGER: It's, it's really—I was stunned by that—

NIXON: Hmm.

KISSINGER: — by, by, by their behavior. Usually, it's extremely unpleasant —

NIXON: [unclear]

KISSINGER: — to sit with them. It was a six-hour meeting, but —

NIXON: Hmm. Goddamn —

KISSINGER: — but they were really — well, they wanted more. I, I broke it off, partly because I had to see Pompidou, but I'll have a real problem keeping this thing going for two days. But I'll come up with enough bravado. We shouldn't make another significant move now.

NIXON: No. We can't —

KISSINGER: We should let them make the move. But, if we hadn't done — it was really — I was very —

[unclear exchange]

KISSINGER: If we hadn't made this — first of all, their offer now washes out our proposal anyway, but if we hadn't made that proposal, that was the one new thing in that, in our —

NIXON: Mm-hmm?

KISSINGER: And it makes no practical difference, and I'm certain that Thieu, now that he sees this whole evolution, sees that we — what Thieu is really afraid of is a cease-fire.

NIXON: He is?

KISSINGER: Yeah. Now, there is this possibility, Mr. President: it may be that they have decided to cave, but that they're not going to cave before — until midnight of the last day that they had set for themselves.

That they say to themselves, they can cave soon enough. That's — I mean, they can cave whenever it — whether they cave at the last second, or two weeks earlier —

NIXON: Mm-hmm.

KISSINGER: — doesn't get them any benefit. Brezhnev said what the Russians did to them. Le Duc Tho was in Moscow Sunday — Sunday night, Monday morning. He saw Mazurov, number fourteen in the Politburo. I saw Brezhnev for twenty-five hours.

NIXON: Geez —

KISSINGER: Brezhnev did not receive Le Duc Tho.

NIXON: Twenty-five hours?

KISSINGER: Twenty-five hours I saw him.

"I know we have to end the war. I know that now."
September 29, 1972, 9:45 a.m.
Richard Nixon, Henry Kissinger, and Bob Haldeman
OVAL OFFICE

Kissinger met with Tho in Paris again in late September and found him continuing his newly productive ways. Several reasons may have accounted for North Vietnam's changing attitude toward peace. The main one arose from America's subtle turn in expectations. At the Moscow summit, Kissinger had explained that "we will not leave in such a way that a Communist victory is guaranteed. However, we are prepared to leave so that a Communist victory is not excluded. . . . I don't know if this distinction is meaningful." It would be meaningful to the North Vietnamese—and to South Vietnamese President Thieu, who saw American support for his regime slipping away. As the secret peace talks continued to make strides, it was Thieu and not Tho who seemed more and more like the enemy of peace. Kissinger discussed that problem when he briefed Nixon about the latest peace talks.

• • •

KISSINGER: See my worry, Mr. President, isn't the election. My worry is that—

NIXON: Oh, I know, I know. That's just what I—just what—Bob agrees with me, and I said exactly that I was prepared, that I'm prepared, and I know we have to end the war. I know that now, but when we really decimate the place, you've got pretty serious problems. But nevertheless, the real question is, it's the old—the old irony: if we don't end it, end it before the election, we've got a hell of a problem. But, if we end it in the wrong way, we've got a hell of a problem—not in the election. As I said, forget the election. We'll win the election. We could—Bob, we could surrender in Vietnam and win the election, because who the hell is going to take advantage of it? McGovern says surrender, right?

HALDEMAN: Yeah—

NIXON: But the point I make—

HALDEMAN: It doesn't affect the election; it affects—

NIXON: It affects what we're going to do later. It affects our world position. [unclear] And, so that's why—why Thieu will. Hell, yes they're hurting—

KISSINGER: Let me—

NIXON: —if we get a landslide.

KISSINGER: Let me make a few things. See, I don't think it is technically possible—even though these silly North Vietnamese think it is—to get all the documents signed by the election.

NIXON: Yeah. Yeah.

KISSINGER: The best we can do by the election is a statement of principles.

NIXON: Right.

KISSINGER: That can absolutely do you no damage, and must help you, because it has—

NIXON: Forget about it—

KISSINGER: —prisoner release in it—

NIXON: It sounds right.

KISSINGER: — cease-fire —

NIXON: Right —

KISSINGER: — with withdrawal —

NIXON: Oh, oh. That's, that's fine, but even if —

KISSINGER: — and no coalition government, and continuation of the GVN.

NIXON: Right.

KISSINGER: And no withdrawal — no resignation of Thieu.

NIXON: Both a Committee of Reconciliation, or a Committee —

KISSINGER: A Commission of National Concord or Commission —

NIXON: Right.

KISSINGER: — of National Reconciliation, and any knowing person — I mean, this will go like SALT, believe me.

NIXON: Yeah. I — I agree with you on that. The question, though, there is what we do require Thieu to do. If we do — if he does get out, does it unravel in South Vietnam, Henry? That's the point.

KISSINGER: That is —

NIXON: Goddamn it, you know, you can't have.

KISSINGER: That, Mr. President, we cannot do.

NIXON: That worries me.

KISSINGER: Me too.

NIXON: Especially.

KISSINGER: And if — because if we had wanted to do that —

NIXON: Yeah. Well, if we'd wanted to do it, also —

KISSINGER: We had —

NIXON: — Henry, the effect, when you didn't see what's happening, if it is happening as always. But what you see is — you know, you know these little Indonesians and all the rest. They'll all come apart at the seams. There is — there is a domino. That's what really —

KISSINGER: Well —

NIXON: — worries me —

KISSINGER: Well, it depends, Mr. President —

NIXON: On how Thieu does it.

KISSINGER: Well, it depends how this thing — this is why he cannot, his resignation can't be written into the agreement. He has to resign —

NIXON: That's all right —

KISSINGER: — after peace is restored, saying he's done everything.

NIXON: Yeah.

KISSINGER: But —

NIXON: Yeah?

KISSINGER: — if this thing is played intelligently, he may never resign. I don't believe this agreement — what I believe this agreement will do, practically, the practical consequence of what we're now working on is — and, there are so many — I may have misled you a little bit yesterday — there are so many technical issues in there —

NIXON: Oh, yeah. I know about that —

KISSINGER: — that it may never even get signed. But assuming it got signed, I believe the practical results will be a cease-fire, an American vindication, and return of prisoners, and everything else in Vietnam —

NIXON: And then it'll end and then it'll sit screwed up.

KISSINGER: And they'll go at each other with Thieu in office. That's what I think.

"He's got to realize that this war has got to stop. I mean, that's all there is to it."
September 29, 1972, 5:15 p.m.
Richard Nixon, Henry Kissinger, and Alexander Haig
OVAL OFFICE

The North Vietnamese had expressed their acceptance of a tripartite election commission to oversee the democratic selection of a new government. It would be composed of officials from each of the Vietnams, along with what were described as "neutral parties." Thieu, however, was adamantly opposed to any involvement of the North Vietnamese and was telling his people in speeches that the only way to peace was to kill Communists. Nixon and Kissinger discussed their plan to send Haig to try to change Thieu's mind, and then they briefed Haig, who was due to leave for Saigon the following day.

• • •

HAIG: I think we don't want to have a breach with the man [Thieu], but I think he's got to know that he's [unclear].

NIXON: Well, I think you could make it, of course, as clear as you possibly can, because, after all, we're his friend and a breach with us is not going to help him. And also, a breach with us would destroy him here in this country. Good God, I mean, he's got no place to go.

KISSINGER: I mean, no one can make it credible that you are betraying a man for whom you risked the summit, Cambodia, Laos —

NIXON: I realize that —

KISSINGER: — bombing, mining.

NIXON: — and he's — he's got to realize that. The other thing is that he's got to realize that this war has got to stop. I mean, that's all there is to it. [unclear] We cannot go along with this sort of dreary business of hanging on for another four years. It's been too long. It's been too long. I'm convinced of this. I'm convinced of it. If I thought — believe me, if I thought, if I was reasonably sure that immediately after [unclear] going all out — I mean after the election, the goddamn war would end, and the president's back and so forth, and you wouldn't be quite as concerned about trying to do something now. But I'm not sure. [unclear]

KISSINGER: We've got to do it. If we can't end it this way, we've got to go all out after the election.

NIXON: I understand that. I know. What I meant is, if I knew that option would work, I would say to hell with this.

KISSINGER: Right.

NIXON: I would try doing it. But I'm not sure it'll work, that's why we've got to try this.

HAIG: I think we have to make an honest effort to do this —

NIXON: Yes.

HAIG: Do all we can without dishonoring ourselves, which I don't think is possible under the arrangements that we've talked at.

KISSINGER: And, you see, if we have made this effort, and then if you have to go all out — the strength of your position up to now has been that we've always been able to present to the American public both strength and moderation. We've always alternated a peace proposal with a tough line. We've never been in the position — you've never been in the position of Johnson, who was bombing mindlessly day after day, without ever making a peace proposal. So if this doesn't work, we haven't — it gives us three, four, six months of, of, of quiet. I don't think anything less than this will work. Al, you've looked over these papers, now what do you think?

HAIG: It doesn't matter what I think. I think it would be awfully difficult to reject what they have given to us in this last session. [unclear] because anybody would [unclear] it seems that they have really given up the objective of [unclear].

NIXON: That's what — and that's what he's got to understand —

KISSINGER: And, therefore the argument of saying they don't want a Communist government there just no longer holds the water —

NIXON: That's the thing that concerns me about our position at this point, that we cannot say that they are insisting on a Communist government. Because they are getting a chance for a non-Communist government to survive, are they not?

KISSINGER: Yeah, of course, what they think is that if they can get Thieu to resign, plus all these changes made, plus keeping their army in the country, that they can create so much chaos that the remnant is going to collapse. And, therefore, our scheme requires that if Thieu agrees to this constituent assembly rule, that then we will require that they have to pull some of their army out of Vietnam, and all of their army out of Cambodia and Laos. And if they don't do that, we wouldn't settle. And on that I think we can stand. I mean, they can't demand both that the constitution be abrogated, and that they can keep their whole army in the country.

NIXON: I would put it to 'em. I guess that you can be just as strong as you want, Al, in this respect. You can be just as tough as you want [unclear]. First, [unclear] make it, make it very clear to him that this has nothing to do with the election.

HAIG: Yes, sir. Absolutely, sir —

NIXON: This is why we're doing it, but that — make it very clear to him, however, that after the election, we've got to live with this problem, and we've got to have a solution to it. That — that our — that after we get in, we cannot just continue to sit there, that this POW thing is a pretty good indication of the enormous buildup that's goddamn [unclear]. And — and that we've got to have a solution, and we're going to find it. And that it isn't going to work that other way, you know what I mean. It's — therefore, we believe that this is the best thing we can do [unclear]. What — how do you have it in mind to present it to him?

HAIG: Well, I was going to structure it just this way. This is why we discussed it. We'll start out talking about what the past four years has represented in terms of our interest for a non-Communist South Vietnam, the risks we have taken. [unclear] Then I'll make it very clear that this is different than 1968, where Johnson had to try to achieve some progress at the negotiating table to help his domestic election chances.

NIXON: That's right.

HAIG: That we are in precisely an opposite position this year, that you don't need this.

NIXON: Uh-huh.

HAIG: But that you want to use your strength, domestically, here, to put pressure on Hanoi for concessions —

NIXON: That's right —

HAIG: — and that they are moving. And that we do have [unclear] some interesting possibilities, it's not yet acceptable. But that's what I want to discuss with them. Then, I want to go through the realities of the strategic picture; what we could hope for if we don't get a settlement; the fact that we are going to have been faced with disabling legislation.

NIXON: But point out that we still wanted — that the last Senate vote should not be reassuring, because it was still a margin of only one vote.

HAIG: We give him that —

NIXON: So, in reality —

HAIG: At a time when you're thirty points ahead in the polls —

NIXON: That's right.

HAIG: — we win a vote for cutoff of funds by two votes.

NIXON: That's right.

HAIG: So, that this is — this is very damaging. And I'm going to recall his discussions with me last October, when he said if he felt there was a true peace in the making that he would step down —

KISSINGER: And he repeated it on May 8.

HAIG: And he repeated it on May 8.

NIXON: [unclear]

KISSINGER: Or May 10, whenever he made it.

HAIG: Then I will go through our counterpunch, which does not yet get him into the proposal that he sent out. We will go through it in the detail, and, of course, the paragraph [unclear] political arrangements is the toughest, and I will discuss those, but, in reality, what they've offered us is a fig leaf for an advisory group that is without power, and that the South Vietnamese government would still control the army, the police, and the territories they currently hold —

NIXON: What I mean is that on this case, what I would like for you to do is to say to the president, if you could say, "Now, Mr. President, [unclear] asked me here. He's a pretty shrewd analyzer — analyzer of these things." Why don't you [unclear]? "It seems to me like this is the way you might be able to see it." In other words, put it out that I've analyzed this thing, and that I wish to call it to his attention. See?

HAIG: That's right, and if he can't select the man — well, I won't get into that —

NIXON: Yeah. That's right —

HAIG: — until we get through the whole proposition.

NIXON: That's right.

HAIG: Now, he'll have problems with that, because it calls for a constituent assembly and a new constitution, and —

KISSINGER: Yeah, but he will, in effect, dominate the election because the electoral law — the election can never take place because its electoral law will be written by a commission —

NIXON: [unclear]

KISSINGER: — which requires unanimity. I don't see how you can ever agree on any actual laws —

NIXON: [unclear] noted his interest in the proposition. And that he — and, therefore, I think that he should be very, very generous, insofar as what happens after that due to the unanimity proposition.

Now, he'll say [unclear]. And, also, how much of this needs to be public at the present time. [unclear] But the main thing, I guess, Al, that I want you to get across to him, is that he can't just assume that because I win the election that we're going to stick with him through hell and high water. This war is not going to go on. Goddamn it, we can't do it.

We're not going to do it. We're not going to have our — we're not gonna have, let alone, our guys getting killed, and our prisoners, so that's just that. We're not going to have him get killed. And we happen to have our relationships with the Russians and the Chinese. There's that, and, also, I'm not going to have it keep us from doing some other things that we need to do. We've got to get the war the hell off our backs in this country. That's all there is to it.

HAIG: And off his people's back.

NIXON: Oh, I feel that, too. Tell him that I know those casualties show three hundred a week being killed. I said, "I take no comfort out of the fact that we — our casualties were one last week when his are three hundred." I said, "To me, that concerns me and that, I doubt that I'd be here." I think you now know, I want you to know you can go very far in saying that I believe that he ought to accept this proposition. That's my view. I wouldn't indicate that I'm not going to press him on it, either. I'd indicate that we might just [unclear].

HAIG: Well, I think—I think once—

NIXON: And, incidentally, I just want it to be arranged so that Al has plenty of time with him. I want to be sure that he has—

KISSINGER: Oh, yes.

NIXON: [unclear]

KISSINGER: Now, we got a cable that he sees him twice. Monday morning—

NIXON: Yeah, yeah.

KISSINGER: —and Tuesday afternoon—

NIXON: Well, look, but you better send a message indicating that I want him to take plenty of time [unclear]—

KISSINGER: Well, I think once he hears the subject, he's going to take plenty of time. It's too much in his interest. I don't think we should get him all stirred up—

NIXON: All right—

KISSINGER: —before Al gets there.

HAIG: [unclear] But I don't think, either, that we should force him into an answer in the first session there, or even the second, necessarily, because this is the kind of thing that he'll want to think out in the greatest detail. He ought to know that we're very strong for him.

NIXON: Whatever, he's got to think. He may not decide at the second session, then you'll get away, and he'll sit down and talk with his own people.

KISSINGER: That doesn't make a difference—

NIXON: [unclear] Huh?

KISSINGER: We'll table this proposal anyway the following week, and it doesn't make any difference what he agrees to.

NIXON: Let's suppose—yeah, let's see. Are you going to tell him that you're going to table his proposal?

HAIG: Tell him we're going to move.

NIXON: How?

HAIG: We intend to move. Of course, if it looks like it could cause a public break—

KISSINGER: We can't. It isn't desirable to have a public break, because—

NIXON: No, that would be bad. A public break would hurt us. That'd hurt us in the election.

KISSINGER: That would. Also you'd be accused by McGovern, then, that you strung along with Thieu, and when it served your interest—

NIXON: Yeah.

KISSINGER: —just before the election, you killed twenty thousand people.

NIXON: That's right.

KISSINGER: So, we should avoid—

NIXON: We can't do that—

KISSINGER: —a public break.

NIXON: What you've got to say there is that this—you've got to point out that this president has stood by him with no support. The House is against him. The Senate is against him. The media has been against him. The students have rioted. All sorts of hell-raising loose.

He's made these tough decisions. And, now, he's got to have something from him, in return. We've got to have [unclear], an agreement, an acceptable proposition that I think he can live with. That's really what you get down to.

KISSINGER: Mr. President, nobody would have believed that they would make a proposal which would keep the Saigon government in power with its own army and police, but without Thieu. Never have they gone that far before. All their previous proposals were that Saigon has to disappear and that the other government, the Provisional Government of National Concord, replaces it. Because that would have led to a sure Communist takeover. And that was easy to reject. We were never tempted for one minute. You could have settled it in July, announced those terms. We were never tempted for thirty seconds by any of those —

NIXON: [unclear]

KISSINGER: But here we are with — confronted with a proposal of a Government of National Concord that has no power, no police, no army, and, moreover, we won't even accept the word "government" for it. We'll call it "Committee" or "Commission for National Reconciliation."

"We've come absolutely to a hard place with the South Vietnamese."
October 6, 1972, 9:30 a.m.
Richard Nixon and Henry Kissinger
OVAL OFFICE

Even as the United States came closer and closer to common ground with its adversary, North Vietnam, it was clear that serious differences existed with its ally, South Vietnam. Haig's visit to Thieu, designed to reassure him, failed to do that. Rather than convince Thieu that the United States would not make peace with North Vietnam without him, privately that is exactly what the United States threatened to do.

• • •

KISSINGER: We've come absolutely to a hard place with the South Vietnamese. It's not, they're not, I've got the transcript of the —

NIXON: [Gives unrelated instruction to assistant who enters and then departs.] You've got Haig's transcript?

KISSINGER: I have Haig's transcript. These guys are scared, and they're desperate. And they know what's coming. And Thieu says that, sure, these proposals keep him going. Somewhere down the road he'll have no chance except to commit suicide.

• • •

KISSINGER: I've had a study. They [unclear] air force, they lied to us again. They substituted planes that they told us were better, and Haig has found out aren't nearly as good. We're dealing with a sick military establishment on top of everything else. They're going to have funding problems in January. But then, the dilemma that additional military operations produce for us, is this. We can improve the situation in South Vietnam drastically, but we can't get our prisoners back. And before they collapse, they will offer us our prisoners for a withdrawal. And in that case, I think at this point, we have to take that.

NIXON: We will. I'd take it today. They're not going to offer it, but I'd take it.

KISSINGER: So that is, well I don't think that we can do it before the election.

NIXON: They're not going to offer it, that's what I mean. When I mean "today," I mean I'd take it November, December, January, anytime.

KISSINGER: Yeah.

NIXON: That's the deal, we have to take it.

KISSINGER: That's right. But that will also collapse the South Vietnamese, except we won't be so responsible for the whole settlement. So as I look down the road, I think there is one chance in four —

NIXON: Well, if they're that collapsible, and if they think this thing is going to collapse, that's another way to look at it, too. We've got to remember: we cannot keep this child sucking at the tit when the child is four years old. You know what I mean? There comes a time.

KISSINGER: What we can get out of a settlement now, I'm not even sure it's going to help you politically. You can judge better whether you will wind up like Churchill, having just —

NIXON: I don't want it for the election, but go ahead.

KISSINGER: Well, if we keep going, you may have no choice, you may get it before the election.

NIXON: Well, let's try our best not to. The more that we can stagger it past the election, the better.

KISSINGER: You do not want it before the election?

NIXON: Well, I don't want it before the election if we have a Thieu blowup. If we do, it's going to hurt us very badly.

KISSINGER: We may be able to avoid a Thieu blowup.

"The deal we got, Mr. President, is so far better than anything we dreamt of."
October 12, 1972, 7:05 p.m.
Richard Nixon, Henry Kissinger, Alexander Haig, and Bob Haldeman
EXECUTIVE OFFICE BUILDING

When Kissinger arrived in Paris for a new round of talks with Tho on October 8, he received — for the first time — a peace agreement composed by the North Vietnamese. A complete document, it gave Kissinger hope that the North Vietnamese were actually ready to sign. During three days of talks honing the draft agreement, Kissinger sent very little information to Nixon. Presumably, he didn't want to be hindered or delayed by a president with other major concerns. And there were plenty; on October 10, the Washington Post *reported that an FBI investigation had found evidence of a campaign of political sabotage by the Nixon forces that was "unprecedented in scope and intensity." When Kissinger returned to Washington, he brought Nixon good news on the diplomatic front.*

• • •

NIXON: Well, it was a long, long day —

KISSINGER: [unclear] Mr. President —

NIXON: Sure.

KISSINGER: Well, you got three out of three, Mr. President [their goal of a China summit, a Soviet summit, and a Vietnam peace agreement]. It's well on the way.

NIXON: You got an agreement? Are you kidding?

KISSINGER: No, I'm not kidding.

NIXON: Did you agree on it? Three out of three?

KISSINGER: Although it's done, we got to —

NIXON: [laughs]

KISSINGER: We got it word for —

NIXON: I see.

KISSINGER: — word. We got a — we got a text.

NIXON: [humorously] Al — I'm going to ask Al, because you're too prejudiced, Henry. You're so prejudiced to the peace camp that I can't trust you. Don't you think so, Al?

HAIG: Yes, sir.

KISSINGER: If it is done —?

NIXON: What about Thieu?

HAIG: It isn't done.

KISSINGER: Well, that's the problem, but it is a commitment.

HAIG: He wanted this agreement.

NIXON: It's not insurmountable. How do we handle it?

KISSINGER: I have to — I have to go up — out — here is what we have to do: I have to go to Paris on Tuesday [October 17] to go over the agreed things word for word with Le [Duc Tho].

NIXON: You could then get it?

KISSINGER: No problem. I think we have an agreed text. I've left a man behind to go over it. Except, but I've — you know, just in case there's any last-minute treachery. Then I go to Saigon to get Thieu aboard. Then I have to go to Hanoi if they're willing [unclear] —

NIXON: I understand.

KISSINGER: That was the price we had to pay.

NIXON: Well, that's no price if we get Thieu aboard. What do you think, Al? When do you get him aboard?

KISSINGER: That's —

HAIG: He's already aboard —

KISSINGER: But the deal we got, Mr. President, is so far better than anything we dreamt of. I mean it was absolutely, totally hard-line with them.

NIXON: Good.

KISSINGER: The deal is [unclear] —

NIXON: Won't it totally wipe out Thieu, Henry?

HALDEMAN: Yeah.

KISSINGER: Oh, no. It's so far better than anything we discussed. He won't like it because he thinks he's winning, but here is the deal, just to give you the main points, then I'll tell you [unclear] —

NIXON: We can do that after.

KISSINGER: All right, afterwards. The cease-fire will go into effect —

NIXON: The more — the more, of course, we think of all this is that we see a lot of the problems, you know, the silly-ass thing of some SAM hitting the French consulate [in Hanoi] and everything raises hell about it. I didn't think it either. Most people would rather kill all the Frenchmen anyway, but the point is —

KISSINGER: [unclear] we had a love fest two hours yesterday.

NIXON: I know. I know. My point is, Henry, I'm thinking of Americans. Most Americans are very cynical about all these things now. But the point is that we can't go on, and on, and on, and on having these things hanging over us either. We can ask — the other thing, are they afraid we're going to nuke 'em? Or just hang on for another ten years?

KISSINGER: Mr. President —

NIXON: You see, Al, that's the problem, isn't it?

KISSINGER: We've done just about everything we can do, but this is a deal, Mr. President, that George Meany could go along with. So we have no problem. I mean this is — if — if you went on television and said you're going to make this as an American proposal, the *New York Times,* the *Washington Post,* and even moderates would fall all over themselves, foaming at the mouth, swearing that this couldn't — that you were indeed out of —

NIXON: Mm-hmm.

KISSINGER: — tough, mean, [unclear].

NIXON: Good. Well, I've got a little saved up.

KISSINGER: I mean, so you — but, first, the cease-fire allows, goes into effect until the thirtieth or thirty-first. We have to settle then. [unclear] withdrawal of our forces in two months.

NIXON: In two months after the cease-fire?

KISSINGER: Two months after the cease-fire.

NIXON: Right.

KISSINGER: And some provisions about military aid to South Vietnam. There's bound to be technical issues as far as whether we can continue military aid.

NIXON: Yeah.

KISSINGER: It says we cannot give military aid except for replacements of what is theirs.

• • •

KISSINGER: The peace we are getting out of this is with honor.

NIXON: Henry, let me tell you this: it has to be with honor. But also it has to be in terms of getting out. We cannot continue to have this cancer eating at us at home, eating at us abroad. Let me say, if these bastards turn on us, I am not beyond [unclear] them. I believe that's, that's what we're up against.

KISSINGER: They don't care if we —

NIXON: I am not going to allow the United States to be destroyed in this thing.

KISSINGER: Mr. President —

NIXON: These little assholes are not going to do it to us —

KISSINGER: Mr. President, if they — if we play this gun-shy — both Al — and Al, as you know, as I told you last week, was very leery about our approach, but —

NIXON: Is that what he told you?

HAIG: He told me, but he told you I'm going to get him [Thieu].

NIXON: Well, that's the only thing.

KISSINGER: I — I think everything I say to you, Al supports one hundred percent. I mean we are — we're getting out with honor, we are saving [unclear] —

NIXON: You use that term, [unclear] "with honor"?

KISSINGER: "With honor."

NIXON: Do you use it? Apprise me, Al. "Honor"?

HAIG: [unclear] exactly. Sure.

NIXON: It is "honor"?

HAIG: Thieu's got his rights to deal with the rest of them.

• • •

NIXON: What's that? He will accept the fact that we will continue to give military aid?

KISSINGER: Yeah. But that he's already accepted in principle, we just have to find the right words for him. Even though they replaced them with the present ones, that all can change.

NIXON: Hah! Don't worry. Don't worry —

KISSINGER: And what we can say is —

NIXON: Just do it.

KISSINGER: — we are permitted to make periodical replacements of armaments [unclear] form that appears equal in quality and quantity to those being replaced.

NIXON: Good. [unclear] That's right on. Right. Right —

• • •

KISSINGER: Then on the political side —

NIXON: Now — now, this is the critical thing [unclear] —

[unclear exchange]

KISSINGER: Mr. President, but with this, Thieu can stay. No side deals.

NIXON: Why can he? How? Under what conditions?

KISSINGER: There are no conditions. Thieu can stay. The only thing we agreed was that Thieu will talk to the other side —

NIXON: Mm-hmm.

KISSINGER: — about setting up something that will be called the National Council for National Reconciliation and Concord.

NIXON: Will talk to them or agree to it? Did we agree to it or did they agree to it?

HAIG: They agreed to it —

KISSINGER: "Immediately after the cease-fire, the two seated South Vietnamese partisans [parties] shall hold consultations in the spirit of national reconciliation and concord, mutual respect, and mutual nonelimination, to set up an administrative structure called the National Council for National Reconciliation and Concord. The two South Vietnamese parties shall do their utmost to accomplish this within three months after the cease-fire comes into effect —"

[unclear exchange]

NIXON: Say that thing again. Suppose — does the release of our prisoners depend upon their agreeing on that?

KISSINGER: This will be decided on after the prisoners are released.

NIXON: The prisoners will be released regardless of the success of that agreement?

HALDEMAN: It was from sixty days to past ninety.

KISSINGER: That's right. Secondly, the cease-fire is of unlimited duration, and I have a verbal assurance in the protocol that the cease-fire provisions are independent of all other points.

NIXON: Why have they gone this far?

KISSINGER: So, all he has to —

[unclear exchange]

KISSINGER: — agree is to negotiate a National Council for Reconstruction [Reconciliation]. But if you consider, Mr. President, there isn't one newsman in this city who believes that this will end with anything other — and the Thieu government, of course, not [unclear].

NIXON: Good.

KISSINGER: Then Thieu will take a beating —

NIXON: They're leaving Thieu in. They're in. And they're supposed to negotiate a national council? Thieu will never agree, they'll never agree, so they screw up, and we support Thieu, and the Communists support them, and they can continue fighting, which is fine. Right, Al? Do you see it that way, Al?

KISSINGER: They will not go this way —

NIXON: Huh?

HAIG: I would have said that in full.

• • •

NIXON: Now, what did you do with regard to reparations and the rest?

KISSINGER: I'll come to that in a —

NIXON: I'm very — you know, as you know, I'm not going to — I'd give them everything because I see those poor —

KISSINGER: [unclear] victor reparations.

NIXON: — North Vietnamese kids burning with napalm and it burns my heart.

KISSINGER: With reparations — with reparations we had to say it.

NIXON: I don't mind them.

KISSINGER: All right, I'll read you the clause we've — we couldn't get around it because that is also our — that is our best guarantee that they will observe the agreement. They are panting for economic aid.

NIXON: Are they?

KISSINGER: Oh.

NIXON: They want it? See, China doesn't want it, Al. China doesn't want economic aid —

[unclear exchange]

KISSINGER: The United States —

NIXON: Henry, you're overlooking the most important point of this offer. This is the first time the North Vietnamese have ever indicated any interest. Do you remember? I said it in the May 8 speech.

KISSINGER: That's right.

NIXON: I mean the May speech — May speech in 1969 [Nixon's May 14, 1969, speech in which he stated support for reconstruction aid for both South and North Vietnam]. They said, "Screw you." Economic aid to Communists is — compromises their morality. It compromises the Chinese morality.

KISSINGER: Well —

NIXON: And they're — they want it? This is great!

KISSINGER: They want a five-year program. What that means is —

NIXON: Good. Give it to them —

KISSINGER: If we give them a five-year program that's part of the agreement.

NIXON: Yep, that's right.

KISSINGER: But if there is a five-year program, this is the best guarantee that they aren't going to start up. If we can get them committed to rebuilding their country —

NIXON: Right.

KISSINGER: — for that period of time, and I'm going to —

NIXON: Concentrating on internal rather than external affairs.

KISSINGER: Exactly. We have more pages on the international control — all of which is bullshit to tell you the truth, but it will read good for the soft-hearts, for the soft-heads. We have four pages of joint commission, a four-party commission, if [unclear] agrees to it, a national commission. It is utter, downright crap because they'd never work, but it's in there. The thing that will — the thing that will work, though, is they're playing to us. Here is what it says about reparations: "The United States expects that this agreement will usher in —"

NIXON: Will usher in how?

KISSINGER: A year from now.

HAIG: That's right with Hanoi.

NIXON: Usher in what?

KISSINGER: "Usher in an era of reconciliation with the Democratic Republic of Vietnam and with all the peoples of Indochina. In pursuance of this traditional policy of the United States to contribute to healing the wounds of wars of both warring parties —"

NIXON: There's no question, no problem. Give 'em — give 'em ten billion, because I believe in this. I really do believe in it. The fact is if we did it with the Germans, we did it with the Japs, why not for these poor bastards? Don't you agree, Henry? Don't you agree, Henry? Goddamn it, I feel for these people. I mean they fought for the wrong reasons, but damn it to hell, I am not — I just feel for people that fight down, and bleed, and get killed.

• • •

NIXON: Let me come down to the nut-cutting, looking at Thieu. What Henry has read to me, Thieu cannot turn down. If he does, our problem will be that we have to flush him, and that will have flushed South Vietnam. Now, how the hell are we going to come up on that?

"But it's really turned out to be a damn good help to us because we can really bludgeon Hanoi for whatever additional nickels we need."

October 22, 1972, 12:22 a.m.

Richard Nixon and Alexander Haig

CAMP DAVID TELEPHONE

On October 21, the North Vietnamese broke a promise made to Kissinger that there would be no publicity about the accord until it was officially announced by all parties. The North Vietnamese premier, however, soon told a reporter from Newsweek *that an agreement would be announced within two days. At the time, Kissinger was in Saigon, where he was having a steep uphill battle convincing Thieu to agree to the basic terms settled in Paris. The news reports on the accord didn't help Kissinger, who stooped to lying in his efforts to persuade Thieu. In Washington, however, Nixon decided it was one leak he could use to his advantage, as he told Haig.*

• • •

HAIG: Hello?

NIXON: Hello.

HAIG: Mr. President?

NIXON: Yeah? I had one thought that in view of Hanoi as having, you know, totally broken their word with regard to publicity and so forth—

HAIG: Right, sir.

NIXON: —don't you think Henry ought to—I mean insist on [unclear] that said we—he'd meet them in Vientiane. You know that the Hanoi ploy I'd—I think they really [unclear] so much that—I know how passionately he wants to go there, but, you know, they've really handled this in a very shameful way.

HAIG: Well, let me tell you what I've done, sir. Dobrynin was in here this afternoon with a strong message from Brezhnev. He called me at about ten.

NIXON: Yeah?

HAIG: I just called him and laced it to him. I said, "You tell your goddamn people in Hanoi that they have broken our agreement, which we considered sacred, that if you want to be helpful in getting this thing settled, you insist to them that there'll be no more of this, and that we expect them to be flexible, or we cannot have a repeat of the '68 situation, and that we may have some additional requirements that they have to understand and meet because we have a very difficult problem."

NIXON: Mm-hmm.

HAIG: Now that they have breaked—broken—

NIXON: Because they—because they broke it? And did he—

HAIG: That's right.

NIXON: What'd he say?

HAIG: For the first time he was very much on the defensive. He was shocked. He said, "This is inexcusable." And I told him who did it—it was the prime minister—and who they gave the leak to, and it's all over the press. And I said, "It's given us an incredible problem, which could sink, delay this thing and require additional negotiating."

NIXON: Right. Good.

HAIG: I've done that to safe-side it.

NIXON: Yeah.

HAIG: And I think we ought to wait on—on the Hanoi—

NIXON: Yeah. Well—

HAIG: —thing, until we get Henry's—Bunker's assessment—

NIXON: Is he going to go from Phnom Penh to Hanoi?

HAIG: No, no. No, he'll come back to Saigon.

NIXON: Oh.

HAIG: And then we have, in effect—

NIXON: Mm-hmm.

HAIG: —all day tomorrow.

NIXON: Oh, good—

HAIG: He'll be in Saigon.

NIXON: Debating with Thieu some more?

HAIG: That's right.

NIXON: Oh, good.

HAIG: And then he would leave Monday our time.

NIXON: Well, when he says he thinks he has braked for them he's still got a day's work.

HAIG: I think so.

NIXON: Yeah. Yeah —

HAIG: And I wouldn't add this burden to him now, until he gets to —

NIXON: I get your point.

HAIG: [unclear]

NIXON: Yeah, yeah, yeah. Okay. That's good. Well, since you've taken that, but you see what our thinking is that —?

HAIG: Oh, absolutely.

NIXON: — that we can't get sucked into this now, Al, on any — and then have it broken off on something.

HAIG: No, if this is a locked agreement, with Thieu on board —

NIXON: Yeah?

HAIG: — I don't think the Hanoi thing's bad at all for us. I think it's damn —

NIXON: No.

HAIG: — good.

NIXON: No.

HAIG: It's positive.

NIXON: No.

HAIG: And end on a high, a very high note.

NIXON: I agree. I agree.

HAIG: Now, I've called Bill Rogers and told him that it looks much better.

NIXON: [chuckles]

HAIG: Just to keep him abreast of anything all day, too.

NIXON: But you told him for — did you tell him where we've laced Dobrynin? Or you didn't?

HAIG: No, I didn't —

NIXON: Well, you didn't need to. But you just told him it looks better and that's that, huh?

HAIG: That's right.

NIXON: But told him to keep shut? I mean —

HAIG: Absolutely. That's why I —

NIXON: Let's don't sound better because, Al, this thing may still blow. You know?

HAIG: Oh, it could still blow.

NIXON: Yeah.

HAIG: He — you see, we've had them working full bore on getting this equipment out there, getting aircraft back from the Koreans —

NIXON: Yeah?

HAIG: — in with the Thais —

NIXON: Right.

HAIG: — and then there's the ChiNats —

NIXON: Right.

HAIG: — and the Iranians. And they've been working like hell over there.

NIXON: At State? [Reference is to Operation Enhance Plus, in which military equipment intended for South Korea, Thailand, and Taiwan was diverted to South Vietnam.]

HAIG: Yes, sir.

NIXON: Well, they must be pleased. Oh, I know we had to tell them, but I just wanted the — I just want them, they ought to know that we don't want to —

HAIG: Well, he doesn't have any of the details.

NIXON: We don't want to leak anything to the — to *Time* or the — or the *Washington Post* or something. Then, well —

HAIG: Oh, no.

NIXON: You know the whole settlement thing is just — if they leak it, that's one thing, but when we do it, it's inexcusable.

HAIG: Well, we've held the line very strongly since this —

NIXON: You understand the reason that I don't want this leaked is not because of the goddamn enemy. The reason I don't want it leaked is because it might hurt us.

HAIG: Very much so. That's right.

NIXON: Mm-hmm.

HAIG: But there's going to be a lot of stories tomorrow on this Hanoi story.

NIXON: I understand —

HAIG: They all have it. They spread it all over town this afternoon.

NIXON: Sure. Sure.

HAIG: But it's really turned out to be a damn good help to us because we can really bludgeon Hanoi for whatever additional nickels we need.

NIXON: Yeah. But doesn't it say "coalition government"?

HAIG: Uh, not really. It says the —

NIXON: What is the story hit at? Yeah?

HAIG: It, essentially, it has the outlines of the political settlement. It's heavy on that Thieu will stay in power, there'll be two governments, and they'll negotiate what will ultimately be a coalition, which is true. We wouldn't put it that way ourselves.

NIXON: Yeah. But now Henry understands now, Al, that that word, as I said, cannot be used.

HAIG: Oh, no.

NIXON: In fact, or, you know —

HAIG: We'll never use it —

NIXON: — or appearance.

HAIG: — in our briefings or —
NIXON: Right.
HAIG: — or discussion of it.
NIXON: Right. Right. Okay.
HAIG: Fine, sir.

"We know that the enemy's hurting, or they wouldn't be talking."
October 22, 1972, 10:10 a.m.
Richard Nixon and Alexander Haig
CAMP DAVID TELEPHONE

As Kissinger continued to negotiate in Saigon, Nixon continued to receive regular updates from Haig.

• • •

NIXON: Have you done any further thinking on —?
HAIG: Yes. I figured —
NIXON: Have you talked to Dobrynin again or not? Or —
HAIG: I've got a call in to him. He went out for [unclear] —
NIXON: Now, the other thing, the only thing that I was thinking there, if you want to play it at a higher level, I almost think I might have to talk to him at this point, in other words, to keep this lid on.
HAIG: Yes.
NIXON: And I will do it. I mean I have a — what I have in mind is this: I think we just simply have to tell him, "Mr. Ambassador, we've — because of what happened in Hanoi, because of what — of your people blowing this, I mean," and then show him the papers — that this is — "Thieu has reacted as we would expect: negatively." We had it all set, because, that is, he was provided, you know, that so he could play a part in it. But they were going to have a victory celebration, they've played this, he put the whole thing out, and now he's thrown up his hands.

"Now, we do not think this is permanent. We think we can handle it, but the main thing is that — two things: one, we will settle on the basis that we have described; two, we have to have a time to settle and you must not push us; but that, but — and, three, you need not be concerned about the election deadline." Remember? Because he knows that —
HAIG: Mm-hmm.
NIXON: — and that's a total commitment that you can pass on.
HAIG: Well, I'm not sure I would —
NIXON: Go far?
HAIG: — make a commitment to go along the route outline, because he knows that without Thieu there is no commitment.
NIXON: Well — oh, I see your point —

HAIG: Well, I think that's the —

NIXON: I mean, that'd be dumping him. Yeah, yeah. Tell him we've got a — we will say that basically, on all the military sides and so forth and so on, that's a deal. And we're ready to —

HAIG: Right. So he's not worried we'll stay —

NIXON: Yeah. And we'll see — and we'll work with you to see what we can work out.

HAIG: Right. That's sensible —

NIXON: We have to — we may have to go our own. We understand that we'll have to go our own way, but we haven't given up on Thieu. We're still working on it.

HAIG: That's right. That's right.

NIXON: We're still working on it, but we've got to put the lid on this thing and hold it.

HAIG: That's right. And we need them to —

NIXON: And we need you — and just say our relations, the two great powers, must not be affected by the fact that these two pipsqueaks are acting the way that they are. And that, now, let's keep our heads. And you keep theirs down and we'll keep his down, but that's the responsibility. I really feel that I had — that if I told him that that could have quite an impact on him.

HAIG: Yes, sir. I do, too. I do, too.

NIXON: So, you think about it and I'll be there at twelve fifteen.

HAIG: Okay.

NIXON: And if we think well of it we'll call him in and just lay it out like that. But we'll talk it through first.

HAIG: All right, sir.

NIXON: Fine. Good. But you had no other thoughts since we've talked? The other thing is that I — I just had lunch with it, doing a little more thinking about one thing: I am just really adamant on Henry not going to Hanoi with this thing in mind because, basically, the way it will look is a complete surrender.

HAIG: Yep.

NIXON: You know what I mean? It'll be played that way. And also it'll look like Ramsey Clark, going to Hanoi, hat in hand, making their deal [reference to his visit in 1972 to Hanoi to protest American bombing]. Sure, we're going to get the prisoners back and sure, you know, but they'll say, "What the hell have we fought for? The prisoners?"

HAIG: I agree.

NIXON: You see the problem?

HAIG: Oh, absolutely. I do.

NIXON: His going to Hanoi can do it now. To do it, I think, another — however, a part of the game plan, he can make a commitment to go to Hanoi later.

HAIG: Later?

NIXON: Yeah. You know, say, "All right, let's meet in Paris." And then he'll come to Hanoi later.

HAIG: Exactly.

NIXON: And then we can. Then there's no problem, but it must not be before the election. It must not be. Third point is this: I strongly feel that if we could make the case that we really would prefer not to do this before the election, I mean not just politically, but not to do it because, basically, one hell of a lot of people in this country and, frankly, in Vietnam — the South, particularly — think that we are doing it, doing the wrong thing, because of the election.

HAIG: Exactly.

NIXON: And I think we just ought to say, you know, we — we're just not going to be able to do it, but I think that point has just got to be made, that this isn't the right time.

HAIG: That's right. No, this is right and in many respects this has pulled us back from what could have been a more troublesome [unclear] —

NIXON: Yeah. Yeah. Who knows? [chuckles]

HAIG: Right, sir.

NIXON: But we're going to work it out in the end. The main point is we've come a long way on these negotiations, as you well know. The war has got to be ended, Al, and we're now at the point where we've got a basis for ending it. We know that the enemy's hurting, or they wouldn't be talking. The Soviets —

HAIG: That's right.

NIXON: The Soviets [are] helping. In other words, they haven't got all the cards either. And we're still bombing. And that's the way it's going to be. And so, therefore, we'll end it. But, I think, the sad part of it is that I just don't know how South Vietnam — I don't see any leadership other than Thieu. I don't see any other horse, looking to the — do you look — do you see this Diem syndrome starting again? [South Vietnamese President Ngo Dinh Diem was assassinated in a military coup in 1963.]

HAIG: No. No, he's going to come out of this very, very strong.

NIXON: Thieu will?

HAIG: Oh, yeah.

NIXON: Yeah. I know. But then what happens? How can he be strong if we cut off assistance to him?

HAIG: Well, what we've got to do is work with the same parameters we've put on the military side and —

NIXON: Yeah.

HAIG: — and keep the economic in, and —

NIXON: Yeah.

HAIG: — and —

NIXON: In other words, keep —

HAIG: — maybe we can work another deal with Hanoi.

NIXON: With Hanoi, without the political?

HAIG: Without the political.

NIXON: Huh. That's true. Well —

HAIG: They're hurting so badly —

NIXON: That may be.

HAIG: — that they may pay the price.

NIXON: Right. Okay.

HAIG: Right, sir.

• • •

Afterword: When Kissinger failed to obtain Thieu's support for the agreement, Nixon reluctantly had to send word to the North Vietnamese that the negotiations would have to continue. At that, Hanoi regarded the entire episode as a political trick on the part of the Americans. Kissinger, with Nixon's support, managed to salvage the situation, and the peace talks began again following the election.

"If . . . the United States . . . were not able to deal with the entity of Vietnam . . . with whom can the United States ever deal successfully?"

October 24, 1972, 11:15 a.m.

Richard Nixon, Fritz G. A. Kraemer, and Henry Kissinger

OVAL OFFICE

Fritz G. A. Kraemer, an attorney and holder of two doctorates, was a Pentagon analyst who discovered young émigré infantryman Heinrich Kissinger during World War II. Kissinger owed his rise to the White House to Kraemer, who served as his longtime mentor. However, they broke off their relationship after this meeting due to differing views over Vietnam. Kraemer believed the United States was giving away too much in the negotiations to end the war in an election-year gambit, causing both American allies and foes to question whether the United States remained a responsible ally and world power. This later became known as the theory of "provocative weakness," a core tenet of neoconservatism.

• • •

KISSINGER: Our difficulty, Kraemer, has been not that we have made concessions before the election. Our difficulty has been to think up demands which could protract it beyond the election because every demand we make —

NIXON: They settle.

KISSINGER: — they meet within twenty-four hours. So we are literally running out of proposals we can make to them.

NIXON: Yeah.

KRAEMER: Make a proposal that they should withdraw from South Vietnam.

KISSINGER: We've made that now. We've made the proposal, for example, that their prisoners have to stay in South Vietnamese jails.

NIXON: Forty thousand.

KISSINGER: Forty thousand political prisoners would stay in South Vietnamese jails, which we thought was unacceptable.

KRAEMER: That's interesting.

KISSINGER: And they have now accepted that their cadres stay in South Vietnamese jails. Now, you know that this is not an easy thing for them to sign a document in which they release our prisoners, [they] have to release South Vietnamese military prisoners, but all [North Vietnamese] civilian prisoners stay in jail.

KRAEMER: Do you perhaps think, that the cease-fire is such an advantage to them for the psychological reason that they are more disciplined, more homogeneous?

NIXON: I think they are fairly confident, but I think there is the other factor, which I think we must have in mind. Remember, we never want to obviously underestimate — that they have taken a hell of a beating. I mean the bombing has hurt, the mining has hurt, the attrition that has occurred in South Vietnam. I mean, when you stop to think of, not just what we have done in the North, but the '52s, those six carriers we've had out there, and everything. We have clobbered the bejeezus out of them. I think, therefore, that they have reached a point, and it is only temporary, I agree, where in their thought there, they may have read Mao. You know, he was always willing to retreat.

KISSINGER: We may have been, in fact, too successful, because we told them, for example, that all communications will be cut off on November 7. Because the president would have to retreat to reorganize the government.

• • •

NIXON: We've fought a pretty good fight up to this point, and we're not caving. Because we see that it's a very difficult war. Success or failure now, not just for the moment — because anything will look good for two or three months — but something that has a chance to survive, shall we say, for two or three years. That is very much a condition that we cannot compromise on.

KRAEMER: May I formulate, say, one strategic sentence —

NIXON: Sure.

KRAEMER: — that maybe summarizes —

NIXON: Sure.

KRAEMER: If it should prove, within a number of fronts, that we, the United States, were not able to deal with the entity of Vietnam, thirty-one million inhabitants, that would be, apart from everything moral, the question will arise — among friend, foe, and entrants — with whom can the United States ever deal successfully? Because this entity of thirty-one million, supported by the Soviets, by China, but not by their manpower —

NIXON: Yeah.

KRAEMER: — is relatively so small that everybody from Rio de Janeiro to Copenhagen, and from Hanoi to Moscow, can draw the conclusion: obviously, the enormous

American power couldn't deal with this. Therefore, as a lawyer, I would say [unclear] since we cannot deal with Vietnam, with whom can we deal?

"I didn't want to let this night go by without calling."

November 8, 1972, 1:31 a.m.
Richard Nixon and Hubert Humphrey
WHITE HOUSE TELEPHONE

Four years after Senator Humphrey called former Vice President Nixon to concede the 1968 presidential election, they spoke again in the early-morning hours following the 1972 presidential election. Despite political differences, their friendship went back to the days when they served in the Senate together more than two decades earlier. Now that they were no longer direct rivals, Humphrey called to congratulate Nixon on his landslide victory over Senator George McGovern. Nixon hinted that he had a Vietnam agreement; at that point, Thieu had not yet scuttled it.

• • •

NIXON: Hubert, how are you?

HUMPHREY: Well, fine, and I wanted to call up just to congratulate you on this historic victory.

NIXON: Well, thank you very much.

HUMPHREY: You really racked 'em up.

NIXON: You've been a very statesmanlike man. As I always, just speaking as friends, people ask me very privately to compare this with '68, and I said, "Well, the difference is, that when Senator Humphrey and I were campaigning and we had this terrible issue of Vietnam, we both put the country first." And I said, "This time, we had a problem where one fellow said any goddamn thing that came in his head."

HUMPHREY: Yeah.

NIXON: For your private information, you should know that for three days, I had the whole thing in my pocket.

HUMPHREY: Yes.

NIXON: [laughs] As you probably guessed.

HUMPHREY: Yes. I had a talk with Henry a couple of days ago.

NIXON: Right.

HUMPHREY: They asked me whether or not we could have got a settlement like this in '69, and I said no.

NIXON: Well, you made a great statement. I asked Henry to call you. I think you should know that —

HUMPHREY: Thank you.

NIXON: — within ten days you will see, it's all fallen into place. And we knew it a week ago, but we couldn't say it. I mean —

HUMPHREY: Well, I understood that.

NIXON: But I felt you had to fight for your man, and I understood why, but I know that you didn't approve of some of the tactics.

HUMPHREY: Well, I'll have a talk with you sometime. I knew, you know, I did what I had to do.

NIXON: Of course you did.

HUMPHREY: If not, Mr. President, this whole defeat would have been blamed on me, and so —

NIXON: That's right. [laughs]

HUMPHREY: I know that.

NIXON: Well, we'll get together and we'll work for the good of the country. That's the important thing.

HUMPHREY: Surely will. And I didn't want to let this night go by without calling.

NIXON: It's so good of you to call.

"Get the very best agreement you can."
November 18, 1972, 12:02 p.m.
Richard Nixon and Henry Kissinger
WHITE HOUSE TELEPHONE

Just ten days after the election, the Vietnam peace agreement began to look shaky. This time, it was American ally South Vietnam that wavered. Kissinger informed President Nixon that he had received a phone call from U.S. Ambassador to South Vietnam Ellsworth Bunker. Bunker said the "news is not good." The South Vietnamese were trying to change the terms for a negotiation session scheduled in Paris.

• • •

KISSINGER: What I wanted to mention and check with you since we now — we had a phone call from Bunker. We haven't got the actual message yet saying that now, apparently the South Vietnamese are beginning to kick over the [traces] again.

NIXON: Oh, Christ.

KISSINGER: And I believe that we just have to continue now and get the best agreement we can —

NIXON: Yeah.

KISSINGER: — and then face them with it afterwards.

NIXON: How are they kicking it over?

KISSINGER: Well, they've apparently submitted a memorandum to him. He just said the news is not good. And their ambassador here has also raised some questions with Sullivan. It's their old pattern. What they always do is they first read what you give them then they raise a few technical objections and they just keep escalating it.

NIXON: Mm-hmm.

KISSINGER: But —

NIXON: Well, shall I send them another letter?

KISSINGER: No, I think we now have to wait, Mr. President, until we get a — until we see at least what's going to happen in Paris.

NIXON: Mm-hmm.

KISSINGER: And once we have the text of an agreement in Paris we'll have a new situation.

NIXON: So, Bunker says that they're kicking over the [traces] and just being unreasonable as hell. Is that it?

KISSINGER: That seems to be the case. But I don't — we can't delay the negotiations and we can't tell Hanoi that we're having trouble.

NIXON: No, sir.

KISSINGER: They're going to play it like an accordion.

NIXON: All right.

KISSINGER: The other —

NIXON: When you really come down to it, though, I just can't see how Thieu has got any other choice. Goddamn it, we've told him we're doing everything we can and that's going to be it —

KISSINGER: Well —

NIXON: — but on the other hand the idea of just making a bilateral thing, Henry, is —

KISSINGER: It's repugnant.

NIXON: It's repugnant because we lose everything we've done. You know what I mean? People said we could have done that years ago.

KISSINGER: Well, if we can get a cease-fire in Laos and Cambodia; and we can, of course, say we've put them in a position where they can defend themselves.

NIXON: Uh-huh.

KISSINGER: But it's going to be a miserable exercise.

NIXON: Well, it may not be. You just can't tell —

KISSINGER: If we do it bilaterally I mean —

NIXON: This is maybe —

KISSINGER: But I — I —

NIXON: This just may be bargaining on their part knowing, knowing that you're going to Paris.

KISSINGER: Basically, I really don't know where the hell they're going to go.

NIXON: Mm-hmm.

KISSINGER: And they're still making all the preparations as if there will be a cease-fire.

NIXON: Right. I noticed that.

KISSINGER: But I just wanted to check with you whether it is in accord with your views that we proceed negotiating. We can't wait any longer for coordinating.

NIXON: Hmm. Well, what would be the choice otherwise? This would mean you —

KISSINGER: Well, but we'd have to —

NIXON: — wouldn't go?

KISSINGER: That's right. And ask for another delay but I think that's almost impossible.

NIXON: Well, we couldn't do that.

KISSINGER: I mean not after—

NIXON: No—

KISSINGER: —we announced it.

NIXON: —but I would, uh—I'd simply go. You mean they—don't you really think they're trying to strengthen the bargaining position before you go to Paris? Isn't that—or—

KISSINGER: Oh, I think that's one possibility. That they're just, uh—

NIXON: Mm-hmm.

KISSINGER: —trying to prove that if they're going to cave they're going to do it afterwards, not before.

NIXON: Mm-hmm.

KISSINGER: And probably that they figure they'll get less than what they agreed to so they better ask for more.

NIXON: Mm-hmm. Mm-hmm. Well, I think you should tell Bunker to play it damn tough. He is, isn't he?

KISSINGER: Oh, yes.

• • •

KISSINGER: And what [exiled former Cambodian Prime Minister] Sihanouk says that, his interests were completely sold out by the North Vietnamese. He said this to the Algerian ambassador—

NIXON: Mm-hmm.

KISSINGER: —that it was one of the most shocking examples, and it's an example of U.S.-Soviet pressure and that it's the Soviets who pressed the North Vietnamese into yielding.

NIXON: Yeah. Yeah. Well, go right ahead on the same track. Do the very best that you can. Haig has no doubts about going ahead now, does he?

KISSINGER: Oh, no. No, no. He's completely with us.

NIXON: And he feels that we have to do it, and, uh—

KISSINGER: Haig is against an open break with them before the negotiation, as I am.

NIXON: Oh, absolutely. Yeah. No, no. Go negotiate now. But they can't go over the [traces]. They're—they're making public statements?

KISSINGER: No. No, no. This is a private communication.

NIXON: Yeah. Yeah. All right. Just go ahead. Do the best—the very best you can. Get the very best agreement you can.

KISSINGER: Right.

NIXON: That's all. Okay?

KISSINGER: Okay, Mr. President.

NIXON: Fine, Henry. Fine.

"'We'll make our own deal and you'll have to paddle your own canoe.'"
November 18, 1972, 12:32 p.m.
Richard Nixon and Bob Haldeman
WHITE HOUSE TELEPHONE

"Peace was at hand," and then it wasn't. As Thieu continued to buck the peace agreement to which he had originally agreed, Nixon gave more thought to making an agreement with North Vietnam only. He did not want to abandon an American ally, but securing the best exit terms for the United States was the primary objective.

• • •

NIXON: Well, Henry says he's having some more problems with Thieu. He's kicking up his heels —

HALDEMAN: Oh, really?

NIXON: — according to a line from Bunker and so forth. He wants to renegotiate this and that and more, a hell of a lot of other things. And I told Henry, "Well, just go right ahead to Paris," get the very best deal he could. And then we're just going to have to, in my opinion, then say to Thieu, "This is it. If you don't want to go, fine. Then we'll make our own deal and you'll have to paddle your own canoe." It's tough, but don't you think that's what we have to do?

HALDEMAN: I don't see what else you can do now.

NIXON: Right.

HALDEMAN: 'Cause, uh —

NIXON: Well, it's a good deal; that's the point. The only thing is that what — the big thing we have here is that if Thieu doesn't go, of course, it poisons the agreement to an extent and so forth and so on, but that, then we have completed Vietnamization, we have dealt with the others, we're getting out, and South Vietnam —

HALDEMAN: Turn it over to him.

NIXON: — is strong enough to defend itself and now it's up to South Vietnam.

HALDEMAN: If he collapses then there we are.

NIXON: I don't think he'll collapse.

HALDEMAN: He's going to ride that out anyway.

NIXON: Well, he will certainly collapse if he plays this dog-in-the-manger theme on that because the Congress is damn well not going to appropriate the money for him.

HALDEMAN: Yep, because we told him that.

NIXON: Yeah, well, we're going to tell him that again.

"They're tough on the points that are almost insoluble."
November 29, 1972, 7:35 p.m.
Richard Nixon and Alexander Haig
WHITE HOUSE TELEPHONE

The problem with the secret talks in Paris was that they did not include all four parties, as did the official talks. While the North Vietnamese were able to speak for the Viet Cong, the absence of the South Vietnamese at the table was a liability. They were told the fate of their country on an as-needed basis, an arrangement that helped lead to the falling-out between Kissinger and Thieu in late October. The South Vietnamese were aware that the first round of secret peace talks after the U.S. presidential election began in Paris on November 20. Further talks were scheduled for December 8. In the interim, the South Vietnamese government sent a special envoy, Nguyen Phu Duc, to Washington. He and the ambassador, Tran Kim Phuong, tried to open what amounted to separate negotiations with Nixon, but he would have none of it.

• • •

NIXON: Now, on the matter today, we've got what I think is — I don't know what more we can do with these clowns but we'll —

HAIG: Yeah, I think we've got a couple of tough nuts to get over here between now and the time they leave. They're still pretty strong on a couple of points and that's what we're working on.

NIXON: Well, they're [chuckles] — they're tough on the points that are almost insoluble. That —

HAIG: That's right. That's right.

NIXON: But we've got to stand firm, you see? We — I mean, they just got to realize it, and it's really true that January 3 is too late. [The U.S. Constitution requires Congress to convene on January 3, unless they have stated plans to do otherwise. Congress did not convene until January 18.]

HAIG: That's right. Well, I think they —

NIXON: Don't you agree?

HAIG: — got that message — yes, sir, and I think they're just hoping beyond hope that they can get some changes, some of which are impossible to get.

NIXON: But don't you think we should stand firm?

HAIG: We have to.

NIXON: Yeah. All right. That's what we'll do then.

HAIG: Right, sir. Well then —

NIXON: And, uh —

HAIG: — it's going to take some work.

NIXON: Are you going to be with Henry in —?

HAIG: In Paris. Yes, sir.

NIXON: Good. Well, you just have to see that he stays right on track, and —

HAIG: Oh, he will. Uh-huh. I'm not worried about —

NIXON: No, he'll do everything he can.

HAIG: Yes, sir.

NIXON: But, in the meantime, what these people — there's really nothing more we can do, you know? Those — they've just got to realize that all this —

HAIG: Exactly, exactly.

NIXON: You know, that —

HAIG: So, they're [unclear] — it's coming through. It's just a traumatic thing for them.

NIXON: I know.

HAIG: They just [unclear].

NIXON: Well, I couldn't have given the message to them stronger today than I did, you know, I think.

HAIG: Oh, no. God. There wasn't any doubt about it. They — they know.

NIXON: Mm-hmm.

HAIG: They know, and I think tomorrow we'll have it sorted down to the manageable two or three pieces.

NIXON: Right.

HAIG: And we'll just put the frosting on the cake.

NIXON: Right. Okay, Al. Fine.

HAIG: Good, sir.

"We've been playing with fire."

November 30, 1972, 12:17 p.m.
Richard Nixon, Bob Haldeman, Henry Kissinger, and Alexander Haig
OVAL OFFICE

The two South Vietnamese diplomats remained in Washington, seeking to insert their nation into the peace talks somehow. Nixon tried to figure out what to do with them — and more important, what to do with the nation they represented.

• • •

KISSINGER: What the little bastard [Nguyen Phu Duc] has now said is that we should go on alone. Just our prisoners for withdrawal and let them continue fighting. I think they have to get it into their heads that, in that case, the Congress, no matter what you intend to do — the North Vietnamese will demand cutting off military and economic aid as a price for that —

NIXON: Why in the hell would they?

HALDEMAN: What the hell are they going to shoot? They won't have any bullets.

KISSINGER: Well, their idea is we continue to give aid, and they'll fight alone.

NIXON: I'm thinking of going that route.

KISSINGER: But tell them that the Congress won't —

• • •

NIXON: No, I'm sorry, but fine, but I have issued — directed that Congress cut off all military and economic aid. And that's it. [unclear]

KISSINGER: But I would just say that the Congress will under no circumstances agree to that.

NIXON: Yeah. I'm not going to worry —

KISSINGER: So then you're not the villain.

NIXON: I'm going to be a villain myself, too.

KISSINGER: Did you get to the Vietnamese?

NIXON: Henry, you must say that you reported to me. I'm not going to listen to it from him.

KISSINGER: No, no.

NIXON: We're going to have it straight out and get it done [unclear]. Well, the hopes that they would start to be reasonable proved to be wrong.

KISSINGER: [unclear] after the agreement is made. They won't be able to say they [unclear] —

NIXON: Yeah.

KISSINGER: [unclear]

NIXON: Well, are you going to then put the thing to him about my meeting at Midway or I'm going to tell him that?

KISSINGER: Well, these guys — the major trouble is, they have this punk kid in the palace, this thirty-year-old suitor [Hoang Duc Nha], who is —

NIXON: Mm-hmm.

KISSINGER: — acting out a Wagnerian drama. I mean, I must say when I went through the agreement this morning, I told Haig afterwards, when you listen to these guys you begin to doubt your sanity.

NIXON: No, it's a good reason.

KISSINGER: [unclear] but it's —

NIXON: [unclear] we'll just go ahead. And, frankly, you go ahead with the North Vietnamese and we will cut off economic aid, but, of course, it means that everything we fought for is lost.

KISSINGER: Well, we can just let Congress do it.

NIXON: Yeah. I think Duc understands it.

KISSINGER: Duc understands it, and the ambassador [Tran Kim Phuong].

NIXON: It's after what I put him through. Christ, he's [unclear] —

KISSINGER: Mr. President, you gave an absolutely magnificent presentation.

NIXON: Did it do any good?

KISSINGER: You could not have —

NIXON: It didn't do any good? That's —

KISSINGER: Oh, no. No, no, no. I — I've dealt with these guys. They — they're going to wait till a minute before midnight.

NIXON: Well what's —

KISSINGER: I mean, this is a lot better than the —

NIXON: Then you'll make the deal on Saturday?

KISSINGER: Right.

NIXON: Then sign, and then what happens? You come back here again, do what?

KISSINGER: And then we'll have to put it to them and say this is it —

NIXON: We'll have him come back here and put it to — to them and say, "Do you want to meet with the president, or not?"

KISSINGER: That's right. That's right.

NIXON: Is that what you say? For the purpose of the agreement, that we're going ahead on this without economic assistance? Fine.

KISSINGER: Well, I'm seeing the North Vietnamese Monday. They are having a message for us now, too. Maybe they are going crazy. They're both nuts. I mean, that's the trouble with these Vietnamese, they're —

NIXON: That's right. Don't worry. Sit down. They'll be here. They'll be here.

KISSINGER: And they're fighting it out —

NIXON: You think — do you think the North — huh, I guess the North Vietnamese can just break off negotiations now, too. No they can't —

KISSINGER: We've — why would — they can, but we've been playing with fire ever since we had this goddamn agreement with these two maniacal parties.

. . .

NIXON: We have no choice with these people now.

HAIG: No, no. We —

NIXON: Goddamn, I know this little guy [Nguyen Phu Duc] understands it and so forth, but if they want to commit suicide that's all there is to it. Are they going to?

HAIG: No. I don't think so. It would be inconceivable. This man isn't suicidal.

NIXON: You don't think so?

HAIG: No.

NIXON: Why did he send that message this morning? Henry came in here [unclear] to the effect that Thieu had laid out, and all it meant for us to go at it alone, and he'd go it alone. Did he really?

HAIG: Not really that way. Well — and that's what he tried to pull away from. What he was saying is, "For God's sake, if I can't get these three principles — "

NIXON: Yeah?

HAIG: "— then try to work out the May 8 proposition, in which we cut the mining and the bombing in return for your prisoners and a cease-fire, and then we'll continue to try to police the cease-fire with your help. And if they break it, then we would hope you could intervene."

NIXON: When it's all done, we can't intervene —

HAIG: It's got to be done. Well, I told him that it would kill us with the Soviets —

NIXON: [unclear] We've got to go ahead. He says he's got a message coming in from the North Vietnamese. Maybe they're going to break off negotiations, Al, do you think they are?

HAIG: No. I don't think so.

NIXON: Why not?

HAIG: They want to settle. That I'm convinced of. But they have [unclear] —

NIXON: What I said to him about the congressional thing is totally true. [unclear] aid for them.

HAIG: Of, course it's true.

NIXON: I got it from, also, Goldwater. Goldwater, Jesus Christ. [unclear] He says, "If this ever becomes public and you don't accept it, you're down the tubes."

HAIG: That's right.

NIXON: And they've got to understand that. I mean, that aid will be cut off like that. [taps table] Like that. [taps table] And they can't do that. I think the meeting at Midway is an excellent idea if he'll do it. If. But understand, a meeting for the purpose only of my — of our agreeing [unclear] is it. I will not go there to talk about the agreement.

HAIG: That's impossible.

NIXON: He'll just [unclear] —

HAIG: They're going to fight and negotiate —

NIXON: Huh?

HAIG: — right to the wire.

NIXON: What's that?

HAIG: They're going to fight right up to the wire. Now, you pulled the wire tight today and that's the end of it. And they now know that.

NIXON: When do you leave?

HAIG: I plan on the fifteenth, sir [Haig intended to leave for Saigon on December 15 to meet with Thieu].

NIXON: Well, you deserve a little rest.

HAIG: [unclear]

NIXON: Henry cannot take the — this heat much longer. You know what I mean? He's — you know what I mean? It's — it's been hard for him. But — an emotional pattern here is —

HAIG: It's worse. Well, I, this past — well, he had three weeks where I thought he lost touch with reality. It started out in Paris, the first round in October. He drove that thing despite all the counsel, all I could give him —

NIXON: Well, and I was trying telling him that, you know, I didn't want the goddamn thing. But you know why he did that? He wanted to make peace before the damn election. There isn't anybody to do it after the election.

HAIG: That's right.

NIXON: For Christ's sakes don't do that. Then what happened?

HAIG: Then in Saigon he really lost touch because here he was sending two messages to the North Vietnamese, agreeing to the [unclear], knowing that Thieu was not on board, and it was going to take some careful working. That's what caused our problem. Now, this week he started to regain himself. And I think he did a very fine job last week.

NIXON: Are you going with him?

HAIG: Yes, sir.

NIXON: Does he have you in on the meetings?

HAIG: Yes, sir. In fact, at the two private meetings I sat there. [Haig was referring to the two private meetings with Le Duc Tho and Xuan Thuy on November 24 and 25.] And we did the right thing. We had to delay. Well, we could never have done this with Thieu around.

NIXON: This has got to give Thieu something. And that meeting with the Joint Chiefs will.

HAIG: That helps. That's right. And, you know, it's conceivable. I just don't think he'll do that. I think he's going to come around. I think he'll come around, and we've got to have that communication completed in the next twenty-four hours.

NIXON: Hmm. In the next twenty-four hours he'll come around and meet with us?

HAIG: We'll just have to drive it to that.

NIXON: I think he's going to wait. Wouldn't you think he'd just wait?

HAIG: See what we get? Well, he'll caveat it in a certain way. But he's got to know —

NIXON: The point is — the point is it's done. I told him now Henry's gone over, he's going to settle the goddamn thing. At the end of the week, they can either come or go. That's my view as to what he'll say. If he says go at it alone, that puts us in a position. What — what kind of a deal could we make with the North Vietnamese? Just prisoners for withdrawal, right?

HAIG: And the end of —

NIXON: You can't reason with them —

HAIG: — the mining and the bombing —

NIXON: Huh?

HAIG: And the end of the mining and the bombing.

NIXON: Why don't we give up the mining, the bombing, for prisoners? [unclear] It's just a hell of a way to end the goddamn war.

"He must play the hard line with them, and, if necessary, . . . we'll have to break off."
December 4, 1972, 7:51 p.m.
Richard Nixon and Richard Kennedy
WHITE HOUSE TELEPHONE

On December 4, Kissinger and Haig flew to Paris for a meeting with Tho. They were warily hopeful that the Vietnam peace talks could be righted, after the fallout of late October. What they found was that Tho was no longer in any hurry, the U.S. presidential election having formerly been a kind of deadline for him. Instead, he was stalling with all of his former recalcitrance. Colonel Kennedy, a staff member at the NSC, relayed the disappointing situation to Nixon. The question of how to shake the North Vietnamese back into productive negotiations wasn't easy, especially in view of the fact that the United

States was then arming the South Vietnamese heavily and quickly, in anticipation of an imminent cease-fire. As Nixon heard Kennedy's report, his mind was on the American people. He felt he couldn't give them any more words on the peace process; it had to be action and results.

· · ·

NIXON: Hello?

KENNEDY: Mr. President?

NIXON: Yes.

KENNEDY: This is Colonel Kennedy, sir.

NIXON: Yes. What is the report from Paris you have?

KENNEDY: Oh, we have — it's a very long one, sir.

NIXON: Yeah.

KENNEDY: And I was going to bring it over to you, or have it brought over to you right away. We're just having it retyped so you could read it easily.

NIXON: Oh, I see. Fine.

KENNEDY: He — they were pretty tough.

NIXON: Well, I expected that.

KENNEDY: And he feels that it just might be that we're going to have to break off negotiations.

NIXON: Mm-hmm.

KENNEDY: That they're just not going to move.

NIXON: Mm-hmm.

KENNEDY: Now he just doesn't [unclear] — it's possible that, in fact, that they're playing a little chicken.

NIXON: Mm-hmm.

KENNEDY: Using us on the assumption that we have a problem here, vis-à-vis Saigon on the one hand, and domestically on the other —

NIXON: Mm-hmm.

KENNEDY: — that they can use to go back, really, beyond the understandings that we'd [unclear] —

NIXON: September [October] 8. Right.

KENNEDY: So, Henry believes that we ought to just go in and be tough and indicate that we're — we want to insist on the changes of last week and boil the remaining two issues down to the correct Vietnamese translation on the administrative structure —

NIXON: Mm-hmm.

KENNEDY: — and one of our formulations — that we had three of them, on the — establishing the principle that the North Vietnamese do not have any legal right to intervene indefinitely in South Vietnam.

NIXON: Mm-hmm.

KENNEDY: Then, we can drop all our other requests in exchange for their dropping their changes on civilian prisoners and U.S. civilian personnel.

NIXON: Mm-hmm. Mm-hmm.

KENNEDY: Now, if they were to buy that, of course, then we would have had some significant gains —

NIXON: Mm-hmm.

KENNEDY: — which would still leave us with some problem with Saigon, but, at least, a wholly defensible position in respect to them.

NIXON: Mm-hmm.

KENNEDY: On the other hand, if they don't, this, he believes, would give us a tenable position domestically. However difficult it will be, nonetheless, we could rightly say that we were tricked in the translation, and we'd always reserved on it, as we said at the beginning —

NIXON: Mm-hmm.

KENNEDY: — and that they're trying to distort the phrase by describing it as a gover — the council as a governmental institution.

NIXON: Mm-hmm.

KENNEDY: And, on the military side, they were in effect trying to produce an agreement, which ratified their continued presence — the presence of their forces in South Vietnam.

NIXON: Mm-hmm. Mm-hmm.

KENNEDY: So, as I say he's [unclear] —

NIXON: Well, I think what we'd better do is to — I really think I can sense from — without having to read the whole message — I mean, going into the details of it — that you'd better message him to the effect that we should stick firmly to our positions. What I — I mean, what you have described —

KENNEDY: Right.

NIXON: — of course, is what we had agreed in advance —

KENNEDY: Right.

NIXON: — that we cannot give — we cannot go back beyond what they've agreed to before. Is that — first.

KENNEDY: Yes.

NIXON: And, second, that he must play the hard line with them, and, if necessary, we — we'll have to break off.

KENNEDY: Right.

NIXON: There's really no other choice, because, basically, we can't just go to Saigon with nothing.

KENNEDY: Well, I think that's exactly his point. If we go the other way, we'd wind up in a situation in which we'd be going back to Saigon, indeed, with having accomplished nothing of what they had been working with us now for the past several weeks.

NIXON: Right.

KENNEDY: And this would — and this would cause, perhaps, some domestic problems, too, because people would see that nothing had been accomplished.

NIXON: Mm-hmm.

KENNEDY: And Thieu, probably — in his view — if we were to do this and cave on it, Thieu would probably simply go down.

NIXON: Yes.

KENNEDY: He couldn't survive —

NIXON: Yeah.

KENNEDY: — such a thing.

NIXON: Well, that's really Henry's point, isn't it? That he — that his point being that we've got to have as a minimum what we've agreed to up to this point. And, uh —

KENNEDY: Yes, sir. That's right —

NIXON: Mm-hmm. Well, you just send him a message that we must stick to the positions that we have previously insisted upon, and that they either have to take it or leave it.

KENNEDY: Right.

NIXON: The choice is theirs, and that we have other choices that we can make, too.

KENNEDY: Now on that — in that, Henry notes that he instructed me earlier today to call Dobrynin and —

NIXON: Right.

KENNEDY: — just lay it out to him in the most categorical terms. That —

NIXON: Right.

KENNEDY: — it's the other side's intransigence which is causing this problem and if —

NIXON: Right.

KENNEDY: — they have any influence, they'd better bring [it] to bear.

NIXON: That's correct.

KENNEDY: I did so.

NIXON: Right.

KENNEDY: He also saw the Chinese ambassador tonight —

NIXON: Yeah.

KENNEDY: — and did the same —

NIXON: Right.

KENNEDY: — in Paris.

NIXON: Right. Okay, well, I think the main thing is that before he meets in the morning, it's now midnight there —

KENNEDY: Yes, sir.

NIXON: — that you just send a message that he's on the right course, to stick to it.

KENNEDY: All right, sir.

NIXON: And that we — we'll have to — but to make the record so that it's their intransigence that breaks it off rather than —

KENNEDY: Yes, sir.

NIXON: — our insistence on changes.

KENNEDY: This is precisely the thrust —

NIXON: And that's —

KENNEDY: — of his approach.

NIXON: And that's really what it is, too —

KENNEDY: Right.

NIXON: — because —

KENNEDY: He feels that if it, in fact, has to be broken off, that, in all probability, that it would — you would have to step out and make a case to the people, again, rallying them again as you've done in the past, with your — with firm and clear, direct appeals. And he outlined some of the points that would be made, precisely along the lines that you've suggested. Making the point that it is their intransigence, and their clear trickery, that's caused this breakdown.

NIXON: Mm-hmm. Well, that's a — somewhat of a weak reed at this point. I mean, I realize that Henry's thinking of past circumstances, of course, where we were able to do so. The difficulty is that we're — well, we may have to do that. That we have to realize that we, ourselves, are boxed somewhat into a corner, here, by reason of the, you know, the hopes that have been raised.

KENNEDY: Oh, yes, sir.

NIXON: You see?

KENNEDY: Yes, sir.

NIXON: So, I think you should indicate that — in the message — that the idea of going to the people is a very — it's a tenuous situation, I would say. I mean, it's a — I don't consider that as being a — as a very viable option. I think that we, probably, are better off to break it off and then just do what we have to do for a while.

KENNEDY: Right. Yes, sir.

NIXON: I mean a — I think Henry must not rely on the fact that he thinks, "Well, we can just go to the people as we did on November 3, in Cambodia, and May 8, and so forth, and it will all come around again," but the situation has changed quite drastically since then, you see, as a result —

KENNEDY: Yes.

NIXON: — of what has happened. And so — but the main point is he has got to stay hard on the course, but don't assume that we can go to the option of my, you know, making a big television speech calling for the bombing —

KENNEDY: Oh, he feels that we'd have to — we'd have to step up the bombing, again as a [unclear] —

NIXON: Oh, I understand that.

KENNEDY: Right.

NIXON: I understand that.

KENNEDY: Sure.

NIXON: We may do that.

KENNEDY: Yes.

NIXON: But I don't think that —

KENNEDY: But without going back —

NIXON: But going on television for the purpose of doing it, and so forth —

KENNEDY: Right.

NIXON: — is not something that I think is too via — is really a viable option. I think we have to do it, and I think he has just got to indicate that, and then the other — the only other course, of course, is to keep the negotiations open any longer, and I guess he can't do that either, can he?

KENNEDY: Well of course, that's what he'd be trying to do with this, with this option.

NIXON: Mm-hmm.

KENNEDY: Going back, again. Cutting down our proposals to those two —

NIXON: Mm-hmm.

KENNEDY: — and insisting that both sides stick with those things that had been agreed last week.

NIXON: That's right. Well that's the thing to say: we will agree — we will stick to those things we've agreed to last week, or else we have no choice but to break off the negotiations. But, be sure to put the message to Henry the fact that he must not assume that we should go on national television for the purpose of doing it. I think we're just going to have to just — just do it this time.

KENNEDY: Right.

NIXON: Because the going on television isn't quite — probably too viable an option. When do they meet again?

KENNEDY: Tomorrow afternoon, Paris time fifteen hundred. That's nine o'clock. No. Yes, nine o'clock, our time.

NIXON: Nine o'clock our time.

KENNEDY: Yes, sir.

NIXON: Mm-hmm. Mm-hmm. Now — well, I really think that that's really all we have to pass on to him tonight, then.

KENNEDY: All right, sir. I'll get it off right away.

NIXON: I mean to — we've got to stick the course, we've got to insist on, as a minimum, the — what we have already agreed to, and if they are not going to go with that, then we will have to assume that they've engaged in deceit and trickery, and we will have to look to our other options, which we are really going to do. But, I don't want him to be under any illusions to the effect — on the point that we'll then go make a big speech, here, in this country. I mean, the domestic situation is one that will not really carry that at this point —

KENNEDY: Yes, sir.

NIXON: — much as we would like to. It just isn't there right now.

KENNEDY: Well it's — it — because of the tremendous pressure the press has put on all this —

NIXON: That's right.

KENNEDY: — it's built up to a crescendo, and —

NIXON: That's right.

KENNEDY: — and the disappointment is going to be there, but —

NIXON: That's correct.

KENNEDY: — on the other hand, I think that —

NIXON: On the other hand — we — understand, I have no question about doing it.

KENNEDY: Right.

NIXON: I'm just questioning the idea of escalating it even further by — in terms of saying, "Well, the negotiations have broken down," announcing it all, "and now we're going back to unlimited bombing," and all that sort of thing.

KENNEDY: Yes, sir.

NIXON: I think the thing to do is just to go back to the bombing, and so forth. That is something that we — we'll go back to what we do, but not — I don't think we can assume that we can go back to simply making a big speech about it.

KENNEDY: Yes, sir.

NIXON: And that he should think about that as he develops it. Okay?

KENNEDY: All right, sir.

NIXON: All right, fine.

KENNEDY: And I'll get this [unclear] right away —

NIXON: Get something along —

KENNEDY: — and the other is just now finished, and I'll have it brought over.

[unclear exchange]

KENNEDY: His message.

NIXON: You can send it over. I don't think it's going to change much. It's just really a [chuckles] blow-by-blow, right?

KENNEDY: Yes, sir. That's right. But, it goes on and elaborates on what we've spoken about.

NIXON: Right, okay.

KENNEDY: All right, sir.

"They're all saying that we're close to a settlement."

December 12, 1972, 5:50 p.m.
Richard Nixon and Alexander Haig
OVAL OFFICE

First, the challenge was to get South Vietnam back on board with the peace agreement. Now, North Vietnam also wavered. With the American election over, the pressure to agree was off for all parties except one: Richard Nixon.

• • •

NIXON: Well, the [unclear] earlier. Have you got Henry's message?

HAIG: No, his message hasn't come in. I called about it. It's very long, very long. He's laid out all kinds of things that we should be doing, and how we should proceed from here; Henry's thoughts on Thieu; Henry's thoughts on the military action; Henry's thoughts on how [it] should be handled publicly, and what we'll have to cope with; how to keep the dialogue going with them to keep from breaking. You know, a lot of the press reporting is — it's encouraging in a way because obviously nobody's telling anybody anything, and these guys are wrong as hell. They're —

NIXON: They're all saying that we're close to a settlement.

HAIG: [chuckles] Yeah.

NIXON: They're all wrong.

HAIG: They're all wrong.

NIXON: But they may be right.

HAIG: They may be right.

NIXON: You know what I mean? They may be right in the broad sense, in the sense that a settlement is inevitable. They are wrong in the timing; a settlement is not inevitable right at this time. That's kind of my feeling about it. What do you think?

HAIG: I think that, sir. I've been through all the intelligence that we've had since the sixth of October, the raw reports. It's just inconceivable to me that Hanoi's going to be able to pick up and go on the way they're going and that they do want this because they've instructed all their cadres, they've reorganized their forces in the South, broken down into small units, everyone's been briefed and oriented.

NIXON: Yeah. So, what does that mean?

HAIG: Well, I think they're going — they're going to play on what they anticipate to be pre-Christmas anxiety on our part, and, we [unclear] —

NIXON: What I mean is this: let me say that I'm talking about Henry's long message and so forth, Al. There is nothing to be gained by going through a tortured examination of what went wrong and this and that and the other thing. You know what I mean is that —

HAIG: Yeah.

NIXON: — just forget that. I am not interested in all that.

HAIG: No, sir.

NIXON: There's nothing to be gained of going over: well, they gave on this, and we gave on that, and they're sons of bitches, and so forth. Just forget all that. All that — all we have to be concerned about now is where to go from here? And the point is that — I told you when I went through this — he's got to go to the meeting tomorrow. You sort of got off — got off to him my thoughts, did you?

HAIG: Yes, sir. I sent that message to him and told him to use it as he sees fit, sees fit —

NIXON: Yes, if he thinks it wise, of course. You can't tell if it's wise unless you're really there, of course.

HAIG: No, that's right.

NIXON: He's got the sense of it. He'll know.

HAIG: He did. He was quite explicit in saying that the thing would be done amicably —

NIXON: Yeah.

HAIG: — which lessens the chance that they'll go public with an attack. Although they've reacted quite sharply with Thieu today. [Haig was referring to the North Vietnamese reaction to Thieu's December 12 speech.]

NIXON: What are they saying?

HAIG: Well, they said this was an unreasonable demand, the United States was responsible for it. Then, Madame Binh did the same thing, except she said that she, that — she sort of implied that we shouldn't allow him to do this, trying to keep his foot between us.

NIXON: Mm-hmm.

HAIG: But Hanoi was a little more —

NIXON: Mm-hmm?

HAIG: — more direct in its attack on both Thieu and ourselves, as they mean being a puppet of ours, and an extension of our view, claiming that we really didn't want to settle, and that we're building up with military supplies, and civilians acting as military — tens of thousands, they say — and that we don't really want peace and that we just want to continue to Vietnamize.

NIXON: Mm-hmm.

HAIG: Which is fairly consistent with their approach to the table.

NIXON: Mm-hmm —

HAIG: They're making these same kinds of —

NIXON: Al, what's your — when you really come down to the fundamental thing, first of all, Henry has got to get the talks moving on tomorrow and then out of the way if possible.

HAIG: That's right.

NIXON: Then he will come back. After he comes back then presumably he will be — there'll be — there will be a letdown here. Everybody will think it was going to go, but that doesn't worry me. I mean, we can take a letdown.

HAIG: Hmm.

NIXON: And so on. And with — do you see, he mustn't think it's the end of the world because the talks don't succeed —

HAIG: No, no.

NIXON: — right now? I mean, I don't think — you left Henry in that frame of mind when he left, or is he —? His hopes were pretty high on Saturday when he left, or even after he got back?

HAIG: They were — they were high Saturday.

NIXON: Because when you came back you obviously were [unclear] —

HAIG: And I must say, based on the session Saturday, it was just a question of whether we bought a compromise, or folded, or —

NIXON: That's right.

HAIG: — they did, but that was it.

NIXON: And then nothing happened.

HAIG: Then nothing happened. They reopened the same issues we had hammered out Friday and Saturday so laboriously.

NIXON: What in the hell do you think happened? I guess nothing in between. I don't know.

HAIG: Well, I—you know, we've done a hell of a lot of things that must be driving them up the wall in an objective sense. I mean, Christ, we have put in a billion dollars' worth of equipment. We had to—

NIXON: [unclear] Come on—now then, though then—so we were disappointed Saturday. Henry obviously got a hell of a letdown on Monday. See, I can tell more by his reactions from this than by reading thirty or forty pages of—

HAIG: Of course.

NIXON: —why—you know what I mean. You can, too. We all know what it is. Now, the reason he's down and discouraged is he raised his hopes high. Now his hopes are dead. Now they're dashed. Well, they should have never been high and they never should have been dashed in my opinion. I think it's always about where it was. Am I wrong or not? If I am, well, then I'll start reading all this stuff.

HAIG: No, I think—

NIXON: [unclear]

HAIG: No, I think you're exactly right, sir. I think this thing, we just got to—all the indications are that they want to settle and I think they will settle. But they're Communists, and every goddamn nickel they can make from us, they're going to try to get. And they don't mind if it takes two months, a month, a week. They're going to get the best deal they can get.

NIXON: So how are we going to position Ziegler tomorrow [unclear]? Did Henry give any guidance on that?

HAIG: Well, he claims that he has guidance in here. I think we should merely say—and I'm sure his guidance will say this—that he's returned for consultations.

NIXON: Well, I'll be in in the morning early enough. As soon as I get in, I'll call you, you come in, we'll have a good talk about it.

HAIG: Yes, sir.

NIXON: You and I will get Ziegler positioned.

HAIG: Right—

NIXON: "He's home for consultation, but there's still some knotty issues remaining." I think, frankly, we ought to say we—no, no, we can't say we've made progress, if they're going to deny it. No, I mean, I don't know. It is true that there has been progress—

HAIG: There has been progress, and I could—I think we could say that—

NIXON: "We have made some progress but there are still some knotty issues to be resolved and we're trying to resolve them."

HAIG: That's right.

NIXON: "He's come home for consultation." "When will they be resumed?" "Just as soon as we — when both sides agree they would serve a useful purpose." That's what I'd say, just like that and get out of the room.

HAIG: Exactly. And then when there's just [unclear] —

NIXON: Now, let me come to the key point: you really don't feel we should bomb again? Don't you? You see the real problem you got there is that if we do, the bastards could use that as an excuse for not talking. And, yes, they might [unclear]. I don't know.

HAIG: No, sir. I'm afraid, depending on what is really the cause of the hang-up, if it's this whole array of things, I think we should start racking 'em. And recognizing it's going to be tough. But, hell, we've taken a lot tougher than this.

NIXON: [unclear]

HAIG: It's not going to be — it's not going to be that tough.

NIXON: N-n-n-no, no. Well, the election is over. Forgetting the election and that sort of thing, sure it's the Christmas season. [unclear] but we'll just say we're doing this because they — we want, we want to get these negotiations going. Look, I don't know. What do we say? Why do we say we're bombing more? What — what's our —?

HAIG: Well, I think we have to —

NIXON: We're not going to say a damn thing; we're just going to start doing it. And they'll say, "Le Duc Tho was over there," and we'll say, "Well, there was a buildup, an enemy buildup."

HAIG: There was a buildup —

NIXON: That's what I'd say.

HAIG: There was a buildup. The talks had gone on for an extended period, beyond what we thought would be necessary. We can't risk dawdling tactics. We're prepared to stop it just as soon as we get a settlement. Of course, it's going to stop.

NIXON: But then we must not stop bombing the North until we get a settlement.

HAIG: Until we have it on the line —

NIXON: That's the point. We must not do it. Now that's the point, the mistake we made, to stop this damn thing before we had a settlement, Al.

HAIG: And we're going to get — we're going to get pressure from Dobrynin. I am confident Henry's going to come back with some theories as to why we shouldn't do it. We have to consider that. He may know something we don't know. Or he may get some assurances from Le Duc Tho that we don't know about.

NIXON: Right.

HAIG: But, my own instincts are that they only understand one thing. And if they're going to try to play us right up to the congressional return, that will be even tougher to start again than when these men are back in town. And we get into a weather problem. The B-52s are great around the clock, sir, but they need escorts and the escorts are weather sensitive. So while it's technical — technically feasible, it's not, not the kind of thing you can do without reason, with some kind of reasonable weather. Hell, we've got another complication as I sat down to try to war-game this: Thieu's calling for a cease-fire. There has habitually been a holiday cease-fire, and we're going to have to wrestle with that one, how to manage that problem. And I think that's, quite frankly, what Hanoi's very conscious of. They don't want us to start bombing. They realize, now, that they've got a gap that can —

NIXON: When does the cease-fire run? From when to when?

HAIG: Well, he offered — ordinarily, they run it Christmas —

NIXON: Through New Year?

HAIG: — midnight the day before Christmas to midnight the day following Christmas. Then they have another one at New Year's. There have been occasions when they've had them longer. They've run them right through the period.

NIXON: [unclear]

HAIG: Thieu offered that today, but that was in conjunction —

NIXON: He offered the longer one?

HAIG: But that was in conjunction with this POW exchange.

NIXON: No shit, he's done it. They're not going to give us any POWs.

HAIG: Now, Henry thinks —

NIXON: That damn thing. He knows better than that.

HAIG: That he knows.

NIXON: Huh?

HAIG: That was the red herring to take the heat off of him and show his magnanimous spirit. Now, we may have to send the vice president out to, still, to brutalize this guy.

NIXON: Yeah. About what [unclear]? I mean even before we have a settlement?

HAIG: To say, "Look —"

NIXON: What will he tell him?

HAIG: "— by God, we want you to know we're going, and are you going to persist in this? That it's going to be your destruction. And we've got to take military action. We've got to concert on that to get maximum pressure on Hanoi." Well, I think we have to think about this. Maybe I should do that, I don't know. But I think Thieu right now is so far off the reservation that it's going to take some more tending.

NIXON: I agree. Maybe you have to do that. Maybe using the vice president for that is —

HAIG: Maybe premature.

NIXON: But Thieu has got to be told in the coldest possible terms. What in the hell, has he paid any attention to this stuff? And, but — well, it's hard. We always knew it was going to be hard. It's just a little harder than we expected. What happened is that Henry got his hopes a little higher than he should have before the election.

HAIG: That's right. That's right —

NIXON: I never thought — I didn't, you know. I didn't, as you know, have very high hopes, and I don't think you did either —

HAIG: You never have, and I never have.

NIXON: Huh? Did you ever have —?

HAIG: I never have.

NIXON: Really? I never did. I remember when Henry came in, remember he said, "Well we got three [for] three over there." [The "three" refers to the three diplomatic triumphs of 1972: China, the Soviet Union, and Vietnam.] I waited — the next morning he cooled off a little. He knew that it was a little bit exuberant. What the hell? You got nothing but a slap on the face from Thieu when you went out there, right? But you know, there comes a time when it must end.

HAIG: That's right. That is absolutely —

NIXON: That was really the theme of Bunker's call, wasn't it?

HAIG: Yeah.

NIXON: As I understood it, he said well —

HAIG: That's right. We've backed this guy. We've given him everything. It's time for him to stand up and face it.

NIXON: That's right. But we really have, Al. Even Abrams, he sits sort of like a silent rock and never says anything, but even he said it on one occasion that I can recall, he said, "Well, we've got to cut him loose to see what he can do. The time has come. He's depended on us too long."

HAIG: Yeah, well, I agree with that —

NIXON: Isn't that really it?

HAIG: Yes, sir. And I agree with him completely. We're just going to have to — have to manage that in turn. But I think we're in a hell of a lot stronger position than they are, sir. I really do.

NIXON: Than the North?

HAIG: I think we're in great shape and we've —

NIXON: Why?

HAIG: — got to stay confident and —

NIXON: Why are we in a better position here?

HAIG: Because they are hurting very badly in the South. They're —

NIXON: Goddamn it, if we just get the bombing going again.

HAIG: That's right. They can't face that.

NIXON: That's why they're being — if they're being amicable, the reason they're being amicable is because of their fear of the bombing. I don't think there's any other damn reason to talk. I want you to get that across to him. I — just tell Henry that I do not want him to do anything that will limit my option, very clear option, to resume intensive bombing in the North. And that — you know, in a sense, that's really better than having to have that option open than to have — than to pay a price to have them say something pleasant as he leaves.

"I do not see why Hanoi would want to settle three weeks from now when they didn't settle this week."

December 14, 1972, 10:08 a.m.

Richard Nixon, Henry Kissinger, and Alexander Haig
OVAL OFFICE

When Kissinger returned to Washington, he reported to Nixon on the failure of the most recent peace talks to reach or even approach a peace accord. The conversation soon moved to a military solution and the imminent instigation of full-force bombing in North Vietnam. Kissinger himself was no longer confident that the peace negotiations would lead to any productive end, without the introduction of another offensive. Contemporaries at the time and historians since have analyzed the attitudes in the White House, believing that the peace accords probably could have been worked out without bombing attacks, yet Hanoi at the time was a volatile place. Many hardliners believed that the war could and should continue. The bombing may have dissuaded them. In what was one of the most important conversations in the effort to end the war, Kissinger and the president redefined the U.S. commitment to South Vietnam, under Thieu, and to the region in the short term.

• • •

KISSINGER: First of all, let me give you my assessment of how these negotiations went. They came back on November—they came here on November 20 determined to settle. When Le Duc Tho arrived at the airport, he said, "It would not be understood if we had a second meeting—if a second meeting was requested." We gave them sixty-nine changes, of which many of them were crap, just to go through the motions of supporting Saigon. Instead of blowing their top, they went through in a very businesslike fashion. They accepted twelve of them; we were down to four.

NIXON: Wait a minute. You're talking about what day?

KISSINGER: The first day, November 20.

NIXON: Oh. That was the time after the election.

KISSINGER: Between November 20 and November 24—

NIXON: That's when you got the twelve concessions.

KISSINGER: That's when we got the first concession — the twelve concessions and, literally, we were within one day of settlement, then. We said, "If we can get two out of three of the other four that were outstanding—"

NIXON: Mm-hmm.

KISSINGER: "—we'll settle." We would have settled for one out of three.

NIXON: Sure.

KISSINGER: It was easy to do.

NIXON: Then?

KISSINGER: At the end of the third day, he got a message, read it at the table, blanched, immediately asked for a recess, and it's never been the same since. Immediately then, the next day, he introduced new demands of his own, which he had not done before. And, from then on, he started dragging things. Now—

NIXON: Huh? What was the message? What's your analysis?

KISSINGER: My analysis of the message is that they probably got a readout of what you said to Duc, and what I said to their local ambassador, which was to say—

NIXON: No, I hadn't seen Duc by that time.

KISSINGER: No, you — oh, no —

NIXON: [unclear]

KISSINGER: — that's what we said to him. Or at any rate, they —

NIXON: Well, we had said it, though. We said we'd need to play a hard line with them —

KISSINGER: Then they got a readout of what I said to their ambassador, which was exactly what I —

NIXON: That was probably it. That was it. I think they're probably infiltrated over there in Paris. That's what I think.

KISSINGER: That's right.

NIXON: [unclear]

KISSINGER: That's even more —

NIXON: Yeah.

KISSINGER: — likely than what you said —

NIXON: That's it. No, not Duc. I don't think Duc would do it, but —

KISSINGER: Well, Duc wouldn't do it himself —

NIXON: But, you see, they got a readout. I think the Paris thing leaks like a sieve. Their rooms are — and those assholes don't know that their rooms are bugged by the Communists, and the Communists passed it back. And, so?

KISSINGER: Whatever the reason is, they then decided that —

NIXON: That's when you showed them, that's when you saw it. That was the turn of events.

KISSINGER: Then, there was a turn of events. Then, he introduced two demands, which he knew we couldn't meet. One, that the political prisoners ought to be released.

NIXON: Hmm.

KISSINGER: And, second, that we should pull out our civilian personnel serving in the technical branches there, which would have the practical consequence of grounding the air force —

NIXON: Yes, of course —

KISSINGER: — and — and grounding the radar, and, in effect, destroying the ARVN. That's when I asked for a recess.

NIXON: Mm-hmm.

KISSINGER: Because I knew —

NIXON: To come home?

KISSINGER: To come home. This was the first session. Still, we were quite optimistic. We thought that if we kept pushing, we could finish it that week, but we had no assurance that we could get Thieu along, so we wanted you —

NIXON: Duc —

KISSINGER: — to talk to Duc.

NIXON: That's when you [unclear] —

KISSINGER: Now, in addition to whatever they may have picked up of what we said to the South Vietnamese, the South Vietnamese behavior was so incredible that that gave them an incentive, because the longer these negotiations went on, the better off they were. The greater the tension between Saigon and us —

NIXON: Mm-hmm.

KISSINGER: — the greater the possibility that we would flush Thieu down the drain.

NIXON: I see.

KISSINGER: Without it — without it. And, the third factor was that every day that I was there on the first trip, Saigon Radio put out the content of the negotiations, which we had given them, and were — was keeping a scorecard on the concessions, so that Hanoi must have decided that any concession they made to us would be played in Saigon as a victory for them. So, for all these three factors —

NIXON: Yeah?

KISSINGER: — they put a quietus on the negotiations. Now, when we came back, it was a roller coaster. Up and down, the whole time.

NIXON: Hmm.

KISSINGER: And, since we thought it should be settled quickly, and since all the evidence up to then was still consistent with settling quickly, it was not easy to tell, at first, what they were up to. For example, on Monday morning, Al and I saw him alone. He gave us —

NIXON: This was the first day?

KISSINGER: The first day.

NIXON: Yeah, the — but before we get that in, we must also throw into the equation the fact that those two — well, there were more than that — the two sessions I had. You had three or four with Duc when he was here.

KISSINGER: That's right, they —

NIXON: It obviously was reported back, because we put that to 'em, and it was put in such unequivocal terms that that undoubtedly got back to 'em.

KISSINGER: That got back to them, but that could have worked either way, Mr. President, because they could have concluded from that, "Let's settle fast, and then the Americans will put the heat on him."

NIXON: Right.

KISSINGER: In the first session —

NIXON: If they wanted to settle?

KISSINGER: In the first session, he always asked me what my schedule was for getting the thing done. When you would go on television. When I would come —

NIXON: Yeah, I know —

KISSINGER: — to Hanoi. When the bombing of the North would stop. But the bombing of the North has dropped off so much now because of these idiots in Defense, that we've practically given it to them for nothing. We had twenty-eight TacAir sorties today — yesterday. That's not to say that they won't pay a price —

NIXON: Well, what'd they say in Paris? They say it's weather holding that off? [unclear] Bullshit.

KISSINGER: So, uh —

NIXON: Go ahead.

KISSINGER: So that was the situation on — at the first session —

NIXON: At the beginning of the sessions, right?

KISSINGER: At the beginning of the sessions, they wanted to know the schedule. When do we go to Hanoi? When is the speech? When is the cease-fire? And they wanted to know all of this because, of course, they're planning their military actions around it. Last week, Monday morning, he gave us a very conciliatory talk.

NIXON: Mm-hmm.

KISSINGER: And, frankly, to show you how naive or wrong we were, we thought the only question was with it — there were only four issues left at that point.

NIXON: I know. You remember, you said before you left, you have two days.

KISSINGER: Yeah. Well, we thought it would be done Monday afternoon. We get in there Monday afternoon, he withdraws every concession he's made two weeks previously and says there're only two choices: to sign the October agreement, or to —

NIXON: Why'd he do that privately, not publicly? Do you think —?

KISSINGER: Well, incidentally —

NIXON: You don't think he got new instructions —

KISSINGER: No.

NIXON: — to be more [unclear] —?

KISSINGER: No, no. No, no. He did it privately to establish the fact that he wanted peace. Then he did it in the afternoon —

NIXON: Well, that's all right. Now, why is he trying to establish the fact that he wants peace? So that we don't go wild? Is that it?

KISSINGER: That's right. That's right. They have two problems. They are at the ragged edge, themselves. They are obviously terrified of what we will do.

NIXON: Yeah.

KISSINGER: On the other hand, they also feel they can play us. And so, their problem was how to get through the week.

NIXON: Mm-hmm.

KISSINGER: Now, they start with this very sharp approach. In the afternoon, he withdraws every concession.

NIXON: Yeah.

KISSINGER: And says if we want them, we have to give them counterconcessions. So then, I canceled the Tuesday meeting in order to be able to work on the Chinese and Russians, and because we cannot go back to the October draft, Mr. President, for a number of reasons. If we go back to the October draft, we'll be overthrowing Thieu.

We've got to get some changes. Secondly, it has now become — their bad faith has now become so self — so evident —

NIXON: Hmm?

KISSINGER: — that many things we could have accepted in October —

NIXON: Hmm?

KISSINGER: — we cannot, now, accept without their being written down. Thirdly, there are many things we could have accepted on a quick schedule for which there's no excuse, whatever, to accept on a slow schedule, like putting international machinery in place. Now — then, Wednesday, we met, and he was conciliatory again, and he gave us back five of those ten changes we made. Thursday was bad again. Friday, he gave us the one real concession he made of — when I talk like this, that's a four-hour session, every day.

NIXON: Mm-hmm.

KISSINGER: Friday, he gave us administrative structure. That was the one big concession he made.

NIXON: Yeah.

KISSINGER: Uh —

NIXON: Then he withdrew it Monday?

KISSINGER: No, administrative structure was never withdrawn, but civilian personnel, he found two things which he knew —

NIXON: Mm-hmm.

KISSINGER: — we couldn't take. One, is the release of political detainees. The other is the withdrawal of civilian personnel. So, every day, they came up in one form or another. And quite diabolically, one day, he said — remember when Al left that Saturday?

NIXON: Mm-hmm.

KISSINGER: He said, "All right, we'll take them out of the agreement." So Monday, he reintroduces them as an understanding, which doesn't do us any good; we still have to withdraw them. We don't give a damn whether they're in the agreement or not; we want them there. Now, they were never in the agreement. We had a full discussion on the subject. It was settled in October. That concession, alone, if we pull out our civilian personnel —

NIXON: It destroys [unclear].

KISSINGER: It's bigger than all the concessions put together he's made to us. So, on Saturday, when Al left, we were down to one issue — the DMZ — or so it seemed. We made another schedule. I said, "I'm sending Al back; he's then going to go with the vice president —"

NIXON: [unclear]

KISSINGER: So, the son of a bitch knew the vice president was ready to leave. So he puts on a fainting spell, says he's getting sick, he's just —

NIXON: Don't you think that was a fainting spell, though?

KISSINGER: Oh, that was a fake —

NIXON: An act?

KISSINGER: Oh, he was — ninety percent acting. He's got a headache. He's got to — he can't meet on Sunday. If they wanted to settle, Mr. President, they would have settled Saturday night, if it had taken till four in the morning.

NIXON: That's why you kept at it, which you were right to do. You see —

KISSINGER: [unclear]

NIXON: — you — you're — you may wonder whether you shouldn't have broken it off the first day, but I think — I think, and I don't know whether Al agrees or not; I never asked — but I think it was just well to just to continue to press, and press, and press, and press. If there's one thing for sure for everybody here, they want the goddamn thing over for a variety of reasons, and many for the wrong reasons, and some for the right reasons. Many think it is over. But, at least, we've got to be — we've got to play our string out so that we make the record. Right, Al?

HAIG: That's right.

NIXON: And that was what you did —

KISSINGER: We — we couldn't break off the first day.

NIXON: If you hadn't, we — well, Christ, you knew. You didn't. You stayed there ten days.

KISSINGER: We had to prove what they were up to, Mr. President. We had to go the extra mile.

NIXON: And to prove it, also, to your colleagues, your loyalists, like Mr. Sullivan, Mr. [unclear], those people, too.

KISSINGER: Well —

NIXON: Did they finally get [unclear] —?

KISSINGER: Oh, Sullivan said he doesn't understand how I stood it, and —

NIXON: Is that right?

KISSINGER: But you had no idea, when I —

NIXON: You left him over there [unclear], I see?

KISSINGER: Well, to work on the protocol; I'll get into that in a minute. So then, on Saturday, we had it down to one issue. It — all we wanted on that issue is that they give us back something they had agreed to three weeks ago. We didn't introduce a new demand. The issue — Al has explained to you the DMZ issue.

NIXON: Oh, sure.

KISSINGER: The way they phrase it, we would not just leave their troops there, we would abolish the dividing line between North and South Vietnam, after which they would have an unlimited right of intervention. They would be the only legitimate government in Vietnam, while there were severe restrictions on the South Vietnamese. That — then, we might just as well overthrow Thieu. I mean, we've got to keep Thieu — not sovereignty, Reston has it completely wrong. [Reston's December 13 column stated, "It is a question of whether the cease-fire . . . will acknowledge in a few simple unambiguous words that the Saigon Government has sovereign right and authority over all the territory of South Vietnam."] Sovereignty's not the issue, because he can have sovereignty with a cease-fire.

NIXON: Reston, I think, he has it wrong. He has it wrong in one sense and right in another sense. That's really that Thieu is salvageable. To us, it isn't — that isn't what worries us. Not at all. But go ahead.

KISSINGER: To us, Mr. President, it seems to me, to sign an agreement which leaves whatever number they've got there — let's say a hundred and fifty thousand, which we think, plus the unlimited right of movement across the border, and, indeed, not just the right to movement across the border, but abolishing the border — that I think is close to a sellout. It's a demand they never made of us. They had agreed to the other proposition three weeks ago, so it's not unthinkable to them.

So, what did they do? On Sunday, we had experts meetings to conform the texts. It's a purely technical thing; third-level people on my staff, third-level people on theirs. In the guise of language changes, they immediately introduced four substantive issues to make goddamn sure we couldn't settle. For example, all week long, we had fought on the issue. They had agreed that the PRG shouldn't be mentioned in the text.

On Friday, we made the concession that it could be mentioned in the preamble. And we had then thought that the — that Saigon would pull off the preamble and sign a document without the preamble. And they agreed to that. So on Sunday, in the language meeting, they put the PRG into the — into three places in the text. I don't want to bore you with all these details —

NIXON: It's important I get the feel on all this —

KISSINGER: It's just to give you the feel —

NIXON: I've got the feel. I've got the feel. I just want to, so I can see what they're doing.

KISSINGER: That — that they immediately introduce something, which guarantees that there could be no settlement on Monday.

NIXON: [unclear]

KISSINGER: On Monday, they told me they had no instructions.

NIXON: Yeah.

KISSINGER: But they —

NIXON: May I ask one question? May I ask one question that troubles me here? As you know, Kennedy, at your instruction, made a call to Dobrynin.

KISSINGER: Yeah —

NIXON: Remember? And we — and which I thought was a good thing to do. And he put it out there, and Dobrynin said he'd convey the message. I got on the phone, briefly, with the same thing, just saying —

KISSINGER: I thought it was excellent. Al told me.

NIXON: — there's one issue, but the whole point is, excellent or not, do we have the Russians screwing us here, too?

KISSINGER: No.

NIXON: You don't think so?

KISSINGER: No, because Al gave me a report which —

NIXON: Yeah, but you were there when I talked to him, and [unclear] —

KISSINGER: No, but Al gave me a report of something Dobrynin told him of where the negotiations stood, which they had been told by Hanoi, which is so — it's partly true, and partly so distorted, that Hanoi is lying to them the way Saigon is lying to us.

NIXON: Do you think Dobrynin is — not Dobrynin, but the Soviet is trying to move them?

KISSINGER: Yeah, definitely.

NIXON: Do you think so, Al?

HAIG: There's something to that, Mr. President.

KISSINGER: Because they know you. Brezhnev wants to come here. There's nothing in it for them. If they wanted to screw you, they'd do it in the Middle East. There's nothing in it for the Russians —

NIXON: All right. All right, I get it. I was troubled by whether we had, you know, put a — played a — made a play there which would hurt us where we have a much bigger game, and I just hate to waste it on these assholes. But you did what you could.

KISSINGER: No, what neither —

NIXON: You saw the Chinese, too?

KISSINGER: Yeah.

NIXON: Was that worthwhile?

KISSINGER: No — well, I don't know. The Chinese never tell us.

NIXON: All right. Come on. Come [unclear] —

KISSINGER: So, Monday —

NIXON: [unclear]

KISSINGER: So, Monday they come in, just to make sure we don't settle, they come in with a signing — new signing proposals. So, I figure out a way by which we can accept it, and tentatively accepted it. The next day, he comes in with a DMZ proposal, which is, however, exactly what they gave us the week before — just moving the sentence one place further — and withdraw the signing proposal they had made the day before, and put it into a form that we can't accept, claiming that he had been overruled in Hanoi. In other words, his communication for that worked very fast.

Then, again, in the form of going through the language of the document, they introduce four other issues. Then — now, this is December 12 — six weeks after I told them we want to bring the protocols into being simultaneously with the agreement, five weeks after they say they want to sign the agreement, they, for the first time, produced their protocol for the international commission and for the other commission, giving us just one night to study it. Now, when you see those protocols, they're an insult to our intelligence.

NIXON: Yeah. I know.

KISSINGER: They have a — they have 250 members in the international commission. They have — each team has liaison offices assigned to it as the same number as the team from the party. All their communications, all their transportation, comes from the party. In other words, the Communists supply all the communications and transportation in their area; they have no right to move out of their building unless the Communists agree to it. We'll never get anyone to serve on it. And, so, the international commission is a total joke, and everything is insulting. They had agreed. All week long, they told us there's a great concession, that there would be a team in the DMZ. So where do they put the DMZ team? On the Cua Viet River. Did you know that?

HAIG: [laughs]

KISSINGER: [laughing] They put the DMZ team on the Cua Viet River, which is at Quang Tri. And then, they have a proposal for a Two-Party Commission, in which they give the Communist member — the international member can't move a — can't go to the bathroom without Communist permission. Then, there's a Two-Party Commission, in which the Communist member can run freely around the country, make any investigation he wants, it's established in every district capital.

In other words, the political — the Two-Party Commission is a way for them to spread the VC all over the country. And then, in the international commission, they introduce this Council of National Reconciliation as one of the parties, as if it were a government.

· · ·

KISSINGER: Less was settled on Tuesday, so, then the only thing we accomplished Tuesday was to go over the language of the agreement. We had it down to two —

NIXON: Yeah.

KISSINGER: There were only two unresolved issues, one of them a total, cheap, miserable trick on their part, again. They had introduced the phrase that "the National Council will direct the other party." We refused to accept "direct," so they said "supervise." We refused to accept "supervise," and we finally bargained them down to the word "promote," which they had accepted. They accepted the English word "promote," but they kept the Vietnamese word "supervise." So, in the text that's going to be circulating in Vietnam [unclear]. All I'm trying to tell you, Mr. President, is here then I was —

NIXON: You were willing to stay there?

KISSINGER: So then I was there on the last day. We had it down to two issues on the text, and one issue of substance. I said, "Let the experts get together and just compare texts once more to make sure we got it right." So they introduced seventeen changes in the form of linguistics, by changing the obligations on Cambodia and Laos, by taking out a word on replacements, what weapons we can replace. We had said, "destroyed, worn out, damaged, or used up." They take out the word "destroyed." I said, "Listen, Mr. Le Duc Tho, why do you take out 'destroyed'?" He said, "Because, if a thing is damaged, you can't destroy it without damaging it, so it's an unnecessary word." So here we go into an hour's debate on the philosophical problem of whether you —

NIXON: [unclear]

KISSINGER: Uh —

NIXON: How many [unclear]?

KISSINGER: But, you know goddamn well. Now, all of this we've already communicated to Saigon. If we take it out — if this were Dobrynin — if this were Gromyko in the last hour of the SALT settlement, I'd run this through and wouldn't quibble. But, you know what their strategy is. If we accept their DMZ language, which would be a disaster, they've got to sign it. If we accept their signing language, they've got the seventeen language changes. If we accept every one of these seventeen language changes, which would destroy again what they granted us three weeks ago on Cambodia and Laos, they've got the protocols. And they are now saying all of these things, and if we accept the protocols, which we — I mean, if we did that, we might just as well overthrow Thieu and leave — then they've got the understandings. On the other hand, he played a very clever game. He's — first of all, their book must say that "Kissinger's a man of great vanity, so keep buttering him up." So, they kept saying to me, "You and I are the only men who understand this war, so you go back to your president, and I'll go back to my Politburo." Here he was sitting with ten little guys all the time, and he kept saying, "You know, I'm trying to settle. I make all these concessions to you, and they overrule me in Hanoi," he says. Now, when a Politburo member tells you he's been overruled in front of ten clerks —

NIXON: That's crazy.

KISSINGER: — you know it isn't true. So, what they've done is quite diabolical. They've got the issue in a stage where, with one phone call to us, they can settle it in an hour. But they're always going to keep it just out of reach, and —

NIXON: Henry, tell me this —

KISSINGER: Now, Laird thinks we can just yield. We can't yield. They won't let us yield —

NIXON: Did you talk to — did you get Laird this morning?

KISSINGER: Well, Laird has sent you a memo.

NIXON: Well, wait a minute. How much does Laird know?

HAIG: He knows that things are going bad, that we're considering other possibilities for reaction —

NIXON: What is he suggesting? To yield?

HAIG: Yeah. Oh, he called. I told you yesterday. He called me the night before and said, "We can't — we can't take military action. I'm going to send a memo over." Well, the memo got here yesterday morning and it just says we've got to settle.

NIXON: So what's new?

KISSINGER: Any terms [unclear].

NIXON: What's new with him? [laughter] Have we ever gotten anything else with him?

KISSINGER: Oh, no. No, no —

NIXON: November 3, Cambodia, May 8. [Nixon sometimes used shorthand to refer to past speeches. "November 3" refers to his "silent majority" speech of 1969, "April 30" was the 1970 announcement of the Cambodian incursion, and "May 8" was his 1972 decision to bomb and mine Hanoi and Haiphong harbor.]

KISSINGER: Mr. President, if —

NIXON: Rogers has stood firm, though, on this, hasn't he?

KISSINGER: He hasn't stood at all as far as I know.

NIXON: Well, no, no, but he's never indicated any moving — movement away. Does Sullivan?

KISSINGER: No, Sullivan is completely —

NIXON: Well, I know. I think he would if there were — you haven't heard from Rogers? Now, you've briefed him a couple times. How's he see it? What has he said? I want to know.

HAIG: He's —

NIXON: This depends on whether we have a meeting or not —

HAIG: [unclear]

NIXON: Huh?

HAIG: He's been absolutely unquestioning on it —

KISSINGER: No —

HAIG: — and what we can do.

KISSINGER: Let me — let me put Sullivan's view fairly. In the text of the agreement, Sullivan would make concessions I would not make. But Sullivan has now accepted the fact —

NIXON: That there's —

KISSINGER: — that no matter what concessions we make in the text, they're not gonna settle. Now, there are a number of possibilities. It is — there's a ten percent chance that Tho is telling the truth that he's going back to Hanoi —

NIXON: No.

KISSINGER: I don't believe it. I just —

NIXON: Yeah —

KISSINGER: [unclear]

NIXON: — there's a ten percent chance. Go ahead —

KISSINGER: In fairness, I have to say there's a second possibility that they now want to see, for a little longer, how that Saigon-Washington split works.

NIXON: Right. Third?

KISSINGER: There's the predominant possibility that there isn't enough pressure on them to make them settle. Now, the reason I wanted to — I — I recommended and am responsible for the accelerated schedule before November 7, is that November 7 gave them a deadline from which they could not — that which they could not evade.

NIXON: Yeah.

KISSINGER: And, therefore, they had to make rapid movements. I — that — what we are seeing now is their normal negotiating habit. They're shits, if I can use a — I mean, they are tawdry, miserable, filthy people. They make the Russians looks good.

NIXON: And the Russians make the Chinese look good, I know.

KISSINGER: And the Russians make the Chinese look good. I mean, it isn't just this crap I'm giving you; it is they never, never do anything that isn't tawdry. Now, November 7 scared the pants off them. Now, I remember talking to Al about it, and I take full responsibility; he was in favor of a slower schedule —

NIXON: He went along with it. He went along with no problem —

KISSINGER: No, I get a lot of credit, exorbitant credit, when things go well. I have to take the blame when things do not —

NIXON: Who remembers [the 1971] India-Pakistan [war] —?

KISSINGER: Well, no. There I was right. India-Pakistan I was right. This one I wasn't necessarily right on.

NIXON: Who knows? Who knows!

KISSINGER: India-Pakistan didn't bother me. On that one, I was right. And that one paid off in China. India-Pakistan was one —

NIXON: What I meant is, at the time — what I'm talking about is, are we going to have enough time? All these assholes in the press said we were wrong. Now, at the present time, the press will say, "We're quite aware we're very, very close to peace, and da-da-da-da-da." They were wrong, and so when it turns the other way, they're going to say, "Peace has escaped da-da-da-da-da," and they're going to be wrong again. And it isn't going to make a goddamn bit of difference. My point is, you've got to remember who the enemy are. The enemy has never changed. The election didn't change it. The only friends we've got, Henry, are a few people of rather moderate education out in this country, and thank God, they're about sixty-one percent of the people, who support us. The left-wingers, most of your friends, and most — and many of mine —

KISSINGER: Some friends of mine —

NIXON: — are against us.

KISSINGER: I'm using the left-wingers, Mr. President —

NIXON: Yeah. They're all through with us, though —

KISSINGER: I —

NIXON: — and we're through with them.

KISSINGER: I have —

NIXON: They don't even know. They don't know what's going to hit them, we believe.

KISSINGER: I have no illusions about the left-wingers. Those sons of bitches are [unclear] —

NIXON: Well, they're so tawdry, right? Now, let's come down to where we've got to go.

KISSINGER: So — but, the difference —

NIXON: I — understand, Henry — you know, I told it — as Al over here will tell you — as

I told you last night. I say, "What difference does it make? It's done." You know, what — whether it was before, we should have done it during the election, and so forth and so on.

Looking back, we probably should have let it wait till the election, and the day after the election: whack! You know? And said — or [unclear], rather than whack, said, "You've got forty-eight hours, kiddies. Either settle, or get awful hurt." That's probably what we should have done, but we didn't.

KISSINGER: That's probably true.

NIXON: That's probably — I mean, from the standpoint of the election, we would probably have done even a little bit better than we did. [laughs] [unclear] It didn't make a difference; we did very well. But nevertheless, nevertheless, there it is. It's an interesting thing. You know, you've got two interesting analyses of the elections. You've got the Lou Harris analysis, who — which thinks that we were quite helped by the idea that we were sort of for peace and progress, and all that sort of thing. You've got the Dick [unclear] analysis, which I think is much closer to the truth — that says, on the other hand, it says [unclear]. He says all these things. He says, "Oh, yes." He says, "It helped the president's image, and the rest. When — but you came right down to the issues, what really won it, was, it was the comparison between a sellout, a repulsive, peace-at-any-price radical against a sound man." They said that was what it was really about. You see, that's why it didn't make any difference whether you settled or not. But the point is, who was to know, then? Now, though, it's over. Now, we've got to look to the future.

KISSINGER: What we had to balance, then —

NIXON: And, what the hell, how are we going to give them another deadline? We — that's our problem.

KISSINGER: What we had to balance, then, was to weigh the advantage of an unchangeable deadline against the danger of an endlessly protracted negotiation while our assets were there.

NIXON: That's right.

KISSINGER: And we lost the gamble. That's what it comes down to. We lost the gamble eighty percent because of Thieu.

NIXON: Thieu, ah! That's right.

KISSINGER: Now, but all of the —

NIXON: If Thieu — if Thieu had gone along, in the first instance, then we could have made the deal quickly that we could have lived with. That was the real problem. That we know.

KISSINGER: Because if that —

NIXON: But that we can't say —

KISSINGER: No.

NIXON: — due to the fact that we know that Thieu's survival is what we're fighting for. Not his, but we know there ain't nobody else to keep the goddamn place —

KISSINGER: That's right.

NIXON: — together at the moment. Now, we're in a real box on that. We all know that. But, you see, so therefore, that's what I mean, Henry. You were basing your whole assumption — we were basing our assumption — on the fact that Thieu would. You remember, when you went to Saigon, you were amazed when you went in and said, "Thieu [unclear]. There is no coalition government. You have veto power." And the son of a bitch says, "No I don't want anything other than — we've got to have total victory."

KISSINGER: Yeah.

NIXON: That was, that was, that was the thing.

KISSINGER: Even there, the bastard misled us. If, on the first day, he had told us he couldn't accept it, we could have still tripped our relations with Hanoi, and avoided some of the dangers. But he led us on for three days, said he might accept it, and only on the last afternoon of the last day towards — but that's water over the dam. I agree —

NIXON: Now, where do we go?

KISSINGER: Well, we are now in this position: as of today, we are caught between Hanoi and Saigon, both of them facing us down in a position of total impotence, in which Hanoi is just stringing us along, and Saigon is just ignoring us. Hanoi — I do not see why Hanoi would want to settle three weeks from now when they didn't settle this week. I do not see what additional factors are going to operate. I'm making a cold-blooded analysis.

NIXON: Right.

KISSINGER: I see no additional factor, if nothing changes —

NIXON: That's right.

KISSINGER: — that will make Hanoi more receptive early in January.

NIXON: [unclear]

KISSINGER: I see no additional factor that will make Saigon more conciliatory. On — in — on the contrary, Saigon, in the process of trying to sabotage the settlement, is going to float so many proposals of its own that it knocks out the few props we've got left. That Christmas truce proposal of Thieu is a disaster, because it removes the few military pressures that we have got left. Therefore, I have come to the reluctant conclusion that we've got to put it to them in Hanoi, painful as it is.

But, we cannot do it anymore from the old platform. We have to do it, now, from the platform of — what we have to do is this, Mr. President, if — my — I've thought about it very hard, now. I think I ought to give a low-key briefing tomorrow of just where the negotiations stand.

NIXON: You think you should?

KISSINGER: Well, Al thinks Ziegler should, but I don't see how anyone else — I went out there and said they were going well. If I hide, now, it is not going —

NIXON: You're not hiding. Let's think. All right, let's think about it. Somebody could give a low-key briefing, so let's start [unclear] —

KISSINGER: I don't think anyone else can do it except I.

NIXON: All right, all right, let's talk [unclear] —

KISSINGER: I was the guy who said, "Peace is at hand —"

NIXON: — let's talk about that later. Let's talk about — somebody should give a low-key briefing. What should the briefing be?

KISSINGER: The briefing should be where were we at the end of October, and why did we think peace was imminent? What has happened in the interval, and what is, now, in prospect? We can explain, very convincingly, that with goodwill, peace was easily achievable. But every time we turned over a rock, we found a worm underneath. That, if they wanted a cease-fire, they should have had an international machinery in place. They didn't do it. That, while they were talking cease-fire to us, we have reams of intelligence reports that ordered them to go into massive action on the first —

NIXON: [unclear]

KISSINGER: — day of the cease-fire —

NIXON: Right.

KISSINGER: — and to go on for —

NIXON: They were going to violate it?

KISSINGER: — three days after. They translated the document in a way that was totally misleading as to the nature of —

NIXON: Whether it was a government or a coalition [unclear] —

KISSINGER: Or whether it had to "direct," or whether it had to "promote." That, the simplest thing —

NIXON: I mean, the way — let me say, if we're going to talk about this — Al, take these words down — the way that it should be done. I mean, I'd have all this so it's done by either Ziegler or [unclear] all these things about the proposed direction. But, the point is, you should say that we had evidence, first, massive intelligence evidence that they were intending to violate the cease-fire and all the understandings.

Second, they insisted on translating the document, and insisted on a change in the document, which would have made it a coalition government, or a Communist — a Communist-coalition government over the people of South Vietnam, something we had insisted we would never agree upon, rather than a Commission of Reconciliation, which had for its purpose [unclear]. In other words, be sure that the violation, the Communist government, that that kind of thing gets into the lead. Go ahead.

KISSINGER: That then —

NIXON: Think of things we could say then.

KISSINGER: That then, even though there was extensive international machinery provided in the agreement, they claimed —

NIXON: They sabotaged the international machinery by making it totally meaningless, so that nobody would even serve.

KISSINGER: But, first, they wouldn't even show it to us till December 12.

NIXON: That's right. In view of the — but even that, just say that the international machinery they totally agree — disagreed to set up international machinery to supervise it all in any meaningful way.

KISSINGER: Then, they told us that the demobilization provision of the agreement would take care of their troops. Every time we try to give it one concrete meaning, through a de facto understanding, through giving it a time limit, through indicating —

NIXON: They were using these negotiations solely for the purpose, not of — that is not [unclear] not for the purpose of ending the war, but of continuing the war in a different form.

KISSINGER: And so, we have come —

NIXON: And not of bringing peace, but of having — continuing war in this terribly difficult part of the country. War in South Vietnam; peace in North Vietnam. Well, that was their proposal: peace for North Vietnam and continuing war in South Vietnam.

KISSINGER: So, we have come to the reluctant conclusion that — you have expressed it very well right now, Mr. President — that this wasn't a peace document. This was a document for perpetual warfare, in which they create —

NIXON: Perpetual warfare in South Vietnam —

KISSINGER: That's right.

NIXON: — and peace in North Vietnam. That's the way to put it.

KISSINGER: That's right —

NIXON: "Peace in North Vietnam and perpetual warfare in South Vietnam, with the United States — and the United States cooperating with them in the —"

KISSINGER: Now —

NIXON: "— in imposing a Communist government on the people of South Vietnam against their will."

KISSINGER: And this is why these negotiations, which could have been very rapid —

NIXON: That's right. Now —

KISSINGER: — and should have been very rapid —

NIXON: — the negotiations: on the other hand, the negotiations — we have had agreements throughout this period of time. We have reached agreement on all these issues, at varying times, from which they have first agreed and then withdrawn. This can be settled in one day —

KISSINGER: That's right.

NIXON: — if they're willing to settle. And we're willing to settle in one day.

KISSINGER: Exactly.

NIXON: No other meetings are needed; just an exchange of messages has been arranged.

KISSINGER: Or —

NIXON: [unclear]

KISSINGER: Or another meeting is necessary. But — so this is — now, we also have to disassociate ourselves from Saigon to some extent. We have to say —

NIXON: Yeah?

KISSINGER: — "It isn't — what is the difference between us and Saigon? Saigon wanted total victory. The president has always said that he would give them a reasonable chance to survive. The difference between us and Hanoi is that they will not give them a reasonable chance to survive. So, Saigon's objections never had a chance." I —

NIXON: And, on the other hand, I would tilt it. I would say we were ready to tilt it very strongly against Hanoi, and very lightly against Hanoi — against Saigon. I would say that North Vietnam — that as far as Saigon is concerned, they — we understandably express concern about the agreement, about the people — the people of South — but, on the other hand, Saigon had agreed, on May 8, at the time we laid down the conditions of a cease-fire, the return of our POWs, and internationally supervised elections, that they would agree to that. And now, they have backed off of that proposal, and are insisting now on a total withdrawal of forces, which, of course, is not consistent —

KISSINGER: But we have to —

NIXON: [unclear]

KISSINGER: We had to back off a bit from Saigon, Mr. President, if Saigon —

NIXON: And that backs off.

KISSINGER: In — I agree. In Saigon's interest, because then, it isn't Saigon that vetoed it, but it is our judgment that the Communists are — have used another guise to impose themselves. Now, I would recommend that we leave open the possibility of this settlement, if the other side meets the very minimum conditions that we have indicated. I would then recommend that we start bombing the bejeezus out of them within forty-eight hours of having put the negotiating record out. And I would then recommend that after about two weeks of that, we offer withdrawal for prisoners, about the time that the Congress comes back —

NIXON: Yeah.

KISSINGER: — and say, "It has now been proved that the — the negotiation's too complex involving all the Vietnamese parties. Let them settle their problems among each other. The South is strong enough to defend itself —"

NIXON: "So we will withdraw." Now, let me ask a critical question. Do you have in this record a clear Q and A, for one thing, where you said, "All right, will you, if we withdraw all of our forces, and stop the bombing and the mining, will you return our prisoners?"

KISSINGER: No —

NIXON: Would you say that they have? See, that's the trouble, because that's —

KISSINGER: No, I'll tell you, Mr. President, why I didn't do that, because, I think that —

NIXON: Well—

KISSINGER: —the one, they won't—they don't want that, now. They want us to [unclear]—

NIXON: Oh, I know they don't, but it's one point that we're interested in hearing, either when we talk—

KISSINGER: But I would—

NIXON: —about—when we talk about going at it alone, without Saigon, Henry, the only basis for our going at it alone is, at this time, the withdrawal of all of our forces, stopping the bombing and the mining, getting our POWs, and continuing to aid South Vietnam—

KISSINGER: That's right.

NIXON: That's the only basis.

KISSINGER: That's right.

NIXON: And, they'll never agree to that.

KISSINGER: Well, Mr. President, they are not all that strong. I think if you are willing to go six months, they're going to crack.

NIXON: Well, but Henry—Henry, I know if I'm willing to go six months it isn't in the cards. Right? I'm willing to go six months, but that I cannot convince the Congress of, in my opinion. I mean, I must say that on that, I would have to respect the judgment of some other people here. We can go for—we can sure go till Christmas. I mean, we can go to till the Congress comes back.

KISSINGER: It's better—

NIXON: We want to remember that we're going to have a period—if you're thinking of bombing North Vietnam for six months, bombing for six months is not going to work.

KISSINGER: Well then we can't—then we've had it.

NIXON: Well then, we have to, then, have a look at our choices.

KISSINGER: Because—because it is possible—

NIXON: Right, but bombing for what? I mean, what do we say?

KISSINGER: Prisoners.

NIXON: We could do that.

KISSINGER: When Congress—

NIXON: But, provided we make the record, which we haven't made that record, have we?

KISSINGER: No, no, but we can easily fix that, Mr. President, by having the two weeks after the bomb—I would like to bomb for two weeks within this framework, because they might accept it by New Year's, if they get a terrific shock, now. If then, by New Year's, they haven't accepted it, we could at the first formal session in Paris after New Year's propose prisoners for withdrawal.

NIXON: Prisoners for withdrawal?

KISSINGER: And—

NIXON: [unclear]

KISSINGER: That's right.

NIXON: [unclear] then say, "Now, Viet" — I meant, the way I would say it: "Vietnamization is now concluded."

KISSINGER: That's right.

NIXON: "The American role is now concluded. For a return of our prisoners of war, we will quit the bombing [unclear]." Yes, you could bomb for six months, I agree —

KISSINGER: You see, my point —

NIXON: — on that basis. But you can't bomb for six months with the idea that we'll go back and have some sort of a settlement —

KISSINGER: I think we're too close on this one —

NIXON: I mean, in other words — your pro — you had that in one of your original proposals last week. But my point is that on this, as far as this one is concerned —

KISSINGER: This one —

NIXON: — I have a feeling it's out the window. I mean, I don't want to —

KISSINGER: No.

NIXON: — sound pessimistic. I — Al's — Al, for the first time, is more optimistic even than you are. Al thinks they want to settle.

KISSINGER: I also think they want to settle, but —

NIXON: Do you think they want to settle?

KISSINGER: Mr. President, they are —

NIXON: Do you think they're going to?

HAIG: Yes, if they get a good kick in the ass.

KISSINGER: They are scared out of their minds that you'll resume bombing. They have taken shit from me that you wouldn't believe. I — here is Le Duc Tho, the number-three man in his country, and the things I have said to him, in front of his people, you would not believe.

NIXON: Like what?

KISSINGER: About, you know, about his tawdry performance; about his extraordinary trickery. And then, just making fun of him. When he came up, I said, "Now we get the daily speech."

NIXON: [unclear] that's something else.

KISSINGER: And —

NIXON: [unclear]

KISSINGER: No, no. The point is, I bluster threats from you. The point I'm making is, Mr. President, the reason they were so nice to me is because their strategy is to make us believe — why do they let their experts meet? Why did he come out every day to shake hands with me, so that I couldn't fight him off? I mean, he just walked up to the guard and stuck out his hand.

NIXON: I understand —

KISSINGER: Why did they do all of this? Because they want to create the impression —

NIXON: That it's still alive.

KISSINGER: — that the peace —

NIXON: And, of course, they're leaking it all to the press.

KISSINGER: That's right.

NIXON: The press is playing it very heavily until today, and now the press is playing it the other way because you've returned, and —

KISSINGER: Yeah, but he's leaving tomorrow, so they're going to play it, again, the other way tomorrow.

NIXON: Well, that he's going home for what? Consultations?

KISSINGER: [unclear] What he's going to say is he's going home for consult —

NIXON: All right, where does Agnew fit into this?

KISSINGER: Well —

NIXON: My own view is very mixed on that. I was —

KISSINGER: Well —

NIXON: I was all for it when we had Agnew with something solid he was to go to talk about. But you — Agnew, to send that unguided missile out there, even with Haig, and to have him sit down there, and to have that clever Thieu start to say, "Well, we've got to have this and this," and Agnew won't even know what the hell hit him. That's what I'm afraid of —

KISSINGER: I'm no longer — if we go the route I've recommended, I'm not so much in favor of sending Agnew. I am in favor of —

NIXON: Sending somebody?

KISSINGER: Of sending somebody, maybe Haig —

NIXON: Yeah.

KISSINGER: — because —

NIXON: I think somebody has to go.

KISSINGER: — we have to shut these guys up.

NIXON: That's right. The point is, I don't want them to think that we've resumed the bombing, and so forth, and that they've gotten their way, Henry. That's the point —

KISSINGER: You see, that's — what we have to navigate, now, is a route in which we disassociate from them, but stay closer to them than to Hanoi; to lay the basis for your withdrawing; for your offering the withdrawal for prisoners early —

NIXON: I'd have to make the offer of withdrawal for prisoners. I feel this, if I could make that offer, before the Congress convenes —

KISSINGER: You can do it the last week of December.

NIXON: I think that's what we have to do.

KISSINGER: The way I would play it —

NIXON: I don't see any other way. I don't see any other way we can survive this whole goddamn thing —

KISSINGER: No.

NIXON: — and, in the meantime, what do we do? Retain the present complement of men there?

KISSINGER: Where?

NIXON: South Vietnam. Twenty-nine thousand [the approximate number of U.S. military personnel still in South Vietnam].

KISSINGER: Yes, I don't think they make any difference.

NIXON: All right.

HAIG: I don't think they make any difference, and I think it'd be a bad sign to draw them down —

NIXON: I understand that. I just want to be sure that we know what the answer is —

KISSINGER: But — but what I would do —

[unclear exchange]

KISSINGER: What I would recommend, Mr. President —

NIXON: I feel the same way.

KISSINGER: — is, first of all, we ought to get Haig over to the Pentagon as quickly as possible. [Haig was scheduled to become vice chief of staff of the army in January 1973.]

NIXON: [laughs]

KISSINGER: He's —

NIXON: What can he do over there?

KISSINGER: What he can do over there is — we should put him in charge of a Vietnamese task force. We've got this chairman of the Joint Chiefs who is a navy lobbyist, and who doesn't give a goddamn about the war in Vietnam, and we ought to put Haig in charge of it over in the Pentagon. We ought to put one man in charge of it in Saigon, because —

NIXON: Who? Whitehouse?

KISSINGER: No. No, no. I mean one military guy. I'd put Vogt in charge.

NIXON: All right.

KISSINGER: And then, we can get some real banging done —

NIXON: When?

KISSINGER: — instead of having North Vietnam carved up into six little areas — [The U.S. military divided North Vietnam into "Route Packages" (1, 2, 3, 4, 5, 6A, and 6B), from south to north, to allocate bombing assignments.]

NIXON: When? When? When? When?

KISSINGER: — and then — now, the way I would play it, is this: assuming we have the press conference tomorrow or Saturday — there's something to be said for having it Saturday, because that gets Le Duc Tho out of Paris, although he'll be out of Paris by the time I'd go on.

NIXON: I'd worry about him.

KISSINGER: Well, I'd just like —

NIXON: You probably think he doesn't have a stage?

KISSINGER: He won't have a stage in Moscow.

NIXON: You mean, not to do the bombing, and so forth?

KISSINGER: No, no. The bombing I would, then, resume within — over the weekend. Say something —

NIXON: While he's still in Paris? What is it that you don't want to do with him? What is it that you want to — don't want to do while he's in Paris?

KISSINGER: I didn't want him — I didn't want to give our version of the negotiations while he's still in Paris —

NIXON: It's a good plan.

KISSINGER: Let him kick off his own propaganda machine —

NIXON: That's right. That's right.

KISSINGER: I'd like to gain the twelve hours it takes to check with him —

NIXON: Yeah.

KISSINGER: — while he's moving, but he's going to leave Paris. If we have our press conference at noon, he'll be out of Paris till six in the evening.

NIXON: Today is Thursday?

KISSINGER: Yeah. We can do it tomorrow —

NIXON: I would not make your press conference, if you do it, I wouldn't make it — I don't know. Al and I talked about it last night, and I wonder if, maybe, we shouldn't do it on the basis of, maybe, more on the Ziegler thing. [unclear]

KISSINGER: I think it's a terrible mistake. Ziegler cannot answer the questions. It will look as if I'm hiding —

NIXON: Let's leave you out of it, whether it looks as if you're hiding or not. [unclear] We may want you to hide for your — for everybody's good. Your own, everybody else's. I mean, what do you think, Al? I don't know. You're the best to do it, there's no question about that —

KISSINGER: No, the bombing announcement —

NIXON: — but my point is — my point is —

KISSINGER: I shouldn't do the bombing announcement. What I think we should do is that I — no one else understands the negotiations well enough to explain. The way —

NIXON: [unclear]

KISSINGER: — we've always snowed the press is by just overwhelming them with technical —

NIXON: All right.

KISSINGER: [unclear]

NIXON: All right. What do you want to have come out?

KISSINGER: What I want to —

NIXON: Think about it. What do you want to have the press report after Kissinger gives his three-hour briefing to the press?

KISSINGER: What we have the press report is, first of all —

NIXON: In other words, what are the points you want the press to report?

KISSINGER: That peace was imminent; that it was Communist bad faith — not Saigon — that has prevented it; that —

NIXON: In other words, you want that they — I'm trying to get at something more fundamental. In other words, the press will report the peace talks have broken down.

KISSINGER: No. No, no. The peace talks are still open —

NIXON: That's right.

KISSINGER: — but that the United States remains willing to settle it. The United States remains convinced that it could be settled —

NIXON: Hmm.

KISSINGER: — in an extraordinarily short time —

NIXON: But you see — but — but then, the point is that — I'm trying to give you — you see, you've got to get — all right, that one point is the peace talks are not broken down; they are at an impasse. The impasse is the fault, primarily, of the North Vietnamese, who are insisting — who have — well, the points I made earlier. The third point is that we're ready to resume at any time, on that. But the — then — then, you've got to get across the fact that we are not simply quibbling over language and translation —

KISSINGER: That's right —

NIXON: — and so forth. But what it is really about is —

KISSINGER: What —

NIXON: It's not only the fate of the South Vietnamese, it's the fate — the fate of peace there. And also, let's understand, we have our POWs there, and they have not — and they have refused. We had hoped to get this done before Christmas. We wanted our POWs, and we are — I'd like to get a flavor of stepping up the bombing at this time for the POW purposes, before he [Le Duc Tho] even comes. You get my point?

KISSINGER: That's right. [unclear]

NIXON: Just stepping up the bombing for the purpose of getting them to talk is not going to be [laughs] a very easy one to wheel.

KISSINGER: But for four years, we have said we would not sell out.

NIXON: I know —

KISSINGER: And what these guys have tried to get us to do — that if they had been willing to implement the agreement of the end of October, it would have been easy.

NIXON: Mm-hmm.

KISSINGER: But every time we try to make it concrete on any issue that would inhibit their military action in the future —

NIXON: Mm-hmm. Mm-hmm.

KISSINGER: — they were impossible. For — on the POWs —

NIXON: I know —

KISSINGER: — we've asked them for a protocol, how the POWs would be —

NIXON: What I'd like for you to do, if you would, would be to sit down, later this afternoon or this evening — you've got plenty of time to think — put down on one sheet of paper, put five or six positive points you want the press to write, to come out of this. This is what we have to do. And then, let everything play around that, rather than giving the press what they would like. And that is simply a gory and brilliant analysis of what they did to us, and what we did to them, and we had it here and there, they had it there and there, and this and that. That will ruin us. That will really ruin us.

If, on the other hand, we can — the public gets the impression that this broke because these bastards were at fault, that they want to impose a Communist government, they're still holding our prisoners, and we want to get them back, and, consequently, the president is going to insist on taking the strong action to get this war over with. This war must end! It must end soon! And if they don't want to talk, we will have to go get 'em. If they won't return our prisoners, we want to hit them soon. We're going to take the necessary military action to get them back. That's what you've got to get across —

KISSINGER: And what I would think, Mr. President, is we should not announce the bombing tomorrow. We should just start it —

NIXON: Announce it?

KISSINGER: — on Saturday.

NIXON: We're not going to ever announce the bombing.

KISSINGER: That's right, and then —

NIXON: Then we've got [to] get — and Laird in?

KISSINGER: Ron [Ziegler] can handle that one.

NIXON: No, just remind them. These have — no, we've always been bombing. We've just — this is fair —

KISSINGER: [unclear]

NIXON: — the weather has been bad. Play that. Let's be a little bit clever. The weather has been bad.

KISSINGER: Well —

NIXON: They don't know better.

KISSINGER: Well —

NIXON: They don't know better —

KISSINGER: — it's known that we stopped north of the twentieth, and I think —

NIXON: All right, fine. Fine. Well —

KISSINGER: And I think we can even use that as an advantage to show our goodwill — faith.

NIXON: All right. Fine.

KISSINGER: But, I think —

NIXON: We've stopped north of the [unclear] —

KISSINGER: But I think we should resume that.

NIXON: I didn't resume that. Why doesn't he say, "We have resumed bombing. We have stepped up bombing"? Why build it up? Why escalate it that way? Just start bombing north of the twentieth.

HAIG: What I meant, it's bound to make a hellish splash, Mr. President.

NIXON: When we do it?

HAIG: When we do it —

NIXON: Then why explain it?

HAIG: I —

KISSINGER: No, he should just answer the questions.

HAIG: The next day [unclear] —

NIXON: And what, then? What does he say, then?

HAIG: Henry should say, "Yes, due to [unclear] —"

NIXON: Yeah.

HAIG: "— the current —"

NIXON: No, see, because of the buildup. That's what I'd say: buildup of the enemy, buildup north of the [unclear]. I'd put it on the basis, because of their buildup north of the twentieth, it appears that they're going to resume —

KISSINGER: No.

NIXON: — activities.

KISSINGER: No, Mr. President, on the —

NIXON: You see my point? Or, something like that. I mean, not on the basis of — if you start the bombing for the purpose, only, of getting them to accept this agreement, that ain't going to work. If you start the bargaining, if the reason for it, after January 1, which it must be, is only for the purpose of getting our prisoners back, that will work. But if you, at the present time, you can start bombing, say, "Because of significant enemy buildup activities north of that" — put it on military grounds, not on political grounds. Don't say that we started bombing because they broke off negotiations. Don't say that. Now, that's just the wrong —

KISSINGER: No —

NIXON: — decision.

KISSINGER: — Mr. President, I think there's a fifty–fifty —

NIXON: They all know why we started.

KISSINGER: I think there's a fifty–fifty chance if we give them a tremendous wallop, particularly not the sort of shit the air force likes to do, if I may use this word —

NIXON: I went over this with them —

KISSINGER: — but if we did —

NIXON: It is shit.

KISSINGER: If we got all their power plants in one day, so that the civilian population would be without light, knocked out all the docks in Haiphong, so that even if the harbor is cleared, they can't unload there for months to come, then they would know it's —

NIXON: What kinds of ships are still left around there? [unclear] aren't there some?

HAIG: Yeah —

KISSINGER: We'd have to do it with smart bombs.

NIXON: Well, can then we knock out docks, then, without knocking out the ships? [unclear]

HAIG: Yes, there are certain dock facilities that can be taken out —

NIXON: [unclear]

KISSINGER: I'd frankly take my chance on the ships. Your great asset, Mr. President —

NIXON: All right. Take a chance on the ships. All right —

KISSINGER: — is your unpredictability —

NIXON: Look, I'm going to do it. Now, the other thing is nobody — I am the only one who seems to be for this. I went over this with Moorer and Rush. Incidentally, he's saying it's fine. Don't worry about him.

KISSINGER: No, Rush is fine.

NIXON: He'll stand fine with us. He — he felt that we should continue, and he thinks that, in the end, that we've got to make a deal, and so forth. But Rush will do. He says, "Whatever you decide on, I —"

KISSINGER: We've got to make a deal.

NIXON: [unclear] but the point about the — the point about the — the reason I say take out all the goddamn airfields, Christ, the Israelis did it and it had quite an effect. Let's do it.

HAIG: [unclear]

NIXON: Everything in the air —

HAIG: Including the civilian ones —

NIXON: — including the big civilian —

HAIG: — the military sides of 'em.

NIXON: Why not the civilian sides of them, too? What kinds of planes do you think —?

HAIG: Well, we could hit a —

KISSINGER: Chinese and Russian.

HAIG: Chinese and Soviets.

NIXON: All right, fine. Can you go down the military side of it?

HAIG: They tell me they can do it —

NIXON: Yeah? When?

HAIG: — using smart bombs.

NIXON: Are we gonna have — are we gonna have, though — are we going to have a delay of four weeks before they get it done? These smart bombs can't be used except in clear weather, isn't that right? Aren't they visual?

HAIG: That's right, sir. And the weather right now is absolutely bad.

NIXON: Oh, shit.

HAIG: So, we've got to —

NIXON: Here we are again, Henry. We went through this last year, as you remember.

HAIG: I think the only way to do it is to give them about a — just tell them they have blanket authority to do it, because the worst thing we could do, is do a half-assed job the first time —

NIXON: I know. I know. I know, but, Al, suppose the weather — let's talk. Suppose the weather stays bad through January 3, when the Congress comes back? What in the hell do we get out of it?

KISSINGER: It's impossible.

HAIG: After that, you can't.

NIXON: Huh?

HAIG: That — that won't be.

KISSINGER: We've got —

NIXON: It won't be bad that long?

HAIG: No.

NIXON: That's all right. Now, the other point is: what about the '52s? Can't they get in there now?

KISSINGER: Yes.

NIXON: Well goddamn it, let's get them in. What's wrong with getting the '52s in?

KISSINGER: Well, we've done —

NIXON: Are we afraid they're going to be shot down?

KISSINGER: Well, no. We've got the problem, Mr. President, let's face it: the Chief — the chairman of the Chiefs is a navy lobbyist; he's not a military commander. The Chiefs —

NIXON: He's [unclear] '52s?

KISSINGER: The Chiefs only give a damn about budget categories. May 8, you put your neck on the line and those bastards carved up Vietnam into areas of jurisdiction. They didn't give one goddamn about the national interest. They gave a damn about their service interest.

NIXON: I know. You remember when Connally [unclear] —

KISSINGER: You were —

NIXON: — [unclear] commander —

KISSINGER: You were right —

NIXON: — so we put that asshole Weyand in there, who was worse than Abrams, if anything. Abrams is a — just a clod. I think he's a good division commander, and everyone —

KISSINGER: We made it.

NIXON: — liked him.

KISSINGER: You were one hundred percent right. We were all wrong —

NIXON: [unclear] mistake, who was right, and who was wrong. But the point is —

KISSINGER: [unclear]

NIXON: — it's done now. We don't have anybody in charge out there.

KISSINGER: Well, Vogt can do it. We were all —

NIXON: I need — I need a [unclear] out there [unclear] —

KISSINGER: Well, but he didn't have the authority, Mr. President —

NIXON: We've got poor little Don Hughes is out there running the fighters. He can't do a goddamn thing —

KISSINGER: Well, because they —

NIXON: You have said it.

KISSINGER: — because they — because there's — there are four different commands bombing North Vietnam, Mr. President —

NIXON: All right, how do we change the four different commands? Can that be done, tomorrow? I'd like it today.

KISSINGER: That can be done the day you give the order. If there'll be —

NIXON: That's got to get done immediately.

KISSINGER: They'll be —

NIXON: We can't fart around.

KISSINGER: There'll be unbelievable screaming.

NIXON: Well, that's the point. They've got to get it done right, for a change. We cannot make these military decisions and take all the heat, and have them screw it up again.

KISSINGER: But we've got to get a guy in the Pentagon who monitors it from a strategic point of view, and not a fiscal point of view. And we've got to get a guy out there who looks at it from a strategic point of view. Now, my judgment is that if you go bold, if we send a message the day the bombing starts saying, "We are ready to resume right away, but we want to warn you that if this agreement is not concluded by January 1, we will not conclude it anymore, and we will work in a different framework." That scares them. We have a fifty–fifty chance, then, of concluding it.

NIXON: Why not?

KISSINGER: I believe a better than fifty–fifty chance.

NIXON: We've had a fifty–fifty so many times before.

KISSINGER: Yeah, but —

NIXON: That's all right. I don't care. I don't care.

KISSINGER: I have to give you —

NIXON: Suppose it's ten to ninety?

KISSINGER: No, no. It's better than ten to ninety. It may be seventy-five to twenty-five, because these guys are on their last legs, too. They are scared to death of exactly what we're talking about now, and they can't take much more. If they will not settle by January 1, then, at the end of December, at the last plenary session in Paris before [the end of] December, I would scrap this proposal and go for a straight prisoner for withdrawal and end of bombing proposal —

NIXON: I know.

KISSINGER: — and then, you'd be in good shape by the time Congress returns.

NIXON: Congress cannot return [unclear].

KISSINGER: But I would not yet do that, because if you do it now —

NIXON: [unclear]

KISSINGER: — then, we missed the chance we have of wrapping up this agreement —

NIXON: [unclear] the proposal last week. The proposal last week said that we would bomb them for six months and just, you know, change the proposal right away.

KISSINGER: That's right.

NIXON: We must not do that. We've got to play this string out. This string must be played out till the bitter end. It's not — it may not be bitter, I don't know. I'm afraid it is, and I'm afraid that they think they've got —

KISSINGER: No, Mr. President —

NIXON: — us in a crack.

KISSINGER: No, if they thought they had us in a crack, they'd break.

NIXON: No, no, no. I think what — no, the reason they don't break, I think, is much more fundamental than that. The reason they don't break is that they know exactly the kind of a conversation — or they fear — is taking place now. If they broke, they'd know that conversation would take place. They think without breaking it, they're going to be stringing us along. It's the same old shit they've been through all the time, and the minute they break, they figure they're going to get bombed.

Well, they're going to get bombed, even without breaking, because, while they haven't broken, we know they have. That's all that. I think — I think the breaking thing, which you, which you're — they want to keep — they want to keep — they feel that by not — by keeping the negotiations open, by having the peaceniks in this country write, "Well, peace is very, very close. Things are going pretty well," this and that, that that is a hell of an inhibiting force on me. You see? On the other hand, if they break, then they are at fault, and then they say, "Oh, Christ, we run the risk of getting bombed." That's why they're not breaking, Henry, I think.

KISSINGER: That's —

NIXON: And you think there may be another reason?

KISSINGER: They still want — they still [unclear] —

NIXON: You think they want peace?

KISSINGER: Yeah.

NIXON: Really?

KISSINGER: Yeah.

NIXON: Why?

KISSINGER: If you read the instructions they've put out to their cadres. They have told their cadres, "Just hang on a little longer."

NIXON: Yeah?

KISSINGER: "It's going — there is going to be peace." I don't think they can stand a long war. The factors that made them settle in October — when the mines start going in tomorrow, on Saturday, and they are — they are going to have one hell of a —

NIXON: Incidentally, do we have to wait too long to get the mines in?

KISSINGER: Well, Saturday's only a day and a half away.

NIXON: Oh, Christ. I'm just trying to think of anything that — well —

KISSINGER: But this is pretty fast action. If you start — if you resume on Sunday — you resume the bombing on Sunday, then I would send Haig out. I don't — I would not send the vice president under —

NIXON: No.

KISSINGER: — these circumstances.

NIXON: No, no. The vice president isn't going out. The vice president can't take this heat. I mean, the vice president will get out there, and what will happen is that Thieu will wrap him right around his little finger. He will, I know. If you send the vice president as a missile with one single objective, with Al there to watch him like a hawk, then he can do it. But the vice president will go out there, and Thieu will say — but he'll show him, you know, that shit he'll go through, and the vice president will come back. He'll say, "All right." He'll say the right things to Thieu there, but he'll come back, and then he'll argue to the president — to me —

KISSINGER: Because —

NIXON: — privately, "Well, we shouldn't do this, and we shouldn't drop this, and we shouldn't do that —"

KISSINGER: Because Thieu's —

NIXON: Trying to make his record for the future.

KISSINGER: Because Thieu's behavior has also been totally unforgivable, Mr. President —

NIXON: Terrible. Never said a goddamn word of thanks for what we've done standing by him, and the rest. He needs to be told that?

KISSINGER: He's —

NIXON: I am fed up with him, totally, right up to the [unclear] —

KISSINGER: He's been incompetent as a war leader —

NIXON: And, incidentally, they're delaying the foundation, for it's going to be withdrawal for prisoners. That's the point. And that, they will — you think, they'll accept withdrawal for prisoners?

KISSINGER: Well, he proposed it in a letter to you.

NIXON: I don't mean Thieu. I don't give a goddamn what he accepts. Will the North accept it?

KISSINGER: Not for three months.

NIXON: Do you agree?

HAIG: I think they're going to have to take some heavy pounding.

KISSINGER: I think there's a better chance that they'll accept this agreement before January 1 —

NIXON: [unclear]

KISSINGER: — than there is that they'll accept withdrawal for prisoners. But, I have laid the basis of our going to withdrawal for prisoners, and —

NIXON: And we know we can't wheel together.

KISSINGER: — and, believe me, it scares them. Every time at the meeting that I say, "Now [unclear] remember one thing, this is your last chance of negotiating in this framework. Don't forget this. Next time, we talk only military." And every time he pulls back from that [unclear].

NIXON: Right.

KISSINGER: This is why I wouldn't play it yet.

NIXON: Well, what should we do with Dobrynin, on this?

KISSINGER: I would just be enigmatic with Dobrynin.

NIXON: Tell him nothing?

KISSINGER: I would say—

NIXON: You're not going to see him?

KISSINGER: I'll see him, briefly. I'll say we are totally fed up.

NIXON: I've got a little problem, you know. Tricia's going to be there. [Nixon's daughter, Tricia Nixon Cox, and her husband, Ed, were then in Europe and expected to be in the Soviet Union during the time North Vietnam would be bombed.]

KISSINGER: They'll treat her marvelously.

NIXON: Should she cancel?

KISSINGER: No.

NIXON: [unclear]

KISSINGER: No, we should keep our good relations with the Russians. We should give the impression that they were screwed just as we were, as indeed they were, Mr. President. The account that Dobrynin gave to Haig is, first of all, one they couldn't have—

NIXON: The main thing to get across when the bombing goes, starts again, Al—remember this is something [unclear] and Ziegler will be talking about—the main point is that I really want this time, Henry, as I said, I don't want a long talking sheet. I just want to see one page, like I do before I do a—

KISSINGER: No, I'll—

NIXON: —very important press thing. What are the points we want to pound into the consciousness of these dumb, left-wing enemies of ours in the press? Pound 'em out. Pound 'em out, and forget about it. Make all the other points, because that dazzles them. But remember, we've got an audience out there that's ours. Talk to the sixty-one percent [the percentage of the popular vote Nixon received in the general election on November 7, 1972]. Talk to—I know, everybody thinks they're dummies—they were smart enough to vote for us.

KISSINGER: Mr. President, they saved us. They're the good [unclear]—

NIXON: [unclear] But they've got to hear it clear and loud and simple. Prisoners, they will understand. Treachery, they will understand. Changes of wording, they will not understand. Dates and da-da-da-da-da-da, they will not understand. But they'll understand treachery, and they'll understand the imposition of a Communist government on the people of South Vietnam. That, they will understand. Thieu's not going along, they'll understand that if it's said in a way more in sorrow than in anger, but, that as far as we're concerned, making it very clear, we are not hostage to either of the Vietnams.

KISSINGER: That—

NIXON: We are the party that wants peace in Vietnam, for both sides. And let the future of this poor, suffering country be determined by the people of South Vietnam and not on the battlefield. That's what our proposal is. We call on the South and we call on the North to agree to this kind of thing. Call on them both to agree. You can—

KISSINGER: I think that they—

NIXON: —make quite a little show you put on out there.

KISSINGER: That's—

NIXON: On the other hand, I think it should be done like today.

KISSINGER: No, I think we should wait till tomorrow. Give Dobrynin a chance to get—so that his people aren't stunned by it.

NIXON: What do you mean Dobrynin?

KISSINGER: I think the Russians shouldn't be stunned.

NIXON: Oh. Why would they be more stunned today than tomorrow?

KISSINGER: Because, today, they've had no preparations. I can tell Dobrynin, today, you're fed up, then Brezhnev will have read it tomorrow, and then, by the time I go on, it will be—also, I—

NIXON: This is not the time when I should tell Dobrynin.

KISSINGER: No, because—I'll tell you why, Mr. President—

NIXON: All right. Don't use him.

KISSINGER: Let me tell you—

NIXON: I don't want to—

KISSINGER: No, let me tell you why not.

NIXON: But understand, I'm ready to—we've got to play the big bullet, and we'll use it—

KISSINGER: No, but Mr. President—

NIXON: —I think that's the only bullet, but I will not play it, not in front of that—in front of these television cameras, again, and make one of these asshole Vietnam speeches. This is not the time.

KISSINGER: You were right. You were right—

NIXON: We can't do it.

KISSINGER: No, you were right.

NIXON: You can't rally people when they're up there already.

KISSINGER: You were [unclear]—

NIXON: You can rally them when they're on their ass.

KISSINGER: —I was wrong.

NIXON: No, you're not right or wrong. It's just a question of what you know.

KISSINGER: But the—

NIXON: Go ahead.

KISSINGER: But the reason you shouldn't —

NIXON: Never.

KISSINGER: — intervene directly is we should not make Vietnam an issue in your relations with Brezhnev.

NIXON: Yeah.

KISSINGER: We should have the Russians in the position where they say, "These crazy, stupid —"

NIXON: Yeah.

KISSINGER: "— lying sons of bitches in Hanoi —"

NIXON: Yeah.

KISSINGER: "— have screwed us again."

NIXON: Well, now, the question: what are you going to do about — what should we do — I asked Al about this yesterday — should we get Rogers, Laird, Moorer, Helms in? And we'd have to have the poor, poor vice president, too. I think he'll listen.

KISSINGER: Yeah. I would do it Saturday morning.

NIXON: Before the bombing?

KISSINGER: Yeah.

NIXON: Yeah, but Laird will — with all the orders [unclear] —

KISSINGER: I wouldn't evade it.

NIXON: Huh?

KISSINGER: I wouldn't evade it. I'd say, "I've got you in, gentlemen, to tell you you're [I'm] commander in chief." Let me give them a brief — a short briefing. I would not ask their advice —

NIXON: Could I ask you — could I ask you —

KISSINGER: Or you could do it tomorrow afternoon.

NIXON: Yeah. Could I ask you, incidentally, you're going to do the briefing for the press, and we'll do it tomorrow afternoon, but could you, Henry, take the time, today, to lay the framework for that by enlisting a few people?

KISSINGER: Absolutely.

NIXON: All right. Now, the ones you should enlist, it seems to me —

KISSINGER: Is the vice president?

NIXON: You should tell the vice president, "Look, the spee — the thing is off," and then say, "The president doesn't want you to get out there on a loser, and at this point, we're not ready. Later on, we may have to use you, because we haven't got an agreement." You understand?

KISSINGER: Right.

NIXON: Now, he'll talk about the fact, "Well, let me go out and negotiate with him." You can say, "No, Mr. Vice President, you don't have a negotiating stroke." [unclear]

KISSINGER: We shouldn't negotiate with either of the Vietnamese —

NIXON: You understand that the real reason is I don't want him negotiating with even

Guatemala, because, as you know, he doesn't have what we know, understand. But you point out if you can see him — or Al can see him, either one, either — the second one —

KISSINGER: Yes.

NIXON: — I think you should see — I think — there's the Rogers thing.

KISSINGER: I'll see him.

NIXON: And I think — I don't know how you handle Rogers. I haven't seen him since the meeting in Camp David, and — but I — but he's not whimpered about everything we've done. So, what do you think? How do you think Rogers should be handled? I just don't want to face Rogers at the meeting —

HAIG: [unclear]

NIXON: I want Rogers as an ally Saturday morning.

HAIG: [unclear]

NIXON: Tell him our whole foreign policy —

KISSINGER: The fact of the matter is Rogers will try to use it to do me in, but he will not necessarily —

NIXON: Yeah?

KISSINGER: There'll be two things happening. Rogers will support you at the meeting —

NIXON: Yeah?

KISSINGER: — and he will leak out stuff that I screwed it up. Now, those are two inevitable —

NIXON: [unclear]

KISSINGER: — results.

NIXON: Let me say, all that doesn't matter. How many times have they done that to both of us?

KISSINGER: That's right. But he'll support you —

NIXON: One time I screwed it up, the other time you screwed up. The main thing is winning, isn't it?

KISSINGER: That's right. I don't give a damn —

NIXON: The main thing is — look, the main thing is how we look four years from now. Four years we're going to be here.

KISSINGER: That's why —

NIXON: Goddamn those bastards. And listen, they don't realize. I mean, you — I mean, I will not do anything foolish. That's why I won't go on the television, or anything like that. I won't do anything foolish. But — I won't say anything foolish — but I will do things that are goddamn rash as hell, 'cause I don't give a goddamn what happens. I don't care. I don't really care —

KISSINGER: Mr. President, it's painful for me, but if you do — if you don't do this, it will be like the EC-121 [an April 1969 incident when North Korean fighter aircraft shot down an EC-121 Warning Star on a reconnaissance mission over the Sea of Japan;

all thirty-one U.S. military personnel on board died]. The Russians — you got more credit with the Russians —

NIXON: That's right.

KISSINGER: — and this —

NIXON: I know that.

KISSINGER: — they'll pay attention to.

NIXON: That's right.

KISSINGER: Now, we're going to take unshirted hell, again, here in this country. I can just see the cartoons and the editorials —

NIXON: Sure.

KISSINGER: — and the news stories —

NIXON: Sure. Sure. And let me tell you, over Christmas period and the rest, it isn't going to make that much difference because they ain't going to have pictures of American casualties, and they aren't going to have — they'll hear about there are a few missing planes in action, but, Henry, the war is a nonissue at the moment. Right, Al?

HAIG: Right. Right —

NIXON: Sure, it's in the headlines about peace, and all that, but that's the assholes like Reston, and the rest like him. But the average person doesn't give a damn.

KISSINGER: Mr. President, everybody will have to believe, that can be convinced, that we made a tremendous effort. If it fails —

NIXON: Yeah.

KISSINGER: [unclear]

NIXON: And that we will not — we will not agree to a peace that is a peace of surrender. Put it that way.

KISSINGER: That was our position —

NIXON: And that we will not agree to a peace that is a peace of surrender. We will not agree to a peace that is a peace that imposes a Communist government. And that we — and you say that, you lay those conditions on it, but that now, on the other hand, we're ready at any time to negotiate for peace. They were willing to negotiate as of three weeks ago. Now, it's time we find out. But that's the end of it. We're not going to be impotent under these circumstances, at a time they are building up. You see, the rationale for the bombing, Al, must be a buildup in the North. Just say that. Christ, everybody's going to think that it's true.

HAIG: It is true.

NIXON: It's true. They've restored the goddamn power plants, and the rest, so we're bombing the North again, because they're building up the North —

KISSINGER: [unclear] they have the biggest — that's another thing, Mr. President. They have the biggest infiltration, a bigger one than last year, going on right now.

NIXON: Don't worry about that at the moment. I mean that's — that's true, but wait, but my point is, without going into infiltration and the rest, we just have to say, "Because of a — there's a big enemy buildup in the war, and they're not going to trick us, so we're going to bomb them." We'll take the heat right over the Christmas period, and then, on January 3, it's prisoners for withdrawal.

KISSINGER: You can do that. I forget when January 1 is. I think —

NIXON: January 1 is a Monday.

KISSINGER: It's a Monday?

NIXON: That's right.

KISSINGER: The Thursday before that, whenever that is, it would be about the twenty-eighth of December, we table in Paris. We scrap this plan and table in Paris: straight prisoner, and withdrawal, and end of bombing — I mean, withdrawal and end of bombing for prisoners.

NIXON: That's right.

KISSINGER: Let them — they'll turn it down right away; we'll be in good shape.

NIXON: Fine. Then we just continue to, continue bombing them. Now, Laird will bitch about the cost of this.

HAIG: Right.

NIXON: Now, what is it? Sure, it's a problem. How much is the cost of this?

KISSINGER: It's pretty high.

HAIG: It —

NIXON: Bombing?

HAIG: The real scrub will be about three billion dollars, if it had to go through till — to June. If it stops short of that, we're talking about one point five.

KISSINGER: I think, Mr. President —

NIXON: You think one point five?

KISSINGER: — these guys —

NIXON: The Defense Department is going to have to swallow it, anyway, because we're not going to continue to have four intelligence departments, and four tactical air forces. That's one thing we're changing over at that goddamn place, when you get there.

KISSINGER: But they were willing to — the other side, we must look at it realistically. The other side was practically on their knees in October. They'd never have gotten as far as they did. It is not a bad agreement. It's a good agreement, if it's observed. If it's observed, the other side will be forced to withdraw. What we have to do, though, is to convince them that we are not easily pushed around. If we cave now, the agreement will be unenforceable, and we will have —

NIXON: Right.

KISSINGER: — signed something that —

[unclear exchange]

NIXON: Well, all right. This is the way. Now, let's — you will go when? You just — last night, we felt that Ziegler should do it. Do you agree Henry should do it now? It's a tough call, isn't it?

HAIG: It is a tough call because there is so much in the business of answering questions and —

NIXON: Well, I think Henry has to do it for another reason, maybe. Look, and we can't claim that he's hiding —

HAIG: It will —

NIXON: — or that I'm hiding —

HAIG: — look contrived.

NIXON: Huh?

HAIG: It will look contrived. It —

NIXON: Or that I —

HAIG: That's right.

NIXON: Now —

KISSINGER: Ron has neither the conviction, nor the authority, Mr. President —

NIXON: Well, he has the conviction.

KISSINGER: But he can't project it because he doesn't know enough.

NIXON: No, no. I know. No, Ron doesn't give a shit about the bombing. He doesn't care. He's sure to go right ahead and do it. Don't have any ideas about [unclear] —

KISSINGER: No, no. He has the convic — no, he's backed the policy —

NIXON: Yeah.

KISSINGER: — but he cannot present the negotiations with —

NIXON: That's right.

KISSINGER: — conviction.

NIXON: I understand.

KISSINGER: I don't present the bombing anyway. That, Ron should do in answer to questions.

HAIG: The morning it happens, he just —

NIXON: Yeah.

HAIG: — says he's not sure.

NIXON: Yeah.

KISSINGER: Tomorrow, all we do —

NIXON: [unclear]

KISSINGER: — is to —

NIXON: I know.

KISSINGER: — is to explain where we stand —

NIXON: I'm not worried about the bombing as some others are. I think you're going to have the heat in the magazines, and so forth and on, and Sevareid, and Rather, and all those jackasses. Cronkite will cry buckets of tears. Everybody says, "Why do the bombing over Christmas? Weather is it, and so forth?" Can we get one message to Thieu: please stop the crap about a Christmas to New Year's truce, right now. Right now.

KISSINGER: Immediately.

NIXON: No — there ain't going to be no truce. Or do we — or shouldn't we do that?

KISSINGER: Absolutely.

NIXON: Because I can't stop this over Christmas.

KISSINGER: Absolutely not.

HAIG: We can stop it Christmas Day. I — I don't know what to do.

KISSINGER: I wouldn't stop it. Once we go, we keep going. Maybe Christmas Day —

NIXON: Now, maybe, Al's got a point. Christmas Day, that's all, but not New Year's. Except for Christmas Day, there will be no — there will be no truce, except for Christmas Day.

KISSINGER: We can get that to —

NIXON: Just say, "Except for Christmas Day, there will be no truce." I don't want anybody flying over Christmas Day. People would not understand that. There's always been a truce; World War I, World War II, and so forth. All right, the main thing is for you to get rested and get ready for all this and go out there and just remember that when it's toughest, that's when we're the best. And remember, we're going to be around and outlive our enemies. And also, never forget, the press is the enemy.

KISSINGER: On that, there's no question —

NIXON: The press is the enemy. The press is the enemy. The establishment is the enemy. The professors are the enemy. Professors are the enemy. Write that on the blackboard a hundred times and never forget it.

KISSINGER: I, on the professors —

NIXON: Always —

KISSINGER: — I need no instruction at all.

NIXON: Always —

KISSINGER: And on the press, I'm in complete agreement with you —

NIXON: It's the enemy. So we use them, at times. But remember, with the exception, now and then, of a — I think [Richard] Wilson, maybe — there are two or three — Howard Smith. Yes, there are still a few patriots, but most of them are — they're very disappointed because we beat 'em in the election. They know they're out of touch with the country. It kills those bastards. They are the enemy, and we're just gonna continue to use them, and never let them think that we think they're the enemy. You see my point? But the press is the enemy. The press is the enemy. That's all.

KISSINGER: Mr. President, if you don't do this —

NIXON: [laughs]

KISSINGER: — you'll be —

NIXON: I'll do it.

KISSINGER: — then you'll really be impotent, and you'll be caught between the liberals and the conservatives. You won't win the liberals. And — and, besides, we'll be totally finished by February. They'll just be chopping the salami.

NIXON: There's another one that you've got to — you've got — that I think is very important, that I want you to — I want to talk, and I want you to get to — I want you to have a private talk with Rush. Rush can work on Laird. And Rush, of course, will be in State, in eventual time. Rush will be loyal.

KISSINGER: Rush is —

NIXON: Rush believed last week, when we got these messages — when Al was coming back — he thought we did — you know, that this is exactly the thing to do, and he analyzed it beautifully. He says the problem is here. He says that Saigon's interests and North Vietnam's interests are different from our own, so we've got to —

[unclear exchange]

NIXON: He's totally right. But the point is, we can't make a deal which plays either interest. But Rush must be sold. Now, what about Moorer?

HAIG: Moorer's a whore.

KISSINGER: He is. He's a whore. He'll do whatever he's told.

NIXON: Helms?

KISSINGER: I'll get him.

NIXON: Helms is going to get a marvelous — oh, incidentally, when he goes to Iran, I want him to roam. Let him roam down onto those goddamn sheikdoms. Let him go around, you know, to see the southeast and the rest. I mean he — he's —

KISSINGER: Helms is a loyalist.

NIXON: He'll do a lot of good. What I mean is, he's going to be an ambassador extraordinary over there. [Helms was recently appointed ambassador to Iran.]

KISSINGER: We won't have any problems with Helms.

"Senator, I know this is a very tragic day for you."
December 19, 1972, 12:21 p.m.
Richard Nixon and Joe Biden
WHITE HOUSE TELEPHONE

President Nixon comforts Senator-elect Joe Biden (D-DE), whose wife and one-year-old daughter had been killed in a tragic car accident the day before. Biden's sons, Beau and Hunter, who survived the accident, remained in the hospital.

• • •

BIDEN: Hello, Mr. President, how are you?

NIXON: Senator, I know this is a very tragic day for you, but I wanted you to know that all of us here at the White House were thinking about you and praying for you, and also for your two children.

BIDEN: I appreciate that very much.

NIXON: I understand you were on the Hill at the time, and your wife was just driving by herself.

BIDEN: Yes, that's right.

NIXON: But in any event, looking at it as you must in terms of the future, because you have the great fortune of being young. I remember I was two years older than you when I went to the House. But the main point is you can remember that she was there when you won a great victory. You enjoyed it together, and now, I'm sure, she'll be watching you from now on. Good luck to you.

BIDEN: Thank you very much, Mr. President.

NIXON: Okay.

BIDEN: Thank you for your call. I appreciate it.

"We've got to continue to crack it up there, so that they know we can still come back."

December 20, 1972, 11:32 a.m.

Richard Nixon, Henry Kissinger, and Bob Haldeman

OVAL OFFICE

On December 18, Nixon had ordered the launch of Operation Linebacker II, an air assault of an intensity not seen since World War II. On the first day, well over a hundred B-52s flew over North Vietnam and dropped bombs on much wider locations than were specified in Linebacker I or any previous U.S. missions. Hanoi and Haiphong were the central targets in what was to have been a three-day campaign. Nixon and his advisors were in a noticeably buoyant frame of mind as they received reports that the assault was going largely as planned. They began their conversation trading notes on Thieu but were more focused on the endgame in both Vietnams.

• • •

NIXON: Well, Henry, are you ready to go?

KISSINGER: Haig has joined the club.

NIXON: What's the matter? [unclear]?

KISSINGER: He got kicked —

NIXON: [unclear]

KISSINGER: He got kicked in the teeth —

NIXON: Yeah?

KISSINGER: Kept waiting for five hours.

NIXON: Has he seen him [Thieu], and then saw him?

KISSINGER: Saw him. Got a letter to you turning it all down. Demands the withdrawal of North Vietnamese forces, totally.

HALDEMAN: Hmm.

KISSINGER: He'll accept the political framework, now, reluctantly. He accepts the national council. He'll no longer call it a coalition government in disguise. All he wants is total withdrawal of North — North Vietnamese forces and two other insane conditions. And — he has to be insane.

NIXON: Well, where does that leave us now?

KISSINGER: That leaves us that we go balls out on January 3 for a separate deal. Under these conditions, Mr. President, it's two — there are only two choices we now have.

NIXON: Uh-huh.

KISSINGER: Actually, I think the North Vietnamese are in a curious pattern. They came to the technical meeting today.

NIXON: They did?

KISSINGER: They didn't cancel it. They condemned us for twenty minutes about the bombing and refused to talk about anything else, but then they proposed another technical meeting for Saturday. Now, that's not a sign of enormous vigor. [laughter] Well, we lost three B-52s this morning, and we hit a Russian ship.

NIXON: We lost three more B-52s? That's six together — altogether?

KISSINGER: Yeah. Yesterday we didn't lose any.

NIXON: What?

KISSINGER: Yesterday we didn't lose any.

NIXON: Oh, that's rough.

KISSINGER: Well, we are scaling down —

NIXON: What do we have to do then?

KISSINGER: Well, tomorrow, we had in any event planned to go down to thirty over Hanoi and scatter the rest over the rest of the country.

NIXON: Mm-hmm.

KISSINGER: And —

NIXON: I wonder what they did to — were these lost over Hanoi —

KISSINGER: Yeah.

NIXON: — these three '52s?

KISSINGER: These SA-2s were designed against B-52s, Mr. President.

NIXON: How much of a flap is going to be developed out of those three B-52s?

KISSINGER: Um, they're starting.

NIXON: Hmm?

KISSINGER: They're starting. Kennedy made a speech last night.

NIXON: What'd he say?

KISSINGER: That Congress says that if you fail —

NIXON: Right.

KISSINGER: — I fail. He took me on, too. He said it's got to be taken out of our hands, and Congress has to legislate us out of the war. Of course, what that son of a bitch Thieu has done to us is criminal. We could have ended the war as an American initiative —

NIXON: How does the — how does Moorer feel about the three B-52s? Does he express concern? Or, Laird? Did you talk to him?

KISSINGER: Well, I talked to Laird, but, you know, they say they expected three for every hundred. That's true.

NIXON: For every strike?

HALDEMAN: Every hundred that you move in —

KISSINGER: Yeah.

HALDEMAN: — expect to lose three.

NIXON: Well, that's what we've been losing.

KISSINGER: But, of course, the trouble is our air force. With — to give you an example, every day, they have flown these missions at exactly the same hour.

HALDEMAN: Yeah.

KISSINGER: Then, I told this to them yesterday. They said, "Well, we got so much other stuff coming in." But these North Vietnamese aren't stupid. They know at seven ten, the goddamn B-52s are coming. That's what I think happened.

NIXON: Hmm.

KISSINGER: That these guys —

NIXON: Well let's come back to the losses again. If they expect three for every hundred, that's what we're losing, is that correct?

KISSINGER: Yeah.

NIXON: We didn't lose that many, though. You didn't lose any the second day, did you?

KISSINGER: No.

NIXON: Well, we mustn't knock it off, though.

KISSINGER: Absolutely not.

NIXON: Laird is not suggesting knocking it off, is he?

KISSINGER: Well, he wouldn't resist such an order, but I think now that we've crossed the Rubicon, Mr. President, the only thing that we can do is total brutality. But, we now have a strategic choice. I think there's a better than fifty–fifty chance that the North Vietnamese will want to go ahead with the agreement, 'cause I don't see any sense in their continuing the technical talks if they didn't want to, to settle. It is now also clear to me, or almost clear, that there's almost no way we can get Thieu to go along without doing a Diem on him.

NIXON: [unclear]?

KISSINGER: No, I know. But I'm just saying what our problem is. We had to scuttle his economic aid; we had to scuttle his military aid. And we can do it. Then, he gets overthrown and — so, what I think we have to do, the only question in my mind, now, is whether we should get to the bilateral —

NIXON: Is Haig on his way back?

KISSINGER: He'll be in Key Biscayne, either tomorrow night or first thing Friday.

NIXON: He's not going to see Thieu again?

KISSINGER: No. There's nothing to talk about. He's now in Bangkok, and he's going to Seoul, and he'll be in Key Biscayne no later than eight o'clock Friday morning. And the only — of course, Thieu kept him waiting for six hours; his schedule is screwed up. That's another outrageous behavior of Thieu. You know, he kept me waiting once for fifteen hours. But let's — that's a different problem. We have two choices now. We can either scrap the peace plan altogether and go immediately to the bilateral, and we then — the North Vietnamese may force on us if they turn it down, too. Or, we can conclude it with the North Vietnamese, if they come along, and, then, if Thieu doesn't buy it, go, go bilateral. That son of a bitch — you know, if we had known that no matter what we did, he wouldn't go along —

NIXON: Yeah.

KISSINGER: — we could have settled the week of November 20. I wouldn't have presented all of his goddamn demands.

NIXON: Mm-hmm. Yeah, but what would we just — what would we have settled?

KISSINGER: Well, we could have gotten — we could have gotten eight or ten changes.

NIXON: No, no, no, no, no. But how could we have settled with them, and still retained —?

KISSINGER: No, what we would have had to do, then, was use the fact of a settlement. I think, domestically, we'll be all right if we get a settlement with Hanoi that Thieu rejects, and then go bilaterally —

NIXON: I agree.

KISSINGER: And then go bilaterally. What's killing us now is that we have neither a settlement with Hanoi, nor a settlement with Thieu. And if that bastard hadn't strung us along — I mean, your instructions to me — I mean, that's not your instructions, but I mean if you — because we had both decided this, my conception was, which I had recommended to you, to do as much as we can in presenting Thieu's position, so that then, get the maximum from the other side, we can take it back to Saigon. If we had known that no matter what we did, it wouldn't make any difference, that he was going to demand unconditional surrender, we could have had some sort of agreement on November 21 or 22. Because you and I recognize that most of these changes are bullshit. They are slight improvements, but what makes this agreement go is what you told Duc.

NIXON: Coming back to the B-52 thing, now. The — we cannot back off of this, now —

KISSINGER: No.

NIXON: — even if that's — if it's three, if they expect three on every one [hundred], that's about what you have to be, have to be prepared for. But I wouldn't think that, that — that they would rush into that every time. It would seem to me that —

KISSINGER: Well, the — there are many other targets in the North. They don't have to hit Hanoi every time.

NIXON: [unclear]

KISSINGER: And, of course, if these sons of bitches had airplanes that could fly —

NIXON: I know. I know. But they don't have, so we've got to [unclear] —

KISSINGER: No, but if they could put a lot of TacAir up with the B-52s, it would confuse the SAMs.

HALDEMAN: If you've lost Thieu, why can't you move right now to settle?

KISSINGER: Well, because now we — they owe us an answer.

NIXON: That's right.

KISSINGER: And I think it's a sign of weakness to send them a note before we've got an answer. That — that note we sent them makes it very easy for them to settle.

NIXON: You say they did agree to the technical talks last — since they got your note [unclear]?

KISSINGER: They continued. The technical talks were scheduled for today.

NIXON: Right.

KISSINGER: They came in and just read a statement denouncing the bombings. That's all right, but then at the end of that statement, they proposed another meeting for Saturday. So far, the Chinese reaction has been very mild. The Soviet reaction has been very mild. We may get an agreement out of this. We may win the Hanoi game.

NIXON: What is the —

KISSINGER: I completely misjudged Thieu. I thought at the end of October, we all thought at the end of October, the reason we held out was because we were all convinced that as soon as your election was over, and he realized it wasn't just an election ploy, he'd come along. And when we sent Haig out the day after your election, we thought then that this would do it.

NIXON: He, in effect, has said [unclear]?

KISSINGER: We'll he's ignored your letters, his usual tactic —

NIXON: Mm-hmm.

KISSINGER: — and stated his demands again. He's made another crap concession: he says he will now accept that national council — it's a great concession of him — if we get the North Vietnamese troops out; if we get a commitment from the North Viet — if we don't recognize; if the PRG isn't mentioned anywhere in the document, including the preamble; and, one other condition, which is —

NIXON: Well, in effect, what he has said, and we must play this very, very close to the vest, is that he wants us to go alone.

KISSINGER: That's right.

NIXON: Now, what we've got to figure out, and have to figure it out in the coolest possible terms: we've got to figure out how we can go it alone with Hanoi, without sinking South Vietnam.

KISSINGER: That — that's right.

NIXON: Now, the question is: will the Congress provide aid to South Vietnam, in the event they don't go along with the settlement? Also, the question is: will Hanoi settle this bilaterally? What the hell can they do, without the condition that we stop aid to South Vietnam?

KISSINGER: Well —

NIXON: I know the other reason is June 8. We answered we would cut aid down, and accept, if the other side does, and so forth, and so on. Well, put yourself in their position. Here, they're sitting on that prisoner thing; they know Thieu won't go along; they know we can't give them a political settlement. What the hell?

KISSINGER: Well, what they get is —

NIXON: What incentive have they got? Well, they get the bombing stopped, for one thing. And they got the mining stopped —

KISSINGER: That's why you've got to keep bombing.

NIXON: I know —

KISSINGER: That's the major reason, now, why you have to keep up the bombing. It gets the bombing stopped. It gets the mining stopped. It gets us out of there. We — they don't have to worry about the DMZ. They don't have to worry about a lot of other restrictions. And they can gamble that Congress will cut off the aid.

NIXON: That's right.

KISSINGER: I mean, it's unlikely that we're going to be able to get eight hundred million dollars of aid a year for South Vietnam.

NIXON: We also hold the — you realize your aid promise to North Vietnam is in jeopardy, too. I can't see the Congress aiding the North and not aiding the South —

KISSINGER: No, we can't give them aid under those conditions, while they're fighting in the South.

HALDEMAN: Wouldn't that be their incentive to let us go on aiding the South?

KISSINGER: Well, they won't — we can't give them aid while they're fighting the South. I think that's the problem —

NIXON: Never. Not as long as there's a war. In other words, there's no cease-fire then.

KISSINGER: No. No cease-fire. But we can make the argument that the North — South Vietnamese can stand on their own feet.

NIXON: That's right. That's right. No, I understand. It's not a very good way to do it, but it's the best we've got.

KISSINGER: Well, it's probably — I think now, Mr. President, if Thieu were not a cheap, self-serving son of a bitch, because that's really what's involved. That bastard can't figure out how he's going to stay in office in a free political contest. If he had embraced the agreements in late October, stood next to you somewhere, it would have been easy to make it work, and proclaim it a victory. But, now, he's made such an issue of it that I don't see — we may wind up getting an agreement, the guy collapses on us six months later, and I don't know why he wouldn't be — not because of the agreement, but because of what he's made out of the agreement.

NIXON: I understand.

KISSINGER: Now, I still don't exclude that this devious son of a bitch, that if we did get an agreement, that maybe — that you could argue that he's making this whole record so that he can say he was raped by us, vis-à-vis his domestic constituents —

NIXON: And that he'd do, if he won.

KISSINGER: — and then, he'll cave at the very last second, reluctantly screaming, bitching. But—

NIXON: Maybe we don't want to play it.

HALDEMAN: But I—that's the question we have to ask ourselves. Supposing we—you make an agreement, which your ally says is imposed on him, and then the son of a bitch collapses a year from now. Whether we aren't better off early in January—

NIXON: I'm not sure, Bob, that the Colson argument is the one we didn't worry too much about. You may not recall what it was. Well, I think it's better. The first thing is going to be damn near moot anyway. His point was that a bilateral agreement, the weakness in it being, well, what the hell, that's just exactly what McGovern offered.

KISSINGER: No. That isn't—

NIXON: And Mansfield, and some of the rest.

HALDEMAN: It's—(a) it's not; (b) it's in a totally different period of time, and after a totally different set of circumstances—

KISSINGER: Because what McGovern offered is a unilateral withdrawal, with a total cutoff of military and economic aid—

NIXON: Well, then Mansfield also cuts off—

HALDEMAN: It's the prisoners—

NIXON: —military and economic aid—

KISSINGER: Well, no, and then we'll get our prisoners.

NIXON: No. No, he didn't get that—

[unclear exchange]

KISSINGER: No, no. He would say after we get out, he was sure they would release our prisoners.

HALDEMAN: It wasn't in his deal.

KISSINGER: But it wasn't part of the deal—

NIXON: We know. The point is, I listened, I argued, I answered it in a different way. In my view, the main thing is to now finish it the best way we can, as honorably as we can. We have made this last pop at 'em, which we had to do.

KISSINGER: And we've got to keep it up, or we'll never get the prisoners.

NIXON: Oh, I understand that. I mean, you've got to keep that bombing of the North, Henry, until you get the prisoners.

KISSINGER: Without that, we'll never get the prisoners. Incidentally, one thing is fascinating to me from my television performance, from Saturday. I have yet to receive one negative letter. I must have two hundred letters by now, or telegrams, all saying, "We are proud of what you're doing. Don't let the Communists push you around."

NIXON: So, you see, that, of course, would militate against a separate deal, too.

KISSINGER: We've got no place to go with a negotiated deal. That's the tragedy.

NIXON: Well, I'm just telling you that the—the point is that it's a—there's no negotiation—

KISSINGER: If Thieu went along, Mr. President, we — by last night, I had come to the view that, on the assumption that Haig could get Thieu's agreement, that you'd be better off sticking with this agreement —

NIXON: I know. We talked about that.

KISSINGER: — and not going the bilateral route. But I don't see how we can go the negotiated route, and then wind up with — unless we just blazed right through — get it, and then let Thieu turn it down. That's another option —

NIXON: What's that?

KISSINGER: We could just stick with the agreement, bomb the bejeezus out of them until we get the agreement, and then let Thieu turn it down, and then go bilaterally.

NIXON: I don't like that.

HALDEMAN: You don't?

KISSINGER: Because, well —

HALDEMAN: That's easier to sell.

KISSINGER: Well, if Thieu turns it down.

NIXON: No —

KISSINGER: My nightmare is that Thieu will then accept it, saying, "I had to accept this, because the Americans betrayed us."

NIXON: I think that, basically, we should say, and I think it's better not to try to get the negotiated agreement, it's better at this point simply to make a separate deal, and with the North saying, we — it's obvious that they won't go along on this sort of thing. We can't feel that, well, we'll stop the bombing, we'll stop the mining, we'll withdraw all of our forces in return for our prisoners of war, and you decide the situation in the South. We'll continue to aid the South. Now, it doesn't do anything for Laos; it doesn't do anything for Cambodia. It's tough on that issue.

KISSINGER: But we can help them bilaterally. What Thieu has done to the structure of Southeast Asia — the one thing in which Harriman was right, unfortunately, is that Thieu is an unmitigated, selfish, psychopathic son of a bitch. I mean, here he's got a deal which we wouldn't have dared to propose it in August, lest McGovern turn it against us.

NIXON: What was Kennedy's — the occasion of his attack?

KISSINGER: B'nai B'rith —

NIXON: The speech he gave?

KISSINGER: The B'nai B'rith [unclear] —

NIXON: Oh, Christ.

KISSINGER: It wasn't an all-out attack; it was a fairly moderate one. But Dole has been popping off. I saw him this morning on television.

NIXON: Again?

HALDEMAN: Really?

KISSINGER: Yeah.

HALDEMAN: What'd he say today?

KISSINGER: He said it is not yet time to take it out of the president's hands, but if this continues, we may have to be concerned. I mean, it was a sort of a half-assed support of you.

. . .

KISSINGER: So Haig closed his cable, he said, "I'm proud to be joining the club now."

NIXON: There's nobody else — it's a good thing we didn't send Agnew, isn't it? What if Agnew had gone? What would have happened then?

KISSINGER: Well, we would have had to go bilateral. You see, what Carver thinks — the CIA expert — Carver thinks that what Thieu expected me to do in October was to go on to Hanoi and sign the goddamn thing, and that what he's been waiting for, is for us to sign it, scream bloody murder, and then go along. He doesn't want to be asked ahead of time.

NIXON: And you think maybe that — you think maybe we should — you really think that maybe we should consider the option of signing an agreement, and having Thieu turn it down? Well, if it could be one where we got an agreement, and, then Thieu said, "I won't go until they're all out." You see, Bob, the position that puts us in politically? That he — he — then there's a great debate in this country that we're signing an agreement that allows Communists to stay in the country.

HALDEMAN: Yeah, but you — you're signing an agreement that's better than any agreement you had hoped to get. [unclear]

KISSINGER: And not different, because that's what we'd always proposed to do —

HALDEMAN: It meant bigger objectives. And, then —

NIXON: And then of course —

HALDEMAN: — we'd go the last mile and —

NIXON: And that would be better —

HALDEMAN: — try to drag Thieu along.

NIXON: And then we say, "Well, under the circ —" But I'll tell you, we could do it as an alternative. What I mean is, I don't want to go down the road to try to get a political agreement, and then — and they all — then, you see, your agreement would have in the aid to North Vietnam, and all the rest. Then, let us suppose Thieu turns it down. Then what do you do?

KISSINGER: Then you have to go bilateral.

NIXON: Then go bilateral.

KISSINGER: Then you'd have to say to Hanoi you'd implement those provisions that he —

NIXON: That we can. Do you think it'd work then? Do you — do you like the idea of Thieu turning it down there?

KISSINGER: Of course, we may have no choice, Mr. President.

HALDEMAN: That forces him to take the damaging action, rather than in this — if you go bilaterally, you're taking it. You're writing Thieu off —

KISSINGER: The tragedy is, I must tell you, if — if I had known on November 20 what we know now, I could have emerged out of the November 20 session with an agreement.

NIXON: A bilateral agreement, you mean?

KISSINGER: Oh, yeah. You know, since he won't accept it anyway, I could have made something, a few changes, come out, get it signed quickly. That son of a bitch has really hazarded our whole domestic structure.

NIXON: Well, it isn't that. Our whole domestic structure has survived other things worse than this.

KISSINGER: I know, but he's doing it for —

NIXON: I know.

KISSINGER: In — all I'm saying is you've got —

NIXON: I know —

KISSINGER: — you've shown us all your faith, I mean. When I say you, I mean the administration, because I'm in total agreement with what you — what we've decided here. In fact, I recommended most of it; all of it.

NIXON: That's right.

KISSINGER: I said it only because the goddamn press is trying to play a split between us.

NIXON: Mm-hmm. I can't figure those three '52s. When I talked to you yesterday, you didn't have this report on it. How could that have —?

KISSINGER: No, no. That's this morning's wave. That's the seven thirty milk run.

NIXON: That's the first wave? Well, we — in other words, we haven't even gotten the results of the whole day then, have we?

KISSINGER: No.

NIXON: They lost three in one run?

KISSINGER: Mr. President, these North Vietnamese are not idiots. When you come at exactly the same hour, every day, they say, "Sure, it's a lot of activity," but they can tell the difference between a B-52 — and it is criminal.

NIXON: Well, is there anything I should do? Should we get Moorer in? Tell him? I mean, after all —

KISSINGER: Well, I think we'll just rattle them. This is the last day which involves his extensive raids in the Hanoi area. We were, in any event, after today —

NIXON: For three days, yeah.

KISSINGER: — going to shift to other targets, because we've used up the targets in the Hanoi area.

NIXON: Have you raised with him, with Moorer, the point of us changing the time?

KISSINGER: I've got to call — I've — yes, I raised it with him yesterday. They say, "Well, they have so many other planes in the area, that they won't be able to know." That's total nonsense. They can tell a B-52 from another plane.

NIXON: Is it too late today to change this, the orders? [unclear] any runs? Well, we'll hope for the best. Maybe there won't be any more today. Maybe there will. But if they do, they do. This is war, Henry—

KISSINGER: There's nothing we can do.

NIXON: That's right.

KISSINGER: It's a brutal business.

NIXON: But we have to realize that Thieu has now cost, as you realize, that if we had, knowing these things, we should have made the deal.

KISSINGER: Mr. President, but we couldn't know these things. If—for the United States to screw an ally, it's not an easy matter. It was the right decision. If we had been totally selfish, we would have, just after November 7, said, "Don't come home on November 24 without a deal under whatever circumstances." Which—I didn't recommend it. We couldn't do it. We wanted to see Duc. In fact, that's why I came back.

NIXON: I know.

KISSINGER: We thought we could get Duc lined up. These sons of bitches, and you spent three and a half hours with his emissary. We've had Haig out there three times. I've been out twice.

NIXON: He won't see Bunker.

KISSINGER: Well, he'll see Bunker, but Bunker has lost his effectiveness, frankly.

NIXON: It's not his fault.

KISSINGER: No. This guy is a maniac. There's one basic reality, Mr. President: there's only one protection for these guys, and that's the confidence of the United States, and the pride the American people have in the settlement, Congress, and the president. They've blown both of these now, and they're haggling around. And all this bullshit about the North Vietnamese forces in the South, that's just putting up a condition, which they know can't be met. They won't push them out of there. They won't put—they had four divisions in Military Region 3, the South Vietnamese. The North Vietnamese have ten thousand men against a hundred and twenty thousand. They won't push them out of Military Region 3. Then they have the nerve to come to us and say, "You negotiate them out." And if they had pushed them out, this issue wouldn't exist. Now, that's thirty miles from Saigon.

NIXON: I know.

KISSINGER: Nor did you make one concession different from what you had stated publicly for two years, which they never objected to.

NIXON: Except for the cease-fire.

KISSINGER: On October [7] '70, you proposed a cease-fire-in-place; on January [25] '72 you proposed a cease-fire-in-place; and May 8 ['72], you proposed a cease-fire-in-place. And that's exactly what you got.

NIXON: I know.

KISSINGER: I mean, no right-winger here can say you made a concession.

NIXON: We're not going to worry about the right-wingers or what anybody else says. The main thing, now, is to really — to end this war and [unclear] —

KISSINGER: Then the goddamn bastard sends you a letter saying —

NIXON: Yeah.

KISSINGER: — he wants to fight the war alone. That not only keeps all the troops in there, it opens up the DMZ, it keeps Laos and Cambodian supply corridors open. So it isn't the troops that bother him.

NIXON: When will the word get out that Haig has been rebuffed?

KISSINGER: Oh, that can't get out, because only Haig and Thieu know. And neither has an interest in getting that word out.

NIXON: No.

KISSINGER: Nor do we have an interest, I think, in getting the word out.

NIXON: No, no. I'll say.

KISSINGER: Because we don't have an agreement.

NIXON: That's right. That'd just make the North tougher.

KISSINGER: Yeah. Well, I don't know about that; it might make the North settle. If they think they have really got us hung out there.

NIXON: Well, we'll see. You should — we've got to continue the bombing of the North. It does not have to be on the, you know, on the massive basis that we've had. You know, the three-day, or whatever it is. We've just got to continue to crack it up there, so that they know we can still come back. That's what they really need.

KISSINGER: Well, Mr. President, it's got to be massive enough so it really hurts them.

NIXON: I meant massive in terms of the Hanoi area, which is —

KISSINGER: Oh. Oh, yeah. No, no. There — there we should scale it down. You're right.

NIXON: [unclear] not going to go in with excessive losses, Henry. It isn't worth it.

KISSINGER: That's right.

NIXON: We're doing this for political purposes and the military effect there is not all that great, as you well know.

KISSINGER: That's right.

NIXON: And the military up there is not all that great, as you well know.

KISSINGER: They've also hit a Russian and a Polish ship. It wasn't one their —

NIXON: In Haiphong?

KISSINGER: In Haiphong, yeah. It wasn't one of their better days.

HALDEMAN: They sink 'em?

KISSINGER: We've already gotten the Russian protest.

NIXON: Well, we've had that before.

KISSINGER: It isn't a bad protest. It's low-key.

NIXON: As long as ships are there, it's a battle zone. Now, goddamn it, they know to expect it.

KISSINGER: Well, actually, I think the Hanoi part of it is working out. That's going almost like May 8, because —

. . .

KISSINGER: But if the North Vietnamese came back to talk to me, I think it would go like May 8. It'd be a great victory.

NIXON: I agree.

KISSINGER: And then we should settle. And then, Thieu refuses, and then we'll just finish it.

NIXON: How do we finish it?

KISSINGER: Go bilateral.

NIXON: Oh, yeah! Yeah. That.

KISSINGER: I have given Haig all sorts of instructions how to work out a common strategy, but the bastard never got around to it. I mean, never permitted it. I don't mean Haig is a bastard. I mean Thieu.

NIXON: Well, Thieu taking that letter and reacting this way, that's it. As far as I'm concerned, there's no other track.

KISSINGER: No.

NIXON: Henry, that's why I'm almost to the view, Bob, and I must say that rather than — rather than making a deal, and then having him publicly turn it down, is to simply say, frankly, publish our letter and his response.

KISSINGER: But then he's finished.

NIXON: Huh?

KISSINGER: Then we'll never get money for him.

NIXON: That's right, too. That's right. You're right. We can't do that.

HALDEMAN: He's worse off with that than he is turning down the peace offer, because he can make a case for turning down the negotiations. His only weakness [unclear].

NIXON: Yeah, because my letter dictates our going alone, doesn't it?

KISSINGER: Oh, yeah. No question.

NIXON: And, therefore, we cannot publish that. No, what we would have to do rather than publishing it, we'd simply say that he prefers not to do it. Just state it, and then go bilateral. I'm trying to think about the game to play.

KISSINGER: We can say —

NIXON: My own view is that, in view of his response to my letter, that there — that trying publicly to drag him along is not a good strategy. I just think that it's not.

KISSINGER: Well, except Hanoi may force it on us.

NIXON: Oh.

KISSINGER: Supposing Hanoi —

NIXON: Says, "We won't make a deal unless —"

KISSINGER: No. But supposing Hanoi replies — if Hanoi turns down our suggestion of Monday, we're in good shape.

NIXON: Mm-hmm.

KISSINGER: Or, but supposing Hanoi accepts it and says, "Let's meet on January 3." Then, my view would be that we should meet, because that would take the heat off. Settle and then just put it to Thieu.

NIXON: That's right. That's what I would do. Put it to Thieu. And, then, what happens? Thieu says, "No, I won't go along—"

KISSINGER: No, Thieu will probably say, "I'm forced; raped; under duress. I'll sign it." That's what he'll do.

NIXON: That's what most people really think, don't they? Even still, with Moorer and all these guys.

KISSINGER: Yeah, but they've all been wrong. I've been wrong. Everybody has been wrong.

NIXON: I don't know [unclear]—

KISSINGER: I mean—I thought, and so did everybody who knew something about this, that he would welcome the terms at the end of October, and that we'd get an agreement with his acquiescence, and enthusiasm, and support. Then, when he kicked us in the teeth at the end of October, we thought, well, maybe that's the recollection of '68, and as soon as your election is in the bag, and he knows—

NIXON: Yeah.

KISSINGER: —you still mean it, then he'll yield. So, we sent Haig out. He played his usual game with Haig. Then we thought, all right, we go through the charade of presenting his demands and getting those turned down, and he'll come along. But he has—just hasn't. He's gotten meaner and meaner.

NIXON: The thing now is to treat him with total silence.

KISSINGER: I agree.

NIXON: Total silence.

KISSINGER: Some of my people think you should give him one more chance. I think that's a mistake. You've given him every—

NIXON: That's the one danger. What—how would you give him one more—?

KISSINGER: Well, we you could say, "On January 5, I'm going to make the following proposal," but that's a sign of weakness, because if he reacts as he did—he's never replied to your proposal to meet him.

NIXON: Right.

KISSINGER: He's never replied to you, before or after. He's replied to every overture of yours by just repeating his old proposition. And, of course, he's created an objective situation now where maybe the South—North Vietnamese can no longer settle, because they've been so weakened in the South. The end of October, the thing was nicely balanced, in which they had enough assets left. The CIA station chief in Saigon thinks they're so weak in the South, now, that they couldn't survive a cease-fire. Then—

NIXON: Well, gloomy as it looks, something may happen.

KISSINGER: Well it isn't — your action on Monday, Mr. President, restored the initiative to you. We can now — this thing has got —

NIXON: We've got something to stop.

KISSINGER: This thing is going to end.

NIXON: Yeah.

KISSINGER: They wouldn't have come to the technical talks if they weren't weak.

NIXON: Well, they only came to the first — well, that —

KISSINGER: No, no, but they don't need the technical talks —

NIXON: I know. They only came for the purpose of making a protest.

KISSINGER: Yeah, but they have a chance tomorrow at the public sessions. This is a — this is secret. No one knows they made a protest.

NIXON: Oh, they agreed, then, to more technical talks?

KISSINGER: And then they — they proposed, at the end of that meeting, to meet again on Saturday.

NIXON: But, I suppose that tomorrow they're going to break off the talks, right?

KISSINGER: I doubt it. Tomorrow would be vituperative. No, I had already thought that in Saigon, if Thieu had caved, we could have sent them a message that said — proposed a fixed date, and say we've now got Saigon's agreement.

NIXON: I know.

KISSINGER: It isn't that gloomy. I think we're going to pull it out in January.

NIXON: Well, we're not going to act on it, at any rate. What's — I am — I want to keep on top of this military situation, however. I don't want the military to do stupid things, you know what I mean? Of all the — the plane losses, though, I think, are predictable. If you send a hundred planes over there, with the SAMs down below, you're going to get some planes.

". . . Then we'll stop the bombing within thirty-six hours."

December 27, 1972, 8:39 p.m.
Richard Nixon and Henry Kissinger
WHITE HOUSE TELEPHONE

The devastation of Linebacker II continued past the original three-day schedule. It stopped on Christmas, so that the planners could reevaluate the targets, and then resumed on December 26. The following day, North Vietnam sent word that it was willing to come to terms. Kissinger didn't wait to tell the president in person but phoned him with the news.

• • •

KISSINGER: We had another message from the North Vietnamese today.

NIXON: Yeah?

KISSINGER: You may have heard from [Richard] Kennedy —

NIXON: No. No, I haven't talked to him.

KISSINGER: Well, the message said—

NIXON: Because I've been at the Truman funeral today. [Former President Harry Truman died on December 26, and the funeral was held in his hometown of Independence, Missouri.]

KISSINGER: Oh, I see. Well, they canceled the technical meeting today—

NIXON: Right. Right.

KISSINGER: But they reaffirmed their offer of meeting on the eighth.

NIXON: Right.

KISSINGER: And—

NIXON: This is all private, nothing public.

KISSINGER: The message?

NIXON: Everything is pub—private on this, nothing public. Because if they go public, we go public.

KISSINGER: Nothing public.

NIXON: Okay.

KISSINGER: And they also reaffirmed that the technical meetings will resume as soon as we stop bombing. Now, I sent them a message yesterday after our talk in which I just said if they confirm all these things with specific dates, then we'll stop the bombing within thirty-six hours.

NIXON: Right.

KISSINGER: And that may give us an announcement as early as Saturday.

NIXON: Yeah. That's good. Because I told you if we could—it's not imperative, but if we could get it before the first, it would be good.

KISSINGER: Well, I think it's certain by Sunday, and there's a fifty–fifty chance of Saturday.

NIXON: Well, we hope so. And if it doesn't—?

KISSINGER: I thought Saturday had the advantage of making the news magazines.

NIXON: [laughs] Yeah. Oh, the hell with them. But, in any event, if it doesn't come for them, that's fine. The main thing is if we could get it by Sunday, even, so that it hits New Year's Day, and all that sort of thing, that would be good. Because if we—I'd rather not have the New Year's bombing halt as just a bombing halt, you see my point?

KISSINGER: Well, there's almost no chance that we won't hear by Saturday. I mean, all they'd have to do is—if we get the message by Saturday morning, then we'll—

NIXON: Right?

KISSINGER: —we'll announce it on Sunday morning.

NIXON: Right.

KISSINGER: And—but I think we'll get the message on Friday, in which case, if you wanted to, we could announce it on Saturday.

NIXON: That's all right, too.

KISSINGER: And make the Sunday—

NIXON: Because we — we gave them a hell of a good bang, you know? And I'm glad we only lost two — two B-52s. That wasn't too bad.

KISSINGER: That's right. Yeah. Yesterday?

NIXON: Yeah.

KISSINGER: Right. I think we lost another two today.

NIXON: Well, I know. That's what we expect, don't we?

KISSINGER: That's right.

NIXON: We're hitting about the average.

KISSINGER: That's about right. That's right.

NIXON: Two out of sixty today.

KISSINGER: Two out of sixty, yes.

NIXON: Well, that's —

KISSINGER: That's less than five percent.

NIXON: Right. But, but, but, they're —

KISSINGER: It's a little more than — a little more than three percent. That's about —

NIXON: But we're — but, on the other hand, we're punishing the hell out of them, aren't we?

KISSINGER: Oh, there's no question about it, absolutely no question. We had — the French foreign minister today showed us a report from his consul-general in Hanoi saying, "I've just lived through the most terrifying hour of my life. An unbelievable raid has just taken place." And — oh, no, there's no question about that.

NIXON: Well, we'll shake them all up, and if we can hold those losses down to two or three a day, that's about all we can hope.

KISSINGER: And I think that we'll — by this weekend, we'll be over the worst of it.

NIXON: Well, we hope so. But we should hear from them by Sunday, I think, huh?

KISSINGER: No question about it. I think we can, unless something new happens. The message is so — it's written to give them the greatest possible incentive to answer fast, because they can control when the bombing stops. We no longer say we stop on Sunday. We say we stop within thirty-six hours of getting their reply.

NIXON: Good.

KISSINGER: So we could stop Saturday already.

NIXON: Right.

KISSINGER: And, frankly, one day's bombing doesn't make any difference.

NIXON: Oh, no. If we do it, we get — all — look, if we stop on Saturday, that gets the advantage. It's just another advantage of having it out of the news, and we've done our damage to them. We — we've got our message across, Henry, that's the important thing —

KISSINGER: We've got our message across, Mr. President, and we've gotten it across before all hell broke loose here, and we've faced down the people again, and you have shown that you are not to be trifled with.

NIXON: [laughs] Hmm. I wouldn't worry about the people here, I mean, their bitching

around, and the news magazines. Don't worry about it, Henry, it's not all that important. The public isn't that much concerned about all this.

KISSINGER: Oh, Mr. President —

NIXON: Do you think so?

KISSINGER: I am certain you will go down in history as having —

NIXON: Well, forget the history. But, I mean, you haven't run into a hell of a lot of flak
out there, have you? People are worrying about your bombing, are they?

KISSINGER: Well, I don't see many people out there.

NIXON: [laughs] I know.

KISSINGER: I'm going to stay out of the social columns on this trip.

NIXON: Well, the point is that don't let them needle you. That's the point.

KISSINGER: Oh, I don't —

NIXON: Right now, the thing is that we're doing the right thing, we just stick right to
our guns, and if we get this — if we can get a response from them, why, that's good.
If we don't, well then, we go to option two. We're all ready.

KISSINGER: Exactly. Actually, it doesn't really make any difference, because the news
magazines close on Friday. I just forgot about that.

NIXON: Well, we don't give a goddamn about them, anyway.

KISSINGER: Exactly.

NIXON: Because if — if something happens before they close, then they're terribly embarrassed.

KISSINGER: Exactly. Exactly.

NIXON: [laughs] Okay?

KISSINGER: [laughs] Right.

NIXON: Well, enjoy yourself. Bye.

KISSINGER: Thank you. Bye.

The capitulation of North Vietnam

December 28, 1972, 4:00 p.m.
Richard Nixon and Henry Kissinger
WHITE HOUSE TELEPHONE

*North Vietnam, which had often dithered in the past, required only twelve hours to agree
to basic terms and a date for a final round of peace talks. The administration was then
left with the problem of Thieu. The week before, in the midst of Linebacker II, Haig had
met with him in Saigon. Haig firmly explained that if Thieu didn't enter into any such
peace agreement as might be submitted to him, the United States would not necessarily
continue to support him and his nation. That didn't move Thieu, who held to his opinion
that the United States was betraying him. With the news that the North Vietnamese were
ready to finalize the peace accords, Nixon and Kissinger were faced with the question of*

whom next to send to Saigon, seeking the cooperation of President Thieu. Eventually, the
president resorted to letters.

· · ·

KISSINGER: Well [Richard] Kennedy told me —

NIXON: Yeah, he said — he just gave me a brief, then said you'd be calling me.

KISSINGER: Right, [unclear] it's gone just as programmed. I mean, just as was proposed.

NIXON: No conditions?

KISSINGER: No. No, no. They — it's all of ours —

NIXON: Right.

KISSINGER: — are accepted. So —

NIXON: Now the question is — how about the time now? How does it —? How do we —? What — how does that work?

KISSINGER: We'll go Saturday.

NIXON: Today is Thursday?

KISSINGER: Yeah.

NIXON: Is that their understanding, too?

KISSINGER: We'll just tell them.

NIXON: Yeah.

KISSINGER: I don't think we should horse around.

NIXON: Yeah, I just want — I want to know what the understanding is.

KISSINGER: Well, their understanding is that we'll notify them whenever we'll do it.

NIXON: Right.

KISSINGER: And we'll do that tomorrow morning.

NIXON: Tomorrow morning, then, you'll have notified them that — what, in effect? What I meant is, I'm trying to think in terms of what — when it becomes public, et cetera.

KISSINGER: [unclear] public — twenty-four hours later. Tomorrow morning, we'll notify them about the halt.

NIXON: Tomorrow morning is Friday, right?

KISSINGER: And we've worked that out with Moorer, and we'll stop it at seven.

NIXON: At seven, when?

KISSINGER: P.m., tomorrow night.

NIXON: Oh, seven p.m. tomorrow night we stop. Oh, I see, okay. I'd — I —

KISSINGER: Then, we announce it at ten a.m. Saturday.

NIXON: [unclear] the public announcement is at ten a.m. Saturday.

KISSINGER: But that, frankly, Mr. President, we won't even ask them. We'll just tell them.

NIXON: Oh, sure. I just want to —

KISSINGER: [unclear] them two hours ahead of time that that's what we're going to do.

NIXON: Yeah, I understand.

KISSINGER: Don't you think? Well, at any rate, I think it's —

NIXON: It's what — I see no reason, no reason to do it otherwise. I mean, what are the arguments here —?

KISSINGER: What they can do about it.

NIXON: Huh?

KISSINGER: What they're going to do about it?

NIXON: Well, I don't know. I — I know —

KISSINGER: Can we exchange another set of messages?

NIXON: No, no. I wouldn't exchange any messages. No.

KISSINGER: I think we'll just tell them.

NIXON: Well, because, basically, they have accepted our proposal, right?

KISSINGER: Exactly.

NIXON: Our proposal was that the — that we would halt on the thirty-first?

KISSINGER: No. Our proposal was that we'd halt within thirty-six hours of an answer.

NIXON: I see. And — so we will be keeping our word? That's all I want to be sure of, up to a point.

KISSINGER: No, no, we'll keep our word by two — we'll be within two hours. We're stopping within thirty-four hours.

NIXON: Mm-hmm. Right.

KISSINGER: But, you know, we got an answer within twelve hours.

NIXON: Right.

KISSINGER: Which shows how anxious, how anxious they are.

NIXON: Hmm. What do you — what significance do you attach to all this?

KISSINGER: Well, I think they are in — practically on their knees.

NIXON: Mm-hmm.

KISSINGER: Because, also in their answer, they said, "We will fix a schedule for the final signing at that next meeting."

NIXON: [laughs] They always want to talk about schedules, don't they?

KISSINGER: Yeah, but this one — in considering what we've done to them —

NIXON: Yep.

KISSINGER: — that they are willing —

NIXON: I must say this: this should have some effect on our brethren in the press, shouldn't it?

KISSINGER: As you know, if they had strung us out — if they could have taken it another week or two, we would have had unshirted hell in this country. So —

NIXON: Right.

KISSINGER: — for them to accept this within twelve hours is a sign of enormous weakness.

NIXON: Mm-hmm. Mm-hmm. Mm-hmm.

KISSINGER: And it's a very conciliatory reply. They said they'll come with a very serious attitude, and they hope we will, too, and that it can be rapidly settled.

NIXON: Mm-hmm.

KISSINGER: Technical meetings are starting Tuesday.

NIXON: Mm-hmm. Okay. Well, that's good. Ten o'clock, then. Public announcement, ten o'clock Saturday morning.

KISSINGER: Right, and I think all we should do is just a very brief one —

NIXON: Right.

KISSINGER: — just saying, "Private meetings will be resumed."

NIXON: Mm-hmm.

KISSINGER: We'll give them the date. "Technical meetings will be resumed." Give the day.

NIXON: Right.

KISSINGER: And then, in answer to a question, which is sure to come, we should say, "Yes, while these talks are going on, we are not bombing north of the twentieth."

NIXON: Mm-hmm. Well, you — but you're going to tell them — they already know that, though.

KISSINGER: They will have known that tomorrow morning.

NIXON: Yeah.

KISSINGER: They'll have known it for thirty-six hours when we announce —

NIXON: So, basically, you would have Ziegler make the announcement, right?

KISSINGER: Well, Warren will have to do it.

NIXON: All right, it doesn't make any difference. He can do it. We'll announce it at —

KISSINGER: At the resumption of the meetings.

NIXON: And then?

KISSINGER: You make a formal announcement of —

NIXON: Then they'll say, "What about the bombing?" That until the — well, you prepare the answer.

KISSINGER: Exactly.

NIXON: That there — there will no — be no bombing until the meetings are concluded, or something?

KISSINGER: That's it. While the — while serious negotiations are going on.

NIXON: Yeah. Mm-hmm. Okay. Fine.

KISSINGER: So this has been another spectacular for you, Mr. President —

NIXON: Yeah. Well, hell, we don't know whether it's that —

KISSINGER: Well, it took terrific courage to do it.

NIXON: Yeah. Well, at least, it pricked the boil, didn't it?

KISSINGER: Mr. President, anything else would have been ruined in the long run.

NIXON: Mm-hmm.

KISSINGER: And all the guys who are now saying, "Well, why do we do it with B-52s?"

NIXON: [laughs]

KISSINGER: These are the people who oppose this thing —

NIXON: What with?

KISSINGER: If you did it with DC-3s, they'd be upset.

NIXON: The point is that, as we know, we couldn't do it with anything but B-52s because, goddamn it, there's nothing else that can fly at this time of year.

KISSINGER: Mr. President, within ten days, you got these guys back to the table, which no other method could have done.

NIXON: Well, that's a — just keep right on and —

KISSINGER: And I think it — this way, it makes the weekend papers, and the excitement is going to die —

NIXON: Boy, it'll make the news magazines, too.

KISSINGER: Yeah.

NIXON: They'll open up for this, don't worry.

KISSINGER: Mac Bundy called me last night. He said he's going to write a letter — write a public letter to you and —

NIXON: I've seen it. Protesting?

KISSINGER: [unclear]

NIXON: Yeah. Well, of course.

KISSINGER: I said, "Why?" And he said, "Because, what am I going to tell my son?" I said, "I'll tell you what you can tell your son: Tell him, 'I got us into this war and now I'm keeping — I'm preventing us from getting out,'" and hung up on him.

NIXON: Good.

KISSINGER: But that New York establishment hasn't —

NIXON: They're done. They're done.

KISSINGER: — hasn't ever come —

NIXON: Well, the main thing now, Henry, is that we have to pull this off, and it's going to be tough titty.

KISSINGER: I think now we're going to turn — we've already got a list of economic pressures —

NIXON: Right.

KISSINGER: — and we're going to start implementing those next week.

NIXON: On?

KISSINGER: Saigon.

NIXON: Well, yes. Right. On Saigon, though, as I see — and I'm talking to Kennedy a little, which he'll fill you in, a little this morning, about, you know, some of the concerns as to the options that we had to be considering, here. That's assuming we go forward with our plan by just talking to the North. My view is, we talk and we settle. Right? With that —?

KISSINGER: Exactly.

NIXON: Now then — then, what do we — at what point do we inform Saigon that we are going to proceed in that way, or that we have proceeded in that way?

KISSINGER: Well, I think this thing is going to happen just before your inauguration. Basically, I'd — I would still send Agnew and Haig out there to give them a face-saving way off. [unclear]

NIXON: Yeah, but, [laughs] suppose he doesn't. That's, I suppose, our problem —

KISSINGER: Then we just proceed and sign the documents.

NIXON: Proceed and sign the documents? But they won't sign if Hanoi doesn't — if Saigon doesn't sign. I'm just trying to raise the questions, you understand?

KISSINGER: [unclear] Well, I think it will wind up with Saigon, at least, implementing it, whether they sign it or not.

NIXON: Mm-hmm. Well, you've got to have that understood with Hanoi then — that they aren't going to say, "Well" — you see, I — I think you wouldn't want to have that happening just before the inauguration, have Saigon —

KISSINGER: That's what I think should happen, Mr. President. If we send Agnew to Saigon before the inauguration, that would get him back by the sixteenth.

NIXON: Yes.

KISSINGER: Then, that I go on the final leg of this exercise, right after the inauguration.

NIXON: Right.

KISSINGER: It stretches it out a little more, and then you could go on around the twenty-ninth or thirtieth.

NIXON: In other words, we would have no announcement before the inauguration.

KISSINGER: No announcement, but obvious activity.

NIXON: Mm-hmm. Well, I don't think, then, I'd send, send — I don't think I would send Agnew out with the possibility of getting a rebuff before the inauguration. I'm inclined to think I would — I'd have the activity if — you see, the problem we have here, which we've got to think about — the problem we have here is that — I — if — we may as well play the inauguration as best we can, and I think you'd better — you may have to string your talk out to shove him past that point. I mean, if we can't, if we aren't going to get it — if we can't get it settled before the inauguration, I don't want him going out there and getting rebuffed before the inauguration. I don't think the risk is worth it.

KISSINGER: I think we can be extra — extraordinarily — I don't think he will be re-buffed.

NIXON: I know, but the point is, if he isn't rebuffed, then we would settle it, right then. I mean, there's no — there's nothing to be gained by having him go out there and just show a lot of activity before the inauguration.

KISSINGER: No, but we —

NIXON: The activity — it's enough for you to go over to Paris, frankly. I'm inclined to think that much up and down is — the only activity that would be worth anything more than your going to Paris is basically something that I said, you see?

KISSINGER: Right. Well —

NIXON: You see, because I won't be able to address the matter of — it's really — see, a lot

of this depends — a lot of this affects the flavor of the inaugural address, you understand? That's the problem.

KISSINGER: Right.

NIXON: And I'm —

KISSINGER: Well I'd hate to have this whole thing — if we —

NIXON: That's why I don't want [laughs] — that's why I don't want Agnew to blow it
before the inauguration. I don't want to — I don't want — I don't plan to — under
these circumstances, I can't say much about it, but I'm going to have to play it very
close to the vest.

KISSINGER: Well, if we have an agreement — well, I said it's dangerous to tie ourselves
to a schedule that culminates just before the inauguration, because if anything goes
wrong with that, we'll be in the same position as we were at the end of October.

NIXON: Well then, let's push Agnew past the inauguration, too, then.

KISSINGER: All right, we can do that.

NIXON: I think that's the best thing. Just — you mean, you'd take, then — you'd take a
whack on the eighth, and then another on the fifteenth? Something like that?

KISSINGER: Well, I think we should conclude it by the eleventh, this time. I just think
it's too dangerous.

NIXON: All right, but you conclude it, it's going to start getting out, and then Saigon
I suppose — you see, my problem — I — I think once it's concluded — well, we can
talk about this later, but you can be thinking about this so that we get a plan — once
this thing is concluded, and we agree, the damn thing is going to get out, and then
Saigon might blow.

   On the other hand, I don't want Agnew going out there and basically provoking
it. If so — I realize there's a risk if he doesn't go, but I think there's even a — at least,
we do not have the confrontation before the inauguration. If Agnew goes before the
inauguration, Henry, you could well have a confrontation and have the whole damn
thing seem to be shattered. So, what we have to do is to work out some sort of a plan,
whereby you do your deal, and then we sort of —

KISSINGER: Well, we could put it into cold storage for ten days and just start it on
inaugural day.

NIXON: I'm afraid that's what we'd better do.

KISSINGER: Although it's a high risk if one leaves these things lying around. But, of
course, we may not finish it by the eleventh.

NIXON: Well, yeah. I understand that. Well, the main thing, you'll have some activity,
and we won't be bombing.

KISSINGER: We can ask Bunker's judgment.

NIXON: Yeah. Well, I don't know. Kennedy seemed to have some views that Thieu
would — was going to be more — might begin to be reasonable, more reasonable,
but I think that's sort of silly, Henry.

KISSINGER: No, I think that's right.

NIXON: Well, we've felt that before, haven't we?

KISSINGER: Yes, but we haven't really. The last time, when Haig was out there, we didn't have a specific proposition to put before him.

NIXON: [laughs] Well, this is going to be goddamn specific, and he isn't going to like it, right?

KISSINGER: But what are his options?

NIXON: Yeah. I know. Well, I'd rather have him blow, Henry, right after the inauguration, than before. You see my problem?

KISSINGER: Of course.

NIXON: The problem being that I don't want to have the — and we'll just tell the North, Look, with the inauguration coming on, we got — we can't do it, then, but you're going to send Agnew right immediately after the inauguration.

KISSINGER: That's right and —

NIXON: That's — I think you could — I think they'd well understand that, if they're not being bombed. Get my point?

KISSINGER: That's right. Getting through with these bastards always is when you let —

NIXON: They might let off — they might get off the hook.

KISSINGER: When you let up the pressure on them, they are again —

NIXON: Mm-hmm.

KISSINGER: — feel confident.

NIXON: On the other hand, we ought to get — hmm —

KISSINGER: But it can easily be done that way, and then we could, perhaps, compress it by having Agnew go to Saigon and have me go to the other places, simultaneously —

NIXON: Yeah. Yeah. Yeah. Yeah.

KISSINGER: I thought there was some advantage in having Agnew come back and then start again.

NIXON: Yeah, but Agnew coming back, I mean, with problems with Thieu and all that, is just not the right story before the inauguration. I mean, I know it's —

KISSINGER: Well, we —

NIXON: — that's too high of a risk from the standpoint of our domestic situation.

KISSINGER: Right.

NIXON: I know the risk on the other side, but I think we'd better take the risk on the other side and delay Agnew for five days.

KISSINGER: We can do that.

NIXON: Well —

KISSINGER: It can be done.

NIXON: — I do think we'd better do it.

KISSINGER: That can be done.

NIXON: Yeah.

KISSINGER: And it may stretch beyond the eleventh, anyway.

NIXON: Yeah. Well, we hope not, but if it does, it does. We just take a little more time.

KISSINGER: Right.

NIXON: And, at least, we'll get the statements about progress out. Okay. Well fine, Henry.

"I am certain, now, he's coming along."

January 21, 1973, 10:33 a.m.
Richard Nixon and Henry Kissinger
WHITE HOUSE TELEPHONE

On January 7, the talks with the North Vietnamese resumed, and on January 13, the parties succeeded in reaching a final agreement on the peace treaty ending the war in Vietnam. As one of the final pieces of business, Nixon and Kissinger continued to look for ways to convince Thieu to commit to the agreement. Kissinger was able to report to the president his optimism that Thieu would embrace the accord. Important locations in North Vietnam had been decimated by Operation Linebacker II, and Thieu, with promises of American support in money and materiel, felt more confident than he had the previous year, in the aftermath of the Easter Offensive.

• • •

NIXON: Hello.

KISSINGER: Mr. President?

NIXON: I wondered what the latest report was?

KISSINGER: Right. We haven't had the Thieu answer; we just have his reactions as he received your letter.

NIXON: The second letter? The third letter?

KISSINGER: The second letter —

NIXON: The third letter?

KISSINGER: The letter we discussed yesterday.

NIXON: Yeah.

KISSINGER: And he said, well, he understands that if you'd make these requests, that there must be a very grave situation here. And he's now, practically, agreed to the agreement. Now, he's yakking about the protocols.

NIXON: Yeah, he's been doing that for all week, of course.

KISSINGER: Well, no, he was still — he's now given up on his objections to the agreement. I am certain, now, he's coming along.

NIXON: Mm-hmm.

KISSINGER: And he is, just now, making the record of having fought every step of the way.

NIXON: Mm-hmm. Mm-hmm. Well, do we expect an answer from him?

KISSINGER: We expect some answer today, yes. Which, in my view, will still leave a little crack open. What he would like to be able to say, for domestic reasons, is that his foreign minister talked to me in Paris and got one crappy little concession.

NIXON: Mm-hmm.

KISSINGER: Now, I have sent Sullivan in to see the North Vietnamese.

NIXON: Mm-hmm.

KISSINGER: And it's just possible that we'll get one.

NIXON: Mm-hmm.

KISSINGER: And I'll know that tonight.

NIXON: Mm-hmm. Mm-hmm.

KISSINGER: But, even without it, I'm certain he'll come along, now.

NIXON: He doesn't have any choice. I mean that, as we all well know. Well, in any event, what — you said you're planning to leave tonight?

KISSINGER: No, tomorrow morning. [Kissinger was to depart for Paris to meet North Vietnamese leader Le Duc Tho.]

NIXON: Tomorrow morning? Mm-hmm. Well —

KISSINGER: And Haig will be coming back this afternoon.

NIXON: Well, what time tomorrow morning?

KISSINGER: I'm leaving at nine.

NIXON: I mean, what time should we get together?

KISSINGER: Oh, anytime you say.

NIXON: Well, what time — you see, I meant what time [unclear] — well, when everything will be in the bag. That's what I want to know. Maybe it would — maybe we'd better wait —

KISSINGER: Well —

NIXON: — wait till tomorrow morning.

KISSINGER: Tomorrow morning, we'll have all the facts.

NIXON: Yeah, there's no use —

KISSINGER: And I can put off the departure by —

NIXON: Mm-hmm.

KISSINGER: — a half an hour.

NIXON: No use to meet before that. Suppose that we plan to meet at, say — say eight thirty tomorrow morning? That gives us a time to — for you to have — you — I mean, you — are you supposed to depart at nine?

• • •

KISSINGER: I think, Mr. President, at the very worst, if I would — could recommend, if he has not given his formal agreement, then, I would just ignore him. I would not make — and he will, then, the next day, certainly come along.

NIXON: Mm-hmm.

KISSINGER: He cannot afford to break with you publicly once you've committed yourself.

NIXON: Mm-hmm. Well, we've told them — him that in the letter, haven't we, Henry?

KISSINGER: We've told him that, but he hasn't broken with you once he realized — once he accepted the fact that you meant business.

NIXON: Yeah. Yeah —

KISSINGER: Every exchange, he moves closer to you.

NIXON: Mm-hmm. Mm-hmm.

KISSINGER: He is not acting like a man digging in.

NIXON: Right. Good, well then, we'll plan — as a matter of fact, we'll meet, then, at eight o'clock in the morning. Let's just make it certain.

KISSINGER: Right.

NIXON: And then, that way, we can get the whole thing fired out of the way.

"The settlement will last only as long as our two governments go forward together."
January 30, 1973, 9:30 a.m.
Richard Nixon, Tran Van Lam, and Henry Kissinger
OVAL OFFICE

The treaty to end the Vietnam War was formally signed by a delegation in Paris on January 27. As with any treaty, the proof would be in the commitment made to it, between the lines. Tran Van Lam, the minister of foreign affairs for South Vietnam and the signatory for his country in Paris, visited Nixon at the White House a few days after the ceremony. He and Nixon tried to put bygones aside and look forward to the future.

• • •

NIXON: We must have an even closer relationship as peacetime allies. The settlement will last only as long as our two governments go forward together. You can count on our continued military and material support and economic support. And spiritual support. We recognize only one government in South Vietnam. The Republic of Vietnam will be recognized and assisted. The key to U.S. policy in Indochina is our continued alliance and friendship with Vietnam. I have sent the vice president to show that we are standing firm with our allies [Agnew planned to tour Southeast Asia from January 30 to February 9]. You have stood firm. We respect you for it. The American press shouldn't discourage you. They don't represent the American people. You should know you have a friend in this office. We all have a responsibility to cool it now; however, China and the USSR will be urged to restrain their friends.

LAM: We are gratified by your approach. Sometimes we gave a hard time to Dr. Kissinger. But we perfectly understand the necessity of sticking together. We had to show we tried to get the maximum we could. But it finally depends on goodwill between us.

NIXON: There is no goodwill on their side. I have no illusions about that. We must create a necessity. A carrot and a stick.

LAM: I would like on behalf of President Thieu and our National Security Council to apologize for any difficulties we may have caused you. Your statement regarding

Saigon as the legitimate government is very helpful to us. I would like to present another point, having to do with the site of the international conference. In Paris we had been assured there would be no demonstrations, but there was one on the day of the ceremonies. We told Schumann it was very hard for the prestige of France. The other side have not insisted on Paris. We prefer elsewhere. In my opinion we prefer some other site.

NIXON: The French must give us an assurance, and unless there is no demonstration we can't go there. To have a demonstration on this historic occasion will be counter to the spirit of the occasion. Schumann is a crook.

LAM: The secretary-general of the UN is among the participants. Therefore it should be in a UN spot.

NIXON: Let me emphasize this: you have the third-largest army in the world. You must be self-confident. I was glad you had a celebration on the day of settlement. We have a stick and a carrot to restrain Hanoi. After all this sacrifice — now is the important point. The key is our strength and our alliance.

LAM: You will be proud of our people. The problem is how to split the NLF from the NVA. We should scrupulously keep the agreement. We should always put the other side in the position of the bad guy. Can you get French support at the conference?

NIXON: Pompidou is a good man. Let us play the game on the conference very carefully.

LAM: How about a conference with President Thieu?

NIXON: I would like to have President Thieu visit in San Clemente at the western White House. Tell him to propose any date convenient to him. Anytime he says after March 1. Anytime between March and June.

Afterword: Within two years, Nixon had resigned from the presidency, the victim of his own activities in the Watergate scandal. Within three years, Lam was in exile in Canberra, Australia, where he eventually made a living running a coffee shop. He had barely gotten out of South Vietnam alive after it fell to the North Vietnamese in April 1975.

TIMELINE OF KEY EVENTS

January 20, 1969: Richard M. Nixon is inaugurated president of the United States at the U.S. Capitol in Washington, DC.

February 23–March 2, 1969: In his first trip overseas, Nixon visits various European allies, including NATO, France, Germany, and the UK. A month into his presidency, Nixon addresses European parliamentarians before he addresses the Congress. On the tour, Nixon discusses the need to improve transatlantic relations (especially with France) and issues such as the Vietnam War, the Soviet Union, and China.

March 14, 1969: Nixon asks Congress to approve a modified antiballistic missile (ABM) system.

March 17, 1969: Nixon orders the secret bombing of Cambodia to destroy North Vietnamese supply routes and base camps, commencing with Operation Breakfast. When the public becomes aware of the bombings later, Nixon is criticized by some for broadening the war despite his stated goal to end it.

May 1969: Nixon orders FBI wiretaps to track the sources of leaks revealing the secret bombing of Cambodia. Nixon defends his use of wiretaps by indicating that his predecessors also used them.

May 21, 1969: Nixon nominates Warren Burger as chief justice of the Supreme Court. The Burger court would rule on several critical issues, including *Roe v. Wade*.

June 8, 1969: Nixon meets with Republic of Vietnam President Nguyen Van Thieu on Midway Island and subsequently announces a reduction of the number of American soldiers in Vietnam by twenty-five thousand.

June 9, 1969: By a vote of seventy-four to three, the Senate confirms the nomination of Warren Burger as chief justice of the Supreme Court.

June 28, 1969: The Stonewall riots in New York City mark the start of the modern gay rights movement in the United States.

July 20, 1969: *Apollo 11* lands on the moon. Astronauts Neil Armstrong and Edwin "Buzz" Aldrin become the first humans to walk on the moon, while crewmate Michael Collins orbits in the *Columbia* command module.

July 25, 1969: In Guam, Nixon greets the returning astronauts. In addition, he outlines what would become known as the Nixon Doctrine whereby the United States would provide arms and aid — but not military forces — to Asian allies, who would provide their own military forces to resist Communist aggression. More generally, the Nixon Doctrine signaled the beginning of a period of reduced American commitments around the world, especially military commitments.

August 8, 1969: Nixon announces the Family Assistance Plan, his welfare reform proposal providing direct payments to the working poor. This marked one of the most progressive social programs embraced by the Nixon White House. Rejected by Congress, the Family Assistance Plan never became law.

August 15–18, 1969: The Woodstock Music and Art Fair takes place in White Lake, New York. It is regarded as one of the most significant events in popular music history, and more than five hundred thousand attended.

October 29, 1969: The Supreme Court orders school integration "at once," in *Alexander v. Holmes County Board of Education,* 396 U.S. 1218 (1969), in order to force holdout schools to end the practice of segregation.

November 3, 1969: Nixon outlines the policy of "Vietnamization" whereby the United States would provide South Vietnam with equipment and financial aid but withdraw American troops. Following the Nixon Doctrine, the United States would continue to provide such assistance, but local forces would carry more of the burden of the fighting. In what may have been the most significant speech of Nixon's presidency, Nixon asks for the support of the "silent majority."

November 9, 1969: A group of Native Americans, led by Richard Oakes, seizes Alcatraz Island, the site of the former prison, in San Francisco. The group holds the island for nineteen months, inspiring a wave of renewed Native American pride and government reform.

November 24, 1969: Nixon signs the Non-Proliferation of Nuclear Weapons Treaty.

January 1, 1970: Nixon signs the National Environmental Policy Act of 1969.

April 1, 1970: Nixon signs the Public Health Cigarette Smoking Act into law, banning cigarette advertisements on television in the United States starting on January 1, 1971.

April 11, 1970: *Apollo 13* is launched toward the moon with a crew of Jim Lovell, Fred Haise, and Jack Swigert. On April 13, an oxygen tank in the spacecraft explodes, forcing the crew to abort the mission. They return safely to Earth on April 17.

April 22, 1970: The first Earth Day is celebrated.

April 30, 1970: Nixon announces the launching of military attacks on enemy sanctuaries in Cambodia. He is criticized by some for what appears to be an expansion of American involvement in Vietnam. The announcement sets off a massive wave of student and antiwar activism, which results in the circling of the White House with buses to prevent a possible march on the grounds of the White House.

May 4, 1970: In Kent, Ohio, National Guardsmen fire on antiwar demonstrators at Kent State University who are protesting the American invasion of Cambodia, killing four and wounding nine students.

May 9, 1970: One hundred thousand people demonstrate in Washington, DC, against the Vietnam War.

July 9, 1970: Expanding his environmental policy agenda, Nixon announces a plan to establish the Environmental Protection Agency (EPA) and the National Oceanic and Atmospheric Administration (NOAA).

December 21, 1970: Nixon meets Elvis Presley in the Oval Office. The visit is kept secret, although a photo of Nixon and Elvis later becomes the most requested document at the National Archives.

December 31, 1970: Nixon signs the Clean Air Act of 1970.

February 8, 1971: The NASDAQ stock market debuts in New York.

February 16, 1971: Nixon begins secretly recording conversations and meetings in the Oval Office and in the Cabinet Room. The system would later be expanded to various White House telephones, the Executive Office Building, and Camp David. While previous presidents going back to Franklin Roosevelt also secretly taped meetings and phone calls, Nixon is the first to comprehensively tape using a sound-activated system that captures 3,700 hours of recordings. Most of Nixon's closest aides are unaware they are being taped until the existence of the taping system is disclosed to the Ervin Committee in July 1973.

April 20, 1971: The Supreme Court rules that busing children as a means of dismantling dual school systems is constitutional, in *Swann v. Board of Education,* 402 U.S. 1 (1971). The Nixon White House is not supportive of the ruling.

April 24, 1971: Five hundred thousand people in Washington, DC, and 125,000 in San Francisco march against the Vietnam War.

June 10, 1971: Nixon quietly ends the U.S.-China trade embargo, which had been in effect for more than two decades, in the process of normalizing relations with the world's most populous country.

June 12, 1971: Daughter Patricia ("Tricia") Nixon marries Edward Ridley Finch Cox at the White House.

June 13, 1971: The *New York Times* begins publishing the Pentagon Papers, a forty-volume study of the Vietnam War based on highly classified Pentagon records from the Kennedy and Johnson administrations. While not directly implicated, the Nixon White House unsuccessfully seeks an injunction to prevent further publication.

June 30, 1971: The Twenty-sixth Amendment to the Constitution is adopted, granting eighteen-, nineteen-, and twenty-year-olds the right to vote.

July 9, 1971: Nixon sends National Security Advisor Henry Kissinger to Beijing, China, to meet with Prime Minister Zhou Enlai. The purpose of the visit is to come to agreement on a future visit by President Nixon.

July 15, 1971: Nixon makes an announcement that he will be the first president of the

United States to visit the People's Republic of China, ending more than two decades of isolation and hostility.

August 15, 1971: Under the authority of the Economic Stabilization Act of 1970 (84 Stat. 799), Nixon announces Phase I of the Economic Stabilization Program, a new economic policy of wage and price controls and a new international economic system that results in the end of the gold standard. One of the most significant postwar economic events, this announcement deals a mortal blow to the Bretton Woods system of fixed exchange rates.

September 3, 1971: The Quadripartite Agreement on Berlin is signed by the United States, the Soviet Union, the United Kingdom, and France. The agreement establishes trade and travel relations between West Berlin and West Germany and communications between East Berlin and West Berlin for the first time, greatly reducing East-West tensions and permitting further cooperation between the two blocs.

November 22–December 16, 1971: The Indo-Pakistani War of 1971 leads to India's victory and the independence of Bangladesh. In what would become known as the "tilt" to Pakistan, the United States supports Pakistan in the conflict, ostensibly because Pakistan is an ally of China. The Soviet Union supports India, despite India's reputation for being the leader of the nonaligned countries.

January 7, 1972: Nixon announces his candidacy for a second presidential term.

February 21–28, 1972: Nixon visits the People's Republic of China, further advancing the effort to normalize relations between the two nations.

May 8, 1972: Nixon announces the bombing and mining of North Vietnamese harbors in Hanoi and Haiphong, jeopardizing the forthcoming summit plans with the Soviet Union.

May 15, 1972: Presidential candidate and governor of Alabama George C. Wallace is shot while campaigning at a shopping mall in Laurel, Maryland. He would never fully recover, and his would-be assassin, Arthur Bremer, would spend more than thirty-five years in prison.

May 20–June 1, 1972: Nixon visits Austria, the Soviet Union, Iran, and Poland. He takes part in one of the key achievements of his presidency, the signing of the Strategic Arms Limitation Treaty (SALT I).

June 17, 1972: Five burglars are arrested inside the Democratic National Committee headquarters in the Watergate office complex in Washington, DC. The burglars would be tied to Nixon's Committee to Re-elect the President.

June 23, 1972: Nixon and Chief of Staff H. R. "Bob" Haldeman discuss the progress of the FBI's Watergate investigation, in particular the tracing of the source of the money found on the burglars. They propose having the CIA order the FBI to halt its investigation of the Watergate break-in by claiming that the break-in was a matter of national security. This conversation would become known as the "smoking gun."

June 29, 1972: The Supreme Court rules that the death penalty is unconstitutional.

August 1, 1972: A $25,000 cashier's check designated for Nixon's Committee to Re-elect the President is found in the bank account of a Watergate burglar. However, Watergate is not a major issue of the 1972 presidential campaign.

August 23, 1972: Nixon accepts the presidential nomination of the Republication National Convention in Miami Beach, Florida.

September 5, 1972: The Olympic Games in Munich are disrupted when Palestinian terrorists kill eleven Israeli athletes.

November 7, 1972: Nixon is reelected to a second term in the largest landslide victory in American political history in terms of the number of votes cast.

December 18–30, 1972: Nixon orders a massive bombing of North Vietnam after the peace agreement reached in October falls apart. The bombing forces the North Vietnamese back to the negotiating table and later becomes known as the "Christmas bombing." Nixon receives major criticism both domestically and internationally for his decision to temporarily resume bombing.

December 30, 1972: Nixon announces a halt to the bombing in North Vietnam.

January 20, 1973: Richard M. Nixon is inaugurated president of the United States at the U.S. Capitol in Washington, DC, and begins his second term of office.

January 22, 1973: The Supreme Court rules in *Roe v. Wade,* 410 U.S. 113 (1973), that the constitutional right to privacy "is broad enough to encompass a woman's decision whether or not to terminate her pregnancy."

January 23, 1973: Nixon announces that an agreement had been reached to end American combat in Vietnam, which also marked the end of the military draft and a transition to an all-volunteer military.

January 27, 1973: The peace treaty ending the Vietnam War is signed in Paris; it requires that all American prisoners of war (POWs) be returned.

January 30, 1973: Watergate burglars James McCord and G. Gordon Liddy are convicted of conspiracy, burglary, and wiretapping.

February 7, 1973: The U.S. Senate creates the Senate Select Committee on Presidential Campaign Activities with Senate Resolution 60, more popularly known as the Ervin Committee for its chairman, Senator Sam Ervin (D-NC).

February 12, 1973: The first group of Vietnam POWs returns to the United States.

March 21, 1973: Nixon, Haldeman, and Counsel to the President John W. Dean III discuss the Watergate break-in and the subsequent cover-up. Dean tells the president that the cover-up is "a cancer on the presidency" that must be excised or his presidency will be in danger.

April 30, 1973: Nixon accepts the resignations of his two closest White House aides, H. R. "Bob" Haldeman and Assistant to the President for Domestic Affairs John D. Ehrlichman, as well as Attorney General Richard Kleindienst and John Dean. Nixon publicly accepts responsibility for Watergate.

May 1, 1973: The U.S. Senate votes in favor of a resolution calling for the appointment of a Watergate special prosecutor.

July 1, 1973: The United States Drug Enforcement Administration (DEA) is founded.

July 12, 1973: The last presidential conversation is recorded on the secret taping system. Chief of Staff Alexander M. Haig Jr. orders the cessation of all taping, but only after 3,700 hours have been recorded.

July 13, 1973: During a private interview with investigators from the Senate Select Committee on Presidential Campaign Activities, otherwise known as the Ervin Committee, Alexander P. Butterfield, administrator of the Federal Aviation Administration and a former White House aide, reveals the existence of the secret White House taping system in advance of his public testimony.

July 16, 1973: During his testimony at the public hearings of the Senate Select Committee on Presidential Campaign Activities, otherwise known as the Ervin Committee, Butterfield reveals the existence of the White House taping system and details specifics of how the system worked.

July 31, 1973: U.S. Representative Robert F. Drinan (D-MA) introduces an impeachment resolution in Congress.

September 22, 1973: Henry A. Kissinger is sworn in as secretary of state.

October 6–24, 1973: An Arab-Israeli war, later known as the Yom Kippur War, commences when a coalition of Arab nations led by Egypt and Syria attacks Israel.

October 10, 1973: Vice President Spiro T. Agnew resigns as a result of corruption charges unrelated to Watergate. The charges stem from activities going back to when he was county executive of Baltimore County, Maryland.

October 12, 1973: Nixon nominates House Minority Leader Gerald R. Ford to replace Spiro T. Agnew as vice president.

October 20, 1973: Attorney General Elliot Richardson and Deputy Attorney General William Ruckelshaus resign rather than fire the Watergate special prosecutor, Archibald Cox, as ordered by President Nixon. However, Acting Attorney General Robert Bork agrees to fire Cox. These events would become known as the "Saturday Night Massacre."

October 24, 1973: Nixon vetoes the War Powers Resolution, which is passed by Congress over his veto. The intent of the War Powers Resolution is to make the president more accountable to the Congress during wartime.

November 17, 1973: Nixon famously says to a gathering of Associated Press managing editors, "People have got to know whether or not their president is a crook. Well, I'm not a crook."

December 6, 1973: Gerald R. Ford becomes vice president.

January 2, 1974: Nixon signs the Emergency Highway Energy Conservation Act, which establishes a national fifty-five-mile-per-hour speed limit.

February 6, 1974: The House of Representatives votes to proceed with its presidential impeachment probe.

April 29, 1974: Nixon announces that he will publish transcripts of forty-six taped conversations subpoenaed by the Watergate special prosecutor and the House Judiciary Committee in the hope that Congress will not subpoena any additional Nixon tapes.

May 7, 1974: Nixon signs the Federal Energy Administration Act of 1974, which represents the first energy policy in the history of the United States.

July 24, 1974: The Supreme Court rules in *U.S. v. Nixon* that President Nixon must hand over subpoenaed tapes to John Sirica, U.S. District Court chief judge.

July 27–30, 1974: The House Judiciary Committee adopts three articles of impeachment against President Nixon.

August 8, 1974: In a television broadcast, Nixon announces to the nation that he will resign effective the next day.

August 9, 1974: Nixon departs the South Grounds of the White House at 10:00 a.m. on *Marine One* for the last time. He flies to Andrews Air Force Base, Maryland. From there, he flies to El Toro Marine Corps Air Station, California, aboard the *Spirit of '76*, the name he gave *Air Force One* to commemorate the forthcoming bicentennial celebration.

September 8, 1974: Nixon accepts a pardon from President Gerald R. Ford "for all offenses against the United States which he, Richard Nixon, has committed or may have committed or taken part in during the period from January 20, 1969 through August 9, 1974." While Nixon would never admit any wrongdoing, many in the public conclude that accepting a pardon suggests that he is in fact guilty of something.

ACKNOWLEDGMENTS

In preparing this book, we stand on the shoulders of our predecessors. More than a decade ago, early pioneers who made portions of the Nixon tapes available to the public include the Department of Agriculture, C-SPAN, George Washington University's National Security Archive, and the Presidential Recordings Program at the University of Virginia's Miller Center of Public Affairs. The latter was then under the control of Tim Naftali, so it was serendipitous that the National Archives selected him in 2006 to be the first director of the federalized Richard Nixon Presidential Library in Yorba Linda, California, where he continued to expand access to the Nixon tapes. The Society for Historians of American Foreign Relations and Professor Peter Hahn of Ohio State University have also been prominent supporters of the tapes, devoting countless sessions at annual conferences to the recordings and the insight they offer on the Nixon foreign policymaking process.

Without the help of Tom Blanton of the National Security Archive and tapes expert Richard Moss, it would not have been possible for Luke A. Nichter to start nixontapes .org. The site was launched with the goal of making a complete, user-friendly, digitized version of the Nixon tapes available as a public service. It had never been attempted before and continues to be a work in progress. Listeners from all over the world visit the site each day, and it remains the only place to access the complete Nixon tapes without traveling to either the Nixon Presidential Library in Yorba Linda or the National Archives in College Park, Maryland.

This book also benefited greatly from the help of many helpful archivists — far too many to name them all — first at what was known as the Nixon Presidential Materials Project, then the Nixon Presidential Library once it became federalized in 2007. Special recognition is due to AV archivist Jon Fletcher for his patience in helping us to find the best photographs. Jimmy Byron of the Nixon Foundation also loaned his expertise at navigating the massive White House photo collection. Of all of the exceptional people at the National Archives, among the most helpful have been David Paynter, Jay Olin, James Mathis, and the Special Access/FOIA staff. Over the years, experts at the Historian's Office of the Department of State have served as an invaluable sounding board.

For as long as the debate continues over where Richard Nixon belongs in our pantheon of presidents, a rigorous field of Nixon studies grows and thrives. Just a sampling of those who have contributed to this debate in recent years as more records from the Nixon White House become available includes Jonathan Aitken, Pierre Asselin, Gary Bass, Carl Bernstein, Conrad Black, Nigel Bowles, William Burr, Len Colodny, Robert Dallek, John Dean, Jack Farrell, Mark Feldstein, Niall Ferguson, J. Brooks Flippen, Jeffrey Frank, Daniel Frick, Don Fulsom, Irwin Gellman, David Greenberg, Jussi Hanhimäki, George Herring, Jeff Himmelman, Joan Hoff, Max Holland, Alistair Horne, Ken Hughes, Walter Isaacson, Marvin Kalb, Laura Kalman, Jeffrey Kimball, Henry Kissinger, Maarja Krusten, Stanley Kutler, Mark Lawrence, Fredrik Logevall, Margaret MacMillan, Thomas Mallon, Allen Matusow, Kevin McMahon, Richard Moss, Lien-Hang Nguyen, Keith Olson, Rick Perlstein, John Prados, Andrew Preston, Lubna Qureshi, Stephen Randolph, Brian Robertson, James Rosen, Thomas Schwartz, Geoff Shepard, Melvin Small, Jeremi Suri, Evan Thomas, Anand Toprani, Jules Witcover, and Bob Woodward.

At Texas A&M University–Central Texas, thanks are due to Marc Nigliazzo, Peg Gray-Vickrey, Russ Porter, Jerry Jones, and Michael Cotten for their support of this project since the beginning. At Houghton Mifflin Harcourt our editor, Bruce Nichols (and his team), was superb. He heroically edited the manuscript to a manageable size, which was no small task. Two of our friends and colleagues — Julie Fenster and Virginia Northington — helped us in a myriad of indespensable ways. Super agent Lisa Bankoff of ICM was a huge booster of this project from the start. Ditto for Lora Wildenthal and Allen Matusow of Rice University. We are grateful.

INDEX OF SUBJECTS

INDEX OF NAMES